JOHN WILLIS

SCREEN WORLD

1994

Volume 45

WITH FULL-COLOR HIGHLIGHTS
OF THE FILM YEAR

Clint Eastwood in *In the Line of Fire*
© Columbia/Castle Rock

Christian Slater, Patricia Arquette in *True Romance*
© Morgan Creek Prods.

Diane Keaton, Woody Allen in *Manhattan Murder Mystery*
© TriStar Pictures

John Candy, Leon, Doug E. Doug, Malik Yoba, Rawle D. Lewis in *Cool Runnings*
© The Walt Disney Co.

Angela Bassett in *What's Love Got To Do With It*
© Touchstone Pictures

Anthony Hopkins, director Richard Attenborough, Debra Winger
in *Shadowlands* © Savoy Pictures

Julia Roberts, Denzel Washington in *The Pelican Brief*
© Warner Bros.

Kurt Russell in *Tombstone*
© Hollywood Pictures

Walter Matthau, Mason Gamble in *Dennis the Menace*
© Warner Bros.

Michael Wincott, Kiefer Sutherland in *The Three Musketeers*
© Walt Disney Pictures

Kate Maberly, Andrew Knott, Heydon Prowse
in *The Secret Garden* © Warner Bros.

Joe Mantegna, Max Pomeranc in *Searching for Bobby Fischer*
© Paramount Pictures

John Lone, Jeremy Irons in *M. Butterfly*
© Geffen Pictures

Thomas Ian Nicholas (c) in *Rookie Of The Year*
© 20th Century Fox

Jesse Bradford in *King Of The Hill*
© Gramercy Pictures

Sylvester Stallone, Janine Turner in *Cliffhanger*
© TriStar Pictures

Marisa Tomei, Christian Slater in *Untamed Heart*
© Metro-Goldwyn-Mayer

Mario Van Peebles, Salli Richardson in *Posse*
© Gramercy Pictures

Matt Dillon in *Mr. Wonderful*
© Warner Bros,

Robert Sean Leonard, Tushka Bergen in *Swing Kids*
© Hollywood Pictures

Sean Astin in *Rudy*
© TriStar Pictures

T.J. Lowther, Kevin Costner in *A Perfect World*
© Warner Bros

Anthony Hopkins, Emma Thompson
in *The Remains Of The Day*
© Columbia Pictures

Jeff Bridges in *Fearless*
© Warner Bros.

Tom Hanks in *Philadelphia*
© Tristar Pictures

Tara Morice, Paul Mercurio in *Strictly Ballroom*
© Miramax Films

Jason Scott Lee in *Dragon*: *The Bruce Lee Story*
© Universal City Studios

Elijah Wood in *The Adventures Of Huck Finn*
© Walt Disney Pictures

Richard Jordan in *Gettysburg*
© New Line Cinema

Director Adrian Lyne, Robert Redford
in *Indecent Proposal* © Paramount Pictures

Michael Keaton, Robert Sean Leonard, Keanu Reeves, Kate Beckinsale, Emma Thompson, Kenneth Branagh, Denzel Washington in *Much Ado About Nothing* © Samuel Goldwyn Co.

Michael Douglas in *Falling Down*
© Warner Bros.

Harrison Ford in *The Fugitive*
© Warner Bros.

Jodie Foster, Richard Gere in *Sommersby*
© Warner Bros.

Arnold Schwarzenegger, Austin O'Brien in *Last Action Hero*
© Columbia Pictures

Robert Duvall, Richard Harris in *Wrestling Ernest Hemingway*
© Warner Bros.

Keiko, Jason James Richter in *Free Willy*
© Warner Bros./Regency Ent.

Stockard Channing in *Six Degrees of Separation*
© Metro-Goldwyn-Mayer

David Huddleston, Michael J. Fox, Christina Vidal, Nathan Lane
in *Life With Mikey* © Touchstone Pictures

Johnny Depp, Darlene Cates in *What's Eating Gilbert Grape*
© Paramount Pictures

Bill Murray, Andie MacDowell, Chris Elliott in *Groundhog Day*
© Columbia Pictures

Jack Noseworthy, David Kriegel in *Alive*
© Touchstone Pictures

Bette Midler in *Hocus Pocus*
© Walt Disney

Vincent D'Onofrio, Tracey Ullman in *Household Saints*
© Fine Line Features

Pierce Brosnan, Matthew Lawrence, Sally Field, Mara Wilson, Lisa Jakub, Robin Williams in *Mrs. Doubtfire* © 20th Century Fox

Daniel Day-Lewis, Michelle Pfeiffer in *The Age Of Innocence* © Columbia Pictures

Jim Varney, Erika Eleniak, Cloris Leachman, Diedrich Bader in *The Beverly Hillbillies* © 20th Century Fox

Christina Ricci, Jimmy Workman in *Addams Family Values* © Paramount Pictures

Kevin Kline, Kevin Dunn, Frank Langella in *Dave* © Warner Bros.

Brad Pitt, Juliette Lewis, Michelle Forbes, David Duchovny
in *Kalifornia* © Gramercy Pictures

Bridget Fonda in *Point of No Return* © Warner Bros.

Reese Witherspoon, Sarel Bok, Ethan Randall in *A Far Off Place*
© Walt Disney Pictures

Rattler, Ben, Tiki in *Homeward Bound: The Incredible Journey*
© Walt Disney Pictures

Janet Jackson in *Poetic Justice* © Columbia Pictures

Al Pacino in *Carlito's Way* © Universal City Studios

Jack Skellington in *The Nightmare Before Christmas* © Touchstone Pictures

Tom Cruise in *The Firm*
© Paramount Pictures

Rory Cochrane in *Dazed And Confused*
© Gramercy Pictures

Jason Patric, Wes Studi in
Geronimo: An American Legend © Columbia Pictures

xv

Heip Thi Le in *Heaven And Earth* © Warner Bros.

Meg Ryan in *Sleepless in Seattle*
© TriStar Pictures

Mel Gibson, Nick Stahl in *The Man Without a Face*
© Warner Bros.

Michael Keaton, Nicole Kidman in *My Life*
© Columbia Pictures

John Willis

Screen World

1994

Volume 45

Associate Editor

BARRY MONUSH

National Velvet 1950's Giant Butterfield 8

Cleopatra The V.I.P.s The Sandpiper Who's Afraid of Virginia Woolf?

1966 Boom! The Only Game in Town Hammersmith Is Out

To
ELIZABETH TAYLOR

A WOMAN WHO HAS CAPTURED THE WORLD'S ATTENTION FOR FIFTY YEARS WITH HER STRIKING BEAUTY, FASCINATING SCREEN PERFORMANCES AND SELFLESS HUMANITARIAN WORK.

FILMS: There's One Born Every Minute (debut, 1942), Lassie Come Home (1943), Jane Eyre (1944), The White Cliffs of Dover (1944), National Velvet (1945), Courage of Lassie (1946), Cynthia (1947), Life With Father (1947) A Date With Judy (1948), Julia Misbehaves (1948), Little Women (1949), Conspirator (1950), The Big Hangover (1950), Father of the Bride (1950), Father's Little Dividend (1951), A Place in the Sun (1951), Callaway Went Thataway (1951; cameo), Love Is Better Than Ever (1952), Ivanhoe (1952) The Girl Who Had Everything (1953), Rhapsody (1954), Elephant Walk (1954), Beau Brummell (1954), The Last Time I Saw Paris (1954), Giant (1956), Raintree County (1957; Academy Award nomination), Cat on a Hot Tin Roof (1958; Academy Award nomination), Suddenly, Last Summer (1959; Academy Award nomination), Butterfield 8 (1960; Academy Award for Best Actress), Cleopatra (1963), The V.I.P.s (1963), The Sandpiper (1965), Who's Afraid of Virginia Woolf? (1966; Academy Award for Best Actress), The Taming of the Shrew (1967), Dr. Faustus (1967), Reflections in a Golden Eye (1967), The Comedians (1967), Boom! (1968), Secret Ceremony (1968), The Only Game in Town (1970), X, Y and Zee (Zee and Company; 1972), Hammersmith Is Out (1972), Under Milk Wood (1973), Night Watch (1973), Ash Wednesday (1973), The Driver's Seat (1973), That's Entertainment! (1974), The Blue Bird (1976), A Little Night Music (1977), Winter Kills (1979; cameo), The Mirror Crack'd (1980), Genocide (1981; narrator), Young Toscanini (1989), The Flintstones (1994).

Night Watch   Ash Wednesday   The Mirror Crack'd   1990's

Ben Kingsley in *Schindler's List* Academy Award for Best Picture
© Universal City Studios/Amblin Entertainment

CONTENTS

EDITOR: JOHN WILLIS
ASSOCIATE EDITOR: BARRY MONUSH

Staff: Marco Starr Boyajian, William Camp, Jimmie Hollifield II, Tom Lynch, Stanley Reeves, John Sala

Acknowledgments: David Christopher, Cline&White, Willa Clinton, Richard D'Attile, Gerard Dapena, Samantha Dean, Donna Dickman, Marcy Engleman, The Film Forum, Frank Gaffney, Jamie Geller, Andrea Hirschon, Doris Hirsch, Lauren Hyman, Terry Kane, Craig Kelemen, Leo Lawrence, David Munro, Lorraine Osmundsen, Greg Rossi, George Scherling, Kimberly Scherling, Sheldon Stone, Dave Zeliff.

1. Clint Eastwood   2. Tom Cruise   3. Robin Williams   4. Kevin Costner

5. Harrison Ford   6. Julia Roberts   7. Tom Hanks   8. Mel Gibson

9. Whoopi Goldberg   10. Sylvester Stallone   11. Meg Ryan   12. Arnold Schwarzenegger

13. Demi Moore   14. Macaulay Culkin   15. Jack Nicholson   16. Al Pacino

TOP BOX OFFICE STARS OF 1993 (Tabulated by Quigley Publications)

17. Denzel Washington

18. Sean Connery

19. Michael Douglas

20. Tommy Lee Jones

1993 RELEASES

January 1 through December 31, 1993

21. Robert Redford

22. Sally Field

23. Gene Hackman

24. Jodie Foster

25. Anthony Hopkins

Kevin Kline

Laura Dern

Liam Neeson

Josh Hamilton, Ethan Hawke

ALIVE

(TOUCHSTONE/PARAMOUNT) Producers, Robert Watts, Kathleen Kennedy; Co-Producer, Bruce Cohen; Director, Frank Marshall; Screenplay, John Patrick Shanley; Based on the book by Piers Paul Read; Photography, Peter James; Designer, Norman Reynolds; Editors, Michael Kahn, William Goldenberg; Music, James Newton Howard; Costumes, Jennifer Parsons; Special Visual Effects, Industrial Light & Magic; Casting, Michael Fenton, Valorie Massalas; a Kennedy/Marshall production; Distributed by Buena Vista Pictures; Dolby Stereo; Technicolor; Rated R; 127 minutes; January release

CAST

Nando Parrado	Ethan Hawke
Antonio Balbi	Vincent Spano
Roberto Canessa	Josh Hamilton
Carlitos Paez	Bruce Ramsay
Antonio "Tintin" Visintin	John Haymes Newton
Gustavo Zerbino	David Kriegel
Roy Harley	Kevin Breznahan
Javier Methol	Sam Behrens
Lilliana Methol	Illeana Douglas
Bobby Francois	Jack Noseworthy
Federico Aranda	Christian Meoli
Alberto Antuna	Jake Carpenter
Rafael Cano	Michael De Lorenzo
Fraga	Jose Zuniga
Hugo Diaz	Danny Nucci
Fito Strauch	David Cubitt
Eduardo Strauch	Gian Di Donna
Daniel Fernandez	John Cassini
Juan Martino	Michael Woolson
Pablo Montero	Chad Willett
Moncho Sabella	Richard Ian Cox
Coche Inciarte	Gordon Currie
Susana Parrado	Ele Keats
Felipe Restano	Joshua Lucas
Alex Morales	Silvio Pollio
Alvaro Mangino	Nuno Antunes
Pancho Delgado	Michael Tayles
Pedro Algorta	Steven Shayler
Victor Bolarich	Jason Gaffney
Co-Pilot	Jerry Wasserman
Pilot	Michael Sicoly
Sra. Alfonsin	Diana Barrington
Eugenia Parrado	Jan D'Arcy
Steward	Frank Pellegrino
Tomas Alonso	Seth James Arnett
Dr. Solana	Auerlio Dinunzio
Sra. Solana	Fiona Roeske
Martinez	Tony Morelli
Jorge Armas	Patrick Ramano

and John Malkovich

Plot Capsule: *True story of a South American soccer team whose plane crashes in the Andes Mountains, forcing them to survive against incredible odds, ultimately using the bodies of the dead passengers for food. Earlier film version of the story was the 1976 Paramount release* Survive!, *from Mexico.*

© Touchstone Pictures/Paramount Pictures

Danny Nucci, Josh Hamilton, Bruce Ramsay, Vincent Spano ABOVE: Richard Ian Cox, Bruce Ramsay, Michael De Lorenzo, Josh Hamilton, David Cubitt

Jack Noseworthy,
Michael Tayles,
Ethan Hawke, Gordon
Currie, Bruce Ramsay

Ethan Hawke, Daniel Fernandez   ABOVE: Ethan Hawke, Josh Hamilton

John Haymes Newton,
Josh Hamilton, Ethan Hawke

9

Anne Archer, Joe Mantegna   BELOW: Willem Dafoe, Madonna

BODY OF EVIDENCE

(MGM) Producer, Dino De Laurentiis; Executive Producers, Stephen Deutsch, Melinda Jason; Director, Uli Edel; Screenplay, Brad Mirman; Photography, Doug Milsome; Designer, Victoria Paul; Costumes, Susan Becker; Music, Graeme Revell; Editor, Thom Noble; Line Producer, Mel Dellar; Co-Producers, Bernd Eichinger, Herman Weigel; Casting, Mary Jo Slater; a Dino De Laurentiis Communications production; Dolby Stereo; Deluxe color; Rated R; 99 minutes; January release

CAST

Rebecca Carlson	Madonna
Frank Dulaney	Willem Dafoe
Robert Garrett	Joe Mantegna
Joanne Braslow	Anne Archer
Sharon Dulaney	Julianne Moore
Dr. Alan Paley	Jurgen Prochnow
Jeffrey Roston	Frank Langella
Charles Biggs	Stan Shaw
Dr. McCurdy	Charles Hallahan
Judge Burnham	Lillian Lehman
Detective Reese	Mark Rolston
Gabe	Jeff Perry
Detective Griffin	Richard Riehle
Andrew Marsh	Michael Forest
Printman	D. Scot Douglas
Technicians	Mario DePriest, John DeLay
Photographer	Ross Huffman-Kerr
Reporter	Mark C. Vincent
Minister	Frank Roberts
Michael Dulaney	Aaron Corcoran
Waitress	Timi Prulhiere
Jamie	Corey Brunish
Dr. Novaro	John Chandler
Jury Foreman	Peter Paul Eastman
Clerk	Bryan Clark

Plot Capsule: *Rebecca Carlson, accused of bringing on the death of a millionaire in hopes of inheriting his money, is defended by lawyer Frank Dulaney, who finds himself drawn to her uninhibited, dangerous ways.*

© Metro-Goldwyn-Mayer Inc.

Joe Mantegna, Jurgen Prochnow, Lillian Lehman

Willem Dafoe, Madonna

Paul Gross, Finola Hughes   ABOVE: Paul Gross, Peter Berg

ASPEN EXTREME

(HOLLYWOOD PICTURES) Producer, Leonard Goldberg; Executive Producer, Fred T. Gallo; Director/Screenplay, Patrick Hasburgh; Photography, Steven Fierberg, Robert Primes; Designer, Roger Cain; Costumes, Karen Patch; Editor, Steven Kemper; Music, Michael Convertino; Casting, Gail Levin; Stunts, Gary Jensen; Presented in association with Touchwood Pacific Partners I; Distributed by Buena Vista Pictures; Dolby Stereo; Technicolor; Rated PG-13; 117 minutes; January release

CAST

T.J. Burke	Paul Gross
Dexter Rutecki	Peter Berg
Bryce Kellogg	Finola Hughes
Robin Hand	Teri Polo
Dave Ritchie	William Russ
Karl Stall	Trevor Eve
Franz Hauser	Martin Kemp
Rudy Zucker	Stewart Finley-McLennan
Gary Eimiller	Tony Griffin
Michelle Proux	Julie Royer
Bill Swanson	Patrick T. Johnson
Todd Pounds	William McNamara
Jinx Stone	Gary Eimiller
Himself	Andy Mill

and Bill Ferrell (Official), Catherine Parks (Karen), Karla Olivares (Kimberly), Valerie Kingston (Kimberly's Mom), Monica Olivares (Suzy), Jeronimo Olivares (Little Boy), Rod McCary (Mr. Hanson), Rae Norman (Mrs. Hanson), Rudi Davis (Kevin Hanson), Ami Reade (Sarah Hanson), Bradley Mott (Morton Hayward), Roger Wilson (Jake Neil), Nicolette Scorsese (Tina), Dennis Holahan (Henri), Claudia Cron (Scarlett), Owen O'Farrell, Brett Porter (Bartenders), Marisa Redanty (Tourist), Steven Brill (Waiter), Kevin Bourland (Roy), Morgan Metzger (Randi), Will MacMillan (Beard), Charles Boswell (Suit), John W. Hardy (Assembly Line Worker), Stan Ivar (Mr. Parker), Reuben Yabuku (Attendant), Ken Oakes (Ski School Supervisor), Chris Hanson, John Goulet (Ski Instructors), Katerina Veisbein (Woman at party), Todd R. Beveridge (Cop), Lynn Bopeley (Robin's Friend), Christopher Tufty (Man on horse)

Plot Capsule: *Two young men head for the famed Aspen resort to become ski instructors, hoping to land some female clientele.*

NOWHERE TO RUN

(COLUMBIA) formerly *Pals*; Producers, Craig Baumgarten, Gary Adelson; Executive Producer, Michael Rachmil; Director, Robert Harmon; Screenplay, Joe Eszterhas, Leslie Bohem, Randy Feldman; Story, Joe Eszterhas, Richard Marquand; Photography, David Gribble; Designer, Dennis Washington; Costumes, Gamila Mariana Fahkry; Editors, Zach Staenberg, Mark Helfrich; Music, Mark Isham; Casting, Jackie Burch; Stunts, Billy Burton; Dolby Stereo; Technicolor; Rated R; 94 minutes; January release

CAST

Sam Gillen	Jean-Claude Van Damme
Clydie	Rosanna Arquette
Mookie	Kieran Culkin
Mr. Dunston	Ted Levine
Bree	Tiffany Taubman
Lonnie	Edward Blatchford
Billy	Anthony Starke
Franklin Hale	Joss Ackland
Bus Driver	Allen Graf
Bus Guard	Leonard Termo
Country Store Clerk	James Greene
Pick-Up Truck Thug	Steve Chambers
Tom Lewis	Stephen Wesley Bridgewater
Sarah Lewis	Christy Botkin
Town Meeting Chairwoman	Luana Anders
Hale's Associates	Kevin Page, Albie Selznick

and Andy Gille, Jack Gill, Gene LeBell, Jeff Ramsey, Randall Widner (Bulldozer Men), Gavin Glennon (Auto Parts Clerk), John Rubinow (Clydie's Husband), Stanley White (Cop in diner), Joseph Menza (Diner Cook), John Finn (Cop in chase), John Kerry (Big Thug "John"), Tony Epper (Fire Thug "Al"), Robert Aprisa, Jophery Brown, Tony Brubaker, Ron Howard George, Voyo Goric, Jack Lucarelli, Peter Malota, Frank Orsatti, Manny Perry, Thomas Rosales, Ron Stein, Sven-Ole Thorsen, Jack Verbois, Chuck Zito (Prisoners)

Plot Capsule: *Action-drama in which bank robber Sam Gillen, recently sprung from prison, hides out with a cache of stolen loot on a farm run by a young widow and her two children.*

Kieran Culkin, Rosanna Arquette, Tiffany Taubman ABOVE: Jean-Claude Van Damme

11

James Villemaire, Cathy Moriarty

Simon Fenton, John Goodman

John Sayles, Dick Miller, John Goodman

MANT

Kellie Martin, Omri Katz ABOVE: John Goodman

Omri Katz, Kellie Martin, James Villemaire (between cops)

MATINEE

(UNIVERSAL) Producer, Michael Finnell; Director, Joe Dante; Screenplay, Charlie Haas; Story, Jerico, Charlie Haas; Photography, John Hora; Designer, Steven Legler; Editor, Marshall Harvey; Co-Producer, Pat Kehoe; Costumes, Isis Mussenden; Music, Jerry Goldsmith; Casting, Gretchen Rennell; Visual Effects Supervisor, Dennis Michelson; Mant/Ant Designer, James McPherson; a Renfield production; Dolby Stereo; Deluxe color; Rated PG; 98 minutes; January release

CAST

Lawrence Woolsey	John Goodman
Ruth Corday	Cathy Moriarty
Gene Loomis	Simon Fenton
Stan	Omri Katz
Sandra	Lisa Jakub
Sherry	Kellie Martin
Dennis Loomis	Jesse Lee
Anne Loomis	Lucinda Jenney
Harvey Starkweather	James Villemaire
Howard, the Theatre Manager	Robert Picardo
Mr. Spector	Jesse White
Herb	Dick Miller
Bob	John Sayles
Jack	David Clennon
Rhonda	Lucy Butler
Dwight	Georgie Cranford
Andy	Nick Bronson
Stan's Friends	Cory Barlog, George Carson, Joe Gonzalez
Stan's Mom	Belinda Balaski
Mr. Elroy	Charlie Haas
Mant/Bill	Mark McCracken
"Mant!" Doctor	William Schallert
"Mant!" Scientist	Robert Cornthwaite
"Mant!" General	Kevin McCarthy

Omri Katz, Kellie Martin, Robert Picardo

and Archie Hahn ("Shopping Cart" Star), Naomi Watts ("Shopping Cart" Starlet), Chris Stacy (Gas Station Attendant), Allison McKay, Glenda Chism (Teachers), Aaron Stormer (Kid near Andy), Lana Bucciarelli ("Eew!" Girl), Richard Rossomme (Shredded Wheat Man), D. Christian Gottshall (Store Clerk), Bernard Blanding, Dennis Neal (Soldiers), Luke Halpin (Man in crowd), Eulan Middlebrooks (Young Man in crowd), Elizabeth Dimon (Theater Cashier), Shane Obedzinski (Bleeding Kid), Summer-Healy Chapin ("Balcony Full" Kid), James Scott Hess (Kid in floor seat), Shawn Edward Watkins (Kid next to Mr. Elroy), Danny Hanemann (Man outside theater), Hesse Zeigler (Kid in line), Andy Isaacs (Faint Kid), Joe Candelora (Fireman), Steve Zurk (Cop), Mary Moriarty (Lady in line), John Paul Lehman (Marine Guard), Jacob Witkin (Dr. Diablo), Tracy Roberts (Screaming Woman), Marc Macaulay ("Shopping Cart" Crook), Timothy Bass, Molly Conole, Jeff Breslauer, Peggy O'Neal, Colette Piceau ("Movie Theatre" Actors), Steve Dumouchel, Kurt Smildsin, Michael T. Kelly ("Mob" Actors), Ike Pappas (Newscaster), Brett Rice (Voice of Gene's Dad)

Plot Capsule: *During the 1962 Cuban Missile Crisis flamboyant horror movie producer Lawrence Woolsey arrives in Key West, Florida to preview his latest opus, Mant!, much to the delight of the local teens.*

John Goodman, Simon Fenton

GUNCRAZY

(MAN RAY ASSOCIATES) Producers, Zane W. Levitt, Diane Firestone; Director, Tamra Davis; Screenplay, Matthew Bright; Co-Producer, Mark Yellen; Photography, Lisa Rinzler; Designer, Abbie Lee Warren; Costumes, Merrie Lawson; Music, Ed Tomney; Casting, Partners in Crime; Presented by Zeta Entertainment in association with First Look Pictures; Ultra-Stereo; Foto-Kem color; Rated R; 93 minutes; January release

CAST

Anita Minteer	Drew Barrymore
Howard Hickok	James LeGros
Mr. Kincaid	Michael Ironside
Joy	Ione Skye
Hank	Billy Drago
Rooney	Joe Dallesandro
Tom	Rodney Harvey
Mr. Sheets	Robert Greenberg
Bill	Jeremy Davies
Chuck	Dan Eisenstein
Sally	James Oseland
Crazy Larry	Lawrence Steven Meyers
Clyde	Herb Weld
Susan	Lee Mary Weilnau
Sheriff	Dick Warlock
Elton	Tracey Walter

and Ida Lee (Parishioner), Willow Tipton (School Girl), Jaid Barrymore (Woman with dog), Roger Jackson (Joe), Sally Norvell (Waitress), Zane W. Levit (Ed Hopper), Leo Lee (Soda Pop), Rowena Guinness (Ruby the Prostitute), Harrison Young (Howard's Dad), Michael Franco (Officer Frank), Damon R. Jones (Damian), Thomas E. Weyer (Guard), Diana Firestone (News Reporter)

Plot Capsule: *Aimless teenager Anita Minteer hooks up with her pen-pal, a paroled prisoner named Howard, a teaming which results in a series of random killings. This movie had its U.S. premiere on Showtime cable tv in October, 1992.*

© Man Ray Associates

Drew Barrymore (also above),
James Le Gros

SNIPER

(TRISTAR) Producer, Robert L. Rosen; Executive Producers, Mark Johnson, Walon Green, Patrick Wachsberger; Co-Producers, James Gorman, Charles J.D. Schlissel; Director, Luis Llosa; Screenplay, Michael Frost Beckner, Crash Leyland; Photography, Bill Butler; Designer, Herbert Pinter; Costumes, Ray Summers; Editor, Scott Smith; Music, Gary Chang; Casting, Louis Di Giaimo; Dolby Stereo; Atlab color; Rated R; 98 minutes; January release

CAST

Sgt. Thomas Beckett	Tom Berenger
Richard Miller	Billy Zane
Chester Van Damme	J.T. Walsh
Doug Papich	Aden Young
El Cirujano	Ken Radley
Senior NSC Officer	Dale Dye
Junior NSC Officer	Richard Lineback
Alvarez	Frederick Miragliotta
Mrs. Alvarez	Vanessa Steele
Raul Ochoa	Carlos Alvarez
Ripoly	Tyler Copin
Ripoly's Friend	Teo Gebert
Mountain Top Pilot	William Curtin
Mountain Top Co-Pilot	Howard Bosse
Mountain Top Sniper	Christos A. Linou
Corporal in pool hall	Christopher Norsley
Shaved Head Private	Donald Battee

and Raj Sidhu (Soldier in barn), Reinaldo Arenas (Cacique), Mario Jurado (Dead Indian), Roy Edmonds (Cabrera), Collin Dragsbeck (Door Gunner), Johnny Raaen (Crew Chief), Patrick Moore (Co-Pilot), Loury Cortez (Father Ruiz), Tony Szeto (Boat Rebel)

Plot Capsule: *Military drama. Professional assassin Thomas Beckett, with National Security Council official Richard Miller in tow, goes on his latest assignment in the jungles of Panama to kill a politician planning a coup d'etat.*

© TriStar Pictures

Tom Berenger, Billy Zane

Olympia Dukakis, Ellen Burstyn, Diane Ladd

THE CEMETERY CLUB

(TOUCHSTONE) Producers, David Brown, Sophie Hurst, Bonnie Palef; Executive Producers, David Manson, Philip Rose, Howard Hurst; Director, Bill Duke; Screenplay, Ivan Menchell, based on his stage play; Photography, Steven Poster; Designer, Maher Ahmad; Costumes, Hilary Rosenfeld; Editor, John Carter; Music, Elmer Bernstein; Associate Producers, Cyrus Yavneh, Eva Fyer; Casting, Terry Liebling; Distributed by Buena Vista Pictures; Dolby Stereo; Technicolor; Rated PG-13; 106 minutes; February release

CAST

Esther Moskowitz	Ellen Burstyn
Doris Silverman	Olympia Dukakis
Lucille Rubin	Diane Ladd
Ben Katz	Danny Aiello
Selma	Lainie Kazan
Paul	Jeff Howell
Jessica	Christina Ricci
John	Bernie Casey
Abe Silverman	Alan Manson
Jake Rubin	Jerry Orbach
Murray Moskowitz	Lee Richardson
Irving Jacobs	Sam Schwartz
Rabbi	Stephen Pearlman
Photographer	Gene Ray
Mel	Allan Pinsker
Rene	Alice Eisner
Al	Hy Anzell
Caretaker	Robert Marinaccio
Man	Ben Tatar
Maitre'D	Glen Z. Gress
Bill	Roger Serbagi
Morty	Robert Costanzo
Larry	Wallace Shawn
Ed Bonfigliano	Louis Guss
Theresa	Irma St. Paule
Nita	Therese Courtney
Judge	Bingo O'Malley
Cantor	Emanuel Matthew Yavne
Customers	Brett James Kennedy, Kathryn Fisher
Detective	Sean E. Markland
Singer	Etta Cox

Plot Capsule: *Three middle-aged friends, all recently widowed, find their daily rituals threatened when one of them is courted by a widower. Menchell's play opened on Broadway in 1990 and starred Eileen Heckart, Elizabeth Franz and Doris Belack.*

© Buena Vista Pictures

Danny Aiello

Diane Ladd

Olympia Dukakis

Ellen Burstyn

HOMEWARD BOUND: THE INCREDIBLE JOURNEY

(WALT DISNEY PICTURES) Producers, Franklin R. Levy, Jeffrey Chernov; Executive Producers, Donald W. Ernst, Kirk Wise; Director, Duwayne Dunham; Screenplay, Caroline Thompson, Linda Woolverton; Based on the novel *The Incredible Journey* by Sheila Burnford; Photography, Reed Smoot; Designer, Roger Cain; Costumes, Karen Patch; Music, Bruce Broughton; Editor, Jonathan P. Shaw; Co-Producer, Mack Bing; Animal Coordinator, Joe Camp; Animal Provider/Trainer, Jungle Exotics; Head Dog Trainer, Gary "Sam" Vaughn; Head Cat Trainer, Tammy Maples; Casting, Susan Bluestein, Marsha Shoenman; Presented in association with Touchwood Pacific Partners I; Distributed by Buena Vista Pictures; Dolby Stereo; Technicolor; Rated G; 84 minutes; February release

CAST

Shadow	Ben
Chance	Rattler
Sassy	Tiki
Bob Burnford	Robert Hays
Laura Burnford	Kim Greist
Kate	Jean Smart
Hope	Veronica Lauren
Jamie	Kevin Chevalia
Peter	Benj Thall
Molly's Father	Don Alder
Desk Sergeant	Ed Bernard
Research Assistant	Anne Christianson
Vet	Ted D'Arms
Forest Ranger "Mark"	Woody Eney
Forest Rangers	Rich Hawkins, Kit McDonough
Caterer	Nurmi Husa
Molly's Mother	Jane Jones
Foote	David MacIntyre
Laura's Mother	Mary Marsh
Hal	Nick Mastrandrea
Minister	Glenn Mazen
Molly	Mariah Milner
Bob's Mother	Janet Penner
Quentin	William Edward Phipps
Peter's Teacher	Dorothy Roberts
Laura's Dad	Frank Roberts
Grace	Virginia Spray
Frank	Gary Taylor
Kirkwood	Mark L. Taylor
Jamie's Teacher	Peggy West
Special Vocal Effects	Frank Welker

Animal Voices Provided by

Chance	Michael J. Fox
Sassy	Sally Field
Shadow	Don Ameche

Plot Capsule: *A cat and two dogs, temporarily left by their vacationing owners with a friend, trek across the wilderness, encountering various wildlife adventures, determined to find their way home. Previous version,* The Incredible Journey, *was released by Disney in 1963.*

Rattler with Bear ABOVE: Tiki, Rattler, Ben

Robert Hays, Kevin Chevalia, Rattler

Benj Thall, Ben

Kathy Ireland, Emilio Estevez

Tim Curry Above: Samuel L, Jackson, Emilio Estevez

NATIONAL LAMPOON'S LOADED WEAPON 1

(NEW LINE CINEMA) Producers, Suzanne Todd, David Willis; Executive Producers, Michel Roy, Howard Klein, Erwin Stoff; Co-Executive Producer, Michael DeLuca; Director, Gene Quintano; Screenplay, Don Holley, Gene Quintano; Story, Don Holley, Tori Tellem; Photography, Peter Deming; Designer, Jaymes Hinkle; Editor, Christopher Greenbury; Costumes, Jacki Arthur; Casting, Ferne Cassel; Produced in association with 3 Arts Entertainment; Dolby Stereo; Film House color; Rated PG-13; 83 minutes; February release

CAST

Jack Colt	Emilio Estevez
Wes Luger	Samuel L. Jackson
Becker	Jon Lovitz
Jigsaw	Tim Curry
Destiny Demeanor	Kathy Ireland
Captain Doyle	Frank McRae
General Mortars	William Shatner
Translator	Dhiru Shah
Hindu	Gokul
Mini-Mart Punks	Tom Bruggeman, Danny Castle
Irv	Lance Kinsey
Police Photographer	Bill Nunn
Coroner	Dr. Joyce Brothers
Witness	Lin Shaye
Armanied Cop	Robert Willis
Tailor	Vito Scotti
Dooley	Ken Ober
Scotty	James Doohan
Police Psychiatrist	Lauren Abels
Prison Attendant	Richard Moll
Harold Leacher	F. Murray Abraham
Valet	Charlie Sheen
Mike McCracken	Denis Leary
Michael Castner	Michael Castner
Megaphone Cop	J.P. Hubbell
Young Cop	Corey Feldman
Comic Cop	Phil Hartman
Desk Clerk	J.T. Walsh
Themselves	Erik Estrada, Larry Wilcox
FBI Agent	Paul Gleason

and Denise Lee Richards, Mary Lynn Naggie, Suzie Hardy, Karman Kruschke (Cindys), Jake Johannsen (Drug Dealer), Mile Lajeunesse (Mr. Jerricho), Sherry Bilsing (Cookie Receptionist), Allyce Beasley (Spinach Destiny), Rick Ducommun (D.A.), Charles Napier, Charles Cyphers (Interrogators), Benjamin Kimball Smith (Kid on bike), Danielle Nicolet (Debbie Luger), Beverly Johnson (Doris Luger), Christopher Shobe (Ted Polansky), Marcus Lasha (Young Luger), Hank Cheyne, Al Watson (Stormtroopers), Whoopi Goldberg (Sgt. York), Bruce Willis (Man whose house is attacked)

Plot Capsule: *Spoof of buddy-cop movies, most specifically the* Lethal Weapon *series, involving drug smuggling and the Wilderness Cookie Girl murder case.*

Emilio Estevez, Samuel L. Jackson, Erik Estrada

SOMMERSBY

(WARNER BROS.) Producers, Arnon Milchan, Steven Reuther; Executive Producers, Richard Gere, Maggie Wilde; Co-Producer, Mary McLaglen; Director, Jon Amiel; Screenplay, Nicholas Meyer, Sarah Kernochan; Story, Nicholas Meyer, Anthony Shaffer; Based on the film *The Return of Martin Guerre*, written by Daniel Vigne and Jean-Claude Carriere; Photography, Philippe Rousselot; Designer, Bruno Rubeo; Costumes, Marilyn Vance-Straker; Editor, Peter Boyle; Music, Danny Elfman; Casting, Billy Hopkins, Suzanne Smith; a Le Studio Canal+, Regency Enterprises, and Alcor Films presentation; Dolby Stereo; Panavision; DuArt/Technicolor; Rated PG-13; 115 minutes; February release

CAST

Jack Sommersby	Richard Gere
Laurel Sommersby	Jodie Foster
Buck	Lanny Flaherty
Travis	Wendell Wellman
Orin Meecham	Bill Pullman
Little Rob	Brett Kelley
Reverend Powell	William Windom
Esther	Clarice Taylor
Joseph	Frankie Faison
Dick Mead	Ronald Lee Ermey
Doc Evans	Richard Hamilton
Mrs. Evans	Karen Krischenbauer
Storekeeper Wilson	Carter McNeese
Tom Clemmons	Dean Whitworth
John Green	Stan Kelly
Mrs. Bundy	Stephanie Weaver
Eli	Khaz B.
Boys	Josh McClerren, Mark Williams
Drifter # 1	Muse Watson
KKK#1/Folsom	Paul Austin
KKK	Frank Taylor, Billy Butch Frank, Dale Stewart
Marshalls	Jake Cress, Doug Sloan
Lawyer Webb	Ray McKinnon
Lawyer Dawson	Maury Chaykin
Judge Issacs	James Earl Jones
Court Bailiff	Stuart Fallen
Clerk	Barry McLerran
Timothy Fry	Richard Lineback
Night Clerk	Dr. Michael Gold
Witness	Joe Basham
Boarding House Manager	Patrick Morse
Auctioneer	Joe Neel
Official	Harry T. Daniel

Plot Capsule: *Drama, set after the Civil War, in which Jack Sommersby, long presumed dead, returns to his farm a changed man, causing his wife Laurel to wonder if this is indeed her husband. Remake of the French film* The Return of Martin Guerre *which starred Gerard Depardieu and Nathalie Baye and was released in the U.S. in 1983 by European International.*

© Regency Enterprises VOF/Le Studio Canal

Bill Pullman ABOVE: James Earl Jones   Jodie Foster, Richard Gere (and above and top)

Kiefer Sutherland, Jeff Bridges TOP RIGHT: Jeff Bridges, Nancy Travis

THE VANISHING

(20th CENTURY FOX) Producers, Larry Brezner, Paul Schiff; Executive Producers, Pieter Jan Brugge, Lauren Weissman; Director, George Sluizer; Co-Producer/Screenplay, Todd Graff; Based upon the novel *The Golden Egg* by Tim Krabbe; Photography, Peter Suschitzky; Designer, Jeannine C. Oppewall; Editor, Bruce Green; Music, Jerry Goldsmith; Costumes, Durinda Wood; Casting, Risa Bramon Garcia, Juel Bestrop; a Morra, Brezner, Steinberg & Tenenbaum production; Dolby Stereo; Deluxe color; Rated R; 110 minutes; February release

CAST

Barney Cousins	Jeff Bridges
Jeff Harriman	Kiefer Sutherland
Rita Baker	Nancy Travis
Diane Shaver	Sandra Bullock
Lynn	Park Overall
Denise Cousins	Maggie Linderman
Helene Cousins	Lisa Eichhorn
Arthur Bernard	George Hearn
Miss Carmichael	Lynn Hamilton
Cop at gas station	Garrett Bennett
Highway Cop	George Catalano
Cop at apartment	Frank Girardeau
TV Host	Stephen Wesley Bridgewater
Colleague	Susan Barnes
Stan	Rich Hawkins
DMV Clerk	Michael Kaufman
Cashier	Sabrena Roddy
Women on the street	Andrea Lauren Herz, Joanne Schmoll
Woman with barrette	Allison Barcott
Young Barney	Aeryk Egan
Pump Attendant	James Chesnutt
Little Girl	Danielle Zuckerman
Man in line	Floyd Van Buskirk
Cook	Marius Mazmanian
Woman in ladies room	Gina Gallante
Denise's Boyfriend	Michael John Hughes
DMV Guard	Howard Matthew Johnson
Waiter	Kristopher Logan

Plot Capsule: *After his girlfriend mysteriously disappears from a road stop Jeff Harriman spends years absorbed in her whereabouts, while her kidnapper, an odd school teacher named Barney, decides to make Jeff aware of his involvement in the crime. Remake of the Dutch thriller* Spoorless *(released in the U.S. in 1990 as* The Vanishing*) which was also directed by George Sluizer.*

Sandra Bullock, Jeff Bridges ABOVE: Jeff Bridges

Andie MacDowell, Bill Murray

Stephen Tobolowsky, Bill Murray ABOVE: Bill Murray

Andie MacDowell, Chris Elliott, Bill Murray

GROUNDHOG DAY

(COLUMBIA) Producers, Trevor Albert, Harold Ramis; Executive Producer, C.O. Erickson; Director, Harold Ramis; Screenplay, Danny Rubin, Harold Ramis; Story, Danny Rubin; Photography, John Bailey; Designer, David Nichols; Costumes, Jennifer Butler; Editor, Pembroke J. Herring; Music, George Fenton; Casting, Howard Feuer; Dolby Stereo; Technicolor; Rated PG; 104 minutes; February release

CAST

Phil Connors	Bill Murray
Rita Hanson	Andie MacDowell
Larry	Chris Elliott
Ned Ryerson	Stephen Tobolowsky
Buster Greene	Brian Doyle-Murray
Nancy Taylor	Marita Geraghty
Mrs. Lancaster	Angela Paton
Gus	Rick Ducommun
Ralph	Rick Overton
Doris the Waitress	Robin Duke
Anchorwoman	Carol Bivins
Phil's Assistant Kenny	Willie Garson
Man in hallway	Ken Hudson Campbell
Old Man	Les Podewell
Groundhog Official	Rod Sell
State Trooper	Tom Milanovich
Bartender	John Watson, Sr.
Piano Teacher	Peggy Roeder
Neurologist	Harold Ramis
Psychiatrist	David Pasquesi
Cop	Lee R. Sellars
Bank Guard Felix	Chet Dubowski
Bank Guard Herman	Doc Erickson
Phil's Movie Date	Sandy Maschmeyer
Fan on street	Leighanne O'Neil
Debbie	Hynden Walsh
Fred	Michael Shannon

and Evangeline Binkley, Samuel Mages, Ben Zwick ("Jeopardy!" Viewers), Timothy Hendrickson (Waiter Bill), Martha Webster (Waitress Alice), Angela Gollan (Piano Student), Shaun Chaiyabhat (Boy in tree), Dianne B. Shaw (E.R. Nurse), Barbara Ann Grimes, Ann Heekin, Lucina Paquet (Flat Tire Ladies), Brenda Pickleman (Buster's Wife), Amy Murdoch (Buster's Daughter), Eric Saiet (Buster's Son), Lindsay Reinsch (Woman with cigarette), Roger Adler (Guitar Player), Ben A. Fish (Bass Player), Don Rio McNichols (Drum Player), Brian Willig (Saxophone Player), Richard Henzel, Rob Riley (D.J. Voices), Scooter (The Groundhog).

Plot Capsule: *Comedy-fantasy in which Phil Connors, a cynical weatherman, finds himself forced to relive the same day, February 2nd, over and over again in the town of Punxsatawney, Pennsylvania.*

Bill Murray, Scooter ABOVE: Bill Murray

Marisa Tomei, Rosie Perez

TOP LEFT: Christian Slater, Marisa Tomei

UNTAMED HEART

(MGM) formerly *The Baboon Heart*; Producers, Tony Bill, Helen Buck Bartlett; Executive Producer, J. Boyce Harman, Jr.; Director, Tony Bill; Screenplay, Tom Sierchio; Photography, Jost Vacano; Designer, Steven Jordan; Editor, Mia Goldman; Music, Cliff Eidelman; Costumes, Lynn Bernay; Associate Producers, Tom Sierchio, Marci Liroff; Casting, Marci Liroff; Dolby Stereo; Deluxe color; Rated PG-13; 102 minutes; February release

CAST

Adam	Christian Slater
Caroline	Marisa Tomei
Cindy	Rosie Perez
Howard	Kyle Secor
Patsy	Willie Garson
Bill #1	James Cada
Bill #2	Gary Groomes
Mother Camilla	Claudia Wilkens
Sister Helen	Pat Clemons
Nuns	Lotis Key, Vanessa Hart
Young Adam	Charley Bartlett
Orphan Boy	Vincent Kartheiser
Orphanage Nurse	Wendy Feder
Caroline's Mom	Nancy Marvy
Steven	Paul Douglas Law
Michael	Josh Schaefer
Mary	Marquetta Senters
Jim	Joe Minjares
Sportscaster	Joe Schmit
Cook	John Beasley
Stromboli	Steve Cochran
Tree Customer	Sally Wingert
Caroline's Father	Richard Grusin
Lottie	Buffy Sedlachek
Ronnie	Tom Sierchio
Nick	Aaron Kjenaas
Police Officer	Isabell Monk
Doctor	Allen Hamilton
Beauty Shop Customer	Kay Bonner Nee
Beauty School Instructor	Lia Rivamonte
Kevin	Greg Sain
Girl in car	Margaret McGraw
Priest	John Paul Gamoke

Plot Capsule: *Caroline, a waitress with bad luck in men, finds herself being attracted to Adam, the strange, shy busboy at the Minneapolis restaurant where they both work.*

Christian Slater ABOVE: Rosie Perez, Christian Slater, Marisa Tomei

THE TEMP

(PARAMOUNT) Producers, David Permut, Tom Engelman; Executive Producer, Howard W. Koch Jr.; Director, Tom Holland; Screenplay, Kevin Falls; Story, Kevin Falls, Tom Engelman; Photography, Steve Yaconelli; Designer, Joel Schiller; Editor, Scott Conrad; Music, Frederic Talgorn; Costumes, Tom Rand; Casting, Elisabeth Leustig, Judith Holstra; Dolby Stereo; Deluxe color; Rated R; 98 minutes; February release

CAST

Peter Derns	Timothy Hutton
Kris Bolin	Lara Flynn Boyle
Roger Jasser	Dwight Schultz
Jack Hartsell	Oliver Platt
Brad Montroe	Steven Weber
Sara Meinhold	Colleen Flynn
Charlene Towne	Faye Dunaway
Lance	Scott Coffey
Dr. Feldman	Dakin Matthews
Sharon Derns	Maura Tierney
Rosemary	Lin Shaye
Mercer	Michael Winters
Nathan Derns	Danny Swanson
Marla Higgins	Demene E. Hall
Larry	Jesse Vint

and Gary Rooney (Bouncer), Bill Johns (Waiter), Don Alder (Office Security Guard), Betsy Toll (Test Lady), Mary Marsh (Shopper), J.W. Crawford (Researcher), Billy Koch (Juice Bartender), Ralph Vanhollebeke (Mr. Henderson), Moultrie Patten (Walt), William Earl Ray (Man in bar), Josh Holland (Gary), Russ Fast (Cop), Shanti Kahn, Elizabeth Richard (Redmont Secretaries), Ralph Archenhold (Samaritan), Glenn Mazen (Minister), Adrian Latourelle (Intern), Lars Wanberg (Lobby Security Guard), Betty Moyer (Receptionist), Rob LaBelle (Bill Lives), Kirk Nieland (Steele), John Raymond Brannen (New Lobby Security Guard), Mary Starrett, Jim Bosley (TV Newscasters)

Plot Capsule: *Junior executive Peter Derns hires mysterious Kris Bolin as his assistant, not realizing she may have a deadly plan for climbing the corporate ladder.*

© Paramount Pictures

Lara Flynn Boyle, Timothy Hutton
ABOVE: Faye Dunaway, Timothy Hutton

MAC

(SAMUEL GOLDWYN CO.) Producers, Nancy Tenenbaum, Brenda Goodman; Director, John Turturro; Screenplay, John Turturro, Brandon Cole; Photography, Ron Fortunato; Designer, Robin Standefer; Editor, Michael Berenbaum; Costumes, Donna Zakowska; Music, Richard Termini, Vin Tese; Casting, Todd Thaler; a Mac Films production; Dolby Stereo; Technicolor; Rated R; 117 minutes; February release

CAST

Mac Vitelli	John Turturro
Vico Vitelli	Michael Badalucco
Bruno Vitelli	Carl Capotorto
Alice Vitelli	Katherine Borowitz
Nat	John Amos
Polowski	Olek Krupa
Oona	Ellen Barkin
Gus	Steven Randazzo
Clarence	Matthew Sussman
Tony Gloves	Nicholas Turturro
Papa	Joe Paparone
Mr. Stunder	Dennis Farina
Mrs. Stunder	Kaiulani Lee
Francis	Richard Spore

and James Madio (Young Mac), Stephi Lineburg (Young Alice), Herbert E. Weitz (Auctioneer), Stretch "Raul Merced" (Joe Brown), Mike Starr (Fireman), Michael Glynn (Bricklayer #1), Harry Bugin (Patient), Angelo Florio (Paulie Bay), Anthony Alessandro (Young Bricklayer), Sandor Tecsy (Fat Joey), Kent Broadhurst (Mr. Tabin), Abe Altman (Mr. Deutscher), Joseph Marino (Joe the Plumber), Jayne Haynes (Bum), Ruth Maleczech (Burgess), Shirley Stoler (Customer), Doris Gramovot (Cook), Katherine Turturro (Gus' Mom), Robert Proscia (Wounded Man), Jeff Braun (Husband), Aida Turturro (Wife), Amedeo Turturro (Child), Patrick Pisano (Young Vico), Anthony Capotorto (Young Bruno), Efren Andaluz (Mac's Son), Judith Roberts (Woman on the bus), Mario Todisco (Joe the Mule), Jared Matesky (Junkman), Jason Dunchin (Mental Patient), Morton Tenenbaum (Mr. Deutscher's Friend)

Plot Capsule: *In 1950's Queens Mac Vitelli quits his construction job to start his own company, setting out to prove that he can build better houses than his ex-boss. Directorial debut of actor John Turturro. Katharine Borowitz is Turturro's real-life wife.*

© Samuel Goldwyn Company

Michael Badalucco, John Turturro
ABOVE: Michael Badalucco, Carl Capotorto, John Turturro

Bruce Campbell, Embeth Davidtz BELPW: The Deadites

ARMY OF DARKNESS

(UNIVERSAL) Producer, Robert Tapert; Co-Producers, Bruce Campbell, Introvision International, Inc.; Director, Sam Raimi; Screenplay, Sam Raimi, Ivan Raimi; Photography, Bill Pope; Designer, Tony Tremblay; Editors, Bob Murawski, R.O.C. Sandstorm; Music, Joseph LoDuca, Danny Elfman; Visual Effects, Introvision International, Inc., William Mesa; Special Makeup Effects, Kurtzman, Nicotero & Berger EFX Group; Ash & Sheila Makeup Effects, Tony Gardner, Alterian Studios Inc.; Casting, Ira Belgrade; a Dino De Laurentiis Communications presentation of a Renaissance Pictures production; Dolby Stereo; Deluxe color; Rated R; 77 minutes; February release

CAST

Ash/Evil Ash	Bruce Campbell
Sheila/Evil Sheila	Embeth Davidtz
Arthur	Marcus Gilbert
Wiseman	Ian Abercrombie
Duke Henry	Richard Grove
Gold Tooth	Michael Earl Reid
Blacksmith	Timothy Patrick Quill
Linda	Bridget Fonda
Possessed Witch	Patricia Tallman
Cowardly Warrior	Theodore Raimi
Tiny Ash #1	Deke Anderson
Tiny Ash #2	Bruce Thomas
Old Woman	Sara Shearer
Pit Deadites	Shiva Gordon, Billy Bryan
Winged Deadite	Nadine Grycan
Deadite Captain	Bill Moseley
Henry's Man	Micheal Kenney
Lieutenants	Andy Bale, Robert Brent Lappin
Tower Guard	Rad Milo
Chief Archer	Brad Bradbury

Plot Capsule: *Ash, with chainsaw and Oldsmobile, is plunked down in the Middle Ages with the mission of finding a sacred book and doing battle with the evil dead. Third installment in the horror series following* The Evil Dead *(New Line Cinema, 1983) and* Evil Dead II *(Rosebud Releasing, 1987) both of which starred Bruce Campbell and were directed by Sam Raimi.*

© Universal City Studios Inc.

EL MARIACHI

(COLUMBIA) Producers/Screenplay, Robert Rodriguez, Carlos Gallardo; Director/Story/Photography/Editor/Sound, Robert Rodriguez; a Los Hooligans production; U.S./Spanish language; Dolby Stereo; Technicolor; Rated R; 82 minutes; February release

CAST

El Mariachi	Carlos Gallardo
Domino	Consuelo Gomez
Azul	Reinol Martinez
Moco	Peter Marquart
El Nino	Oscar Fabila

Plot Capsule: *Action-comedy. In a small Mexican border town an innocent mariachi singer is mistaken for a dangerous killer named Azul, both of them being in possession of identical guitar cases.*

This film received a special award from the NY Film Critics.

© Columbia Pictures Industries

Peter Marquart ABOVE: Carlos Gallardo

Barbara Hershey, Joey Hope
Singer, Robert Duvall

Michael Douglas,
Barbara Hershey

FALLING DOWN

(WARNER BROS.) Producers, Arnold Kopelson, Herschel Weingrod, Timothy Harris; Executive Producer, Arnon Milchan; Director, Joel Schumacher; Screenplay, Ebbe Roe Smith; Photography, Andrzej Bartkowiak; Designer, Barbara Ling; Editor, Paul Hirsch; Co-Producer, Dan Kolsrud, Stephen Brown, Nana Greenwald; Music, James Newton Howard; Costumes, Marlene Stewart; Casting, Marion Dougherty; Associate Producers, William S. Beasley, Ebbe Roe Smith, John J. Tomko; Presented in association with Le Studio Canal+, Regency Enterprises and Alcor Films; Dolby Stereo; Panavision; Technicolor; Rated R; 115 minutes; February release

CAST

D-Fens	Michael Douglas
Det. Martin Prendergast	Robert Duvall
Beth	Barbara Hershey
Sandra	Rachel Ticotin
Mrs. Prendergast	Tuesday Weld
Surplus Store Owner	Frederic Forrest
D-Fens' Mother	Lois Smith
Adele (Beth's Child)	Joey Hope Singer
Guy on freeway	Ebbe Roe Smith
Mr. Lee	Michael Paul Chan
Captain Yardley	Raymond J. Barry
Detective Lydecker	D.W. Moffett
Detective Brian	Steve Park
Detective Jones	Kimberly Scott
Detective Keene	James Keane
Detective Graham	Macon McCalman
Detective Sanchez	Richard Montoya
Police Clerk	Bruce Beatty
Officer at station	Mathew Saks
Gang Members	Agustin Rodriguez, Eddie Frias, Pat Romano, Fabio Urena
Angie	Karina Arroyave
Angie's Mother	Irene Olga Lopez
Uniformed Officer at Beth's	Benjamin Mouton
Uniformed Officer's Partner	Dean Hallo

and James Morrison (Construction Sign Man by bus stop), John Fleck (Seedy Guy in park), Brent Hinkley (Rick - Whammyburger), Dedee Pfeiffer (Sheila — Whammyburger), Carol Androsky (Woman who throws up at Whammyburger), Margaret Medina (Lita the Waitress), Vondie Curtis-Hall (Not Economically Viable Man), Mark Frank (Annoying Man at phone booth), Peter Radon, Spencer Rochfort (Gay Men), Carole Ita White (2nd Officer at Beth's), Russell Curry (2nd Officer's Partner), John Fink (Guy behind Woman Driver), Jack Kehoe (Street Worker), Valentino D. Harrison (Kid with missile launcher), Jack Betts (Frank - Golfer), Al Mancini (Jim - Golfer), John Diehl (Dad at back yard party), Amy Morton (Mom at back yard party), Abbey Barthel (Trina at back yard party), Susie Singer (Suzie the Stripper), Wayne Duvall (Paramedic), Valisha Jean Malin (Prendergast's Daughter)

Plot Capsule: *A seemingly mild-mannered businessman leaves his car in the middle of a Los Angeles traffic jam and goes on a rampage of destruction throughout the hostile environment of the city.*

Michael Douglas

ABOVE: Rachel Ticotin

© Warner Bros.

Michael Douglas

ABOVE: Frederic Forrest

Albert Finney, Jill Clayburgh TOP RIGHT: Kathryn Erbe, Ethan Hawke

RICH IN LOVE

(MGM) Producers, Richard D. Zanuck, Lili Fini Zanuck; Co-Producers, David Brown, Gary Daigler; Director, Bruce Beresford; Screenplay, Alfred Uhry; Based on the novel by Josephine Humphreys; Photography, Peter James; Designer, John Stoddart; Costumes, Colleen Kelsall; Editor, Mark Warner; Music, Georges Delerue; Casting, Shari Rhodes; a Zanuck Company production; Dolby Stereo; Deluxe color; Rated PG-13; 105 minutes; March release

CAST

Warren Odom	Albert Finney
Helen Odom	Jill Clayburgh
Lucille Odom	Kathryn Erbe
Billy McQueen	Kyle MacLachlan
Vera Delmage	Piper Laurie
Wayne Frobiness	Ethan Hawke
Rae Odom	Suzy Amis
Rhody Poole	Alfre Woodard
Tick	J. Leon Pridgen II
Parnell Meade	David Hager
Sharon	Ramona Ward
Sam Poole	Wayne Dehart
Inn Receptionist	D.L. Anderson
Bookstore Clerk	Janell McLeod
Horse Carriage Driver	Jennifer Banco
Singer	Anthony Burke
Terry	Terry Park
Laura Migo	Stephanie Legette

Plot Capsule: *Comedy-drama, set in South Carolina. When Helen Odom walks out on her husband of 27 years her teenage daughter Lucille tries to hold the remaining family together.*

Alfre Woodard, Kyle MacLachlan

Kathryn Erbe, Suzy Amis ABOVE: Kyle MacLachlan, Suzy Amis

AMOS & ANDREW

(COLUMBIA) Producer, Gary Goetzman; Co-Producers, Jack Cummins, Marshall Persinger; Director/Screenplay, E. Max Frye; Photography, Walt Lloyd; Designer/Costumes, Patricia Norris; Music, Richard Gibbs; Editor, Jane Kurson; a Castle Rock Entertainment in association with New Line Cinema presentation; Dolby Stereo; Technicolor; Rated PG-13; 94 minutes; March release

CAST

Amos Odell	Nicolas Cage
Andrew Sterling	Samuel L. Jackson
Phil Gillman	Michael Lerner
Judy Gillman	Margaret Colin
Chief of Police Cecil Tolliver	Dabney Coleman
Officer Donnie Donaldson	Brad Dourif
Earl	Chelcie Ross
Waldo Lake	I.M. Hobson
Ernie	Jeff Blumenkrantz
Stan	Todd Weeks
Riley	Jordan Lund
Wendy Wong	Jodi Long
Reporters	Michael Burgess, Leonor Anthony
Anchorman	Walter Raymond
The Reverend Fenton Brunch	Giancarlo Esposito
Ula	Loretta Devine
Dr. R.A. "Roy" Fink	Bob Balaban
Sherman	Ron Taylor
Stacy	Aimee Graham
State Police Captain	Ernie Garrett
Bloodhound Bob	Tracey Walter
Anchorwoman	Allison Mackie
Mainland Gatekeeper	Eric Paisley
Mrs. Andrew Sterling	Kim Staunton

Plot Capsule: *Satirical comedy. When black author Andrew Sterling is mistaken for a burglar in his own home the town's police officer tries to cover-up any racist implications by asking white criminal Amos Odell to pose as Sterling's kidnapper.*

Michael Lerner, Margaret Colin
ABOVE: Samuel L. Jackson, Nicolas Cage

Giancarlo EspositoTOP: Dabney Coleman, Brad Dourif

SWING KIDS

(HOLLYWOOD PICTURES) Producers, Mark Gordon, John Bard Manulis; Executive Producers, Frank Marshall, Christopher Meledandri; Co-Producer, Harry Benn; Director, Thomas Carter; Screenplay, Jonathan Marc Feldman; Photography, Jerzy Zielinski; Designer, Allan Cameron; Editor, Michael R. Miller; Music, James Horner; Choreographer, Otis Sallid; Costumes, Jenny Beavan; Casting, Deborah Aquila; Presented in association with Touchwood Pacific Partners I; Distributed by Buena Vista Pictures; Dolby Stereo; Technicolor; Rated PG-13; 113 minutes; March release

CAST

Peter Muller	Robert Sean Leonard
Thomas Berger	Christian Bale
Arvid	Frank Whaley
Frau Muller	Barbara Hershey
Major Knopp	Kenneth Branagh
Evey	Tushka Bergen
Willi Muller	David Tom
Frau Linge	Julia Stemberger
Otto	Jayce Bartok
Emil	Noah Wyle
Herr Schumler	Johan Leysen
Hinz	Douglas Roberts
Bannfuhrer	Martin Clunes
Helga	Jessica Stevenson
HJ Thug	Carl Brincat
Mama Klara	Mary Fogarty
Bismarck Owner	Karel Belohradsky
Bismarck Bandleader	Peter Baikie
Swing Girl with Thomas	Jennifer Chamberlain
Swing Girl with Peter	Lucie Vackarova
Evey's School Friends	Katerina Dankova, Magdalena Chrzova
Jewish Boy	Jiri Malek

and Metin Yenal (Customer in bookshop), Arthur White (Alberti), Marek Libert (Whistling HJ), Nada Konvalinkova (Pastry Shop Woman), Petr Jakl (Policeman in marketplace), David Robb (Dr. Berger), Ciaran Madden (Frau Berger), John Streitburger (Dr. Keppler), Hana Cizkova (Frau Keppler), Petr Lepsa (Cafe Trichter Owner), Warnar Van Eeden (Trichter Bandleader), Andrew Kitchen (Gestapo at Trichter), Jeremy Bulloch (Small Club Owner), Joseph Bennett, Roman Janousek (Luftwaffe Pilots), Richard Hanson (HJ Fink), Sean Pertwee (Gestapo Arresting Berger), Sarka Horcikova (Berger's Maid), Jochen Horst (Speaker at HJ Rally), Vladimir Matejcek (Funeral Pastor), John Duval (Gestapo with ashes), Marie Vorlova (First Woman with ashes), Eliza Clark (Girl with ashes), Kate Buffery (Woman with ashes), Sabine Skala (Cafe Bismarck Singer), Billy Burke, Sven Daum, Gregory Garrison, Ulf Garrizmann, Ideal Getinkaya, Ines Goritz, Bettina Heyroth, Dita Kalibova, Dana Kopacova, Britta Krause, Ivan Landa, Tomas Mesner, Anna Montanaro, Cathy Murdoch, Vaclav Muska, Melinda O'Connor, Julie Oram, Tessa Pattani, Lenka Pesatova, Simon Shelton, Tini Stoll, Pavel Svoboda, Freya Tampert, Klara Vejvodova (Featured Dancers)

Plot Capsule: *German teenagers Peter and Thomas, fans of American swing music, find themselves being forced to join the Hitler youth movement, little realizing their country's oncoming danger and the slow disintegration of their freedom.*
© Hollywood Pictures Company

Christian Bale, Robert Sean Leonard (and above)

Robert Sean Leonard, Tushka Bergen

Christian Bale, Robert Sean Leonard, Frank Whaley, Jayce Bartok

Robert Sean Leonard, Christian Bale

Robert Sean Leonard, Kenneth Branagh

Robert Sean Leonard, Barbara Hershey, David Tom

Christian Bale, Lucie Vackarova ABOVE: Christian Bale,
Frank Whaley, Robert Sean Leonard, Jayce Bartok

Bill Murray TOP RIGHT: Uma Thurman, Robert De Niro

MAD DOG AND GLORY

(UNIVERSAL) Producers, Barbara De Fina, Martin Scorsese; Executive Producer/Screenplay, Richard Price; Director, John McNaughton; Photography, Robby Muller; Editors, Craig McKay, Elena Maganini; Music, Elmer Bernstein; Designer, David Chapman; Costumes, Rita Ryack; Co-Producer, Steven A. Jones; Casting, Todd Thaler; Dolby Stereo; Technicolor; Rated R; 96 minutes; March release

CAST

Wayne "Mad Dog" Dobie	Robert De Niro
Glory	Uma Thurman
Frank Milo	Bill Murray
Mike	David Caruso
Harold	Mike Starr
Andrew	Tom Towles
Lee	Kathy Baker
Shooter	Derek Anunciation
Driver	Doug Hara
Dealer in car	Evan Lionel
Pavletz	Anthony Cannata
Shanlon	J.J. Johnston
Cop	Guy Van Swearingen
Tommy	Jack Wallace
M.C./Comic	Richard Belzer
Guy at table	Clem Caserta
Frank's Gang	Fred Squillo, Chuck Parello
Detectives at crime scene	Tony Fitzpatrick, Eric Young, Bruce Jarchow
Uniform Cop	Bob Rice
Dealers in the park	William King, Kevin Hurley
Detective in restaurant	Richard Price
Dispatcher	John J. Polce
Saul	Dick Sollenberger
Irene	Paula Killen
Big John	Eddie "Bo" Smith

Plot Capsule: *Comedy-drama. After saving the life of gangster Frank Milo, mousey criminal photographer Wayne "Mad Dog" Dobie is presented with Frank's girlfriend, Glory, as a "gift."*

© Universal City Studios Inc.

Uma Thurman, Robert De Niro
ABOVE: Bill Murray, Robert De Niro

FIRE IN THE SKY

(PARAMOUNT) Producers, Joe Wizan, Todd Black; Executive Producer, Wolfgang Glattes; Co-Producers, Tracy Torme, Robert Strauss, Nilo Rodis-Jamero; Director, Robert Lieberman; Screenplay, Tracy Torme; Based upon the book *The Walton Experience* by Travis Walton; Photography, Bill Pope; Designer, Laurence Bennett; Editor, Steve Mirkovich; Costumes, Joe I. Tompkins; Music, Mark Isham; Casting, Rick Pagano, Sharon Bialy, Debi Manwiller; Alien Sequence Designer/Visual Effects Supervisor, Michael Owens, Industrial Light & Magic; Dolby Stereo; Panavision; Deluxe color; Rated PG-13; 108 minutes; March release

CAST

Travis Walton	D.B. Sweeney
Mike Rogers	Robert Patrick
Allan Dallis	Craig Sheffer
David Whitlock	Peter Berg
Greg Hayes	Henry Thomas
Bobby Cogdill	Bradley Gregg
Blake Davis	Noble Willingham
Katie Rogers	Kathleen Wilhoite
Frank Watters	James Garner
Dana Rogers	Georgia Emelin
Dan Walton	Scott MacDonald
Cyrus Gilson	Wayne Grace
Buck	Kenneth White
Ray Melendez	Robert Covarrubias
Dennis Clay	Bruce Wright
Ellis	Robert Biheller
Dr. Wilson	Tom McGranahan, Sr.
Dr. Cayle	Julie Ariola
Ramon	Peter Mark Vasquez
George	Gordon Scott
Mary Rogers	Mical Shannon Lewis
Emily Rogers	Courtney Esler
Cathy	Holly Hoffman
Nurse	Marcia MacLaine
Geiger Counter Man	Glen Lee
Bill Grant	Vernon Barkhurst
Citizens	Jerry Basham, Teresa Fox, Travis Walton
Anchorwoman	Susan Castillo
Lurae Jenkins	Jane Ferguson
Cathy's Mom	Nancy Neifert
Jarvis Powell	Charley Lang
Ida	Lynne Marie Sager

and Mari Padron (Thelma), John Breedlove (Balding Man), Frank Chavez (Orlando), Louis A. Lotorto, Jr. (Paramedic), Ronald Lee Marriott (Digger), Shinichi Mine (Japanese Reporter), Scott M. Seekins (Emergency Room Doctor), Eric Wilsey (Claude)

Plot Capsule: *A group of lumberjacks is accused of murdering their friend Travis Walton, whom they all insist was abducted by an alien vehicle. This sci-fi drama is based on a true incident which occured in 1975 in Northeastern Arizona.*

Craig Sheffer   Henry Thomas   Robert Patrick ABOVE: D.B. Sweeney
TOP: James Garner

CB4

(UNIVERSAL) Producer, Nelson George; Executive Producers, Sean Daniel, Brian Grazer; Co-Producers, William Fay, Chris Rock; Director, Tamra Davis; Screenplay, Chris Rock, Nelson George, Robert Locash; Story, Chris Rock, Nelson George; Photography, Karl Walter Lindenlaub; Designer, Nelson Coates; Editor, Earl Watson; Music Supervisor, Bill Stephney; Music, John Barnes; Casting, Kimberly Hardin; Dolby Stereo; Deluxe color; Rated R; 86 minutes; March release

CAST

Albert Brown/MC Gusto	Chris Rock
Euripides Smalls/Dead Mike	Allen Payne
Otis O. Otis/Stab Master Arson	Deezer D
A. White	Chris Elliott
Virgil Robinson	Phil Hartman
Gusto	Charlie Murphy
Sissy	Khandi Alexander
Albert Sr.	Arthur Evans
Eve	Theresa Randle
Trustus	Willard E. Pugh
40 Dog	Tyrone Granderson Jones
Daliha	Rachel True
Lt. Davenport	Victor Wilson
Baa Baa Ack	Richard Gant
Ben	J.D. Daniels
Wacky Dee	Stoney Jackson
Grandma	La Wanda Page

and Louisa Abernathy (Mrs. Otis), Sharisse Jackson (Tamika), Daphne Jones (Tashana), Saba Shawel (Tawana), Vanessa Lee Chester (Talona), Chasiti Hampton (Tee Tee), Wayne Ward (Biscuit Diner), John Walcutt (Director), Jeremiah Birkett (Malik), Christopher Keene (Accountant), Lance Crouther (Well Dressed Man), Shirley Hemphill (976-Sexy), Mari J. Sahley (976-Piss), Al Clegg (976-Diss), Laverne Anderson, Sonee Thompson (Video Set Dancers), Gerard G. Williams, Melvin Jones (Inmates), Cathy Giannone, Bill Haller, Kenneth Menard, Loretta Jean Crudup (Diners), Mary Oedy (Sun), Robin Tasha Ford (Shine), Renee Tenison, Rosie Tenison (Twins), Niketa Calame (Albertina), Jedda Jones (Waitress), Ice T, Ice Cube, Halle Berry, Flavor Flav, Eazy E, Shaquille O'Neal (Themselves)

(Plot Capsule) *Comedy. Three middle-class friends pass themselves off as a streetwise, cutting edge rap group called CB4 (Cell Block 4).*

TOP LEFT: Chris Rock, Deezer D, Allen Payne   © Universal City Studios Inc.

ETHAN FROME

(MIRAMAX) Producer, Stan Wlodkowski; Executive Producers, Lindsay Law, Richard Price; Director, John Madden; Screenplay, Richard Nelson; Based on the novel by Edith Wharton; Photography, Bobby Bukowski; Designer, Andrew Jackness; Editor, Katherine Wenning; Music, Rachel Portman; Costumes, Carol Oditz; Casting, Billy Hopkins, Suzanne Smith; an American Playhouse Theatrical Films presentation, produced in association with Richard Price/BBC Films; Dolby Stereo; DuArt Color; Rated PG; 99 minutes; March release

CAST

Ethan Frome	Liam Neeson
Zeena Frome	Joan Allen
Mattie Silver	Patricia Arquette
Reverend Smith	Tate Donovan
Mrs. Hale	Katharine Houghton
Ned Hale	Stephen Mendillo
Denis Eady	Jay Goede
Jotham	George Woodard
Young Ruth Hale	Debbon Ayer
Young Ned Hale	Ron Campbell
Gow	Burt Porter
Mr. Varnum	Robert Nutt
Mrs. Varnum	Louise DeCormier
Mrs. Homan	Patty Smith

and Tom Todoroff (Conductor 1910), Rusty De Wees, Paul Donlon (Men), Darri Johnson (Customer), William Graves (Denis Eady's Father), Phil Garran (Mr. Howe), Virginia Smith (Mrs. Howe), Marcie Vaughan (1st Young Woman), Joanne Rathgeb (1st Mother), Deborah Bremer (Funeral Woman), W. Clark Noyes (Funeral Man), Howard Boardman (Funeral Guest), Gil Rood (Conductor 1885), Dennis Mientka (Ned Hale's Father), Edsel Hughes (Ruth's Father, 1880's), David Dellinger (Minister), Kristin Collins, Annie C.Z. Nesson, Sarah Yorra (Hale Party)

Plot Capsule: *In turn of the century, snowbound New England Ethan Frome finds himself falling in love with the cousin of his domineering, bedridden wife.*

© Miramax Films

Liam Neeson, Patricia Arquette (and above)

A FAR OFF PLACE

(WALT DISNEY PICTURES) Producers, Eva Monley, Elaine Sperber; Executive Producers, Kathleen Kennedy, Frank Marshall, Gerald R. Molen; Director, Mikael Salomon; Screenplay, Robert Caswell, Jonathan Hensleigh, Sally Robinson; Based on the books *A Story Like the Wind* and *A Far Off Place* by Laurens van der Post; Photography, Juan Ruiz Anchia; Designer, Gemma Jackson; Editor, Ray Lovejoy; Music, James Horner; Costumes, Rosemary Burrows; Distributed by Buena Vista Pictures; an Amblin Entertainment co-presentation, presented in association with Touchwood Pacific Partners I; Dolby Stereo; Widescreen; Technicolor; Rated PG; 107 minutes; March release

CAST

Nonnie Parker	Reese Witherspoon
Harry Winslow	Ethan Randall
John Ricketts	Jack Thompson
Xhabbo	Sarel Bok
Paul Parker	Robert Burke
Elizabeth Parker	Patricia Kalember
John Winslow	Daniel Gerroll
Col. Mopani Theron	Maximilian Schell
Jardin	Miles Anderson
Tracker	Fidelis Cheza
Warden Robert	Taffy Chihota
Doctor	Anthony Chinyanga
Store Keeper	Brian Cooper
Nuin-Tara	Magdalene Damas
Bamuthi	John Indi
Children on sand dune	Sebastian Klein, Kessia Randall
Poacher	Isaac Mabikwa
Koba	Bertha Msora
Carfax	Japan Mthembu
Mr. Tang	Charles Pillai
Warden Gerald	Andrew Whaley
Matabele Dancers	King George Ziki Moyo Group

Plot Capsule: *Their parents slaughtered by poachers, two American teenagers enlist the aid of a friendly Bushman named Xhabbo to lead them across the African desert to safety. This adventure-drama marked the directorial debut of cinematographer Mikael Salomon.*

© The Walt Disney Co./Amblin Entertainment

Top Left: Maximilian Schell, Sarel Bok, Ethan Randall, Reese Witherspoon
LEFT: Ethan Randall, Sarel Bok, Reese Witherspoon

Reese Witherspoon,
Ethan Randall, Sarel Bok

Sarel Bok, Reese Witherspoon, Ethan Randall

Gabriel Byrne, Bridget Fonda

POINT OF NO RETURN

(WARNER BROS.) Producer, Art Linson; Co-Producer, James Herbert; Director, John Badham; Screenplay, Robert Getchell, Alexandra Seros; Based on Luc Besson's film *Nikita*; Photography, Michael Watkins; Designer, Philip Harrison; Music, Hans Zimmer; Editor, Frank Morriss; Associate Producers, D.J. Caruso, David Sosna; Costumes, Marlene Stewart; Casting, Bonnie Timmermann; Dolby Stereo; Panavision; Technicolor; Rated R; 109 minutes; March release

Bridget Fonda

CAST

Maggie	Bridget Fonda
Bob	Gabriel Byrne
J.P.	Dermot Mulroney
Kaufman	Miguel Ferrer
Amanda	Anne Bancroft
Angela	Olivia D'Abo
Fahd Bahktiar	Richard Romanus
Victor the Cleaner	Harvey Keitel
Beth	Lorraine Toussaint
Drugstore Owner	Geoffrey Lewis
Cop	Mic Rogers
Big Stan	Michael Rapaport
Burt	Ray Oriel
Johnny D	Spike McClure
Johnny's Mom	Lieux Dressler
Detective	John Capodice
Judge	Carmen Zapata
Computer Instructor	Calvin Levels
Weapons Instructor	Michael Runyard
Karate Instructor	Bill M. Ryusaki
Kaufman's Assistant	Jan Speck
Waiter in restaurant	Francesco Messina
Guard in booth	Peter Mark Vasquez
Shopping Woman	Wendy L. Davies
Operative	James Handy
Guy with gun	Lee Dupree
Operative with headset	David Sosna
New Orleans Thug	Bruce Barnes
VIP Woman	Jacqueline Koch
Angela's Bodyguards	Kenny Endoso, Gary Kasper
Maid	Rosalind Jue
Valet	Eric Cohen
Building Security Guard	Francois Chau
Hassan	Joe Garcia
Policeman	Frank Girardeau
Students	Clark Heathcliffe Brolly, Jodie Markell
Police Detective	Robert Harvey
Venice Guitar Player	Harry Perry

Harvey Keitel   Anne Bancroft

Plot Capsule: *A dangerous female criminal is given a reprieve from execution and trained by a secret organization to become an assassin. This action-drama is a remake of director Luc Besson's film* Nikita *which was released in the U.S. in 1991 by the Samuel Goldwyn Company as* La Femme Nikita *and starred Anne Parillaud.*

Gabriel Byrne, Bridget Fonda

TEENAGE MUTANT NINJA TURTLES III

(NEW LINE CINEMA) Producers, Thomas K. Gray, Kim Dawson, David Chan; Executive Producer, Raymond Chow; Co-Producer, Terry Morse; Director/Screenplay, Stuart Gillard; Based on characters created by Kevin Eastman, Peter Laird; Photography, David Gurfinkel; Designer, Roy Forge Smith; Editors, William D. Gordean, James R. Symons; Music, John Du Prez; Martial Arts Choreographer/Stunts, Pat. E. Johnson; Chief Puppeteer, Gordon Robertson; Creature Effects, All Effects Company; a Golden Harvest presentation in association with Gary Propper; Dolby Stereo; Technicolor; Rated PG; 95 minutes; March release

CAST

Casey Jones/Whit	Elias Koteas
April O'Neal	Paige Turco
Walker	Stuart Wilson
Lord Norinaga	Sab Shimono
Mitsu	Vivian Wu
Leonardo	Mark Caso
Raphael	Matt Hill
Donatello	Jim Raposa
Michaelangelo	David Fraser
Splinter	James Murray
Kenshin	Henry Hayashi

and John Aylward (Niles), Mak Takano (Benkei - Honor Guard #1), Steven Getson Akahoshi, Kent Kim, Ken Kensei (Honor Guards), Travis A. Moon (Yoshi), Tad Horino (Grandfather), Glen Chin (Jailer), Koichi Sakamoto (Young Priest), Tracy Patrick Conklin (Sam), Edmund Stone (Dave), Jeff Kawasugi (Murata), Phil Chong (Rider), Yeon Kim (Blacksmith); Voices: Robbie Rist (Michaelangelo), Brian Tochi (Leonardo), Tim Kelleher (Raphael), Corey Feldman (Donatello); Animatronic Puppeteers: Rick Lyon (Donatello), Gordon Robertson (Michaelangelo), Noel MacNeal (Raphael), Jim Martin (Leonardo), James Murray, Lisa Aimee Sturz, Tim Lawrence (Splinter)

Plot Capsule: *Four crime fighting turtles and their human friend April swap places with five 17th Century samurai warriors and find themselves on an adventure in feudal Japan. Third "Turtles" film following the New Line Cinema releases* Teenage Mutant Ninja Turtles *(1990) and* Teenage Mutant Ninja Turtles II: The Secret of the Ooze *(1991). Paige Turco repeats her role from the second film while Elias Koteas reprises his character from the first.*

© New Line Cinema

Elias Koteas, Splinter
ABOVE: John Aylward, with the Turtles

JUST ANOTHER GIRL ON THE I.R.T.

(MIRAMAX) Producers, Erwin Wilson, Leslie Harris; Director/Screenplay, Leslie Harris; Photography, Richard Connors; Editor, Jack Haigis; Designer, Mike Green; Music Producer/Supervisor, Eric Sadler; Costumes, Bruce Brickus; Casting, Tracey Moore; a Truth 24 F.P.S. production; Color; Rated R; 92 minutes; March release

CAST

Chantel	Ariyan Johnson
Tyrone	Kevin Thigpen
Natete	Ebony Jerido
Paula	Chequita Jackson
Cedrick	William Badget
Gerard	Jerard Washington
Debra Mitchell	Karen Robinson
Owen Mitchell	Tony Wilkes
Mr. Weinberg	Johnny Roses
Andre	Shawn King
Lavonica	Kisha Richardson
Denisha	Monet Dunham
Mr. Moore	Wendall Moore

and Laura Ross (Customer), Rashmella (Woman in welfare office), Ron L. Cox (Clinic Doctor), Richie Carter (Rashawn), Mwata Carter (Amiri), Gary Perez (Store Manager), Lynn Franklin (Social Worker), Erwin Wilson, Louis Thomas Jr. (Policemen), Nicholas B. Carter (Child who opens bag), Jasmine Thomas (Chantel's & Ty's Baby), Moise Dominique (New Born Baby)

Plot Capsule: *Brooklyn-set drama follows the undisciplined life of Chantel, a smart-mouthed 17 year-old who sets her sights on getting out of her dead-end neighborhood but winds up pregnant instead.*

© Miramax Films

Ariyan Johnson

Cynthia Stevenson

John C. McGinley, Jon Tenney, Tom Sizemore,
Peter Gallagher © Skouras Pictures

John C. McGinley

Peter Gallagher

Suzy Amis

Lili Taylor

Jon Tenney

WATCH IT

(SKOURAS) Producers, Thomas J. Mangan IV, J. Christopher Burch, John C. McGinley; Executive Producers, David Brown, William S. Gilmore; Director/Screenplay, Tom Flynn; Photography, Stephen M. Katz; Editor, Dorian Harris; Designer, Jeff Steven Ginn; Costumes, Jordan Ross; Music, Stanley Clarke; Casting, Shari Rhodes; Line Producer, Fran Roy; an Island World presentation in association with the Manhattan Project of a River One Films production; Dolby Stereo; Technicolor; Rated R; 102 minutes; March release

CAST

John Casey	Peter Gallagher
Anne	Suzy Amis
Rick	John C. McGinley
Michael	Jon Tenney
Ellen	Cynthia Stevenson
Brenda	Lili Taylor
Danny	Tom Sizemore
Denise	Terri Hawkes
Call Girl	Jordana Capra
Girl on videotape	Taylor Render
Fan at ballpark	Lorenzo Clemons
Jewelry Salesman	Mark Grapey
Sharon	Jeannine Welles
Deborah	Gina Raffin
Denise's Boyfriend	Scott Haven
Delivery Boy	Bill Cusack
Waiter	Marty Higgenbotham
Minister	Del Roy
Danny's Girl	Maria Stevens
Girl with Rick	Tricia Munford
Girl at party	Emily Hopper
Bill Clark	Michael Hughes
Todd Black	Tony Difalco
Ellen's Dinner Guests	Lee R. Sellers, Eva Black

Plot Capsule: *A comic look at four male friends in their late 20's, their relationships with women and their obsession with a game from their college days called "watch it."*

BORN YESTERDAY

(HOLLYWOOD PICTURES) Producer, D. Constantine Conte; Executive Producer, Stratton Leopold; Director, Luis Mandoki; Screenplay, Douglas McGrath; Based on the play by Garson Kanin; Photography, Lajos Koltai; Designer, Lawrence G. Paull; Editor, Lesley Walker; Costumes, Colleen Atwood; Music, George Fenton; Co-Producer, Stephen Traxler; Casting, Amanda Mackey, Cathy Sandrich; Associate Producer, Chris Soldo; Presented in association with Touchwood Pacific Partners I; Distributed by Buena Vista Pictures; Dolby Stereo; Technicolor; Rated PG; 101 minutes; March release

CAST

Billie Dawn	Melanie Griffith
Harry Brock	John Goodman
Paul Verrall	Don Johnson
Ed Devery	Edward Herrmann
JJ	Max Perlich
Phillipe	Michael Ensign
Secretary Duffee	Benjamin C. Bradlee
Beatrice Duffee	Sally Quinn
Senator Kelley	William Frankfather
Senator Hedges	Fred Dalton Thompson
Mrs. Hedges	Celeste Yarnall
Cynthia Schreiber	Nora Dunn
Mrs. Kelley	Meg Wittner
Senator Duker	William Forward
Bindy Duker	Mary Gordon Murray
Cynthia's Assistant	Ted Raimi
Victoria Penny	Rondi Reed
Congressman Hulse	Matthew Faison
Mrs. Hulse	Kate McGregor-Stewart
Man at party	Arthur Leeds
Senator Welch	John Wesley
Mrs. Welch	Andi Chapman
Senator Dorn	Drew Snyder
Mrs. Dorn	Terri Hanauer
Senator Banks	John Achorn
Mrs. Banks	Ann Hearn
Jewelry Store Owner	Gordon Reinhart
Lois	Selma Archerd
Valerie	Catherine Hausman
Maid	Freda Foh Shen
Waitress	Marisol Massey
Dr. Playle	Dr. Leroy Perry, Jr.
Barber	Tony Palladino
Manicurist	Amanda Hendon
Jose Perical	Fritz Sperberg
Hansom Cab Driver	Robyn Renner
Bellman	Paul Guyot

Plot Capsule: *Wealthy junk tycoon Harry Brock arrives in Washington to do some political wheeling and dealing, his beautiful but dumb mistress, Billie Dawn, in tow. To avoided embarrassment he hires a writer, Paul Verrall, to become Billie's tutor. Remake of the 1950 Columbia Pictures comedy-drama which starred Judy Holliday (Billie), Broderick Crawford (Harry), and William Holden (Paul).*

© Hollywood Pictures Company

Melanie Griffith, John Goodman, Max Perlich, Edward Herrmann, Don Johnson ABOVE: John Goodman, Melanie Griffith
TOP: Edward Herrmann, Don Johnson, Melanie Griffith, John Goodman

Mary Stuart Masterson, Robert Sean Leonard

(standing) Mary Stuart Masterson, Robert Sean Leonard, Stockard Channing, Beau Bridges, (seated) Cybill Shepherd, Ron Silver

MARRIED TO IT

(ORION) Producer, Thomas Baer; Executive Producers, Peter V. Herald, John L. Jacobs; Director, Arthur Hiller; Screenplay, Janet Kovalcik; Photography, Victor Kemper; Designer, Robert Gundlach; Editor, Robert C. Jones; Associate Producers, Erica Hiller, Janet Kovalcik; Costumes, Julie Weiss; Music, Henry Mancini; Casting, Howard Feuer; Dolby Stereo; Deluxe color; Rated R; 112 minutes; March release

CAST

John Morden	Beau Bridges
Iris Morden	Stockard Channing
Chuck Bishop	Robert Sean Leonard
Nina Bishop	Mary Stuart Masterson
Claire Laurent	Cybill Shepherd
Leo Rothenberg	Ron Silver
Sol Chamberlain	Don Francks
Lucy Rothenberg	Donna Vivino
Marty Morden	Jimmy Shea
Kenny Morden	Nathaniel Moreau
Madelein Rothenberg	Diane D'Aquila
Dave	Chris Wiggins
Jeremy Brimfield	Paul Gross
Arthur Everson	Gerry Bamman
Mrs. Foster	Djanet Sears
Murray	George Sperdakos
Mullaney	Larry Reynolds
Himself	Ed Koch
Romero	Louis Dibianco
Lawyers	George Guidall, John Ottavino
Newscasters	David L. King, Jamie Deroy
Blonde at ballet	Nancy Cser
Dudley	Ian Neeson
Students	Chris Bickford, Jason Pechet
Banker	Charles Kerr
Secretary	Susan Henley
Burly Mover	Howard Jerome
Older Woman	Marilyn Boyle
Ross	Marc Gomes
Limo Driver	Philip Akin
Cafe Waiter	Gregory Jbara
Trendy Waiter	Silvio Oliviero
Arresting Officers	Larry Aubrey, Harry Booker
Reporter	D. Garfield Andrews
Muriel	Monique Cousineau
Students	Melissa Claputo, Allison Scott, Steven Lederri

Plot Capsule: *Comedy-drama.* *Three diverse New York couples find themselves becoming unlikely friends when the wives meet at a school gathering.*

© Orion Pictures

Beau Bridges, Stockard Channing
ABOVE: Cybill Shepherd, Ron Silver

HEAR NO EVIL

(20th CENTURY FOX) Producer, David Matalon; Executive Producer, David Streit; Director, Robert Greenwald; Screenplay, R.M. Badat, Kathleen Rowell; Story, R.M. Badat, Danny Rubin; Photography, Steven Shaw; Designer, Bernt Capra; Editor, Eva Gardos; Music, Graeme Revell; Casting, Glenn Daniels; Dolby Stereo; Technicolor; Rated R; 97 minutes; March release

CAST

Jillian Shanahan	Marlee Matlin
Ben Kendall	D.B. Sweeney
Lt. Philip Brock	Martin Sheen
Mickey O'Malley	John C. McGinley
Grace	Christina Carlisi
Cooper	Greg Elam
Wiley	Charley Lang
Mrs. Kendall	Marge Redmond
Tim Washington	Billie Worley
Roscoe	George Rankins
Nadine Brock	Karen Trumbo
Police Interpreter	Candice Kingrey
Mrs. Paley	Mary Marsh
Porsche Driver	Ron Graybeal
Doctor	Bill Pugin
Ms. Younger	Pat Codekas

and Mary Ann Marino (Museum Guard), Clay Luper (FBI Cotton Candy Vendor), Joe Ivy, Rick Jones (FBI Agents), Mahon Kelly (Alex), Marvin LaRoy Sanders (Grocery Checker), Kathy McCurdy (Sign Language Instructor), Merrilee Dale (Museum Guide)

Plot Capsule: *Drama-thriller. A deaf physical trainer finds herself in danger when a client secretly slips into her beeper a valuable coin that someone would kill to get their hands on.*

D.B. Sweeney, Marlee Matlin   © Twentieth Century Fox

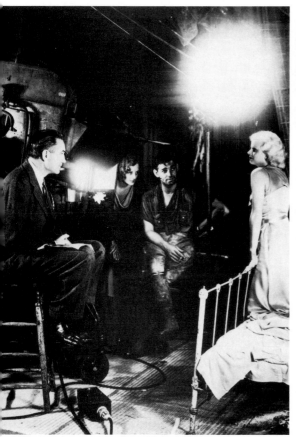

director of photography Harold Rosen,
director Victor Fleming, Clark Gable,
Jean Harlow on the set of "Red Dust"

Greta Garbo, Robert Taylor, director George Cukor, director of photography
William Daniels on the set of "Camille"

VISIONS OF LIGHT

(KINO INTERNATIONAL) Producer, Stuart Samuels; Executive Producers, Terry Lawler, Yoshiki Nishimura; Co-Producer/Editor, Arnold Glassman; Directors, Arnold Glassman, Todd McCarthy, Stuart Samuels; Screenplay, Todd McCarthy; Photography, Nancy Schreiber; an American Film Institute-NHK/Japan Broadcasting co-production; Color/black and white; Not rated; 91 minutes; April release

WITH

Nestor Almendros, John Alonzo, John Bailey, Michael Ballhaus, Stephen Burum, Bill Butler, Michael Chapman, Allan Daviau, Caleb Deschanel, Ernest Dickerson, Frederick Elmes, William Fraker, Conrad Hall, James Wong Howe, Victor Kemper, Laszlo Kovacs, Charles Lang, Sven Nykvist, Lisa Rinzler, Owen Roizman, Charles Rosher Jr., Sandi Sissel, Vittorio Storaro, Haskell Wexler, Robert Wise, Gordon Willis, Vilmos Zsigmond

Plot Capsule: *A documentary on motion picture cinematography featuring clips from dozens of films from the silent era to the present.*

Winner of the best documentary award from the NY Film Critics and National Society of Film Critics.

© Kino Intl. Corp.

Miko Hughes, Danny DeVito, Robert J. Steinmiller Jr.

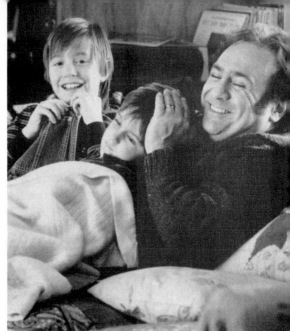

Robert J. Steinmiller Jr., Miko Hughes, Danny DeVito

JACK THE BEAR

(20th CENTURY FOX) Producer, Bruce Gilbert; Executive Producer, Ron Yerxa; Director, Marshall Herskovitz; Screenplay, Steven Zaillian; Based on the novel by Dan McCall; Photography, Fred Murphy; Designer, Lilly Kilvert; Editor, Steven Rosenblum; Associate Producer, Peter Burrell; Music, James Horner; Costumes, Deborah L. Scott; Casting, Mary Goldberg; an American Filmworks/Lucky Dog production; Dolby Stereo; System 35 Widescreen; Deluxe color; Rated PG-13; 99 minutes; April release

CAST

John Leary	Danny DeVito
Jack Leary	Robert J. Steinmiller, Jr.
Dylan Leary	Miko Hughes
Norman Strick	Gary Sinise
Mr. Festinger	Art LaFleur
Grandpa Glickes	Stefan Gierasch
Grandma Glickes	Erica Yohn
Elizabeth Leary	Andrea Marcovicci
Peggy Etinger	Julia Louis-Dreyfus
Karen Morris	Reese Witherspoon
Mr. Mitchell	Bert Remsen
Gordon Layton	Carl Gabriel Yorke
Mrs. Festinger	Lee Garlington
Mrs. Mitchell	Lorinne Vozoff
Dexter Mitchell	Justin Mosley Spink
Michael	Jahary Bennett
Mrs. Sampson	Lillian Hightower Domio
Edward Festinger	Troy Slaten
Katie Festinger	Jessica Steinmiller
Ray	Douglas Tolbert
Vince Buccini	Christopher Lawford
Detective Marker	Cliff Bemis
Mr. Strick	Charles Dugan
Mrs. Strick	Marion Dugan
Mr. Morris	Sam Freed
Mrs. Morris	Dorothy Lyman
Cop	Kevin McDermott
Construction Worker	Rob Dunn
Nursery School Teacher	Christy Botkin
Nurse	Vonna Bowen
Studio Technician	Steven McCall
Street Workers	Paul S. Wilson, Scott Thomson
Backhoe Driver	George E. Clayton, Jr.
Sondra	Monica Calhoun
Fireman	Kelly Connell

Plot Capsule: *The host of a late night tv horror show, whose wife has recently been killed in a car accident, uses his childlike imagination to raise his two sons, trying to protect them from the terrors of the real world.*

© Twentieth Century Fox

Miko Hughes, Robert J. Steinmiller Jr.

Reese Witherspoon, Robert J. Steinmiller Jr., Julia Louis-Dreyfus, Miko Hughes, Danny DeVito

Norman D. Golden II, Burt Reynolds

Burt Reynolds BELOW: Ruby Dee, Norman D. Golden II

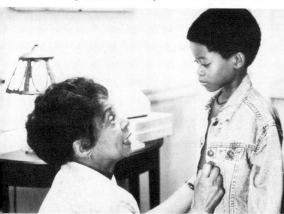

Thom McCleister, Norman D. Golden II, Frank Sivero

COP AND A HALF

(UNIVERSAL) Producer, Paul Maslansky; Executive Producer, Tova Laiter; Director, Henry Winkler; Screenplay, Arne Olsen; Photography, Bill Butler; Designer, Maria Caso; Editors, Daniel Hanley, Roger Tweten; Costumes, Lillian Pan; Music, Alan Silvestri; Casting, Meg Liberman/Mark Hirschfeld; Associate Producer, Elaine Hall; an Imagine Films Entertainment presentation; Dolby Stereo; Deluxe Color; Rated PG; 93 minutes; April release

CAST

Nick McKenna	Burt Reynolds
Devon Butler	Norman D. Golden II
Rachel	Ruby Dee
Captain Rubio	Holland Taylor
Fountain	Ray Sharkey
Raymond	Sammy Hernandez
Chu	Frank Sivero
Quintero	Rocky Giordani
Waldo	Marc Macaulay
Rudy	Tom McCleister
McPhail	Ralph Wilcox
Jenkins	Tom Kouchalakos
Rio	Carmine Genovese
McNally	Sean Evan O'Neal
Boy in bathroom	Max Winkler
Mr. Fleming	Steve Carlisle
Mrs. Boyle	Annabelle Weenick
Purse Thief	Paul Vroom
Bobo #1 Artist	Tim Goodwin
Bobo #2	Mike Benitez
Mrs. Bobo #2	Maria Canals
Bob #3 Thug	Nils Stewart
Bartender	Chester Grimes
Homeowner #3	Claudette McAdoo
Martha	Becky Kluzek
Katy	Amanda Seales
Boys	Nicholas Caruso, Shane Obedzinski
Jump Rope Twins	Jennifer and Ashley Howard
Maria	Malia Tuaileva
Passing Cop	Kenneth Taylor
Watching Cop #1	Nicole Bradley
Mr. Perm	Bill Cordell
Police Dispatcher	Sandra Itzin Gallo
Lady with groceries	Amy Stephen Wilder
Attorney (tv show)	Alan Landers
District Attorney	Judy Clayton
Skateboard Kid	Andrew Reynolds
TV Reporter	Debra Becker

Plot Capsule: *Action-comedy. Devon Butler, an eight year-old who fantasizes about being a policeman, gets his wish when he witnesses a murder and is teamed with detective Nick McKenna, in hopes of solving the case.*

© Universal City Studios Inc.

Dana Ivey, Elijah Wood

Elijah Wood, Courtney B. Vance

Ron Perlman

Robbie Coltrane, Jason Robards, Elijah Wood, Courtney B. Vance

Robbie Coltrane, Jason Robards

THE ADVENTURES OF HUCK FINN

(WALT DISNEY PICTURES) Producer, Laurence Mark; Executive Producers, Barry Bernardi, Steve White; Director/Screenplay, Stephen Sommers; Based on the novel *The Adventures of Huckleberry Finn* by Mark Twain; Co-Producer, John Baldecchi; Photography, Janusz Kaminski; Designer, Richard Sherman; Editor, Bob Ducsay; Costumes, Betsy Faith Heimann; Music, Bill Conti; Casting, Mary Goldberg; Distributed by Buena Vista Pictures; Dolby Stereo; Technicolor; Rated PG; 108 minutes; April release

CAST

Huck Finn	Elijah Wood
Jim	Courtney B. Vance
The Duke	Robbie Coltrane
The King	Jason Robards
Pap Finn	Ron Perlman
Widow Douglas	Dana Ivey
Mary Jane Wilks	Anne Heche
Deputy Hines	James Gammon
Harvey Wilks	Paxton Whitehead
Dr. Robinson	Tom Aldredge
Susan Wilks	Laura Bundy
Country Jake	Curtis Armstrong
Miss Watson	Mary Louise Wilson
Scrawny Shanty Lady	Frances Conroy
Ben Rodgers	Daniel Tamberelli
Book Worm	Denman Anderson
Bully	Mickey Cassidy
Joe Rodgers	Alex Zuckerman
Levi Bell	Marian Zinser
Julia Wilks	Renee O'Connor
Shanty Lady's Husband	Leon Russom
Billy Grangerford	Garette Ratliff Henson
Colonel Grangerford	Richard Anders
Miss Sophie Grangerford	Elaine Fjellman
Mother Grangerford	Janet Shea
Sirus	Jay R. Unger
Sheriff	Dion Anderson
Campfire Man	Paul Kropfl
William Wilks	Mark Allen Branson
Abe Turner	John Henry Scott
Curmudgeon	Hoskins Deterly
Joe Turner	Mike Watson

and Gary Lee Davis, Ben R. Scott (Fighting Men), Russell Paul Parkerson (The Fishing Boy), Kimberly Latrice Hall (Louise), Paul Dewees (Auctioneer), Evelyn B. Bunch (Jingo Lady)

Plot Capsule: *Mark Twain's classic tale of a rustic boy from the Mississippi who takes off on a raft with a runaway slave, engaging in assorted adventures that bind their friendship. Previous film versions of the novel were released in 1919 (Paramount with Lewis Sargent as Huck), 1931 (Paramount, Junior Durkin), 1939 (MGM, Mickey Rooney), 1960 (MGM, Eddie Hodges), 1974 (UA,* © The Walt Disney Company

THE SANDLOT

© Twentieth Century Fox

(20th CENTURY FOX) Producers, Dale de la Torre, William S. Gilmore; Executive Producers, Mark Burg, Chris Zarpas, Cathleen Summers; Director, David Mickey Evans; Screenplay, David Mickey Evans, Robert Gunter; Photography, Anthony B. Richmond; Designer, Chester Kaczenski; Costumes, Grania Preston; Editor, Michael A. Stevenson; Music, David Newman; Casting, Shari Rhodes; Presented in association with Island World; Dolby Stereo; Panavision; Deluxe color; Rated PG; 101 minutes; April release

Mike Vitar, Tom Guiry, James Earl Jones

CAST

Scotty Smalls	Tom Guiry
Benjamin Franklin Rodriguez	Mike Vitar
Hamilton "Ham" Porter	Patrick Renna
Michael "Squints" Palledorous	Chauncey Leopardi
Alan "Yeah-Yeah" McClennan	Marty York
Kenny DeNunez	Brandon Adams
Bertram Grover Weeks	Grant Gelt
Tommy "Repeat" Timmons	Shane Obedzinski
Timmy Timmons	Victor DiMattia
"The Babe"	Art La Fleur
Bill	Denis Leary
Mom	Karen Allen
Mr. Mertle	James Earl Jones
Wendy	Marlee Shelton
Young Mr. Mertle	Herb Muller
Police Chief	Garret Pearson
Thieves	Ed Mathews, Keith Campbell
Phillips	Wil Horneff
Little League Punk #2	Tyson Jones
Schoolyard Pitcher	Karl Simmons
Coach	Maury Wills
Older Benny	Pablo P. Vitar
Home Plate Umpire	Bob Apisa
Third Base Umpire	Robbie T. Robinson
Giants Catcher	Chuck Fick
Giants Pitcher	Tim Page
Giants Third Baseman	Dennis Williams
Mother at pool	Cynthia Windham
Toddler	Shane Lavar Smith
Older Scotty	Arliss Howard
Voice of Older Scotty	David Mickey Evans

Tom Guiry, Karen Allen

Plot Capsule: *In the summer of 1962 new kid in town Scotty Smalls, despite his lack of athletic skills, joins a sandlot baseball team and, with his new friends, does battle with the junkyard dog on the other side of the playing field fence.*

Patrick Renna, Victor DiMattia, Shane Obedzinski, Mike Vitar, Marty York,
Tom Guiry, Chauncey Leopardi, Grant Gelt, Brandon Adams

Robert Redford, Demi Moore BELOW: Demi Moore, Woody Harrelson
RIGHT: Woody Harrelson, Demi Moore

INDECENT PROPOSAL

(PARAMOUNT) Producer, Sherry Lansing; Executive Producers, Tom Schulman, Alex Gartner; Co-Producer, Michael Tadross; Director, Adrian Lyne; Screenplay, Amy Holden Jones; Based on the novel by Jack Engelhard; Photography, Howard Atherton; Designer, Mel Bourne; Costumes, Bobbie Read, Bernie Pollack, Beatrix Aruna Pasztor; Music, John Barry; Casting, Victoria Thomas; Dolby Stereo; Deluxe color; Rated R; 117 minutes; April release

CAST

John Gage	Robert Redford
Diana Murphy	Demi Moore
David Murphy	Woody Harrelson
Mr. Shackleford	Seymour Cassel
Jeremy	Oliver Platt
Day Tripper	Billy Bob Thornton
Mr. Langford	Rip Taylor
Auction Emcee	Billy Connolly
Realtor	Joel Brooks
Van Buren	Pierre Epstein
Screenwriters	Danny Zorn, Kevin West
David's Girlfriend	Pamela Holt
David's Father	Tommy Bush
David's Mother	Mariclare Costello
David's Boss	Curt Odle
Craps Women	Jedda Jones, Myra J., Edwonda White
Craps Stick Man	James Migliore
Croupier	Nick Georgiade
Dress Shop Saleslady	Ritamarie Kelly
Sam	Sam Micco
Pit Boss	Joseph Ruskin
High Roller	Joe La Due
Roulette Croupier	Ben W. Fluker
Coffee Shop Waitress	Carleen Sbordone
High Roller Card-man	Toru Nagai
Craps Pit Boss	Steven Dean
Craps Box Man	Frank J. Allison
Jeremy's Secretary	Dana Williams
Craps Dealer	David Cousin
Wine Goddess	Catlyn Day

and Irene Olga Lopez (Gage's Maid), Dru Davis (Bernice), Rudy Morrison (Maitre D'), Richard B. Livingston (Mike), Joe Bays (Jeffrey), David Rees (Businessman), Francoise Bush (Woman in restaurant), Elizabeth Gardner (Real Estate Receptionist), Art Cabrera, Israel Juarbe, Lydia Nicole, Iqbal Theba, Maurice Sherbanee, Yasemin Baytok, Elsa Raven (Citizenship Students), Matthew Barry, Chi-Muoi Lo, Art Chudabala, Michelle C. O'Brien, Hilary Reynolds, Rebecca Howard (Architecture Students), Selma Archerd, Katherine Pope, Jerome Rosenfeld, Nancy Thom (Auction Bidders), Sheena Easton, Herbie Hancock (Themselves)

Plot Capsule: *In this romantic drama a couple, down on their luck in Las Vegas, are offered one million dollars by a millionaire if the wife will consent to one night of sex with him.*

© Paramount Pictures

Woody Harrelson, Robert Redford,
Demi Moore, Seymour Cassel

Leonardo DiCaprio, Robert De Niro

Ellen Barkin, Leonardo DiCaprio

Ellen Barkin, Leonardo DiCaprio, Robert De Niro

THIS BOY'S LIFE

(WARNER BROS.) Producer, Art Linson; Executive Producers, Peter Guber, Jon Peters; Co-Producer, Fitch Cady; Director, Michael Caton-Jones; Screenplay, Robert Getchell; Based on the book by Tobias Wolff; Photography, David Watkin; Designer, Stephen J. Lineweaver; Editor, Jim Clark; Music, Carter Burwell; Costumes, Richard Hornung; Casting, Owens Hill, Rachel Abroms; Dolby Stereo; Panavision; Technicolor; Rated R; 114 minutes; April release

CAST

Dwight Hansen	Robert De Niro
Caroline Wolff	Ellen Barkin
Toby Wolff	Leonardo DiCaprio
Arthur Gayle	Jonah Blechman
Pearl	Eliza Dushku
Roy	Chris Cooper
Norma	Carla Gugino
Skipper	Zack Ansley
Kathy	Tracey Ellis
Marian	Kathy Kinney
Arch Cook	Bobby Zameroski
Chuck Bolger	Tobey Maguire
Jerry Huff	Tristan Tait
Psycho	Travis MacDonald
A&P Manager	Richard Liss
Terry Taylor	Michael Bacall
Terry Silver	Adam Sneller
Mr. Howard	Gerrit Graham
Geiger Counter Vendor	Thomas Kopache
Principal Shippy	Lee Wilkof
Jimmy Voorhees	Sean Murray
Oscar Booker	Jason Horst
Silver Sisters	Deanna Milligan, Morgan Brayton
Ticket Seller	Robert Munns
Vice Principal	Bill Dow
A&P Employee	Shawn MacDonald
Truck Driver	Frank C. Turner
Minister	John R. Taylor
Target Ranger	Stephen E. Miller
Voice in crowd	Dwight McFee
2nd Place Shooter	Ken Camroux
Score Caller	Ross Chaston
Crash Witness	Scott Woodmansee

Plot Capsule: *Caroline Wolff and her son Toby arrive in Concrete, Washington hoping to start life anew. Trouble begins when Caroline decides to marry a brutish and abusive man who makes life hell for Toby.*

Leonardo DiCaprio received the New Generation Award from the Los Angeles Film Critics for his performance in this film (and What's Eating Gilbert Grape*).*

© Warner Bros.

Robert De Niro, Leonardo DiCaprio

BODIES, REST & MOTION

(FINE LINE FEATURES) Producers, Allan Mindel, Denise Shaw, Eric Stoltz; Executive Producer, Joel Castleberg; Director, Michael Steinberg; Screenplay, Roger Hedden, based on his play; Photography, Bernd Heinl; Editor, Jay Cassidy; Music, Michael Convertino; Costumes, Isis Mussenden; Designer, Stephen McCabe; Casting, Sunny Seibel; a co-presentation of August Entertainment; Dolby Stereo; Deluxe color; Rated R; 93 minutes; April release

CAST

Carol	Phoebe Cates
Beth	Bridget Fonda
Nick	Tim Roth
Sid	Eric Stoltz
Elizabeth	Alicia Witt
Yard Sale Lady	Sandra Lafferty
TV Customer	Sidney Dawson
Station Attendant	Jon Proudstar
Chip	Scott Johnson
Dineh Woman	Kezbah Weidner
Motorcycle Rider	Peter Fonda
Waitress	Amaryllis Borrego
Elizabeth's Grandfather	Rich Wheeler
TV Store Kid	Scott Frederick
Radio Preacher's Voice	Warren Burton

Plot Capsule: *In the small Arizona town of Enfield, Nick walks out on his girlfriend Beth who soon develops a relationship with housepainter Nick. Roger Hadden's dramatic play opened Off-Broadway in 1986.*

© Fine Line Features

Phoebe Cates, Tim Roth

Bridget Fonda, Eric Stoltz

BOILING POINT

(WARNER BROS.) formerly *Money Men*; Producers, Marc Frydman, Leonardo De La Fuente; Executive Producers, Rene Bonnell, Olivier Granier; Co-Producer, Patrick Beaufront; Co-Executive Producer, Philippe Maigret; Director/Screenplay, James B. Harris; Based on the novel *Money Men* by Gerald Petievich; Photography, King Baggot; Music, Cory Lerios, John D'Andrea; Designer, Ron Foreman; Costumes, Molly Maginnis; Casting, Al Guarino; a Hexagon Films production; Dolby Stereo; Technicolor; Rated R; 90 minutes; April release

CAST

Jimmy Mercer	Wesley Snipes
Red Diamond	Dennis Hopper
Vikki	Lolita Davidovich
Ronnie	Viggo Mortensen
Leach	Seymour Cassel
Max	Jonathan Banks
Carol	Christine Elise
Dio	Tony Lo Bianco
Mona	Valerie Perrine
Levitt	James Tolkan
Transaction Man	Paul Gleason
Connie	Lorraine Evanoff
Sally	Stephanie Williams
Roth	Tobin Bell
Steve	Bobby Hosea
Brady	Dan Hedaya
Henderson	George Gerdes

and James Pickens, Jr. (Prison Officer), Keith Hickles (Cook), Rick Dean (Bartender), John Petievich (Hotel Security Officer), Mark Phelan (Banner), Nancy Sullivan (Clerk), John Lander (Coroner's Deputy), Lisa Kaseman (Ballroom Dancer), Janet May (Vocalist)

Plot Capsule: *Treasury agent Jimmy Mercer searches Hollywood to find the killers of a fellow agent. Meanwhile one of the men he seeks, Red Diamond, tries to find the $50,000 he owes another gangster.*

© Warner Bros.

46   Dennis Hopper, Wesley Snipes ABOVE: Wesley Snipes

Aidan Quinn

Johnny Depp, Mary Stuart Masterson

BENNY & JOON

(MGM) Producers, Susan Arnold, Donna Roth; Executive Producer, Bill Badalato; Director, Jeremiah Chechik; Screenplay, Barry Berman; Story, Barry Berman, Leslie McNeil; Photography, John Schwartzman; Designer, Neil Spisak; Editor, Carol Littleton; Costumes, Aggie Guerard Rodgers; Music, Rachel Portman; Casting, Risa Bramon Garcia, Heidi Levitt; Dolby Stereo; Deluxe color; Rated PG; 98 minutes; April release

CAST

Sam	Johnny Depp
Joon Pearl	Mary Stuart Masterson
Benny Pearl	Aidan Quinn
Ruthie	Julianne Moore
Eric	Oliver Platt
Dr. Garvey	C.C.H. Pounder
Thomas	Dan Hedaya
Mike	Joe Grifasi
Randy Burch	William H. Macy
Claudia	Liane Alexandra Curtis
Mrs. Smail	Eileen Ryan
UPS Man	Don Hamilton
Walter	Waldo Larson
Orderlies	Irvin Johnson, Shane Nilsson
Admitting Nurse	Leslie Laursen
Video Customer	Faye Killebrew
Video Clerk	Ramsin Amirkhas
Customer	Lynette Walden
Young Joon	Amy Elizabeth Sanford
Young Benny	Brian Keevy
Policeman	John Grant Phillips
Local	Tony Lincoln
Patrons	Noon Orsatti, Dan Kamin

Plot Capsule: *A mentally ill young woman falls for an odd-ball street entertainer much to the dismay of her overly-protective brother.*

© Metro-Goldwyn-Mayer

Mary Stuart Masterson ABOVE: Johnny Depp

Johnny Depp ABOVE: Aidan Quinn

WHO'S THE MAN?

(NEW LINE CINEMA) Producers, Charles Stettler; Executive Producer, Suzanne de Passe; Director, Ted Demme; Screenplay, Seth Greenland; Photography, Adam Kimmel; Designer, Ruth Ammon; Costumes, Karen Perry; Editors, Jeffrey Wolf, John Gilroy; Music, Andre Harrell, Michael Wolff; Casting, Jaki Brown; from Tin Pan Apple/de Passe Entertainment/Thomas Entertainment; Dolby Stereo; Technicolor; Rated R; 87 minutes; April release

CAST

Doctor Dre	Doctor Dre
Ed Lover	Ed Lover
Lionel	Badja Djola
Teesha Braxton	Cheryl "Salt" James
Nick Crawford	Jim Moody
Lamar	Andre Blake
Griles	Rozwill Young
Frankie Flynn	Colin Quinn
Shorty	Todd 1
Forty	Bowlegged Lou (from Full Force)
G-George	Bernie Mack
K.K.	Bill Bellamy
Bubba	T-Money
Sgt. Cooper	Denis Leary
Homeboy #1	Garfield
Albert	High L. Hurd
Charlie	Roger Robinson
Brenda	Maggie Rush
Demetrius	Richard Bright
Gustave	Dennis Vestunis
Officer Barnes	James Cavanagh Burke
Roscoe	Lee Drakeford
Boogie	Curtis Carrott
Model/Kelly	Caron Bernstein
Rev. Green	Randy Frazier
Fuji	Kim Chan
Tony Como	Vinny Pastore
Captain Reilly	Joe Lisi
Receptionist	Lorena Mann
Sheneequa	Leslie Segar
Girl #1	Jenay Nurse
Korean Merchant	Glenn Kubota
TV Reporter	Ralph McDaniels
Nurse	Linque Ayoung
Drill Man #1	Gavin O'Connor
Cop	Ali Abdul Wahha
Bartender	Afrika Bambatta
Bubba Worker	Apache, Eric B.
Jose	B-Real (of Cypress Hill), Black Sheep, Brand Nubian
Junkie	Bushwick Bill, D-Nice, Da Youngstas
Kid #2	Del Tha Funkee Homosapien
Day	Delroy
Themselves	Fab 5 Freddy, Flavor Flav
Bartender	Freddy Foss, Fu Schnickens, Grand Puba
Lorenzo	Guru (from Gangstarr), Heather B., Heavy D
Mike, Steve, Billy	House of Pain
Club Doorman	Humpty Hump
Nighttrain	Ice-T, Isis, Jamalski
Micah & Karim	Kris Kross
Rashid	KRS-One
Kid #1	Kwame
Homeboy, Jawaan	Leaders of the New School, Little Daddy Shane
Roberto	Kurt Loder
Vanessa	Monie Love
Naughty By Nature	Naughty By Nature, Nice & Smooth, Nikki D.
Bernstein	Ken Ober
Sherisse	Pepa (of Salt 'n Pepa)
Gerald	Phife (from Tribe Called Quest)
Dana	Queen Latifah, Q-Tip (from Tribe Called Quest)
Robbers #1 & 2	Pete Rock & C.L. Smooth
Detectives	Run DMC, Mark Sexx, Show Biz & A.G., Smooth B.
Benny	Stretch (from Live Squad), Too Short, D.J. Wiz (from Kid 'n Play)
Woman	Yo-Yo

Plot Capsule: *Comedy-drama about two barbers-turned-police officers who set out to expose the evil real estate developer who is buying up their neighborhood.*

© New Line Cinema

Top Left: Ed Lover, Yolanda Whitaker, Doctor Dre
Center: Christopher Smith, Ed Lover, Christopher Kelly, Doctor Dre

Doctor Dre, Ed Lover

Timothy Hutton, Amy Madigan

Timothy Hutton

THE DARK HALF

(ORION) Producer, Declan Baldwin; Executive Producer/Director/Screenplay, George A. Romero; Based on the novel by Stephen King; Photography, Tony Pierce-Roberts; Designer, Cletus Anderson; Costumes, Barbara Anderson; Associate Producer, Christine Romero; Casting, Terry Liebling; Make-up Effects, John Vulvich, Everett Burrell; Music, Christopher Young; Editor, Pasquale Buba; Visual Effects Producer, VCE/Peter Kuran; a Dark Half production; Dolby Stereo; Deluxe color; Rated R; 122 minutes; April release

CAST

Thad Beaumont/George Stark	Timothy Hutton
Liz Beaumont	Amy Madigan
Sheriff Alan Pangborn	Michael Rooker
Reggie Delesseps	Julie Harris
Fred Clawson	Robert Joy
Mike Donaldson	Kent Broadhurst
Shayla Beaumont	Beth Grant
Miriam Cowley	Rutanya Alda
Rick Cowley	Tom Mardirosian
Homer Gamache	Glenn Colerider
Annie Pangborn	Chelsea Field
Digger Holt	Royal Dano
Young Thad Beaumont	Patrick Brannan
Doc Pritchard	Larry John Meyers
Little Girl	Christina Romero
Dr. Albertson	Rohn Thomas
Hilary	Molly Renfroe
Head Nurse	Judy Grafe
Male Nurse	John Machione
Student	Erik Jensen
Trudy Wiggins	Christine Forrest
Pangborn's Receptionist	Nardi Novak
Norris Ridgewick	Zachery "Bill" Mott
Officer Hamilton	William Cameron
Troopers	David Butler, Curt De Bor
Dodie	Drinda Lalumia
NYC Cops	Lamont Arnold, Lee Hayes
Todd Pangborn	John Ponzio
Man in the hallway	Jack Skelly
Donaldson Cops	Marc Field, Rik Billock
Officers	Bruce Kirkpatrick, David Early
Wes	Jeff Monahan
Dave	Jeffery Howell
Rosalie	Melissa Papp
Garrison	J. Michael Hunter
Receptionist	Therese Courtney
Young Officer	Marty Roppelt
Wendy & William Beaumont	Sarah & Elizabeth Parker

Plot Capsule: *Writer Thad Beaumont has only succeeded in the literary market by publishing trashy books under the name of George Stark. When he attempts to "kill off" his alter-ego, Stark suddenly materializes to seek revenge.*

© Orion Pictures

Timothy Hutton, with Sarah & Elizabeth Parker
ABOVE: Michael Rooker

(front row) Diane Lane, Alan Arkin, Elizabeth Perkins, Kevin Pollak; (back row) Kimberly Williams, Matt Craven, Bill Paxton, Vincent Spano, Julie Warner, Sam Raimi

INDIAN SUMMER

(TOUCHSTONE) formerly *Tamakwa*; Producers, Jeffrey Silver, Robert Newmyer,; Co-Producer, Caroline Baron, Jack Binder; Director/Screenplay, Mike Binder; Photography, Tom Sigel; Editor, Adam Weiss; Designer, Craig Stearns; Costumes, Jane Robinson; Music, Miles Goodman; Casting, Richard Pagano, Sharon Bialy, Debi Manwiller; an Outlaw Production; Distributed by Buena Vista Pictures; Dolby Stereo; Panavision; Technicolor; Rated PG-13; 97 minutes; April release

CAST

Unca Lou Handler	Alan Arkin
Jamie Ross	Matt Craven
Beth Warden/Claire Everett	Diane Lane
Jack Belston	Bill Paxton
Jennifer Morton	Elizabeth Perkins
Brad Berman	Kevin Pollak
Stick Coder	Sam Raimi
Matthew Berman	Vincent Spano
Kelly Berman	Julie Warner
Gwen Daugherty	Kimberly Williams
Sam Grover	Richard Chevolleau
Man in canoe	Robert Feldmann
Cook	Anne Holloway
Ranger Thadeus Clay	Cliff Woolner
Young Jennifer	Emily Creed
Young Jamie	Brad Deutch
Adam Randall	Jesse Felsot
Young Rick	Gabriel Gunsberg
Young Matthew	Brian La Pointe
Young Brad	Jeremy Linson
Young Kelly	Heidi Marshall
Young Jack	Noah Plener
Young Beth	Rebecca Rumsey
Ida Heinken	Ashley Williams

Plot Capsule: *Comedy in which seven adults are invited by their former counselor to spend a few days reliving the old routine at their childhood summer camp.*

© Touchstone Pictures

Vincent Spano, Julie Warner, Matt Craven, Kevin Pollak, Diane Lane, Kimberly Williams, Elizabeth Perkins, Bill Paxton

Elizabeth Perkins, Diane Lane, Kevin Pollak, Matt Craven

THE PICKLE

(COLUMBIA) Producer/Director/Screenplay, Paul Mazursky; Executive Producer, Patrick McCormick; Co-Producer/Editor, Stuart Pappe; Photography, Fred Murphy; Designer, James Bissell; Costumes, Albert Wolsky; Music, Michel Legrand; Casting, Carrie Frazier, Shani Ginsberg; Special Effects Coordinator, Michael L. Wood; Dolby Stereo; Technicolor; Rated R; 103 minutes; April release

CAST

Harry Stone	Danny Aiello
Ellen Stone	Dyan Cannon
Francoise	Clotilde Courau
Yetta	Shelley Winters
Ronnie Liebowitz	Barry Miller
Phil Hirsch	Jerry Stiller
Gregory Stone	Chris Penn
President	Little Richard
Yakimoto Yakimura	Jodi Long
Carrie	Rebecca Miller
Mike Krakower	Stephen Tobolowsky
Nancy Osborne	Caroline Aaron
Grandmother	Rita Karin
Bernadette	Linda Carlson
Patti Wong	Kimiko Cazanov
Molly-Girl	Ally Sheedy
"The Pickle" Cast	Dudley Moore, Isabella Rossellini, Griffin Dunne
Young Harry	J.D. Daniels
Dr. Spalding	Spalding Gray
Russian Cab Driver	Elya Baskin
Mission Control Farmer	Michael Greene
Electronics Store Clerk	Robert Cicchini
Chauffeur	John Rothman
Jose Martinez	Castulo Guerra
Young Yetta	Caris Corfman
Father	Arthur Taxier
Grandfather	Sol Frieder
Butch Levine	Paul Mazursky
Young Butch	Michael Shulman
Pinnie	Brandon Danziger
Irwin	Louis Falk
Little Boy 1945	Ben Diskin
Clem	Geoffrey Blake
Farm Boys	Brent Hinkley, Eric Edwards, Richmond Arquette, Stephen Polk
Kareem	Paul Bates
Concierge	Marcus Naylor
Doorman	Joe Pecoraro
Pharmacy Clerk	Betsy Mazursky
David	Michael Harris
Molly	Anna Maria & Caroline Clark
Car Man	Arthur French
Man with beer	Erik King
Woman in window	Davenia McFadden
Boy who stopped	Lawrence Gilliard, Jr.
Boy who also stopped	Sharrieff Pugh
FX Man	Billy Jaye
Alberto	Sergio Premoli
Clapper Boy	Mark Deakins
1st A.D.	Brooke Smith
Mr. Aronowitz	Andre Philippe
Mr. Shacknoff	Fyvush Finkel
Uncle Morris	Nathanial Katzman

and Chuck Flores, Bob Harrison, Michael Asher (Band), Waldemar Kalinowski (Crying Man), Twink Caplan (Crying Woman), Tony Conferti (Crying Man in candy store), Stephen Cody (Tractor Man), Jill Mazursky (Tractor Woman), Zeljko Negovetic (Wagon Driver), Chris Vecchione (Farm Girl), Scott Wulff (Adam), Jacklynn Jill Evans (Eve), Hap Lawrence (Gothic Man), Patricia Place (Gothic Woman), Michael Ashe (Elegant Man), Tiffany Salerno (Elegant Woman), Richard Coate (Plaza Hotel Waiter), Josif Shikhil (Russian Man - Coney Island), Donald Trump (Himself)

Plot Capsule: *A noted Hollywood director, suffering from a string of flops, questions his life while awaiting the release of his latest movie, an atypical sci-fi epic about a flying pickle.*

© Columbia Pictures Industries

Top: Clotilde Courau, Danny Aiello, Chris Penn
Middle: Danny Aiello, Shelley Winters
Bottom: Barry Miller, Stephen Tobolowsky, Chris Penn, Shelley Winters, Rebecca Miller, Dyan Cannon, Michael Harris, Kimiko Cazanov, Jerry Stiller

BOUND BY HONOR

(HOLLYWOOD PICTURES) formerly *Blood In, Blood Out*; Producers, Taylor Hackford, Jerry Gershwin; Executive Producers, Jimmy Santiago Baca, Stratton Leopold; Director, Taylor Hackford; Screenplay, Jimmy Santiago Baca, Jeremy Iacone, Floyd Mutrux; Story, Ross Thomas; Photography, Gabriel Beristain; Designer, Bruno Rubeo; Editors, Fredric Steinkamp, Karl F. Steinkamp; Costumes, Shay Cunliffe; Music, Bill Conti; Co-Executive Producer, Rene Sheridan; Casting, Richard Pagano/Sharon Bialy; Associate Producer, Gina Blumenfeld; Presented in association with Touchwood Pacific Partners I; Dolby Stereo; Technicolor; Rated R; 170 minutes; April release

CAST

Miklo Velka	Damian Chapa
Cruz Candelaria	Jesse Borrego
Paco Aguilar	Benjamin Bratt
Montana Segura	Enrique Castillo
Magic Mike	Victor Rivers
Bonafide	Delroy Lindo
Red Ryder	Tom Towles
Popeye	Carlos Carrasco
Wallace	Teddy Wilson
Chuey	Raymond Cruz
Frankie	Valente Rodriguez
Big Al	Lanny Flaherty
Lightning	Billy Bob Thornton
Carlos	Geoffrey Rivas
Dolores	Karmin Murcelo
Lupe	Jenny Gago
Juanito	Noah Verduzco
Carmen	Lupe Ontiveros
Smokey	Gary Cervantes
Mano	Victor Mohica
Rollie	Tom Wilson
Spider	Ray Oriel
Sgt. Devereux	Mike Genovese
Cyclone	Steven Anthony Jones
Pockets	Harold J. Surratt
Janis	Natalija Nogulich
Ivan	Ving Rhames

and Danny Trejo (Geronimo), Jimmy Santiago Baca (Gato), Peter Mark Vasquez (Chivo), Judith Verduzco (Alicia), Sonia Rodriguez (Victoria), Roberto Contreras (Cruz' Grandfather), Evelyn Guerrero (Luisa), Gary Tacon (Clavo), Luis Contreras (Realthing), Paul Tocha (Apache), Freddy Negrete (Freddy), David Dunard (Gill), Steve Eastin (Hollenbeck Captain), Alina Arenal (Perla), Julie Zamaryonov (Belinda), Daniel McDonald (Gallery Asst.), Gibby Brand (Jared Levinson), Elizabeth Austin (Lois Levinson), Adan Hernandez (Gilbert), Richard E. Butler (Frank Velka), Michael Bofshever (Salesman), Art Snyder (Councilman Snyder), Robert Pescovitz (Surgeon), Primitivo Tapia (Street Kid), Robert J. Juarez (Priest), Eddie Perez (Joker), Claudia Gabriella Colin (Joker's Girl), David Labiosa (Coolaide), Rudy Barrios (Tres Puntos Gangmember), Juan Charles, Charles Guillermo, Eugen Barrios, Jimmy Chavez (Vatos Locos), Rene Bontana (5 Puntos Counterman), Dan Vasquez (Warden), Michael McFall, Donald E. Lacy, Jr. (Transvestites), Zandra Hill (Black Cook), George Pereira (Old Con), Angel Romero (Parole Board Member), Joe Schloss (Prison Escort), Chris Chloupek (Prison Photographer), Gill Montie (AV Inmate), Vanessa Marquez (Montana's Daughter), Martin McDermott (Delano Guard), Martha Cardenas (Landlady), Catherine Price (Newscaster), Jerry Perea (Tattooed Lipped Partier), Lindsay Ginter (Officer Young), Victor Koliacos (PCP Kid), Christine Avila (Mother of PCP Kid), Robert Padgett (Doctor to PCP Kid), Rio Hackford (PCP Intern)

Plot Capsule: *A dramatic look at the disparate lives of three Latino youths from East Los Angeles as Miklo turns criminal and spends time in jail, Cruz falls into a life of drug addiction and Paco becomes an undercover cop.*

© Hollywood Pictures Company

TOP: Benjamin Bratt, Jesse Borrego, Damian Chapa
MIDDLE: Damian Chapa, Benjamin Bratt
BOTTOM: Jesse Borrego, Benjamin Bratt

William Baldwin, Sherilyn Fenn

Kelly Lynch, Sherilyn Fenn, William Baldwin

William Baldwin, Kelly Lynch

Kelly Lynch, Sherilyn Fenn, William Baldwin

THREE OF HEARTS

© New Line Cinema Corp.

(NEW LINE CINEMA) Producers, Joel B. Michaels, Matthew Irmas; Executive Producer, David Permut; Co-Producer, Hannah Hempstead; Director, Yurek Bogayevicz; Screenplay, Adam Greenman, Mitch Glazer; Story, Adam Greenman; Photography, Andrzej Sekula; Designer, Nelson Coates; Costumes, Barbara Tfank; Music, Joe Jackson; Editor, Dennis M. Hill; Casting, Penny Perry, Annette Benson; Dolby Stereo; Deluxe color; Rated R; 105 minutes; April release

CAST

Joe Casella	William Baldwin
Connie Czapski	Kelly Lynch
Ellen Armstrong	Sherilyn Fenn
Mickey Poliare	Joe Pantoliano
Yvonne	Gail Strickland
Allison	Cec Verrell
Isabella	Claire Callaway
Gail	Marek Johnson
Daphne	Monique Mannen
Ralph	Timothy D. Strickney
Patient	Frank Ray Perilli
Harvey	Tony Amendola
Frankie	Keith MacKechnie
Woman auditioning	Ann Ryerson
Operators	Gloria Gifford, Jill Jarress, Ken Magee, Lin Shaye
Photographer	Joshua Grenrock
Priest	Jan A.P. Kaczmarek
Bride	Aleksandra Kaniak
Groom	Stanislaw Dziedzic
Bride's Mother	Maria Heggnes
Bride's Father	Ebyslaw Kogut
Lead Singer	Liliana Overman
Elevator Operator	Mitchell Group
Woman in bar	Tawny Kitaen
Nurse	Julie Lott
Student	Lynn A. Henderson

Plot Capsule: *New York-set romantic triangle. Connie attempts to regain her recently departed female lover, Ellen, by hiring Joe, a male escort, to date Ellen, make her life miserable and turn her off men.*

Kevin Anderson   Jeanne Tripplehorn

THE NIGHT WE NEVER MET

Annabella Sciorra, Matthew Broderick

(MIRAMAX) Producer, Michael Peyser; Executive Producers, Sidney Kimmel, Bob Weinstein, Harvey Weinstein; Co-Producer, Rudd Simmons; Director/Screenplay, Warren Leight; Photography, John A. Thomas; Designer, Lester Cohen; Costumes, Ellen Lutter; Editor, Camilla Toniolo; Casting, Billy Hopkins, Suzanne Smith; a Sidney Kimmel presentation of a Michael Peyser production; Dolby Stereo; Film House color; Rated R; 99 minutes; April release

CAST

Sam Lester	Matthew Broderick
Ellen Holder	Annabella Sciorra
Brian McVeigh	Kevin Anderson
Pastel	Jeanne Tripplehorn
Janet Beehan	Justine Bateman
Aaron Holder	Michael Mantell
Lucy	Christine Baranski
Nosy Neighbors	Doris Roberts, Dominic Chianese
Kenneth	Tim Guinee
Todd	Bradley White
Eddie	Greg Germann
Inga	Dana Wheeler-Nicholson
Mrs. Winkler	Louise Lasser
Shep	Bill Campbell
Leslie	Michelle Hurst
Marty Holder	Lewis Black
Cabbie	Ranjit Chowdhry
French Cheese Shopper	Naomi Campbell
Bartender	Richard Poe
Less/More Cheese Lady	Katharine Houghton
Chuck Barber	David Slavin
Catha	Brooke Smith
Pharmacy Clerk	Bitty Schram
Doorman	Billy Strong
Deli Customer	Catherine Lloyd Burns
Triple Creme Cheese Shopper	Michael Mastrototaro
Cleaning Customers	Michael Imperioli, Suzanne Dottino
"My Name Is Eduardo"	Jose Evelio Alvarez
Sparrow's Nest Salesman	Paul Guilfoyle
Foreign Film Actor	Davidson Thomson
"Excuse Me" Shopper	Kathryn Rossetter
Yogurt Eating Date	Mary B. McCann
3rd Cheese Man	Steven Goldstein
Shep's New Date	Suzanne Lanza
Dental Patient	Garry Shandling

Plot Capsule: *Romantic comedy about three New Yorkers who agree to share an apartment at alternate times, therefore never meeting each other and leading to some mistaken identities.*

© Miramax Films

Annabella Sciorra, Matthew Broderick
Above: Annabella Sciorra

Lauren Holly, Jason Scott Lee TOP RIGHT: Jason Scott Lee

DRAGON: THE BRUCE LEE STORY

(UNIVERSAL) Producer, Raffaella De Laurentiis; Executive Producer, Dan York; Director, Rob Cohen; Screenplay, Edward Khmara, John Raffo, Rob Cohen; Based on the book *Bruce Lee: The Man Only I Knew* by Linda Lee Caldwell; Photography, David Eggby; Designer, Robert Ziembicki; Editor, Peter Amundson; Music, Randy Edelman; Costumes, Carol Ramsey; Fight Choreographer, John Cheung; Casting, Jane Jenkins, Janet Hirshenson; Co-Producer, Rick Nathanson; Associate Producers, Kelly Breidenbach, Hester Hargett; Dolby Stereo; Panavision; Deluxe color; Rated PG-13; 121 minutes; May release

CAST

Bruce Lee	Jason Scott Lee
Linda Lee	Lauren Holly
Bill Krieger	Robert Wagner
Vivian Emery	Michael Learned
Gussie Yang	Nancy Kwan
Philip Tan	Kay Tong Lim
Bruce's Father	Ric Young
Yip Man	Luoyong Wang
Jerome Sprout	Sterling Macer
The Demon	Sven-Ole Thorsen
Johnny Sun	John Cheung
Luke Sun	Ong Soo Han
Joe Henderson	Eric Bruskotter
Principal Elder	Aki Aleong
Elder	Chao-Li Chi
Brandon	Iain M. Parker
Young Bruce	Sam Hau
Shannon	Michelle Tennant
History Teacher	Clyde Kusatsu
April	Alicia Tao
Mr. Ho	Kong Kwok Keung
Chefs	Johnny Cheung, Anthony Carpio, Chan Tat Kwong
Nunnemacher	John Lacy
Benny Sayles	Harry Stanback
Tad Overton	Michael Cudlitz
Green Hornet	Forry Smith
"Green Hornet" Director	Van Williams
Assistant Director	Sean Faro

and Alan Eugster (Propman), Paul Raci (Bad Guy), Ed Parker, Jr. (Ed Parker), Shannon Lee (Party Singer), Robert D. Garrett (Krieger's Butler), Lala Sloatman (Sherry Schnell), Fu Suk Han (Cha Cha Dancer), Nick Brandon (Boswain), Louis Turenne (Maitre d'), Paul Mantee (Doctor), Jonathan Penner (Studio Executive), Calvin Bartlett (Stunt Coordinator), Jan Solomita, Shannon Uno (Hecklers), Lau Pak Lam ("Big Boss" Director), Rob Cohen ("Enter the Dragon" Director)

Plot Capsule: *True story of martial arts master Bruce Lee and his rise to international film stardom before his untimely death at the age of 32.*

© Universal City Studios Inc.

John Cheung, Jason Scott Lee
ABOVE: Jason Scott Lee, Forry Smith

Sigourney Weaver, Kevin Kline

DAVE

(WARNER BROS.) Producers, Lauren Shuler-Donner, Ivan Reitman; Executive Producers, Joe Medjuck, Michael C. Gross; Director, Ivan Reitman; Screenplay, Gary Ross; Photography, Adam Greenberg; Designer, J. Michael Riva; Editor, Sheldon Kahn; Music, James Newton Howard; Associate Producer, Gordon Webb; Costumes, Richard Hornung; Casting, Michael Chinich, Bonnie Timmermann; a Northern Lights Entertainment/Donner/Shuler-Donner production; Dolby Stereo; Technicolor; Rated PG-13; 112 minutes; May release

CAST

Dave Kovic/Bill Mitchell	Kevin Kline
Ellen Mitchell	Sigourney Weaver
Bob Alexander	Frank Langella
Alan Reed	Kevin Dunn
Duane Stevensen	Ving Rhames
Vice-President Nance	Ben Kingsley
Murray Blum	Charles Grodin
Alice	Faith Prince
Randi	Laura Linney
White House Tour Guide	Bonnie Hunt
Senate Majority Leader	Parley Baer
House Majority Leader	Stefan Gierasch
Mrs. Travis	Anna Deavere Smith
Policeman	Charles Hallahan
Jerry	Tom Dugan
Lola	Alba Oms
Secret Service #1	Steve Witting
David	Kellen Sampson
White House Guard	Lexie Bigham
Don Durenberger	Stephen Root
Girl at Durenberger's	Catherine Reitman
Mom at Durenberger's	Dawn Arnemann
Clara	Marianna Harris
Diane	Sarah Marshall
White House Barber	Ralph Manza
President's Physician	George Martin
White House Nurse	Laurie Franks
Trauma Doctor	Tom Kurlander
Trauma Nurse	Dendrie Taylor
Japanese Prime Minister	Joe Kuroda
Vice-President's Wife	Genevieve Robert
Vice-President's Son	Jason Reitman
Secretary of Education	Ruth Goldway
Director of OMB	Frank Birney
Secretary of Treasury	Paul Collins
Secretary of Commerce	Peter White
Postmaster General	Robin Gammell

and Heather Hewitt (Judy), Gary Ross (Policeman #2), Jeff Joseph (Ellen's Aide), Bonnie Bartlett (Senator), Robert V. Walsh (Speaker of the House), William Pitts (Congressional Doorkeeper), Dan Butler (Reporter), Frederic W. Barnes, Ronald Brownstein, Eleanor Clift, Senator Christopher Dodd, Senator Tom Harkin, Bernard Kalb, Larry King, Michael Kinsley, Morton Kondracke, Jay Leno, Frank Mankiewicz, Christopher Matthews, John McLaughlin, Senator Howard Metzenbaum, Justice Abner J. Mikva, Robert D. Novak, Thomas P. "Tip" O'Neill, Richard Reeves, Arnold Schwarzenegger, Senator Paul Simon, Senator Alan Simpson, Ben Stein, Oliver Stone, Kathleen Sullivan, Jeff Tackett, Helen Thomas, Nina Totenberg, Sander Vanocur, John Yang (Themselves), Wendy Gordon, Ben Patrick Johnson, Steve Kmetko (Announcers).

Plot Capsule: *Comedy-satire about a mild-mannered employment agent who is asked to impersonate his lookalike, the President of the United States, when the latter suffers a stroke.*

Gary Ross received an Academy Award nomination for his original screenplay.

© Warner Bros.

Kevin Dunn, Kevin Kline
ABOVE: Kevin Kline

Kevin Dunn, Kevin Kline, Frank Langella

Kevin Dunn, Faith Prince, Ben Kingsley, Kevin Kline, Ving Rhames,
Sigourney Weaver, Charles Grodin, Frank Langella

...in Kline (and above)

Kellen Sampson, Kevin Klin...

Edward Furlong, Jeff Bridges, Lucinda Jenny
TOP RIGHT: Jeff Bridges, Edward Furlong

AMERICAN HEART

(TRITON PICTURES) Producers, Rosilyn Heller, Jeff Bridges; Executive Producer, Cary Brokaw; Director, Martin Bell; Screenplay, Peter Silverman; Story, Peter Silverman, Martin Bell; Co-Producer, Neil Koenigsberg; Photography, James R. Bagdonas; Editor, Nancy Baker; Designer, Joel Schiller; Costumes, Beatrix Aruna Pasztor; Music, James Newton Howard; Casting, Reuben Cannon & Associates, Cecily Adams; Color; Rated R; 113 minutes; May release

CAST

Jack Kelson	Jeff Bridges
Nick Kelson	Edward Furlong
Charlotte	Lucinda Jenney
Rainey	Don Harvey
Molly	Tracey Kapisky
Freddie	Margaret Welsh
Terry Cosmos	Marcus Chong
Rollie	Christian Frizzell
Normandy	Melvyn Hayward
Diane	Shareen J. Mitchell
Young Jack	Greg Sevigny
Monique	Jayne Entwistle
Lisa	Wren Walker
Flo	Charlotte London
Vernon the Bartender	Loyd Catlett
Moose	Francisco Arenas
Stony	Sam Strange
Nicole	Barbara Irvin

and John Boylan (Janitor), Willie Williams, Roosevelt Franklin (The Gospel Fireballs), Kit McDonough (Landlady), Cristine McMurdo-Wallis (School Administrator), Richard Joffray (Taxi Dispatcher Voice), Benjamin & Jared Hinkle (Roy), Flapjack (Creamo), Michelle Matlock (Bandit), Mark Namer (Pool Bar Guy), Burke Pearson (Jack's Bum), Apollo Dukakis (Steve), Laura Bobovski (Girl in food store), John DeLay (Building Supervisor), Gary Lee Dansenburg (Suburban Son), Todd Jamieson (Suburban Father)

Plot Capsule: *Jack Kelson, newly released from prison, is given the burden of having to start his life anew with his estranged teenage son, in this drama set in Seattle.*

© Triton Pictures

Edward Furlong, Tracey Kapisky
ABOVE: Jeff Bridges

Mercedes Ruehl, Richard Dreyfuss

Irene Worth

Brad Stoll, Mike Damus

NEIL SIMON'S
LOST IN YONKERS

(COLUMBIA) Producer, Ray Stark; Executive Producer, Joseph M. Caracciolo; Director, Martha Coolidge; Screenplay, Neil Simon, based on his play; Photography, Johnny E. Jensen; Designer, David Chapman; Editor, Steven Cohen; Music, Elmer Bernstein; Co-Producer, Emanuel Azenberg; Costumes, Shelley Komarov; a Rastar production; Dolby Stereo; Technicolor; Rated PG; 113 minutes; May release

CAST

Louie Kurnitz	Richard Dreyfuss
Bella Kurnitz	Mercedes Ruehl
Grandma Kurnitz	Irene Worth
Jay Kurnitz	Brad Stoll
Arty Kurnitz	Mike Damus
Johnny	David Strathairn
Hollywood Harry	Robert Guy Miranda
Eddie Kurnitz	Jack Laufer
Gert	Susan Merson
Harry's Crony	Illya Haase
Gas Station Attendant	Calvin Stillwell
Truck Driver	Dick Hagerman
Danny	Jesse Vincent
Kid in store	Howard Newstate
Cop	Peter Gannon
Teresa	Lori Schubeler
Flo	Jean Zarzour
Celeste	Mary Scott Gudaitis

Plot Capsule: *During World War II two young boys are forced to stay with their domineering grandmother and their emotionally unstable aunt. Mercedes Ruehl and Irene Worth repeat their Tony Award-winning roles from the original 1991 Broadway production.*

© Columbia Pictures Industries

David Strathairn, Mercedes Ruehl

Mercedes Ruehl, Irene Worth

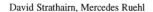

59

Big Daddy Kane, Stephen Baldwin, Mario Van Peebles, Tiny Lister, Charles Lane, Tone Loc

POSSE

(GRAMERCY PICTURES) Producers, Preston Holmes, Jim Steele; Co-Producer, Jim Fishman; Executive Producers, Tim Bevan, Eric Fellner; Co-Executive Producers, Paul Webster, Bill Fishman; Director, Mario Van Peebles; Screenplay, Sy Richardson, Dario Scardapane; Photography, Peter Menzies, Jr.; Designer, Catherine Hardwicke; Music, Michel Colombier; Editor, Mark Conte; Casting, Pat Golden; a Polygram Filmed Entertainment release in association with Gramercy Pictures of a Working Title Films production; Dolby Stereo; Panavision; Technicolor; Rated R; 109 minutes; May release

CAST

Jesse Lee	Mario Van Peebles
Little J	Stephen Baldwin
Weezie	Charles Lane
Obobo	Tiny Lister
Father Time	Big Daddy Kane
Colonel Graham	Billy Zane
Carver	Blair Underwood
Papa Joe	Melvin Van Peebles
Lana	Salli Richardson
Angel	Tone Loc
Old Man	Woody Strode
Vera	Vesta
King David	Robert Hooks
Cable	Isaac Hayes
Mayor Bigwood	Paul Bartel
Sheriff Bates	Richard Jordan
Preston	Reginald Vel Johnson
Jimmy Love	Stephen J. Cannell
Reporters	Reginald Hudlin, Warrington Hudlin
Phoebe	Pam Grier
Snopes	Nipsey Russell
Walker	James Bigwood
Deputy Buntzman	Mark Buntzman
Spanish Soldier	Ismael Calderon
Susan	Tracy Lee Chavis
Town Drunk	James E. Christopher
Cook	Lawrence Cook
Deputy Tom	Richard Edson
Doubletree	Richard Gant

and Thomas Steven Hall (Deputy Errol), Clabe Hartley (Klikai), Sandra Ellis Lafferty (Big Kate), Jeffrey Lloyd Layne (Little Joseph), Robert May (John, The Blacksmith), T.J. McClain (Monty), Christopher Michael (Izzy), Bob Minor (Alex), Aaron Neville (Railroad Singer), Steve Reevis (Two Bears), Sy Richardson (Shepherd), Dario Scardapane (Photographer), Frank A. Soto (Aaron), David Jean Thomas (Head Rower), Mark Twogood (Wallace), Karen Williams (Dilsey), Geo Cook, Michel Cook, I. Keith Cunningham, Andrew J. Gregory, Will "Nahkohe" Strickland (Iron Brigade), Badd Boyz of the Industry, Eugene Brooks, Shon Evans, Shydi Evans, Damian Johnson, Anthony R. Walker (Street Performers)

Plot Capsule: *Hoping to avenge his father's murder Jessie Lee engages a band of deserters from the Spanish-American war to trek to the town of Freesmansville. This western, featuring a principally black cast, marked the first theatrical release from Gramercy Pictures.*

© Gramercy Pictures

Billy Zane

Salli Richardson

Blair Underwood

Director Mario Van Peebles

Sharon Stone, William Baldwin

SLIVER

(PARAMOUNT) Producer, Robert Evans; Executive Producers, Howard W. Koch, Jr., Joe Eszterhas; Director, Phillip Noyce; Screenplay, Joe Eszterhas; Based on the novel by Ira Levin; Photography, Vilmos Zsigmond; Designer, Paul Sylbert; Editors, Richard Francis-Bruce, William Hoy; Co-Producer, William J. MacDonald; Music, Howard Shore; Casting, Amanda Mackey, Cathy Sandrich; Dolby Stereo; Deluxe color; Rated R; 106 minutes; May release

Sharon Stone

CAST

Carly Norris	Sharon Stone
Zeke Hawkins	William Baldwin
Jack Landsford	Tom Berenger
Vida Jordan	Polly Walker
Judy	Colleen Camp
Samantha	Amanda Foreman
Alex Parsons	Martin Landau
Lt. Victoria Hendrix	CCH Pounder
Mrs. McEvoy	Nina Foch
Gus Hale	Keene Curtis
Peter Farrell	Nicholas Pryor
Jackie Kinsella	Anne Betancourt
Martin Kinsella	Tony Peck
Doorman	Frantz Turner
Dr. Palme	Dr. Melvyn Kinder
Dmitri	Radu Gavor
Naomi Singer	Allison Mackie
Detective Corelli	Jose Rey
Detective Ira	Jim Beaver
Janitor Rodrigues	Gilbert Rosales
Security Guards	Mik Scriba, Steve Carlisle
Waiter	Mark Bramhall
Doctor	Christine Avila
Mr. Anderson	Sid McCoy
Ted Weisberger	Alexander Gutman
Mrs. Ballinger	Robin Groves
Mr. Ballinger	Matthew Faison
Ballinger's Daughter	Marne Patterson
Gloria Alden	Katharine Pope
Reporters	Christine Toy, Philip Hoffman, Nicole Orth-Pallavicini
Waspy Man	Arthur Eckdahl
Waspy Woman	Patricia Allison
Minister	Bernie McInerney
Doormen	James Noah, Eduardo N.T. Andrade
Detective Howard	Robert Miano
Detective Phillip	Steve Eastin
Man brushing teeth	Phillip Noyce

Keene Curtis

Nina Foch

Plot Capsule: *Following the mysterious death of a previous occupant, Carly Norris moves into a sleek Manhattan apartment building, where all of the tenants are unknowingly watched by way of a sophisticated surveillance set-up. Mystery adapted from the best selling novel by Ira Levin.*

Sharon Stone, Tom Berenger

HOT SHOTS!
PART DEUX

(20th CENTURY FOX) Producer, Bill Badalato; Executive Producer, Pat Proft; Director, Jim Abrahams; Screenplay, Jim Abrahams, Pat Proft; Photography, John R. Leonetti; Designer, William A. Elliott; Editor, Malcolm Campbell; Music, Basil Poledouris; Associate Producers, Greg Norberg, Michael McManus; Costumes, Mary Malin; Casting, Jackie Burch; Visual Effects Supervisor, Erik Henry; Dolby Stereo; Deluxe color; Rated PG-13; 87 minutes; May release

CAST
(in order that you should know their names)

Topper Harley	Charlie Sheen
Tug Benson	Lloyd Bridges
Ramada Rodham Hayman	Valeria Golino
Colonel Denton Walters	Richard Crenna
Michelle Rodham Huddleston	Brenda Bakke
Harbinger	Miguel Ferrer
Dexter Hayman	Rowan Atkinson
Saddam Hussein	Jerry Haleva
Gerou	David Wohl
Gray Edwards	Mitchell Ryan
Williams	Michael Colyar
Rabinowitz	Ryan Stiles
Lavinia Rodham Benson	Rosemary Johnston
The Captain	Gregory Sierra
Rufshaad	Andreas Katsulas
Prime Minister Soto	Clyde Kusatsu

and Ben Lemon (Team 2 Leader), Buck McDancer (Richard Nixon), Larry Lindsey (Gerald Ford), Ed Beheler (Jimmy Carter), Daniel T. Healy (George Bush), Jay Koch (Ronald Reagan), Charlie Haugk (Navy Seal), Dian Kobayashi (Mrs. Rodham Soto), Bob Vila (Himself), Stuart Proud Eagle Grant (Geronimo), J.D. DeKranis (Michael Corleone Look-Alike), Bob Legionnaire (Capt. McCluskey Look-Alike), Corey Rand (Sollozzo Look-Alike), Tony Edwards (Limo Driver), James Lew (Kick Boxer Opponent), Gerald Okamura (Corrupt Kick Boxing Referee), Chi-Muoi Lo (Thai Kick Boxing Sportscaster), Ron Pitts (Black Kick Boxing Sportscaster), Norm Compton (Phil), Kelly Connell (Radio Operator), Wayne Satz (News Anchorman), Pat Harvey (News Reporter), Joseph V. Perry (Singing Waiter), Oz Tortora (Singing Busboy), Judith Kahan (Veiled Woman), Shaun Toub (Sleeping Guard), Mark Steen (Adrian Messenger), Carey Tall, Sr. (Train Conductor), Don Miloyevich (Cab Driver), Edward Nassaney (Iraqi Door Guard), Andy Siegel (Iraqi Soldier), C. Ransom Walrod (Iraqi Boat Driver) John Arthur Escobar (Necktie Guard), Scott Reeves, Christopher Lindsay, Daniel Herold, Thomas Temple, Lindsay Kough, Dennis Barglof, Michael Templeton, Andrew Link, Keith Woulard, Dan Jessee, Chris Sweeney, Timothy Henkel (Navy Seals), Melanie Asistores, Tiaraya Soo, Haeran Park, Carol Tong (Raker Girls), Nancy Abrahams (Mother whose baby is snatched), Charlie Abrahams (Snatched Baby), Jane Butenhoff (Slim Woman at banquet), Louise Yaffe, Eleanor Schiff (Gray Edwards' Concubines), Pamela Thompson, Karen "Boom Boom" Proft, Nancy Sheen (Nuns Not in This Movie), Don Gruenberg, Alice Gruenberg, Jamie Abrahams (Backyard Family), Joseph "Bambi" Abrahams (Basketball Player), Alison Anne Abrahams (Chain Skimmer), Jack Benstein (Cop), Deborah Hwang-Marriott (Kickboxing Mother), William Haig Marriott (Kickboxing Child), Siren, Zap (American Gladiators), Martin Sheen (Capt. Willard)

Plot Capsule: *Sequel to the 1991 comedy* Hot Shots *follows Topper Harley on a dangerous rescue mission, spoofing the* Rambo *films specifically and war movies in general.*

© Twentieth Century Fox

TOP LEFT: Charlie Sheen, Valeria Golino
MIDDLE: Charlie Sheen
BOTTOM LEFT: Ryan Stiles, Miguel Ferrer, Michael Colyar

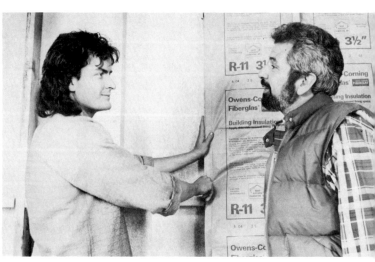

Charlie Sheen, Bob Vila

Tyrin Turner, Larenz Tate, MC Eiht

MENACE II SOCIETY

(NEW LINE CINEMA) Producer, Darin Scott; Directors, The Hughes Brothers (Allen Hughes, Albert Hughes); Screenplay, Tyger Williams; Story/Co-Producers, Allen and Albert Hughes, Tyger Williams; Executive Producer, Kevin Moreton; Photography. Lisa Rinzler; Desinger, Penny Barrett; Costumes, Sylvia Vega-Vasquez; Music, QD III; Editor, Christopher Koefoed; Casting, Tony Lee; a New Line production; Dolby Stereo; Foto Kem color; Rated R; 107 minutes; May release

CAST

Tyrin Turner (C)

Caine Lawson	Tyrin Turner
Ronnie	Jada Pinkett
O-Dog	Larenz Tate
Grandpapa	Arnold Johnson
Sharif	Vonte Sweet
Grandmama	Marilyn Coleman
A-Wax	MC Eiht
Chauncy	Clifton Powell
Pernell	Glenn Plummer
Lew-Loc	Too $hort
Detective	Bill Duke
Tat Lawson	Samuel L. Jackson
Mr. Butler	Charles S. Dutton
Doc	Pooh Man
Anthony	Jullian Roy Doster
Stacy	Ryan Williams
Harold Lawson	Reginald Saafir Mohamed
Lloyd	Christopher M. Brown
Junior	Garen Holman
Deena	Stacy Arnell

and Dave Kirsch (Insurance Man), Erin Leshawn Wiley (Ilena), Samuel Monroe, Jr. (Guy, Ilena's Cousin), June Kyoko Lu (Grocery Store Woman), Toshi Toda (Grocery Store Man), Brandon Hammond (5 year old Caine), Reginald Ballard (Clyde), Khandi Alexander (Karen Lawson), Eugene Lee, James Pickins, Jr. (Men), Nancy Cheryl Davis (Teacher), Cynthia Calhoun (Jackee), Joy Matthews (Nurse #1), Dwayne Barnes (Basehead), Alvin Mears (K-9 Police Officer), Robert R. Gonzales (Car Dealer), Martin Davis (Car-Jack Victim), Charles J. Grube (Officer Fassel), Mike Kelly (Officer Gadd), Rolando Molina, Clifton Gonzalez Gonzalez, Tony Valentino, Danny Villarreal (Vatos), Yo Yo (Girl at party)

Plot Capsule: *Involved in a shooting at a convenience store, Caine, an L.A. teenager, sees his life descend further into the nightmare world of drugs and violence. This drama marked the directorial debut of brothers Albert and Allen Hughes.*

© New Line Cinema

Tyrin Turner, Julian Roy Doster

Sylvester Stallone, Janine Turner

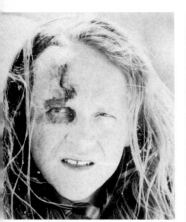

Denis Forest

Craig Fairbrass

Gregory Scott Cummins   Sylvester Stallone   Leon

John Lithgow, Caroline Goodall
TOP RIGHT: Michael Rooker, Ralph Waite

CLIFFHANGER

(TRISTAR) Producers, Alan Marshall, Renny Harlin; Executive Producer, Mario Kassar; Director, Renny Harlin; Screenplay, Michael France, Sylvester Stallone; Story, Michael France, based on a premise by John Long; Photography, Alex Thomson; Designer, John Vallone; Editor, Frank J. Urioste; Music, Trevor Jones; Costumes, Ellen Mirojnick; Associate Producers, Tony Munafo, Jim Davidson; Co-Producers, Gene Patrick Hines, James R. Zatolokin, David Rotman; Co-Executive Producer, Lynwood Spinks; Casting, Mindy Martin; Stunts, Joel Kramer; Visual Effects Producer, Pamela Easley; Visual Effects Supervisors, Neil Krepela, John Bruno; Aerial Unit Coordinator, Marc Wolff; a Carolco/Le Studio Canal+/Pioneer Production, in association with RCS Video; Dolby Stereo; Panavision; Technicolor; Rated R; 114 minutes; May release

CAST

Gabe Walker	Sylvester Stallone
Qualen	John Lithgow
Hal Tucker	Michael Rooker
Jessie Deighan	Janine Turner
Travers	Rex Linn
Kristel	Caroline Goodall
Kynette	Leon
Delmar	Craig Fairbrass
Ryan	Gregory Scott Cummins
Heldon	Denis Forest
Sarah	Michelle Joyner
Evan	Max Perlich
Walter Wright	Paul Winfield
Frank	Ralph Waite
Brett	Trey Brownell
Davis	Zach Grenier
Matheson	Vyto Ruginis
Stuart	Don Davis
Agent Hayes	Scott Hoxby
Agent Michaels	John Finn
Treasury Agent	Bruce McGill
Treasury Secretary	Rosemary Dunsmore
Treasury Jet Pilot	Kim Robillard
Pilot	Jeff McCarthy
Co-Pilot	Mike Weis
Treasury Helicopter Pilot	Duncan Prentice
Ray	Kevin Donald
Marvin	Jeff Blynn
Thor	Thor

Plot Capsule: *Adventure drama in which a criminal mastermind and his cohorts force a pair of Colorado mountain climbers to help them locate three cases containing a stolen fortune in cash.*

The film received Academy Award nominations for special visual effects, sound and sound effects editing.

© TriStar Pictures Inc.

Rex Linn, John Lithgow

Sylvester Stallone, Janine Turner

65

MADE IN AMERICA

(WARNER BROS.) Producers, Arnon Milchan, Michael Douglas, Rick Bieber; Executive Producers, Nadine Schiff, Marcia Brandwynne; Co-Executive Producer, Steven Reuther; Co-Producer, Patrick Palmer; Director, Richard Benjamin; Screenplay, Holly Goldberg Sloan; Story, Marcia Brandwynne, Nadine Schiff, Holly Goldberg Sloan; Photography, Ralf Bode; Designer, Evelyn Sakash; Costumes, Elizabeth McBride; Editor, Jacqueline Cambas; Music, Mark Isham; Casting, Reuben Cannon & Assocs.; a Le Studio Canal+, Regency Enterprises and Alcor Film presentation of a Stonebridge Entertainment/Kalola Productions, Inc./Arnon Milchan production; Dolby Stereo; Deluxe color; Rated PG-13; 111 minutes; May release

Ted Danson, Whoopi Goldberg

CAST

Sarah Mathews	Whoopi Goldberg
Hal Jackson	Ted Danson
Tea Cake Walters	Will Smith
Zora Mathews	Nia Long
Jose	Paul Rodriguez
Stacy	Jennifer Tilly
Alberta	Peggy Rea
Bob Takashima	Clyde Kusatsu
Teddy	David Bowe
James	Jeffrey Joseph
Diego	Rawley Valverde
Bruce	Fred Mancuso
Paula	Charlene Fernetz
Dwayne	Shawn Levy
Clinic Nurse	Lu Leonard
Hospital Doctor	Joe Lerer
Hospital Nurse	Janice Edwards
Hospital Intern	Michael McFall
White Women	Phyllis Avery, Frances Bergen
Rocky	O'Neal Compton
Stew	Michael Halton
P.A.s	William John Murphy, Ross Benjamin
Principal Rockwell	Mel Stewart
Mr. Alden	David E. Kazanjian
Person at car lot	Jim Cranna
Wife at car lot	Shannon Orrock
Child at car lot	Alexandra Joy Cuccia
Japanese Women	Chikako Felper, Patricia Jow
Woman in sushi bar	Raquel Osborne
Man with beer	James Anthony Cotton
Sushi Waitress	Miyuki Takei
Sushi Chef	Akihide "Bo" Fujiyama
Rappers	Y-T Style: Gregory Fields, Meashell McCann, Antoine Foote, Jeffrey Russell

Plot Capsule: *Breaking into the records at a sperm bank a young black girl is dismayed to find out that her biological father is white.*

© Regency Enterprises V.O.F./Le Studio Canal

Will Smith, Nia Long

Will Smith, Whoopi Goldberg

Sally the Chimp, Ted Danson

Dennis Hopper

John Leguizamo, Bob Hoskins

SUPER MARIO BROS.

(HOLLYWOOD PICTURES) Producers, Jake Eberts, Roland Joffe; Co-Producer, Fred Caruso; Directors, Rocky Morton, Annabel Jankel; Screenplay, Parker Bennett, Terry Runte, Ed Solomon; Based on the concept and characters created by Shigeru Miyamoto and Takashi Tezuka of Nintendo; Photography, Dean Semler; Designer, David L. Snyder; Editor, Mark Goldblatt; Visual Effects Design and Supervision, Christopher Francis Woods; Costumes, Joseph Porro; Music, Alan Silvestri; Associate Producer, Brad Weston; Casting, Mali Finn, Donn Finn; Stunts, Gary Jensen; a Lightmotive/Allied Filmmakers presentation in association with Cinergi Productions; Distributed by Buena Vista Pictures; Dolby Stereo; Technicolor; Rated PG; 104 minutes; May release

CAST

Mario Mario	Bob Hoskins
Luigi Mario	John Leguizamo
King Koopa	Dennis Hopper
Daisy	Samantha Mathis
Iggy	Fisher Stevens
Spike	Richard Edson
Lena	Fiona Shaw
Daniella	Dana Kaminski
Toad	Mojo Nixon
Scapelli	Gianni Russo
Bertha	Francesca Roberts
The King	Lance Henriksen
Old Lady	Sylvia Harman
Angelica	Desiree Marie Velez
Brooklyn Girls	Andrea Powell, Heather Pendergast, Melanie Salvatore
Goomba Toad	John Fifer
Sgt. Simon	Don Lake
Hat Check Girl	Terry Finn
Goombas	Thomas Merdis, Michael Harding, Michael Lynch, Scott Mactavish, Wallace Merck
Nuns	Mona B. Fierro, Karen Brigman, Christi Work, Joy Rees, Lucy Alpaugh
T.V. Announcer	Robert Raiford
Reporters	Harry Murphy, Patt Noday
Scapelli Bodyguards	Robert Lee Edwards, Ronald Lou Edwards
Pizza Delivery Boy	Matthew Zachary Hopkins
Egon	Robert Faulkner Priester
James	Preston Lane
Japanese Businessmen	Jim Asaki, Matt Nikko
Devo Controller	Kevin West
Devo Technician	Jeffrey Pillars
Creature Voices	Frank Welker
Narrator	Dan Castellenetta

Plot Capsule: *Sci-fi fantasy adapted from the popular video game. A pair of New York plumbers enter an alternate universe to rescue a princess and save the destruction of the world.*

© Allied Filmmakers N.V./Nintendo

Richard Edson, Fisher Stevens, with Goombas
ABOVE: Goomba, Samantha Mathis, Yoshi

Michael J. Fox, Christina Vidal, Nathan Lane

LIFE WITH MIKEY

(TOUCHSTONE) Producers, Teri Schwartz, Scott Rudin; Director, James Lapine; Screenplay/Co-Producer, Marc Lawrence; Photography, Rob Hahn; Designer, Adrianne Lobel; Editor, Robert Leighton; Costumes, William Ivey Long; Music, Alan Menken; Songs: "Cold Enough to Snow" by Alan Menken (music), Stephen Schwartz (lyrics)/ performed by Jennifer Warnes, "Life With Mikey Theme" by Alan Menken (music), Jack Feldman (lyrics); Casting, John Lyons; Distributed by Buena Vista Pictures; Dolby Stereo; Technicolor; Rated PG; 93 minutes; June release

CAST

Michael Chapman	Michael J. Fox
Angie Vega	Christina Vidal
Ed Chapman	Nathan Lane
Geena Briganti	Cyndi Lauper
Barry Corman	David Krumholtz
Mr. Corcoran	David Huddleston

and Victor Garber (Brian Spiro), Frances Chaney (Mrs. Cantrell), Kathryn Grody (Mrs. Corman), Mary Alice (Mrs. Gordon), Annabelle Gurwitch (Debbie), Kathleen McNenny (Allison Jones), Jonathan Charles Kaplan (George), Tony Hendra (Cookie Commercial Director), Mario Todisco (Driver), Michael Rupert (Harrison), Christine Baranski (Carol), Sean Power (Lenny), Laura Bundy (Courtney Aspinall), Chris Durang (Santa), Barbara Walsh (Commercial Mother), Brenda Currin (George's Mom), Heather MacRae (Mrs. Tobin), Wendy Wasserstein (Mrs. Wasserman), Ryan Kent (Evan), Tim Progosh (Norman Feller), Aida Turturro (Officer Moran), Paula Garces (Janice), Ralph Small (Mr. Wasserman), Kevin Zegers (Little Mikey), Tracy Spindler (Cynthia), Dylan Baker (Mr. Burns), Kate Burton (Mrs. Burns), Stephen Bogardus, William Finn (Men), Ann Lawrence (Concerned Woman), Kelli Fox (Marilyn), Robin Byrd (Bambi), Hrant Alianak (Cereal Commercial Director), Jerry Lawler (The Lobotomizer), Jeff Jarrett (Evil Eye), Anaysha Figueroa (Kimberly Denise Jackson), Michelle Moffat (Kimberly's Mom), Frank Crudele (Passerby), Carlton Watson (Galaxy Waiter), Sandra Caldwell (Corcoran Receptionist), Eve Crawford (Courtney's Mom), Marcell Rosenblatt (Tiffany's Mom), Silvio Oliverio (Marker), Janet Metz (Employee), Mandy Patinkin (Irate Man), BETTY: Alyson Palmer, Amy Ziff, Bitzi Ziff (Street Singing Trio), Barbara Hollander (Judy Wasserman), Giannetta Savarino (Baton Twirler), Shayna Rossin (Tiffany), Richard James MacDonald (Impressionist), Samson Benen (Boy), Joey Allen (Hockey Player), Holly Bohl, Kristen Bohl (Tobin Twins), Vanessa Wilson (Ventriloquist), Ashley Brown (Eric the Magician), Chantel LeBlanc (Cristin), Tara Pearson (Erin), Elan Rivera (Spanish Singer), Jessica Wilson (New York Singer), Phoebe Lapine, Anna Rose Menken, Ali Caplan (Andrews Sisters), Jacob Reynolds (Baseball Boy), Kristen Simpson (Bluebird Singer), Shatim Welch, Kai Reevey, Ashley Canterna (Rap Kids), Damian Gryski (Juggler), Veronica Wappel, Victoria Wappel (Hippie Sisters), Chelsie Lamie (Violinist), Syreeta Neal (Street Drummer), Blake McGrath, Tina Pereira (Acrobats), Soliella Cole, Angela Cole (Stilt Walkers), Billy Joel Ablaza (Party Boy), Stephanie Berntson (Opera Singer), Stefanie Gnys (Tap Dancer), Adrienne Canterna (Belly Dancer), Erica Yamada (Erica), Camille Harrison, Christine Muir, Gigi Uson (Cookie Dancers), Karen Greene, Caitlin Lee Lockwood, Bronwen Roach, Martha Schabas, Kate Scheuer (Ballerinas), Ruben Blades (Angie's Father)

Plot Capsule: *New York-based comedy. Former child star Michael Chapman hopes to revive his failing talent agency by representing a streetwise 10 year-old girl*

© Touchstone Pictures

David Krumholtz, Christina Vidal

Christina Vidal, Michael J. Fox

Christina Vidal, Michael J. Fox

Michael J. Fox

William Finn, Ann Lawrence, Christina Vidal, Michael J. Fox

Christina Vidal, Cyndi Lauper, Michael J. Fox

Joel Grey, Mandy Patinkin, James Spader, Charles Durning

Mandy Patinkin, James Spader

THE MUSIC OF CHANCE

James Spader, Charles Durning

(I.R.S. RELEASING) Producers, Frederick Zollo, Dylan Sellers; Executive Producers, Miles Copeland III, Paul Colichman, Lindsay Law; Co-Producer, Kerry Orent; Director, Philip Haas; Screenplay, Philip Haas, Belinda Haas; Based on the novel by Paul Auster; Photography, Bernard Zitzermann; Designer, Hugo Luczyc-Wyhowski; Costumes, Rudy Dillon; Music, Phillip Johnston; Casting, Bonnie Timmermann; an I.R.S./Trans Atlantic Entertainment and American Playhouse Theatrical Films presentation; Dolby Stereo; Foto-Kem color; Rated R; 97 minutes; June release

CAST

Jack Pozzi	James Spader
James Nashe	Mandy Patinkin
Calvin Murks	M. Emmet Walsh
Bill Flower	Charles Durning
Willie Stone	Joel Grey
Tiffany	Samantha Mathis
Floyd	Christopher Penn
Louise	Pearl Jones
Floyd Jr.	Jordan Spainhour
Driver	Paul Auster

Plot Capsule: *Two drifters decide to accept an offer to play poker with a pair of eccentric millionaires, with unexpected consequences.*

© I.R.S./Trans Atlantic

Mandy Patinkin, James Spader

GUILTY AS SIN

(HOLLYWOOD PICTURES) formerly *Beyond Innocence;* Producer, Martin Ransohoff; Executive Producers, Don Carmody, Bob Robinson; Director, Sidney Lumet; Screenplay, Larry Cohen; Photography, Andrzej Bartkowiak; Designer, Philip Rosenberg; Costumes, Gary Jones; Editor, Evan Lottman; Music, Howard Shore; Casting, Lynn Stalmaster; Associate Producers, Lilith Jacobs, Jolene Moroney; Distributed by Buena Vista Pictures; Dolby Stereo; Technicolor; Rated R; 106 minutes; June release

Don Johnson, Rebecca De Mornay

CAST

Jennifer Haines	Rebecca De Mornay
David Greenhill	Don Johnson
Phil Garson	Stephen Lang
Moe Plimpton	Jack Warden
Judge Tompkins	Dana Ivey
Diangelo	Ron White
Emily	Norma Dell'Agnese
Nolan	Sean McCann
Lt. Bernard Martinez	Luis Guzman
Caniff	Robert Kennedy
McMartin	James Blendick
Heath	Tom Butler
Miriam Langford	Christina Baren
Esther Rothman	Lynne Cormack
Kathleen Bigelow	Barbara Eve Harris
Mr. Loo	Simon Sinn
Ed Lombardo	John Kapelos
Ray Schiff	Tom McCamus
Judge Steinberg	Harvey Atkin
Ken Powell	Anthony Sherwood
Arraignment Judge	Chris Benson
Receptionist	Melanie Nicholls-King
Clerk	Johnie Chase
Rita Greenhill	Brigit Wilson
Plasterer	Alberto De Rosa
Woman at cleaners	Yanira Contreras
Woman at supper club	Shelley Young
Postal Supervisor	Sandi Ross
Handwriting Expert	Peter Blais
Lab Technician	Denis Akiyama
Nurse	Lili Francks
Intern	Roland Rothchild
Jury Foreman	Jack Newman
Security Guard	Gene Mack
Squash Player	Tom Quinn

Plot Capsule: *Drama in which attorney Jennifer Haines reluctantly takes on the case of arrogant ladies' man David Greenhill, accused of killing his wife for her money.*

© Hollywood Pictures Co.`

Rebecca De Mornay, Don Johnson

Don Johnson, Rebecca De Mornay, Jack Warden

Khandi Alexander, Vanessa Bell Calloway, Laurence Fishburne, Angela Bassett

WHAT'S LOVE GOT TO DO WITH IT

(TOUCHSTONE) Producers, Doug Chapin, Barry Krost; Executive Producers, Roger Davies, Mario Iscovich; Director, Brian Gibson; Screenplay, Kate Lanier; Based upon the book *I, Tina* by Tina Turner and Kurt Loder; Photography, Jamie Anderson; Designer, Stephen Altman; Editor, Stuart Pappe; Costumes, Ruth Carter; Choreographer, Michael Peters; Music, Stanley Clarke; Co-Producer: Pat Kehoe; Casting, Reuben Cannon & Associates; Distributed by Buena Vista Pictures; Dolby Stereo; Technicolor; Rated R; 118 minutes; June release

CAST

Tina Turner	Angela Bassett
Ike Turner	Laurence Fishburne
Jackie	Vanessa Bell Calloway
Zelma Bullock	Jenifer Lewis
Alline Bullock	Phyllis Yvonne Stickney
Darlene	Khandi Alexander

and Rae'ven Kelly (Young Anna Mae), Virginia Capers (Choir Mistress), Cora Lee Day (Grandma Georgiana), Sherman Augustus (Reggie), Chi (Fross), Terrence Riggins (Spider), Gene "Groove" Allen (Club Announcer), Pamala Tyson (Leanne), Penny Johnson (Lorraine), Rob LaBelle (Phil Spector), Elijah Saleem (Ike Jr., age one), Tyrandis Holmes (Young Ike, Jr.), Jamaine Harrington (Young Michael), Devon Davison (Young Ronnie), Eric Thomas (Young Craig), Richard T. Jones (Ike Turner, Jr.), Michael David Simms (Ike's Lawyer), John Fink (Anna's Lawyer), James Reyne (Roger Davies), Dorothy Thornton, Juanita Allen, Natalie Wilson, David McKinney, Maurice O'Niel, Monroe Howard, Wakeen Best, Francis Cheaton, Bell Dawn Best, Billie Barnum, Jeanne Steele, Cassandra Thames, Demetrice Cheaton, Helen Marie Lovelace, Seymour Daniel, Jayd Stanfield, Frank Raspberry, Serist Roberts, Michelle Jackson, Dena Ellerbee, Maggie McGee, Alfie Silas, Oren Waters, Valetta Barber (Choir Members), Rev. Emery Shaw (Organ Player), Morris O'Connor, Larry Washington, Joe Allen, Michael Sessions, L. Van Taylor (The Kings of Rhythm), Jennifer Leigh Warren, Sonya Hensley, Leslie Thurston, Eartha Robinson (Audience Members), Kate Lanier (Stripper on balcony), Jacqueline Woolsey (Boutique Clerk), Mayah McCoy (Young Hairdresser), Barry "Shabaka" Henley (El Paso Doctor), Michael Colyar (Apollo Announcer), Patricia Sill (Spector's Assistant), Ronnie Turner, Michael Butler, Greg Cook, Michael Smith, Brian Cayle, Darrel Richards, Walter Davis (The Revue), Barry O'Neill, Ali Glazer, Julie Phillips (Kids), Bob Kane (Dance Show Host), Shavar Ross (Michael Turner), Damon Hines (Ronnie Turner), Suli McCullough (Craig Turner), Daniel McDonald (London Announcer), Wyonna Smith, Rosemarie Jackson (Ikettes), Rudolph Willrich (Judge), Irene DeBari (ICU Nurse), Terrance Evans (Bus Driver), Richard Stay, Nelson Parks, Matt Kirkwood (Party Goers), Javi Mulero (Bellhop), Joe Vant (Hotel Clerk), O'Neal Compton (Ramada Inn Manager), Michael Monks (Hotel Porter), James Ralston (Guitarist), Timmy Cappello (Keyboards), Jack Bruno (Drummer), Bob Feit (Bass Player), Kenny Moore (Piano Player), Daniel Allan Carlin (Conductor), Dean Minerd (Stagehand), Fred Ponzlov, Tom De Carlo, Richard B. Livingston, Louis Mawcinitt (Managers), Owen Bush, Herb Muller, David Fresco (Old Men), Sparkle, Helen Brown (Old Women), Page Moseley (Ritz Announcer), Lorna Scott (Nurse), Rick Felkins (Stage Manager), Robert Lesser (Fairmount MC)

Plot Capsule: *True story of singer Tina Turner's rise to stardom and her turbulent marriage to musician Ike Turner. Angela Bassett's vocals were dubbed by Tina Turner, who appears in a concert clip at the film's end.*

Angela Bassett received the Golden Globe Award for Best Actress in a Musical or Comedy; Bassett also received an Academy Award nomination for best actress while Laurence Fishburne was also nominated by the Academy for best actor.

© Touchstone Pictures

Rob LaBelle, Angela Bassett, Laurence Fishburne

Tina Turner, Angela Bassett

Angela Bassett

Laurence Fishburne, Angela Bassett

Laurence Fishburne, Angela Bassett

Angela Bassett, Laurence Fishburne

Angela Bassett, Laurence Fishburne

Jeff Goldblum, Richard Attenborough, Laura Dern, Sam Neill

Joseph Mazzello, Sam Neill, Ariana Richards

JURASSIC PARK

(UNIVERSAL) Producers, Kathleen Kennedy, Gerald R. Molen; Director, Steven Spielberg; Screenplay, Michael Crichton, David Koepp; Based on the novel by Michael Crichton; Photography, Dean Cundey; Designer, Rick Carter; Editor, Michael Kahn; Music, John Williams; Associate Producers, Lata Ryan, Colin Wilson; Full-Motion Dinosaurs, Dennis Muren; Live Action Dinosaurs, Stan Winston; Dinosaur Supervisor, Phil Tippett; Special Dinosaur Effects, Michael Lantieri; Full Motion Dinosaurs and Special Visual Effects, Industrial Light & Magic; Casting, Janet Hirshenson, Jane Jenkins; an Amblin Entertainment production; Dolby Stereo; Deluxe color; Rated PG-13; 123 minutes; June release

CAST

Alan Grant	Sam Neill
Ellie Sattler	Laura Dern
Ian Malcolm	Jeff Goldblum
John Hammond	Richard Attenborough
Robert Muldoon	Bob Peck
Donald Gennaro	Martin Ferrero
Dr. Wu	B.D. Wong
Tim	Joseph Mazzello
Lex	Ariana Richards
Arnold	Samuel L. Jackson
Dennis Nedry	Wayne Knight
Harding	Jerry Molen
Rostagno	Miguel Sandoval
Dodgson	Cameron Thor
Volunteer #1	Christopher John Fields
Volunteer Boy	Whit Hertford
Mate	Dean Cundey
Worker in Raptor pen	Jophery Brown
Helicopter Pilot	Tom Mishler
"Mr. D.N.A." Voice	Greg Burson
Worker at Amber Mine	Adrian Escober
Jurassic Park Tour Voice	Richard Kiley

Plot Capsule: *Fantasy-thriller from the best selling book about an island theme park featuring genetically cloned Dinosaurs and the eventual havoc that ensues when the park's power is shut down. This film became the highest grossing movie released in 1993.*

1993 Academy Award winner for Best Special Visual Effects, Sound and Sound Effects Editing.

© Universal City Studios/Amblin Entertainment

Laura Dern, Richard Attenborough, Martin Ferrero,
Jeff Goldblum, Sam Neill

Ariana Richards, Sam Neill, Joseph Mazzello

Joseph Mazzello, Laura Dern,
Ariana Richards, Sam Neill

Laura Dern, Jeff Goldblum, Bob Peck
ABOVE: Ariana Richards, Sam Neill

Robert Prosky, Austin O'Brien
TOP RIGHT: Arnold Schwarzenegger

LAST ACTION HERO

(COLUMBIA) Producers, Steve Roth, John McTiernan; Co-Producers, Robert E. Relyea, Neal Nordlinger; Executive Producer, Arnold Schwarzenegger; Director, John McTiernan; Screenplay, Shane Black, David Arnott; Story, Zak Penn, Adam Leff; Photography, Dean Semler; Designer, Eugenio Zanetti; Editor, John Wright; Visual Effects Consultant, Richard Greenberg; Music, Michael Kamen; Costumes, Gloria Gresham; Casting, Jane Jenkins, Janet Hirshenson; Stunts, Fred M. Waugh, Joel Kramer, Vic Armstrong; a Steve Roth/Oak production; Dolby Stereo; Panavision; Technicolor; Rated PG-13; 130 minutes; June release

CAST

Jack Slater/Arnold Schwarzenegger	Arnold Schwarzenegger
John Practice	F. Murray Abraham
Frank	Art Carney
Benedict	Charles Dance
Dekker	Frank McRae
The Ripper/Tom Noonan	Tom Noonan
Nick	Robert Prosky
Tony Vivaldi	Anthony Quinn
Mrs. Madigan	Mercedes Ruehl
Danny Madigan	Austin O'Brien
Death	Sir Ian McKellen
Tough Asian Man	Professor Toru Tanaka
Teacher	Joan Plowright
Lieutenant Governor	Jason Kelly
Rookie	Noah Emmerich
The Mayor	Tina Turner
SWAT Cop	Billy Lucas
Andrew Slater	Ryan Todd
Polonius	Apollo Dukakis
Punk	Patrick Flanagan
Monoghan	Donald C. Llorens
Monroe	Michael Chieffo
Cop in LA station	Mike Muscat
Watch Commander	John Finnegan
Video Babes	Bobbie Brown-Lane, Angie Everhart
Whitney/Meredith	Bridgette Wilson
Skeezy	Jeffrey Braer
Cop at Ex-Wife's House	Anthony Peck
Cop #2 in LA station	Paul Gonzales
Cop in station	Anna Navarro

and Dex Sanders (Mitchell), Nick Dimitri (Doctor at funeral), Sven-Ole Thorsen (Gunman), Rick Ducommun (Ripper's Agent), Wendle Josepher (Candy Girl), Michael V. Gazzo (Torelli), Lee Reherman (Krause), R.C. Bates (Rabbi), Colleen Camp (Ratcliff), Donna Borghoff (Hooker), John McTiernan, Sr. (Cigar Stand Man), Tiffany Puhy (Autograph Seeker), Keith Barish, Jim Belushi, Chevy Chase, Chris Connelly, Karen Duffy, Larry Ferguson, Leeza Gibbons, Hammer, Little Richard, Robert Patrick, Maria Shriver, Sharon Stone, Jean-Claude Van Damme, Melvin Van Peebles, Damon Wayans (Cameos), Danny DeVito (Voice of Whiskers)

Plot Capsule: *A teenager finds a magic movie ticket that allows him to be a part of the latest Jack Slater action thriller, in this tongue-in-cheek adventure.*

© Columbia Pictures Industries

Arnold Schwarzenegger, Mercedes Ruehl
ABOVE: Austin O'Brien, Tom Noonan

HOUSE OF CARDS

(MIRAMAX) Producers, Dale Pollock, Lianne Halfon, Wolfgang Glattes; Executive Producer, Vittorio Cecchi Gori; Co-Executive Producer, Gianni Nunnari; Co-Producer, Jonathan Sanger; Director/Screenplay, Michael Lessac; Story, Michael Lessac, Robert Jay Litz; Photography, Victor Hammer; Designer, Peter Larkin; Editor, Walter Murch; Music, James Horner; Costumes, Julie Weiss; Casting, Mali Finn; from Penta Films; Dolby Stereo; Deluxe color; Rated PG-13; 108 minutes; June release

CAST

Ruth Matthews	Kathleen Turner
Dr. Jake Beerlander	Tommy Lee Jones
Sally Matthews	Asha Menina
Michael Matthews	Shiloh Strong
Adelle	Esther Rolle
Lillian Huber	Park Overall
Stoker	Michael Horse
Judge	Anne Pitoniak
Sectenel	Joaquin Martinez
Joey's Mother	Jacqueline Cassel
Bart Huber	John Henderson
Roy Huber	Craig Fuller
Frank Stearson	Rick Marshall
Reuben	Reuben Valiquette Murray
Emily	Emily Russell
Joey	Joseph Michael Sipe, Jr.
Melissa	Yvette Thor
Teacher	Connie Mashburn
Samuel	Samuel David Miller
Michael	Michael McDaniel
Robert	Robert W. Lyon
Luchera	LuChera Huntley
Issac	Issac J. Banks
Eric	Eric Coble

Plot Capsule: *Psychological drama in which Ruth Matthews attempts to find help for her six year- old daughter who has retreated into her own imaginary world.*

© PentAmerica Communications Inc.

Asha Menina, Tommy Lee Jones

Asha Menina

Kathleen Turner, Asha Menina

Tommy Lee Jones, Kathleen Turner

Dewey Weber, Holly Marie Combs, Tim Guinee

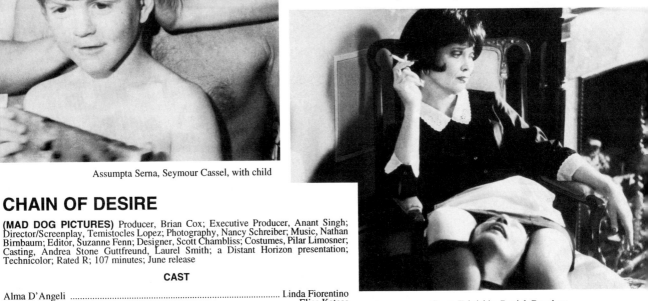

Assumpta Serna, Seymour Cassel, with child

CHAIN OF DESIRE

(MAD DOG PICTURES) Producer, Brian Cox; Executive Producer, Anant Singh; Director/Screenplay, Temistocles Lopez; Photography, Nancy Schreiber; Music, Nathan Birnbaum; Editor, Suzanne Fenn; Designer, Scott Chambliss; Costumes, Pilar Limosner; Casting, Andrea Stone Guttfreund, Laurel Smith; a Distant Horizon presentation; Technicolor; Rated R; 107 minutes; June release

CAST

Alma D'Angeli	Linda Fiorentino
Jesus	Elias Koteas
Isa	Angel Aviles
Jerald Buckley	Patrick Bauchau
Linda Bailey	Grace Zabriskie
Hubert Bailey	Malcolm McDowell
Keith	Jamie Harrold
Ken	Tim Guinee
David Bango	Dewey Weber
Diana	Holly Marie Combs
Mel	Seymour Cassel
Cleo	Assumpta Serna
Joe	Kevin Conroy
Angie	Suzzanne Douglas
M.C.	Joseph McKenna
Dancers	Karole Armitage, Michael Puleo, Rachel Tucker, Alicia Ho, Edward Jenkins
Woman in church	Iraida Polanco
Boy in church	Joshua Robert Kaplan
Jesus' Mother	Antonia Rey
Santera	Teodorina Bello
Procurer	Mickey Cottrell
Diana's Friend in gallery	Sabrina Lloyd
Tommy	York Bergin
Boy in window	Todd Bailey
Girl at ticket counter	Sarah Newhouse

and Edgar Oviedo Sandoval, John Schnall (Radio Announcers), "All the President's Women": Brooks Rogers (Sgt. Landom), Lynn Frazen-Cohn (Gloria Insburg), Rica Martens (Woman in pearls), Ebony Jo-Ann (Laughing Woman)

Plot Capsule: *A series of dramatic and comical vignettes focusing on several disparate New Yorkers, each segment linked by a random sexual encounter.*
© Mad Dog Pictures

Grace Zabriskie, Patrick Bauchau

Malcolm McDowell

DENNIS THE MENACE

(WARNER BROS.) Producers, John Hughes, Richard Vane; Executive Producer, Ernest Chambers; Director, Nick Castle; Screenplay, John Hughes; Based on characters created by Hank Ketcham; Photography, Thomas Ackerman; Designer, James Bissell; Music, Jerry Goldsmith; Editor, Alan Heim; Costumes, Ann Roth, Bridget Kelly; Associate Producer, William Ryan; Casting, Jane Jenkins, Janet Hirshenson; from Warner Bros. Family Entertainment; Dolby Stereo; Technicolor; Rated PG; 96 minutes; June release

CAST

George Wilson	Walter Matthau
Dennis Mitchell	Mason Gamble
Martha Wilson	Joan Plowright
Switchblade Sam	Christopher Lloyd
Alice Mitchell	Lea Thompson
Henry Mitchell	Robert Stanton
Margaret Wade	Amy Sakasitz
Joey	Kellen Hathaway
Chief of Police	Paul Winfield
Polly	Natasha Lyonne
Mickey	Devin Ratray
Gunther	Hank Johnston
Andrea	Melinda Mullins
Edith Butterwell	Billie Bird
Edward Little	Bill Erwin
Photographer	Arnold Stang
Gaggle Ladies	Ethel Gerstein, Rebecca C. Hogan, Leona Toppel, Peggy Goldberg
Gaggle Man	Jack McGuigan
Mike	Corey Vane
Hide and Seeker	Casey Gamble
Babysitter	Diana Campeanu
Broken Arm Babysitter	Robert A. Saunders
Elderly Babysitter	Beverly J. O'Donnell
Boss	Ben Stein
Ruff	Betty

Walter Matthau, Joan Plowright

Plot Capsule: *A precocious five year-old innocently creates mayhem for his retired neighbor, Mr. Wilson, and proves a formidable foe to a mysterious tramp named Switchblade Sam. The first production from Warner Bros. newly established Family Entertainment Division. The "Dennis the Menace" comic strip first appeared in newspapers in March of 1951.*

© Warner Bros.

Robert Stanton, Ruff, Lea Thompson, Mason Gamble

Christopher Lloyd

Walter Matthau, Mason Gamble, Ruff

Amy Sakasitz, Mason Gamble, Kellen Hathaway

Ross Malinger, Tom Hanks

SLEEPLESS IN SEATTLE

(TRISTAR) Producer, Gary Foster; Executive Producers, Lynda Obst, Patrick Crowley; Director, Nora Ephron; Screenplay, Nora Ephron, David S. Ward, Jeff Arch; Story, Jeff Arch; Photography, Sven Nykvist; Designer, Jeffrey Townsend; Costumes, Judy Ruskin; Music, Marc Shaiman; Editor, Robert Reitano; Music Supervision, Marc Shaiman, Nicholas Meyers; Associate Producer, Delia Ephron; Casting, Juliet Taylor; Song: "A Wink and a Smile" by Marc Shaiman, Ramsey McLean/performed by Harry Connick, Jr.; Dolby Stereo; Technicolor; Rated PG; 104 minutes; June release

CAST

Sam Baldwin	Tom Hanks
Annie Reed	Meg Ryan
Walter Jackson	Bill Pullman
Jonah Baldwin	Ross Malinger
Jay	Rob Reiner
Becky	Rosie O'Donnell
Jessica	Gaby Hoffman
Greg	Victor Garber
Suzy	Rita Wilson
Maggie Baldwin	Carey Lowell
Rob	Tom Riis Farrell
Barbara Reed	Le Clanche Du Rand
Cliff Reed	Kevin O'Morrison
Dennis Reed	David Hyde Pierce
Betsy Reed	Valerie Wright
Irene Reed	Frances Conroy
Harold Reed	Tom Tammi
Uncle Milton	Calvin Trillin
Dr. Marcia Fieldstone	Caroline Aaron
Loretta	Linda Wallem
Harriet	LaTanya Richardson
Keith	Tom McGowan
Wyatt	Stephen Mellor
Baltimore Waitress	Marguerite Schertle
Claire	Dana Ivey
Bob	Brian McConnachie
Mailman	Matt Smith
Clarise	Amanda Maher
Victoria	Barbara Garrick
Seattle Maitre D'	Victor Morris
Seattle Waiter	Philip Mihalski
Seattle Detective	Donald J. Lee, Jr.
Nervous Woman on airplane	Mary A. Kelly
Tiffany Saleswoman	Diane Sokolow

and Hannah Cox (Jessica's Mother), Rich Hawkins (Jessica's Father), Tamera Plank (Stewardess), Mike Badalucco, Jeff Mazzola (New York Taxi Dispatchers), Philip Levy (Taxi Driver), Julie Janney (Cynthia), Tony Zazula (Maitre D'), John Boylan, Robert Livingston (Elevator Men), Butch Stevenson (Valet), Sidney Armus (Information Booth Man)

Plot Capsule: *Romantic comedy in which recent widower Sam Baldwin's call-in to a radio talk show proves an irresistible attraction to newly-engaged Annie Reed, thousands of miles away in Baltimore. The film received Academy Award nominations for original screenplay and song ("A Wink and a Smile").*

© TriStar Pictures Inc.

Meg Ryan, Bill Pullman

Meg Ryan

Brian McConnachie, Tom Hanks, Rob Reiner

Meg Ryan, Rosie O'Donnell

Tom Hanks

Meg Ryan

Rob Reiner, Tom Hanks

Tom Hanks, Ross Malinger, Victor Garber, Rita Wilson

Ross Malinger

TOP LEFT: Gene Hackman, Tom Cruise, TOP RIGHT: David Strathairn

Terry Kinney

John Beal

Gary Busey, Holly Hunter, Tom Cruise

Hal Holbrook, Gene Hackman

Steven Hill

THE FIRM

(PARAMOUNT) Producers, Scott Rudin, John Davis, Sydney Pollack; Director, Sydney Pollack; Executive Producers, Michael Hausman, Lindsay Doran; Screenplay, David Rabe, Robert Towne, David Rayfield; Based upon the novel by John Grisham; Photography, John Seale; Designer, Richard MacDonald; Editors, William Steinkamp, Frederic Steinkamp; Music, Dave Grusin; a John Davis/Scott Rudin/Mirage production; Dolby Stereo; Deluxe color; Rated R; 154 minutes; June release

CAST

Mitch McDeere	Tom Cruise
Abby McDeere	Jeanne Tripplehorn
Avery Tolar	Gene Hackman
Oliver Lambert	Hal Holbrook
Lamar Quinn	Terry Kinney
William Devasher	Wilford Brimley
Wayne Tarrance	Ed Harris
Tammy Hemphill	Holly Hunter
Ray McDeere	David Strathairn
Eddie Lomax	Gary Busey
F. Denton Voyles	Steven Hill
The Nordic Man	Tobin Bell
Kay Quinn	Barbara Garrick
Royce McKnight	Jerry Hardin
Thomas Richie	Paul Calderon
Sonny Capps	Jerry Weintraub
Barry Abanks	Sullivan Walker
Young Woman on beach	Karina Lombard
Nina Huff	Margo Martindale
Nathan Locke	John Beal
The Squat Man	Dean Norris
Frank Mulholland	Lou Walker
Rental Agent	Debbie Turner
Wally Hudson	Tommy Cresswell
Randall Dunbar	David Kimball
Attorneys	Don Jones, Michael D. Allen
Restaurant Waiter	Levi Frazier, Jr.
Telephone Installer	Brian Casey
Minister	Rev. William J. Parham
Cafe Waiter	Victor Nelson
Congressman Billings	Richard Ranta
Madge	Janie Paris
Judge	Frank Crawford
Dutch	Bart Whiteman
Prison Guard	David Dwyer
FBI Agents	Mark Johnson, Jerry Chipman
Technician	Jimmy Lackie
Cotton Truck Drivers	Afemo Omilami, Clinton Smith
River Museum Guides	Susan Elliott, Erin Branham
Pilot	Ed Connelly
Ruth	Joey Anderson
Quinn's Maid	Deborah Thomas
Elvis Hemphill	Tommy Matthews
Lawyer Recruiters	Chris Schadrack, Jeffrey Ford, Jonathan Kaplan
Young Woman at Patio Bar	Rebecca Glenn
Woman dancing with Avery	Terri Welles
Vietnam Veteran	Gregory Goossen
Car Rental Agent	Jeane Aufdenberg
Seaplane Pilot	William R. Booth
Peabody Musicians	The Lannie McMillan Quartet
Restaurant Singer	Ollie Nightingale
Restaurant Lead Guitarist	Teenie Hodges
Memphis Street Musician	Little Jimmy King
Singer at Hyatt	James White
Morolto	Paul Sorvino

Tom Cruise, Ed Harris

Plot Capsule: *Drama from the number-one best seller. Recent Harvard law school graduate Mitch McDeere accepts an offer from a small Memphis firm, only to find out that they are involved in illegal and deadly operations from which there appears to be no escape.*

The movie received Academy Award nominations for supporting actress Holly Hunter and original music score.

© Paramount Pictures

CENTER RIGHT: Wilford Brimley, BOTTOM RIGHT: Jeanne Tripplehorn, Tom Cruise

Pauly Shore, Lane Smith, Cindy Pickett, Carla Gugino, Patrick Renna, Mason Adams

SON-IN-LAW

(HOLLYWOOD PICTURES) Producers, Michael Rotenberg, Peter M. Lenkov; Executive Producer, Hilton Green; Director, Steve Rash; Screenplay, Fax Bahr, Adam Small, Shawn Schepps; Story, Patrick J. Clifton, Susan McMartin, Peter M. Lenkov; Photography, Peter Deming; Designer, Joseph T. Garrity; Editor, Dennis M. Hill; Costumes, Molly Maginnis; Music, Richard Gibbs; Casting, Cheryl Bayer; Distributed by Buena Vista Pictures; Dolby Stereo; Technicolor; Rated PG-13; 95 minutes; July release

CAST

Crawl	Pauly Shore
Rebecca Warner	Carla Gugino
Walter Warner	Lane Smith
Connie Warner	Cindy Pickett
Walter Warner, Sr.	Mason Adams
Zack Warner	Patrick Renna
Theo	Dennis Burkley
Tracy	Tiffani-Amber Thiessen
Travis	Dan Gauthier
Carol	Ria Pavia
Lisa	Lisa Lawrence
Principal	Graham Jarvis
Mud Wrestling Announcer	Nick Light
Horace	Ernie Kinney
Cowboy	Troy Shire
Indian	Adam Goldberg

and Robert Koch (Country Club Waiter), Ryk O. (Halloween Fairy), Garret Sato (Hairdresser), Emily Dole (Thumper), John Hatton (Fiddle Player), Jim Henken (Guitar), Lynn Coulter (Drums), Mike George (Bass), Jay Leach (Musician)

Plot Capsule: *Comedy in which a South Dakota farm girl returns home for Thanksgiving break with her oddball college boyfriend from L.A.*

© Hollywood Pictures Co.

Carla Gugino, Pauly Shore

Carla Gugino, Pauly Shore

Cindy Pickett, Pauly Shore, Lane Smith

ROOKIE OF THE YEAR

(20th CENTURY FOX) Producer, Robert Harper; Executive Producers, Jack Brodsky, Irby Smith; Director, Daniel Stern; Screenplay, Sam Harper; Photography, Jack Green; Designer, Steven Jordan; Editors, Donn Cambern, Raja Gosnell; Music, Bill Conti; Costumes, Jay Hurley; Casting, Linda Lowy; Associate Producer, Joan Aguado; Dolby Stereo; Deluxe color; Rated PG; 103 minutes; July release

CAST

Henry Rowengartner	Thomas Ian Nicholas
Chet Steadman	Gary Busey
Sal Martinella	Albert Hall
Mary Rowengartner	Amy Morton
Larry "Fish" Fisher	Dan Hedaya
Jack Bradfield	Bruce Altman
Bob Carson	Eddie Bracken
Clark	Robert Gorman
George	Patrick LaBrecque
Phil Brickma	Daniel Stern
Jeff Murdoch	John Candy
Becky	Colombe Jacobsen-Derstine
Tiffany	Kristie Davis
Edith	Tyler Ann Carroll
Heddo	Tom Milanovich
Dr. Kersten	Ross Lehman
Derkin	John Gegenhuber

and James "Ike" Eichling (Little League Coach), Josh Wagner (Little League Fielder), Erik Vandersteuyf (Windemere), James Andelin (Wizard of Wrigley), Andrew Mark Berman (Ernie), Mark Doran (Richards, Cubs Catcher), Neil Flynn (Okie, Cubs 1st Base), E. Milton Wheeler (Suarez, Cubs 2nd Base), Sam Sanders (Fern, Cubs Short Stop), Neil Fiala (Mullens, Cubs 3rd Baseman), W. Earl Brown (Frick, Bullpen Catcher), Frank L. Wiltse (Peyton, Cubs Pitcher), Barry L. Bonds, Bobby Bonilla, Pedro Guerrero (Three Big Whiffers), Jerry Saslow, Mike Bacarella (Bleacher Bums), Don Forston (Big Bum), Ken Earl (Pepsi Executive), Anthony Diaz-Perez (Rude Hot Dog Vendor), Mike Houlihan (Carson's Hot Dog Vendor), Tim Stoddard (Dodger Pitcher), B.J. Sanabria (Chicken Runner), Cristian Mendez (Other Mets Runner), Mike Daughtry (Mets 3rd Base Coach), Toney Howell (Surprised Expos Runner), Blake Hammond (Screaming Patient), Ian Gomez (Odd Bellman), R.A. Bauer (Bellman), Mathew Dunne (Commercial Director), Askia Bantu (Mr. Banks), Robert Harper (Confused Teacher), Peter Bankins (Flower Shop Customer), Cindy Becker (Receptionist), Dan Conway, Ron Beattie, Sunnie Hikawa, Al Joyner (Press Conference Reporters), Christopher Howe, Karen L. Stephens (Airport Reporter), Jon Hilario, Michael Keeney (Phys Ed Dweebs), Kimberly Dal Santo (Kid Autograph Seeker), Phillip J. Maxwell, Tom Brennan, Arnie Silberman, Larry Brelsford, Dave Slickenmeyer, George H. Drenth (Umpires)

Plot Capsule: *After breaking his arm 12 year-old Henry Rowengartner discovers he can throw a baseball with lightning speed. In no time he is signed-up by the Chicago Cubs as their star pitcher. Actor Daniel Stern makes his theatrical directorial debut with this comic-fantasy.*

© Twentieth Century Fox

Thomas Ian Nicholas, Gary Busey

Patrick LaBrecque, Robert Gorman, Thomas Ian Nicholas

Thomas Ian Nicholas, Daniel Stern

Eddie Bracken, Dan Hedaya, Thomas Ian Nicholas

Thomas Ian Nicholas

Rene Russo, Clint Eastwood

John Malkovich

IN THE LINE OF FIRE

(COLUMBIA) Producer, Jeff Apple; Executive Producers, Wolfgang Petersen, Gail Katz, David Valdes; Director, Wolfgang Petersen; Screenplay, Jeff Maguire; Photography, John Bailey; Designer, Lilly Kilvert; Editor, Anne V. Coates; Music, Ennio Morricone; Costumes, Erica Edell Phillips; Casting, Janet Hirshenson, Jane Jenkins; Co-Producer, Bob Rosenthal; from Castle Rock Entertainment; Dolby Stereo/Sony Dynamic Digital Sound; Panavision; Technicolor; Rated R; 130 minutes; July release

CAST

Frank Horrigan	Clint Eastwood
Mitch Leary	John Malkovich
Lilly Raines	Rene Russo
Al D'Andrea	Dylan McDermott
Bill Watts	Gary Cole
Harry Sargent	Fred Dalton Thompson
Sam Campagna	John Mahoney
Matt Wilder	Greg Alan-Williams
President	Jim Curley
First Lady	Sally Hughes
Jack Okura	Clyde Kusatsu
Tony Carducci	Steve Hytner
Mendoza	Tobin Bell
Jimmy Hendrickson	Bob Schott
Raul	Juan A. Riojas
Booth's Landlady	Elsa Raven
Paramedic	Arthur Senzy
Pam Magnus	Patrika Darbo
Sally	Mary Van Arsdel
LAPD Brass	Ryan Cutrona
FBI Technician	Lawrence Lowe
FBI Supervisor	Brian Libby
Young Agent	Eric Bruskotter
Political Speaker	Patrick Caddell
Professor Riger	John Heard
Walter Wickland	Alan Toy
CIA Agent Collins	Carl Ciarfalio
Hunters	Walt MacPherson, Robert Peters
Police Captain Howard	Tyde Kierney
FBI Official	Anthony Peck
Bartender	Rick Hurst
DC News Anchor	Doris E. McMillon
Bellboy	Robert Sandoval
Agent Chavez	Joshua Malina
Sanford Riggs	William G. Schilling
Computer Technician/Bates	Michael Kirk
Party Fat Cat	Richard Camphuis
Marge	Marlan Clarke

And Robert Alan Beuth (Man at Bank), Susan Lee Hoffman (Woman at Bank), Donna Hamilton (Reporter at Dulles), Bob Jimenez (Reporter at Hotel), Cylk Cozart (Agent Cozart), Michael Zurich (Agent Zurich), Rich DiDonato, Jeffrey Kurt Miller (Undercover Agents), Kirk Jordan (Agent), Steve Railsback (CIA)

Plot Capsule: *Secret Service agent Frank Horrigan has never forgiven himself for failing to save President Kennedy's life in Dallas, 1963. Thirty years later a professional assassin taunts Horrigan with a plot to kill the current president.*

The movie received Academy Award nominations for supporting actor John Malkovich, original screenplay and film editing.

© Columbia PicturesIndustries/Castle Rock

Rene Russo, Clint Eastwood

John Malkovich

John Malkovich

Clint Eastwood

Dylan McDermott

Clint Eastwood, Rene Russo

87

Jason James Richter, August Schellenberg, Lori Petty, Keiko

Jason James Richter, Keiko

Jason James Richter, Keiko

FREE WILLY

(WARNER BROS.) Producers, Jennie Lew Tugend, Lauren Shuler-Donner; Executive Producers, Richard Donner, Arnon Milchan; Co-Producers, Penelope L. Foster, Richard Solomon, Jim Van Wyck; Director, Simon Wincer; Screenplay, Keith A. Walker, Corey Blechman; Story, Keith A. Walker; Photography, Robbie Greenberg; Designer, Charles Rosen; Music, Basil Poledouris; Editor, O. Nicholas Brown; Associate Producers, Mark Marshall, Douglas C. Merrifield; Costumes, April Ferry; Casting, Judy Taylor, Lynda Gordon; Whale Effects Supervisor, Walt Conti; Animatronic Whales Created by Edge Innovations; Underwater Photography, Pete Romano, Marty Snyderman; Supervising Whale Trainer, Scott Sharpe; Presented in association with Le Studio Canal+, Regency Enterprises and Alcor Films; from Warner Bros. Family Entertainment; Dolby Stereo; Panavision; Technicolor; Rated PG; 111 minutes; July release

CAST

Jesse	Jason James Richter
Rae Lindley	Lori Petty
Annie Greenwood	Jayne Atkinson
Randolph Johnson	August Schellenberg
Glen Greenwood	Michael Madsen
Dial	Michael Ironside
Wade	Richard Riehle
Dwight Mercer	Mykelti Williamson
Perry	Michael Bacall
Gwenie	Danielle Harris
Vector	Isaiah Malone
Passerbys	Betsy Toll, Rob Sample, Merrilyn Jones
Waiter	Mickey Gaines
Fish Throwers	Justin R. Hall, Robert M. Duque, Sam Samson
Fish Vendor	Willis Van Dusen
Brody	Tom Lasswell
Homeless Men	Moultrie Patten, Ed Murphy
Announcer	Jim Michaels
Willy	Keiko

Plot Capsule: *In the Pacific Northwest a delinquent boy finds meaning to his life when he tends to a captured killer whale at an aquatic amusement park.*

Keiko, Jason James Richter

HOCUS POCUS

(WALT DISNEY PICTURES) Producers, David Kirschner, Steven Haft; Executive Producer, Ralph Winter; Director, Kenny Ortega; Screenplay, Mick Garris, Neil Cuthbert; Story, David Kirschner, Mick Garris; Photography, Hiro Narita; Designer, William Sandell; Editor, Peter E. Berger; Co-Producer, Bonnie Bruckheimer; Co-Executive Producer, Mick Garris; Costumes, Mary Vogt; Music, John Debney; Song: *I Put a Spell on You* by Jay Hawkins/performed by Bette Midler; Casting, Mary Gail Artz, Barbara Cohen; Choreographers, Peggy Holmes, Kenny Ortega; Visual Effects Supervisor, Peter Montgomery; Visual Effects, Buena Vista Visual Effects; Talking Cat Animation, Rhythm & Hues, Inc.; Makeup, John M. Elliott, Jr., Lee C. Harman; Distributed by Buena Vista Pictures; Dolby Stereo; Technicolor; Rated PG; 93 minutes; July release

CAST

Winifred Sanderson	Bette Midler
Sarah Sanderson	Sarah Jessica Parker
Mary Sanderson	Kathy Najimy
Max Dennison	Omri Katz
Dani Dennison	Thora Birch
Allison	Vinessa Shaw
Emily	Amanda Shepherd
Ernie ("Ice")	Larry Bagby III
Jay	Tobias Jelinek
Jenny	Stephanie Faracy
Dave	Charles Rocket
Billy Butcherson	Doug Jones
Headless Billy Butcherson	Karyn Malchus
Thackery	Sean Murray
Elijah	Steve Voboril
Thackery's Father	Norbert Weisser
Miss Olin	Kathleen Freeman
Firemen	D.A. Pawley, Ezra Sutton
Bus Driver	Don Yesso
Cop	Michael McGrady
Cop's Girlfriend	Leigh Hamilton
Little Girl "Neat Broom"	Devon Reeves
Singer	Joseph Malone
Little Angel	Jordan Redmond
Lobster Man	Frank Del Boccio
Boy in class	Jeff Neubauer
Calamity Jane	Teda Bracci
Dancer	Peggy Holmes
"Satan"	Garry Marshall
"Satan's" Wife	Penny Marshall

Plot Capsule: *Comical fantasy . Three Salem witches, hanged in 1693, return 300 years later on Halloween night to take revenge on the town's children. Three kids race against time to put a stop to the evil doings.*

© The Walt Disney Company

Thora Birch, Bette Midler

Bette Midler, Omri Katz

Bette Midler, Sarah Jessica Parker

Kathy Najimy, Bette Midler, Sarah Jessica Parker

Tupac Shakur, Janet Jackson

Janet Jackson

POETIC JUSTICE

(COLUMBIA) Producers, Steve Nicolaides, John Singleton; Director/Screenplay, John Singleton; Photography, Peter Lyons Collister; Designer, Keith Brian Burns; Editor, Bruce Cannon; Music, Stanley Clarke; Song: *Again* by Janet Jackson, James Harris III, Terry Lewis/performed by Janet Jackson; Poetry by Maya Angelou; Casting, Robi Reed; Dolby Stereo; Technicolor; Rated R; 110 minutes; July release

CAST

Justice	Janet Jackson
Lucky	Tupac Shakur
Iesha	Regina King
Chicago	Joe Torry
Jessie	Tyra Ferrell
Heywood	Roger Guenveur Smith
Aunt June	Maya Angelou
Markell	Q-Tip
J Bone	Tone Loc
Maxine	Miki Howard
Dexter	Keith Washington
Gena	Mikki Val
Dina	Dina D.
Baha	Baha Jackson
Simone	Khandi Alexander
Thugs	Che J. Avery, Lloyd Avery II
Kim	Kimberly Brooks
Ticket Taker	Rico Bueno
Shante	Maia Campbell
Panhandler	Michael Colyar
Cousin	Kina V. Cosper
Uncle Earl	John Cothran, Jr.
Aunt May	Norma Donaldson
Truck Driver	Kelly Joe Dugan,
Last Poets	Suliamen El Hadi, Omar Ben Hassan, Jalal Nuriddin, Daoud Spencer
E.J.	Rene Elizondo
Crackhead	Benjamin I. Ellington
Lloyd	Dedrick Gobert
Mailroom Supervisor	Clifton Gonzalez Gonzalez
Gangsta	Ricky Harris
Patricia	Patricia Y. Johnson
Keisha	Shannon Johnson
Rodney's Girlfriend	La Keisha M. Jones
Cop	Kirk Kinder
Angry Customer	Vashon LeCesne
Beauty College Instructor	Jennifer Leigh
Annie	Jenifer Lewis
Cousin Pete	Special K McCray
Rita	Sarena Mobley
Antonio	Kahlil Gibran Nelson
Penelope	Lori Petty
Cashier	Denney Pierce
Woman with Baby	Renato Powell
Fighting Man	Jimmy Ray, Jr.
Dock Worker	Michael Rapaport
Aunt April	Ernestine Reed
Woman on couch	Robi Reed
Angel	Crystal A. Rodgers
Uncle Herb	Eugene Tate
Concession Stand Man	David Villafan
Cousin Dion	Dion Blake Vines
Aunt Audrey	Rose Weaver
Rodney	Anthony Wheaton
Colette	Yvette Wilson
Brad	Billy Zane
Policemen	Jeff Cantrel, Joe Dalu, Judd Dunning, Randall C. Heyward, Mike James, Mark Miller, Al Murray

Plot Capsule: *In South Central L.A. a postal worker finds himself attracted to a beautician who fancies herself a poet. Together they and a pair of friends embark on a journey to Northern California, in this dramatic love story. Singer Janet Jackson makes her motion picture acting debut.*

The film received an Academy Award nomination for original song ("Again").
© Columbia Pictures Industries

LEFT: Tupac Shakur, Regina King,
Joe Torry, Janet Jackson

Richard Dreyfuss, Emilio Estevez

Richard Dreyfuss, Emilio Estevez

Emilio Estevez, Richard Dreyfuss

Rosie O'Donnell, Marcia Strassman, Dennis Farina

Emilio Estevez, Richard Dreyfuss, Rosie O'Donnell

ANOTHER STAKEOUT

(TOUCHSTONE) Producers, Jim Kouf, Cathleen Summers, Lynn Bigelow; Executive Producer/Director, John Badham; Co-Producer, D.J. Caruso; Screenplay, Jim Kouf, based on his characters; Photography, Roy H. Wagner; Designer, Lawrence G. Paull; Editor, Frank Morris; Music, Arthur B. Rubinstein; Costumes, Stephanie Nolin; Casting, Carol Lewis; Associate Producers, Justis Greene, Kristine J. Schwarz; Dolby Stereo; Technicolor; Rated PG-13; 109 minutes; July release

CAST

Chris Lecce	Richard Dreyfuss
Bill Reimers	Emilio Estevez
Gina Garrett	Rosie O'Donnell
Brian O'Hara	Dennis Farina
Pam O'Hara	Marcia Strassman
Lu Delano	Cathy Moriarty
Thomas Hassrick	John Rubinstein
Tony Castellano	Miguel Ferrer
Barbara Burnside	Sharon Maughan
McNamara	Christopher Doyle
Tilghman	Sharon Schaffer
Van Agents	Rick Seaman, Jan Speck
Vegas Police Captain	Gene Ellison
Vegas Investigators	Frank DeAngelo, J.R. West
Unlucky	Frank C. Turner
Killer	Steven Lambert
Captain Coldshank	Dan Lauria
Desk Sergeant	Denalda Williams
Garage Attendant	Larry B. Scott
Blonde Date	Christi Brasher
Gaetano	Sammy Jackson
Seattle Det. Wills	Blu Mankuma
Seattle Det. Gilliam	Thomas Mitchell
Reynaldo	Scott Anderson
Michael	Michael DeLano
Pizza Man	Al Goto
Neighbor Frank	Steve Bacic
Ronnie Burnside	Taylor Estevez
Cops	Bruce Barbour, Rick Blackwell
Paramedic	Michael Steve Jones
Doctor	Chris Shoemaker
Nurses	Nancy Sosna, Cammie Ann Crier
Coroner	Martin Rogers
Maria	Madeleine Stowe

Plot Capsule: *Two Seattle police detectives and an assistant D.A. pose as a family to stakeout a neighborhood, hoping that a missing trial witness might show up. A comedy-adventure sequel to the 1987 Touchstone Pictures film* Stakeout *which also starred Richard Dreyfuss and Emilio Estevez.*

David Stepkin, Michael Artura

Patrick McGaw, Mira Sorvino

AMONGST FRIENDS

(FINE LINE FEATURES) Producer, Matt Blumberg; Director/Screenplay/Executive Producer, Rob Weiss; Co-Producer, Mark Hirsch; Photography, Michael Bonvillain; Designer, Terrence Foster; Music, Mick Jones; Editor, Leo Trombetta; a Last Outlaw Films production presented in association with Islet; Color; Rated R; 88 minutes; July release

CAST

Early Eighties

Young Andy	Chris Santos
Young Trevor	Michael Leb
Young Billy	Christian Thom
Andy's Father	Lou Cantelmo
Andy's Grandfather	Jerry Leonard
Jack Trattner	David Stepkin
Poker Players	Greg Bernardi, Lou Bernardi, Charles Mattina
Kids in fight	Adam Montalbano, Michael Sorvino
Billy's Father	Jay Gordon
Drug Dealer	Michael Weiss

Late Eighties

Billy	Joseph Lindsey
Kid at door	Andy Weiss
Trevor	Patrick McGaw
Andy	Steve Parlavecchio
Girl on couch	Hayley Guzman
Laura	Mira Sorvino
Driver Narc	Richard Mangogna
Passenger Narc	James Biberi
Judge	Joseph Sciarrotta
Stenographer	Maddi Amato
Attorney	Mort Carr
Beating Victim	Steve Kaplan

1992

Friend	Brett Lambson
Bodega Owner	Julio Barrier
Michael	Michael Artura
Guy outside of bakery	Bob Graziano
Louis	Don Damico
Sal	Michael Ringer
Vic	Frank Medrano
Eddie	Louis Lombardi
Billy's Crew	Jimmy Natale, Howard Goodman, Richie "The Boxer", Chris "The Mayor" McMahon

and Steve "Buddha" Rosenbluth (Nicky), Michael Blak (Craig), Jeff Sternhell (Ernie), Rob Weiss (Bobby), Shawn A. English(Monte), James Rich (Ricky), Tommy Colmer (Tommy) Huey Friedman (U-Mel), Steven Miller (Bouncer Shot), Sammy Pugliese(Bartender), Kim Carlucci (Crying Girl), Paul Badome, Al Marrero (Abused Bouncers), Tony Fatone, Martin Haber (Jack's Crew), Ford Sorvino (Fish), Lou Mastantuono (Rubber), Matt Schultz (Biker Crew Member), Howard Cotler (Laura's Father), Amy Pierce (Countergirl), Chris James (Mitch the dealer), Steve Proto (Dave), Lora Zuckerman (Leslie), Peter Papageorgiou (Young Wiseguy), Vincent Bandille, Al Lopez (Wiseguys in lot), Robert Canaan (Tony - Young Wiseguy), Bernard Jaffe (Philly Valicio), Stan Schwartz (Arnie the Jeweler), Sara Sloves (Andy's Girl), Sybil Temtchine (Laura's Friend), Pete Traina (Arson), Danielle Givner, Shashana Ami, Jaime Baron, Linda Gerstman (Girls on beach)

Plot Capsule: *Drama about three friends from the affluent Five Towns section of Long Island who become drug-dealing criminals.*
© Fine Line Features

Steve Parlavecchio

Brett Lambson, Steve Parlavecchio, Patrick McGaw

Michelle Burke, Dan Aykroyd, Jane Curtin,
Top Right: Jason Alexander, Chris Farley, Dan Aykroyd

CONEHEADS

(PARAMOUNT) Producer, Lorne Michaels; Executive Producer, Michael Rachmil; Director, Steve Barron; Screenplay, Tom Davis, Dan Aykroyd, Bonnie Turner, Terry Turner; Photography, Francis Kenny; Designer, Gregg Fonseca; Editor, Paul Trejo; Costumes, Marie France; Music, David Newman; Co-Producers, Dinah Minot, Barnaby Thompson, Bonnie Turner; Casting, Lora Kennedy; Conehead Makeup Designer & Creator, David B. Miller; Visual Effects Supervisor, John Scheele; Dolby Stereo; Deluxe color; Rated PG; 86 minutes; July release

Laraine Newman

Michael McKean

CAST

Beldar Conehead	Dan Aykroyd
Prymaat Conehead	Jane Curtin
Conjab "Connie" Conehead	Michelle Burke
Gorman Seedling	Michael McKean
Eli Turnbull	David Spade
Ronnie	Chris Farley
Larry Farber	Jason Alexander
Lisa Farber	Lisa Jane Persky
Gladys Johnson	Jan Hooks
Motel Clerk	Michael Richards
Otto	Sinbad
Marlax	Phil Hartman
Carmine	Adam Sandler
Khoudri	Shishir Kurup
Christina	Joey Adams
Stephanie	Parker Posey
Senator	Kevin Nealon
Principal	Julia Sweeney
Coach	Ellen Degeneres
Ron	Todd Susman
Harv	James Keane
Captain Orecruiser	Garrett Morris
Highmaster	Dave Thomas
Highmaster Mentot	Peter Aykroyd
Laarta	Laraine Newman
Dentist	Jon Lovitz
Golfer	Tom Arnold

Dan Aykroyd, Michael Richards

and Robert Knott (Air Traffic Controller), Jonathan Penner (Captain Air Traffic), Whip Hubley (F-16 Pilot), Howard Napper (Ang Pilot), Eddie Griffin (Customer), Grant Martell, Art Bonilla (Hispanic Men), Rosa Briz (Hispanic Woman), Cooper Layne (Engineer), Sarah Levy (Hygenist), Drew Carey (Taxi Passenger), Sydney Coberly (Nurse), Barry Kivel (Doctor), Terry Turner (Sketch Artist), McNally Sagal, Richard M. Comar (Agents), Danielle Aykroyd (3 year old Connie), Nicolette Harnish (10 year old Connie), Walt Robles (Fire Marshall), Sam Freed (Master of Ceremonies), Tom Davis (Supplicant), Nils Allen Stewart (Guard), Tim Meadows (Athletic Cone), Mitchell Bobrow (Garthok Combatant), Laurence Bilzerian (Cone Battle Commander), Topper Lilien (Cone Pilot)

Plot Capsule: *Two pointy-headed extra-terrestrials land on Earth hoping to fit seamlessly into society. Sci-fi comedy based on sketches from tv's* Saturday Night Live, *which also starred Dan Aykroyd and Jane Curtin.*

© Paramount Pictures

Bottom Left: David Spade, Bottom Right: Dave Thomas

ROBIN HOOD: MEN IN TIGHTS

(20th CENTURY FOX) Producer/Director, Mel Brooks; Executive Producer, Peter Schindler; Screenplay, Mel Brooks, Evan Chandler, J. David Shapiro; Story, J. David Shapiro, Evan Chandler; Photography, Michael D. O'Shea; Designer, Roy Forge Smith; Editor, Stephen E. Rivkin; Costumes, Dodie Shepard; Music, Hummie Mann; Associate Producer, Evan Chandler; Casting, Lindsay D. Chag, Bill Shepard; a Brooksfilm production in association with Gaumont; Dolby Stereo; Deluxe color; Rated PG-13; 105 minutes; July release

CAST

Robin Hood	Cary Elwes
Prince John	Richard Lewis
Sheriff of Rottingham	Roger Rees
Marian	Amy Yasbeck
Blinkin	Mark Blankfield
Ahchoo	Dave Chappelle
Asneeze	Isaac Hayes
Broomhilde	Megan Cavanagh
Little John	Eric Allan Kramer
Will Scarlet O'Hara	Matthew Porretta
Latrine	Tracey Ullman
King Richard	Patrick Stewart
Don Giovanni	Dom DeLuise
The Abbot	Dick Van Patten
The Hangman	Robert Ridgley
Rabbi Tuckman	Mel Brooks
Filthy Luca	Steve Tancora
Dirty Ezio	Joe Dimmick
Tax Assessor	Avery Schreiber
Villager	Chuck McCann
Dungeon Maitre D'	Brian George
Head Saracen Guard	Zitto Kazann
Assistant Saracen Guard	Richard Assad
Sheriff's Guard	Herman Poppe
Fire Marshall	Clive Revill

and Joe Baker (Angry Villager), Carol Arthur (Complaining Villager), Kelly Jones (Buxom Lass), Clement Von Franckenstein (Royal Announcer), Corbin Allred (Young Lad), Chase Masterson (Giggling Court Lady), Don Lewis (Mime), Roger Owens (Peanut Vendor), Patrick Valenzuela (Lead Camel Jockey), Steffon, Dante Henderson, Bryant Baldwin, Diesko Boyland Jr., Edgar Godineaux Jr. (Sherwood Forest Rapper-Dancers), Johnny Dean Harvey, Keith Diorio, Joseph R. McKee, Nathan Prevost, Don Hesser, Bill Bohl, Chris Childers, Raymond Del Barrio (Merry Men Dancers), Malcolm Danare, Edwin Hale, Nick Jameson, Peter Pitofsky, Nicholas Rempel (Inept Archers), Rudy De Luca, Matthew Saks, Robin Shepard, Dee Gubin (Party Guests), Johnny Cocktails, Lisa Cordray, Laurie Main, Elaine Ballace, Stuart Schreiber (Wedding Guests), James Van Patten, Ira MIller, David DeLuise, Lillian D'Arc, Patrick Brymer, Robert Noble, Henry Kaiser, Tony Tanner, Diana Chesney, James Glaser, Ronny Graham (Villagers)

Plot Capsule: *Spoof of the legend of English outlaw Robin Hood, his band of Merry Men and their fight against the evil Sheriff of Rottingham.*

© Twentieth Century Fox

Amy Yasbeck, Mel Brooks, Cary Elwes, Mark Blankfield

Cary Elwes, Dave Chappelle

Eric Allan Kramer, Cary Elwes

Richard Lewis, Roger Rees

Anthony LaPaglia

Mike Myers, Nancy Travis

Amanda Plummer

Mike Myers, Nancy Travis

Brenda Fricker, Mike Myers

SO I MARRIED AN AXE MURDERER

(TRISTAR) Producers, Robert N. Fried, Cary Woods; Executive Producer, Bernie Williams; Co-Producer, Jana Sue Memel; Director, Thomas Schlamme; Screenplay, Robbie Fox; Photography, Julio Macat; Designer, John Graysmark; Editors, Richard Halsey, Colleen Halsey; Music, Bruce Broughton; Music Supervisor, Danny Bramson; Costumes, Kimberly Tillman; Casting, Mindy Marin; a Fried/Woods production; Dolby Stereo; Technicolor; Rated PG-13; 93 minutes; July release

CAST

Charlie Mackenzie/Stuart Mackenzie	Mike Myers
Harriet Michaels	Nancy Travis
Tony Giardino	Anthony LaPaglia
Rose Michaels	Amanda Plummer
May Mackenzie	Brenda Fricker
Heed	Matt Doherty
Commandeered Car Driver	Charles Grodin
Park Ranger - Vickie	Phil Hartman
Tony's Girlfriend - Susan	Debi Mazar
Pilot	Steven Wright
Cafe Roads Performer	Patrick Bristow
Cafe Roads M.C.	Cintra Wilson
Butcher shop Customers	Al Nalbandan, George Mauricio, Kiki Douveas, Lillie Lowe, Maria Dos Remedios
Police Records Officer	Luenell Campbell
Policeman	Kelly Christmas
Russian Sailors	Ilya Brodsky, Eugene Buick
"A Current Affair" Anchorwoman	Maureen O'Boyle
"A Current Affair" Reporter	Steve Dunleavy
Obituary Employees	Michael G. Hagerty, Michael Richards
Marriage Desk Employee	Adele Proom
Serenade Musicians	David Knowles, Carl Rusk, Paul Sanchez
Ralph	Jessie Nelson
Auntie Molly	Wanda McCaddon
Uncle Angus	Glen Vernon
Tony's Dance Partner	Maggy Myers Davidson
Scottish Minister	Robert Nichols
Wedding Reception Musicians	JFK Cunningham, Robert Black, John Taylor
Walter the Plumber	Ken Johnson
Master Cho	Kelvin Han Yee
Police Captain	Alan Arkin

and Joe Bellan (Man with Bimbo), Keith Selvin (Young Stuart), Poets' Corner: Greg Germann (Desk Clerk), Kenneth Grantham (Maitre D'), Bob Sarlatte (M.C.), Cynthia Frost (Mrs. Levenstein), Fred Ornstein (Mr. Levenstein), John X. Heart (Waiter), Frederick Walsh (Bellboy)

Plot Capsule: *In this comedy-thriller San Francisco poet Charlie Mackenzie suspects that the woman of his dreams may be a husband killer.*

© TriStar Pictures Inc.

95

Sean Connery, Wesley Snipes

RISING SUN

(20th CENTURY FOX) Producer, Peter Kaufman; Executive Producer, Sean Connery; Director, Philip Kaufman; Screenplay, Philip Kaufman, Michael Crichton, Michael Backes; Based upon the novel by Michael Crichton; Line Producer, Ian Bryce; Photography, Michael Chapman; Designer, Dean Tavoularis; Editors, Stephen A. Rotter, William S. Scharf; Music, Toru Takemitsu; Costumes, Jacqueline West; Casting, Donna Isaacson; a Walrus & Associates Ltd. production; Dolby Stereo; Deluxe color; Rated R; 129 minutes; July release

Wesley Snipes, Harvey Keitel

CAST

John Connor .... Sean Connery
Web Smith .... Wesley Snipes
Tom Graham .... Harvey Keitel
Eddie Sakamura .... Cary-Hiroyuki Tagawa
Bob Richmond .... Kevin Anderson
Yoshida-san .... Mako
Senator John Morton .... Ray Wise
Ishihara .... Stan Egi
Phillips .... Stan Shaw
Jingo Asakuma .... Tia Carrere
Willy "the Weasel" Wilhelm .... Steve Buscemi
Cheryl Lynn Austin .... Tatjana Patitz
Greg .... Peter Crombie
Rick .... Sam Lloyd
Julia .... Alexandra Powers
Chief Olson/Interrogator.............................. Daniel Von Bargen
Zelly .... Lauren Robinson
Hsieh .... Amy Hill
Jim Donaldson .... Tom Dahlgren
Tanaka .... Clyde Kusatsu
Fred Hoffman .... Michael Chapman
Young Japanese Negotiators .... Joey Miyashima, Nelson Mashita
Lauren .... Tamara Tunie
Doorman Guard .... Tony Ganios
Jeff .... James Oliver Bullock
and Michael Kinsley, Eleanor Clift, Clarence Page, Pat Choate (TV Panel Members), Steven C. Clemons (Show Moderator), Dan Butler (Ken Shubik), Toshishiro Obata (Guard at Imperial Arms), Tylyn John (Redhead), Shelley Michelle (Blonde), Michele Ruiz (TV Interviewer), Patricia Ayame Thomson (Accident Reporter), Jeff Imada, Max Kirishima (Eddie Sakamura's Yakuza), Larry O. Williams, Jr. (Younger Brother), Scot Anthony Robinson (First Brother), Keith Leon Hickles (Another Brother), Carl A. McGee (Guy at window), Quincy Adams, Jr. (Mean Face), Cecil Brown (Big Guy), Meagen Fay (Hamaguri Receptionist), Max Grodenchik (Club Manager), Gunnar Peterson (Valet), Jessica Tuck (Senator Morton's Aide), Masa Watanabe (Japanese Elevator Guard), Minnie Summers Lindsey (Grandma Otis), Paul Fujimoto (Iwabuchi), Kenji (Tempura Chef), Michael Leopard (Cop), Dennis Ota, Raymond Kitamura (Nakamoto Yakuza), Rita Weibel (Girl at Eddie's Party), Seiichi Tanaka (Taiko Drum Master)

Plot Capsule: *American investigators John Connor and Web Smith explore the Japanese influence over the United States' business industry when they look into the murder of a young woman at the opening of an L.A. office tower. Based on Michael Crichton's best-selling thriller.*

Stan Egi, Mako

Sam Lloyd, Kevin Anderson, Peter Crombie

Wesley Snipes, Tia Carrere

Wesley Snipes, Sean Connery

Cary-Hiroyuki Tagawa

Wesley Snipes, Harvey Keitel, Sean Connery

Tommy Lee Jones

Harrison Ford

THE FUGITIVE

(WARNER BROS.) Producer, Arnold Kopelson; Executive Producers, Roy Huggins, Keith Barish; Co-Producer, Peter MacGregor-Scott; Director, Andrew Davis; Screenplay, Jeb Stuart, David Twohy; Story, David Twohy; Based on characters created by Roy Huggins; Photography, Michael Chapman; Designer, Dennis Washington; Editors, Dennis Virkler, David Finfer, Dean Goodhill, Don Brochu, Richard Nord, Dov Hoenig; Music, James Newton Howard; Costumes, Aggie Guerard Rodgers; Casting, Amanda Mackey, Cathy Sandrich; Dolby Stereo; Technicolor; Rated PG-13; 127 minutes; August release

CAST

Dr. Richard Kimble	Harrison Ford
Samuel Gerard	Tommy Lee Jones
Helen Kimble	Sela Ward
Dr. Anne Eastman	Julianne Moore
Cosmo Renfro	Joe Pantoliano
Sykes	Andreas Katsulas
Dr. Charles Nichols	Jeroen Krabbe
Biggs	Daniel Roebuck
Poole	L. Scott Caldwell
Newman	Tom Wood
Detective Kelly	Ron Dean
Detective Rosetti	Joseph Kosala

and Miguel Nino, Tony Fosco (Chicago Cops), John Drummond (Newscaster), Joseph F. Fisher (Otto Sloan), James Liautuad (Paul), David Darlow (Dr. Lentz), Tom Galouzis M.D., James F. McKinsey M.D. (Surgeons), Mark D. Espinoza (Resident), John E. Ellis (Anesthesiologist), Gene Barge, Thomas C. Simmons (11th District Cops), Joseph Guzaldo (Prosecutor), Dick Cusack (Walter Gutherie), Nick Kusenko (Assist. Defense Attorney), Joan Kohn (Asst. Prosecuting Attorney), Joe D. Lauck (Forensic Technician), Joseph V. Guastaferro (Coroner), Andy Romano (Judge Bennett), Richard Riehle (Old Guard), Thom Vernon (Carlson), Ken Moreno (Partida), Eddie "Bo" Smith, Jr. (Copeland), Frank Ray Perilli, Otis Wilson (Jail Officers), Pancho Demmings (Young Guard), Jim Wilkey (Bus Driver), Danny Goldring (Head Illinois State Trooper), Nick Searcy (Sheriff Rawlins), Kevin Crowley (State Trooper), Michael James (Head Welder), Michael Skewes (Highway Patrolman), Ila Cathleen Stallings (Duty Nurse), Linda Casaletto (Rural Hospital Nurse), Cody Glenn (Paramedic), Cynthia Baker (Woman in car), Johnny Lee Davenport (Marshal Henry), Mike Bacarella (Marshal Stevens), Bill Cusack (Tracing Technician), David Hodges (Marshal David), Lillie Richardson (Copeland's Girlfriend), Peter J. Caria IV (Billy), Tighe Barry (Windshield Washer), Monika Chabrowski (Polish Landlady), Lonnie Sima (Landlady's Son), Oksana Fedunyszyn (Myoelectric Receptionist), Orlando Garcia (Desmondo), Afram Bill Williams (Salesman), Bruce L. Gewerz M.D. (Dr. Bruce), Jane Lynch (Dr. Kathy Wahlund), Joseph Rotkvich (Officer Joseph), Steven Lilovich (Officer Steve), Noelle Bou-Sliman (Myoelectric Technician), Roxanne Roberts, Alex Hernandez (Trauma Doctors), Theron Touche Lykes (Orderly), Joel Robinson (Boy Patient), Greg Hollimon (Skating Orderly), Cheryl Lynn Bruce (O.R. Doctor), Marie Ware (Nurse Gladys), Bernard McGee (Man), Ann Whitney (Myoelectric Director), Lily Monkus, Willie Lucas (Desk Clerks), Turk Muller (Clearing Officer), Ana Maria Alvarez (La Cubana), Eugene F. Crededio (Visitation Guard), Maurice Person (Clive Driscoll), Terry Hard (Officer Hormel), Pam Zekman, David Pasquesi, Lester Holt, Jay Levine (Newscasters), Brent Shaphren, Stephen A. Landsman, B.J. Jones (Doctors at bar), Drucilla A. Carlson (Gerard's Secretary), Margaret Moore (Nichol's Asst.), Manny Lopez (Seminar Doctor), John M. Watson, Sr. (Bones Roosevelt), Kirsten Nelson (Betty), Juan A. Ramirez (Man on "El"), Neil Flynn (Transit Cop), Allen Hamilton (Host), Eric Fudala (Hotel Security Guard)

Plot Capsule: *Dr. Richard Kimble, falsely accused of murdering his wife, escapes on his way to death row, then sets out to find the real killer, with U.S. Marshal Samuel Gerard in hot pursuit. Action thriller based on the ABC tv series which starred David Janssen and Barry Morse and ran from 1963-1967.*

Tommy Lee Jones received the Academy Award as Best Supporting Actor of 1993.

Tommy Lee Jones won best supporting actor awards from the Los Angeles Film Critics and the Hollywood Foreign Press Assn. (Golden Globes).

The movie received Academy Award nominations for picture, cinematography, film editing, sound, original score, and sound effects editing.

© Warner Bros.

LEFT: Tommy Lee Jones

TOP LEFT: Harrison Ford, TOP RIGHT: Joe Pantoliano, Daniel Roebuck, Tommy Lee Jones

Sela Ward

Andreas Katsulas

Jeroen Krabbe

Harrison Ford, BOTTOM RIGHT: Joe Pantoliano

Top: Ben Kingsley, Max Pomeranc, CENTER LEFT: Michael Nirenberg, CENTER RIGHT: Max Pomeranc,
BOTTOM: Laurence Fishburne, Joe Mantegna, Max Pomeranc

SEARCHING FOR BOBBY FISCHER

(PARAMOUNT) Producers, Scott Rudin, William Horberg; Executive Producer, Sydney Pollack; Co-Producer, David Wisnievitz; Director/Screenplay, Steven Zaillian; Based upon the book by Fred Waitzkin; Photography, Conrad L. Hall; Designer, David Gropman; Editor, Wayne Wahrman; Costumes, Julie Weiss; Music, James Horner; a Scott Rudin/Mirage production; Dolby Stereo; Deluxe color; Rated PG; 110 minutes; August release

Josh Waitzkin, Max Pomeranc

CAST

Josh Waitzkin	Max Pomeranc
Fred Waitzkin	Joe Mantegna
Bonnie Waitzkin	Joan Allen
Bruce Pandolfini	Ben Kingsley
Vinnie	Laurence Fishburne
Jonathan Poe	Michael Nirenberg
Poe's Teacher	Robert Stephens
Kalev	David Paymer
Morgan	Hal Scardino
Russian Park Player	Vasek Simek
Tunafish Father	William H. Macy
Tournament Director	Dan Hedaya
School Teacher	Laura Linney
Fighting Parent	Anthony Heald
Man of many signals	Steven Randazzo
Katya Waitzkin	Chelsea Moore
Chess Club Regulars	Josh Mostel, Josh Kornbluth
Chess Club Member	Tony Shalhoub
Asa Hoffman	Austin Pendleton
Reporters	Tom McGowan, Ona Fletcher
Themselves	Kamran Shirazi, Joel Benjamin, Roman Dzindzichashvili
Park Player	Jerry Poe McClinton
Night Park Player	Matt De Matt Reines
Washington Square Patzers	Vincent Smith, Jerry Rakow
Statistician	William Colgate
Journalist	Tony De Santis
Final Tournament Director	R.D. Reid
Park Dealer	Anthony McGowan
82nd Girl	Katya Waitzkin
Petey	Ryder Fleming-Jones
Running Chess Kid	Harris Krofchick
Gym Parents	John Bourgeois, Maria Ricossa
Screaming Mom	Caroline Yeager
Josh's Syracuse Opponent	Andrew Sardella
Josh's Teammate	Nathan Carter
Birthday Friends	Nicholas Taylor, Jonathan Fazio, Nicky Mellina, Philip Neiman, Elizabeth Gropman

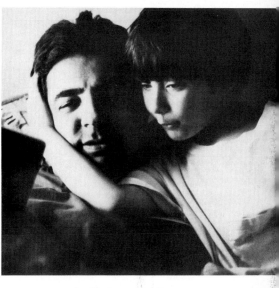

Joe Mantegna, Max Pomeranc

Plot Capsule: *The true story of 7 year-old Josh Waitzkin and his exceptional talent for playing chess which motivates his father to enter the boy in the national children's championships.*

The movie received an Academy Award nomination for cinematography.

© Paramount Pictures

Joan Allen

Max Pomeranc (c, right)

TOP LEFT: Eddie Griffin, Robert Townsend, Marla Gibbs, Asia Dos Reis, Robert Guillaume, TOP RIGHT: Bill Cosby

THE METEOR MAN

Stephanie Williams

James Earl Jones

(MGM) Producer, Loretha C. Jones; Director/Screenplay, Robert Townsend; Photography, John A. Alonzo; Designer, Toby Corbett; Editors, Adam Bernardi, Richard Candib, Andrew London, Pam Wise; Music, Cliff Eidelman; Costumes, Ruth Carter; Casting, Eileen Mack Knight; Visual Effects Supervisor, Bruce Nicholson; Special Visual Effects, Industrial Light & Magic; a Tinsel Townsend production; Dolby Stereo; Panavision; Deluxe color; Rated PG; 100 minutes; August release

CAST

Jefferson Reed	Robert Townsend
Mrs. Reed	Marla Gibbs
Michael	Eddie Griffin
Mr. Reed	Robert Guillaume
Mr. Moses	James Earl Jones
Simon	Roy Fegan
Mrs. Harris	Cynthia Belgrave
Mrs. Walker	Marilyn Coleman
Goldilocks	Don Cheadle
Uzi	Bobby McGee
Marvin	Bill Cosby
Pirate	Big Daddy Kane
Byers	Frank Gorshin
Malik	Sinbad
Mrs. Laws	Nancy Wilson
Jamison	Luther Vandross
Jr. Lords	Another Bad Creation: Romelle "Ro Ro" Chapman, Demetrius "Red" Pugh, Marliss "Mark" Pugh, Christopher Sellers, David "Li'l Dave" Shelton, Adrian "G.A." Witcher
Digit	Tiny Lister
Mrs. Williams	Jenifer Lewis
Stacy	Stephanie Williams
Bloods	Naughty by Nature: Vinnie, Treach, Kaygee
Crips	Cypress Hill: Louis Freese, Larry Muggerud, Senen Reyes
Drug Workers	Biz Markie, Don Reed
Doctor	Beverly Johnson
Old Nurse	LaWanda Page
Vanessa	Lela Rochon
Mr. Little	Wallace Shawn
Clarence James Carter III	John Witherspoon
Janice Farrell	Charlayne Woodard
Officer Patterson	Tommy R. Hicks
Squirrel	Asia Dosreis
Dre	Sam Jackson
Dre's Mother	Barbara Montgomery

and Turean Butler, Reginald Davis, Raynard Holman, Darren Overton, Bryan Young, Jason Young (Baby Lords), George S. Allen III (Man), Janice Garcia (Screaming Woman), Deborah Lacey (T.V. Housewife), Faizon Love (Husband), Stu Gilliam (Head Physician), Greg Littman (Doctor #1), Angela Robinson (Nurse), Joel Weiss (Orderly), Larry A. Wiggs II (Karate Kid), Shirley Jenkins (Bystander #1), Clayton Lebouef (Junkie), Dierk Torsek (T.V. Newscaster)

Plot Capsule: *Sci-Fi adventure-comedy about an inner city teacher who is struck by a magical meteor, giving him super powers and the ability to fly.*

LaWanda Page

Sinbad

Nancy Wilson

Frank Gorshin

© Metro-Goldwyn-Mayer

HEART AND SOULS

(UNIVERSAL) Producers, Nancy Roberts, Sean Daniel; Executive Producers, Cari-Esta Albert, James Jacks; Director, Ron Underwood; Screenplay/Screen Story, Brent Maddock, S.S. Wilson, Gregory Hansen, Erik Hansen; Photography, Michael Watkins; Designer, John Muto; Editor, O. Nicholas Brown; Music, Marc Shaiman; Song: *Walk Like a Man* by Bob Crewe and Bob Gaudio; Costumes, Jean-Pierre Dorleac; Co-Producers, Erik Hansen, Gregory Hansen; Line Producer, Dirk Petersmann; Associate Producer, Dixie J. Capp; Visual Effects Producer, Julia Gibson; Visual Effects Supervisor/Pacific Data Images, Inc., Jamie Dixon; an Alphaville/Stampede Entertainment production; Dolby Stereo/Digital DTS; Panavision; Deluxe color; Rated PG-13; 103 minutes; August release

Kyra Sedgwick, Robert Downey Jr., David Paymer

CAST

Thomas Reilly	Robert Downey, Jr.
Harrison Winslow	Charles Grodin
Penny Washington	Alfre Woodard
Julia	Kyra Sedgwick
Milo Peck	Tom Sizemore
Hal the Bus Driver	David Paymer
Anne	Elisabeth Shue
Frank Reilly	Bill Calvert
Eva Reilly	Lisa Lucas
Woman at audition	Shannon Orrock
Singer at audition	Michael Zebulon
Shirley Washington (age 7)	Chasiti Hampton
Diane Washington (age 8)	Wanya Green
Agnes Miller	Janet MacLachlan
Billy Washington (age 4)	Javar David Levingston
Bob Newhart	Robert William Newhart
John McBride	Sean O'Bryan
Himself	B.B. King

and Steven Clawson (Bartender), Joan Stuart Morris (Wanda), George Maguire (Music Director), Marc Shaiman (Piano Accompanist), Richard Portnow (Max Marco), Jacob Kenner (Duane Dortmueller - age 10), Janette Caldwell (Woman in cadillac), Eric Lloyd (Thomas Reilly - age 7), Janet Rotblatt (Mrs. Brodsky), Bill Capizzi (Race Track Ticket Clerk), Will Nye (Frank's Football Buddy), Eric Poppick (Mr. Polito), Susan Kellermann (Noelle), Robert Parnell (Mitchell), Ed Hooks (Jim), Michael Halton (Motorcycle Cop), Wren T. Brown (Sgt. Wm. Barclay), Lorinne Dills-Vozoff (Anne's Mom), Richard Roat (Anne's Dad), Bob Amaral (Duane Dortmueller), Luana Anders (Records Bureaucrat), John Goodwin (Security Guard), John Durbin (Stage Manager), Walter King, Melvin Jackson, Leon Warren, James Toney, Michael Doster, Calep Emphrey Jr., Tony Coleman (B.B. King's Band), Kymberly Newberry (Angela Barclay), Jamilah Adams Mapp (Samantha Barclay - age 3), Tony Genaro (Man at farmhouse), Kurtwood Smith (Businessman).

Plot Capsule: *Comedy-drama in which the souls of four people, killed in a bus accident in San Francisco in 1959, become lifelong secret guardians to Thomas Reilly. Before time runs out they enlist the grown-up Thomas to help them each resolve the one task they left unfinished when they died.*

© Universal City Studios Inc.

CENTER: Elisabeth Shue, Robert Downey Jr., BOTTOM: Alfre Woodard,
Kyra Sedgwick, Robert Downey Jr., Charles Grodin, Tom Sizemore

Andrew Knott

Andrew Knott, Heydon Prowse, Kate Maberly

THE SECRET GARDEN

(WARNER BROS.) Producers, Fred Fuchs, Fred Roos, Tom Luddy; Executive Producer, Francis Ford Coppola; Director, Agnieszka Holland; Screenplay, Caroline Thompson; Based on the book by Frances Hodgson Burnett; Photography, Roger Deakins; Designer, Stuart Craig; Editor, Isabelle Lorente; Music, Zbigniew Preisner; Song: *Winter Light* by Zbigniew Preisner, Linda Ronstadt, Eric Kaz/performed by Linda Ronstadt; Costumes, Marit Allen; Casting, Karen Lindsay-Stewart; an American Zoetrope production; from Warner Bros. Family Entertainment; Dolby Stereo; Technicolor; Rated G; 101 minutes; August release

CAST

Mary Lennox	Kate Maberly
Colin Craven	Heydon Prowse
Dickon	Andrew Knott
Mrs. Medlock	Maggie Smith
Martha	Laura Crossley
Lord Craven	John Lynch
Ben Weatherstaff	Walter Sparrow
Mary's Mother/Lilias Craven	Irene Jacob
Government Official	Frank Baker
Cook	Valerie Hill
Betty Butterworth	Andrea Pickering
Will	Peter Moreton
John	Arthur Spreckley
Major Lennox	Colin Bruce
Ayah	Parsan Singh
Grandmother at dock	Eileen Page
Grandfather at dock	David Stoll
Girl at dock	Tabatha Allen

Plot Capsule: *Orphan Mary Lennox, forced to stay at her Uncle's gloomy English mansion, is drawn to her bedridden cousin Colin and an untended garden on the estate's grounds. Earlier film version of the drama-fantasy starred Margaret O'Brien as Mary and was released by MGM in 1949.*

LA Film Critics Award to Zbigniew Preisner for best music score (with "Olivier Olivier" and "Blue")

© Warner Bros.

Maggie Smith

Kate Maberly, Andrew Knott

Andrew Knott, Heydon Prowse, Kate Maberly

Heydon Prowse, Kate Maberly, Andrew Knott

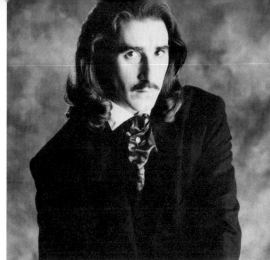

John Lynch

Kate Maberly

Andrew Knott, Heydon Prowse, Kate Maberly, Laura Crossley

Heydon Prowse

Diane Keaton, Woody Allen

MANHATTAN MURDER MYSTERY

(TRISTAR) Producer, Robert Greenhut; Executive Producers, Jack Rollins, Charles H. Joffe; Director, Woody Allen; Screenplay, Woody Allen, Marshall Brickman; Photography, Carlo DiPalma; Designer, Santo Loquasto; Editor, Susan E. Morse; Costumes, Jeffrey Kurland; Co-Producers, Helen Robin, Joseph Hartwick; Associate Producer, Thomas Reilly; Casting, Juliet Taylor; Dolby Stereo; Technicolor; Rated PG; 107 minutes; August release

CAST

Larry Lipton	Woody Allen
Carol Lipton	Diane Keaton
Paul House	Jerry Adler
Lillian House	Lynn Cohen
Sy	Ron Rifkin
Marilyn	Joy Behar
Jack, the Super	William Addy
Neighbors	John Doumanian, Sylvia Kauders
EMS Doctor	Ira Wheeler
Ted	Alan Alda
Marcia Fox	Anjelica Huston
Helen Moss	Melanie Norris
Mrs. Dalton	Marge Redmond
Nick Lipton	Zach Braff
"21 Club" Staff	George Manos, Linda Taylor
Hotel Day Clerk	Aida Turturro
Policemen	John A. Costelloe, Frank Pellegrino, Philip Levy, Wendell Pierce, Steve Randazzo
Hotel Night Clerk	Yanni Sfinias
Hotel Maid	Gloria Irizarry
Lillian's Sister	Ruth Last
Theater Auditioner	Suzanne Raffaelli

Plot Capsule: *New Yorkers Larry and Carol Lipton befriend the Houses, an elderly couple residing in their apartment building, only to have Mrs. House pass away shortly thereafter. Carol suspects that she may have been murdered and begins her own brand of private investigating. This comedy re-teamed Woody Allen with former writing partner Marshall Brickman and ex-co-star Diane Keaton.*

Woody Allen, Diane Keaton, Jerry Adler

Alan Alda, Diane Keaton

Anjelica Huston, Woody Allen

Ron Rifkin, Diane Keaton, Woody Allen,
Anjelica Huston, Joy Behar

Jean-Claude Van Damme

HARD TARGET

(UNIVERSAL) Producers, James Jacks, Sean Daniel; Executive Producers, Moshe Diamant, Sam Raimi, Robert Tapert; Line Producer, Daryl Kass; Co-Producers, Chuck Pfarrer, Terence Chang; Director, John Woo; Screenplay, Chuck Pfarrer; Photography, Russell Carpenter; Designer, Phil Dagort; Editor, Bob Murawski; Music, Graeme Revell; an Alphaville/Renaissance production; Dolby Stereo/Digital DTS; Deluxe color; Rated R; 92 minutes; August release

CAST

Chance Boudreaux	Jean-Claude Van Damme
Emil Fouchon	Lance Henriksen
Natasha Binder	Yancy Butler
Pik Van Cleaf	Arnold Vosloo
Uncle Douvee	Wilford Brimley
Carmine Mitchell	Kasi Lemmons
Binder	Chuck Pfarrer
Mr. Lopacki	Bob Apisa
Marie	Lenore Banks
Frick	Douglas Forsythe Rye
Frack	Michael D. Leinert
Elijah Roper	Willie Carpenter
Waitress	Barbara Tasker
Shop Steward	Randy Cheramie
Randal Poe	Eliott Keener
Police Detective	Robert Pavlovich
Dr. Morton	Marco St. John
Ismal Zenan	Joe Warfield
Madam	Jeanette Kontomitras
Man on the street	Ted Raimi
Stephan	Sven Thorsen
Jerome	Tom Lupo
Peterson	Jules Sylvester
Billy Bob	Dave Efron

Plot Capsule: *Natasha Binder enlists the help of merchant sailor Chance Boudreaux to find her missing father, unaware that he was the latest victim of a deadly organized "game" wherein people pay to hunt homeless veterans. This action-thriller marked the American film debut of Hong Kong director John Woo.*

© Universal City Studios Inc.

Lance Henriksen

Jean-Claude Van Damme, Wilford Brimley, Yancy Butler

Arnold Vosloo

John McConnell, Jesse Bradford, Adrien Brody

Cameron Boyd, Jesse Bradford

Jesse Bradford

KING OF THE HILL

(GRAMERCY PICTURES) Producers, Albert Berger, Barbara Maltby, Ron Yerxa; Executive Producer, John Hardy; Director/Screenplay, Steven Soderbergh; Based on the memoirs of A.E. Hotchner; Photography, Elliot Davis; Designer, Gary Frutkoff; Costumes, Susan Lyall; Casting, Deborah Aquila; a Wildwood/Bona Fide production; Dolby Stereo; Panavision; Film House color; Rated PG-13; 102 minutes; August release

CAST

Aaron Kurlander	Jesse Bradford
Mr. Kurlander	Jeroen Krabbe
Mrs. Kurlander	Lisa Eichhorn
Ben	Joseph Chrest
Mr. Mungo	Spalding Gray
Lydia	Elizabeth McGovern
Miss Mathey	Karen Allen
Lester	Adrien Brody
Sullivan Kurlander	Cameron Boyd
Billy Thompson	Chris Samples
Christina Sebastian	Katherine Heigl
Ella McShane	Amber Benson
Patrolman Burns	John McConnell
Mr. Sandoz	John Durbin
Elevator Operator	Lauryn Hill
Principal Stellwater	Remak Ramsey

Plot Capsule: *With his father on the road, his mother institutionalized and his brother sent to live elsewhere, 12-year-old Aaron Kurlander is forced to survive life in a depression era St. Louis hotel by his own means.*

© Gramercy Pictures

John McConnell, Jesse Bradford

Spalding Gray, Elizabeth McGovern

Karen Allen, Jesse Bradford

Adrien Brody, Jesse Bradford

Jesse Bradford, Lisa Eichhorn, Cameron Boyd, Jeroen Krabbe

Cameron Boyd, Jesse Bradford

Rene Auberjonois, Suzy Amis

Suzy Amis

Suzy Amis, Bo Hopkins

THE BALLAD OF LITTLE JO

(FINE LINE FEATURES) Producers, Fred Berner, Brenda Goodman; Executive Producers, Ira Deutchman, John Sloss; Director/Screenplay, Maggie Greenwald; Photography, Declan Quinn; Designer, Mark Friedberg; Music, David Mansfield; Editor, Keith Reamer; Costumes, Claudia Brown; Casting, Judy Claman, Jeffery Passero; a Polygram Filmed Entertainment presentation of a Fred Berner/JoCo production; Dolby Stereo; Color; Rated R; 120 minutes; August release

CAST

Little Jo Monaghan	Suzy Amis
Frank Badger	Bo Hopkins
Percy Corcoran	Ian McKellen
Tinman Wong	David Chung
Ruth Badger	Carrie Snodgress
Streight Hollander	Rene Auberjonois
Mary Addie	Heather Graham
Jasper Hill	Sam Robards
Shop Keeper	Ruth Maleczech
Elvira	Olinda Turturro
Russian Mother	Irina Pasmur
Mr. Henry Grey	Anthony Heald
Mrs. Grey	Melissa Leo
Young Henry Grey	Sean Murphy
Sam	Jeffrey Andrews
Mrs. Addie	Cathy Haase
Mr. Addie	Peadair S. Addie, Sr.
Helen Monaghan	Jenny Lynch
Amos Monaghan	Vince O'Neil
Farmwife	Karen Johnson
Soldiers	Troy Smith, Keith Kamppinen
Duke Billy	Rusty Pegar
Wilkins	Robert Erickson
Russian Father	Michael Rudd
9 year-old Nick	David Ruben Plowman
14 year-old Nick	Sasha Pasmur
Photographer	Renee Tafoya
Laundress	Barbara Jean Marsh
Travelling Judge	Richard Osterman
Mortician	Dennis McNiven

Plot Capsule: *Posing as a man to avoid the abuse and restrictions given women of the time, Josephine Monaghan arrives at the frontier town of Ruby City to set up her own life and seek her independence. This western drama was filmed in Southern Montana.*

© Fine Line Features

Suzy Amis, Ian McKellen

Samantha Mathis, Sandra Bullock

THE THING CALLED LOVE

(PARAMOUNT) Producer, John Davis; Executive Producer, George Folsey Jr.; Director, Peter Bogdanovich; Screenplay, Carol Heikkinen; Photography, Peter James; Designer, Michael Seymour; Editor, Terry Stokes; Costumes, Rita Riggs; Co-Producer, Darlene K. Chan; Casting, Dianne Crittenden; Dolby Stereo; Deluxe color; Rated PG-13; 116 minutes; August release

CAST

James Wright	River Phoenix
Miranda Presley	Samantha Mathis
Kyle Davidson	Dermot Mulroney
Linda Lue Linden	Sandra Bullock
Lucy	K.T. Oslin
Billy	Anthony Clark
Ned	Webb Wilder
Floyd	Earl Poole Ball
Themselves	Deborah Allen, Jimmie Dale Gilmore, Katy Moffatt, Jo-El Sonnier, Pam Tillis, Kevin Welch, Trisha Yearwood
R.C.	Wayne Grace
Mary	Micole Mercurio
Selma	Starletta Dupois

and Larry Black (Taxicab Driver), O'Neal Compton (Singing Cop), Zoe Cassavetes, Lenae King (Bluebird Waitresses), Barry "Shabaka" Henley (Reverend Raymond), Paul Hampton (Doug Siskin), Carol Grace Anderson (Diner Waitress), Larry K. Hirsch (Studio Engineer), Kevin Bourland (Publisher), Tom Nolan (Desk Cop), Edward Richbourg (Stan the Barber), Vernon Oxford (Tom the Barber), Merri Biechler (Truck Stop Waitress), Barbara Harrington (Auditioner), Anna Thea Bogdanovich, Cliff Brown, Rosie Flores, Jason Klassi (Writer's Circle Participants), Valeri Ross (Doctor), Carol Wade (Nurse), Lisa De Caro (Joy), Erica Rezac (Little Girl), Gregory H. Alpert (Graceland Guard), Jack Verbois (Rear-ended Driver), Angel Cook, Rick Hall, George Olsey, Michael Andrew Shure (Onlookers), Bret Graham (Cowboy at bus station), Steven Hebert, Susan Ahulii (Congratulators), Deirdre McGill, Steve Cottrell (Bluebird Patrons), Ledge Musselman (Bartender), Ron Deskins, Erik Moncarz (Cooks)

Plot Capsule: *Miranda Presley arrives in Nashville hoping to make it on the country music scene. This drama was the last completed feature of actor River Phoenix (who died on Oct. 31, 1993), although his previous film,* Silent Tongue, *was withheld for release until 1994.*

© Paramount Pictures

LEFT: River Phoenix, Samantha Mathis, Dermot Mulroney

INSIDE MONKEY ZETTERLAND

(I.R.S. RELEASING) Producers, Tani Cohen, Chuck Grieve; Executive Producers, Louis J. Pearlman, Jefery Levy; Director, Jefery Levy; Screenplay, Steven Antin; Additional Voice Over & Dialogue, John Boskovich; Co-Producers, Steven Antin, Greta von Steinbauer; Photography, Christopher Taylor; Designer, Jane Stewart; Editor, Lauren Zuckerman; Costumes, Stephen Earabino, Hayley Marcus; Music, Rick Cox, Jeff Elmassian; Color, Panavision; Not rated; 92 minutes; August release

CAST

Monkey Zetterland	Steven Antin
Grace Zetterland	Patricia Arquette
Imogene	Sandra Bernhard
Cindy	Sofia Coppola
Brent Zetterland	Tate Donovan
Sasha	Rupert Everett
Honor Zetterland	Katherine Helmond
Mike Zetterland	Bo Hopkins
Bella	Ricki Lake
Daphne	Debi Mazar
Sofie	Martha Plimpton
Waitress	Robin Antin
Grandma	Frances Bay
Boot Guy	Luca Bercovici
Guy at taco stand	Chuck Grieve
Psychiatrist	Lance Loud
Speaker	Joan Marchinko
Young Monkey	Nicholas Matus

and Chris Nash (Policeman), Louis J. Pearlman (Warden), Suzanne Potts (Policewoman), Robert Russell (Hasidic Jew), Sparkle Stillman (Blue Rinsed Lady), Blair Tefkin (Brent's Assistant), Marc Lafia, Melissa Lechner, Louis J. Pearlman, Lauren Zuckerman (Observation Psychiatrists)

Plot Capsule: *Dramatic-comical look into the daily life of part-time actor/writer Monkey Zetterland and his various eccentric relationships.*

© I.R.S. Releasing

Steven Antin, Rupert Everett, Patricia Arquette

111

THE MAN WITHOUT A FACE

(WARNER BROS.) Producer, Bruce Davey; Executive Producer, Stephen McEveety; Director, Mel Gibson; Screenplay, Malcolm MacRury; Based on the novel by Isabelle Holland; Photography, Donald M. McAlpine; Designer, Barbara Dunphy; Editor, Tony Gibbs; Costumes, Shay Cunliffe; Music, James Horner; Co-Producer, Dalisa Cohen; Associate Producers, Donald Ginsberg, Bob Schulz; Special Makeup Creator, Greg Cannom; Casting, Marion Dougherty; an Icon production; Dolby Stereo; Technicolor; Rated PG-13; 116 minutes; August release

CAST

Justin McLeod	Mel Gibson
Catherine	Margaret Whitton
Gloria	Fay Masterson
Megan	Gaby Hoffman
Chief Stark	Geoffrey Lewis
Carl	Richard Masur
Chuck Norstadt	Nick Stahl
Douglas Hall	Michael DeLuise
Mr. Lansing	Ethan Phillips
Mrs. Lansing	Jean De Baer
Mr. Cooper	Jack De Mave
Mrs. Cooper	Viva
Rob Lansing	Justin Kanew
David Taylor-Fife	Sean Kellman
Scott Pearson	Chris Lineburg
Amy Banks	Kelly Wood
Signy Eaton	Jessica Taisey
Chuck's Father	David A. McLaughlin
Sam the Barber	George Martin
Gus	Timothy Sawyer
Bob	Lawrence Wescott, Jr.
Mr. Cameron	Michael Currie
Mrs. Cameron	Stanja Lowe
Dr. Talbot	Zach Grenier
Judge Sinclair	William Meisle
Mr. McDowell	Robert Hitt
Miss Fletcher	Mary Lamar Mahler
Chuck at age 17	Robert DeDiemar, Jr.
Ferry Crew Member	Drew Guenett
Holyfield Masters	Gene Leverone, Malcolm MacRury
Speaker at graduation	George D. Fuller
Neighbor	Harriette C. Henninger
Husband #6	Edmond Genest
Chuck's Friend	John B. Guptill
Pedestrian	Michael Forte
Ferry Passenger	Elizabeth S. Clarke
Mickey	Rocky

Plot Capsule: *In 1968 Maine troubled, 12 year-old Chuck Norstadt befriends a lonely, facially scarred recluse, Justin McLeod, who becomes the boy's tutor. This drama, based on the 1972 novel by Isabelle Hollman marked, Mel Gibson's directorial debut.*

© Garthrope Inc.

Nick Stahl, Mel Gibson

Mel Gibson

Gaby Hoffman

Margaret Whitton

Mel Gibson

Nick Stahl, director Mel Gibson

Richard Masur

Fay Masterson

Nick Stahl

WILDER NAPALM

(TRISTAR) Producers, Mark Johnson, Stuart Cornfeld; Executive Producer, Barrie M. Osborne; Director, Glenn Gordon Caron; Screenplay, Vince Gilligan; Photography, Jerry Hartleben; Designer, John Muto; Costumes, Louise Frogley; Editor, Artie Mandelberg; Music, Michael Kamen; Casting, Louis DiGiaimo; a Baltimore Pictures production; Dolby Stereo; Technicolor; Rated PG-13; 110 minutes; August release

CAST

Vida Foudroyant	Debra Winger
Wallace Foudroyant	Dennis Quaid
Wilder Foudroyant	Arliss Howard
Fire Chief	M. Emmet Walsh
Rex	Jim Varney
Snake Lady	Mimi Lieber
Deputy Sheriff Spivey	Marvin J. McIntyre
Young Wilder	Justin LeBlanc
Young Wallace	Lance Lee Baxley
Horace Braintree	Peter Willie
Harrison	Daniel Hagen
Maurice	Eric Whitmore
Deputy Sheriff Day	Robert Peters
Tall Man	Buck Nolan
Bingo Lady	Rae L. Lawrence
Singing Firemen	The Mighty Echoes:
Arnold	Charles Gideon Davis
Matt	John Hostetter
Bud	Jonathan Rubin
Moe	Harvey Shield

Plot Capsule: *Drama-comedy about a pair of estranged brothers, Wallace and Wilder Foudroyant, who both possess the power to set things on fire with mere thought.*

© TriStar Pictures Inc.

Debra Winger, Dennis Quaid

Roberto Benigni, Burt Kwouk

Herbert Lom, Claudia Cardinale, Roberto Benigni

SON OF THE PINK PANTHER

(MGM) Producer, Tony Adams; Executive Producer, Nigel Wooll; Director/Story, Blake Edwards; Screenplay, Blake Edwards, Madeline Sunshine, Steve Sunshine; Photography, Dick Bush; Designer, Peter Mullins; Music, Henry Mancini; Costumes, Emma Porteous; Editor, Robert Pergament; Main Title Sequence, Desert Music Pictures; a United Artists presentation in association with Filmauro S.R.L.; Dolby Stereo; Deluxe color; Rated PG; 93 minutes; August release

CAST

Jacques Gambrelli/ Jacques Clouseau Jr.	Roberto Benigni
Commissioner Dreyfus	Herbert Lom
Maria Gambrelli	Claudia Cardinale
The Queen	Shabana Azmi
Princess Yasmin	Deborah Farentino
Yussa	Jennifer Edwards
Hans Zarba	Robert Davi
Arnon	Mark Schneider
Hanif	Mike Starr
Garth	Kenny Spalding
Chief Lazar	Anton Rodgers
Cato	Burt Kwouk
Dr. Balls	Graham Stark
King	Oliver Cotton
General Jaffar	Aharon Ipale
Rima	Natasha Pavlova
Jacqueline	Nicoletta Braschi
Anchorman Andre	Henry Goodman
Franscois	Dermot Crowley
Jean Claude	Sputare Tanney
Madame Balls	Liz Smith
Doctor	Joe James
Customs Official	Sylvestre Tobias
Lugash Agent	Nadim Sawalha
Colonel Al-Durai	Jon Paul Morgan

and Andrew Hawkins (French Agent), Badi Uzzaman (Wasim), Mozaffar Shafeie (Omar), Arnold Yarrow (Uncle Idris), Harry Audley (Pilot), Jacinta Mulcahy (Louise Chauvin), Steven Crossley, Elisabeth Barat (Reporters), Bill Wallis (President), John Francis (Yacht Captain), Simon De Selva (Co-Pilot), Ahmed Khalil (Otter Pilot), Joumana Al Awar (Queen's Secretary), Hossam Ramzy (Burly Arab), Sheila Hyde (Wafiyyah), Tony Kirkwood (Marcel Langois), Andy Scourfield (Clouseau's Ghost), Elizabeth Banks (Nurse)

Plot Capsule: *The illegitimate son of bumbling Inspector Jacques Clouseau joins forces with Clouseau's exasperated ex-boss, Commissioner Dreyfus, to rescue the kidnapped Princess Yasmin of Lugash. The eighth Inspector Clouseau/Pink Panther comedy directed by Blake Edwards. The series began with* The Pink Panther *(United Artists, 1964), which starred Peter Sellers as Clouseau. Claudia Cardinale repeats her role from that film.*

© United Artists Prods.

NEEDFUL THINGS

(COLUMBIA) Producer, Jack Cummins; Executive Producer, Peter Yates; Director, Fraser C. Heston; Screenplay, W.D. Richter; Based on the novel by Stephen King; Photography, Tony Westman; Designer, Douglas Higgins; Editor, Rob Kobrin; Music, Patrick Doyle; Costumes, Monique Prudhomme; Associate Producer/Production Manager, Gordon Mark; Casting, Mary Gail Artz, Barbara Cohen; a Castle Rock Entertainment in association with New Line Cinema production; Dolby Stereo; Technicolor; Rated R; 120 minutes; August release

CAST

Leland Gaunt	Max von Sydow
Sheriff Alan Pangborn	Ed Harris
Polly Chalmers	Bonnie Bedelia
Nettie Cobb	Amanda Plummer
Danforth Keeton III	J.T. Walsh
Deputy Norris Ridgewick	Ray McKinnon
Hugh Priest	Duncan Fraser
Wilma Jerzyk	Valri Bromfield
Brian Rusk	Shane Meier
Father Meehan	W. Morgan Sheppard
Reverend Rose	Don S. Davis
Frank Jewett	Campbell Lane
Henry Beaufort	Eric Schneider
Pete Jerzyk	Frank C. Turner
Myrtle Keeton	Gillian Barber
Myra	Deborah Wakeham
Sheila Ratcliff	Tamsin Kelsey
John LaPointe	Lochlyn Munro
Andy Clutterbuck	Bill Croft
Eddie Warburton	Dee Jay Jackson
Ruth Roberts	Ann Warn Pegg
George Cobb	Gary Paller
14 year-old Girl	Sarah Sawatsky
Lester Pratt	Robert Easton
Young Hugh	Mike Chute
Baseball Announcer	Mel Allen
Race Track Announcer	Trevor Denman
Raider	K-Gin

Plot Capsule: *Horror thriller from the best selling Stephen King novel. A mysterious stranger, Leland Gaunt, opens Needful Things, an antique shop, in the town of Castle Rock, Maine, where customers can find items to fulfill their deepest desires.*

© Castle Rock Entertainment

Max von Sydow

J.T. Walsh

Max von Sydow, Amanda Plummer

Ed Harris, Bonnie Bedelia

CALENDAR GIRL

(COLUMBIA) Producers, Debbie Robins, Gary Marsh; Executive Producers, Penny Marshall, Elliot Abbott; Director, John Whitesell; Screenplay, Paul W. Shapiro; Photography, Tom Priestley; Designer, Bill Groom; Editor, Wendy Greene Bricmont; Costumes, Erica Edell Phillips; Music, Hans Zimmer; a Parkway Production; Dolby Stereo; Technicolor; Rated PG-13; 91 minutes; September release

CAST

Roy Darpinian	Jason Priestley
Ned Bleuer	Gabriel Olds
Scott Foreman	Jerry O'Connell
Harvey Darpinian	Joe Pantoliano
Roy's Father	Steve Railsback
Arturo Gallo	Kurt Fuller
Antonio Gallo	Stephen Tobolowsky
Becky O'Brien	Emily Warfield
Marilyn Monroe	Stephanie Anderson
Man in bathrobe	Maxwell Caulfield
Himself	Chubby Checker
Photographer	Michael Quill
Ned's Mother	Leslie Wing
Six year-old Ned	Blake McIver Ewin
Six year-old Scott	Michael David Kaye
Six year-old Roy	Sean Fitzgerald
Six year-old Becky	Maggie Simman
12 year-old Ned	Sean Fox
12 year-old Scott	Timothy Heath
12 year-old Roy	Kevin Michaels

and Elizabeth Quill, Emily Whitesell (Howdy Doody Moms), Irene Roseen (Nurse), Jerry Brutsche (Pipsqueak), Jason Brown (Young Boxer), Candi Brough, Randi Brough (Twins), Liz Vessey (Sylvia), Lisa Walters (Delphine), Rae Allen (Mrs. Macdonald), Tuesday Knight (Nude Woman), Phil Reeves, Sean Whitesell (Officers), Steve Carlisle (Farmer), Joe Dietl, Todd Lemisch (Ushers), Jay S. York (Tattoo Artist), Harry S. Murphy (PCH Officer), Christine Joan Taylor (Melissa Smock), Cortney Page (Marilyn Monroe's Voice)

Plot Capsule: *In 1962 three 18 year-old friends, about to go their separate ways, decide to have one final adventure together and take off for Hollywood in the hopes of getting a date with Marilyn Monroe.*

© Columbia Pictures Industries

Jerry O'Connell, Gabriel Olds, Jason Priestley

KALIFORNIA

(GRAMERCY PICTURES) Producers, Steve Golin, Aris McGarry, Joni Sighvatsson; Executive Producers, Lynn Bigelow, Jim Kouf, Michael Kuhn; Co-Producers, Mitch Sacharoff, Kristine Sena; Director, Dominic Sena; Screenplay, Tim Metcalfe; Photography, Bojan Bazelli; Designer, Michael White; Editor, Martin Hunter; Costumes, Kelle Kutsugaras; Music, Carter Burwell; a Polygram Filmed Entertainment presentation in association with Viacom Pictures of a Propaganda Films production; Dolby Stereo; Widescreen; Deluxe color; Rated R; 120 minutes; September release

CAST

Early Grayce	Brad Pitt
Adele Corners	Juliette Lewis
Brian Kessler	David Duchovny
Carrie Laughlin	Michelle Forbes
Mrs. Musgrave	Sierra Pecheur
Walter Livesy	Gregory Mars Martin
Driver	David Milford
Little Girl	Marisa Raper
Teenage Girl	Catherine Larson
Middle-Aged Farmer	Bill Crabbe
Officers	Loanne Bishop, Ron Kuhlman
Police Officer	Brett Rice
Bar Waitress	Sarah Sullivan
Carol	Patricia Sill
John Diebold	J. Michael McDougal
Old Man	Tommy Chappelle
Parole Officer	Judson Vaughn
Peter	John Zarchen
Eric	David Rose
Mr. Musgrave	John Dullaghan
Young Cracker	Eric Stenson
Waitress	Mary Ann Hagan
Newscaster	Patricia Hunte
Gas Station Attendant	Jerry G. White

Plot Capsule: *Drama about a young couple, studying the sites of noted serial killings, who unknowingly ask a deranged murderer and his girlfriend to rideshare with them on their cross country trip.*

© Gramercy Pictures

Brad Pitt, Juliette Lewis

Michelle Forbes, David Duchovny

Stanley Tucci, Dennis Quaid

Dennis Quaid, Michelle Schuelke, Kathleen Turner

UNDERCOVER BLUES

(MGM) formerly *Cloak & Diaper*; Producer, Mike Lobell; Executive Producers, Herbert Ross, Andrew Bergman; Director, Herbert Ross; Screenplay, Ian Abrams; Photography, Donald E. Thorin; Designer, Ken Adam; Editor, Priscilla Nedd-Friendly; Music, David Newman; Costumes, Wayne Finkelman; Casting, Hank McCann; a Lobell/Bergman/ Hera production; Dolby Stereo; Deluxe color; Rated PG-13; 90 minutes; September release

CAST

Jane Blue	Kathleen Turner
Jeff Blue	Dennis Quaid
Novacek	Fiona Shaw
Muerte	Stanley Tucci
Det. Sgt. Halsey	Larry Miller
Lt. Theodore Sawyer	Obba Babatunde
Vern Newman	Tom Arnold
Bonnie Newman	Park Overall
Leamington	Ralph Brown
Axel	Jan Triska
Sikes	Marshall Bell
Frank	Richard Jenkins
Foster	Dennis Lipscomb
Mr. Ferderber	Saul Rubinek
Police Captain	Dakin Matthews
Jane Louise Blue	Michelle Schuelke
Col. Kenton	Michael Greene
Zubic	Olek Krupa
Cab Driver	Jenifer Lewis
Burt	Chris Ellis
The Drunk	Eliott Keener
Ozzie	David Chappelle
Bag Lady	Katherine Gaskin
Nun	Marion Zinser
Getaway Driver	Eddie Braun
Bartender	M. Randall Jordan
Waiter	Robert Adams
Baby Newman	Nicholas Wertz
Party Guest	Spencer Henderson
Bank Clerk	Diana Boylston
Soniat House Manager	Robert R. Colomes

and Roger Willis (Napoleon Bartender), Phillip S. Blunt, Louis Robinson (Bar Patrons), John Austin, Brett S. Barre, Larry Lesslir (Policemen), Barry Bedig (Mariner), James Lew, Julius LeFlore, Bill McIntosh (Novacek's Men)

Kathleen Turner, Fiona Shaw

Plot Capsule: *Ex-spies Jane and Jeff Blue, on vacation in New Orleans with their new baby, are forced back into business to foil an international terrorist ring in this comedy-adventure.*

© Metro-Goldwyn-Mayer Inc.

Kieu Chinh

Tsai Chin

France Nuyen

Lisa Lu

Kieu Chinh, Ming-Na Wen, Tamlyn Tomita, Tsai Chin, France Nuyen, Lauren Tom, Lisa Lu, Rosalind Chao

Ming-Na Wen

Tamlyn Tomita

Lauren Tom

Rosalind Chao

THE JOY LUCK CLUB

(HOLLYWOOD PICTURES) Producers, Wayne Wang, Amy Tan, Ronald Bass, Patrick Markey; Executive Producers, Oliver Stone, Janet Yang; Director, Wayne Wang; Screenplay, Amy Tan, Ronald Bass; Based on the novel by Amy Tan; Photography, Amir Mokri; Designer, Donald Graham Burt; Editor, Maysie Hoy; Music, Rachel Portman; Casting, Heidi Levitt, Risa Bramon Garcia; an Oliver Stone production in association with Ronald Bass; Distributed by Buena Vista Pictures; Dolby Stereo; Technicolor; Rated PG-13; 138 minutes; September release

CAST

Suyuan	Kieu Chinh
Lindo	Tsai Chin
Ying Ying	France Nuyen
An Mei	Lisa Lu
June	Ming-Na Wen
Waverly	Tamlyn Tomita
Lena	Lauren Tom
Rose	Rosalind Chao
June's Father	Chao-Li Chi
June (age 9)	Melanie Chang
Old Chong	Victor Wong
Singing Girl	Lisa Connolly
Waverly (age 6-9)	Vu Mai
Lindo (age 4)	Ying Wu
Lindo's Mother	Mei Juan Xi
Huang Tai Tai	Guo-Rong Chen
Matchmaker	Hsu Ying Li
Lindo (age 15)	Irene Ng
Lindo's Father	Qugen Cao
Lindo's Brother	Anle Wang
Lindo's Brother 2	Yan Lu
Pedicab Driver	Boffeng Liang
Tyan Yu	William Gong
Lindo's Servant	Diana C. Weng
Matchmaker's Friend	Yuan-Ho C. Koo
Huang Tai Tai Servant	Zhi Xiang Xia
Servant's Boyfriend	Dan Yi
Rich	Christopher Rich
Hairdresser	Nicholas Guest
Mrs. Chew	Kim Chew
Waverly's Brother	Jason Yee
Lindo's Husband	Ya Shan Wu
Shoshana	Samantha Haw
Ying Ying (age 16-25)	Yu Fei Hong
Lin Xiao	Russell Wong
Lin Xiao's Opera Singer	Grace Chang
Harold	Michael Paul Chan
Ken	Phillip Moon
Jennifer	Melissa Tan
An Mei (age 9)	Yi Ding
An Mei (age 4)	Emmy Yu
An Mei's Mother	Vivian Wu
Popo	Lucille Soong
An Mei's Uncle	You Ming Chong
Aunties	Fen Tian, Lena Zhou, Jeanie Lee Wu
Ted Jordan	Andrew McCarthy
Mr. Jordan	Jack Ford
Mrs. Jordan	Diane Baker
Wu Tsing	Tian Ming Wu
Second Wife	Elizabeth Sung
An Mei's Nanny	Eva Shen
Suyuan's Twin Daughters	Sheng Yu Man, Sheng Wei Ma

Yu Fei Hong, Russell Wong

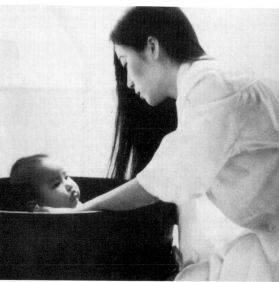

Yu Fei Hong

Plot Capsule: *Four Chinese mothers and their four American-born daughters look back on the relationships, triumphs and struggles in their lives that made them develop into stronger women.*

© Buena Vista Pictures

Kieu Chinh

119

TOP LEFT: Christian Slater, TOP RIGHT: Michael Rapaport,
Christian Slater, Patricia Arquette, Bronson Pinchot

Dennis Hopper

Gary Oldman

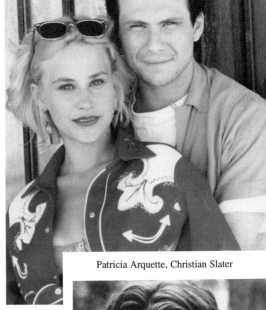

Patricia Arquette, Christian Slater

Michael Rapaport, Patricia Arquette, Saul Rubinek

Brad Pitt

Christopher Walken

Bronson Pinchot

TRUE ROMANCE

(WARNER BROS.) Producers, Bill Unger, Steve Perry, Samuel Hadida; Executive Producers, James G. Robinson, Gary Barber, Bob Weinstein, Harvey Weinstein, Stanley Margolis; Director, Tony Scott; Screenplay, Quentin Tarantino; Photography, Jeffrey L. Kimball; Designer, Benjamin Fernandez; Editors, Michael Tronick, Christian Wagner; Music, Hans Zimmer; Costumes, Susan Becker; Casting, Risa Bramon Garcia, Billy Hopkins; a Morgan Creek production, in association with Davis Film; Dolby Stereo; Panavision; Foto-Kem color; Rated R; 118 minutes; September release

Dennis Hopper, Chris Penn, Patricia Arquette,
Christian Slater, Val Kilmer, Bronson Pinchot

CAST

Clarence Worley	Christian Slater
Alabama Whitman	Patricia Arquette
Clifford Worley	Dennis Hopper
Mentor	Val Kilmer
Drexl Spivey	Gary Oldman
Floyd (Dick's Roommate)	Brad Pitt
Vincenzo Coccotti	Christopher Walken
Elliot Blitzer	Bronson Pinchot
Big Don	Samuel L. Jackson
Dick Ritchie	Michael Rapaport
Lee Donowitz	Saul Rubinek
Mary Louise Ravencroft	Conchata Ferrell
Virgil	James Gandolfini
Lucy	Anna Thomson
Lenny	Victor Argo
Marty	Paul Bates
Nicky Dimes	Chris Penn
Cody Nicholson	Tom Sizemore
Burger Man	Said Faraj
Burger Stand Customer	Gregory Sporleder
Kandi	Maria Pitillo
Frankie	Frank Adonis
Marvin	Kevin Corrigan
Luca	Paul Ben-Victor
Wurlitzer	Michael Beach
Police Radio Operator	Joe D'Angerio
Detective	John Bower
Squad Cop #1	John Cenatiempo
Boris	Eric Allan Kramer
Monty	Patrick John Hurley
Lobby Cops	Dennis Garber, Scott Evers
Running Cop	Hilary Klym
I.A. Officer	Steve Gonzales
Floyd "D"	Laurence Mason
Police Captain	Ed Lauter

Christian Slater, Dennis Hopper

Plot Capsule: *Newlyweds Clarence and Alabama take off for California with a suitcase full of cocaine which Clarence has stolen from Alabama's pimp. Unbeknownst to them the mob is soon on their trail.*

© Morgan Creek Productions Inc.

Christian Slater

THE REAL McCOY

(UNIVERSAL) Producers, Martin Bregman, Willi Baer, Michael S. Bregman; Executive Producers, Ortwin Freyermuth, William Davies, William Osborne, Gary Levinsohn; Director, Russell Mulcahy; Screenplay, William Davies, William Osborne; Co-Producer, Louis A. Stroller; Photography, Denis Crossan; Designer, Kim Colefax; Editor, Peter Honess; Music, Brad Fiedel; Casting, Mary Colquhoun; a Bregman/Baer production; Dolby Stereo; Eastman color; Rated PG-13; 106 minutes; September release

CAST

Karen McCoy	Kim Basinger
J.T. Barker	Val Kilmer
Jack Schmidt	Terence Stamp
Gary Buckner	Gailard Sartain
Patrick	Zack English
Baker	Raynor Scheine
Cheryl Sweeney	Deborah Hobart
Kelly	Pamela Stubbart
Mr. Kroll	Andy Stahl
Lewis	Dean Rader-Duval
Hoke	Norman Max Maxwell
Karl	Marc Macaulay
Guards	Peter Turner, David Dwyer, Frank Roberts
Prison Guards	Robert Glover, Claude File
Businessman	David Hart
Cashier	Henry Stram
Parole Officer	Larry Black
Personnel Woman	Rebecca Wackler
Waitress	Saundra Franks
Beautician	Rebecca Koon
Woman at laundry	Stephanie Astalos-Jones
Accountant	Jack Wilkes
Salesperson	Tom Even
Lawyer	Jill Jane Clements
Mr. Katanich	Al Hamacher
Neighbor	Edith Ivey
Bank Guard	Eric Ware
Radly	Alex Van
Newscaster	Joe Washington
Stewardess	Polly W. Le Porte
Dispatcher	Bill Crabb
Schmidt's Girlfriend	Megan Hughes
Old Timer	Seneca W. Foote
Convenience Store Customer	Lois Hanevold
Maitre d'	W. Clifford Klenk
Roy Sweeney	Nick Searcy
Cab Dispatcher	Afemo Omilami

Plot Capsule: *Cat burglar Karen McCoy, recently released from jail, hopes to go straight but criminal Jack Schmidt kidnaps her son to ensure that she will help him pull off an Atlanta bank heist.*

© Universal City Studios, Inc.

Val Kilmer, Kim Basinger, Dean Rader-Duval, Terence Stamp, Raynor Scheine

Zack English, Kim Basinger

Val Kilmer, Kim Basinger

TOP LEFT: Michael Rispoli, Vincent D 'Onofrio, Victor Argo, Joe Grifasi,
TOP RIGHT: Judith Malina, Tracey Ullman

HOUSEHOLD SAINTS

(FINE LINE FEATURES) Producers, Richard Guay, Peter Newman; Executive Producer, Jonathan Demme; Director, Nancy Savoca; Screenplay, Nancy Savoca, Richard Guay; Based on the novel by Francine Prose; Photography, Bobby Bukowski; Editor, Beth Kling; Designer, Kalina Ivanov; Costumes, Eugenie Bafaloukos; Casting, John Lyons, Julie Madison; a Jones Entertainment Group/Newman-Guay production; Dolby Stereo; Eastman color; Rated R; 124 minutes; September release

CAST

Catherine Falconetti	Tracey Ullman
Joseph Santangelo	Vincent D'Onofrio
Teresa	Lili Taylor
Carmela Santangelo	Judith Malina
Nicky Falconetti	Michael Rispoli
Lino Falconetti	Victor Argo
Leonard Villanova	Michael Imperioli
Young Teresa	Rachael Bella
Evelyn Santangelo	Illeana Douglas
Frank Manzone	Joe Grifasi
Father Matthias	Dale Carmen
Augie Santangelo	John DiBenedetto
Rita	Marie DeCicco
Cindy Zagarella	Nancy Marie
Lorraine	Sam Josepher
Fran	Elizabeth Bracco
Young Cindy Zagarella	Jessica DiCicco
Judy	Mabel McKeown
Host	Robert Stoke
Sr. Cupertino	Marianne Leone
Vincenzo Santangelo	Thomas A. Ford
Mr. Shen	George Teng
Mrs. Harris	Mary Porster
Pat Shen	Dzeni Teng
Mary	Elizabeth D'Onofrio
Sr. John Xavier	Phyllis Wenderlich
Sr. Agnes	Schelli Barbaro

and Ann Tucker (Sr. Philomena), Sebastian Roche (Jesus), Dorothy Hughes (Mrs. Angela Linari), Beatrice Boyle (Nun/Receptionist), Chalotz Lagola (Johnny), Dawn Saito (Mme. Butterfly), Loretta Bassani (Antoinette), Caterina D'Alessio (Rossina), Marta Fensore (Maria), Calogero Savoca (Louis), Anthony Manzo, Vincent Fensore (Neighbors); Storytellers: Irma St. Paul (Mary), Leonardo Cimino (Mario), Rosemary De Angeles (Older Mother), Dianna Salvanto (Younger Mother), Max Fetner (Little Boy), Christina Rosa, Gabriella Rosa (Baby)

Plot Capsule: *Drama set in New York's little Italy follows the marriage of Catherine Falconetti to Joseph Santangelo, who wins her in a card game, and the eventual religious obsession of their daughter, Teresa.*

© Fine Line Features

Lili Taylor, Michael Imperioli

Vincent D'Onofrio, Tracey Ullman

Daniel Day-Lewis, Winona Ryder, Miriam Margolyes

Michelle Pfeiffer, Daniel Day-Lewis

THE AGE OF INNOCENCE

(COLUMBIA) Producer, Barbara De Fina; Director, Martin Scorsese; Screenplay, Jay Cocks, Martin Scorsese; Based upon the novel by Edith Wharton; Photography, Michael Ballhaus; Designer, Dante Ferretti; Editor, Thelma Schoonmaker; Costumes, Gabriella Pescucci; Music, Elmer Bernstein; Title Sequence Design, Elaine & Saul Bass; Co-Producer, Bruce S. Pustin; Associate Producer, Joseph Reidy; Casting, Ellen Lewis; a Cappa/De Fina production; Dolby Stereo; System 35 Widescreen; Technicolor; Rated PG; 136 minutes; September release

CAST

Newland Archer	Daniel Day-Lewis
Ellen Olenska	Michelle Pfeiffer
May Welland	Winona Ryder
Opera Singers	Linda Faye Farkas, Michael Rees Davis, Terry Cook
Larry Lefferts	Richard E. Grant
Sillerton Jackson	Alec McCowen
Mrs. Welland	Geraldine Chaplin
Regina Beaufort	Mary Beth Hurt
Julius Beaufort	Stuart Wilson
Beaufort Guest	Howard Erskine
Party Guests	John McLoughlin, Christopher Nilsson
Mrs. Mingott	Miriam Margolyes
Mrs. Archer	Sian Phillips
Janey Archer	Carolyn Farina
Henry van der Luyden	Michael Gough
Louisa van der Luyden	Alexis Smith
The Duke	Kevin Sanders
Mr. Urban Dagonet	W.B. Brydon
Gertrude Lefferts	Tracey Ellis
Countess Olenska's Maid	Cristina Pronzati
Florist	Clement Fowler
Mr. Letterblair	Norman Lloyd
Stage Actress	Cindy Katz
Stage Actor	Thomas Gibson
Herself	Zoe
Photographer	Martin Scorsese
Riviere	Jonathan Pryce
Mingott Maid	June Squibb
Katie Blenker	Domenica Scorsese
Archer Maid	Mac Orange
Philip	Brian Davies
Archer Guest	Thomas Barbour
Bishop	Henry Fehren
Mary Archer	Patricia Dunnock
Ted Archer	Robert Sean Leonard
Narrator	Joanne Woodward

Plot Capsule: *In 1870's New York lawyer Newland Archer finds himself falling hopelessly in love with the ostracized Countess Olenska, despite his upcoming marriage to her cousin, May Welland. Based on the 1921 Pulitzer Prize-winning novel, this was the final film appearance of actress Alexis Smith. Previously filmed by RKO in 1934 with Irene Dunne (Ellen) and John Boles (Newland)*

1993 Academy Award winner for Best Costume Design.

The film received Academy Award nominations for supporting actress (Winona Ryder), adapted screenplay, art direction, and original score. Winona Ryder was named best supporting actress by the Holllwood Foreign Press (Golden Globes).

© Columbia Pictures Industries

Stuart Wilson, Richard E. Grant, Daniel Day-Lewis

Michelle Pfeiffer, Geraldine Chaplin, Winona Ryder

Winona Ryder, Daniel Day-Lewis

Daniel Day-Lewis, Michelle Pfeiffer

Michelle Pfeiffer, Daniel Day-Lewis

Michelle Pfeiffer, Michael Gough, Alexis Smith, Kevin Sanders

STRIKING DISTANCE

(COLUMBIA) formerly *Three Rivers*; Producers, Arnon Milchan, Tony Thomopoulos, Hunt Lowry; Executive Producer, Steven Reuther; Director, Rowdy Herrington; Screenplay, Rowdy Herrington, Martin Kaplan; Photography, Mac Ahlberg; Designer, Gregg Fonseca; Editors, Pasquale Buba, Mark Helfrich; Co-Producer, Carmine Zozzora; Music, Brad Fiedel; Costumes, Betsy Cox; Dolby Stereo; Technicolor; Rated R; 102 minutes; September release

Bruce Willis, Sarah Jessica Parker

CAST

Tom Hardy	Bruce Willis
Jo Christman	Sarah Jessica Parker
Nick Detillo	Dennis Farina
Danny Detillo	Tom Sizemore
Det. Eddie Eiler	Brion James
Jimmy Detillo	Robert Pastorelli
Tony Sacco	Timothy Busfield
Vince Hardy	John Mahoney
Frank Morris	Andre Braugher
Fred Hardy	Tom Atkins
Don Penderman	Mike Hodge
Kim Lee	Jodi Long
Det. Sid McClelland	Roscoe Orman
Kesser	Robert Gould
Chick	Gareth Williams
Gunther	Ed Hooks
Bailiff	Lawrence Mandley
Judge	Julianna McCarthy
Cop	John T. Bower
Newscasters	Sally Wiggin, Andrea Martin, Suzanne Vafiadis, Ken Rice
Gary Hardy	Michael Canavan
Jerry Hobart	Scott Kloes
W.C. Fields	Bruce Kirkpatrick
Officer Luffey	Edward Gero
Officer Schultz	Andrew May
Paula Puglisi	Sigrid Adrienne
Nurse Debbie	Elva Branson
Bartender	Jack Pashkin
Drug Runner	Erik Jensen
Dispatcher	Jeffrey J. Stephan
Himself	Bob the Cat

Sarah Jessica Parker

Plot Capsule: *Pittsburgh cop Tom Hardy, ostracized from the police force for inform-ing on his partner, is demoted to working on the city's river rescue squad where he finds that a serial killer's victims are all people he once knew.*

© Columbia Pictures Industries

Bruce Willis

Bruce Willis, Dennis Farina, John Mahoney

AIRBORNE

(WARNER BROS.) Producers, Bruce Davey, Stephen McEveety; Director, Rob Bowman; Screenplay, Bill Apablasa; Story, Stephen McEveety, Bill Apablasa; Photography, Daryn Okada; Designer, John Myhre; Editor, Harry B. Miller III; Music, Stewart Copeland; Costumes, Abigail Murray; Casting, Robert J. Ulrich, Eric Dawson; an Icon production; Dolby Stereo; Technicolor; Rated PG; 90 minutes; September release

CAST

Mitchell Goosen	Shane McDermott
Wiley	Seth Green
Nikki	Brittney Powell
Jack	Chris Conrad
Aunt Irene	Edie McClurg
Uncle Louie	Patrick O'Brien
Augie	Jack Black
Gloria	Alanna Ubach
Snake	Jacob Vargas
Blane	Owen Stadele
Walt	Chris Edwards
Tony Banducci	Daniel Betances
Mark Banducci	David Betances
Mr. Goosen	Jim Jansen
Mrs. Goosen	Louan Gideon

and Chick Hearn (Basketball Announcer), Brian Winkler (Sean), Jessica Boevers (Alexis), Katrina Fiebig (Debbie), Bill Apablasa (Mr. Cauley), Laketa O'Bannon (Stacey), Napiera Groves (Molly Ryan), Jay Herold (Clyde), Jason Smith (Rosenblat), Larry Bagby III (Jimbo), Pat Parnell (Prep), Paul Kennedy (Examiner), Cean Heidt (Supervisor), Jim Trimble (Jimmy)

Plot Capsule: *California surfer Mitchell Goosen, forced to live with relatives in Cincinnati, finds himself at odds with his hockey-obsessed fellow classmates, eventually showing off his own skating prowess in a citywide rollerblade competition.*

TOP AND CENTER RIGHT: Shane McDermott

Turkish whirling dervishes

BARAKA

(SAMUEL GOLDWYN CO.) Producer, Mark Magidson; Supervising Producer, Alton Walpole; Director/Photography, Ron Fricke; Concept & Scenario, Ron Fricke, Mark Magidson, Bob Green; Musical Director/Music, Michael Stearns; Editors, Ron Fricke, Mark Magidson, David E. Aubrey; Dolby Stereo; Todd A-O 70 mm; Color; Not rated; 96 minutes; September release

Plot Capsule: *A world-wide odyssey, photographed in 24 countries, using images, sound and music, but no dialogue.*

Japanese snow monkey

Alfre Woodard, Maynard Eziashi, Danny Glover

Danny Glover, Peter Kampila

Marius Weyers

Malcolm McDowell

BOPHA!

(PARAMOUNT) Producer, Lawrence Taubman; Executive Producer, Arsenio Hall; Director, Morgan Freeman; Screenplay, Brian Bird, John Wierick; Based on the play by Percy Mtwa; Photography, David Watkin; Designer, Michael Philips; Editor, Neil Travis; Co-Producer, Lori McCreary; Music, James Horner; Associate Producer, Michael I. Games; an Arsenio Hall Communications production in association with Taubman Entertainment Group; Dolby Stereo; Deluxe color; Rated PG-13; 117 minutes; September release

CAST

Micah Mangena	Danny Glover
De Villiers	Malcolm McDowell
Rosie Mangena	Alfre Woodard
Van Tonder	Marius Weyers
Zweli Mangena	Maynard Eziashi
Pule Rampa	Malick Bowens
Solomon	Michael Chinyamurindi
Naledi Machikano	Christopher John Hall
Thokozile Machikano	Grace Mahlaba
Reteif	Robin Smith
Lucy Van Tonder	Julie Strijdom
Nonsizi	Peter Kampila
Magubane	Sello Maake Ka-Ncube
Bantebe	Eric Miyeni
Mandla	Tshepo Nzimande
Nkeala	Wilfred Tongarepi
Samuel	Innocent Ngavaira
White Policemen	Gavin Mey, Stan Leih
Black Policeman	Joseph Munyama
Teacher	Zilla Mamansi
Philomen	Gift Burnett
Priest	Ackim Mwale
Police Commissioner	Eric Nobbs
Josiah Machikano	Fidelis Cheza
Mrs. Machikano	Anna Manyewe
Thandi Machikano	Portleen Ben
Nomah	Mary Makwangwalala
Mothers	Bertha Msora, Jane Nhukarume
Old Woman	Winnie Ndemera
Child in Police Station	Beauty Mamere
Solomon's Henchmen	Kizito Gamaliel, Alec Ziko

and Sam Banda, Novas Piyo, Gibson Sarare, Rayford Mshanga, Gift Handiradi, Charles Thole, Peter Mudzingwa, Louis Chedemana, June Stanford (Police Cadets)

Plot Capsule: *In 1980 South African police officer Micah Mangena comes into conflict with his son Zweli as the boy begins to see the injustice of apartheid in his country. This drama marked the directorial debut of actor Morgan Freeman.*

© Paramount Pictures:

Danny Glover, Maynard Eziashi

Rory Cochrane, Jason London, Sasha Jenson

Milla Jovovich

Sasha Jenson, Matthew McConaughey

Wiley Wiggins (left)

Christine Harnos, Deena Martin, Michelle Burke

DAZED AND CONFUSED

(GRAMERCY) Producers, James Jacks, Sean Daniel, Richard Linklater; Director/Screenplay, Richard Linklater; Co-Producer, Anne Walker-McBay; Photography, Lee Daniel; Editor, Sandra Adair; Designer, John Frick; Costumes, Katherine (K.D.) Dover; Casting, Don Phillips; an Alphaville production in association with Detour Filmproduction; Dolby Stereo; Color; Rated R; 104 minutes; September release

CAST

Pink	Jason London
Simone	Joey Lauren Adams
Michelle	Milla Jovovich
Pickford	Shawn Andrews
Slater	Rory Cochrane
Mike	Adam Goldberg
Tony	Anthony Rapp
Don	Sasha Jenson
Cynthia	Marissa Ribisi
Shavonne	Deena Martin
Jodi	Michelle Burke
Benny	Cole Hauser
Kaye	Christine Harnos
Mitch	Wiley Wiggins
Tommy	Mark Vandermeulen
Carl	Esteban Powell
Hirschfelder	Jeremy Fox
O'Bannion	Ben Affleck
Melvin	Jason O. Smith
Sabrina	Christin Hinojosa
Darla	Parker Posey
Wooderson	Matthew McConaughey
Julie	Catherine Morris
Clint	Nicky Katt

Plot Capsule: *Comedy follows the various interactions of several teenagers on the last day of school, in 1976, as they aimlessly party away the hours.*
© Gramercy Pictures

Elijah Wood, David Morse

Elijah Wood, Macaulay Culkin

THE GOOD SON

(20th CENTURY FOX) Producers, Mary Anne Page, Joseph Ruben; Executive Producers, Ezra Swerdlow, Daniel Rogosin; Director, Joseph Ruben; Screenplay, Ian McEwan; Photography, John Lindley; Designer, Bill Groom; Editor, George Bowers; Music, Elmer Bernstein; Costumes, Cynthia Flynt; Casting, Deborah Aquila; Dolby Stereo; Deluxe color; Rated R; 87 minutes; September release

CAST

Henry Evans	Macaulay Culkin
Mark Evans	Elijah Wood
Susan Evans	Wendy Crewson
Jack Evans	David Morse
Wallace Evans	Daniel Hugh Kelly
Alice Davenport	Jacqueline Brookes
Connie Evans	Quinn Culkin
Janice	Ashley Crow
Arizona Doctor	Guy Strauss
Doctor in Blackport	Keith Brava
Factory Worker	Jerem Goodwin
Reporter	Andria Hall
Axe Man	Bobby Huber
Ice Man	Mark Stefanich
Woman at rescue	Susan Hopper
Richard in picture	Rory Culkin

Plot Capsule: *Following the death of his mother Mark Evans is sent to live with his relatives, including his cousin Henry, a twelve year-old with possible homicidal tendencies.*
© Twentieth Century Fox

Wendy Crewson, Elijah Wood

Elijah Wood, Macaulay Culkin

Elijah Wood, Quinn Culkin

Craig Sheffer, James Caan

Halle Berry, Omar Epps

THE PROGRAM

(TOUCHSTONE/SAMUEL GOLDWYN) Producer, Samuel Goldwyn, Jr.; Executive Producers, Duncan Henderson, Tom Rothman; Director, David S. Ward; Screenplay, David S. Ward, Aaron Latham; Photography, Victor Hammer; Designer, Albert Brenner; Editors, Paul Seydor, Kimberly Ray; Costumes, Tom Bronson; Music, Michel Colombier; Casting, Lynn Stalmaster; Distributed by Buena Vista Pictures; Dolby Stereo; Technicolor; Rated R; 114 minutes; September release

CAST

Coach Sam Winters	James Caan
Autumn Haley	Halle Berry
Darnell Jefferson	Omar Epps
Joe Kane	Craig Sheffer
Camille Schaeffer	Kristy Swanson
Bud-Lite Kaminski	Abraham Benrubi
Alvin Mack	Duane Davis
Bobby Collins	Jon Maynard Pennell
Louanne	Joey Adams
Joe's Father	J.C. Quinn
Steve Lattimer	Andrew Bryniarski
Ray Griffen	J. Leon Pridgen II
Coach Humes	Mike Flippo
Reporter #1	Jeff Portell
Coach Clayton	Ernest Dixon
Coach Myers	George Rogers
Reverend Wallace	Bernard Mixon
Alvin's Mother	Mary Holloway
Joe's Brother	Steven Griffith
Advisor Smith	George Nannarello
Athletic Director Howard	Jason Byce
Sharon Braver	Mindy Bell
Nichols	Jim Fyfe
Alvin's Tutor	Jason Jenks
Brad Harvey	Bob Neal

and Albert Haynes (Mississippi Tailback), Andre Farr (Mississippi Tackle), Jed Oldenburg (History T.A.), Lynn Swann, Bo Schembechler, Chris Berman, Steve Zabriskie (Themselves), Robert Fuller (Tim Waymen), Al Wiggins (Mr. Haley), Lynelle Lawrence (Leslie), Julia Miller (Debbi), Patrick Smith (Debbi's Boyfriend), Dan Hannafin (Regent Chairman), Charles Portney (Richard Fowler), John Bennes (Edward Learnihan), Charles Lawlor (Charles Shane), Deanna Perry (Rehab Nurse), Tim Parati (Steroids Dealer), Robert D. Raiford (Chancellor Wilson), George Lee (Fat Cat Alumnus), Leslie Broucker, Robert Hook (Trainers), Roger Bright (E.S.U. Doctor), J. Don Ferguson (Referee), Rhoda Griffis (Reporter #3), John R. Murphy (History Professor), Tracy Fowler (Orderly)

Plot Capsule: *Drama following the personal obstacles faced by four diverse college football players at Eastern State University. A sequence showing Craig Sheffer and his teammates lying in the middle of a busy road was deleted during the film's theatrical run after some copycat incidents resulted in tragedy.*
© Touchstone Pictures/Samuel Goldwyn Co.

Andrew Bryniarski, Omar Epps, Duane Davis, Abraham Benrubi

A BRONX TALE

(SAVOY PICTURES) Producers, Jane Rosenthal, Jon Kilik, Robert De Niro; Executive Producer, Peter Gatien; Director, Robert De Niro; Screenplay, Chazz Palminteri, based on his play; Photography, Reynaldo Villalobos; Designer, Wynn Thomas; Costumes, Rita Ryack; Associate Producer, Joseph Reidy; Music Supervisor, Jeffrey Kimball; Editors, David Ray, R.Q. Lovett; Casting, Ellen Chenoweth; a Price Entertainment in association with Penta Entertainment presentation of a Tribeca production; Dolby Stereo; Technicolor; Rated R; 122 minutes; September release

CAST

Lorenzo Anello	Robert De Niro
Sonny	Chazz Palminteri
Calogero Anello (age 17)	Lillo Brancato
Calogero Anello (age 9)	Francis Capra
Jane	Taral Hicks
Rosina	Kathrine Narducci
Jimmy Whispers	Clem Caserta
Bobby Bars	Alfred Sauchelli, Jr.
Danny K.O.	Frank Pietrangolare
Carmine	Joe Pesci
Tony Toupee	Robert D'Andrea
Eddie Mush	Eddie Montanaro
JoJo The Whale	Fred Fischer
Frankie Coffeecake	Dave Salerno
Slick (age 17)	Joseph D'Onofrio
Aldo (age 17)	Luiji D'Angelo
Crazy Mario (age 17)	Paul Perri
Ralphie (age 17)	Dominick Rocchio
Slick (age 9)	Patrick Boriello
Crazy Mario (age 9)	Louis Vanaria
Phil the Peddler	Tommy A. Ford
Driver (Hey Marie!)	Rocco Parente
Murdered Man	Joe Black

and Louis Gioia (Last Rites Priest), Mitch Koplan (Detective Belsik), Phil Foglia (Detective Vella), Richard DeDomenico (Priest), Max Genovino (Louie Dumps), Ralph Napolitano (Gino), Steve Kendall (Red Beard), A.J. Ekoku (A.J.), Sobe Bailey (Willy), Dominick Lombardozzi (Nicky Zero), Frank Caserta, Sr. (Old Gee), Ed Derian (Fight Announcer) Larry Lederman (Racetrack Announcer), Gianna Ranaudo (Tina), Philip Garbarino (Sonny's Killer), Nicky Blair (Jerry), Joe Calvacca Jr., Anthony Etergineoso, Louis Etergineoso, Joe Laham, Alan Lange (Doop Wop Group - Street), Darell Grant, Demond Webber, Rhaman Thomas, Kacy Brooks, Jason Meighan (Doo Wop Group - School), Steve Pendelton, John Tanuzzo, Jr., Steve Bonge, Greg Domey, Mark Cafariella, Butch Garcia, Sonny Hurst (Satan's Messengers), David Batiste, Derrick Simmons, Ali S. Abdul Wahhab (Angry Neighbors), Albert Attanasio, Pat Vacaro (Capos), Rocco "Girffe" Matra, Frank Caserta, Jr. (Soldiers), Richie Ranieri (Bodyguard), Sal Cestaro (Coffeemaker), Larry Liedy (Bartender), Macky Anannlin, Garry Blackwood, Beansie, Johnny Motts, Mike Morigi, Anthony Corozzo, Emily Degrass, Linda Lalicata (Chez Bippy Customers), Elizabeth Abbassi (Lady in window), Ida Bernardini (Fish Store Customer), Frank Conti (Fish Store Owner), Clem Caserta, Jr. (Pizza Man), Sonny Hurst (Biker), Chris Antley, Anthony Cordero, Jean Cruguet, Antonio Graell, Richard Migliore, Johnny Velazquez (Jockeys)

Plot Capsule: *Growing up in the Bronx during the 1950's and 60's Calogero Anello is torn between the influence of his hard-working bus driver father and Sonny, a powerful neighborhood gangster. This drama, based on Chazz Palminteri's one-man Off-Broadway play (in which Palminteri starred), marked the directorial debut of Robert De Niro and the first production released by Savoy Pictures.*
© Savoy Pictures

Robert De Niro

Chazz Palminteri, Clem Caserta, Robert De Niro

Lillo Brancato

Chazz Palminteri

Michael J. Fox

Michael J. Fox, Gabrielle Anwar

Michael J. Fox, Anthony Higgins

Fyvush Finkel, Michael J. Fox

FOR LOVE OR MONEY

(UNIVERSAL) formerly *The Concierge*; Producer, Brian Grazer; Executive Producer, David T. Friendly; Co-Producer, Graham Place; Director, Barry Sonnenfeld; Screenplay, Mark Rosenthal, Lawrence Konner; Photography, Oliver Wood; Designer, Peter Larkin; Editor, Jim Miller; Costumes, Susan Lyall; Music, Bruce Broughton; Casting, John Lyons; an Imagine Films Entertainment presentation; Dolby Stereo; Deluxe color; Rated PG; 95 minutes; October release

CAST

Doug Ireland	Michael J. Fox
Andy Hart	Gabrielle Anwar
Christian Hanover	Anthony Higgins
Mr. Wegman	Michael Tucker
Mr. Drinkwater	Bob Balaban
Julian Russell	Isaac Mizrahi
Gary Taubin	Patrick Breen
Mr. Himmelman	Udo Kier
Albert	Simon Jones
Gloria	Dianne Brill
Gene Salvatore	Dan Hedaya
Milton	Fyvush Finkel
Charlie	Mike G.
Carmen	Saverio Guerra
Vincent	Daniel Hagen
Nora	La Chanze
Mrs. Vigusian	Paula Laurence
Eleanor Hanover	Donna Mitchell
Mrs. Wegman	Debra Monk
Marie	Sandra Reaves-Phillips
Charlotte	Susan Blommaert
Julian Russell Girl	Nicole Beach
Mrs. Brinkerhoff	Susan Ringo
Mr. Brinkerhoff	John Cunningham
Mrs. Nimkoff	Ann McDonough
Mr. Bailey	Richmond Hoxie
Mrs. Bailey	Alice Playten
Benny	Erick Avari
Freddy	Douglas Seale

and David Lipman (Man in elevator), le Clanche du Rand (Woodsy Woman), Anne Lange (Tiffany Saleswoman), Salem Lugwig (Customer), Louis Cantarini (Cab Driver), Hikari Takano (Leon), Jed Krascella (Stage Manager), Gabor Morea (Maitre D'), Beverly Peer, Robert Scott (Musicians), Mark Zimmerman (Pilot), Al Cerullo, Jr. (Co-Pilot), Dan Brennan (Tiffany Guard), Francis Dumaurier (Husband), Bobby Short (Himself), Suzann O'Neill (Tatiana), Tim Gallin (Eliot), Steven Randazzo, Steve Ames, Harry Bugin (Gangsters), Alvin Alexis (Bicyclist), Nick Cosco (Piano Player), Jane Deacy (Traffic Policeman)

Plot Capsule: *Doug Ireland, the concierge at a posh Manhattan hotel, convinces a wealthy financier to front the money for the luxury hotel Doug dreams of building. Troubles arise when Doug finds out that the girl of his dreams is the investor's mistress.*
© Universal City Studios Inc.

Jeremy Irons, John Lone

M. BUTTERFLY

(WARNER BROS.) Producer, Gabriella Martinelli; Director, David Cronenberg; Screenplay, David Henry Hwang, based on his play; Photography, Peter Suschitzky; Designer, Carol Spier; Editor, Ronald Sanders; Music, Howard Shore; Costumes, Denise Cronenberg; Casting, Deirdre Bowen; Make-up Artist for Mr. Lone, Suzanne Benoit; a Geffen Pictures presentation; Dolby Stereo; Color; Rated R; 100 minutes; October release

CAST

Rene Gallimard	Jeremy Irons
Song Liling	John Lone
Jeanne Gallimard	Barbara Sukowa
Ambassador Toulon	Ian Richardson
Frau Baden	Annabel Leventon
Comrade Chin	Shizuko Hoshi
Embassy Colleague	Richard McMillan
Agent Etancelin	Vernon Dobtcheff
Intelligence Officers	David Hemblen, Damir Andrei, Antony Parr
Song's Maid	Margaret Ma
Defense Attorney	Tristram Jellinek
Prosecution Attorney	Philip McGough
Judge	David Neal
Ambassador's Aide	Sean Hewitt
Diplomat at party	Peter Messaline
Drunk in Paris bar	Michael Mehlmann
Critic at garden party	Barbara Chilcott
Mall Trustee	George Jonas
Surveillance Technician	Carl Zvonkin
Marshal	Viktor Fulop
Accordian Player	Cadman Chui
Beijing Opera Performers	The Beijing Opera Troupe
Paris Opera Madama Butterfly	Maria Teresa Uribe

Plot Capsule: *French Diplomat Rene Gallimard falls in love with Beijing Opera diva Song Liling during a performance of* Madama Butterfly, *never foreseeing the strange, unexpected complications of their relationship. The original Broadway production, which premiered in 1988, starred John Lithgow (Gallimard) and B.D. Wong (Song Liling), and won the Tony Award for best play.*

© Geffen Pictures

John Lone, Jeremy Irons

Jeremy Irons, John Lone

John Lone

Anne Bancroft

Nicole Kidman, Bill Pullman

George C. Scott

MALICE

(COLUMBIA) Producers, Rachel Pfeffer, Charles Mulvehill, Harold Becker; Executive Producers, Michael Hirsh, Patrick Loubert; Director, Harold Becker; Screenplay, Aaron Sorkin, Scott Frank; Story, Aaron Sorkin, Jonas McCord; Photography, Gordon Willis; Designer, Philip Harrison; Editor, David Bretherton; Music, Jerry Goldsmith; a Castle Rock Entertainment in association with New Line Cinema presentation; Dolby Stereo; Technicolor; Rated R; 107 minutes; October release

CAST

Dr. Jed Hill	Alec Baldwin
Tracy Safian	Nicole Kidman
Andy Safian	Bill Pullman
Det. Dana Harris	Bebe Neuwirth
Dr. Kessler	George C. Scott
Ms. Kennsinger	Anne Bancroft
Dennis Riley	Peter Gallagher
Lester Adams	Josef Sommer
Earl Leemus	Tobin Bell
Dr. George Sullivan	William Duff-Griffin
Tanya	Debrah Farentino
Paula Bell	Gwyneth Paltrow
Dr. Matthew Robertson	David Bowe
Ms. Worthington	Diana Bellamy
Neighbor Boy	Michael Hatt
Neighbor Boy's Mother	Paula Plum
Girl on bike	Sara Melson
Code Blue Operator	Ken Cheeseman
Anesthesiologist	Richard Rho, M.D.
Resident	Joshua Malina
Scrub Nurse	Christine Wheeler
Circulating Nurse	Sharon Albright
Bartender	Tom Kemp
Dart Players	Robin Joss, Patricia Dunnock
Claudia	Brenda Strong
Desk Sergeant	Michael Bofshever
Desk Clerk	Laura Langdon
Cab Driver	David Candreva
Waitress	Ann Cusack

Plot Capsule: *Amid a series of attacks on female students at a New England college campus, surgeon Jed Hill moves in with old college friend Andy Safian and his wife Tracy, resulting in a devestating series of events.*
© Castle Rock Entertainment

Alec Baldwin, Nicole Kidman

Bebe Neuwirth

Peter Gallagher

Malik Yoba, Leon, Doug E. Doug, Rawle D. Lewis

Leon (right)

Doug E. Doug, Malik Yoba, Rawle D. Lewis, John Candy, Leon

Leon, Rawle D. Lewis, Malik Yoba, Doug E. Doug

COOL RUNNINGS

(WALT DISNEY PICTURES) Producer, Dawn Steel; Executive Producers, Christopher Meledandri, Susan B. Landau; Director, Jon Turteltaub; Screenplay, Lynn Siefert, Tommy Swerdlow, Michael Goldberg; Story, Lynn Siefert, Michael Ritchie; Photography, Phedon Papamichael; Editor, Bruce Green; Costumes, Grania Preston; Casting, Chemin Sylvia Bernard, Jaki Brown-Karman; Stunts, Jacob Rupp; Distributed by Buena Vista Pictures; Dolby Stereo; Technicolor; Rated PG; 98 minutes; October release

CAST

Derice Bannock	Leon
Sanka Coffie	Doug E. Doug
Junior Bevil	Rawle D. Lewis
Yul Brenner	Malik Yoba
Irv	John Candy
Kurt Hemphill	Raymond J. Barry
Josef Grool	Peter Outerbridge
Roger	Paul Coeur
Larry	Larry Gilman
Whitby Bevil, Sr.	Charles Hyatt
Coolidge	Winston Stona
Joy Bannock	Bertina Macauley
Momma Coffie	Pauline Stone Myrie
Winston	Kristoffer Cooper
Registration Official	Bill Dow
Kroychzech	Jay Brazeau
Shindler	Campbell Lane
German Official	Matthew Walker
British Official	Christopher Gaze
Gremmer	Jack Goth
Swiss Captain	David Lovgren
Boys	Kerwin Kerr, Deamion Robinson
Ladies	Beverly Brown, Cyrene Tomlinson
Joseph	Oliver Hunter
Uncle Ferte	Fitz Weir
Drunk	Teddy Price
Cops	Charles Harvey, Clive Anderson
Heckler	Michael London
Push Cart Darby Starter	Lloyd Roache
Hotel Clerk	Cheryl Kroeker
Line Dancer	Karyn J. Scott
Bobsled Starter	Craig Lehto
Themselves	Al Trautwig, John Morgan

Plot Capsule: *Comedy inspired by the true story of a team of Jamaican bobsledders who entered the 1988 Olympic Games against all opposition.*
© The Walt Disney Company

Doug E. Doug, Leon, John Candy

Malik Yoba, Doug E. Doug, Leon

Bruce Davison, Zane Cassidy, Andie MacDowell

SHORT CUTS

(FINE LINE FEATURES) Producer, Cary Brokaw; Executive Producer, Scott Bushnell; Director, Robert Altman; Screenplay, Robert Altman, Frank Barhydt; Based on the writings of Raymond Carver; Photography, Walt Lloyd; Designer, Stephen Altman; Editor, Geraldine Peroni; Music, Mark Isham; Costumes, John Hay; a Cary Brokaw/Avenue Pictures production, presented in association with Spelling Films International; Dolby Stereo; Panavision; Deluxe color; Rated R; 189 minutes; October release

CAST

Ann Finnigan	Andie MacDowell
Howard Finnigan	Bruce Davison
Paul Finnigan	Jack Lemmon
Casey Finnigan	Zane Cassidy
Marian Wyman	Julianne Moore
Dr. Ralph Wyman	Matthew Modine
Claire Kane	Anne Archer
Stuart Kane	Fred Ward
Lois Kaiser	Jennifer Jason Leigh
Jerry Kaiser	Chris Penn
Joe Kaiser	Joseph C. Hopkins
Josette Kaiser	Josette Maccario
Honey Bush	Lili Taylor
Bill Bush	Robert Downey, Jr.
Sherri Shepard	Madeleine Stowe
Gene Shepard	Tim Robbins
Sandy Shepard	Cassie Friel
Will Shepard	Dustin Friel
Austin Shepard	Austin Friel
Doreen Piggot	Lily Tomlin
Earl Piggot	Tom Waits
Betty Weathers	Frances McDormand
Stormy Weathers	Peter Gallagher
Chad Weathers	Jarrett Lennon
Tess Trainer	Annie Ross
Zoe Trainer	Lori Singer
Andy Bitkower	Lyle Lovett
Gordon Johnson	Buck Henry
Vern Miller	Huey Lewis
Aubrey Bell	Danny Darst
Dora Willis	Margerie Bond
Knute Willis	Robert DoQui
Joe Robbins	Darnell Williams
Jim Stone	Michael Beach
Harriet Stone	Andi Chapman
Barbara	Deborah Falconer
Nancy	Susie Cusack
Wally Littleton	Charles Rocket

and Jane Alden (Mrs. Schwartzmeier), Christian Altman (Jimmy Miller), Willie Marlett (Jimmy's Friend), Dirk Blocker (Diner Customer), Suzanne Calvert (Tarmac Secretary), Natalie Strong (Mourner), Jay Della (Bartender), Jeruth Persson (Club Owner), Derek Webster, Nathaniel H. Harris III (Joe Robbins' Pals), Alex Trebek, Jerry Dunphy (Themselves)

Plot Capsule: *Comedy-drama follows the lives of 22 different inhabitants of the Los Angeles area, their actions often unknowingly linking them to each other.*

Robert Altman received an Academy Award nomination for his direction; Madeleine Stowe was given the best supporting actress award from the National Society of Film Critics, while the entire ensemble cast was bestowed with a special Golden Globe Award from the Hollywood Foreign Press Association.
© Fine Line Features

Madeleine Stowe, Tim Robbins, with children

Lily Tomlin, Tom Waits

Anne Archer, Fred Ward

Lori Singer, Annie Ross

Chris Penn, Jennifer Jason Leigh, with children

Matthew Modine, Julianne Moore

Robert Downey Jr., Lili Taylor

Lyle Lovett

Jack Lemmon, Bruce Davison

139

Martin Sheen, Tom Berenger

Pickett's Charge

GETTYSBURG

(NEW LINE CINEMA) Producers, Robert Katz, Moctesuma Esparza; Director/ Screenplay, Ronald F. Maxwell; Based on the novel *The Killer Angels* by Michael Shaara; Co-Producer, Nick Lombardo; Photography, Kees Van Oostrum; Designer, Cary White; Music, Randy Edelman; Editor, Corky Ehlers; Makeup Supervisor, Allan Apone; Costumes, Michael T. Boyd; Casting, Joy Todd; a Turner Pictures and Mace Neufeld/Robert Rehme presentation of an Esparza/Katz production; Dolby Stereo; Foto-Kem color; Rated PG; 254 minutes; October release

CAST

Confederate Cast

Lieutenant General James Longstreet	Tom Berenger
General Robert E. Lee	Martin Sheen
Major General George E. Pickett	Stephen Lang
Brigadier General Lewis A. Armistead	Richard Jordan
Brigadier General Richard B. Garnett	Andrew Prine
Henry T. Harrison	Cooper Huckabee
Major General John Bell Hood	Patrick Gorman
Major Walter H. Taylor	Bo Brinkman
Lieutenant Colonel Arthur Freemantle	James Lancaster
Major General Isaac R. Trimble	Morgan Sheppard
Major G. Moxley Sorrell	Kieran Mulroney
Colonel E. Porter Alexander	Patrick Stuart
Major Charles Marshall	Tim Ruddy
Brigadier General James L. Kemper	Royce Applegate
Captain Thomas J. Goree	Ivan Kane
Major General Henry Heth	Warren Burton
Major General Jubal A. Early	MacIntyre Dixon
Major General J.E.B. Stuart	Joseph Fuqua
Lieutenant General Richard S. Ewell	Tim Scott
Brigadier General J. Johnston Pettigrew	George Lazenby
Major Hawkins	Alex Harvey
Brigadier General William Barksdale	Charles Lester Kinsolving
Confederate Lieutenant	Ted Kozlosky
Lee's Aide	Henry Atterbury
Major General Robert E. Rodes	Graham Winton
Another Officer	Curtiss Bradford
Confederate Officer	Daniel Chamblin
Lieutenant General Ambrose Powell Hill	Patrick Falci
Officer	Ted Turner

and Greg Ginther (Rodes' Courier), George Heffner (Another Officer), Tom Landon, Curtis Utz (Texas Soldiers), Michael Tennessee Lee (Rebel Prisoner), Rick Leisenring (Confederate Voice), Steve Leone (An Officer), Tom Mays (Early's Courier), Frank McGurgan (Old Sergeant), Peter Miller (Pender's Courier), Arnold Nisley (Sergeant), Ted Rebich (Dr. Cullen), C. George Werner (Another Officer), Joe Ayer, Eric Ayer (Banjo and Guitar Players)

(back row) James Lancaster, Royce Applegate, Tim Ruddy, Richard Jordan, Ivan Kane, Tom Berenger, Kieran Mulroney, Cooper Huckabee; (front row) Stephen Lang, Martin Sheen, Bo Brinkman

Federal Cast

Colonel Joshua Lawrence Chamberlain	Jeff Daniels
Brigadier General John Buford	Sam Elliott
Lieutenant Thomas D. Chamberlain	C. Thomas Howell
Sergeant "Buster" Kilrain	Kevin Conway
Major General Winfield Scott Hancock	Brian Mallon
Colonel William Gamble	Buck Taylor
Private Bucklin	John Diehl
Colonel James C. Rice	Josh Mauer
Major General John F. Reynolds	John Rothman
Major General George G. Meade	Richard Anderson
Lieutenant Pitzer	William Campbell
Colonel Thomas C. Devin	David Carpenter
Colonel Strong Vincent	Maxwell Caulfield
Captain Ellis Spear	Donal Logue
Captain Brewer	Dwier Brown
Sergeant Andrew J. Tozier	Herb Mitchell
Brigadier General John Gibbon	Emile O. Schmidt
Private #2	Daniel Bauman
Hancock's Aide	Ken Burns
Bearded Man	Michael Callahan
Captain Atherton W. Clark	Scott Allan Campbell
Buford's Aide	David Cole
Privates	Mark Z. Danielewski, Vee Gentile
Cocky Lieutenant	Brian Egen
2nd Maine Man	Tom Fife
Courier	David Fiske
Old 2nd Maine Man	John Fitzpatrick
Union Rider (Voice #1)	Gary Gilmore
Vincent's Courier	John Hadfield
Sergeant Charles H. Veil	John Heffron
Officers	Con Horgan, Russel Starlin
Devin's Aide	Richard Kiester
Young 2nd Maine Man	Matthew Letscher
Guard, 118th Pennsylvania	Robert Lucas
Private Jim Merrill	Reid Maclean
Private Bill Merrill	Jonathan Maxwell
2nd Maine Soldier	Barry McEvoy
Lieutenant, Buford's Staff	Scott Mehaffey
Sergeant Owen	Mark Moses
Corporal George F. Estabrook	Leonard Termo

and Frank Moseley, Brian Resh, Lawrence Sangi, Michael Phillips, Adam Brandy (Soldiers, 20th Maine), Sandy Mitchell, John Durant (Fiddle and Guitar Players)

Plot Capsule: *An epic recreation of the battle of Gettysburg which began on July 1, 1863 and proved to be the turning point of the Civil War. Michael Shaara's original novel,* The Killer Angels, *won the 1975 Pulitzer Prize for literature. This was the last film appearance of actor Richard Jordan who died on Aug. 30, 1993.*
© New Line Cinema Corp.

Jeff Daniels, Kevin Conway

Sam Elliott

(standing) John Heffron, John Henry Kurtz, C. Thomas Howell, Kevin Conway, Jeff Daniels, Brian Pohanka, Ken Burns, Dale Fetzer, Jack Thompsen; (seated) David Jurgella, Brian Mallon

Lena Olin, Richard Gere

Delroy Lindo, Richard Gere

Anne Bancroft

Richard Gere

MR. JONES

(TRISTAR) Producers, Alan Greisman, Debra Greenfield; Executive Producers, Richard Gere, Jerry A. Baerwitz; Director, Mike Figgis; Screenplay, Eric Roth, Michael Cristofer; Story, Eric Roth; Photography, Juan Ruiz-Anchia; Designer, Waldemar Kalinowski; Editor, Tom Rolf; Music, Maurice Jarre; Costumes, Rita Ryack; Casting, Carrie Frazier, Shani Ginsberg; a Rastar production; Dolby Stereo; Technicolor; Rated R; 114 minutes; October release

CAST

Mr. Jones	Richard Gere
Dr. Libbie Bowen	Lena Olin
Dr. Catherine Holland	Anne Bancroft
Patrick Shea	Tom Irwin
Howard	Delroy Lindo
David	Bruce Altman
Amanda Chang	Lauren Tom
Susan	Lisa Malkiewicz
Mr. Wilson	Thomas Kopache
Dr. Rosen	Peter Jurasik
Hot Dog Vendor	Leon Singer
Judge Harris	Anna Maria Horsford
Bellboy	Edward Padilla
Son	Baha Jackson
Daughter	Epatha Harris
Therapist	Anne Lange
Kelli	Kelli Williams
Richard	Mark Lowenthal
Nurses	Joyce Guy, Marjorie Lovett
Henry	Sal Lopez
Conrad	Scott Thomson
Worker	Bill Moseley
Piano Salesman	Barry Neikrug
Arnie/Violent Patient	Thomas Mikal Ford
Lisa	Lela Ivey
Orderly	Valente Rodriguez
Registrar	Dinah Lenney
Young Girl	Laura O'Loughlin
Girlfriend	Marguerite Pini
Bank Supervisor	Peter Vogt
Saleswoman	Deryn Warren

and David Brisbin (Mr. Warner), Dana Lee (Mr. Chang), Irene Tsu (Mrs. Chang), Kathy Kinney (Homeless Lady), Annie McEnroe (Crying Woman), Maury Efrems (Crying Man), Albert Henderson, John Durbin (Patients), Roman Cisneros (Public Defender), Lucinda Jenney (Christine), Donald Barra (Orchestra Conductor), Taylor Negron (Motorcycle Man), Bill Pullman (Foreman)

Plot Capsule: *Mr. Jones, following a series of disruptive outbursts, is diagnosed as a bipolar manic depressive by Dr. Libbie Bowen, in this dramatic character study.*
© TriStar Pictures

Allison Dean, Ashley Judd

RUBY IN PARADISE

(OCTOBER FILMS) Line Producer, Keith Crofford; Executive Producer, Sam Gowan; Director/Screenplay/Editor, Victor Nunez; Photography, Alex Vlacos; Music, Charles Engstrom; Costumes, Marilyn Wall-Asse; Casting, Judy Courtney; a Full Crew/Say Yeah production in association with Longstreet Prods.; Dolby Stereo; DuArt color; Not rated; 115 minutes; October release

CAST

Ruby Lee Gissing	Ashley Judd
Mike McCaslin	Todd Field
Ricky Chambers	Bentley Mitchum
Rochelle Bridges	Allison Dean
Mildred Chambers	Dorothy Lyman
Debrah Ann	Betsy Douds
Persefina	Felicia Hernandez
Indian Singer	Divya Satia
Wanda	Bobby Barnes
TV Weather Anchor	Sharon Lewis
TV Evangelist	Paul E. Mills
Jimmy	Brik Berkes
Canadian Tourist	Abigail McKelvey
Bar Manager	Kristina Daman
Spinnaker DJ	Mark Limmer
Fisherman	J.D. Roberts
Bar Dancer	Jean Garrido
Ed	Al Mast
Homeless Family	Michele Worthington, George Clark, Carl Brunczek, Kamon Hill
Tennessee Boyfriend	Donovan Lee Carroll
Tampa Lady in red	Kathryn Grubbs
Laundry Manager	Bud Floyd
New Store Employees	Molly Hayslip, Dee Dee Alberts
Nursery Family	Daryl Symore, Pamela Symore, Sarah Luther, Andy Anderson
Parking Lot Couple	Lorie Gene Saye, David Ballasso
Dairy Twist Employee	Jeanette Martin
Donut Shop Employee	Olis Sage
Safe Sex Women	Genny Hayden, Sandi Sherzer
Work Applications	Jim Pigneri, Kenneth Mathews, Lucille Pierce, Ken Schaeffer, Robert D. Reimer
Navy Recruiters	Drew Peterson, Theresa Cronenberger
Trade Fair Salesman	Woody Isom
Tampa Businessman	Gary Martin
Motel Owner	Indira Satia
Sandcastle Builder	Jadonn Sowell

Plot Capsule: *A young girl, bored with her life in a small Tennessee town, ends up working in a souvenir shop at a Florida beach resort where she catches the attention of two very different men.*
© October Films

Ashley Judd, Todd Field

Ashley Judd

Ashley Judd, Bentley Mitchum

Sylvester Stallone

Sylvester Stallone, Wesley Snipes

Wesley Snipes

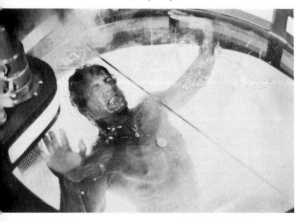

Sylvester Stallone

DEMOLITION MAN

(WARNER BROS.) Producers, Joel Silver, Michael Levy, Howard Kazanjian; Executive Producers, Steven Bratter, Faye Schwab; Co-Producers, James Herbert, Jacqueline George; Director, Marco Brambilla; Screenplay, Daniel Waters, Robert Reneau, Peter M. Lenkov; Story, Peter M. Lenkov, Robert Reneau; Photography, Alex Thomson; Designer, David L. Snyder; Editor, Stuart Baird; Music, Elliot Goldenthal; Title song written and performed by Sting; Associate Producer, Tony Munafo; Costumes, Bob Ringwood; Casting, Joy Todd, Ferne Cassel; Visual Effects, Micheal J. McAlister, Kimberly K. Nelson; Stunts, Charles Picerni, Steve Picerni; a Silver Pictures production; Dolby Stereo; Panavision; Technicolor; Rated R; 114 minutes; October release

CAST

John Spartan	Sylvester Stallone
Simon Phoenix	Wesley Snipes
Lenina Huxley	Sandra Bullock
Dr. Raymond Cocteau	Nigel Hawthorne
Alfredo Garcia	Benjamin Bratt
Chief George Earle	Bob Gunton
Associate Bob	Glenn Shadix
Edgar Friendly	Denis Leary
Zachary Lamb (Young)	Grand L. Bush
Helicopter Pilot	Pat Skipper
Captain Healy	Steve Kahan
TFR Officer	Paul Bollen
Warden William Smithers (Young)	Mark Colson
Warden William Smithers (Aged)	Andre Gregory
Prisoner	John Enos
Tough Cop	Troy Evans
Prison Guard	Don Charles McGovern
Zachary Lamb (Aged)	Bill Cobbs
Police Officers	Patricia Rive, Anneliza Scott, Dean Minerd
Troubled Guy	Kristopher Logan
Squad Leader	Paul Perri
TV Reporter	Susan Lentini
Little Girl	Casey Wallace
Boggle Guard	Michael Tennessee Lee
Museum Guards	Chris Durand, Brett Jones
Taco Bell Entertainer	Dan Cortese
Taco Bell Patrons	Lara Harris, Sam Nehira, Claude Oatts
Taco Bell Scrap	Alex Chapman
Fiber Op Girl	Brandy Sanders
Hamburger Stand Scrap	Rosemarie Lagunas
Irwin	Rob Schneider

and Ken Baldwin, Jack Black, Michael Buice, Carlton Wilborn (Wasteland Scraps), Charles Glass, Ben Jurand, Billy Lucas, Rhino Michaels, Toshishiro Obata, Jesse Ventura (CryoCons)

Plot Capsule: *Sci-fi adventure. Following a bungled rescue attempt in which innocent people are killed, LAPD Sgt. John Spartan and his nemesis, criminal Simon Phoenix, are frozen in a cryogenic prison. They both wake up 70 years in the future in a crime-free metropolis called San Angeles*
© Warner Bros.

Wesley Snipes

Denis Leary

Nigel Hawthorne, Glenn Shadix

Wesley Snipes, Sylvester Stallone

Sylvester Stallone, Sandra Bullock

Wesley Snipes

Sean Astin, Greta Lind

Sean Astin

RUDY

(TRISTAR) Producers, Robert N. Fried, Cary Woods; Executive Producer, Lee R. Mayes; Co-Producer/Screenplay, Angelo Pizzo; Director, David Anspaugh; Photography, Oliver Wood; Designer, Robb Wilson King; Editor, David Rosenbloom; Music, Jerry Goldsmith; Costumes, Jane Anderson; Casting, Richard Pagano, Sharon Bialy, Debi Manwiller; a Fried/Woods Films production; Dolby Stereo; Technicolor; Rated PG; 113 minutes; October release

CAST

Rudy Ruettiger	Sean Astin
D-Bob	Jon Favreau
Daniel Ruettiger	Ned Beatty
Mary	Greta Lind
Frank Ruettiger	Scott Benjaminson
Betty	Mary Ann Thebus
Fortune	Charles S. Dutton
Sherry	Lili Taylor
Pete	Christopher Reed
Young Sherry	Deborah Wittenberg
7 year old Mark	Christopher Erwin
9 year old Bernie	Kevin Duda
11 year old Mark	Robert Benirschke
13 year old Rudy	Luke Massery
13 year old Pete	Robert J. Steinmiller, Jr.
13 year old Bernie	Jake Armstrong
15 year old Frank	John Duda
17 year old Johnny	Joey Sikora
Father Ted	Gerry Becker
Father Zajak	Bob Swan
Father Cavanaugh	Robert Prosky
Classroom Priest	Leonard Kuberski
Locker Room Priest	Father James Riehle
Johnny	Robert Mohler
Boy in neighborhood	Todd Spicer
Ara Parseghian	Jason Miller
Fran	Jean Plumhoff
Coach Gillespie	Spyridon Stratigos
Coach Warren	John Beasley
Coach Yonto	Ron Dean
Coach	Paul Bergan
High School Assistant Coaches	Lorenzo Clemons, Sean Grennan
Football Trainer	John Whitmer

and Scott A. Boyd, William Bergen (Linemen), Kevin Thomas (Player from sidelines), Tom Dennin (Announcer), Michael Sassone (Guard), Marie Anspaugh (Librarian), Chris Olson (Dan Dorman), Vincent Vaughn (Jamie), Peter Rausch (Steve), Kevin White (Roland), Jennie Israel (Rhonda), Amy Pietz (Melinda), Mitch Rouse (Jim), Lauren Katz (Elza), Chelcie Ross (Dan Devine), Christine Failla, Donna Cihak, Colleen Moore (Pretty Girls), Diana James, Mindy Hester, Casey Cooper, Jenna Chevigny (Pick-Up Girls), Beth Behrends (Girl in Cafeteria), Corelle Banjoman (Walk-on), Pablo Gonzales (Groundskeeper), Spencer Grady, Kellie Malczynski (Maintenance Workers), Theodore Hesburgh, Edmund Joyce (Priests), Kent Hunsley (Mill Worker), Dennis McGowan (Barkeeper), Jennifer Patricia Phelps, Michael Scarsella (Friends), George Poorman (Professor), Daniel "Rudy" Ruettiger (Fan in stands), Bob Zillmer (Usher), Scott Denny (Rick)

Plot Capsule: *The true story of Daniel "Rudy" Ruettiger who battled endless opposition in his determination to be accepted into Notre Dame and play on the football team.*
© TriStar Pictures Inc

Sean Astin, Jon Favreau

Sean Astin (c), Jason Miller (r)

Ned Beatty, Sean Astin

Christopher Reed, Sean Astin

Charles S. Dutton, Sean Astin

Sean Astin (c)

Robert Prosky, Sean Astin

Jack Skellington

Zero, Jack Skellington

Sally

Shock, Barrel, Santa

Jack Skellington

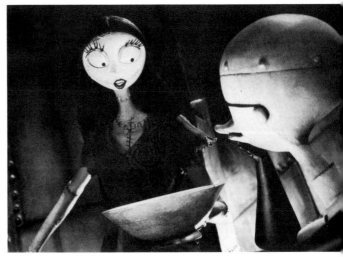

Shock, Barrel, Lock

Sally, Evil Scientist

Sally, Jack Skellington

Oogie Boogie

Shock, Barrel, Lock

TIM BURTON'S
THE NIGHTMARE BEFORE CHRISTMAS

(TOUCHSTONE) Producers, Tim Burton, Denise Di Novi; Co-Producer, Kathleen Gavin; Director, Henry Selick; Screenplay, Caroline Thompson; Based on a story and characters by Tim Burton; Adaptation, Michael McDowell; Photography, Pete Kozachik; Music/Lyrics/Original Score/Associate Producer, Danny Elfman; Animation Supervisor, Eric Leighton; Art Director, Deane Taylor; Editor, Stan Webb; Animators, Trey Thomas, Timothy Hittle, Michael Belzer, Anthony Scott, Owen Klatte, Angie Glocka, Justin Kohn, Eric Leighton, Paul Berry, Joel Fletcher, Kim Blanchette, Loyd Price, Richard C. Zimmerman, Stephen A. Buckley; Storyboard Supervisor, Joe Ranft; Casting, Mary Gail Artz, Barbara Cohen; Distributed by Buena Vista Pictures; Dolby Stereo; Technicolor; Rated PG; 75 minutes; October release

VOICE CAST

Jack Skellington (Singing Voice)/ Barrel/Clown With the Tear Away Face	Danny Elfman
Jack Skellington (Speaking Voice)	Chris Sarandon
Sally/Shock	Catherine O'Hara
Evil Scientist	William Hickey
Mayor	Glenn Shadix
Lock	Paul Reubens
Oogie Boogie	Ken Page
Santa	Ed Ivory
Big Witch/W.W.D.	Susan McBride
Corpse Kid/Corpse Mom/Small Witch	Debi Durst
Harlequin Demon/Devil/Sax Player	Gregory Proops
Man Under Stairs/Vampire/Corpse Dad	Kerry Katz
Mr. Hyde/Behemoth/Vampire	Randy Crenshaw
Mummy/Vampire	Sherwood Ball
Undersea Gal/Man Under the Stairs	Carmen Twillie
Wolfman	Glenn Walters

and Mia Brown, Ann Fraser, Jesse McClurg, Robert Olague, Elena Praskin, Judy Durand, Daamen Krall, David McCharen, David Randolph, L. Peter Callender, Jennifer Levey, John Morris, Bobbi Page, Trampas Warman, Doris Hess, Christina MacGregor, Gary Raff, Gary Schwartz (Additional Voices)

Plot Capsule: *Stop-action animation fantasy . Jack Skellington, no longer thrilled by his position as the Pumpkin King of Halloweentown, stumbles upon Christmas. He decides to kidnap Santa Claus and give the holiday a Halloween touch.*

The movie was nominated for an Academy Award for its special visual effects.
© Touchstone Pictures

Mayor, Jack Skellington

Lea Thompson, Rob Schneider

Jim Varney, Erika Eleniak

Lily Tomlin, Jim Varney, Erika Eleniak, Cloris Leachman,
Diedrich Bader, Duke, Dabney Coleman

THE BEVERLY HILLBILLIES

(20th CENTURY FOX) Producers, Ian Bryce, Penelope Spheeris; Director, Penelope Spheeris; Screenplay, Lawrence Konner, Mark Rosenthal, Jim Fisher, Jim Staahl; Story, Lawrence Konner, Mark Rosenthal; Based upon the television series created by Paul Henning; Photography, Robert Brinkman; Designer, Peter Jamison; Editor, Ross Albert; Music, Lalo Schifrin; Song: *Ballad of Jed Clampett* by Paul Henning/performed by Jerry Scoggins; Costumes, Jami Burrows; Casting, Glenn Daniels; Dolby Stereo; Deluxe color; Rated PG; 93 minutes; October release

CAST

Jethro Bodine/Jethrine	Diedrich Bader
Mr. Drysdale	Dabney Coleman
Elly May Clampett	Erika Eleniak
Granny	Cloris Leachman
Tyler	Rob Schneider
Laura	Lea Thompson
Miss Jane Hathaway	Lily Tomlin
Jed Clampett	Jim Varney
Barnaby Jones	Buddy Ebsen
Themselves	Zsa Zsa Gabor, Dolly Parton
Aunt Pearl	Linda Carlson
Margaret Drysdale	Penny Fuller
Morgan Drysdale	Kevin Connolly
Chief Gallo	Lyman Ward
Miss Arlington	Leann Hunley
Briggs	Ernie Lively
Danforth	David L. Crowley
Waters	Mike Cassidy
Mr. Mackey	David Byrd
Reverend Mason	Patrick Cranshaw
Fat Elmer	Eric "Sparky" Edwards
Spittin' Sam	Mickey Jones
Mayor Amos Jasper	Robert Easton
Billy Bob	Don McNatt
Derek	James Schmid
Jake	Branden R. Morgan
Lance	Charlie Heath

and James O'Sullivan (Coach), Annalee Spheeris (Girl in car), Amy Golden (Girl in bathroom), Eddie De Harp (Guard at wedding), John Ashker (Guy in jeep), Tony Duenas (Gang Member), Nina Beesley (Clampett Maid), Ronan O'Casey (Man at party), Gary Cervantes (Carlos), Gregory Wallace (Male Nurse), Sid Neiman (Gabe), Taylor Gilbert, Marti Muller (Women at party), Shawn Modrell (Flight Attendant), Gordon Ross (Hank), Carmen Filpi (Frank)

Plot Capsule: *After striking it rich Ozark hillbilly Jed Clampett and his family move to Beverly Hills with no intention of altering their backwoods lifestyle. Comedy based on the CBS tv series which ran from 1962 to 1971 and starred Buddy Ebsen, Irene Ryan, Donna Douglas, Max Baer Jr., Raymond Bailey, and Nancy Kulp.*

© Twentieth Century Fox

Cloris Leachman

JUDGMENT NIGHT

(UNIVERSAL) Producer, Gene Levy; Executive Producers, Lloyd H. Segan, Marilyn Vance; Director, Stephen Hopkins; Screenplay, Lewis Colick; Story, Lewis Colick, Jere Cunningham; Photography, Peter Levy; Designer, Joseph Nemec III; Editor, Timothy Wellburn; Costumes, Marilyn Vance; Music, Alan Silvestri; Associate Producers, Christopher Mollo, Kristen Wiseman McIntyre; Casting, Judy Taylor, Lynda Gordon; a Largo Entertainment presentation in association with JVC Entertainment; Dolby Stereo; Panavision; Deluxe color; Rated R; 109 minutes; October release

Emilio Estevez, Stephen Dorff

CAST

Frank Wyatt	Emilio Estevez
Mike Peterson	Cuba Gooding, Jr.
Fallon	Denis Leary
John Wyatt	Stephen Dorff
Ray Cochran	Jeremy Piven
Sykes	Peter Greene
Rhodes	Erik Schrody
Travis	Michael Wiseman
Kid	Michael DeLorenzo
Dre	Relioues Webb
Charley	Will Zahrn
Buck	Eugene Williams
Linda Wyatt	Christine Harnos
Clarissa	Galyn Gorg
Rita	Angela Alvarado
Angie	Lauren Robinson
Freeway Driver	Doug Wert
Driver's Girlfriend	Rachel Watt
Neighbor	Diedre Kelly
Bus Driver	Kathleen Perkins
Rent-a-Cops	David L. Crowley, Stuart Abramson
Cops	Mark Phelan, Nigel D. Gibbs
Announcer	Sean O'Grady
Shop Owner	Lydell Cheshier
Kid on swing	Donovan D. Ross
Policeman	Michael Scranton
Paramedics	Robert S. Neville, Hank McGill

Plot Capsule: *Four friends on their way to a boxing match in Chicago are thrown into a nightmare when they get lost in a desolate area of the city, witness a murder and are hunted down by a gang of criminals*
© Largo Entertainment

Denis Leary

Cuba Gooding Jr., Jeremy Piven, Emilio Estevez,
Stephen Dorff, Michael DeLorenzo

Emilio Estevez, Cuba Gooding Jr.,
Jeremy Piven, Stephen Dorff

Rosie Perez, Jeff Bridges

FEARLESS

(WARNER BROS.) Producers, Paula Weinstein, Mark Rosenberg; Director, Peter Weir; Screenplay, Rafael Yglesias, based upon his novel; Photography, Allen Daviau; Designer, John Stoddart; Editor, William Anderson; Co-Producers, Robin Forman, William Beasley; Music, Maurice Jarre; Costumes, Marilyn Matthews; Associate Producers, Christine A. Johnston, Alan B. Curtiss; Special Effects Coordinator, Ken Pepiot; Casting, Howard Feuer; a Spring Creek production; Dolby Stereo; Technicolor; Rated R; 121 minutes; October release

CAST

Max Klein	Jeff Bridges
Laura Klein	Isabella Rossellini
Carla Rodrigo	Rosie Perez
Brillstein	Tom Hulce
Dr. Bill Perlman	John Turturro
Manny Rodrigo	Benicio Del Toro
Nan Gordon	Deirdre O'Connell
Jeff Gordon	John De Lancie
Jonah Klein	Spencer Vrooman
Byron Hummel	Daniel Cerny
Gail Klein	Eve Roberts
Sarah	Robin Pearson Rose
Alison	Debra Monk
Cindy Dickens	Cynthia Mace
Peter Hummel	Randle Mell
Jennifer Hummel	Kathryn Rossetter

and Craig Rovere, Doug Ballard (FBI Agents), Molly Cleator (IHOP Waitress), Rance Howard (Bald Cabby), Schylar Gholson (Sam Gordon), Trevor Gholson (Benjamin Gordon), Anne Kerry Ford (Mother of Baby), Michael Mulholland (Red Cross Volunteer), Cliff Gober, Jr. (Paramedic), Sally Murphy (Jackie), Steven Culp (Emergency Doctor), John Towey (Wilkenson), Stephanie Erb (Lisa), Cordis Heard (Flight Attendant), Paul Ghiringhelli (Reporter), Ryan Tomlinson (Jonah's Friend), Eric Menyuk (Sears Salesman), Don Amendolia, Rondi Reed (Survivors), Elsa Raven (Grey Haired Lady), William Newman (Elderly Man), Jeanine Jackson (Redhead), Don Boughton (Middle Aged Man), David Carpenter (Young Man in group), Rome Owens ("Bubble" Rodrigo), Kevin Brophy (TV Reporter), Joe Paulino (Reporter #2), Michael Ching (Doorman), Roger Hernandez (Priest), Antoinette Peragine (Laura's Sister), Ramoncita Hernandez (Abuela), Isabel R. Martinez (Tia), I. Rodrigo Martinez (Tio), Mel Gabel (Reflecting Can Hobo), Jama Smith, Donna Keegan, Trisha Brittenham, Linda Lee, Daryl Hemmerich (Flight Attendants), Gerald L. Kersey (Pilot), Randy Danekas (Co-Pilot), Gene DeAngelis (Intercity Captain), Danielle Clegg (Young Survivor), Joan Murphy (Ice Cream Mom), Shannon Ratigan (Harassed Husband), Adelaide M. Wolf (Harassed Wife), Loyd Catlett (Texan), Rebecca Hardt (Ballet Student), Suzanne Q. Burdeau (Danielle's Mother), Maria Bembenek (Jackie's Sister), Richard Blum, Ashley Cemo, Norman Fessler, Lisbeth Rasmussen, Ken Mofhitz, James E. Flannigan, LaVina Wilkerson (Passengers)

Plot Capsule: *Max Klein, after surviving a devestating airplane crash, feels a sense of invulnerability, becoming determined to search out other passengers whose lives were spared and find the reason for his fate.*

Rosie Perez received the Los Angeles Film Critics' Award for best supporting actress; Perez was also nominated for an Academy Award in the supporting category.

© Warner Bros.

Jeff Bridges

Jeff Bridges, Isabella Rossellini

Jeff Bridges

Isabella Rossellini, Rosie Perez

Isabella Rossellini, Jeff Bridges

Tom Hulce, Spencer Vrooman, Jeff Bridges, Isabella Rossellini, John Turturro

Matt Dillon, Dan Hedaya, Luis Guzman, Bruce Kirby

Matt Dillon

Matt Dillon, Annabella Sciorra

Mary-Louise Parker, Matt Dillon

TOP LEFT: Matt Dillon, TOP RIGHT: Matt Dillon, Annabella Sciorra

MR. WONDERFUL

(WARNER BROS.) Producer, Marianne Moloney; Director, Anthony Minghella; Screenplay, Amy Schor, Vicki Polon; Photography, Geoffrey Simpson; Designer, Doug Kraner; Costumes, John Dunn; Editor, John Tintori; Music, Michael Gore; Co-Producer, Steven Felder; Casting, David Rubin, Debra Zane; a Samuel Goldwyn Company production; Dolby Stereo; Technicolor; Rated PG-13; 98 minutes; October release

CAST

Gus DeMarco	Matt Dillon
Leonora	Annabella Sciorra
Rita	Mary-Louise Parker
Tom	William Hurt
Dominic	Vincent D'Onofrio
Pope	David Barry Gray
Dante	Bruce Kirby
Harvey	Dan Hedaya
Juice	Luis Guzman
Couple on train	Jennifer Alonzi, Frank E. Smurlo, Jr.
Mr. Wonderful	Bruce Altman
Harry	Peter Appel
Marlon	Paul Bates
Lecturers	James Bulleit, Raymond Michael Karl
Botanic Garden Worker	Bernard Currid
Patti	Arabella Field
Mike	James Gandolfini
Background Singers	Tanesha Marie Gary, Myreah Moore
Muriel Manner's Husband	William Goldberg
Joe the Waiter	Geoffrey Grider
Mr. Christie	William Duff-Griffin
Man #1 (Paul)	Saverio Guerra
Betty	Angela Hall
Funny Face	Jessica Harper
Emergency Room Nurse	Carol Honda
Organist	Wallace Hornady
Miller	John Christopher Jones
Woman in elevator	Mare Kenney
George	Eric Kollegger
Kevin Klassic	Adam Lefevre
Hannah	Renee Lippin
Man #2 (Joe)	James Lorinz
Martin	Bruce MacVittie
Loretta	Joanna Merlin
Credit Union Officer	Harsh Nayyar
Building Super	Joe Paparone
Man in elevator	Frank Pellegrino
Ralph	John Rothman
Jan	Brooke Smith
Marie	Vanessa Aspillaga Vazquez
M.C.	Floyd Vivino
Muriel Manners	Mary Louise Wilson
Boy Soprano	Hans Zarins

Plot Capsule: *Gus DeMarco's dream of part-ownership in a bowling alley is sidetracked by his alimony payments to ex-wife Leonora. His solution is to act as matchmaker and find her the perfect man to marry.*
© Warner Bros.

Annabella Sciorra, William Hurt

Annabella Sciorra, Matt Dillon

Brendan Fraser, Elisabeth Shue

TWENTY BUCKS

(TRITON PICTURES) Producer, Karen Murphy; Director, Keva Rosenfeld; Screenplay, Leslie and Endre Boehm; Photography, Emmanuel Lubezki; Designer, Joseph T. Garrity; Editor, Michael Ruscio; Costumes, Susie DeSanto; Music, David Robbins; Line Producer, Jason Clark; Ultra-Stereo; Deluxe color; Rated R; 91 minutes; October release

CAST

Angeline	Linda Hunt
Baker	David Rasche
Jack Holiday	George Morfogen
Anna Holiday	Sam Jenkins
Sam	Brendan Fraser
Buddha	Bubba Baker
Aunt Dotty	Rosemary Murphy
Sam's Mother	Concetta Tomei
Aunt Zosia	Peggy Miley
Ghada Holiday	Shohreh Aghbashloo
Uncle Stash	David Fresco
Mark	Noah Margetts
Stripper/Funeral Director	Melora Walters
Mrs. McCormac	Gladys Knight
Patrick	Willie Marlett
Peggy	Amber Wilson
Emily Adams	Elisabeth Shue
Frank	Steve Buscemi
Jimmy	Christopher Lloyd
Bobby McCormac	Kamal Holloway
Liquor Store Clerk	Valente Rodriguez
Long Haired Shoplifters	Larry Greenstein, Skooter Fein
Melanie	Vanessa Marquez
Gary Adams	Kevin Kilner
Clerk	Jeremy Piven
Property Clerk	William H. Macy
Neil	David Schwimmer
Ruth Adams	Diane Baker
Bruce Adams	Alan North
Grocery Store Cashier	Ave Maria Green
Rich Woman	Trudye Bremner
Ex-Hippie	Edward Blatchford
Patrick's Friend	Adam Ryen
Chuck, Receding Bingo Winner	Matt Frewer
Bowling Alley Provocateur	Ned Bellamy
Priest	Spalding Gray
Bingo Caller	John Gamoke
Relative at wake	Nancy Gormley
Bank Teller	Nina Siemaszko

Plot Capsule: *The story of one twenty dollar bill and the people's lives it effects, dramatically and comically, as it is passed from person to person. The first draft of this screenplay was written by the late Endre Boehm in 1935 and finally brought to fruition by his son, Leslie.*

© Triton Pictures

Linda Hunt

RIGHT: Christopher Lloyd, Steve Buscemi

Sherilyn Fenn

Sean Young

Kate Nelligan

Kate Nelligan, Armand Assante

Christopher McDonald, Kate Nelligan

FATAL INSTINCT

(MGM) formerly *Triple Indemnity*; Producers, Katie Jacobs, Pierce Gardner; Executive Producer, Pieter Jan Brugge; Director, Carl Reiner; Screenplay, David O'Malley; Photography, Gabriel Beristain; Designer, Sandy Veneziano; Editors, Bud Molin, Stephen Myers; Music, Richard Gibbs; Costumes, Albert Wolsky; Casting, Renee Rousselot; Dolby Stereo; Deluxe color; Rated PG-13; 89 minutes; October release

CAST

Ned Ravine	Armand Assante
Laura	Sherilyn Fenn
Lana Ravine	Kate Nelligan
Lola Cain	Sean Young
Frank Kelbo	Christopher McDonald
Max Shady	James Remar
Judge Skanky	Tony Randall
Clarence	Clarence Clemons
Laura's Husband	Michael Cumpsty
Arch	John Witherspoon
Milo Crumley	Blake Clark
Restroom Patron	Edward Blanchard
Restroom Stall Patron	David Greenlee
Guy in bumper car	Tim Frisbie
Freckled-Faced Kid	Michael MacLeod
Judge Ben Arugula	Carl Reiner
Frightened Woman	Laurie Lapinski
First Trial Judge	Eartha Kitt
Blind Guy	Harvey Levine
Prison Guard	Christopher Darga
Flower Delivery Man	Jacob Vargas
Jeff	Alex Zuckerman
Conductor	Ronnie Schell
Train Passenger	Bunny Summers
Sportscaster	Bob Uecker
Sports Announcer	Mark Anthony
Bailiff	Kevin Michael Richardson
Lana's Prosecutor	Susan Angelo
Court Clerk	Gregory Sporleder
Jury Foreman	Joseph Attanasio
Juror	Savannah Smith Boucher

and Steve Houska (Courtroom Usher), Roger Reid (Court Reporter), Barry Eisen (Press Room Reporter), George Lopez, Keith Campbell (Murder Investigators), Doc Severinsen (Guest Musician), Vito Mirabella (Hot Dog Vendor), Bernard Hiller, Lucy Lin, Jane Lynch, Casey King (Prison Reporters), Judy Nagy, Julie Donatt, Pauline Arthur Lomas, Suli McCullough (Reporters)

Plot Capsule: *Comic spoof of erotic thrillers in which cop/lawyer Ned Ravine becomes the target of a plot to do him in by his wife and her lover.*
© Metro-Goldwyn-Mayer Inc.

THE WAR ROOM

(OCTOBER FILMS) Producers, R.J. Cutler, Wendy Ettinger, Frazer Pennebaker; Executive Producers, Wendy Ettinger, Frazer Pennebaker; Directors, DA Pennebaker, Chris Hegedus; Photography, Nick Doob, DA Pennebaker, Kevin Rafferty; Editors, Chris Hegedus, Erez Laufer, DA Pennebaker; Associate Producer, Cyclone Films; Dolby Stereo; Color; Not rated; 92 minutes; November release

WITH

James Carville, George Stephanopoulos, Heather Beckel, Paul Begala, Bob Boorstin, Michael C. Donilon, Jeff Eller, Stan Greenberg, Mandy Grunwald, Harold Ickes, Mickey Kantor, Mary Matalin, Mitchell Schwartz, and the entire war room crew

Plot Capsule: *Documentary on the 1992 Democratic Convention and Bill Clinton's successful bid for the nomination for President of the United States.*

Cited as best documentary by the National Board of Review; the film was also nominated for an Academy Award for feature-length documentary.
© October Films

James Carville

COMBINATION PLATTER

(ARROW RELEASING) Producer/Director, Tony Chan; Co-Producers, Ulla Zwicker, Bluehorse Films Inc.; Executive Producers, Jenny Lee, Man Fuk Chan; Screenplay, Edwin Baker, Tony Chan; Photography, Yoshifumi Hosoya; Art Director, Pat Summa; Music, Brian Tibbs; Editors, Tony Chan, James Y. Kwei; Casting, Amanda Ma; Color; Not rated; 84 minutes; November release

George Stephanopoulos, James Carville

CAST

Robert	Jeff Lau
Claire	Colleen O'Brien
Sam	Lester "Chit-Man" Chan
Benny	Colin Mitchell
Andy	Kenneth Lu
Mr. Lee	Thomas K. Hsiung
Dishwasher	Jia Fu Liu
Jennie	Ellen Synn
Glasshead	Nathanael Geng
Stanley	Peter Kwong
Noriko	Eleonora Kihlberg
James	James Dumont
Chef Chan	Lu Yu
Chef Fong	Bo Z. Wang
Chef Tsui	Vincent H.H. Kuo
Spareribs	Kwan Chack Lau
Michelle	Juliet Leong
Joey I	Doug Rand
Joey II	Sean Grover
Cranky Customers	Ann D'Agnillo, Shira Levin
Immigration Officers	Luke Valerio, Susan Sterman, Larry Weissman, Joe Pantano
Street Kids	Edwin Baker, Bryen Adler
Angry Customer	Joe Litto
New Dishwasher	John Yung
Illegal Restaurant Worker	Alvin Eng
Waitress	Christine Pentelost
Mah Jong Players	Al Flash Kong, Young Tian, Lin Zmi Jian

Plot Capsule: *Comedy-drama looks at the day-to-day activities of a Brooklyn-based Chinese restaurant through the eyes of its new employee, a young Chinese man determined to secure his green card.*
© Arrow Releasing

RIGHT: Jeff Lau

Kathy Bates, Tony Campisi

A HOME OF OUR OWN

(GRAMERCY PICTURES) Producers, Dale Pollock, Bill Borden; Executive Producer/Screenplay, Patrick Duncan; Director, Tony Bill; Photography, Jean Lepine; Designer, James Schoppe; Editor, Axel Hubert; Costumes, Lynn Bernay; Music, Michael Convertino; a Polygram Filmed Entertainment presentation; Dolby Stereo; Color; Rated PG; 103 minutes; November release

CAST

Frances Lacey	Kathy Bates
Shayne Lacey	Edward Furlong
Mr. Munimura	Soon-Teck Oh
Norman	Tony Campisi
Lynn Lacey	Clarissa Lassig
Faye Lacey	Sarah Schaub
Murray Lacey	Miles Feulner
Annie Lacey	Amy Sakasitz
Craig Lacey	T.J. Lowther
Father Tomlin	Melvin Ward
Mr. Hilliard	Dave Jensen
Mr. King	H.E.D. Redford
Doctor	Tony Bill

Plot Capsule: *Drama set in 1962. Frances Lacey, after losing her job in L.A., takes her six kids and heads to Idaho where they find a ramshackle old house and set out to make it into something liveable.*
© Gramercy Pictures

Edward Furlong, Kathy Bates

Clarissa Lassig, Soon-Teck Oh, Miles Fuelner

(clockwise, from top) Edward Furlong, Clarissa Lassig, Sarah Schaub, Amy Sakasitz, Miles Fuelner

FLESH AND BONE

(PARAMOUNT) Producers, Mark Rosenberg, Paula Weinstein; Executive Producer, Sydney Pollack; Co-Producer, G. Mac Brown; Director/Screenplay, Steve Kloves; Photography, Philippe Rousselot; Designer, Jon Hutman; Editor, Mia Goldman; Costumes, Elizabeth McBride; Music, Thomas Newman; Casting, Risa Bramon-Garcia; a Mirage/Spring Creek production; Dolby Stereo; Deluxe color; Rated R; 128 minutes; November release

CAST

Sarah Willlets	Julia Mueller
Clem Willets	Ron Kuhlman
Young Arlis	Jerry Swindall
Scotty Willets	Ryan Bohls
Roy Sweeney	James Caan
Arlis Sweeney	Dennis Quaid
Boy in suit	Ez Perez
Tiny Ted	Craig Erickson
Cindy	Barbara Alyn Woods
Ginnie	Gwyneth Paltrow
Plump Man	Joe Berryman
Kay Davies	Meg Ryan
Elliot	Scott Wilson
Woody	James N. Harrell
Juan	Gerard Johnson
Nestor	Hector Garcia
Peg	Betsy Brantley
Groom	John Hawkes
Pudge Riley	Vic Polizos
Earl	Nik Hagler
Sullen Kid	Travis Baker
Reese Davies	Christopher Rydell
Woman with crying baby	Angie Bolling
Kyle	Joe Stevens
Waitress	Libby Villari
Emma	Gail Cronauer

Plot Capsule: *Arlis Sweeney, haunted by murders committed by his father when Arlis was a boy, hooks up with a drifter named Kay Davies just as his father reappears in his life.*

© Paramount Pictures

Dennis Quaid, Meg Ryan

Meg Ryan, Dennis Quaid

Dennis Quaid, Meg Ryan

Gwyneth Paltrow

James Caan

Al Pacino, Penelope Ann Miller, Sean Penn

CARLITO'S WAY

(UNIVERSAL) Producers, Martin Bregman, Willi Baer, Michael S. Bregman; Executive Producers, Louis A. Stroller, Ortwin Freyermuth; Director, Brian DePalma; Screenplay, David Koepp; Based on the novels *Carlito's Way* and *After Hours* by Edwin Torres; Photography, Stephen H. Burum; Designer, Richard Sylbert; Editors, Bill Pankow, Kristina Boden; Music, Patrick Doyle; Costumes, Aude Bronson-Howard; Casting, Bonnie Timmermann; an Epic Productions presentation; DTS Stereo/Dolby; Panavision; Deluxe color; Rated R; 141 minutes; November release

CAST

Carlito Brigante .... Al Pacino
David Kleinfeld .... Sean Penn
Gail .... Penelope Ann Miller
Benny Blanco .... John Leguizamo
Steffie .... Ingrid Rogers
Pachanga .... Luis Guzman
Norwalk .... James Rebhorn
Vinnie Taglialucci .... Joseph Siravo
Lalin .... Viggo Mortensen
Pete Amadesso .... Richard Foronjy
Saso .... Jorge Porcel
Tony Taglialucci .... Frank Minucci
Frankie .... Adrian Pasdar
Guajiro .... John Agustin Ortiz
Walberto .... Angel Salazar
Rolando .... Al Israel
Quisqueya .... Rick Aviles
Rudy .... Jaime Sanchez
Battaglia (Big Guy) .... Edmonte Salvato
Judge Feinstein .... Paul Mazursky
Club Date .... Tera Tabrizi
Kid .... Victor Sierra
Barber .... Caesar Cordova
and Jon Seda, Ruben Rivera (Dominicans), Sherie Mambru, Brenda Hernandez (Girlfriends), Elliot Santiago (Knifeman), Frank Ferrara (Manzanero), John Hoyt, Chuck Zito, Steven Puente, Tony Cucci (Club Bouncers), Alfred Sauchelli, Jr., Anthony Catanese, Sam Weber, Sonny Zito (Bodyguards), Walter T. Meade (Jackson Corrections Officer), Michael Hadge, Richard Council (Diamond Room Men), Lindsey Lombardi (Diamond Room Dancer), James Bulleit (Louie), Crystal Haney (Estate Party Woman), Gregory Misciagno (Italian at Copa), Mel Gorham (Pachanga's Date), Rocco Sisto (Panama Hatman), John Finn (Duncan), Brian Tarantina (Speller), Jaime Tirelli (Valentin), Owen Hollander (Cab Driver), John Michael Bolger, Ralph Destino, Jr., Vincent Jerosa, Luke Toma, Frank Pietrangolare, Mike Sheehan (Cops), Dean Rader-Duval (Med Tech), Gene Canfield (Train Conductor), Sharmagne Leland-St. John (Woman at Grand Central), Rene Rivera, Orlando Urdaneta (Bartenders), Troy A. Hawkes (Solicitor at Go-Go Club), Kim Rideout (Gail's Friend at dance studio), Drita Barak, Christopher Bregman, Natalia Rey, Joe Conzo, Gaetano "Tom" Lisi, Debra Niewald (Club Patrons), Christina Murphy, Juliette Ortega, Mary C. Hammett (Waitresses), Debbie Benitez, Roberta Mathes, Freddy Rios, Mike Ramos (Dancers), Yelba Matamoros (Blanco's Girlfriend), Nelson Vasquez (Blanco Associate), Jason Daryn (Party Waiter), Dan Brennan, Michael Moran (Party Guests), Vinny Pastore, Garry Blackwood (Copa Wiseguys), Cynthia Lamontagne (Woman at elevator), Bo Dietl, Kato (Casino Men), James V. Miller (Black Jack Dealer), Marc Antony (Latin Band at disco)

Plot Capsule: *Carlito Brigante, fresh out of prison, opens a nightclub with the intention of making enough money to lead a straight life. However, his past involvement with the criminal world and his loyalty to his shady lawyer make it difficult for him to stay out of trouble.*
© Universal City Studios, Inc

Al Pacino

Al Pacino, John Leguizamo

Al Pacino, Sean Penn

Kiefer Sutherland, Charlie Sheen, Chris O'Donnell, Oliver Platt

Tim Curry, Rebecca De Mornay

Chris O'Donnell, Michael Wincott

THE THREE MUSKETEERS

(WALT DISNEY PICTURES) Producers, Joe Roth, Roger Birnbaum; Executive Producers, Jordan Kerner, Jon Avnet; Co-Producers, Ned Dowd, William W. Wilson III; Director, Stephen Herek; Screenplay, David Loughery; Based on the novel by Alexandre Dumas; Photography, Dean Semler; Designer, Wolf Kroeger; Costumes, John Mollo; Editor, John F. Link; Music, Michael Kamen; Song: *All for Love* by Bryan Adams, Robert John "Mutt" Lange, Michael Kamen/performed by Bryan Adams, Rod Stewart, Sting; Stunts, Paul Weston; Distributed by Buena Vista Pictures; Dolby Stereo; Technicolor; Rated PG; 105 minutes; November release

CAST

Aramis	Charlie Sheen
Athos	Kiefer Sutherland
D'Artagnan	Chris O'Donnell
Porthos	Oliver Platt
Cardinal Richelieu	Tim Curry
Milady	Rebecca De Mornay
Queen Anne	Gabrielle Anwar
Rochefort	Michael Wincott
Girard/Jussac	Paul McGann
Constance	Julie Delpy
King Louis	Hugh O'Conor
Henri	Christopher Adamson
Parker	Philip Tan
Peasant	Erwin Leder
Musketeer	Axel Anselm
Seneschals	Bruno Thost, Oliver Hoppa
Damsel	Emma Moore
Innkeeper	Herbert Fux
Barmaid	Nichola Cordey
Armand de Winter	Sebastian Eckhardt

Plot Capsule: *In 17th Century France D'Artagnan journeys to Paris to join the King's musketeers only to discover that they have been dismissed by the evil Cardinal Richelieu who plots to take over the throne. Three defiant musketeers refuse to lay down arms and vow to battle the Cardinal, with D'Artagnan as their comrade. Previous English-language feature film versions of the 1844 novel: (United Artists, 1921, with Douglas Fairbanks), (20th Century Fox, 1935, Walter Abel), (20th Century Fox, 1939, Don Ameche), (MGM, 1948, Gene Kelly), (20th Century Fox, 1974, Michael York).*
© The Walt Disney Company

Oliver Platt

Tim Curry

Kiefer Sutherland

Charlie Sheen, Chris O'Donnell, Oliver Platt, Kiefer Sutherland

Charlie Sheen

Rebecca DeMornay

Chris O'Donnell

MY LIFE

(COLUMBIA) Producers, Jerry Zucker, Bruce Joel Rubin, Hunt Lowry; Executive Producer, Gil Netter; Director/Screenplay, Bruce Joel Rubin; Photography, Peter James; Designer, Neil Spisak; Editor, Richard Chew; Costumes, Judy Ruskin; Music, John Barry; Casting, Janet Hirshenson, Jane Jenkins, Roger Mussenden; Presented in association with Capella Films, from Zucker Brothers productions; Dolby Stereo; Technicolor; Rated PG-13; 112 minutes; November release

Michael Keaton

CAST

Bob Jones	Michael Keaton
Gail Jones	Nicole Kidman
Paul Ivanovich	Bradley Whitford
Theresa	Queen Latifah
Bill Ivanovich	Michael Constantine
Rose Ivanovich	Rebecca Schull
Dr. Mills	Mark Lowenthal
Carol Sandman	Lee Garlington
Doris	Toni Sawyer
Mr. Ho	Haing S. Ngor
Anya Stasiuk	Romy Rosemont
Young Bobbie	Danny Rimmer
Young Rose	Ruth DeSosa
Young Bill	Richard Schiff
Young Paul	Stephen Taylor Knot
Baby Brian	Andrew & Brian Camuccio
Little Boy Brian	Colby Sawyer Garabedian
Miss Morgenstern	Mary Ann Thebus
Laura	Brenda Strong
George	Rudi Davis
Sam	Mark Holton
Deborah	Lisa Walters
Walter	Bruce Jarchow
Dorothy	Jane Morris
Dr. Califano	Kenneth Tigar
Dr. Altman	Ray Reinhardt
Arnold Sherman	Frank DiElsi

and Billy L. Sullivan (Rollercoaster Boy), Michael Gallagher, Christopher Miranda (Rollercoaster Friends), Nora Taylor (Little Girl), Dianne B. Shaw (Detroit Mother), Sondra Rubin (Aunt Sophia), Sylvia Kauders (Aunt Tekla), Sharon Conley (Lida Stasiuk), James R. Sweeney (Nestor Stasiuk), Vasek C. Simek (Uncle Henry), Magda Harout (Aunt Sonia), Mark Zingale, Jonathan Fish (Delivery Men), James Rubin (Uncle Jimmy), Jennifer Flackett (Childbirth Teacher), Gary Rubin (Man at wedding), Susan Breslau, Wendy Sax, Charlotte Zucker, Blanche Rubin, Ari Rubin (Guests at wedding), John Steciw (Band Leader), Fr. Walter Klimchuk (Priest), Peggy Roeder, Treva Tegtmeier, Oksana Fedunyszyn, Lynn Baber (Cousins)

Queen Latifah

Plot Capsule: *During his wife's pregnancy Bob Jones discovers that he has cancer and may not live to see his baby's birth. He is determined to videotape his day to day life so that his child has an idea of what he was like.*

© Columbia Pictures Industries

Haing S. Ngor

Nicole Kidman, Michael Keaton

Matt Dillon, Ving Rhames

Danny Glover, Matt Dillon

Matt Dillon, Danny Glover

Matt Dillon

THE SAINT OF FORT WASHINGTON

(WARNER BROS.) Producers, David V. Picker, Nessa Hyams; Executive Producers, Lyle Kessler, Carl Clifford; Director, Tim Hunter; Screenplay, Lyle Kessler; Photography, Frederick Elmes; Designer, Stuart Wurtzel; Editor, Howard Smith; Music, James Newton Howard; Costumes, Claudia Brown; Casting, Nessa Hyams; produced in association with Carrie Productions; Dolby Stereo; Technicolor; Rated R; 102 minutes; November release

CAST

Jerry	Danny Glover
Matthew	Matt Dillon
Rosario	Rick Aviles
Tamsen	Nina Siemaszko
Little Leroy	Ving Rhames
Spits	Joe Seneca
Arthur	Harry Ellington
Jason	Ralph Hughes
Gloria	Bahni Turpin
Ex-Pharmacist	Robert Beatty, Jr.
Greek Man	Reuben Schaefer
Ennis	Louis Williams
John	Adam Trese
Peter	Kevin Corrigan
Fred	Brian Tarantina
Neighbor Lady	Irma St. Paul
State Employee	Aida Turturro
Sandwich Man	Marvin Gardener
Extra Smoke Man	Edward Wise
Dime Tipper	Alison Mackie
River Banks Woman	Liz Larsen
Woman in window	Frances Chaney
Hooker in car	Octavia St. Laurent
Her Manager	Damon Chandler
Rosie	Rosaleen Linehan
Black 47 Lead Singer	Larry Kirwan
Black 47	Chris Byrne, Geoffrey Blythe, Fred Parcells, Thomas Hamlin
Morning Star	Mary Courtney, Carmel Johnston, Margie Mulvihill
Bellevue Doctor	Mark Lotito
Coffin Handler	Garfield!
Boat Captain	Daniel Von Bargen

and Evelyn Solann (Bird Lady), Walter Meade (Drill Floor Guard), Ellis Williams (Metal Detector Guard), Cortez Nance, Jr. (Clemente Shelter Guard), Philip Gray (Check-in Guard), Stephen Mendillo, Micheal Badalucco (Bridge Cops), Joseph Pentangelo, Douglas Crosby (Arrest Cops), Mansoor Najeeullah (Billie Sweetwater), Victor Slezak, Michael Waldron (Drivers), Peter Appel (Demolition Man)

Plot Capsule: *Drama in which Jerry, a Vietnam vet, and Matthew, a schizophrenic, form an unlikely friendship after meeting at New York's Fort Washington homeless shelter.*

© Warner Bros.

Kaitlyn/Kristen Hooper

Anjelica Huston, Raul Julia

Peter MacNicol, Christine Baranski

Jimmy Workman, Carol Kane, Christina Ricci

ADDAMS FAMILY VALUES

(PARAMOUNT) Producer, Scott Rudin; Executive Producer, David Nicksay; Director, Barry Sonnenfeld; Screenplay, Paul Rudnick; Based on the characters created by Charles Addams; Photography, Donald Peterman; Designer, Ken Adam; Editors, Arthur Schmidt, Jim Miller; Music, Marc Shaiman; *Addams Family Theme* by Vic Mizzy; Visual Effects Supervisor, Alan Munro; Costumes, Theoni V. Aldredge; "Thing" and "Pubert" Puppets and Prosthetics Creator, David B. MIller Studios; Casting, David Rubin, Debra Zane; Dolby Digital Stereo; Deluxe color; Rated PG-13; 94 minutes; November release

CAST

Morticia Addams	Anjelica Huston
Gomez Addams	Raul Julia
Fester Addams	Christopher Lloyd
Debbie Jelinsky	Joan Cusack
Wednesday Addams	Christina Ricci
Granny	Carol Kane
Pugsley Addams	Jimmy Workman
Pubert Addams	Kaitlyn & Kristen Hooper
Lurch	Carel Struycken
Joel Glicker	David Krumholtz
Thing	Christopher Hart
Margaret	Dana Ivey
Gary Granger	Peter MacNicol
Becky Granger	Christine Baranski
Amanda Buckman	Mercedes McNab
Don Buckman	Sam McMurray
Ellen Buckman	Harriet Sansom Harris
Mrs. Glicker	Julie Halston
Mr. Glicker	Barry Sonnenfeld
Desk Sergeant	Nathan Lane
Cousin It	John Franklin
Cousin Aphasia	Charles Busch
Cousin Ophelia	Laura Esterman
Flora Amor	Maureen Sue Levin
Fauna Amor	Darlene Levin
Dementia	Carol Hankins
Donald	Steven M. Martin
Dexter	Douglas Brian Martin
Lumpy Addams	Ryan Holihan
Delivery Nurse	Lois deBanzie
Forceps Nurse	Vicilyn Reynolds
Heather	Cynthia Nixon
Mrs. Montgomery	Edye Byrde
Delivery Room Doctor	David Hyde Pierce
Obnoxious Girl	Andreana Weiner
Host	Peter Graves

and Rick Scarry (Lawyer), Monet Mazur (Flirting Woman), Francis Coady (Flirting Man), Ian Abercrombie (Driver), Chris Ellis (Moving Man), Camille Saviola (Concetta), Zach Phifer (Passport Clerk), Tony Shalhoub (Jorge), Jeffrey Van Hoose (Irwin), Micah Winkelspecht (Mordecai), Matthew Beebe (Wheelchair Camper), Micah Hata (Yang), Joey Wilcots (Jamal), Jason Fife, Karl David-Djerf (Campers), Haley Peel (Young Debbie)

Plot Capsule: *After the arrival of their new baby, Pubert, the Addams Family hires a nanny who sets out to marry and murder Uncle Fester for his fortune. A sequel to the 1991 Paramount comedy with most of the principals repeating their roles. Carol Kane replaces Judith Malina as Granny.*

Nominated for an Academy Award for art direction.
© Paramount Pictures

Jimmy Workman, Christina Ricci, David Krumholtz

Christopher Lloyd, Joan Cusack

John Franklin, What, Dana Ivey

Christina Ricca, Raul Julia, Anjelica Huston, Carel Sruycken, Joan Cusack, Christopher Lloyd, Carol Kane, Jimmy Workman, Thing

Madonna, James Russo

DANGEROUS GAME

(MGM) formerly *Snake Eyes*; Producer, Mary Kane; Executive Producers, Freddy DeMann, Ron Rotholz; Director, Abel Ferrara; Screenplay, Nicholas St. John; Photography, Ken Kelsch; Designer, Alex Tavoularis; Editor, Anthony Redman; Music, Joe Delia; Costumes, Marlene Stewart; Casting, Randy Sabusawa; a Mario & Vittorio Cecchi Gori presentation of a Maverick Production; Dolby Stereo; Deluxe color; Rated R; 105 minutes; November release

CAST

Eddie Israel	Harvey Keitel
Sarah Jennings	Madonna
Francis Burns	James Russo
Madlyn	Nancy Ferrara
Tommy	Reilly Murphy
Director of Photography	Victor Argo
Prop Guy	Leonard Thomas
Blonde	Christina Fulton
Stewardess	Heather Bracken
Burns' Buddy	Glenn Plummer
Girl in trailer	Niki Munroe
Bar Patron	Juliette Hohnen
Morton's Waitress	Julie Pop

and Lori Eastside, John Snyder, Adina Winston, Dylan Hundley (Party Guests), Lili Barsha, Robyn B. Ashley (Flight Attendants), Anthony Redman (Swinger), Noga Isackson (1st AD), Randy Sabusawa (Producer), Mindy Eshelman (Wardrobe), Jesse Long (Script Supervisor), Linda Murphy (Boom Operator), Marta Bukowski (Video Tape Monitor), Bill Pope, Martin Schaer (Camera Operators), Jim Fitzgerald (1st Assistant Camera), Hiram Ortiz (Hair), Patton Howell Caldwell IV (2nd Assistant Director), Phil Nielson (Stunt Coordinator), Richard Belzer, Annie McEnroe, Sammy Jack Pressman (Cameos), Steve Albert (Boxing Announcer)

Plot Capsule: *Director Eddie Israel oversees the difficult filming of his new movie, dealing with a volatile leading man and a leading lady with whom he has an affair.*
© Eye Films, Inc.

BELOW: MAX, Ally Sheedy

Madonna, Harvey Keitel

MAN'S BEST FRIEND

(NEW LINE CINEMA) Producer, Bob Engelman; Executive Producers, Robert Kosberg, Daniel Grodnik; Director/Screenplay, John Lafia; Photography, Mark Irwin; Designer, Jaymes Hinkle; Editor, Michael N. Knue; Music, Joel Goldsmith; Costumes, Beverly Hong; Associate Producer, Kelley Smith; Special Make-up Effects Creator, Kevin Yeager; Animal Trainer, Clint Rowe; Casting, Valorie Massalas; a Roven-Cavallo Entertainment production; Dolby Stereo; Deluxe color; Rated R; 87 minutes; November release

CAST

Lori Tanner	Ally Sheedy
Dr. Jarret	Lance Henriksen
Det. Kovacs	Robert Costanzo
Perry	Fredric Lehne
Det. Bendetti	John Cassini
Rudy	J.D. Daniels
Ray	William Sanderson
Annie	Trula M. Marcus
Judy Sanders	Robin Frates
Mailman	Rick Barker
Chet	Bradley Pierce
Emax Security Guard	Robert Arentz
Dog Catchers	Cameron Arnett, Adam Carl
Mugger	Tom Rosales, Jr.
KCBG Security Guard	Ray Lynkins
Paper Boy	Mickey Cassidy

and L.E. Moko (Mobile Mechanic), Caroline Cornell (KCGB Receptionist), Del Zamora (Rudy's Dad), Arlen Stuart (Mrs. Barclay), Frank Cavestani (Policeman), Paul Hayes (2nd Mechanic), Peter Georges (Truck Driver), Olivia Brown (Lab Assistant), Lisa Cavallo (Friday), Frank Welker (Special Vocal Effects)

Plot Capsule: *Sci-Fi thriller in which TV reporter Lori Tanner unwittingly befriends MAX, a DNA-engineered guard dog with deadly instincts.*
© New Line Cinema Corp

RIGHT: Lance Henriksen

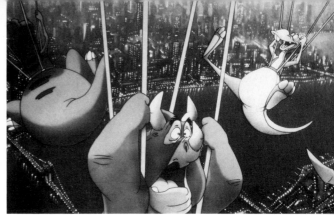

TOP LEFT : Elsa, Woog, Rex, Dweeb, TOP RIGHT: Rex, Woog, Dweeb

Vorb, Dweeb, Louie, Cecilia, Rex, Prof. Screweyes, Elsa,Woog

WE'RE BACK!
A DINSOSAUR'S STORY

(UNIVERSAL) Producer, Stephen Hickner; Executive Producers, Steven Spielberg, Frank Marshall, Kathleen Kennedy; Directors, Dick Zondag, Ralph Zondag, Phil Nibbelink, Simon Wells; Screenplay, John Patrick Shanley; Based on the book by Hudson Talbott; Music, James Horner; Song: *Roll Back the Rock* by James Horner, Thomas Dolby; Co-Producer, Thad Weinlein; Art Director, Neil Ross; Character Designer, Carlos Grangel; Supervising Animators, Jeffrey J. Varab, Bibo Bergeron, Kristof Serrand, Rob Stevenhagen, Thierry Schiel, Sahin Ersoz, Borge Ring; Supervising Editors, Sim Evan-Jones, Nick Fletcher; a Steven Spielberg presentation of an Amblin Entertainment production; Dolby Stereo; Deluxe color; Rated G; 72 minutes; November release

VOICE CAST

Rex	John Goodman
Buster	Blaze Berdahl
Mother Bird	Rhea Perlman
Vorb	Jay Leno
Woog	Rene LeVant
Elsa	Felicity Kendall
Dweeb	Charles Fleischer
Captain NewEyes	Walter Cronkite
Louie	Joey Shea
Dr. Bleeb	Julia Child
Prof. ScrewEyes	Kenneth Mars
Cecilia	Yeardley Smith
Stubbs the Clown	Martin Short
Himself	Larry King

Plot Capsule: *Inventor Captain NewEyes transports a group of dinosaurs to modern day New York where they are befriended by some kids .*
© Universal City Studios Inc..

Rex

Rex, Captain Neweyes, Dweeb, Woog

Robin Williams

Robin Williams, Matthew Lawrence

Matthew Lawrence, Lisa Jakub, Robin Williams, Mara Wilson, Sally Field

Lisa Jakub, Robin Williams,
Mara Wilson, Matthew Lawrence

Scott Capurro, Robin Williams, Harvey Fierstein

MRS. DOUBTFIRE

Robin Williams, Sally Field

(20th CENTURY FOX) Producers, Marsha Garces Williams, Robin Williams, Mark Radcliffe; Executive Producer, Matthew Rushton; Co-Producer, Joan Bradshaw; Director, Chris Columbus; Screenplay, Randi Mayem Singer, Leslie Dixon; Based upon the book *Alias Madame Doubtfire* by Anne Fine; Photography, Donald McAlpine; Designer, Angelo Graham; Editor, Raja Gosnell; Music, Howard Shore; Costumes, Marit Allen; Special Makeup Creator, Greg Cannom; Casting, Janet Hirshenson, Jane Jenkins; a Blue Wolf production; Dolby Stereo; Panavision; Deluxe color; Rated PG-13; 125 minutes; November release

CAST

Daniel Hillard/Mrs. Doubtfire	Robin Williams
Miranda Hillard	Sally Field
Stu	Pierce Brosnan
Frank	Harvey Fierstein
Gloria	Polly Holliday
Lydia Hillard	Lisa Jakub
Chris Hillard	Matthew Lawrence
Natalie Hillard	Mara Wilson
Mr. Lundy	Robert Prosky
Mrs. Sellner	Anne Haney
Jack	Scott Capurro
Bus Driver	Sydney Walker
TV Boss	Joe Bellan
Justin Gregory	Martin Mull
ADR Director Lou	Terence McGovern
Employees	Karen Kahn, Eva Gholson, James Cunningham
Cop	Ralph Peduto
Judge	Scott Beach
Miranda's Attorney	Juliette Marshall
Daniel's Attorney	Drew Letchworth
Miranda's Mother	Jessica Myerson
Alice	Sharon Lockwood
Thug	Jim Cullen
Staring Boys	Kenneth Loo, Jeff Loo
Stunning Woman	Betsy Monroe
Delivery Boy	Joseph Narducci
Ron	James S. Cranna
Dr. Toad	Todd Williams
Lundy's Secretary	Adele Proom

and Rick Overton (Maitre'D), Dan Spencer (Cook), Paul Guilfoyle (Head Chef), Molly McClure (Housekeeper), Andrew L. Prosky (TV Director), William Newman (Mr. Sprinkles), Chris Pray (Puppeteer), Geoff Bolt (Lundy's Waiter), Dick Bright (Stu's Waiter), Adam Bryant (Man in men's room), Tavia Cathcart (Tanya the Hostess), C. Beau Fitzsimons, Jeff Moeller (Valets), Benne Alder (Woman in restroom).

Robin Williams

Plot Capsule: *Daniel Hillard, disturbed that his divorce agreement gives him so little time with his children, disguises himself as a woman to land a job as the kids' new nanny.*

1993 Academy Award winner for Best Makeup.

Golden Globe Award winner for best picture (comedy or musical), and best actor (comedy or musical) Robin Williams.

© 20th Century Fox

Lisa Jakub, Mara Wilson, Robin Williams, Matthew Lawrence

Mara Wilson, Robin Williams, Matthew Lawrence, Lisa Jakub

Kevin Costner

Kevin Costner, T.J. Lowther

Clint Eastwood (left)

Kevin Costner, director Clint Eastwood

A PERFECT WORLD

(**WARNER BROS.**) Producers, Mark Johnson, David Valdes; Director, Clint Eastwood; Screenplay, John Lee Hancock; Photography, Jack N. Green; Designer, Henry Bumstead; Editors, Joel Cox, Ron Spang; Music, Lennie Niehaus; Costumes, Erica Edell Phillips; Casting, Phyllis Huffman, Liz Keigley; a Malpaso production; Dolby Stereo; Panavision; Technicolor; Rated PG-13; 138 minutes; November release

CAST

Butch Haynes	Kevin Costner
Red Garnett	Clint Eastwood
Sally Gerber	Laura Dern
Phillip Perry	T.J. Lowther
Terry Pugh	Keith Szarabajka
Tom Adler	Leo Burmester
Dick Suttle	Paul Hewitt
Bobby Lee	Bradley Whitford
Bradley	Ray McKinnon
Gladys Perry	Jennifer Griffin
Naomi Perry	Leslie Flowers
Ruth Perry	Belinda Flowers
Mr. Hughes	Darryl Cox
Superman	Jay Whiteaker
Tinkerbell	Taylor Suzanna McBride
Dancing Skeleton	Christopher Reagan Ammons
Larry	Mark Voges
Prison Guard	Vernon Grote
Oldtimer	James Jeter
Fred Cummings	Ed Geldart
Paul Saunders	Bruce McGill
General Store Manager	Nik Hagler
Local Sheriff	Gary Moody
Farmer	George Haynes
Farmer's Wife	Marietta Marich
Mr. Willits	Rodger Boyce
Lucy	Lucy Lee Flippin
Paula	Elizabeth Ruscio
Newscaster	David Kroll
Officer Terrance	Gabriel Folse
Officer Pete	Gil Glasgow
Governor	Dennis Letts
Governor's Aide	John Hussey
Trick 'r Treat Lady	Margaret Bowman
Bob Fielder	John M. Jackson
Bob's Wife	Connie Cooper
Bob Fielder Jr.	Cameron Finley
Patsy Fielder	Katy Wottrich
Road Block Officer	Marco Perella
Eileen	Linda Hart

and Brandon Smith (Office Jones), George Orrison (Officer Orrison), Wayne Dehart (Mack), Mary Alice (Lottie), Kevin Woods (Cleveland), Tony Frank (Arch Andrews), Woody Watson (Lt. Hendricks), James W. Gavin, Craig Hosking (Helicopter Pilots)

Plot Capsule: *Escaped convict Butch Haynes takes seven year-old Phillip Perry as hostage, making his way across Texas with ranger Red Garnett in pursuit.*

© Warner Bros.

172

Clint Eastwood, Laura Dern

Clint Eastwood

Kevin Costner, T.J. Lowther

Kevin Costner, T.J. Lowther

Kevin Costner

Macaulay Culkin (C)

The Snowflakes

George Balanchine's
THE NUTCRACKER

(WARNER BROS.) Producers, Robert A. Krasnow, Robert Hurwitz; Executive Producer, Arnon Milchan; Director, Emile Ardolino; Adapted from the stage production by Peter Martins; Story, E.T.A. Hoffman; Narration Written by Susan Cooper; Photography, Ralf Bode; Designer/Scenery, Rouben Ter-Arutunian; Music, Peter Ilyitch Tschaikovsky; Choreographer, George Balanchine; Line Producer, Catherine Tatge; Co-ordinating Producer, Merrill Brockway; Lighting Designer, Alan Adelman; Costumes, Karinska; an Elektra Entertainment/Regency Enterprises presentation of a Krasnow/Milchan/Hurwitz production; Dolby Stereo; Technicolor; Rated G; 92 minutes; November release

CAST

The Sugarplum Fairy	Darci Kistler
Her Cavalier	Damian Woetzel
Dewdrop	Kyra Nichols
Coffee	Wendy Whelan
Marzipan	Margaret Tracey
Tea	Gen Horiuchi
Candy Cane	Tom Gold
Hot Chocolate	Lourdes Lopez, Nilas Martins
Mother Ginger	William Otto
Fritz	Peter Reznick
Grandparents	Karin von Arnoldingen, Edward Bigelow
Dr. Stahlbaum	Robert LaFosse
Frau Stahlbaum	Heather Watts
Herr Drosselmeier	Bart Robinson Cook
Marie	Jessica Lynn Cohen
The Nutcracker	Macaulay Culkin
Narrator	Kevin Kline
Toys: Harlequin and Columbine	Katrina Killian, Roma Sosenko
Soldier	Michael Byars
Mouse King	Robert Lyon

and The Guests: Helene Alexopoulos, Lauren Hauser, Melinda Roy, Stephanie Saland, Simone Schumacher, Deborah Wingert, Lindsay Fischer, Kipling Houston, Peter Naumann, Alexandre Proia, Jock Soto, Erlends Zieminch (Parents), Kimberly Cortes, Eve Harrison, Petra Hoerner, Miriam Peterson, Ashley Siebert, Kielley Young, Misha Braun, Alexander Levine, Igor Odessky, Andrei Vitoptov, Alex Wiesendanger (Children), Priscilla Pellecchia, Robert Wersinger (Teenagers), Zippora Karz, Julie Michael (The Maids); Emily Coates, Wendy Drapala, Elizabeth Drucker, Amanda Edge, Michele Gifford, Pauline Golbin, Dena Kinstlinger, Margo Krody, Anna Liceica, Andrea Long, Zoe Mackler, Deanna McBrearty, Catherine Ryan, Pascale Van Kipnis, Elizabeth Walker, Miranda Weese (Snowflakes), Janey McGeary, Sabrina Pillars, Teresa Reyes, Santhe Tsetsilas, Albert Evans, Russell Kaiser, Gordon Stevens, Runsheng Ying (Hot Chocolate), Miriam Mahdaviani, Inmaculada Velez (Tea), Yvonne Borree, Jennifer Fuchs, Isabel Kimmel, Jennifer Tinsley (Shepherdesses), Stacey Calvert, Kathleen Tracey, Jade Adams, Samantha Allen, Aura Dixon, Tatiana Garcia-Stefanovich, Michele Gifford, Dana Hanson, Lydia Harmsen, Heather Hawk, Romy Karz, Sherri LeBlanc, Monique Meunier, Jenifer Ringer (Flowers), Alexandra Ansanelli, Ellen Barr, Natalia Boesch, Charnie Carter, Tatiana Grigorenko, Scheherazade Madan, Priscilla Pellecchia, Carrie Lee Riggins (Candy Canes), Kira Boesch, Sarah Brodsky, Alexis Doktor, Dana Genshaft, Brynn Jinnett, Glenn Keenan, Marina Squerciati, Halley Zien (Polichinelles), Kimberly Cortes, Jessica Goodrich, Danielle Gordon, Eve Harrison, Petra Hoerner, Sarah Mendell, Abigail Mentzer, Annie Ostrager, Rachel Paukman, Ashley Siebert, Kielley Young, Zoe Zien (Angels), Christopher Boehmer, James Fayette, Espen Giljane, Arch Higgins, Jerome Kipper, Richard Marsden, Bruce Padgett, Todd Williams, Kira Boesch, Sarah Brodsky, Alexis Doktor, Alexander Levine, Igor Odessky, Marina Squerciati, Andrei Vitoptov, Halley Zien (Mice), Jennifer Barton, Vivian Chin, Kimberly Cortes, Katherine Daines, Lauren D'Avella, Dana Genshaft, Jessica Goodrich, Danielle Gordon, Brynn Jinnett, Scarlett Johnson, Glenn Keenan, Sarah Mendell, Abigail Mentzer, Annie Ostrager, Rachel Paukman, Miriam Peterson, Jenny Raim, Diana Townsend-Butterworth, Zoe Zien (Soldiers)

Macaulay Culkin, Jessica Lynn Cohen, Bart Robinson Cook

Plot Capsule: *On Christmas Eve young Marie falls asleep and dreams fantastic images of the nutcracker presented to her by her Uncle Dosselmer in this ballet set to the music of Tschaikovsky. The ballet was last presented on screen in the 1986 Atlantic release* Nutcracker: The Motion Picture.

© Elektra Entertainment

Robert Lyon, Macaulay Culkin, Jessica Lynn Cohen

A DANGEROUS WOMAN

(GRAMERCY) Producer/Screenplay, Naomi Foner; Based on the novel by Mary McGarry Morris; Executive Producer, Kathleen Kennedy; Director, Stephen Gyllenhaal; Photography, Robert Elswit; Designer, David Brisbin; Costumes, Susie DeSanto; Music, Carter Burwell; Editor, Harvey Rosenstock; Casting, Amanda Mackey, Cathy Sandrich; a Rollercoaster production, presented in association with Island World; Dolby Stereo; Foto-Kem color; Rated R; 99 minutes; December release

CAST

Martha Horgan	Debra Winger
Frances	Barbara Hershey
Mackey	Gabriel Byrne
Getso	David Strathairn
Birdy	Chloe Webb
Steve Bell	John Terry
Make-up Girl	Jan Hooks
Tupperware Salesman	Paul Dooley
Mercy	Viveka Davis
John	Richard Riehle
Anita	Laurie Metcalf
Patsy	Maggie Gyllenhaal
Edward	Jacob Gyllenhaal
Paul	Myles Sheridan
Wesley	Brad Blaisdell
Gately	Warren Munson
Checker	Rebecca Arthur
Young Man	Philip McNiven
Heidi	Breon Gorman
Singer	Anna Mathias
Bandleader	Jack Riley
Caterer	Brandis Kemp
In-Mate	Charyl Wright-Roberts
Security Guards	Martine Wood, Joel Randel
Martha's Daughter	Cassidy Ann Thomas, Chelsea Thomas

Plot Capsule: *Martha, a mentally challenged woman incapable of telling a lie, spends her uneventful life working at a cleaners and living with her aunt until she finds herself witnessing a robbery and becoming involved with a wayward handyman.*
© Gramercy Pictures

Jan Hooks, Debra Winger

Barbara Hershey, Debra Winger

Debra Winger

Gabriel Byrne, Debra Winger

Donald Sutherland, Stockard Channing, Bruce Davison, Mary Beth Hurt

Stockard Channing, Donald Sutherland, Ian McKellen

Catherine Kellner, Stockard Channing

SIX DEGREES OF SEPARATION

(MGM) Producers, Fred Schepisi, Arnon Milchan; Executive Producer, Ric Kidney; Director, Fred Schepisi; Screenplay, John Guare, based on his play; Photography, Ian Baker; Designer, Patrizia von Brandenstein; Editor, Peter Honess; Music, Jerry Goldsmith; Costumes, Judianna Makovsky; Casting, Ellen Chenoweth; a Maiden Movies/New Regency production; Dolby Stereo; Panavision; Deluxe color; Rated R; 111 minutes; December release

CAST

Ouisa Kittredge	Stockard Channing
Paul	Will Smith
Flan Kittredge	Donald Sutherland
Geoffrey	Ian McKellen
Kitty	Mary Beth Hurt
Larkin	Bruce Davison
Dr. Fine	Richard Masur
Trent	Anthony Michael Hall
Elizabeth	Heather Graham
Rick	Eric Thal
Ben	Anthony Rapp
Woody	Osgood Perkins
Tess	Catherine Kellner
Doug	Jeffrey Abrams
Police Officer	Joe Pentangelo
Hustler	Lou Milione
Connie	Brooke Hayward Duchin
Sandy	Peter Duchin
Carter	Sam Stoneburner
Polly	Maeve McGuire
Adele	Kelly Bishop
John	John Cunningham
Frank the Doorman	Vasek Simek
Andy	Chuck Close
Jeannie	Kazuko
Paula	Adele Chatfield-Taylor

and Maggie Burke, Edmond Genest, Michael Stanley Kirby (Loft Party Guests), David Callegati (Art Dealer), Daniel Von Bargen (Detective), John Rowe (Usher), Elizabeth Rossa (Bride), Diane Hartford (Julia), Frank O'Brien (Eddie), Ann McDongouh (Teacher), Jose Rabelo (Elevator Man #2), Todd Alcott, Joanna Noble (Concert Goers), Miriam Fond (Nurse), Annie Meisels (Doug's Girl), Mitch Koplan (Policeman), Michele Greco (Workman), Tony Zazaula (Rainbow Room Captain), Arthur McGill (Hansom Cab Driver), Susan Tabor, Paul Schmidt (Posh Couple), Carolyn Groves, Jeannine Moore, Tim Saunders, David Tice (Cocktail Party Guests), Redman Maxfield (Fred), Margaret Eginton (Mary), Margaret Thomson (Grandmother at baptism), Vince O'Brien (Grandfather at baptism), Anne Swift, Richmond Hoxie (Guests at baptism), Kitty Carlisle Hart (Mrs. Bannister), Madhur Jaffrey (Guest of honor), Arthur Brooks, Jacqueline Bertrand, Lisa Crosby, Nancy Duerr, Brian McConnachie, Angela Thornton, Robert Thumbull, Richard Whiting (Mrs. Bannister's Guest), Cleo King (Lieutenant Price)

Plot Capsule: *Comedy-drama about a young man who shows up at the posh Manhattan apartment of Ouisa and Flan Kittredge, claiming to be both a college friend of their children and the son of actor Sidney Poitier. Stockard Channing and Anthony Rapp repeat their roles from the original 1990 Broadway production.*

Stockard Channing was nominated for an Academy Award for her performance.
© Metro-Goldwyn-Mayer Inc.

Anthony Rapp, Catherine Kellner, Jeffrey Abrams, Osgood Perkins

Stockard Channing, Donald Sutherland

Heather Graham, Eric Thal

Donald Sutherland, Stockard Channing, Will Smith

Donald Sutherland, Ian McKellen, Stockard Channing, Will Smith

Mike Myers, Dana Carvey

Mike Myers, James Hong

WAYNE'S WORLD 2

(PARAMOUNT) Producer, Lorne Michaels; Executive Producer, Howard W. Koch Jr.; Co-Producers, Dinah Minot, Barnaby Thompson; Director, Stephen Surjik; Screenplay, Mike Myers, Bonnie Turner, Terry Turner; Based on characters created by Mike Myers; Photography, Francis Kenny; Designer, Gregg Fonseca; Editor, Malcolm Campbell; Music, Carter Burwell; Dolby Stereo; Deluxe color; Rated PG-13; 94 minutes; December release

CAST

Wayne Campbell	Mike Myers
Garth Algar	Dana Carvey
Bobby Cahn	Christopher Walken
Cassandra	Tia Carrere
Del Preston	Ralph Brown
Honey Hornee	Kim Basinger
Milton	Chris Farley
Mr. Wong	James Hong
Aerosmith	Steven Tyler, Joseph Perry, Brad Whitford, Thomas Hamilton, Joseph Kramer
Terry	Lee Tergesen
Neil	Dan Bell
Burning hair Guy at concert	Richard Epper
Topless Girl at concert	Jennifer Miller
Concert Security Guys	Duke Valenti, Benny Graham
Scott	Gavin Grazer
Gate Security Guy	Googy Gress
Themselves	Heather Locklear, Rip Taylor, Jay Leno
Concert Nerds	Bob Odenkirk, Robert Smigel
Naked Indian	Larry Sellers
Jim Morrison	Michael Nickles
Chicken Guy	Joe Liss
Watermelon Guy	Bobby Slayton
Lead Guitarist	George Foster
Studio Recording Engineer	Paul Raczkowski
Mr. Big	Frank DiLeo
Mikita's Waitress	Sydney Coberly
Jerry Segel	Kevin Pollak
Betty Jo	Olivia D'Abo
Tool Box DJ	Ron Litman
Roadies	Matt Kenna, Sean Michael Guess
Bjergen Kjergen	Drew Barrymore
Handsome Dan	Harry Shearer
Mr. Scream	Ted McGinley
Sammy Davis Jr.	Tim Meadows
Heavy Metallers	Scott Coffey, Lance Edwards
Bad Actor	Al Hansen
Good Actor	Charlton Heston
Wedding Minister	Bob Larkin
Mikita's Manager, Glen	Ed O'Neill

Plot Capsule: *Cable-access tv host Wayne Campbell and his partner Garth Algar hope to put on a marathon rock concert called Waynestock. Sequel to the 1992 Paramount Pictures comedy* Wayne's World *which also featured Myers, Carvey, Carrere, Bell, Tergesen, Farley, DiLeo, and O'Neill.*
© Paramount Pictures

Christopher Walken

(front) Dana Carvey, Mike Myers, with
(back) Aerosmith: Joe Perry, Tom Hamilton,
Steven Tyler, Brad Whitford, Joey Kramer

Jason Patric, Wes Studi

GERONIMO:
AN AMERICAN LEGEND

(COLUMBIA) Producer, Walter Hill, Neil Canton; Executive Producer, Michael S. Glick; Director, Walter Hill; Screenplay, John Milius, Larry Gross; Story, John Milius; Photography, Lloyd Ahern; Designer, Joe Alves; Editor, Freeman Davies, Carmel Davies, Donn Aron; Costumes, Dan Moore; Music, Ry Cooder; Casting, Rueben Cannon; Sony Dynamic Digital Sound/Dolby Stereo; Panavision; Technicolor; Rated PG-13; 115 minutes; December release

Matt Damon, Robert Duvall

CAST

Lt. Charles Gatewood	Jason Patric
Brig. Gen. George Crook	Gene Hackman
Al Sieber	Robert Duvall
Geronimo	Wes Studi
Lt. Britton Davis	Matt Damon
Mangas	Rodney A. Grant
Brig. Gen. Nelson Miles	Kevin Tighe
Chato	Steve Reevis
Sgt. Turkey	Carlos Palomino
Ulzana	Victor Aaron
Sgt. Dutchy	Stuart Proud Eagle Grant
Schoonover	Stephen McHattie
Capt. Hentig	John Finn
City Marshal Hawkins	Lee De Broux
Old Nana	Rino Thunder
Billy Pickett	Hoke Howell
Apache Medicine Man	Richard Martin, Jr.
Hawkins' Deputy	J. Young
Yaqui Dave	Raleigh Wilson
Apache Vision Woman	Jackie Old Coyote
Dead Shot	Monty Bass
The Dreamer	Pato Hoffmann
Courier at ball	Scott Crabbe
Woman at ball	Patricia Pretzinger
Sgt. Mulrey	Roger Callard
Bronco Apache	Juddson Keith Linn
Afraid Miner	Mark Boone Junior
Unafraid Miner	M.C. Gainey
Chaplain	Michael Rudd
Dandy Jim	Michael Minjarez
Skip-Hey	Burnette Bennett
Dead Shot's Wife	Davina Smith

Wes Studi, Rino Thunder, Rodney A. Grant

and Jonathan Ward (C.S. Fly), Luis Contreras (Rurale Officer), Jaquelin Lee (Apache Woman), Jim Manygoats (Ailing Apache), Scott Wilson (Redondo), Eva Larson (Cantina Waitress), Greg Goossen, Sonny Skyhawk, Michael Adams, Walter Robles, Anthony Schmidt (Schoonover Gang), Jim Beaver (Proclamation Officer)

Plot Capsule: *In 1885 Lt. Britton Davis joins the army's campaign to put an end to Indian resistance and bring about the mighty warrior Geronimo's surrender. Previous film portrayals of Geronimo include Chief Thundercloud in both* Geronimo *(Paramount, 1938), and* I Killed Geronimo *(UA, 1950), Jay Silverheels in both* The Battle at Apache Pass *(Universal, 1952), and* Walk the Proud Land *(Universal, 1956), and Chuck Connors in* Geronimo *(UA, 1962).*

The film was nominated for an Academy Award for sound.
© Columbia Pictures Industries, Inc.

Robert Duvall (left), Gene Hackman, Steve Reevis

Barnard Hughes, James Coburn, Whoopi Goldberg

Wendy Makkena, Kathy Najimy, Whoopi Goldberg

SISTER ACT 2: BACK IN THE HABIT

(TOUCHSTONE) Producers, Dawn Steel, Scott Rudin; Executive Producers, Laurence Mark, Mario Iscovich; Director, Bill Duke; Screenplay, James Orr, Jim Cruickshank, Judi Ann Mason; Photography, Oliver Wood; Designer, John DeCuir, Jr.; Editors, John Carter, Pem Herring, Stuart Pappe; Costumes, Francine Jamison-Tanchuck; Co-Executive Producer, Christopher Meledandri; Choreographer, Michael Peters; Music, Miles Goodman; Music Supervisor, Marc Shaiman; Casting, Aleta Chapelle; Distributed by Buena Vista Pictures; Dolby Stereo; Technicolor; Rated PG; 106 minutes; December release

CAST

Deloris Van Cartier (Sister Mary Clarence)	Whoopi Goldberg
Sister Mary Patrick	Kathy Najimy
Father Maurice	Barnard Hughes
Sister Mary Lazarus	Mary Wickes
Mr. Crisp	James Coburn
Father Ignatius	Michael Jeter
Sister Mary Robert	Wendy Makkena
Florence Watson	Sheryl Lee Ralph
Joey Bustamente	Robert Pastorelli
Father Wolfgang	Thomas Gottschalk
Mother Superior	Maggie Smith
Rita Watson	Lauryn Hill
Father Thomas	Brad Sullivan
Maria	Alanna Ubach
Ahmal	Ryan Toby
Sketch	Ron Johnson
Margaret	Jennifer "Love" Hewitt
Frankie	Devin Kamin
Tyler Chase	Christian Fitzharris
Tanya	Tanya Blount
Marcos	Mehran Marcos Sedghi

and Valeria Andrews, Dionna Brooks-Jackson, Monica Calhoun, Martha Gonzales, Deondray Gossett, Frank Howard, David Kater, Kimberlee Kramer, Deedee Magno, Patrick Malone, Alex Martin, Jermaine Montell, Sacha Thomas, Ashley Thompson (Classroom Kids), Pat Crawford Brown, Susan Browning, Georgia Creighton, Edith Diaz, Ellen Albertini Dow, Beth Fowler, Prudence Wright Holmes, Sheri Izzard, Susan Johnson-Kehn, Ruth Kobart, Darlene Koldenhoven, Rose Parenti, Carmen Zapata (Choir Nuns), Andrea Robinson (The "Singing Voice" of Sister Mary Robert), Jenifer Lewis, Pamala Tyson, Sharon Brown (Backup Singers), Regan Patno, Kevin Alexander Stea, John Jacquet Jr., Sebastian Lacause, Luca Tommassini, Michael Gregory Gong, Gabriel Trupin, Raymond G. del Barrio, Frank Williams, Lacy Darryl Phillips (Dancers), Paul Thorpe (Dancer "Postman"), Paul Genick (Dancer "Sugar Pie"), Aaron Baker (Dancer "Teeny Bikini"), Warren Frost, Robin Gammell, Revalyn Golde (Archdiocese Persons), Yolanda Whitaker (Sondra), Bill Duke (Mr. Johnson), Sydney Lassick (Competition Announcer), Michael "Bear" Taliferro (Security Guard), Kai Bowe (Stage Manager), William S. Turchyn II (Assistant Stage Manager), John Fontana, Michael A. Tice, Robert Simokovic (Flying Techs), Iris Graves, Pamela Taylor, Robert J. Benson, Juliette Hagerman, Christina Royster, Kwaku A. James, Roy M. Crayton, Kwame James, Latesha Crayton, Erica Atkins, Jennifer Reeves (The Iris Choir), William D. Hall (Chapman Choir Leader)

Plot Capsule: *Lounge singer Deloris Van Cartier goes undercover as a nun in order to turn the tough kids at an inner-city high school into a presentable choir. Sequel to the 1992 Touchstone film "Sister Act" with most of the cast repeating their roles.*
© Touchstone Pictures

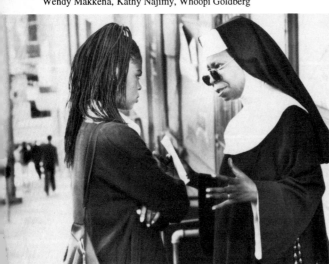

Lauryn Hill, Whoopi Goldberg

Brad Sullivan, Michael Jeter, Kathy Najimy, Whoopi Goldberg, Wendy Makkena, Mary Wickes

Robert Culp, Tony Goldwyn   Denzel Washington, Julia Roberts

Sam Shepard

Stanley Tucci

Hume Cronyn

THE PELICAN BRIEF

(WARNER BROS.) Producers, Alan J. Pakula, Pieter Jan Brugge; Director/Screenplay, Alan J. Pakula; Based on the novel by John Grisham; Photography, Stephen Goldblatt; Designer, Philip Rosenberg; Editors, Tom Rolf, Trudy Ship; Music, James Horner; Costumes, Albert Wolsky; Associate Producer, Donald Laventhal; Casting, Alixe Gordon; Dolby Stereo; Technicolor; Rated PG-13; 141 minutes; December release

CAST

Darby Shaw	Julia Roberts
Gray Grantham	Denzel Washington
Thomas Callahan	Sam Shepard
Gavin Verheek	John Heard
Fletcher Coal	Tony Goldwyn
Denton Voyles	James B. Sikking
Bob Gminski	William Atherton
President	Robert Culp
Khamel	Stanley Tucci
Justice Rosenberg	Hume Cronyn
Smith Keen	John Lithgow
Marty Velmano	Anthony Heald
Stump	Nicholas Woodeson
Edwin Sneller	Stanley Anderson
Matthew Barr	John Finn
Alice Stark	Cynthia Nixon
Charles Morgan (a.k.a. Garcia)	Jake Webber
Eric East	Casey Biggs
Rupert	Christopher Murray
Sarge	Sonny Jim Gaines
K.O. Lewis	Kevin Geer
Song and Dance Man from bar	Joseph Chrest
Managing Editor	Richard Bauer
Sara Ann Morgan	Michelle O'Neill
Edward Linney	Peter Carlin
Justice Jensen	Ralph Cosham

and Terrence P. Currier (Rosenberg's Nurse), Edwin Newman, Magee Hickey (Themselves), Helen Carey (Federal Clerk), Howard Shalwitz (Washington Herald Journalist), Kyle Prue (News Desk Reporter), Jewell Robinson, Kim Peter Novac, Norman Aronovic (Senior Washington Herald Editors), Carl Palmer (Cop in cowboy boots), Carol Sutton (New Orleans Policewoman), Scott Jefferson (Lt. Olsen), Daniel Kamin (Hooten), Mark McLaughlin, Robert Pavlovich (CIA Agents in hotel room), Constance Yelverton (Clerk at Sheraton Hotel), Kim Kettle (Gavin Verheek's Wife), Ellie K. Wang (Reporter at National Cathedral), Fran Dorn (University Registrar), Karen Bralove (University Placement Clerk), Teagle F. Bougere, Carey Varner (University Students), Saundra Quarterman (Laura Kass), Cynthia Hood (Parklane Receptionist), Alan Wade (Parklane Administrator), Harold J. Surratt (Parklane Security Officer), Paul Morella (White & Blazevich Attorney), Ed Johnson (White & Blazevich Security Guard), Jurian Hughes (White & Blazevich Receptionist), Dick Stillwell (White & Blazevich Security), Tom Quinn (Sara Ann Morgan's Father), Beverly Brigham (Safe Deposit Teller), Liza Sweeney Coleman, Douglas R. Coleman (Pursuers with guns), Michael Port, Shanna Connell (Tulane Law Students), Gene Babb, Kyle D. Duvall, Karl Warren, Carrie Boren, James Earl Reed (Reporters)

Plot Capsule: *Drama based on the best selling novel by John Grisham. Law student Darby Shaw writes a legal brief speculating on who may have murdered two supreme court justices. When the document begins circulating through Washington, Darby realizes her life is now in danger.*

© Warner Bros.

James B. Sikking

John Heard

John Lithgow

(counter clockwise, from top) Juliette Lewis, Johnny Depp, Laura Harrington, Leonardo DiCaprio, Mary Kate Schellhardt, Darlene Cates

Leonardo DiCaprio, Johnny Depp

Mary Steenburgen

Leonardo DiCaprio, Johnny Depp, Juliette Lewis

WHAT'S EATING GILBERT GRAPE

(PARAMOUNT) Producers, Meir Teper, Bertil Ohlsson, David Matalon; Executive Producers, Lasse Hallstrom, Alan C. Blomquist; Director, Lasse Hallstrom; Screenplay, Peter Hedges, based on his novel; Photography, Sven Nykvist; Designer, Bernt Capra; Editor, Andrew Mondshein; Music, Alan Parker, Bjorn Isfalt; a Matalon Teper Ohlsson production; Dolby Stereo; Deluxe color; Rated PG-13; 118 minutes; December release

CAST

Gilbert Grape	Johnny Depp
Arnie Grape	Leonardo DiCaprio
Becky	Juliette Lewis
Betty Carver	Mary Steenburgen
Momma	Darlene Cates
Amy Grape	Laura Harrington
Ellen Grape	Mary Kate Schellhardt
Mr. Carver	Kevin Tighe
Tucker Van Dyke	John C. Reilly
Bobby McBurney	Crispin Glover
Becky's Grandma	Penelope Branning
Mr. Lamson	Tim Green
Mrs. Lamson	Susan Loughran
Reverend	Rev. Robert B. Hedges
Todd Carver	Mark Jordan
Doug Carver	Cameron Finley
Sheriff Farrel	Brady Coleman
Deputy	Tim Simek
Boys	Nicholas Stojanovich, Daniel Gullahorn
Waitress	Libby Villari
Police Secretary	Kay Bower
Burger Barn Manager	Joe Stevens
Bakery Worker	Mona Lee Fultz
Dave	George Haynes

Plot Capsule: *Gilbert Grape wants desperately to escape from the dead-end town of Endora, Iowa, and leave behind his eccentric family, which includes his 500-pound mother and mentally retarded brother. An offbeat girl named Becky comes along offering Gilbert some hope.*

Leonardo DiCaprio received an Academy Award nomination and a National Board of Review Award for best supporting actor; in addition he was given the L.A. Film Critics New Generation Award for this film (and This Boy's Life).

© Paramount Pictures

Leonardo DiCaprio, Johnny Depp, Juliette Lewis

Debi Mazar, Chris Penn, Beethoven

Ashley Hamilton, Nicholle Tom

BEETHOVEN'S 2ND

(UNIVERSAL) Producers, Michael C. Gross, Joe Medjuck; Executive Producer, Ivan Reitman; Co-Producer, Gordon Webb; Director, Rod Daniel; Screenplay, Len Blum; Photography, Bill Butler; Designer, Lawrence Miller; Editors, Sheldon Kahn, William D. Gordean; Associate Producer, Sheldon Kahn; Costumes, April Ferry; Music, Randy Edelman; Song: *The Day I Fall in Love* by Carole Bayer Sager, James Ingram, Clif Magness/performed by Dolly Parton, James Ingram; Beethoven's Trainer, Karl Lewis Miller; Casting, Steven Jacobs; Dolby Stereo; Deluxe color; Rated PG; 88 minutes; December release

CAST

George Newton	Charles Grodin
Alice Newton	Bonnie Hunt
Ryce Newton	Nicholle Tom
Ted Newton	Christopher Castile
Emily Newton	Sarah Rose Karr
Regina	Debi Mazar
Floyd	Chris Penn
Taylor	Ashley Hamilton
Seth	Danny Masterson
Janie	Catherine Reitman
Cliff Klamath	Maury Chaykin
Michelle	Heather McComb
Banker	Scott Waara
Janitor	Jeff Corey
Chemistry Teacher	Virginia Capers
Baseball Captains	Devon Gummersall, Jason Perkins
Newspaper Boy	Jordan Bond
Party Guys	Robert Cavanaugh, Randall Slavin
Bully	Dion Zamora
Teen Hecklers	Damien Rapp, Todd Kolker
Heather	Adena Bjork
Arthur Lewis	Pat Jankiewicz
Hot Dog Vendor	Tom Dugan
Window Dresser	Holly Wortell
Window Display Manager	Don Lake

and Beethoven

Plot Capsule: *St. Bernard Beethoven meets and mates with his newly found dog love, leaving a litter of puppies with the Newton Family. Sequel to the 1992 Universal Pictures comedy with Grodin, Hunt, Tom, Castile, and Carr repeating their roles.*

The song "The Day I Fall in Love" was nominated for an Academy Award.
© Universal City Studios Inc.

Sarah Rose Karr, Nicholle Tom, Bonnie Hunt, Charles Grodin, Christopher Castile, with Missy and Beethoven

Robert Duvall, Richard Harris

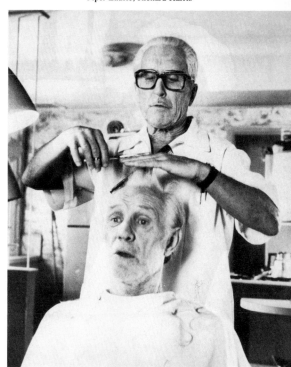

Piper Laurie, Richard Harris

WRESTLING ERNEST HEMINGWAY

(WARNER BROS.) Producers, Todd Black, Joe Wizan; Director, Randa Haines; Screenplay, Steve Conrad; Photography, Lajos Koltai; Designer, Waldemar Kalinowski; Editor, Paul Hirsch; Music, Michael Convertino; Co-Producer, Jim Van Wyck; Costumes, Joe I. Tompkins; Casting, Lora Kennedy; Dolby Stereo; Technicolor; Rated PG-13; 122 minutes; December release

CAST

Walter	Robert Duvall
Frank	Richard Harris
Helen	Shirley MacLaine
Elaine	Sandra Bullock
Bernice	Micole Mercurio
Ned Ryan	Marty Belafsky
Sleeper	Harold Bergman
Georgia	Piper Laurie
Henry's Dad	Ed Amatrudo
Henry	Jag Davies
Umpire	Rudolph X. Herrera
Woman in stands	Persephone Felder
Leo Peetes	Stephen G. Anthony
Sid Showenstein	Greg Paul Meyers
Girls in park	Aquilla Owens, Danika Daly
Mom in park	Doris Carey
Nurse	Jody Wilson
Bus Driver	Anthony Rene Jones
Third Baseman	Richard Jasen
Carl Burney	William Marquez
Cinema Cashier	Ilse Earl
Weatherman	Kent Ehrhardt
Singing Woman	Eleonora L. Vescera
Officer Mickey	Daryl Matthews

(Plot Capsule) *Two senior citizens biding their time in Florida, Frank, a former sailor, and Walter, a retired barber, slowly and reluctantly become friends in this comedy-drama.*
© Warner Bros.

Richard Harris, Robert Duvall

Shirley MacLaine, Richard Harris

Robert Duvall, Sandra Bullock

Antonio Banderas, Tom Hanks

Tom Hanks

PHILADELPHIA

(TRISTAR) Producers, Edward Saxon, Jonathan Demme; Executive Producers, Gary Goetzman, Kenneth Utt, Ron Bozman; Director, Jonathan Demme; Screenplay, Ron Nyswaner; Photography, Tak Fujimoto; Editor, Craig McKay; Designer, Kristi Zea; Music, Howard Shore; Songs: *Streets of Philadelphia* written and performed by Bruce Springsteen, *Philadelphia* written and performed by Neil Young; Costumes, Colleen Atwood; Casting, Howard Feuer; a Clinica Estetico production; Dolby Stereo; DuArt/Technicolor; Rated PG-13; 125 minutes; December release

CAST

Andrew Beckett	Tom Hanks
Joe Miller	Denzel Washington
Charles Wheeler	Jason Robards
Belinda Conine	Mary Steenburgen
Miguel Alvarez	Antonio Banderas
Bob Seidman	Ron Vawter
Walter Kenton	Robert Ridgley
Judge Garnett	Charles Napier
Lisa Miller	Lisa Summerour
Sarah Beckett	Joanne Woodward
Jerome Green	Obba Babatunde
Young Man in pharmacy	Andre B. Blake
Bud Beckett	Robert Castle
Clinic Storyteller	Daniel Chapman
Mr. Laird	Roger Corman
Jill Beckett	Ann Dowd
Bruno	David Drake
Dr. Gillman	Karen Finley
Kenneth Killcoyne	Charles Glenn
Peter/Mona Lisa	Peter Jacobs
Dr. Klenstein	Paul Lazar
Matt Beckett	John Bedford Lloyd
Judge Tate	Roberta Maxwell
Mr. Finley	Warren Miller
Juror	Harry Northup
Randy Beckett	Dan Olmstead
Filko	Joey Perillo
Iris	Lauren Roselli
Dr. Armbruster	Bill Rowe
Anthea Burton	Anna Deavere Smith
Shelby	Lisa Talerico
Jury Foreman	Daniel von Bargen
Librarian	Tracey Walter
Jamey Collins	Bradley Whitford
Chandra	Chandra Wilson
Melissa Benedict	Kathryn Witt

and Buzz Kilman ("Crutches"), Mark Sorensen, Jr. (Clinic Patient); Jeffrey Williamson (Tyrone), Stephanie Roth (Rachel Smilow), Ford Wheeler (Alan), Freddie Foxxx, Paul Moore (Hospital Patients), Jane Moore (Lydia Glines), Dennis Radesky (Santa Claus), Glen Hartell (Library Guard), John Ignarri, Richard Ehrlich (Young Men in library), Julius Erving (Himself), Katie Lintner (Alexis), Peg French, Ann Howard (The Bronte Sisters), Meghan Tepas (Meghan), Molly Hickok (Molly Beckett), Elizabeth Roby (Elizabeth Beckett), Adam Le Fevre (Jill's Husband), Gary Goetzman (Guido Paonessa), Melissa Fraser Brown, Jordan Cael, Dodie Demme, Patricia Greenwell, Donovan Mannato, Steven Scales, Billy Ray Tyson, Kenneth Utt, Steve Vignari, Lawrence T. Wrentz (The Jury), James B. Howard (Dexter Smith), Charles Techman (Ralph Peterson), Jim Roche ("Not Adam and Steve"), Donna Hamilton (Angela Medina), Mayor Edward Rendell (Himself), Daniel Wolff (Filko's Buddy), John T. O'Connell (Macho Barfly), Edward Kirkland (Cousin Eddie), Tony Fitzpatrick (Bartender), Debra H. Ballard (Court Stenographer), Ira Flitter (Andrew's Friend), Gene Borkan (Bailiff), Jon Arterton, Michael Callen, Aurelio Font, Jimmy Rutland, Cliff Townsend (The Flirtations), Q Lazzarus (Party Singer), Lucas Platt (Robert), Lewis Walker ("Punchline"), Carmen Mahiques (Miguel's Mom), Jose Castillo (Miguel's Dad), Leigh Smiley (Young Sarah Beckett), Philip Joseph "PJ" McGee (Child Andrew)

Plot Capsule: *A gay lawyer, Andrew Beckett, fired from his law firm, enlists the help of homophobic lawyer Joe Miller. Together they bring descrimination charges against the firm, certain that Beckett was dismissed from his job because he has AIDS.*

1993 Academy Award winner for Best Actor (Tom Hanks) and original song ("Streets of Philadelphia")

Tom Hanks received a Golden Globe Award as best actor. The film received Academy Award nominations for the original screenplay, title song, and makeup.
© TriStar Pictures

Mary Steenburgen, Obba Babatunde

Denzel Washington

Joanne Woodward, Robert Castle

Robert Ridgely, Ron Vawter, Jason Robards, Tom Hanks, Charles Glenn

HEAVEN AND EARTH

(WARNER BROS.) Producers, Oliver Stone, Arnon Milchan, Robert Kline, A. Kitman Ho; Executive Producer, Mario Kassar; Director/Screenplay, Oliver Stone; Based upon the books *When Heaven and Earth Changed Places* by Le Ly Hayslip, with Jay Wurts, and *Child of War, Woman of Peace* by Le Ly Hayslip, with James Hayslip; Photography, Robert Richardson; Designer, Victor Kempster; Editors, David Brenner, Sally Menke; Co-Producer, Clayton Townsend; Music, Kitaro; Costumes, Ha Nguyen; Casting, Risa Bramon Garcia, Billy Hopkins, Heidi Levitt; Presented in association with Regency Enterprises, Le Studio Canal+ and Alcor Films; an Ixtlan/New Regency/Todd-AO/TAE production; Dolby Stereo; Panavision; Technicolor; Rated R; 142 minutes; December release

Haing S Ngor, Hiep Thi Le

CAST

Le Ly	Hiep Thi Le
Sgt. Steve Butler	Tommy Lee Jones
Mama	Joan Chen
Papa	Haing S. Ngor
Eugenia	Debbie Reynolds
Sau	Dustin Nguyen
Bernice	Conchata Ferrell
Madame Lien	Vivian Wu
Larry	Dale Dye
Viet Cong Captain	Liem Whatley
Paul	Robert Burke
Interrogator	Michael Paul Chan
Big Mike	Timothy Carhart
Young Sergeant	Tim Guinee
Bar Girl	Catherine Ai
Anh	Long Nguyen

Hiep Thi Le, Stephen Polk

and Bussaro Sanruck (Le Ly - age 5), Supak Pititam (Buddhist Monk), Thuan K. Nguyen (Uncle Luc), Lan Nguyen Calderon (Ba), Thuan Le (Kim), Mai Le Ho (Hai), Vinh Dang (Bon), Khiem Thai (Brother in law), Michelle Vynh Le (Viet Cong Cadre Woman), Tuan Tran (Rapist), Aron Starrat (Helicopter Soldier), Peter Duong (Republican Colonel), Hieu Van Vu (Teacher), Phil Neilson (Marine in helicopter), Michael Lee (Ky La Wizard), Thanh Vo (Grenade Girl), George Roarke (U.S. Advisor), Dave Cooper (Bald Onlooker), Irene Ng, Thuc-Hanh Tran (Torture Girls), Vu Anh Phan (Snakeman), Mai Le (Steward), Term Saefam (Herbalist), Stephen Polk, Keith Smith, Brad Rea (G.I.s), Tran Huy (Danang Cop), Yeun Yong Dumda (Jimmy - age 1), Kevin Gallagher (Tall Marine), Brian Helmick (Short Marine), Somsak Hormsombat (Siclo Driver), Nuttikit (Jimmy - age 3), Don Ho, Jr. (Tommy - age 2), Phuong Huu Le (Jimmy - age 6), Scott Barkwill (Staff Sergeant at Embassy), Jennifer Low Sauer, Gina Sheri Tavizon (Supermarket Shoppers), Chitra Mojtabai (Supermarket Check-out Girl), Annie McEnroe, Marianne Muellerleile, Marshall Bell (Dinner Guests), Le Ly Hayslip (Jewelry Broker), Huynh Cao Nguyen (Landlord), Willie Nark-Orn (Tommy - age 5), Lester Gopaoco (Jimmy - age 8), Toby Vu (Alan - age 2), Andy Reeder (Alan - age 4), Chau Mao Doan (California Monk), Vivien Straus (Neighbor's Wife), Mai Nguyen (California Wizard), Melinda Renna (Police Woman), Robert F. Marshall (Detective), Tai Thai (Jimmy - age 20), Tom Nam Ly (Tommy - age 15), Jeffrey Jones (Priest).

Plot Capsule: *The true story of Le Ly, covering her childhood in Vietnam, the devastation of her village during the war and her eventual marriage to an American soldier who takes her to California.*

Golden Globe Award winner for best original music score.
© Warner Bros./Regency Enterprises/Le Studio Canal+

Tommy Lee Jones, Hiep Thi Le, Debbie Reynolds

Hiep Thi Le, Joan Chen

Ann-Margret, Walter Matthau

Jack Lemmon, Walter Matthau

GRUMPY OLD MEN

(WARNER BROS.) Producers, John Davis, Richard C. Berman; Executive Producer, Dan Kolsrud; Director, Donald Petrie; Screenplay, Mark Steven Johnson; Photography, John E. Jensen; Designer, David Chapman; Music, Alan Silvestri; Editor, Bonnie Koehler; Costumes, Lisa Jensen; Casting, Sharon Howard-Field; a John Davis/Lancaster Gate production; Dolby Stereo; Technicolor; Rated PG-13; 104 minutes; December release

CAST

John Gustafson	Jack Lemmon
Max Goldman	Walter Matthau
Ariel Truax	Ann-Margret
Grandpa Gustafson	Burgess Meredith
Melanie Gustafson	Daryl Hannah
Jacob Goldman	Kevin Pollak
Chuck	Ossie Davis
Elliott Snyder	Buck Henry
Mike	Christopher McDonald
Weatherman	Steve Cochran
Pharmacist	Joe Howard
Nurse	Isabell Monk
Punky	Buffy Sedlacheck
Moving Man	John Carroll Lynch
Fishermen	Charles Brin, Ollie Osterberg

Plot Capsule: *A 56 year-old feud between two Minnesota neighbors is further ignited when Ariel, an attractive college professor, moves in across the street. This comedy marked the fifth teaming of Jack Lemmon and Walter Matthau, following their pairings in* The Fortune Cookie *(1966),* The Odd Couple *(1968),* The Front Page *(1974), and* Buddy Buddy *(1981).*
© Warner Bros.

Jack Lemmon, Walter Matthau

Jack Lemmon, Burgess Meredith, Daryl Hannah

Dana Delany

Kurt Russell, Charlton Heston

Val Kilmer, Sam Elliott, Kurt Russell, Bill Paxton

Michael Biehn

Jason Priestley

Powers Boothe, Michael Biehn, Stephen Lang, Bill Paxton,
Kurt Russell, Joanna Pacula, Val Kilmer

TOMBSTONE

(HOLLYWOOD PICTURES) Producers, James Jacks, Sean Daniel, Bob Misiorowski; Executive Producers, Buzz Feitshans, Andrew G. Vajna; Director, George P. Cosmatos; Screenplay, Kevin Jarre; Photography, William A. Fraker; Designer, Catherine Hardwicke; Editors, Frank J. Urioste, Roberto Silvi, Harvey Rosenstock; Costumes, Joseph Porro; Music, Bruce Broughton; Associate Producers, William A. Fraker, John Fasano; an Andrew G. Vajna presentation of a Sean Daniel, James Jacks, Cinergi production; Dolby Stereo; Panavision; Technicolor; Rated R; 127 minutes; December release

Val Kilmer, Kurt Russell

CAST

Wyatt Earp	Kurt Russell
Doc Holliday	Val Kilmer
Johnny Ringo	Michael Biehn
Curly Bill	Powers Boothe
Frank McLaury	Robert Burke
Josephine	Dana Delany
Virgil Earp	Sam Elliott
Ike Clanton	Stephen Lang
Mayor Clum	Terry O'Quinn
Kate	Joanna Pacula
Morgan Earp	Bill Paxton
Billy Breckenridge	Jason Priestley
Sherman McMasters	Michael Rooker
Behan	Jon Tenney
Mattie Earp	Dana Wheeler-Nicholson
Mr. Fabian	Billy Zane
Turkey Creek Jack Jackson	Buck Taylor
Marshal Fred White	Harry Carey, Jr.
Frank Stillwell	Tomas Arana
Billy Clanton	Thomas Haden Church
Barnes	John Corbett
The Priest	Pedro Armendariz, Jr.
Ed Bailey	Frank Stallone
Johnny Tyler	Billy Bob Thornton
Lucinda Hobbs	Cecil Hoffmann
Henry Hooker	Charlton Heston
Allie Earp	Paula Malcomson
Louisa Earp	Lisa Collins
Milt Joyce	Pat Brady
Florentino	Paul Ben Victor
Tom McLaury	John Philbin

and Wyatt Earp (Billy Claiborne), W.R. Bo Gray (Wes Fuller), Forrie J. Smith (Pony Deal), Peter Sherayko (Texas Jack Vermillion), Charles Schneider (Professor Gillman), Gary Clark (Crawley Dake), Billy Joe Patton (Deputy), Bobby Joe McFadden (1st Gambler), Rurale Captain/Groom .. Michael N. Garcia (Rurale Captain/Groom), Grant Wheeler (Drunk), Jim Dunham (Miner), Stephen Foster (Hank Swilling), Grant James (Dr. Goodfellow), Don Collier (High Roller), Charlie Ward (Clark Ray (Cowboys), Chris Mitchum (Ranch Hand), Sandy Gibbons (Father Feeney), Evan Osborne (Piano Player), Shane McCabe (Audience Member), Robert Mitchum (Narrator)

Plot Capsule: *Wyatt Earp and his family arrive in the western town of Tombstone hoping to live a peaceful life. However, the town's unruly violence causedby the McLaurys and Clantons, draws Earp back into a life of law enforcement. Earlier films involving Wyatt Earp and the gunfight at the O.K. Corral include* Tombstone: The Town Too Tough to Die *(Paramount, 1942, with Richard Dix as Earp)*, My Darling Clementine *(20th Century Fox, 1946, Henry Fonda)*, Gunfight at the O.K. Corral *(Paramount, 1957, Burt Lancaster)*, Hour of the Gun *(UA, 1967, James Garner)*, and Doc *(UA, 1970, Harris Yulin)*.

© Cinergi Productions

Kurt Russell

Val Kilmer

Buck Taylor, Val Kilmer, Kurt Russell,
Michael Rooker, Peter Sherayko

Daniel Baldwin, Tom Skerritt, Christopher Lambert
in *Knight Moves* © InterStar

Arye Gross, Claudia Christian in *Hexed*
© Columbia Pictures Industries

KNIGHT MOVES (InterStar Releasing) Producers, Ziad El Khoury, Jean Luc Defait; Executive Producers, Christopher Lambert, Brad Mirman; Co-Producer, Dieter Geissler; Director, Carl Schenkel; Screenplay, Brad Mirman; Photography, Dietrich Lohmann; Editor, Norbert Herzner; Designer, Graeme Murray; Costumes, Deborah Everton, Trish Keating; a Republic Pictures presentation; Panavision; Color; Rated R; 96 minutes; January release. **CAST:** Christopher Lambert (Peter Sanderson), Diane Lane (Kathy Sheppard), Tom Skerritt (Chief of Police Frank Sedman), Daniel Baldwin (Andy Wagner), Ferdinand Mayne (Jeremy Edmonds), Katharine Isobel (Erica Sanderson), Charles Baily-Gates (David Willerman), Arthur Brauss (Viktor Yurilivich), Codie Lucas Wilbee (David, nine years old), Josh Murray (Peter, 14 years old), Frank C. Turner (Doctor), Don Thompson (Father), Megan Leitch (Mother), Alex Diakun (Grandmaster Lutz), Mark Wilson (Newscaster), Kehli O'Byrne (Debi Rutledge), Blu Mankuma (Steve Nolan), Monica Marko (Miss Greenwell), Walter Marsh (Chess President), Suzy Carby (Desk Clerk), Sam Making (Dr. Fulton), Elizabeth Baldwin (Christie Eastman), Dwight McFee (Technician), Pat Bermel, Holly Chester (Officer), Elizabeth Barclay (Lorraine Olson), Rebecca Toolan (Mayor), Aundrea MacDonald (Mary Albert), Freda Perry (Attractive Girl), Marilyn Norry (Homesearcher), Donna Yamamoto (Reporter), Tom Heaton (Detective), Rachel Hayward (Last Victim), Kymberley Sheppard (Janet McLellan), Deryl Hayes (Officer Harton)

HEXED (Columbia) Producers, Marc S. Fischer, Louis G. Friedman; Executive Producers, Bernie Brillstein, Howard Klein; Director/Screenplay, Alan Spencer; Photography, James Chressanthis; Music, Lance Rubin; Editor, Debra McDermott; Designer, Brenton Swift; Casting, Cathy Henderson, Tom McSweeney; a Price Entertainment/Brillstein-Grey production; Dolby Stereo; Technicolor; Rated R; 91 minutes; January release. **CAST:** Arye Gross (Matthew Welsh), Claudia Christian (Hexina), Adrienne Shelly (Gloria O'Connor), Ray Baker (Victor Thummell), R. Lee Ermey (Det. Ferguson), Michael Knight (Simon Littlefield), Robin Curtis (Rebecca), Brandis Kemp (Ms. Strickland), Norman Fell (Herschel Levine), Pamela Roylance (Jennifer), Billy Jones (Larry), John Davies (Henry Pratt), Fred Mata (Bellman), Marilyn Staley (Nurse), Julio Cedillo (Officer Sanchez), Woody Watson (Officer Gillis), Randy Means (Policeman), Phyllis Cicero (Officer Novak), Tasha Auer (Officer Turner), Terry Poland (Mime), Joe Berryman (Southern Businessman),

Gil Glasgow (Priest), Jonathan Dorn, Erin Kempe (Teens), Mark Walters, Tony Brownrigg (Cops), Spencer Lucas, Bob Hess (Detectives), Roy Metcalf (Junkie), Francis Silmon (Singing Dishwasher), Hector Garcia, Alan Ackles, Suzanne Moss (Newscasters), Elaine Long, Linda Edwards, Maria Arita, Laura Banks, David Sederholm, Teresa Ganzel, Michele Russell (Reporters), Geoffrey Garza (Party Bartender), John William Galt (Obese Slob), Gary Moody (Desk Sgt.), John B. Wells (SWAT Commander), Doug Small (Bus Driver), Lisa E. Seyfert (Deaf Woman in bar), Georgia Lambron (Pedestrian)

NEMESIS (Imperial Entertainment) Producers, Ash R. Shah, Eric Karson, Tom Karnowski; Executive Producers, Sundip R. Shah, Anders P. Jensen, Sunil R. Shah; Director, Albert Pyun; Screenplay, Rebecca Charles; Photography, George Mooradian; Designer, Colleen Saro; Costumes, Lizz Wolf; Editors, David Kern; Music, Michel Rubini; Special Visual Effects, Fantasy II Film Effects, Mark Conte; System 35 Widescreen; Color; Rated R; 95 minutes; January release. **CAST:** Olivier Gruner (Alex Rain), Tim Thomerson (Farnsworth), Cary-Hiroyuki Tagawa (Angie-Liv), Merle Kennedy (Max Impact), Yuji Okumoto (Yoshiro Han), Marjorie Monaghan (Jared), Nicholas Guest (Germaine), Vince Klyn (Michel), Thom Mathews (Marion), Marjean Holden (Pam), Brion James (Maritz), Deborah Shelton (Julian), Jennifer Gatti (Rosaria/2nd Woman), Borovnisa Blervaque (1st Woman), Tom Janes (Billy), Jackie Earle Haley (Einstein), Adriana Miles (German National), Rhino Michaels (Bar Patron), Robert Carlton (Waiter), Mabel Falls (Old Woman), Jack Thomerson (Technician), Thunderwolf (Columbian Man), Branscombe Richmond (Mexican Man), Barbara C. Adside

LEPRECHAUN (Trimark) Producer, Jeffrey B. Mallian; Co-Producers, Michael Prescott, David Price, Williams Sachs; Executive Producer, Mark Amin; Director/Screenplay, Mark Jones; Supervising Producer, Jim Begg; Photography, Levie Isaacks; Music, Kevin Kiner; Editor, Christopher Roth; Designer, Naomi Slodki; Special Effects/Makeup, Atlantic West Effects, Gabe Z. Bartalos, Dave Kindlon; Costumes, Holly Davis; Casting, Lisa London; CFI color; Rated R; 92 minutes; January release. **CAST:** Warwick Davis (Leprechaun), Jennifer Aniston (Tory), Ken Olandt (Nathan), Mark Holton (Ozzie), Robert Gorman (Alex), John Sanderford (J.D.), Shay Duffin (Dan O'Grady), John Volstad (Pawnshop Owner), Pamela Mant (Leah

Olivier Gruner in *Nemesis*
© Scanbox Danmark AS

Warwick Davis in *Leprechaun*
© Vidmark Inc.

Jordan Christopher Michael in *Motorama*
© Planet Productions Corp.

Ryan Bollman in *Children of the Corn II*
© Dimension

O'Grady), William Newman (Sheriff Cronin), David Permenter (Deputy Tripet), Raymond Turner (Dispatcher)

MOTORAMA (Two Moon Releasing) Producer, Donald P. Borchers; Executive Producers, Lauren Graybow, Barry Shils, Steven Bratter, Barbara Ligeti; Director, Barry Shils; Screenplay/Story, Joseph Minion; Photography, Joseph Yacoe; Designers, Vincent Jefferds, Cathlyn Marshall; Editor, Peter Verity; Costumes, Dana Allyson; Music, Andy Summers; Casting, Linda Francis; a Planet Productions Corp. presentation; Color; Not rated; 90 minutes; January release. **CAST:** Jordan Christopher Michael (Gus), Martha Quinn (Bank Teller), Michael Naegel (Boy at Wagon Wheel), Susan Tyrrell (Bartender), Harper Flaherty (Old Man at Wagon Wheel), John Laughlin (Man at Wagon Wheel), Kurt Bryant (Another Man), John Diehl (Phil), Robert Picardo (Jerry the Policeman), Jack Nance (Motel Clerk), Cynthia R. King (Girl in backseat), Garrett Morris (Andy), Michael J. Pollard (Lou), Flea (Busboy), Sandy Baron (Kidnapping Husband), Mary Woronov (Kidnapping Wife), Paul Willson (Cook), Rick Taylor (Manager), Vince Edwards (Doctor), Drew Barrymore (Fantasy Girl), Dan Quinn (Billy), Meat Loaf (Vern), Jacob Kenner (Boy at picnic), Sandy Williams (Boy's Mother at picnic), Dick Miller (Horseshoe Player), George Salazar (Chimera Attendant), Charles Tyner (Dying Man), Irwin Keyes (Hunchback Attendant), Marvin Elkins (Chimera Security Guard), Allyce Beasley (Chimera Receptionist), Robin Duke (Miss Lawton), Shelley Berman (Million Dollar Driver)

TRUSTING BEATRICE (Castle Hill) formerly *Claude*; Producers, Mark Evan Jacobs, Cindy Lou Johnson; Co-Producer, Diana Philips; Director/Screenplay, Cindy Lou Johnson; Photography Bernd Heinl; Editor, Camilla Toniolo; Music, Stanley Myers; Color; Not rated; 86 minutes; January release. **CAST:** Mark Evan Jacobs (Claude Dewey), Irene Jacob (Beatrice de Lucio), Charlotte Moore (Mrs. Dewey), Pat McNamara (Al Dewey), Leonardo Cimino (Daddy V.J.), Nady Meas (Seap Sok), Steve Buscemi (Danny), Stephen Perlman (Mr. Gold)

MONEY MAN (Milestone Films) Producers, Philip Haas, Belinda Haas; Director, Philip Haas; Photography, Tony Wilson; Editor, Belinda Haas; Music, Philip Johnston; Color; Not rated; 60 minutes; January release. Documentary on counterfeiter J.S.G. Boggs and his

journey to Washington D.C. to battle with the U.S. Treasury Department.

CHILDREN OF THE CORN II: THE FINAL SACRIFICE (Dimension) Producers, Scott Stone, David Stanley, Bill Froelich; Executive Producer, Lawrence Mortoff; Director, David Price; Screenplay, A.L. Katz, Gil Adler; Based on the short story by Stephen King; Photography, Levie Isaacks; Designer, Greg Melton; Editor, Barry Zetlin; Casting, Geno Havens; Special Visual Effects, Calico Ltd., Rob Burton; a Fifth Avenue Entertainment presentation of a Stone Stanley production; Ultra-Stereo; Foto-Kem color; Rated R; 92 minutes; January release. **CAST:** Terence Knox (John Garrett), Paul Scherrer (Danny Garrett), Rosalind Allen (Angela Casual), Christie Clark (Lacey), Ned Romero (Red Bear), Ryan Bollman (Micah), Ted Travelstead (Mordechai), Ed Grady (Dr. Appleby), John Bennes (Hollings), Wallace Merck (Sheriff Blaine), Joe Inscoe (Simpson), Marty Terry (Mrs. Burke/West), Dean Bridgers (Jedediah), Aubrey Dollar (Naomi), Kristy Angell (Ruth), David Hains (Fraser), Leon Pridgen (Bobby), Kelly Benett (Mary Simpson), Rob Treveiler (McKenzie)

RAIN WITHOUT THUNDER (Orion Classics) Producers, Nanette Sorensen, Gary Sorensen; Executive Producers, Rick Callahan, Mike Mihalich; Director/Screenplay, Gary Bennett; Photography, Karl Kases; Designer, Ina Mayhew; Costumes, Gail Bartley; Music, Randall Lynch, Allen Lynch; Editors, Mallory Gottlieb, Suzanne Pillsbury; a TAZ Pictures production; Technicolor; Rated PG-13; 85 minutes; February release. **CAST:** Betty Buckley (Beverly Goldring), Jeff Daniels (Jonathan Garson), Frederic Forrest (Robert Simka), Graham Greene (Harold Shafley), Linda Hunt (Marilyn Yastrow), Robert Earl Jones (Lawrence Conracky), Carolyn McCormick (Reporter), Iona Morris (Andrea Murdoch), Austin Pendleton (Father Gallagher), Ali Thomas (Allison Goldring), Steve Zahn (Jeremy Tanner), Katharine Crost (Walker Point Guard #1), Stuart Burney (Spencer Goldring), Eliza Clark (Piper Goldring), Heather Lilly (Micka Goldring), Helen Lloyd Breed (Alice Kappelhoff), Katherine Selverstone (Abra Russell), Charles E. Gerber (Grover Cole), Bahni Turpin ("Baby Bomb" Prisoner), Ming-Na Wen ("Uudie" Prisoner), John Scott, Andrew Spencer, Jay Hargrove, Linda Igarashi (Health Officials), Joseph Dophin ("Baby Bomb" Dealer), Fred Fagen (Doctor with probe), Dana Smith (Walker Point Nurse), Lisa Langford ("In Profile"

Mark Evan Jacobs, Nady Meas, Irene Jacob
in *Trusting Beatrice* © Castle Hill Prods.

Heather Lilly, Stuart Burney, Ali Thomas, Betty Buckley,
Eliza Clark in *Rain Without Thunder* © Orion Classics

Peter Weller in *Fifty/Fifty* © Cannon Pictures

Mark Massi, Tom Joslin in *Silverlake Life* © Zeitgeist Films

THE JUDAS PROJECT (RS Entertainment) Producers, James Nelson, Ervin Melton; Executive Producers, James H. Barden, Edward A. Teraskiewicz; Director/Screenplay/Music, James H. Barden; Photography, Bryan England; Editor, Noreen Zepp Linden; a Judas Project production; Color; Rated PG-13; 97 minutes; February release. **CAST:** John O'Banion (Jesse), Ramy Zada (Jude), Richard Herd, Gerald Gordon, Jeff Corey

FIFTY/FIFTY (Cannon) Producers, Maurice Singer, Raymond Wagner; Director, Charles Martin Smith; Screenplay, Dennis Shryack, Michael Butler; Photography, David Connell; Designer, Errol Kelly; Music, Peter Bernstein; Line Producer, Peter Shepherd; Editor, James Mitchell; Color; Rated R; 101 minutes; February release. **CAST:** Peter Weller (Jake Wyer), Robert Hays (Sam French), Charles Martin Smith (Martin Sprue), Ramona Rahman (Suleta), Kay Tong Lim (Akhantar), Dom Magwili (Gen. Bosavi), Azmil Mustapha (Col. Kota), Dharma Al Rashidai Harun (Sentul), OS (Jamik), Rohmat Juraimi (Rebel Leader), Ursala Martin (Liz Powell), Sharudeen Tamby (Col. Seng), M. Rasuli (Subaltern), Kenji Sevai (Helmsman), Ismail Bin Raimli (Elephant Man), Neelawthura Wijewardene (Plane Mechanic), Anna Lim (Maid), Helmy B.H.M. Salleh (Treasurer), Farah Esmilia Ramli (Girl with grenade), Hussein Abu Hassan (Bus Driver), Giuseppe Pollini (Waiter in Rome), Alessandra Filotei (Girl in Rome)

BEST OF THE BEST 2 (20th Century Fox) Producers, Peter E. Strauss, Phillip Rhee; Co-Producers, Marlon Staggs, Deborah Scott; Executive Producers, Frank Giustra, Peter E. Strauss; Director, Robert Radler; Screenplay, Max Strom, John Allen Nelson; Photography, Fred Tammes; Designer, Gary Frutkoff; Music, David Michael Frank; Editor, Bert Lovitt; Stunts, Simon Rhee; Dolby Stereo; Color; Rated R; 100 minutes; March release. **CAST:** Eric Roberts (Alex Grady), Phillip Rhee (Tommy Lee), Christopher Penn (Travis Brickley), Edan Gross (Walter Grady), Ralph Moeller (Brakus), Meg Foster (Sue), Sonny Landham (James), Wayne Newton (Weldon), Betty Carvalho (Grandma), Simon Rhee (Dae Han), Claire Stansfield (Greta), Hayward Nishioka (Sae Jin Kwon), Ken Nagayama (Yung June), Frank Salsedo (Charlie), Stephanos Miltsakaki (Stavros), Myung Kue Kim (Khan), Patrick Kilpatrick (Finch), Mike Genovese (Gus), Nicholas Worth (Sick Humor), Matt Thomas (Soft Voice), Edward Bunker (Spotlight Operator), David Rody (Slimy Man), John Charles Sheehan (Front Doorman), Kane Hodder (Back Doorman),

Randy Gomes (Policeman), Robert Radler (Floor Manager), Harry Hauss (Helicopter Pilot), Buckley Norris (Gambler), Rain Ivana (Teller), Cliff Emmich (Texan), Alex Desir (Andre Marais), Lionel Washington (Hammer), Amanda Barry (Bartender), Albie Selznick (Man in crowd), Melissa Holgate (Woman in crowd), Christine Soustre (Woman at bar), Manny Perry (Gunman in desert), Christy Thom (Girl at restaurant), Randy Falcon (Native Indian), Bob Lewis (Minister), Rusty Meyers (TV Reporter), Jonathan Strauss (Boy Basketball Player), Jeff Olan, Gunter Zeigler (Security Guards), Kelly Clayton, Chris Carnel, Todd Mark, James Choi, Andre Lima (Brakus' Sparring Partners)

LOVE YOUR MAMA (Hemdale) Producer/Director/Screenplay/Casting, Ruby L. Oliver; Photography, Ronald Courtney; Editor, Joy L. Rencher; Music, John Van Allen Jr., Markian Fedorowycz; an Oliver Productions Film; Color; Rated PG-13; 92 minutes; March release. **CAST:** Carol E. Hall (Leola), Audrey Morgan (Mama), Andre Robinson (Wren), Earnest III Rayford (Sam), Kearo Johnson (Willie), Artavia Wright (Lois), Jacqueline Williams (Barbara), Kevin C. White (Bob), Norman D. Hoosier (Zeek), Glenn B. Collins (Jimmy), Linda Roberson (Helena), Mario Andre (Bartender), Pat "Soul" Scaggs (Candy), Darryl A. Reed (Dr. Penn)

SILVERLAKE LIFE: THE VIEW FROM HERE (Zeitgeist) Producers/Directors, Tom Joslin, Peter Friedman; Co-Producers, Doug Block, Jane Weiner; Photography, Tom Joslin, Mark Massi, Elaine Mayes, Peter Friedman; Editor, Peter Friedman; Music, Lucia Hwong; Produced in association with Channel 4 Television and J.P. Weiner production inc.; Color; Not rated; 99 minutes; March release. Documentary chronicles the last days of filmmaker Tom Joslin and his companion Mark Massi, both stricken with AIDS.

STREET KNIGHT (Cannon) Producer, Mark DiSalle; Executive Producers, Yoram Globus, Christopher Pearce; Co-Producer, Peggy DiSalle; Director, Albert Magnoli; Screenplay/Associate Producer, Richard Friedman; Photography, Yasha Sklansky; Music, David Michael Frank; Editor, Wayne Wahrman; Dolby Stereo; Panavision; Color; Rated R; 88 minutes; March release. **CAST:** Jeff Speakman (Jake Barett), Christopher Neame (Franklin), Lewis Van Bergen (Lt. Bill Crowe), Jennifer Gatti (Rebecca), Bernie Casey (Raymond), Richard Coca (Carlos), Stephen Liska (Santino), Grainger Hines (Murphy), Sal Landi

Edan Gross, Eric Roberts in *Best of the Best 2*
© Twentieth Century Fox

Patti LuPone, Anne Archer, Julianne Michelle in *Family Prayers*
© Arrow Releasing

Courteney Cox, Arye Gross in *The Opposite Sex*
© Miramax Films

Alicia Silverstone, Cary Elwes in *The Crush*
© Morgan Creek Productions

(Parker), Hank Stone (Cruise), Tom Magee (Baby Huey), Robert Dryer (Ostrow), Mario Roberts (Lovinger), Bob Liles (Kane), Ramon Franco (Cisco), G. Adam Gifford (Jesus), Claudio Martinez (Latin Lord #1), Kamar Reyes (Smokey), Joey Naber (Little Man), Lil Moe (Peewee), Richard Allen, Jeremiah Birkett, Angel Vargas, Theo Forsett, Mushond Lee, James "J.T." Moye (Blades), Marco Rodriguez (Jack Fernandez), Ketty Lester (Lucinda), Santos Morales (Emilio), Mark DiSalle (Security Guard), Richard Grove (Madman), Julianne Michelle (Hostage), Joycelyn Engle (Hostage's Mother), Ann Fairlie (Homeless Woman)

FAMILY PRAYERS (Arrow Releasing) Producers, Mark Levinson, Bonnie Sugar; Executive Producer, Larry Sugar; Director, Scott Rosenfelt; Screenplay, Steven Ginsberg; Photography, Jeff Jur; Designer, Chester Kaczenski; Costumes, Johnny Foam; Music, Steve Tyrell; Editor, Susan R. Crutcher; a Sugar presentation; Ultra-Stereo; Color; Rated PG; 105 minutes; March release. **CAST:** Joe Mantegna (Martin Jacobs), Anne Archer (Rita Jacobs), Paul Reiser (Dan Linder), Patti LuPone (Aunt Nan), Tzvi Ratner-Stauber (Andrew Jacobs), Julianne Michelle (Faye Jacobs), Conchata Ferrell (Ms. Romeyo), Allen Garfield (Cantor), David Margulies (Uncle Sam)

LAST CALL AT MAUD'S (Maud's Project Prod.) Producers, Karen Kiss, Paris Poirier; Director, Paris Poirier; Photography, Cheryl Rosenthal, Gary Sanders; Editors, Paris Poirier, Elaine Trotter; Music, Tim Horrigan; Color; Not rated; 74 minutes; March release. *Documentary on San Francisco's oldest Lesbian bar, Maud's;* wit Gween Craig, Jo Daly, Sally Gearhart, Judy Grahn, JoAnn Loulan, Phyllis Lyon, Del Martin, Pat Norman, Rikki Streicher, Mary Wings.

THE OPPOSITE SEX (AND HOW TO LIVE WITH THEM) (Miramax) Producers, Stanley M. Brooks, Robert Newmyer; Executive Producer, Jeffrey Silver; Director, Matthew Meshekoff; Screenplay, Noah Stern; Photography, Jacek Laskus; Designer, Alex Tavoularis; Music, Ira Newborn; Editor, Adam Weiss; a Once Upon a Time and Outlaw production; Dolby Stereo; CFI color; Rated R; 86 minutes; March release. **CAST:** Arye Gross (David Crown), Courteney Cox (Carrie Davenport), Kevin Pollak (Eli), Julie Brown (Zoe), Mitch Ryan (Kenneth Davenport), Phil Bruns (Irv Crown), Mitzi McCall (Freida Crown), B.J. Ward (Gisella Davenport), Jack Carter (Rabbi), David DeCastro (Beer Vendor), Donald Brown (Crackerjack Vendor), Aaron Lustig (Movie Bully), Connie Sawyer (Waitress from Hell), Steven Brill (George), David Guggenheim (Pitcher), Craig Alan Edwards (1st Baseman), John Demita (Chipper), Lisa Waltz (Lizbeth), Kimberlin Brown (Leeza), Kimber Sissons (Tracy), Kevin West (Tour Guide), Justin Shenkaro (Bobby), Mindy Mittleman (Cindy), Tess Foltyn (Hanna), Jensen Daggett (Cheerleader), Andrea Evans (Jules), Frank Birney (Priest), Carrie Cline (Periscope Girl)

ROCK HUDSON'S HOME MOVIES (Couch Potato Inc.) Producer/Director/ Screenplay/Editor, Mark Rappaport; Photography, Mark Daniels; Color; Not rated; 63 minutes; April release. Documentary with Eric Farr

THE CRUSH (Warner Bros.) Producer, James G. Robinson; Executive Producer, Gary Barber; Director/Screenplay, Alan Shapiro; Photography, Bruce Surtees; Editor, Ian Crafford; Designer, Michael Bolton; Costumes, Sharon Purdy; Associate Producers, Marci Liroff, Joel Segal; a Morgan Creek production; Dolby Stereo; Technicolor; Rated R; 89 minutes; April release. **CAST:** Cary Elwes (Nick Eliot), Alicia Silverstone (Darian Forrester), Jennifer Rubin (Amy Maddik), Amber Benson (Cheyenne), Kurtwood Smith (Cliff Forrester), Gwynyth Walsh (Liv Forrester), Matthew Walker (Michael)

SIDEKICKS (Triumph Releasing) Producer, Don Carmody; Executive Producers, Chuck Norris, Linda McIngvale, Jim McIngvale; Director, Aaron Norris; Screenplay, Donald G. Thompson, Lou Illar; Story, Lou Illar; Photography, Joao Fernandes; Designer, Rueben Freed; Editors, David Rawlins, Bernard Weiser; Music, Alan Silvestri; Associate Producers, Jordan Yospe, Lou Illar; Casting, Annette Benson, Penny Perry Davis; a Gallery Films presentation; Dolby Stereo; Color; Rated PG; 100 minutes; April release. **CAST:** Chuck Norris (Himself), Beau Bridges (Jerry Gabrewski), Jonathan Brandis (Barry Gabrewski), Mako (Mr. Lee), Julia Nickson-Soul (Noreen Chen), Joe Piscopo (Stone), Danica McKellar (Lauren), John Buchanan (Randy Cellini), Richard Moll (Horn)

UNBECOMING AGE (Castle Hill) Producers/Directors, Alfredo Ringel, Deborah Taper Ringel; Screenplay, Meredith Baer, Geof Prysirr; Photography, Harry Mathias; Editor, Alan James Geik; Music, Jeff Lass; a Ringelvision Entertainment production; Color; Rated PG-13; 91 minutes; April release. **CAST:** Diane Salinger (Julia), John Calvin (Charles), Adam Ryen (Junior), Lyndsay Riddell (Vanessa/Julia at age 4), Priscilla Pointer (Grandma), Wallace Shawn (Dr. Block), George Clooney (Mac), Colleen Camp (Deborah), Anthony Peck (Jake), Betsy Lynn George (Angel), Dayle Haddon (Susan), Shera Danese (Letty), Nicholas Guest (Dooley), Michael Greene (Leonard), Kurt Fuller (Coach Granger), Loyda Ramos (Consuela), Patrick LaBrecque (Pinky), Bryan Clark (Sam), Eleanor Zee (Aggie), Michael Boatman (Robert), Irene Tsu (R.J.), Ann Travolta (Checker), Charles Solomon (Blackjack Dealer), Don Diamont (Alfredo), Bill Erwin (Old Man), Judith Weston (Receptionist), Esther Larner, Frances Marshall (Ladies), Steve Curtis (Umpire), Alison Rockwell (Mrs. Granger)

HOW U LIKE ME NOW (Shapiro Glickenhaus Entertainment) Producer/Director/Screenplay, Darryl Roberts; Executive Producer, Bob Woolf; Photography, Michael Goi; Music, Kahil El Zabar, Chuck Webb; Editor, Tom Miller; Art Director, Kathy Domokos; an Avant Garde production in association with Woolf Vision Enterprises; Dolby Stereo; Foto-Kem color; Rated R; 109 minutes; April release. **CAST:** Darnell Williams (Thomas Clark), Salli Richardson (Valerie Young), Daniel Gardner (Spoony), Raymond Whitefield (Alex), Debra Crable (Michelle), Darryl Roberts (B.J.), Byron Stewart (Pierre), Jonelle Kennedy (Sharon), Charnele Brown (Paula Murray)

RIGHT: Chuck Norris, Jonathan Brandis in *Sidekicks* © Vision International

Salena and J.C. Barone in
Nitrate Kisses © Strand Releasing

Gina Gershon, Richard Edson in
Joey Breaker © Skouras Pictures

NITRATE KISSES (Strand Releasing) Producer/Director / Screenplay/Photography/Editor, Barbara Hammer; Black and white; Not rated; 63 minutes; April release. Documentary on gay lifestyles and history.

STAR TIME (Northern Arts) Producer/Director/Screenplay, Alexander Cassini; Co-Producer, Megan Barnett; Photography, Fernando Arguelles; Music, Blake Leyh; Designers, Carey Meyer, David Jensen; Editor/Associate Producer, Stan Salfas; Ultra-Stereo; Foto-Kem color; Not rated; 85 minutes; April release. **CAST:** John P. Ryan (Sam Bones), Michael St. Gerard (Henry Pinkle), Maureen Teefy (Wendy), Thomas Newman (Guard), Dana Dantine, Duncan Roulend, Robert Resnick, Angel Santana (Newscasters), Reza Mizbani (Iranian Anchorman), Andy Hart (Boy), Sandra Lee (Girl), Alexander Cassini (Anchorman), Nancy Kaufman (Dead Julie), Simone Fievez (Game Show Hostess), Kathy Andrews (Final Anchorwoman), Paul Kaufman, Rory Aylward, Chuck Hart (Dead People at dinner table), Maggie Schmidt (Woman in house), Larry Goodhue, John Provost (Paramedics), Terry Mitchell, Lisa Malkiewicz (Donut Commercial Girls)

BY THE SWORD (Movie Group/Hansen Entertainment) Producers, Peter E. Strauss, Marlon Staggs; Supervising Producer, Deborah Scott; Executive Producers, Phillip Rose, Robert Straight, Frank Giustra; Director, Jeremy Kagan; Screenplay, John McDonald, James Donadio; Photography, Arthur Albert; Designer, Gary Frutkoff; Music, Bill Conti; Costumes, Susan Nininger; Editor, David Holden; Casting, Joy Todd; a Foil/Film Horizon production, presented in association with SVS Pictures; Dolby Stereo; Deluxe color; Rated R; 91 minutes; May release. **CAST:** F. Murray Abraham (Suba), Eric Roberts (Villard), Mia Sara (Clavelli), Chris Rydell (Trebor), Elaine Kagan (Rachel), Brett Cullen (Gallagher), Doug Wert (Hobbs), Sherry Hursey (Tanos), Stoney Jackson (Johnson), Caroline Barclay (Tatiana), Peter Cohl (Calder), Stephen Polk (Williams), Ennalls Berl (Dana), Dharvi Darrelle (Landlady), Eve Laura Kagan (Daughter), Jonathan Strauss (Son), Diane Erickson (Woman), John Sheehan (Doorman), Joseph Socolof (Young Suba), Nate McCoy (Young Villard), Cathy Gallagher (Mrs. Villard), Mark Ivie (Mr. Villard)

JOEY BREAKER (Skouras) Producers, Amos Poe, Steven Starr; Line Producer, Louis Tancredi; Director/Screenplay, Steven Starr; Photography, Joe DeSalvo; Designer, Jocelyne Beaudoin; Editor, Michael Schweitzer; Music, Paul Aston; Costumes, Jessica Haston; Casting, Deborah Aquila; a Poe production; DuArt color; Rated R; 92 minutes; May release. **CAST:** Richard Edson (Joey Breaker), Cedella Marley (Cyna Worthington), Fred Fondren (Alfred Moore), Erik King (Hip Hop Hank), Gina Gershon (Jennie Chaser), Philip Seymour Hoffman (Wiley McCall), Mary Joy (Esther Trigliani), Sam Coppola (Sid Kramer), Michael Imperioli (Larry Metz), Olga Bagnasco (Karina Danzi), Laurence Mason (Lester White), Seth Gilliam (Jeremy Brasher), John Costelloe (Randy Jeter), Sunday Theodore (Morissa Marker), George Bartenieff (Dean Milford), Parker Posey (Irene Kildare), Christopher Logan Healy (Mike Dale), James Dickson (Hollywood Producer), Alison Moir (Actress on street), Joe Gioco (Karina's Manager), Larry Mart (Agent in audience), Beverly Burchett (Mineola Waitress), Anthony Ventola (Astro Waiter)

DELIVERED VACANT (Islet) Producer/Director/Photography/Editor, Nora Jacobson; Color; Not rated; 118 minutes; May release. Documentary on the 1980's gentrification of Hoboken, New Jersey.

CHILDREN OF FATE (First Run Features) Producer, Adam Friedson; Executive Director/Executive Producer, Robert M. Young; Directors, Andrew Young, Susan Todd; Color/black and white; Not rated; 85 minutes; May release. Documentary on Cortile Cascino, a poor section of Palermo, incorporating footage from the un-televised 1961 tv documentary Cortile Cascino, directed by Robert M. Young and Michael Roemer.

HAPPILY EVER AFTER (First National Film) Producer, Lou Scheimer; Director, John Howley; Sequence Directors, Gian Celestri, Kamoon Song, Larry White; Screenplay, Robby London, Martha Moran; Photography, Fred Ziegler; Editor, Jeffrey C. Patch, Joe Gall; Music, Frank W. Becker; Art Director, John Grusd; a Filmation presentation; Dolby Stereo; CFI color; Rated G; 74 minutes; May release. **VOICE CAST:** Irene Cara (Snow White), Edward Asner (Scowl), Carol Channing (Muddy), Dom DeLuise (Looking Glass), Phyllis Diller (Mother Nature), Zsa Zsa Gabor (Blossom), Jonathan Harris (Sunflower), Michael Horton (Prince), Sally Kellerman (Sunburn), Malcolm McDowell (Lord Maliss), Tracey Ullman (Moonbeam/Thunderella), Frank Welker (Batso)

F. Murray Abraham, Eric Roberts in
By the Sword © The Movie Group

Children of Fate © First Run Features

Thomas Ian Griffith in *Excessive Force*
© New Line Cinema Corp.

Charleen Swansea, Ross McElwee in *Time Indefinite*
© First Run Features

EXCESSIVE FORCE (New Line Cinema) Producers, Thomas Ian Griffth, Erwin Stoff, Oscar L. Costo; Director, Jon Hess; Executive Producer, Michael Harpster; Screenplay, Thomas Ian Griffith; Photography, Donald M. Morgan; Editor, Alan Baumgarten; Designer, Michael Z. Hanan; Music, Charles Bernstein; Presented in association with Ian Page productions and 3 Arts productions; Dolby Stereo; Deluxe Color; Rated R; 90 minutes; May release. **CAST:** Thomas Ian Griffith (Terry McCain), Charlotte Lewis (Anna Gilmour), James Earl Jones (Jake), Tony Todd (Frankie Hawkins), Lance Henriksen (Devlin), Burt Young (Sal DiMarco), Paula Anglin (Yvonne), Bobby Bass (Limo Driver), W. Earl Brown (Vinnie DiMarco), Steve Chambers (Thug #2), Cark Giarfalio, Mario Roberts (Guards), Antoni Corone (Fat Tommy), Liza Cruzat (Hooker), Leon Delaney, Tony Epper (Hitmen), Christopher Garbrecht (Red), Ian Gomez (Lt. Landry/ Lucas), Tom Hodges (Dylan), Marie Jagger (Waitress), Brian Leahy (Irish Leader), Monica McCarthy (Sam Atwell), Turk Miller (DiMarco's Thug), Charles Picerni, Jr. (News Reporter), Randy Popplewell (Tony), James Ryder (Make-up Artist), Dick Sollenberger (Dexter), Lisa Soule (Club Girl), Susan Wood (Lisa)

SEX IS... (Outsider Prod.) Producers, Marc Huestis, Lawrence Helman; Director, Marc Huestis; Photography, Fawn Yacker; Editors, Lara Mac, Hrafnhildur Gunnarsdottir; Music, Donny Viscuso, Pussy Tourette; Color/Black and white; Not rated; 80 minutes; May release. Documentary in which several gay men and lesbians talk of their sexual experiences.

INVADER (21st Century) Produer, John R. Ellis; Executive Producers, Menahem Golan, Ami Artzi; Director/Screenplay/Photography/Editor, Philip J. Cook; Music, David Bartley; Color; Rated R; 95 minutes; May release. **CAST:** Hans Bachmann (Frank McCall), A. Thomas Smith (Capt. Harry Anders), Rick Foucheux (Col. Robert Faraday), John Cooke (Gen. John Anheiser), Robert Biedermann (Harvey Briggs), Ralph Bluemke (Rogers), Allison Sheehy (Sandy), Jim Byrnes (Powell), George Stover (Burke), Brown Cardwell (Kelly)

CARNOSAUR (Concorde) Producer, Mike Elliott; Executive Producer, Roger Corman; Director/Screenplay, Adam Simon; Based on the novel by Harry Adam Knight; Photography, Keith Holland; Designer,

Aaron Osborne; Editor, Richard Gentner; Music, Nigel Holton; Visual Effects Supervisor, Alan Lasky; Creature Designer/Creator, John Carl Buechler, Magical Media Industries; a co-production of New Horizons Corp.; Color; Rated R; 82 minutes; May release. **CAST:** Diane Ladd (Dr. Jane Tiptree), Raphael Sbarge ("Doc" Smith), Jennifer Runyon (Thrush), Harrison Page (Sheriff), Clint Howard (Trucker)

TIME INDEFINITE (First Run Features) Producer/Director/ Photography/Editor, Ross McElwee; Color; Not rated; 117 minutes; May release. Documentary on life and death in McElwee's family.

EQUINOX (I.R.S. Releasing) Producer, David Blocker; Executive Producers, Nicolas Stiliadis, Syd Cappe, Sandy Stern; Director/Screenplay, Alan Rudolph; Photography, Elliot Davis; Designer, Steven Legler; Editor, Michael Ruscio; Costumes, Sharen Davis; Casting, Pam Dixon; an SC Entertainment International presentation; Alpha Cine color; Rated R; 110 minutes; June release. **CAST:** Matthew Modine (Henry Petosa/Freddy Ace/Immanuel), Lara Flynn Boyle (Beverly Franks), Fred Ward (Paris), Tyra Ferrell (Sonya Kirk), Marisa Tomei (Rosie Copa), Kevin J. O'Connor (Russell Franks), Tate Donovan (Richie Nudd), Lori Singer (Sharon Ace), M. Emmet Walsh (Pete Petosa), Gailard Sartain (Dandridge), Tony Genaro (Eddie Gutierrez), Angel Aviles (Anna Gutierrez), Dirk Blocker (Red), Kristen Ellickson (Young Helena), Pat Clemons (Helena), Debra Dusay (Judith Hamner), Les Podewell (Jerome Hamner), Megan Lee Ochs (Bess), Carlos Sanz (Harold), Lenora Finley (Maye), Diane Wheeler-Nicholson (Self Defense Victim/Drunk), Isabell Monk (Apartment Manager), Billy Silva (Sabujii), Tom Kasat (I.M. Stong), Paul Meshejian (Ralph), Robert Gould (Mel), Shirley Venard (Villa Capri Waitress), Willie Burks II (Willie), Pancho Demmings (Morgue Worker), Jack Walsh (Newspaper Man), Martin Marinaro (Attendant), Elizabeth Ann Gray (Large Woman on bus), Wayne A. Evenson (Large Woman's Companion), Randy Gust, Jeff Warner (Punks), Matthew Dudley, John Sargent (Toughs), Dale P. Dunham (Co-Worker), Frank Davis (Marsh), Mark Modine (Cook), Ken Earl (Banker), VInnie Curto (Gangster), Chris George (Villa Capri Pianist), Kerry Hoyt (Kerry), Rebecca Sabot (Paris' Girlfriend), Suzette Tarzia (Charlene)

Carnosaur © Concorde

Matthew Modine, M. Emmet Walsh
in *Equinox* © I.R.S. Releasing

Michelle, Cornelius in *Once Upon a Forest* © Twentieth Century Fox

ONCE UPON A FOREST (20th Century Fox) Producers, David Kirschner, Jerry Mills; Executive Producers, William Hanna, Paul Gertz; Director, Charles Grosvenor; Screenplay, Mark Young, Kelly Ward; Based on the story by Rae Lambert; Music, James Horner; Casting, Mike Fenton, Judy Taylor, Allison Cowitt; Animation Director, Dave Michener; Art Director, Carol Holman Grosvenor; Supervising Film Editor, Pat A. Foley; a Hanna-Barbera production produced in association with HTV Cymru/Wales; Dolby Stereo; CFI color; Rated G; 80 minutes; June release. **VOICE CAST:** Michael Crawford (Cornelius), Ben Vereen (Phineas), Ellen Blain (Abigail), Ben Gregory (Edgar), Paige Gosney (Russell), Elizabeth Moss (Michelle), Paul Eiding (Abigail's Father), Janet Waldo (Edgar's Mom), Susan Silo (Russell's Mom), Wil Nipper (Willy), Charlie Adler (Waggs), Rickey Collins (Bosworth), Angel Harper (Bosworth's Mom), Don Reed (Marshbird), Robert David Hall (Truck Driver), Benjamin Smith (Russell's Brother), Haven Hartman (Russell's Sister)

Jonathan Silverman, Terry Kiser, Troy Beyer,
Andrew McCarthy in *Weekend at Bernie's II*
© TriStar Pictures

WEEKEND AT BERNIE'S II (TriStar) Producers, Victor Drai, Joseph Perez; Executive Producer, Angiolo Stella; Director/Screenplay, Robert Klane; Co-Producer, Don Carmody; Photography, Edward Morey III; Designer, Michael Bolton; Editor, Peck Prior; Music, Peter Wolf; Costumes, Fionn; Casting, Jason LaPadura; an ArtimM production; Dolby Stereo; Deluxe color; Rated PG; 89 minutes; July release. **CAST:** Andrew McCarthy (Larry Wilson), Jonathan Silverman (Richard Parker), Terry Kiser (Bernie Lomax), Troy Beyer (Claudia), Barry Bostwick (Hummel), Tom Wright (Charles), Steve James (Henry), Novella Nelson (Mobu), Phil Coccioletti, Gary Dourdan (Cartel Men), James Lally (Morgue Attendant), Michael Rogers (Island Cop), Stack Pierce (Claudia's Dad), Constance Shulman (Tour Operator), Jennie Moreau (Brenda), Curt Karibalis (Hotel Manager), Peewee Piemonte (Arnold), Christine Nerfin (Hotel Hostess), John Hodge (Band Member), Samantha Phillips (Pretty Young Thing), Rudy Warner (Jitney Driver), Caitlin Klane (Little Girl with radio), David Lipman (Movie Patron), Lyle Howry, Ben Lemon, Filippo Cassinelli (New York Cops), Winston de Lugo (Mr. Jennings), J.C. Scott-Klane (Secretary), Cedric Bones (Bank Executive), William Lucas (Store Clerk), Lance Durham (Hotel Beach Employee), Hillel E. Silverman (Maitre'd), Matt Locker (Porter), Ernestine Elena Vanterpool (Woman in store), Robert R. Wilis (EMS Worker)

ROAD SCHOLAR (Samuel Goldwyn Co.) Producer/Director, Roger Weisberg; Screenplay, Andrei Codrescu; Photography/Co-Director, Jean de Segonzac; Editor, Alan Miller; Associate Producer, Daniel Klein; Music, North Forty Music/Wave Band Sound; Color; Not rated; 81 minutes; July release. Documentary of radio commentator Andrei Codrescu's drive across America.

Andrei Codrescu (left) in *Road Scholar*
© Samuel Goldwyn Co

FROM HOLLYWOOD TO HANOI (Friendship Bridge Prods.) Producer/Director/Screenplay, Tiana Thi Thanh Nga; Photography, Michael Dodds, Bruce Dorfman, Jamie Maxtone-Graham; Supervising Editor, Pam Wise; Music, Allan Gus; Color; Not rated; 78 minutes; July release. Filmmaker Tiana Thi Thanh Nga documents her life from Saigon to the U.S. where she journeyed to Hollywood to become an actress.

I'LL LOVE YOU FOREVER ... TONIGHT (Headliner Prods.) Producer/Director/ Screenplay, Edgar Michael Bravo; Photography, Jeff Crum; Designer, John Edgar Bledsoe; Music, Robert Cairns; a Cinema Bravo production; Color; Not rated; 80 minutes; July release. **CAST:** Paul Marius (Ethan), Jason Adams (Dennis), David Poynter (Peter), Roger Shank (Steve), Miles Wilshire (Jeff), Tom Janes (Joe), Steve Bollinger (Roger), Troy Bryant (2nd Man outside bar), Brian Tso (Young Man in bar), Chuck Schuelke (Elder Man at resort), Alejandro D. Wagmeister (Ethan as a child)

Jason Adams, Paul Marius in *I'll Love You Forever Tonight*
© Headliner Prods.

CHEATIN' HEARTS (Trimark) Producers, Rod McCall, Catherine Wanek; Executive Producers, Sally Kirkland, James Brolin; Director/Screenplay, Rod McCall; Photography, Barry Markowitz; Editor, Curtis Edge; Designer, Susan Brand; Music, George S. Clinton; Supervising Producer, Howard Worth; a King/Moonstone presentation; Color; Not rated; 90 minutes; July release. **CAST:** James Brolin (Henry), Sally Kirkland (Jenny), Pamela Gidley (Samantha), Kris Kristofferson (Tom), Laura Johnson (Patsy), Michael Moore (Bill), Renee Estevez (Kat), Mickey Cottrell (Brady), Mark Voltura (Ronny), Jim Magee (Bartender), Gary Naylor (Chuck), Jackson D. Kane (Wesley), Ed Ostertag (Preacher), Lewisa Goggin (Girl in bar), Paula Baz (Dairy Queen Girl), Martha Ostertag (Girl in pickup), Francisco Topete (Hotel Clerk)

James Brolin, Sally Kirkland in *Cheatin' Hearts* © Trimark

TOM AND JERRY: THE MOVIE (Miramax) Producer/Director, Phil Roman; Executive Producers, Roger Mayer, Jack Petrik, Hans Brockmann, Justin Ackerman; Creative Consultants, Joseph Barbera, David Simone; Screenplay, Dennis Marks; Based on characters created by William Hanna and Joseph Barbera; Songs, Henry Mancini, Leslie Bricusse; Music Score, Henry Mancini; Sequence Directors, John Sparey, Monte Young, Bob Nesler, Adam Kuhlman, Eric Daniels, Jay Jackson, Skip Jones; Supervising Editor, Sam Horta; Art Directors, Michael Peraza, Jr., Michael Humphries; a Live Entertainment and Turner Entertainment Company in association with WMG presentation of a Film Roman production; Dolby Stereo; Color; Rated G; 80 minutes; July release. **VOICE CAST:** Richard Kind (Tom), Dana Hill (Jerry), Charlotte Rae (Aunt Pristine Figg), Tony Jay (Lickboot), Henry Gibson (Dr. Applecheek), Rip Taylor (Captain Kiddie), Howard Morris (Squawk), Michael Bell (Ferdinand), Edmund Gilbert (Puggsy), David L. Lander (Frankie da Flea), Anndi McAfee (Robyn Starling)

Jerry, Tom in *Tom and Jerry: The Movie* © Miramax Films

BENEFIT OF THE DOUBT (Miramax) Producers, Michael Spielberg, Brad M. Gilbert; Executive Producers, Bob Weinstein, Harvey Weinstein; Co-Producer, Dieter Geissler; Director, Jonathan Heap; Screenplay, Jeffrey Polman, Christopher Keyser; Story, Michael Lieber; Photography, Johnny Jensen; Music, Hummie Mann; Editor, Sharyn L. Ross; Art Director, David Seth Lazan; Costumes, Ann Foley; Casting,

Rachel Abroms, Owens Hill; a Monument Pictures production co-presented in association with CineVox Entertainment; Ultra Stereo; Deluxe color; Rated R; 90 minutes; July release. **CAST:** Donald Sutherland (Frank), Amy Irving (Karen), Rider Strong (Pete), Christopher McDonald (Dan), Graham Greene (Calhoun), Theodore Bikel (Gideon Lee), Gisele Kovach (Susanna), Ferdinand Mayne (Mueller), Julie Hasel (Young Karen), Patricia Tallman (Karen's Mom), Ralph McTurk (Trooper), Shane McCabe (Wayland), Margaret Johnson (Waitress), Heinrich James (Marina Guard), Jean Fowler (Examiner), Steve Easterling (Coach), John Bachelder (Young Guy), Don Collier (Charlie), Douglas Deane (Turner), David Hammond (Jimmy), Dustin Leighton (Luke), Tanner (Pete's Dog)

Donald Sutherland, Amy Irving, Rider Strong in
Benefit of the Doubt © Miramax Films

HOLD ME, THRILL ME, KISS ME (Mad Dog Pictures) Producer, Travis Swords; Executive Producer, Martin Ira Rubin; Supervising Producer, Alain Silver; Director/ Screenplay, Joel Hershman; Photography, Kent Wakeford; Editor, Kathryn Himoff; Designer, Dominic Wymark; Costumes, Cathy Cooper, Bradley Bayou; Music, Gerald Gouriet; Casting, Doreen Lane; Color; Not rated; 92 minutes; July release. **CAST:** Adrienne Shelly (Dannie), Max Parrish (Eli/Bud/Fritz), Sean Young (Twinkle), Diane Ladd (Lucille), Andrea Naschak (Sabra), Bela Lehoczky (Laszlo), Ania Suli (Olga), Timothy Leary (Mr. Jones), Vic Trevino (Julio), Allan Warnick (Pet Mortician), Joseph Anthony Richards (Duane), Martha Shaw (Social Security Clerk), Frank Noon (Braindead Biker), Mary Lanier (Lucille's Mother), Bruce E. Morrow (Justice of the Peace), Jo Farkas (Justice's Wife), Toshi Toda (Asian Passenger), Cynthia Whitney (Waitress at Illusions), Travis Swords (2nd Cop), John Auxier (Krush), Beauregard (Clock Buyer), George Ontiveros, Jr. (Tattoo Artist), Terri Laird (Tattooed Dancer), Robert Hoover (Illusions Patron), Alain Joel Silver (Omar), Nicole Sassaman (Girl on a leash), Gus the Dog (Himself)

Adrienne Shelly in *Hold Me Thrill Me Kiss Me*
© Mad Dog Pictures

Brion James, Geoffrey Lewis in *Wishman* © Curb Esquire

Juliette Lewis, C. Thomas Howell in *That Night*
© Regency Enterprises V.O.F. /Le Studio Canal⁺

WISHMAN (Curb Esquire/Monarch) Producer, Lon Tinney; Director/Screenplay, Michael Marvin; Photography, Steve Shaw; Editor, John Orland; Color; Rated PG; 89 minutes; July release. **CAST:** Paul LeMat (Basil "Basie" Banks), Geoffrey Lewis (Leggett "Hitch" Hitchcock), Brion James (Jack Rose), Quinn Kessler (Lily Andon), Paul Gleason (Joshua Silverstein), Rance Howard (Detective Sturgis)

JASON GOES TO HELL: THE FINAL FRIDAY (New Line Cinema) Producer, Sean S. Cunningham; Director, Adam Marcus; Screenplay, Dean Lorey, Jay Huguely; Story, Jay Huguely, Adam Marcus; Photography, William Dill; Designer, W. Brooke Wheeler; Special Makeup Effects, Kurtzman, Nicotero and Berger EFX Group; Special Visual Effects, Al Magliochetti; Music, Harry Manfredini; Editor, David Handman; Casting, Hughes/Moss, C.S.A., David Giella; Dolby Stereo; Deluxe color; Rated R; 88 minutes; August release. **CAST:** John D. LeMay (Steven Freeman), Kari Keegan (Jessica Kimble), Kane Hodder (Jason Voorhees), Steven Williams (Creighton Duke), Steven Culp (Robert Campbell), Erin Gray (Diana Kimble), Rusty Schwimmer (Joey B), Richard Gant (Coroner), Leslie Jordan (Shelby), Billy Green Bush (Sheriff Landis), Kipp Marcus (Randy), Andrew Bloch (Josh), Adam Cranner (Ward), Allison Smith (Vicki), Julia Michaels (Elizabeth Marcus, FBI), James Gleason (Agent Abernathy), Dean Lorey (Asst. Coroner), Tony Ervolina (FBI Agent), Diana Georger (Edna, Josh's Girlfriend), Adam Marcus (Officer Bish), Mark Thompson (Officer Mark), Brian Phelps (Officer Brian), Blake Conway (Officer Andell), Madelon Curtis (Officer Ryan), Michelle Clunie (Deborah, the blonde camper), Michael Silver (Luke, the boy camper), Kathryn Atwood (Alexis, the dark haired camper)

THAT NIGHT (Warner Bros.) formerly *One Hot Summer*; Producers, Arnon Milchan, Steven Reuther; Executive Producers, Julie Kirkham, Elliott Lewis; Director/ Screenplay, Craig Bolotin; Based upon the novel by Alice McDermott; Photography, Bruce Surtees; Designer, Maher Ahmad; Editor, Priscilla Nedd-Friendly; Costumes, Carol Ramsey; Music, David Newman; Casting, Mali Finn, Don Finn; a Le Studio Canal+, Regency Enterprises and Alcor Films presentation; Dolby Stereo; Technicolor; Rated PG-13; 89 minutes; August release. **CAST:** C. Thomas Howell (Rick), Juliette Lewis (Sheryl O'Conner), Helen Shaver (Ann O'Conner), Eliza Dushku (Alice Bloom), J. Smith-Cameron (Carol Bloom), John Dossett (Larry Bloom), Katherine Heigl (Kathryn), Sarah

Joy Stevenson (Barbara), Ben and Thomas Terzulli (Mickey and Max Meyer), Michael Costello (Don O'Conner), Kathryn Meisle (Mrs. Carpenter), Adam Lefevre (Mr. Carpenter), Carolyn Swift (Mrs. Rossi), Charles Musumeci (Mr. Rossi), Debora Robertson (Mrs. Meyer), John Healey, Jr. (Mr. Meyer), Becky Ann Baker (Mrs. Bell), Paul Morella (Mr. Bell), Sabrina Lloyd (Jeanette), Thompson Hunt (Coleman), Rick Schatz (Vitelli), Duncan Hood, Paul Hjelmervik (Men at wake), Celia Clark (Wife at wake), Andrea Monter (Little Girl), Danny Kroff (Danny the Date), Luci Roucis (Young Nun), Barbara Barry (Sister Lorraine), Desiree Marie, Jennifer Albright (Girls), Sarah Rose (Pam), Lem Wills (Bus Driver)

MY BOYFRIEND'S BACK (Touchstone) formerly *Johnny Zombie*; Producer, Sean S. Cunningham; Director, Bob Balaban; Screenplay, Dean Lorey; Photography, Mac Ahlberg; Designer, Michael Hanan; Editor, Michael Jablow; Music, Harry Manfredini; Associate Producer, Deborah Hayn-Cass; Costumes, Kimberly Tillman; Makeup Artist, Kimberly Greene; Distributed by Buena Vista Pictures; Dolby Stereo; Technicolor; Rated PG-13; 84 minutes; August release. **CAST:** Andrew Lowery (Johnny Dingle), Traci Lind (Missy McCloud), Danny Zorn (Eddie Denver), Edward Herrmann (Mr. Dingle), Mary Beth Hurt (Mrs. Dingle), Jay O. Sanders (Sheriff McCloud), Libby Villari (Camille McCloud), Matthew Fox (Buck Van Patten), Philip Hoffman (Chuck Bronski), Paul Dooley (Big Chuck), Austin Pendleton (Dr. Bronson), David Womack Galewsky (Young Johnny), Zachary Lefenfeld (Young Eddie), Nicholas Waggoner (Young Buck), Zack Steeg (Young Chuck), Brooke Adams (Young Missy), Bob Dishy (Murray the Gravedigger), Cloris Leachman (Maggie the Zombie Expert), Paxton Whitehead (Judge in Heaven), Jane Simoneau (Lady with apple pie), Delray Cordell (Kid on bike), Eunice Clark (Johnny's School Teacher), Michael Petty (Gerald the Nerdy Student), Larry Strub (Referee), Joe Stevens (Robber at convenience store), Jerry Haynes (Minister at funeral), Phil Ross (Scientist in horror film/French Waiter), Oliver Tull, Matthew McConaughey (Guys), Zeke Mills, Netha Stanton (Movie Goers), Melissa Taub (Beefy Girl in library), Nan Brown (Reporter Brenda), Christian Burrows (Little Chuck), Brandi Burkett (Brandi), LaBrooke Brannon (Staci), Stephanie Wing (Vanna), Jimmy Bennett III (Kid on trike), Gary Graves, Edwin Neal (Big Chuck's Henchmen), Denise Montgomery, Carole Zenner Clester, Nancy Moore, Diane Perella, Mike "TJ" Kennedy, Marco Perella, Paul Menzel, Jack Craig (Townspeople)

Allison Smith, Steven Culp in
Jason Goes to Hell © New Line Cinema Corp.

Traci Lind, Andrew Lowery in
My Boyfriend's Back © Touchstone Pictures

SURF NINJAS (New Line Cinema) Producer, Evzen Kolar; Executive Producers, Sara Risher, Dan Gordon, Kevin Moreton; Director, Neal Israel; Screenplay, Dan Gordon; Photography, Arthur Albert, Victor Hammer; Editor, Tom Walls; Designer, Michael Novotny; Costumes, Deborah La Gorce Kramer; Music, David Kitay; Associate Producer, Ernie Reyes, Jr.; Casting, Annette Benson; Stunts/Martial Arts Coordinator, Philip Tan; Martial Arts Choreography, Ernie Reyes, Sr.; Dolby Stereo; Deluxe color; Rated PG; 87 minutes; August release. **CAST:** Ernie Reyes, Jr. (Johnny McQuinn), Rob Schneider (Iggy), Tone Loc (Lt. Spence), John Karlen (Mac McQuinn), Ernie Reyes, Sr. (Zatch), Nicolas Cowan (Adam McQuinn), Keone Young (Baba Ram), Kelly Hu (Ro-May), Leslie Nielsen (Colonel Chi), Oliver Mills (Moto Surfer), Jonathan Schmock (School Cop), Neal Israel (Mr. Dunbar), Vladimir Parra, Brandon Karrer, Dathan Aragon, Philip Bayless (Backup Singers), Phillip Tan (Capt. Ming), Romy Walthall (Miss Robertson), Rachel Kolar (Rachel), Yoni Gordon (Wendell), Sritao Thepchasoon (Dungeon Guard), Nathan Jung (Manchu), Thep Thien-Chai (Gong Man), Sa-Ngud (Prisoner), Sheng Meng (Major Snee), Tanin Tapmongkol (King), Montatip Kaewprasert (Queen), Rick Dorio (Sgt. Bork), Jim Vallely, Mitch Horowitz (Surf Dudes), Mark Dutt, Desi Singh (Squad Car Cops), Tad Horino (Gum-Bey), Young Jue (Patu Sani Man), Marisa Theodore (Surf Babe), Pete Antico, Robert Terry Lee (Cops), Bowman Chung (Victim)

Robert Downey Jr. in *The Last Party* © Triton Pictures

Ernie Reyes Jr., Rob Schneider, Nicolas Cowan
in *Surf Ninjas* © New Line Cinema Corp.

THE LAST PARTY (Triton Pictures) Producers, Eric Cahan, Donovan Leitch, Josh Richman; Executive Producers, Samuel D. Waksal, Elliott Kastner; Directors, Mark Benjamin, Marc Levin; Photography, Mark Benjamin; Editor, Wendey Stanzler; Co-Producer, Garth Stein; Color; Not rated; 96 minutes; August release. Documentary following actor Robert Downey Jr. as he reports on the country's political situation during the 1992 presidential campaign, with Bill Clinton, Ann Palmer, Hilary Anderson, Patti Davis, Robert Downey Sr., Josh Richman, Curtis Sliwa, Spike Lee, Tracy Gray, Vanessa Warner, Jerry Brown, Kate Barnhart, Joey DiPaolo, Roger Clinton, AZ, Oliver Stone, TKAE, AVON TC5, DOZE TC5, Al Sharpton, Shane Clay, Dave Mustaine, Steven Badagliacco, Suzanne Soderberg, Pasha Jovahopi-Saatchi, Mike Evans, Richard Lewis, Vanessa Vadim, Deborah Falconer, B-Real, G. Gordon Liddy, Mark Levin, Sean Penn, David Baerwald, Mike Ruppert, Senator John Kerry, Representative Dana Rohrabacher, William F. Hamilton III, Michael Kehr, Alvin High School Band, Peter Jennings, Jerry Falwell, TRQ, Allison H. Daniel, Fred R. Bartlett Jr., Mary Stuart Masterson, Guillermo Flores, Steve and Susan Stepanski, Sara and Brian Johnson, The Spatterdashes, Oliver North, Quanell X, Willie D., Daniel Lopez, Matt Dentino, James Learned, Eric Cahan, Connie Benesch, Laura Downey

FATHER HOOD (Hollywood Pictures) Producers, Nicholas Pileggi, Anant Singh, Gillian Gorfil; Executive Producers, Jeffrey Chernov, Richard H. Prince; Director, Darrell James Roodt; Screenplay, Scott Spencer; Photography, Mark Vicente; Designer, David Barkham; Editor, David Heitner; Costumes, Donfeld; Music, Patrick O'Hearn; Casting, Michael Fenton, Allison Cowitt; Distributed by Buena Vista Pictures; Dolby Stereo; Technicolor; Rated PG-13; 94 minutes; August release. **CAST:** Patrick Swayze (Jack Charles), Halle Berry (Kathleen Mercer), Sabrina Lloyd (Kelly Charles), Brian Bonsall (Eddie Charles), Michael Ironside (Jerry), Diane Ladd (Rita), Bob Gunton (Lazzaro), Adrienne Barbeau (Celeste), Georgann Johnson (Judge), Marvin J. McIntyre (Skinny Guy), William Bumiller (Travis), Vanessa Marquez (Delores),

Martha Velez-Johnson (Mrs. Carter), Ray De Mattis (Lawyer), Joshua Lucas (Andy), Vic Bordelon (Guzman), Gregory Cooke, Kamar de los Reyes (Drug Dealers), John Biondi (Benny the Bailiff), Casey Coleman (Young Kid), Jerry Gaona, James Brown III (Foster Kids), Jennifer Banko (Teenage Girl), Cathy Celario (Dealer), Raymond "Reno" Lee Nichols (Businessman), Michael Delano (Pit Boss), Gene Jones (Security Guard), David Pressman, Daryn Holland (Gamblers), Randy Crow (Highway Cop), Bob Thompson (Counterman), Christine Poole (Reporter), Don Hohman (Youth Worker), Scott Eddo, John Manca (Detectives), Gary Epper (Trucker), Ignacio "Nacho" Pineda, Jr. (Sheriff at caves), Eric Glenn (Young Cop), Celso I. Martinez (Cop #2), Rick Zumwalt (Burly Guy), Steve Picerni (Swat Leader), Charles Picerni, Sr., Jeff Dashnaw (Body Guards), Dell Aldrich, Bill Sutherland (Panel Members), Michael Moody (Driver), Ransom Walrod (Blind Driver)

112TH & CENTRAL: THROUGH THE EYES OF THE CHILDREN (Flatfield Prods.) Producers, Jim Chambers, Hal Hisey, Vondie Curtis-Hall; Director, John Chambers; Photography, John Simmons; Fujicolor; Not rated; 108 minutes; August release. Documentary about the effects of the April 1992 Los Angeles riots on the children of South Central L.A. featuring Lorna Anozie, J. Lisa Chang, Kasi Lemmons, Virginia Madsen, Maya McLaughlin, Mimi Savage, Robert Walker, Josie Wechsler, Darnell Williams.

SPACE IS THE PLACE (Rhapsody Films) Producer, Jim Newman; Director, John Coney; Screenplay, Joshua Smith, Sun Ra, Christopher Brooks, Jim Newman; Editor, Mark Gorney; Color; Not rated; 63 minutes; August release. Documentary on musician Sun Ra.

Brian Bonsall, Sabrina Lloyd, Patrick Swayze
in *Father Hood* © Hollywood Pictures

Mark Dacascos, Joselito Santo in *Only the Strong*
© Twentieth Century Fox

ONLY THE STRONG (20th Century Fox) Producers, Samuel Hadida, Stuart S. Shapiro, Steven G. Menkin; Executive Producer, Victor Hadida; Director, Sheldon Lettich; Screenplay, Sheldon Lettich, Luis Esteban; Photography, Edward Pei; Designer, J. Mark Harrington; Editor, Stephen Semel; Costumes, Patricia Field; Music, Harvey W. Mason; Casting, James F. Tarzia; Presented in association with Freestone Pictures & Davis Films; Dolby Stereo; Eastman color; Rated PG-13; 96 minutes; August release. **CAST:** Mark Dacascos (Louis Stevens), Stacey Travis (Dianna), Geoffrey Lewis (Kerrigan), Paco Christian Prieto (Silverio), Todd Susman (Cochran), Jeffrey Anderson Gunter (Philippe - Jamaican Gang Leader), Richard Coca (Orlando), Roman Cardwell (Shay), Ryan Bollman (Donovan), Christian Klemash (Eddie), John Fionte (Cervantes), Joselito "Amen" Santo (Javier), John Gregory Kasper (Coach Kasper), Phyllis Sukoff (Mrs. Esposito), Antoni Corone (Green Beret Sgt.), Mellow Man Ace (Student Rapper), Felipe Savahge, Luis Esteban (Brazilians), Jim Vickers (Police Sgt.), Mark Salem (Cop #1), Joann Dukes (Newscaster), David Luther (School Security Guard), Adeniri S. Ajamu (Chief Ajamo), Alan Jordan (Chop Shop Foreman), Frank Dux (Welder), Tony De Leoni (Mechanics), Diego Perez (Mechanics), Diane Fraind, Henry Fraind (Teachers), Salvador Levy (Cuban Coffee Drinker), Junior Biggs (Jamaican Dealer), Iseline Celestin (Haitian Woman), Donna Kimball (Donovan's Mother), Steven G. Menkin (Doctor), Stuart S. Shapiro (John), Sergio Pereira, Michael F. Lagapa (Silverio's Bodyguards), Marq Withers (Philippe's Bodyguard #1)

Chris Young, Julian Sands in *Warlock: The Armageddon*
© Vidmark Inc.

WARLOCK: THE ARMAGEDDON (Trimark) Producers, Robert Levy, Peter Abrams; Director, Anthony Hickox; Screenplay, Sam Bernard, Kevin Rock; Story, Kevin Rock; Based on characters created by D.T. Twohy; Photography, Gerry Lively; Designer, Steve Hardie; Editor, Chris Cibelli; Costumes, Leonard Pollack; Casting, Alison Kohler; Associate Producer, Sam Bernard; Visual Effects, Bob Bailey; Dolby Stereo; Color; Rated R; 98 minutes; September release. **CAST:** Julian Sands (Warlock), Chris Young (Kenny Travis), Paula Marshall (Samantha), Steve Kahan (Will Travis), Charles Hallahan (Ethan Larson), R.G. Armstrong (Franks), Micole Mercurio (Kate), Craig Hurley (Andy), Bruce Glover (Ted Ellison), Dawn Ann Billings (Amanda Sloan), Zach

Galligan (Douglas), Joanna Pacula (Paula Dare), Wren Brown (Assistant), Gary Cervantes (Cabbie), Bryan Smith (Jimmy), "Michu" Meszaros (Augusto), Richard Zobel (Barker), Michelle Moffatt (Celine), Jeanne Mori (Receptionist), Mark L. Taylor (Drama Coach), Lawrence Mortorff (Druid #1), Michael Villella (Older Man), Ferdinand Mayne (One-Eyed Man), Shannon Kies (Young Woman), Sheryl Mary Lewis (Church Woman)

CACHAO... COMO SU RITMO NO HAY DOS (LIKE HIS RHYTHM THERE IS NO OTHER) (Cineson/Atlantico) Producers, Fausto Sanchez, Andy Garcia; Director, Andy Garcia; Photography, Al "Tiko" Lopez; Editor, Alan Geik; Color; Not rated; 111 minutes; September release. Documentary on mambo composer-performer Israel Lopez Cachao, featuring Israel Lopez Cachao, Andy Garcia, Paquito d'Rivera, Nestor Torres, Jose "Chomb" Silva, Alfredo "Chocolate" Armenteros.

ME AND VERONICA (Arrow Releasing) Producers, Mark Linn-Baker, Max Mayer, Nellie Nugiel, Leslie Urdang; Director, Don Scardino; Screenplay, Leslie Lyles; Photography, Michael Barrow; Editor, Jeffrey Wolf; Designer, John Arnone; Costumes, Patricia Mc-Gourty; Casting, Sheila Jaffe, Georgianne Walken; from True Pictures; Color; Rated R; 97 minutes; September release. **CAST:** Elizabeth McGovern (Fanny), Patricia Wettig (Veronica), Michael O'Keefe (Michael), John Heard (Frankie), Scott Renderer (Boner), Will Hare (Red).

Patricia Wettig, Elizabeth McGovern in *Me & Veronica*
© Arrow Releasing

SPLIT (E.F.T.) Producer, Ellen Fisher Turk; Directors, Ellen Fisher Turk, Andrew Weeks; Screenplay, Dan Chayefsky; Photography, Jacqueline Escolar, Mirjana Gall, Nick Manning, Josh Pease, Hank Rifkin, Ellen Fisher Turk; Editors, Peter Ringer, Keith Brown; Narrator, Wes Kent; Color; Not rated; 60 minutes; September release. Documentary on the life of drag queen International Crysis, with Brian Belovitch, David Burns, Amy Coleman, Jimmy Camica, Justin Davis, Michael Degenhardt, Gerald Duval, David Glamamore, Ron Jones, Codie Leone, Jeremiah Newton, Teri Paris, Rodney Pridgen, Maggie Ruzo

Salvador Dali, International Crysis in *Split* © E.F.T

Debi Mazar, John Cusack in *Money for Nothing*
© Hollywood Pictures

MONEY FOR NOTHING (Hollywood Pictures) formerly *Joey Coyle*; Producer, Tom Musca; Executive Producers, David Permut, Gordon Freedman, Matthew Tolmach; Director, Ramon Menendez; Screenplay, Ramon Menendez, Tom Musca, Carol Sobieski; Photography, Tom Sigel; Designer, Michelle Minch; Editor, Nancy Richardson; Music, Craig Safan; Costumes, Zeca Seabra; Co-Producer, Cyrus Yavneh; Casting, Victoria Thomas; Distributed by Buena Vista Pictures; Technicolor; Rated R; 100 minutes; September release. **CAST:** John Cusack (Joey Coyle), Debi Mazar (Monica Russo), Michael Madsen (Det. Laurenzi), Benicio Del Toro (Dino Palladino), Michael Rapaport (Kenny Kozlowski), Maury Chaykin (Vincente Goldoni), James Gandolfini (Billy Coyle), Fionnula Flanagan (Mrs. Coyle), Elizabeth Bracco (Eleanor Coyle), Ashleigh Dejon (Katie Coyle), Lenny Venito (Hrbek), Philip S. Hoffman (Cochran), Currie Graham (Dunleavy), Frankie Faison (Madigan), Ed Pansullo (Carini), Benji Schulman (Tough Kid), Sam Coppola (Bartender Lindey), Jeanne McCarthy (Red-Headed Waitress), Don Brockett (Beer Belly), Nicholas Giordano, Victoria Thomas (Detectives), Lonzo Green (Homeless Man), Bernie Canepari (Mr. Kozlowski), Iva Saraceni (Mrs. Kozlowski), Elizabeth Zajko (Bartender), Hank Stratton (Yuppie), Thomas N. Levine (Pool Player), Scott Kloes (Investment Counselor), Alice Drummond (Mrs. Breen), Della Crews (Lois Bowden), Don Cannon (TV News Anchor), Lenora Nemetz (Middle Aged Woman), Harish Saluja (Newstand Vendor), Kate Young (Neighbor), Joseph R. Gannascoli (Charlie DiSalvo), Monty Cox (Frogman), Joseph W. Bonacci (Thug), Robert Bella (Junior Bookie), Pete Ferry (Senior Bookie), Marty Kassab (Goldoni's Sweetie), Pete Iole (Airport Ben Franklin), David Norona (U.S. Air Ticket Clerk), Bingo O'Malley (Older Man), Ana De La Cruz (Airline Security Guard), Jeffrey Paul Johnson (Convenience Store Clerk), Betsy Molina (U.S. Air Flight Attendant), Bill Dalzell III, Barbara Russell (Travelers)

BOXING HELENA (Orion Classics) Producers, Carl Mazzocone, Philippe Caland; Executive Producers, James R. Schaeffer, Larry Sugar; Director/Screenplay, Jennifer Chambers Lynch; Story, Philippe Caland; Photography, Frank Byers; Editor, David Finfer; Music, Graeme Revell; Casting, Ferne Cassel; a Main Line Pictures presentation; Dolby Stereo; Technicolor; Rated R; 105 minutes; September release. **CAST:** Julian Sands (Dr. Nick Cavanaugh), Sherilyn Fenn (Helena), Bill Paxton (Ray O'Malley), Kurtwood Smith (Dr. Alan Harrison), Art Garfunkel (Dr. Lawrence Augustine), Betsy Clark (Anne Garrett), Nicolette Scorsese (Fantasy Lover/Nurse), Meg Register (Marion Cavanaugh), Bryan Smith (Russell), Marla Levine (Patricia), Kim Lentz (Nurse Diane), Lloyd T. Williams (Sam the Clerk), Carl Mazzocone Sr. (Pastor), Erik Shoaff (Uncle Charlie), Lisa Oz (Flower Shop Girl), Ted Manson (Mailman), Adele K. Schaeffer, Amy Levin (Flashback Party Women), Matt Berry (Young Nick Cavanaugh)

MORNING GLORY (Academy Entertainment) Producer, Michael Viner; Executive Producer, Jerry Leider; Director, Steven Hilliard Stern; Screenplay, Charles Jarrot, Deborah Raffin; Based on the novel by LaVyrle Spencer; Photography, Laszlo George; Costumes, Maureen Hiscox; Art Director, David Hiscox; Music, Jonathan Elias; a Dove Audio production; Color; Rated PG-13; 95 minutes; September release. **CAST:** Christopher Reeve (Will Parker), Deborah Raffin (Elly Dinsmore), Lloyd Bochner (Bob Collins), Nina Foch (Miss Beasley), Helen Shaver (Lula Peaks), J.T. Walsh (Sheriff Reese Goodloe)

Helen Shaver, Christopher Reeve in *Morning Glory*
© Academy Entertainment

EYE OF THE STRANGER (Silver Lake Intl.) Producer/Director/Screenplay, David Heavener; Executive Producer, Gerald Milton; Photography, Paul Edwards; Editor, Chris Roth; Music, Robert Garrett; Art Director, George Peirson; a Hero Films production; Color; Rated R; 96 minutes; September release. **CAST:** David Heavener (Stranger), Martin Landau (Mayor Howard Baines), Sally Kirkland (Lori), Don Swayze (Rudy), Stella Stevens, Sy Richardson, Joe Estevez, John Pleshette

THE CURE SHOW (I.R.S. Releasing) Producer, Steve Swartz; Executive Producers, Chris Parry, Marcus Peterzell, Veronica Gretton; Directors, Aubrey Powell, Leroy Bennett; Photography, Jeff Zimmerman; Editors, Nick Wickham, Robert Smith, Ian Mallett, Liam Hall; a Fiction Films in association with Polygram Video International Ltd. presentation; Dolby Stereo; Color; Not rated; 97 minutes; October release. Concert of the rock group The Cure, with Robert Smith, Simon Gallup, Porl Thompson, Boris Williams, Perry Bamonte.

Julian Sands, Sherilyn Fenn in *Boxing Helena* © Orion Classics

Robert Smith in *Cure Show* © Rank/PolyGram

Half Japanese in *HalfJapanese* © Film Forum

Derek McGrath, Alex Winter, Megan Ward, Michael Stoyanov in *Freaked*
© Twentieth Century Fox

HALF JAPANESE: The Band That Would Be King (Independent/Film Forum)
Producer/Director, Jeff Feuerzeig; Photography, Fortunato Procopio; Editor, Peter Sorcher; Color; Not rated; 90 minutes; October release. Documentary on the underground band Half Japanese, with Jad and David Fair, Penn Jillette, Maureen Tucker, Byron Coley, Gerard Cosloy, David Greenberger, Phil Milstein, Don Fleming.

MR. NANNY (New Line Cinema)
Producer, Bob Engelman; Executive Producers, Benni Korzen, Michael Harpster; Director, Michael Gottlieb; Screenplay, Edward Rugoff, Michael Gottlieb; Photography, Peter Stein; Designer, Don De Fina; Editors, Earl Ghaffari, Michael Ripps; Music, David Johansen, Brian Koonin; Casting, Fern Champion, Mark Paladini; Dolby Stereo; Deluxe color; Rated PG; 85 minutes; October release. **CAST:** Terry "Hulk" Hogan (Sean Armstrong), Sherman Hemsley (Burt Wilson), Austin Pendleton (Alex Mason, Sr.), David Johansen (Tommy Thanatos), Robert Gorman (Alex Mason, Jr.), Madeline Zima (Kate Mason), Mother Love (Corinne), Peter Kent (Wolfgang), Afa Anoai "Alfa", Brutus Beefcake, George "The Animal" Steele (Themselves), Butch Brickell (Phone Man), James Coffey (Repo Man), Dondi Dahlin (Receptionist), David Mandel, Dennis DeVeaugh, Joe Hess, John F. Hoye (Guards), Kelly Erin-Welton (Nanny), Joshua Santiago, Danny Fotou (Bullies), Artie Malesci (Skipper), Marc Mercury (Security Guard), Sandy Mielke (Principal), Jeff Moldovan (Jocko), Raymond O'Connor (Frank Olsen), Fred Ornstein (Cabbie), Darci Osiecky (Teacher), Jen Sung Outerbridge (Kojiro), Hope Pomerance (Secretary), Timothy A. Powell (Lieutenant)

FREAKED (20th Century Fox)
formerly *Hideous Mutant Freekz*; Producers, Harry J. Ufland, Mary Jane Ufland; Co-Producers/Screenplay, Tim Burns, Tom Stern, Alex Winter; Directors, Tom Stern, Alex Winter; Line Producer, Ginny Nugent; Photography, Jamie Thompson; Designer, Catherine Hardwicke; Costumes, Malissa Daniel; Editor, Malcolm Campbell; Music, Kevin Kiner, Paul Leary, Butthole Surfers, Blind Idiot God; Creature Makeup Effects, Screaming Mad George, Steve Johnson, Alterian Studios, Inc.; Creature & Visual Effects Supervisor, Thomas C. Rainone; Casting, Artz & Cohen; a Tommy production; Dolby Stereo; Deluxe color; Rated R; 79 minutes; October release. **CAST:** Alex Winter (Ricky Coogin/Sensitive Man #1), Randy Quaid (Elijah C. Skuggs), Michael Stoyanov (Ernie), Megan Ward (Julie), Mr. T. (Bearded Lady), William Sadler (Dick Brian), Brooke Shields (Skye Daley), Eduardo Ricard (George Ramirez #1), Henry Carbo (George Ramirez #2), Deepy Roy (George Ramirez #3), Mihaly "Michu" Meszaros (George Ramirez #4), Brian Brophy (Kevin), Morgan Fairchild (Stewardess), Alex Zuckerman (Stuey Gluck), Jaime Cardriche (Toad), Nicholas Cohn (Bob Vila Look-a-Like), Derek McGrath (Worm), Jeff Kahn (Nosey), John Hawkes (Cowboy), Karyn Malchus (Sockhead), Lee Arenberg (The Eternal Flame), Patti Tippo (Rosie the Pinhead), Tim Burns (Frogman), Bobcat Goldthwait (Sockhead as Tourist/Voice of Sockhead), Keanu Reeves (Ortiz the Dog Boy), Don Stark (Editor), Arturo Gil (Clown), Tom Stern (Sensitive Man #2/Milkman), Gibson J. Haynes (Cheese Wart), Pamela Mant (Nun), Joe Baker (Prof. Nigel Crump), L.S. Kruse, Marilyn Garcia (Peasant Women), Rick Le Clair (Screaming Hippie), Georgina Valdez (Screaming Woman), Calvert DeForest (Larry "Bud" Melman), Michael Gilden (Eye), Joseph Griffo (N. Eye), Jack Yates (Security Guy), Ray Baker (Bill Blazer), J.D. Silvester (Biker), Jon M. Chu (Giant Stuey Monster), Vincent Hammond (Giant Rick Monster), David Bowe (EES Asst.), Chuck Bulot (FBI Chief), David Roberson (FBI Guy), James Baxter Rogers (Another FBI Guy)

ME AND THE KID (Orion)
Producers, Lynn Loring, Dan Curtis; Director, Dan Curtis; Screenplay, Richard Tannenbaum; Based on the novel *The Taking of Gary Feldman* by Stanley Cohen; Photography, Dietrich Lohmann; Designer, Veronica Hadfield; Editor, Bill Blunden; Music, Bob Cobert; Costumes, Deborah Lancaster; Associate Producer, Tracy Curtis; Casting, Mary Jo Slater; Ultra-Stereo; CFI Color; Rated PG; 94 minutes; October release. **CAST:** Danny Aiello (Harry Banner), Alex Zuckerman (Gary Feldman), Joe Pantoliano (Roy Walls), Cathy Moriarty (Rose Farrell), David Dukes (Victor Feldman), Anita Morris (Isobel Feldman), Rick Aiello (Agent Pasetta), Demond Wilson (Agent Schamper), Ben Stein (Fred Herbert), Robin Thomas (Dr. Berman), Abe Vigoda (Pawn Broker), Todd Bryant (J.P.), Alaina Reed Hall (Sarah), Mowava Pryor (Janeeta), Joseph Pecoraro (Man in phonebooth), Eric Wylie (Boy in pick up), Richard Zavaglia (Puppy Man), Rosie Zuckerman (Puppy Girl), Rick Cicetti (State Police Captain), Gary Munch (FBI Agent #1), Richard Palmer, Thomas Moriarty (Cops), Georgio Kokosin (Boy in parking lot)

Sherman Hemsley, Hulk Hogan in *Mr. Nanny* © New Line Cinema

Danny Aiello, Alex Zuckerman in *Me and the Kid* © Orion Pictures

Trevor Edmond, Mindy Clarke in *Return of the Living Dead 3*
© Vidmark Inc.

Michael Biehn, Sarah Trigger, Nicolas Cage
in *DeadFall* © Vidmark Inc.

RETURN OF THE LIVING DEAD 3 (Trimark) Producers, Gary Schmoeller, Brian Yuzna; Executive Producers, Roger Burlage, Lawrence Steven Meyers; Director, Brian Yuzna; Screenplay, John Penney; Photography, Gerry Lively; Designer, Anthony Tremblay; Editor, Christopher Roth; Music, Barry Goldberg; Special Effects, Steve Johnson, Tim Ralston, Kevin Brennan, Christopher Nelson, Wayne Toth; Executive in Charge of Production, David Tripet; Color; Rated R; 97 minutes; October release. **CAST:** Mindy Clarke (Julie), J. Trevor Edmond (Curt Reynolds), Kent McCord (Lt. Col. John Reynolds), Basil Wallace (Riverman), Fabio Urena (Mogo), Mike Moroff (Scratch/Santos), Pia Reyes (Alicia), Sal Lopez (Felipe/Musco), James T. Callahan (Colonel), Sarah Douglas (Sinclair)

SURE FIRE (Strand Releasing) Producer, Henry S. Rosenthal; Director/Screenplay/ Photography/Editor, Jon Jost; Music, Erling Wold; a Complex Corp. production; TVC Color; Not rated; 86 minutes; October release. **CAST:** Tom Blair (Wes), Robert Ernst (Larry), Kristi Hager (Bobbi), Kate Dezina (Ellen), Phillip R. Brown (Phillip), Dennis R. Brown (Dennis), Rick Blackwell (Dick), Robert Nalwalker (Sheriff), Haley Westwood (Haley), Kaye Evans (Kaye), Henry M. Blackwell, J.T. Reynolds, Thomas D.A. Smith, John Betenson (Cowboys)

BLACK DIAMOND RUSH (Warren Miller Entertainment) Producers/Director, Kurt Miller, Peter Speek; Screenplay/Narrator, Warren Miller; Photography, Don Brolin; Editors, Katie Hedrich, Kim Schneider; Associate Producer, Max Bervy, Jr.; Music Supervisor, Peter Afterman; Color; Not rated; 90 minutes; October release. Skiing documentary.

DECEPTION (Miramax) formerly *Ruby Cairo*; Producer, Lloyd Phillips; Director, Graeme Clifford; Screenplay, Robert Dillon, Michael Thomas; Story, Robert Dillon; Executive Producer, Haruki Kadokawa; Photography, Laszlo Kovacs; Designer, Richard Sylbert; Editor, Caroline Biggerstaff; Costumes, Ruby Dillon; Casting, Jennifer Shull; Dolby Stereo; Technicolor; Rated PG-13; 90 minutes; October release. **CAST:** Andie MacDowell (Bessie Faro), Liam Neeson (Fergus Lamb), Viggo Mortensen (Johnny Faro), Jack Thompson (Ed), Paul Spencer (Johnny Faro - Boy), Chad Power (Niles Faro), Monica Mikala (Alexandria Faro),

Kaelynn & Sara Craddick (Cleo Faro), Luis Cortes (Hermes #1), Amy Van Nostrand (Marge Swimmer), Pedro Gonzalez-Gonzalez (Uncle Jorge), Lucy Rodriguez (Tia Lupe), Jeff Corey (Joe Dick), Miriam Reed (Renee Dick), Kimberley LaMarque (Mailwoman), Francine Lee (Lily), Alberto Estrella (Hermes #2), Jorge Fegan (Undertaker), Paco Mauri (Coroner), Sylvia Short, Sage Allen, Montrose Hagins (Fergus Groupies), Lolo Navarro (Hotel Proprietress), Rodrigo Puebla, Juan Antonio Llanes (Bank Tellers - Veracruz), Gunter Meisner (Herr Bruchner), Thomas Frey (Bank Teller - Berlin), Monica Simon (EDK Receptionist), Natassa Manisalli (Melina), Nikos Kouros (Kolatos), Aristidis Nikoloudis (Hotel Concierge), Lydia Lenossi (Miss Abousief), Mandana Marino (Miss Hakim), Hosni Hasham Zahram (Taxi Driver), Salh Abu El Asem (Warehouse Foreman), Maisa El Rafai (Woman in church), Negm El Deen Mohammed Afifi (Imam - mosque), Robin Lee (Priest at funeral), Hannaa Hamed Ibrahim (Young Mother - crypt)

ON THE BRIDGE (Direct Cinema) Producer/Director, Frank Perry; Executive Producer/Editor, Emily Paine; Photography, Kevin Keating; Music, Toni Childs; Associate Producer, Esther B. Cassidy; Color; Not rated; 95 minutes; October release. Documentary on director Frank Perry's fight against prostate cancer.

DEADFALL (Trimark) Producers, Ted Fox, Christopher Coppola; Director/Screenplay, Christopher Coppola; Line Producer, Bob Engelman; Screenplay, Nick Vallelonga; Photography, Maryse Alberti; Designer, Clare Scarpulla; Costumes, Jacqui De La Fontaine; Color; Rated R; 99 minutes; October release. **CAST:** Michael Biehn (Joe Donan), James Coburn (Mike Donan/Lou Donan), Nicolas Cage (Eddie), Sarah Trigger (Diane), Charlie Sheen (Steve), Talia Shire (Sam), Angus Scrimm (Dr. Lyme), Peter Fonda (Pete), J. Kenneth Campbell (Huey), Adrienne Stout (Holly), Nick Vallelonga (Patsy), Micky Dolenz (Bart), Clarence Williams III (Dean), Michael Constantine (Frank), Ron Taylor (The Baby), Gigi Rice (Blanche), Marc Coppola (Bob), Brian Donovan (Mitch), Clarence Landry (Larry), Heather Wickham (Barmaid)

BELOW LEFT: *Black Diamond Rush* © Max Bervy
BELOW RIGHT: Liam Neeson, Andie MacDowell in *Deception*
© Miramax Films

Rocks, Daphne in *Look Who's Talking Now* © TriStar Pictures

Miguel Ferrer, Leilani Sarelle in *The Harvest* © Arrow Releasing

BOUND & GAGGED: A LOVE STORY (Northern Arts) Producer, Dennis J. Mahoney; Director/Screenplay, Daniel Appleby; Photography, Dean Lent; Music, Willie Murphy; Editor, Kaye Davis; from Cinescope Productions; Foto-Kem color; Not rated; 96 minutes; October release. **CAST:** Ginger Lynn Allen (Leslie), Chris Denton (Cliff), Elizabeth Saltarrelli (Elizabeth), Chris Mulkey (Steve), Karen Black (Carla), Mary Ella Ross (Lida), Abdul Salaam El Razzac (Santa Adbul), Andrea Scarpa (Italian Lover), Gene Larche (Soaring Eagle), Phyllis Wright (Nurse/Clerk), Bill Schoppert (Molester), Hal Atkinson (Doctor), Joe Minjares (Davis), Peter Williams (Mr. Williams), Randy Schmidt (Bodybuilder), Sarah Todd (Hassled Waitress), Travis James, Garth Schumacher (Sleazy Diners), Patty Shaw (Meter Maid), Pete Jackson (Bar Cop), Anton Stifter, M.D. (E.R. Doctor), Lisa Jensen (Biker Woman), Leonard Rabatin (Bus Ticket Clerk), Michael Bodine (Bus Driver), Julia Tehven, Michael De Leon (Alley Lovers), Kelly Till, Ann Marie Strand (Fighting Women), Elizabeth Campbell, Billy Jaap (Bar Room Dancers), Victor Propokov, Randy Adamsick, Pesoth Pin (Failed Suicide Patients), Paul Tomczyk (Accordian Player)

(Dog Catcher), Roger Cross, Ryan Michael, Phil Hayes (Pilots), Miriam Smith (Tipsy Secretary), Robert Wisden, J.B. Bivens (Rangers), Tegan Moss (Girl with puppy), Chilton Crane (Girl's Mommy), Alicia Bradsen (Mollie at 12), Gina Chiarelli (Young Rosie), Ghislaine Crawford, Justine Crawford (Reindeer Girls), Andrew Airlie (Co-Pilot), Andrea Nemeth (Babysitter), Campbell Lane (Mollie's Dad), Bob Bergen, Peter Iacangelo, Nick Jameson, Patricia Parris, Pat Pinney, Rodney Saulsberry, Jeff Winkless (Dog and Wolf Voices)

ROBOCOP 3 (Orion) Producer, Patrick Crowley; Director, Fred Dekker; Screenplay, Frank Miller, Fred Dekker; Story, Frank Miller; Based on characters created by Edward Neumeier, Michael Miner; Co-Producer, Jane Bartelme; Photography, Gary B. Kibbe; Designer, Hilda Stark; Music, Basil Poledouris; Costumes, Ha Nguyen; Editor, Bert Lovitt; RoboCop Designer/Creator, Rob Bottin; Stop Motion Animation, Phil Tippett; Casting, Steven Jacobs; Dolby Stereo; Deluxe color; Rated PG-13; 105 minutes; November release. **CAST:** Robert John Burke (RoboCop), Nancy Allen (Anne Lewis), Rip Torn (The CEO), John Castle (McDaggett), Jill Hennessy (Dr. Marie Lazarus), CCH Pounder (Bertha), Mako (Kanemitsu), Robert DoQui (Sgt. Reed), Remy Ryan

Robert John Burke in *RoboCop 3* © Orion Pictures

Jim Varney in *Ernest Rides Again* © Emshell

LOOK WHO'S TALKING NOW (TriStar) Producer, Jonathan D. Krane; Executive Producer, Leslie Dixon; Director, Tom Ropelewski; Screenplay, Tom Ropelewski, Leslie Dixon; Based on characters created by Amy Heckerling; Photography, Oliver Stapleton; Designer, Michael Bolton; Editors, Michael A. Stevenson, Harry Hitner; Music, William Ross; Costumes, Molly Maginnis, Mary E. McLeod; Co-Producers, Amy Heckerling, Fitch Cady; Casting, Michelle Allen, Lynne Carrow; Animal Supplier/ Coordinator, Mark Watters; Dolby Stereo; Technicolor; Rated PG-13; 97 minutes; November release. **CAST:** John Travolta (James Ubriacco), Kirstie Alley (Mollie Ubriacco), David Gallagher (Mikey Ubriacco), Tabitha Lupien (Julie Ubriacco), Lysette Anthony (Samantha), Olympia Dukakis (Rosie), Danny DeVito (Voice of Rocks), Diane Keaton (Voice of Daphne), George Segal (Albert), Charles Barkley (Himself), John Stocker (Sol), Elizabeth Leslie (Ruthie), Caroline Elliott, Vanessa Morley (Kids at schoolyard), Sandra Grant (Accountant), Sheila Paterson (Old Waitress), Amos Hertzman (Pimply Faced Kid), Mark Acheson (Burly Dad), Gerry Rousseau (Homeless Guy), Kylie Fairlie (Kid on Santa's lap), Victoria Brooks (Bratty Girl), Ron Gabriel (Seedy Santa), Frank Turner (Dave), Serge Houde (Maitre D'), Michael Puttonen

(Nikko), Bruce Locke (Otomo), Stanley Anderson (Zack), Stephen Root (Coontz), Daniel Von Bargen (Moreno), Felton Perry (Johnson), Bradley Whitford (Fleck), Mario Machado (Casey Wong), Jodi Long (Nikko's Mom), John Posey (Nikko's Dad), S.D. Nemeth (Bixby Snyder), Edith Ivey (Elderly Woman in bathrobe), Curtis Taylor (Rehab #1), Judson Vaughn (Seltz), Ken Strong (Rehab Patrol), Kenny Raskin (Security Monitor), Blaise Corrigan (Officer at ordinance depot), Jeff Garlin (Donut Clerk), Lee Arenberg (Hold-Up Man), Randy Randolph (Cop in donut shop), Shane Black (Donnelly), John Nesci (Jensen), Randall Taylor (Starkweather), James Lorinz (Upset Driver), Bryan Mercer, Kenny Jones (Splatterpunks), Doug Yashuda (Kanemitsu's Aide), Mark Gowan (Sleazy Lawyer), Thomas Boyd (Hooker), Eddie Billups (Man at booking desk), Mark Gordon (Techie in Robochamber), Angie Bolling (Ellen Murphy), Graciela Marin (Cop with body armor), Michael Moss (Unfortunate Rehab), Dianne Butler (Woman on vidphone), David De Vries (Informative Yuppie), Gary Bullock (Gas Station Clerk), Wilbur Fitzgerald (Rebel with weapons cart), Beth Burns (Teen Prostitute), Lonnie Smith (1st Rehab at hotel), Tommy Chappelle (Hotel Desk Clerk),

Jacob Tierney, Noah Fleiss in *Josh and S.A.M.*
© Castle Rock Entertainment

Miriam Margolyes, Steve Buscemi in *Ed and His Dead Mother*
© ITC Entertainment Group

Rick Seaman (Rehab Driver), Ronn Leggett (Pimp), Eva La Rue (Debbie Dix), Alex Van (Rehab in war room)

THE HARVEST (Arrow Releasing) Producers, Morgan Mason, Jason Clark; Executive Producers, Carole Curb, Ron Stone; Director/Screenplay, David Marconi; Photography, Emmanuel Lubezki; Designer, Rae Fox; Costumes, Ileane Meltzer; Editor, Carlos Puentes; a Curb Musifilm/Mie Curb & Lester Korn presentation in association with Ron Stone Prods.; Ultra-Stereo; CFI color; Rated R; 97 minutes; November release. **CAST:** Miguel Ferrer (Charlie Pope), Leilani Sarelle (Natalie), Harvey Fierstein (Bob Lakin), Anthony John Denison (Noel Guzman), Henry Silva (Detective Topo), Tim Thomerson (Steve), Mike Vendrell (Vent), Matt Clark (Hank), Mario Ivan Martinez Morales (Alex), Angelica Espinosa Stransky (Dr. Emma), Jose Francisco Lavat Pacheco (Doctor), Juan Antonio Gonzales Llames (Desk Clerk), Randy Walker (Border Guard), Rafael Valdez G. Conde (Lagno), Alejandro Rojas Brando (Kind Eyes), J. Jorge Zepeda Palacios (Roman Morales), David Villapando Cazares (Cabbie), Jose Guillermo Avalino Rios (Local), David Ralph, Schmid Gorfido (Pock Marks), Georges E. Belanger (Customs Agent)

THE ICE RUNNER (Borde Film Releasing) Producer, Jeffrey M. Sneller; Executive Producer, Samuel S. Sneller; Director, Barry Samson; Screenplay, Joyce Warren, Clifford Coleman, Joshua Stallings; Photography, Brian Capener; Editors, Roy Watts, Joshua Stallings; Designers, Victor Zenkov, Eric Davies; Costumes, Svetlana Borborova; a Gold Leaf Intl. and Johan Schotte presentation of a Monarch Picture; Ultra-Stereo; Foto-Kem color; Rated R; 116 minutes; November release. **CAST:** Edward Albert (Jeffrey West), Victor Wong (Fyodor), Olga Kabo (Lena), Eugene Lazarev (Kolya), Alexander Kuznitsov (Petrov), Basil Hoffman (J.C. Kruck), Bill Bordy (Ed Ross), Sergei Ruban (Gorsky)

ERNEST RIDES AGAIN (Emshell Producers Group) Producer, Stacy Williams; Executive Producer, Coke Sams; Co-Producer, Tom Rowe; Director, John R. Cherry III: Screenplay, John R. Cherry III, William M. Akers; Photography, David Geddes; Editor, Craig Bassett; Music, Bruce Arntson, Kirby Shelstad; Designer, Chris August; Costumes, Martha Snetsinger; Casting, Sid Kozak; CFI color; Rated PG; 92 minutes; November release. **CAST:** Jim Varney (Ernest P. Worrell), Ron K. James (Abner Melon), Linda Kash (Nan Melon), Tom Butler (Dr. Glencliff), Duke Ernsberger (Frank), Jeffrey Pillars (Joe)

JOSH AND S.A.M. (Columbia) Producer, Martin Brest; Executive Producer, Arne L. Schmidt; Co-Producers, Alex Gartner, Frank Deese; Director, Billy Weber; Screenplay, Frank Deese; Photography, Don Burgess; Designer, Marcia Hinds-Johnson; Editor, Chris Lebenzon; Music, Thomas Newman; Costumes, Jill M. Ohannesson; Casting, Carrie Frazier, Shani Ginsberg; a Castle Rock Entertainment in association with New Line Cinema presentation of a City Lights Films productions; Dolby Stereo; Technicolor; Rated PG-13; 98 minutes; November release. **CAST:** Jacob Tierney (Josh Whitney), Noah Fleiss (Sam Whitney), Martha Plimpton (Alison), Stephen Tobolowsky (Thom Whitney), Joan Allen (Caroline), Chris Penn (Derek Baxter), Maury Chaykin (Pizza Man), Ronald Guttman (Jean-Pierre), Udo Kier (Tanning Salon Manager), Sean Baca (Curtis Coleman), Jake Gyllenhaal (Leon Coleman), Anne Lange (Ellen Coleman), Ann Hearn (Teacher), Christian Clemenson (Policeman), Allan Arbus (Businessman on plane), Kayla Allen (Annette at reunion), Nada Despotovich (Susan at reunion), Brent Hinkley (Bill at reunion), Jay McNally, Daniel Tamberelli (Red Haired Kids), Don R. McManus (Calgary Airline Officer), Amy Wright (Waitress), Tyler Gurciullo (Kickball Pitcher), Raye Birk (Hotel Manager), Susan Norfleet (Reunion Coordinator), Annie McEnroe (Woman at laundromat), Pamella D'Pella (Daughter on bus), Harry Caesar (Father on bus), Frank Dent (Canadian Father), Kate Benton (Canadian Mother), Valerie Wildman (Dallas Airline Officer), Bill Dunlevy (Dallas Desk Attendant), Bonnie Burgess (Flight Attendant #1),

John Voldstad (Gas Station Attendant), Dhiru Shah (Bus Driver), Jason Edwards (Truck Driver), Deryn Warren (Calgary Ticket Agent)

THE PHILADELPHIA EXPERIMENT 2 (Trimark) Producers, Mark Levinson, Doug Curtis; Executive Producer, Mark Amin; Director, Stephen Cornwell; Screenplay, Kevin Rock, Nick Paine; Photography, Ronn Schmidt; Music, Gerald Couriet; Designer, Armin Ganz; Costumes, Eileen Kennedy; Special Effects, Frank Ceglia; Dolby Stereo; Color; Rated PG-13; 97 minutes; November release. **CAST:** Brad Johnson (David Herdeg), Marjean Holden (Jess), Gerrit Graham (Dr. William Mailer/Friederich Mahler), James Greene (Professor Longstreet), Geoffrey Blake (Logan), Cyril O'Reilly (Decker), John Christian Grass (Benjamin Herdeg)

ED AND HIS DEAD MOTHER (I.R.S. Releasing) formerly *Bon Appetit Mama*; Producer, Wm. Christopher Gorog; Director, Jonathan Wacks; Screenplay, Chuck Hughes; Photography, Francis Kenny; Music, Mason Daring; Designer, Eve Cauley; from I.T.C.; Color/black and white; Rated PG-13; 90 minutes; November release. **CAST:** Steve Buscemi (Ed Chilton), Ned Beatty (Uncle Benny), Miriam Margolyes (Mother), John Glover (A.J. Pattle), Sam Jenkins (Storm Reynolds)

BATMAN: MASK OF THE PHANTASM (Warner Bros.) Producers, Benjamin Melniker, Michael Uslan; Executive Producer, Tom Ruegger; Co-Producers, Alan Burnett, Eric Radomski, Bruce W. Timm; Directors, Eric Radomski, Bruce W. Timm; Sequence Directors, Kevin Altieri, Boyd Kirkland, Frank Paur, Dan Riba; Screenplay, Alan Burnett, Paul Dini, Martin Pasko, Michael Reaves; Story, Alan Burnett; Based on the DC Comics characters created by Bob Kane; Music, Shirley Walker; Editor, Al Breitenbach; Casting/Voice Supervisor, Andrea Romano; Dolby Stereo; Technicolor; Rated PG; 76 minutes; December release. **VOICE CAST:** Kevin Conroy (Batman), Dana Delany (Andrea Beaumont), Hart Bochner (Arthur Reeves), Stacy Keach Jr. (Phantasm/Carl Beaumont), Abe Vigoda (Salvatore Valestra), Dick Miller (Chuckie Sol), John P. Ryan (Buzz Bronski), Efrem Zimbalist, Jr. (Alfred), Bob Hastings (Commissioner Gordon), Robert Costanzo (Detective Bullock), Mark Hamill (The Joker)

Batman in *Batman: Mask of the Phantasm*
©D.C. Comics Inc.

Michael Dudikoff, Stephen Dorff in *Rescue Me*
© Cannon Pictures Inc.

Wil Horneff, Karen Allen in *Ghost in the Machine*
© Twentieth Century Fox

RESCUE ME (Cannon) Producer, Richard Alfieri; Executive Producers, Jere Henshaw, David A. Smitas; Director, Arthur Allan Seidelman; Screenplay, Mike Snyder; Photography, Hanania Baer; Designer, Elayne Barbara Ceder; Editor, Bert Glatstein; Music, David Waters; Presented in association with Apollo Pictures; Stereo; Color; Rated PG-13; 90 minutes; December release. **CAST:** Michael Dudikoff (Daniel "Mac" McDonald), Stephen Dorff (Fraser Sweeny), Ami Dolenz (Ginny Grafton), Peter DeLuise (Rowdy), William Lucking (Kurt), Dee Wallace Stone (Sarah Sweeny), Liz Torres (Carney), Danny Nucci (Todd), Kimberly Kates (Cindy), Ty Hardin (Sheriff Gilbert), Caroline Schlitt (Dawn Johnson), Jefferey Craig Harris (Johnny - TORSO Lead Singer), Jason Kristofer (Billy), Lisa Sawrence (Hillary Samuels), Paul Joynt (Stamp Buyer), John Miranda (Hector), Jimmy Carville (Hector), Joan Kelly (Principal), Cristi Harris (Cathy), Robert Glen Keith (Karl), Natalie Barish (Chemistry Teacher), Samantha Phillips (Cherie), Cheryl Paris (Hannah), Rick Fitts (State Trooper), Peter Gonneau (Mr. Grafton), Gary Bisig (FBI Agent), Dean Minerd, Gus Corrado, Pamela Kay Davis, Bob Tootle, Jane West (Reporters), Dennis Henning (Gas Station Mechanic), Christopher Cary (Bum), Joey Carson, Shawn Harris, Jimmy Pollock, Mikki Willis (TORSO), Paula Messina (Harriet), Jimmy Shannon (Sarge), Sadie Veraldi (School Secretary), William Hedge (Football Coach), Eric Norris, Eddie Braun, Dennis Madalone (Thugs), Tarmo Semper Urb, Thomas Urb (Folk Singers)

VEGAS IN SPACE (Troma) Producer/Director, Phillip R. Ford; Executive Producer/ Designer, Doris Fish; Screenplay, Doris Fish, Miss X, Phillip R. Ford; Based on the party by Ginger Quest; Photography, Robin Clark; Editors, Ed Jones, Phillip R. Ford; Music, Bob Davis; a Lloyd Kaufman & Michael Herz presentation; Monaco Labs color; Not rated; 88 minutes; December release. **CAST:** Doris Fish (Capt. Dan Tracy/Capt. Tracy Daniels), Miss X (Empress Vel Croford/Queen Veneer), Ginger Quest (Empress Nueva Gabor), Ramona Fischer (Lt. Mike Shadows/Lt. Sheila Shadows), Lori Naslund (Lt. Steve Dane/Lt. Debbie Dane), Timmy Spence (Lt. Dick Hunter), "Tippi" (Princess Angel), Freida Lay (Jane the Computer/La La Galaxy), Arturo Galster (Noodles Nebula), Silvana Nova (Wynetta Whitehead), Sandelle Kincaid (Babs Velour), Tommy Pace (Mrs. Velour), Jennifer Blowdryer (Futura Volare, KUN-TV), John Canalli (Princess Jaundice), Janice Sukaitis (Martian Lady Driver), Jeanette Szudy (National Orbit Reporter/Veneer's Prisoner), Ida Lee (Nueva's Handmaid), Tracy Hughes (Odessa), Susan Strong (Shirelle), Matthew Barton (Zorna Virga), Daniel Crone (Altila Zadora), Norman Schrader (Luna), Susan Kay (Tour Guide), Miss Abood (Princess Eggy)

BANK ROBBER (I.R.S. Releasing) Producer, Lila Cazes; Executive Producers, Jean Cazes, Miles A. Copeland III; Director/Screenplay, Nick Mead; Photography, Andrej Sekula; Designer, Scott Chambliss; Music, Stewart Copeland; Editors, Richard E. Westover, Maysie Hoy; Costumes, Dana Allyson; Casting, Donald Paul Pemrick; Color; Rated NC-17; 91 minutes; December release. **CAST:** Patrick Dempsey (Billy), Lisa Bonet (Priscilla), Judge Reinhold (Officer Gross), Forest Whitaker (Officer Battle), Olivia D'Abo (Selina), Paula Kelly (Mother), Mariska Hargitay (Marissa Benoit), Michael Jeter, Joe Alaskey (Night Clerks), Andy Romano (Police Captain), Warren Munson (Bank Manager), Don Perry (Assistant Manager), Lisa Marie Spikerman (Candy), James Garde (Chris), Stephen McDonough (Andy), Miles A. Copeland III (TV Evangelist), Josh De Bear (Delivery Boy), Michael Wyle (Drug Dealer), Mark Pellegrino (Motorcycle Cop), Ivan Kane (Bar Man), John Chappoulis (Pizza Man), Scott Kaske (Transvestite), Bill Zuckert (Old Man), David Millbern (Wiretapper), James Schendel (Engineer), Eadie Del Rubio, Milly Del Rubio, Elena Del Rubio (Singing Triplets), James Baxter Rogers (Security Guard)

GHOST IN THE MACHINE (20th Century Fox) Producer, Paul Schiff; Co-Producers, William Osborne, William Davies, Barry Sabath; Director, Rachel Talalay; Screenplay, William Davies, William Osborne; Line Producer, Aron Warner; Photography, Phil Meheux; Designer, James Spencer; Editors, Janice Hampton, Erica Huggins; Music, Graeme Revell; Costumes, Isis Mussenden; Visual Effects Producers, VIFX, Rhonda C. Gunner, Gregory L. McMurry, John C. Wash; Special Effects Makeup, Alterian Studios; Makeup Effects/Animatronics, Tony Gardener; Casting, David Rubin, Debra Zane; Dolby Stereo; Deluxe color; Rated R; 95 minutes; December release. **CAST:** Karen Allen (Terry Munroe), Chris Mulkey (Bram Walker), Ted Marcoux (Karl Hochman), Wil Horneff (Josh Munroe), Jessica Walter (Elaine Spencer), Brandon Quintin Adams (Frazer), Rick Ducommun (Phil), Nancy Fish (Karl's Landlord), Jack Laufer (Elliott), Shevonne Durkin (Carol), Richard McKenzie (Frank Mallory), Mimi Lieber (Marta), Mickey Gilbert (Mickey the Driver), Ken Thorley (Salesman), Carl Gabriel Yorke (Safety Technician), Richard Schiff (Scanner Technician), Clayton Landey (Mel), Walter Addison (Veteran Cop), Matthew Glave (Rookie), Carlease Burke, Michael Laguardia, Charles Haugk (Cops), Chris Ellis (Lieutenant), Robert Lamar Kemp (Yuppie), Dom Magwili (Doctor), Haunani Minn (Nurse), Charles Stransky (Cop at police station), Alix Koromzay (Punk Girl), Helen Greenberg (Customer), Nigel Gibbs (Detective), Andrew Woodworth (Home Security Man), Zack Phifer (Priest), Don Keith Opper (Man in office), Mitchell R. Parnes (Bartender), Edwina Moore (Newswoman), Rick Scarry (Newsman)

Patrick Dempsey, Lisa Bonet in *Bank Robber* © I. R. S. Releasing

PROMISING NEW ACTORS OF 1993

SANDRA BULLOCK
(*The Vanishing, The Thing Called Love, Demolition Man,*
Wrestling Ernest Hemingway)

LEONARDO DICAPRIO
(*What's Eating Gilbert Grape, This Boy's Life*)

RALPH FIENNES
(*Schindler's List*)

WENDY CREWSON
(*The Good Son*)

JOSH HAMILTON
(*Alive*)

JULIANNE MOORE
(*Body of Evidence, Benny & Joon, The Fugitive, Short Cuts*)

ROSIE O' DONNELL
(*Sleepless in Seattle, Another Stakeout*)

JASON SCOTT LEE
(*Dragon: The Bruce Lee Story, Map of the Human Heart*)

PAUL MERCURIO
(*Strictly Ballroom*)

JEANNE TRIPPLEHORN
(*The Firm, The Night We Never Met*)

JANINE TURNER
(*Cliffhanger*)

WILL SMITH
(*Six Degrees of Separation, Made in America*)

TOP 100 BOX OFFICE FILMS RELEASED IN 1993

Sylvester Stallon in *Cliffhanger* ©TriStar Pictures

1. Jurassic Park (Jun/Univ) $346,260,000
2. Mrs. Doubtfire (Nov/20th) $219,140,000
3. The Fugitive (Aug/WB) $183,410,000
4. The Firm (June/Par) $158,350,000
5. Sleepless in Seattle (Jun/TriS) $126,500,000
6. Indecent Proposal (Apr/Par) $106,100,000
7. In the Line of Fire (Jul/Col) $102,320,000
8. The Pelican Brief (Dec/WB) $100,770,000
9. Schindler's List (Dec/Univ) $96,150,000
10. Cliffhanger (May/TriS) $84,100,000
11. Free Wilfy (Jul/WB) $77,640,000
12. Philadelphia (Dec/TriS) $77,240,000
13. Groundhog Day (Feb/Col) $70,820,000
14. Grumpy Old Men (Dec/WB) $70,180,000
15. Cool Runnings (Oct/BV) $68,670,000
16. Dave (May/WB) $63,280,000
17. Rising Sun (Jul/20th) $62,490,000
18. Demolition Man (Oct/WB) $58,100,000
19. Sister Act 2: Back in the Habit (Dec/BV) $55,980,000
20. Tombstone (Dec/BV) $55,920,000

Sam Neill, Joseph Mazzello, Ariana Richards in *Jurassic Park*
© Universal Pictures/Amblin Entertainment

21. The Three Musketeers (Nov/BV) $53,460,000
22. Rookie of the Year (Jul/20th) $53,130,000
23. Beethoven's 2nd (Dec/Univ) $51,640,000
24. Dennis the Menace (Jun/Dec) $51,280,000
25. The Nightmare Before Christmas (Oct/BV) $50,110,000
26. Sommersby (Feb/WB) $50,100,000
27. Last Action Hero (Jun/Col) $49,660,000
28. Addams Family Values (Nov/Par) $46,300,000
29. Malice (Oct/Col) $46,110,000
30. Wayne's World 2 (Dec/Par) $46,100,000

31. Made in America (May/WB) $44,950,000
32. The Good Son (Sep/20th) $44,560,000
33. The Beverly Hillbillies (Oct/20th) $42,310,000
34. Homeward Bound: Incredible Journey (Feb/BV) $41,650,000
35. Teenage Mutant Ninja Turtles 3 (Mar/NL) $41,280,000
36. Snow White & the 7 Dwarfs (reissue: Jul/BV) $41,270,000
37. Falling Down (Feb/WB) $40,910,000
38. The Piano (Nov/Mir) $40,100,000
39. Hocus Pocus (Jul/BV) $39,370,000
40. What's Love Got to Do With It (Jun/BV) $38,930,000

Tom Hanks in *Sleepless in Seattle* ©TriStar Pictures

41. Hot Shots Part Deux (May/20th) $37,620,000
42. Carlito's Way (Nov/Univ) $36,520,000
43. Son-in-Law (Jul/BV) $36,450,000
44. Alive (Jan/BV) $36,300,000
45. Sliver (May/Par) $36,290,000
46. Robin Hood: Men in Tights (Jul/20th) $34,990,000
47. Dragon: The Bruce Lee Story (May/Univ) $34,780,000
48. The Joy Luck Club (Sep/BV) $32,750,000
49. The Age of Innocence (Sep/Col) $31,830,000
50. The Sandlot (Apr/20th) $31,780,000

Alec Baldwin, Bill Pullman in *Malice*
© Castle Rock Entertainment

51. Hard Target (Aug/Univ) $31,670,000
52. A Perfect World (Nov/WB) $31,170,000
53. The Secret Garden (Aug/WB) $31,150,000
54. Cop and a Half (Apr/Univ) $30,400,000
55. Point of No Return (Mar/WB) $30,100,000
56. National Lampoon's Loaded Weapon 1 (Feb/NL)........ $27,980,000
57. Menace II Society (May/NL) $27,740,000
58. My Life (Nov/Col) $27,560,000
59. Poetic Justice (Jul/Col) $27,460,000
60. Shadowlands (Dec/Savoy) $25,840,000

The Nightmare Before Christmas © Touchstone Pictures

76. Another Stakeout (Jul/BV) $20,110,000
77. Untamed Heart (Feb/MGM) $18,770,000
78. Sniper (Jan/TriS) $18,580,000
79. Geronimo: An American Legend (Dec/Col) $18,300,000
80. Posse (May/Gram) $18,180,000
81. Born Yesterday (Mar/BV) $17,660,000
82. CB4 (Mar/Univ) $17,650,000
83. A Bronx Tale (Sep/Savoy) $17,300,000
84. Sidekicks (Apr/Triumph) $17,240,000
85. Heart and Souls (Aug/Univ) $16,480,000
86. Jason Goes to Hell: Final Friday (Aug/NL) $15,500,000
87. Needful Things (Aug/Col) $15,130,000
88. Indian Summer (Apr/BV) $14,720,000
89. Body of Evidence (Jan/MGM) $13,550,000
90. The Crush (Apr/WB) $13,540,000

Kevin Kline, Sigourney Weaver in *Dave* © Warner Bros.

61. In the Name of the Father (Dec/Univ) $25,100,000
62. The Man Without a Face (Aug/WB) $24,730,000
63. The Adventures of Huck Finn (Apr/BV) $23,870,000
64. Striking Distance (Sep/Col) $23,790,000
65. Benny & Joon (Apr/MGM) $23,140,000
66. The Program (Sep/BV) $23,100,000
67. The Remains of the Day (Nov/Col) $22,930,000
68. Guilty as Sin (Jun/BV) $22,630,000
69. Rudy (Oct/TriS) $22,600,000
70. Much Ado About Nothing (May/Gold) $22,540,000
71. Nowhere to Run (Jan/Col) $21,930,000
72. Like Water for Chocolate (Feb/Mir) $21,610,000
73. Fire in the Sky (Mar/Par) $21,340,000
74. Super Mario Bros. (May/BV) $20,850,000
75. Coneheads (Jul/Par) $20,720,000

Tom Cruise in *The Firm* © Paramount Pictures

Maggie Smith in *The Secret Garden* © Warner Bros.

91. The Vanishing (Feb/20th) $13,530,000
92. Man's Best Friend (Nov/NL) $12,980,000
93. A Far Off Place (Mar/BV) $12,900,000
94. Life With Mikey (Jun/BV) $12,350,000
95. True Romance (Sep/WB) $12,290,000
96. Undercover Blues (Sep/MGM) $12,200,000
97. Judgment Night (Oct/Univ) $12,110,000
98. Weekend at Bernie's II (Jul/TriS) $11,750,000
99. Strictly Ballroom (Feb/Mir) $11,660,000
100. So I Married an Axe Murderer (Jul/TriS) $11,590,000

Julie Andrews

George Burns

Patty Duke

Michael Caine

PREVIOUS ACADEMY AWARD WINNERS

1927-28: (1) "Wings," (2) Emil Jannings in "The Way of All Flesh," (3) Janet Gaynor in "Seventh Heaven," (6) Frank Borzage for "Seventh Heaven", (7) Charles Chaplin.

1928-29: (1) "Broadway Melody," (2) Warner Baxter in "In Old Arizona," (3) Mary Pickford in "Coquette," (6) Frank Lloyd for "The Divine Lady."

1929-1930: (1) "All Quiet on the Western Front," (2) George Arliss in "Disraeli," (3) Norma Shearer in "The Divorcee," (6) Lewis Milestone for "All Quiet on the Western Front."

1930-31: (1) "Cimarron," (2) Lionel Barrymore in "A Free Soul," (3) Marie Dressler in "Min and Bill," (6) Norman Taurog for "Skippy."

1931-32: (1) "Grand Hotel," (2) Fredric March in "Dr. Jekyll and Mr. Hyde" tied with Wallace Beery in "The Champ," (3) Helen Hayes in "The Sin of Madelon Claudet," (6) Frank Borzage for "Bad Girl."

1932-33: (1) "Cavalcade," (2) Charles Laughton in "The Private Life of Henry VIII," (3) Katharine Hepburn in "Morning Glory," (6) Frank Lloyd for "Cavalcade."

1934: (1) "It Happened One Night," (2) Clark Gable in "It Happened One Night," (3) Claudette Colbert in "It Happened One Night," (6) Frank Capra for "It Happened One Night," (7) Shirley Temple.

1935: (1) "Mutiny on the Bounty," (2) Victor McLaglen in "The Informer," (3) Bette Davis in "Dangerous," (6) John Ford for "The Informer," (7) D.W. Griffith

1936: (1) "The Great Ziegfeld," (2) Paul Muni in "The Story of Louis Pasteur," (3) Luise Rainer in "The Great Ziegfeld," (4) Walter Brennan in "Come and Get It," (5) Gale Sondergaard in "Anthony Adverse," (6) Frank Capra for "Mr. Deeds Goes to Town."

1937: (1) "The Life of Emile Zola," (2) Spencer Tracy in "Captains Courageous," (3) Luise Rainer in "The Good Earth," (4) Joseph Schildkraut in "The Life of Emile Zola," (5) Alice Brady in "In Old Chicago," (6) Leo McCarey for "The Awful Truth," (7) Mack Sennett, Edgar Bergen.

1938: (1) "You Can't Take It with You," (2) Spencer Tracy in "Boys Town," (3) Bette Davis in "Jezebel," (4) Walter Brennan in "Kentucky," (5) Fay Bainter in "Jezebel," (6) Frank Capra for "You Can't Take It with You," (7) Deanna Durbin, Mickey Rooney, Harry M. Warner, Walt Disney.

1939: (1) "Gone with the Wind," (2) Robert Donat in "Goodbye, Mr. Chips," (3) Vivien Leigh in "Gone with the Wind," (4) Thomas Mitchell in "Stagecoach," (5) Hattie McDaniel in "Gone with the Wind," (6) Victor Fleming for "Gone with the Wind," (7) Douglas Fairbanks, Judy Garland.

1940: (1) "Rebecca," (2) James Stewart in "The Philadelphia Story," (3) Ginger Rogers in "Kitty Foyle," (4) Walter Brennan in "The Westerner," (5) Jane Darwell in "The Grapes of Wrath," (6) John Ford for "The Grapes of Wrath," (7) Bob Hope

1941: (1) "How Green Was My Valley," (2) Gary Cooper in "Sergeant York," (3) Joan Fontaine in "Suspicion," (4) Donald Crisp in "How Green Was My Valley," (5) Mary Astor in "The Great Lie," (6) John Ford for "How Green Was

My Valley," (7) Leopold Stokowski, Walt Disney.

1942: (1) "Mrs. Miniver," (2) James Cagney in "Yankee Doodle Dandy," (3) Greer Garson in "Mrs. Miniver," (4) Van Heflin in "Johnny Eager," (5) Teresa Wright in "Mrs. Miniver," (6) William Wyler for "Mrs. Miniver," (7) Charles Boyer, Noel Coward.

1943: (1) "Casablanca," (2) Paul Lukas in "Watch on the Rhine," (3) Jennifer Jones in "The Song of Bernadette," (4) Charles Coburn in "The More the Merrier," (5) Katina Paxinou in "For Whom the Bell Tolls," (6) Michael Curtiz for "Casablanca."

1944: (1) "Going My Way," (2) Bing Crosby in "Going My Way," (3) Ingrid Bergman in "Gaslight," (4) Barry Fitzgerald in "Going My Way," (5) Ethel Barrymore in "None but the Lonely Heart," (6) Leo McCarey for "Going My Way," (7) Margaret O'Brien, Bob Hope.

1945: (1) "The Lost Weekend," (2) Ray Milland in "The Lost Weekend," (3) Joan Crawford in "Mildred Pierce," (4) James Dunn in "A Tree Grows in Brooklyn," (5) Anne Revere in "National Velvet," (6) Billy Wilder for "The Lost Weekend," (7) Walter Wanger, Peggy Ann Garner.

1946: (1) "The Best Years of Our Lives," (2) Fredric March in "The Best Years of Our Lives," (3) Olivia de Havilland in "To Each His Own," (4) Harold Russell in "The Best Years of Our Lives," (5) Anne Baxter in "The Razor's Edge," (6) William Wyler for "The Best Years of Our Lives," (7) Laurence Olivier, Harold Russell, Ernst Lubitsch, Claude Jarman, Jr.

1947: (1) "Gentleman's Agreement," (2) Ronald Colman in "A Double Life," (3) Loretta Young in "The Farmer's Daughter," (4) Edmund Gwenn in "Miracle on 34th Street," (5) Celeste Holm in "Gentleman's Agreement," (7) James Baskette, (8) "Shoeshine," (Italy).

1948: (1) "Hamlet," (2) Laurence Olivier in "Hamlet," (3) Jane Wyman in "Johnny Belinda," (4) Walter Huston in "The Treasure of the Sierra Madre," (5) Claire Trevor in "Key Largo," (6) John Huston for "The Treasure of the Sierra Madre," (7) Ivan Jandl, Sid Grauman, Adolph Zukor, Walter Wanger, (8) "Monsieur Vincent," (France).

1949: (1) "All the King's Men," (2) Broderick Crawford in "All the King's Men," (3) Olivia de Havilland in "The Heiress," (4) Dean Jagger in "Twelve O'Clock High," (5) Mercedes McCambridge in "All the King's Men," (6) Joseph L. Mankiewicz for "A Letter to Three Wives," (7) Bobby Driscoll, Fred Astaire, Cecil B. DeMille, Jean Hersholt, (8) "The Bicycle Thief," (Italy).

1950: (1) "All about Eve," (2) Jose Ferrer in "Cyrano de Bergerac," (3) Judy Holliday in "Born Yesterday," (4) George Sanders in "All about Eve," (5) Josephine Hull in "Harvey," (6) Joseph L. Mankiewicz for "All about Eve," (7) George Murphy, Louis B. Mayer, (8) "The Walls of Malapaga," (France/Italy).

1951: (1) "An American in Paris," (2) Humphrey Bogart in "The African Queen," (3) Vivien Leigh in "A Streetcar Named Desire," (4) Karl Malden in "A Streetcar Named Desire," (5) Kim Hunter in "A Streetcar Named Desire," (6) George Stevens for "A Place in the Sun," (7) Gene Kelly, (8) "Rashomon," (Japan).

Goldie Hawn

John Gielgud

Jessica Lange

Karl Malden

1952: (1) "The Greatest Show on Earth," (2) Gary Cooper in "High Noon," (3) Shirley Booth in "Come Back, Little Sheba," (4) Anthony Quinn in "Viva Zapata," (5) Gloria Grahame in "The Bad and the Beautiful," (6) John Ford for "The Quiet Man," (7) Joseph M. Schenck, Merian C. Cooper, Harold Lloyd, Bob Hope, George Alfred Mitchell, (8) "Forbidden Games," (France).

1953: (1) "From Here to Eternity," (2) William Holden in "Stalag 17," (3) Audrey Hepburn in "Roman Holiday," (4) Frank Sinatra in "From Here to Eternity," (5) Donna Reed in "From Here to Eternity," (6) Fred Zinnemann for "From Here to Eternity," (7) Pete Smith, Joseph Breen, (8) no award.

1954: (1) "On the Waterfront," (2) Marlon Brando in "On the Waterfront," (3) Grace Kelly in "The Country Girl," (4) Edmond O'Brien in "The Barefoot Contessa," (5) Eva Marie Saint in "On the Waterfront," (6) Elia Kazan for "On the Waterfront," (7) Greta Garbo, Danny Kaye, Jon Whitley, Vincent Winter, (8) "Gate of Hell," (Japan).

1955: (1) "Marty," (2) Ernest Borgnine in "Marty," (3) Anna Magnani in "The Rose Tattoo," (4) Jack Lemmon in "Mister Roberts," (5) Jo Van Fleet in "East of Eden," (6) Delbert Mann for "Marty," (8) "Samurai," (Japan).

1956: (1) "Around the World in 80 Days," (2) Yul Brynner in "The King and I," (3) Ingrid Bergman in "Anastasia," (4) Anthony Quinn in "Lust for Life," (5) Dorothy Malone in "Written on the Wind," (6) George Stevens for "Giant," (7) Eddie Cantor, (8) "La Strada," (Italy).

1957: (1) "The Bridge on the River Kwai," (2) Alec Guinness in "The Bridge on the River Kwai," (3) Joanne Woodward in "The Three Faces of Eve," (4) Red Buttons in "Sayonara," (5) Miyoshi Umeki in "Sayonara," (6) David Lean for "The Bridge on the River Kwai," (7) Charles Brackett, B.B. Kahane, Gilbert M. (Bronco Billy) Anderson, (8) "Nights of Cabiria," (Italy).

1958: (1) "Gigi," (2) David Niven in "Separate Tables," (3) Susan Hayward in "I Want to Live," (4) Burl Ives in "The Big Country," (5) Wendy Hiller in "Separate Tables," (6) Vincente Minnelli for "Gigi," (7) Maurice Chevalier, (8) "My Uncle," (France).

1959: (1) "Ben-Hur," (2) Charlton Heston in "Ben-Hur," (3) Simone Signoret in "Room at the Top," (4) Hugh Griffith in "Ben-Hur," (5) Shelley Winters in "The Diary of Anne Frank," (6) William Wyler for "Ben-Hur," (7) Lee de Forest, Buster Keaton, (8) "Black Orpheus," (Brazil).

1960: (1) "The Apartment," (2) Burt Lancaster in "Elmer Gantry," (3) Elizabeth Taylor in "Butterfield 8," (4) Peter Ustinov in "Spartacus," (5) Shirley Jones in "Elmer Gantry," (6) Billy Wilder for "The Apartment," (7) Gary Cooper, Stan Laurel, Hayley Mills, (8) "The Virgin Spring," (Sweden).

1961: (1) "West Side Story," (2) Maximilian Schell in "Judgment at Nuremberg," (3) Sophia Loren in "Two Women," (4) George Chakiris in "West Side Story," (5) Rita Moreno in "West Side Story," (6) Robert Wise for "West Side Story," (7) Jerome Robbins, Fred L. Metzler, (8) "Through a Glass Darkly," (Sweden).

1962: (1) "Lawrence of Arabia," (2) Gregory Peck in "To Kill a Mockingbird," (3) Anne Bancroft in "The Miracle Worker," (4) Ed Begley in "Sweet Bird of Youth," (5) Patty Duke in "The Miracle Worker," (6) David Lean for "Lawrence of Arabia," (8) "Sundays and Cybele," (France).

1963: (1) "Tom Jones," (2) Sidney Poitier in "Lilies of the Field," (3) Patricia Neal in "Hud," (4) Melvyn Douglas in "Hud," (5) Margaret Rutherford in "The V.I.P.'s," (6) Tony Richardson for "Tom Jones," (8) "8 1/2," (Italy).

1964: (1) "My Fair Lady," (2) Rex Harrison in "My Fair Lady," (3) Julie Andrews in "Mary Poppins," (4) Peter Ustinov in "Topkapi," (5) Lila Kedrova in "Zorba the Greek," (6) George Cukor for "My Fair Lady," (7) William Tuttle, (8) "Yesterday, Today, and Tomorrow," (Italy).

1965: (1) "The Sound of Music," (2) Lee Marvin in "Cat Ballou," (3) Julie Christie in "Darling," (4) Martin Balsam in "A Thousand Clowns," (5) Shelley Winters in "A Patch of Blue," (6) Robert Wise for "The Sound of Music," (7) Bob Hope, (8) "The Shop on Main Street," (Czech).

1966: (1) "A Man for All Seasons," (2) Paul Scofield in "A Man for All Seasons," (3) Elizabeth Taylor in "Who's Afraid of Virginia Woolf?," (4) Walter Matthau in "The Fortune Cookie," (5) Sandy Dennis in "Who's Afraid of Virginia Woolf?," (6) Fred Zinnemann for "A Man for All Seasons," (8) "A Man and a Woman," (France).

1967: (1) "In the Heat of the Night," (2) Rod Steiger in "In the Heat of the Night," (3) Katharine Hepburn in "Guess Who's Coming to Dinner," (4) George Kennedy in "Cool Hand Luke," (5) Estelle Parsons in "Bonnie and Clyde," (6) Mike Nichols for "The Graduate," (8) "Closely Watched Trains," (Czech).

1968: (1) "Oliver!" (2) Cliff Robertson in "Charly," (3) Katharine Hepburn in "The Lion in Winter," tied with Barbra Streisand in "Funny Girl," (4) Jack Albertson in "The Subject Was Roses," (5) Ruth Gordon in "Rosemary's Baby," (6) Carol Reed for "Oliver!," (7) Onna White for "Oliver!" choreography, John Chambers for "Planet of the Apes" makeup, (8) "War and Peace," (USSR).

1969: (1) "Midnight Cowboy," (2) John Wayne in "True Grit," (3) Maggie Smith in "The Prime of Miss Jean Brodie," (4) Gig Young in "They Shoot Horses, Don't They?," (5) Goldie Hawn in "Cactus Flower," (6) John Schlesinger for "Midnight Cowboy," (7) Cary Grant, (8) "Z," (Algeria).

1970: (1) "Patton," (2) George C. Scott in "Patton," (3) Glenda Jackson in "Women in Love," (4) John Mills in "Ryan's Daughter," (5) Helen Hayes in "Airport," (6) Franklin J. Schaffner for "Patton," (7) Lillian Gish, Orson Welles, (8) "Investigation of a Citizen Above Suspicion," (Italy).

Jack Nicholson

Eva Marie Saint

Sidney Poitier

Sissy Spacek

Peter Ustinov

Barbra Streisand

1971: (1) "The French Connection," (2) Gene Hackman in "The French Connection," (3) Jane Fonda in "Klute," (4) Ben Johnson in "The Last Picture Show,"(5)Cloris Leachman in "The Last Picture Show," (6) William Friedkin for "The French Connection," (7) Charles Chaplin, (8) "The Garden of the Finzi-Continis," (Italy).

1972: (1) "The Godfather," (2) Marlon Brando in "The Godfather," (3) Liza Minnelli in "Cabaret," (4) Joel Grey in "Cabaret," (5) Eileen Heckart in "Butterflies Are Free," (6) Bob Fosse for "Cabaret," (7) Edward G. Robinson, (8) "The Discreet Charm of the Bourgeoisie," (France).

1973: (1) "The Sting," (2) Jack Lemmon in "Save the Tiger," (3) Glenda Jackson in "A Touch of Class," (4) John Houseman in "The Paper Chase," (5) Tatum O'Neal in "Paper Moon," (6) George Roy Hill for "The Sting," (8) "Day for Night," (France).

1974: (1) "The Godfather Part II," (2) Art Carney in "Harry and Tonto," (3) Ellen Burstyn in "Alice Doesn't Live Here Anymore," (4) Robert DeNiro in "The Godfather Part II," (5) Ingrid Bergman in "Murder on the Orient Express," (6) Francis Ford Coppola for "The Godfather Part II," (7) Howard Hawks, Jean Renoir, (8) "Amarcord," (Italy).

1975: (1) "One Flew Over the Cuckoo's Nest," (2) Jack Nicholson in "One Flew Over the Cuckoo's Nest," (3) Louise Fletcher in "One Flew Over the Cuckoo's Nest," (4) George Burns in "The Sunshine Boys," (5) Lee Grant in "Shampoo," (6) Milos Forman for "One Flew Over the Cuckoo's Nest," (7) Mary Pickford, (8) "Dersu Uzala," (U.S.S.R.), (9) "The Man Who Skied Down Everest."

1976: (1) "Rocky," (2) Peter Finch in "Network," (3) Faye Dunaway in "Network," (4) Jason Robards in "All the President's Men," (5) Beatrice Straight in "Network," (6) John G. Avildsen for "Rocky," (8) "Black and White in Color," (Ivory Coast), (9) "Harlan County, U.S.A."

1977: (1) "Annie Hall," (2) Richard Dreyfuss in "The Goodbye Girl," (3) Diane Keaton in "Annie Hall," (4) Jason Robards in "Julia," (5) Vanessa Redgrave in "Julia," (6) Woody Allen for "Annie Hall," (7) Maggie Booth (film editor), (8) "Madame Rosa," (France), (9) "Who Are the DeBolts?"

1978: (1) "The Deer Hunter," (2) Jon Voight in "Coming Home," (3) Jane Fonda in "Coming Home," (4) Christopher Walken in "The Deer Hunter," (5) Maggie Smith in "California Suite," (6) Michael Cimino for "The Deer Hunter," (7) Laurence Olivier, King Vidor, (8) "Get Out Your Handkerchiefs," (France), (9) "Scared Straight."

1979: (1) "Kramer vs. Kramer," (2) Dustin Hoffman in "Kramer vs. Kramer," (3) Sally Field in "Norma Rae," (4) Melvyn Douglas in "Being There," (5) Meryl Streep in "Kramer vs. Kramer," (6) Robert Benton for "Kramer vs. Kramer," (7) Robert S. Benjamin, Hal Elias, Alec Guinness, (8) "The Tin Drum," (Germany), (9) "Best Boy."

1980: (1) "Ordinary People," (2) Robert DeNiro in "Raging Bull," (3) Sissy Spacek in "Coal Miner's Daughter," (4) Timothy Hutton in "Ordinary People," (5) Mary Steenburgen in "Melvin and Howard," (6) Robert Redford for "Ordinary People," (7) Henry Fonda, (8) "Moscow Does Not Believe in Tears," (Russia), (9) "From Mao to Mozart: Isaac Stern in China."

1981: (1) "Chariots of Fire," (2) Henry Fonda in "On Golden Pond," (3) Katharine Hepburn in "On Golden Pond," (4) John Gielgud in "Arthur," (5) Maureen Stapleton in "Reds," (6) Warren Beatty for "Reds," (7) Fuji Photo Film Co.,

Barbara Stanwyck, (8) "Mephisto," (Hungary), (9) "Genocide."

1982: (1) "Gandhi," (2) Ben Kingsley in "Gandhi," (3) Meryl Streep in "Sophie's Choice," (4) Louis Gossett, Jr. in "An Officer and a Gentleman," (5) Jessica Lange in "Tootsie," (6) Richard Attenborough for "Gandhi," (7) Mickey Rooney, (8) "Volver a Empezar (To Begin Again)," (Spain), (9) "Just Another Missing Kid."

1983: (1) "Terms of Endearment," (2) Robert Duvall in "Tender Mercies," (3) Shirley MacLaine in "Terms of Endearment," (4) Jack Nicholson in "Terms of Endearment," (5) Linda Hunt in "The Year of Living Dangerously," (6) James L. Brooks for "Terms of Endearment," (7) Hal Roach, (8) "Fanny and Alexander," (Sweden), (9) "He Makes Me Feel Like Dancin'."

1984: (1) "Amadeus," (2) F. Murray Abraham in "Amadeus," (3) Sally Field in "Places in the Heart," (4) Haing S. Ngor in "The Killing Fields," (5) Peggy Ashcroft in "A Passage to India," (6) Milos Forman for "Amadeus," (7) James Stewart, (8) "Dangerous Moves," (Switzerland), (9) "The Times of Harvey Milk."

1985: (1) "Out of Africa," (2) William Hurt in "Kiss of the Spider Woman," (3) Geraldine Page in "The Trip to Bountiful," (4) Don Ameche in "Cocoon," (5) Anjelica Huston in "Prizzi's Honor," (6) Sydney Pollack for "Out of Africa," (7) Paul Newman, Alex North, (8) "The Official Story," (Argentina), (9) "Broken Rainbow."

1986: (1) "Platoon," (2) Paul Newman in "The Color of Money," (3) Marlee Matlin in "Children of a Lesser God," (4) Michael Caine in "Hannah and Her Sisters," (5) Dianne Wiest in "Hannah and Her Sisters," (6) Oliver Stone for "Platoon," (7) Ralph Bellamy, (8) "The Assault," (Netherlands), (9) "Artie Shaw: Time Is All You've Got" tied with "Down and Out in America."

1987: (1) "The Last Emperor," (2) Michael Douglas in "Wall Street," (3) Cher in "Moonstruck," (4) Sean Connery in "The Untouchables," (5) Olympia Dukakis in "Moonstruck," (6) Bernardo Bertolucci for "The Last Emperor," (8) "Babette's Feast," (Denmark), (9) "The Ten-Year Lunch: The Wit and Legend of the Algonquin Round Table."

1988: (1) "Rain Man," (2) Dustin Hoffman in "Rain Man," (3) Jodie Foster in "The Accused," (4) Kevin Kline in "A Fish Called Wanda," (5) Geena Davis in "The Accidental Tourist," (6) Barry Levinson for "Rain Man," (8) "Pelle the Conqueror," (Denmark), (9) "Hotel Terminus: The Life and Times of Klaus Barbie."

1989: (1) "Driving Miss Daisy," (2) Daniel Day-Lewis in "My Left Foot," (3) Jessica Tandy in "Driving Miss Daisy," (4) Denzel Washington in "Glory," (5) Brenda Fricker in "My Left Foot," (6) Oliver Stone for "Born on the Fourth of July," (7) Akira Kurosawa, (8) "Cinema Paradiso," (Italy), (9) "Common Threads."

1990: (1) "Dances With Wolves," (2) Jeremy Irons in "Reversal of Fortune," (3) Kathy Bates in "Misery," (4) Joe Pesci in "GoodFellas," (5) Whoopi Goldberg in "Ghost," (6) Kevin Costner for "Dances With Wolves," (7) Sophia Loren, Myrna Loy, (8) "Journey of Hope," (Switzerland), (9) "American Dream."

1991: (1) "The Silence of the Lambs," (2) Anthony Hopkins in "The Silence of the Lambs," (3) Jodie Foster in "The Silence of the Lambs," (4) Jack Palance in "City Slickers," (5) Mercedes Ruehl in "The Fisher King," (6) Jonathan Demme for "The Silence of the Lambs," (7) Satyajit Ray, (8) "Mediterraneo," (Italy), (9) "In the Shadow of the Stars."

1992: (1) "Unforgiven," (2) Al Pacino in "Scent of a Woman," (3) Emma Thompson in "Howards End," (4) Gene Hackman in "Unforgiven," (5) Marisa Tomei in "My Cousin Vinny", (6) Clint Eastwood for "Unforgiven," (7) Federico

Caroline Goodall, Liam Neeson

Adi Nitzan, Jonathan Sagalle

Steven Spielberg directs Liam Neeson

Liam Neeson (c) *SCHINDLER'S LIST*
© Universal City Studios/Amblin Entertainment

Ben Kingsley, Liam Neeson, Caroline Goodall

Liam Neeson (l)

SCHINDLER'S LIST

(UNIVERSAL) Producers, Steven Spielberg, Gerald R. Molen, Branko Lustig; Executive Producer, Kathleen Kennedy; Director, Steven Spielberg; Screenplay, Steven Zaillian; Based on the novel by Thomas Keneally; Photography, Janusz Kaminski; Editor, Michael Kahn; Designer, Allan Starski; Music, John Williams; Violin Solos, Itzhak Perlman; Co-Producer, Lew Rywin; Costumes, Anna Biedrzycka-Sheppard; Casting, Lucky Englander, Fritz Fleischhacker, Magdalena Szwarcbart, Tova Cypin, Liat Meiron, Juliet Taylor; DTS Digital Stereo; Black and white/with Deluxe color sequences; Rated R; 195 minutes; December release

CAST

Oskar Schindler	Liam Neeson
Itzhak Stern	Ben Kingsley
Amon Goeth	Ralph Fiennes
Emilie Schindler	Caroline Goodall
Poldek Pfefferberg	Jonathan Sagalle
Helen Hirsch	Embeth Davidtz

and Malgoscha Gebel (Victoria Klonowska), Shmulik Levy (Wilek Chilowicz), Mark Ivanir (Marcel Goldberg), Beatrice Macola (Ingrid), Andrzej Seweryn (Julian Scherner), Friedrich Von Thun (Rolf Czurda), Krzysztof Luft (Herman Toffel), Harry Nehring (Leo John), Norbert Weisser (Albert Hujar), Adi Nitzan (Mila Pfefferberg), Michael Schneider (Juda Dresner), Miri Fabian (Chaja Dresner), Anna Mucha (Danka Dresner), Albert Misak (Mordecai Wulkan), Michael Gordon (Mr. Nussbaum), Aldona Grochal (Mrs. Nussbaum), Jacek Wojcicki (Henry Rosner), Beata Paluch (Manci Rosner), Piotr Polk (Leo Rosner), Ezra Dagan (Rabbi Menasha Levartov), Beata Nowak (Rebecca Tannenbaum), Rami Hauberger (Josef Bau), Leopold Kozlowski, Jerzy Nowak (Investors), Uri Avrahami (Chaim Nowak), Adam Siemion (OD/Chicken Boy), Magdalena Dandourian (Nuisa Horowitz), Pawel Delag (Dolek Horowitz), Shabtai Konorti (Garage Mechanic), Oliwia Dabrowska (Red Genia), Henryk Bista (Mr. Lowenstein), Tadeusz Bradecki (DEF Foreman), Wojciech Klata (Lisiek), Elina Lowensohn (Diana Reiter), Ewa Kolasinska (Irrational Woman), Bettina Kupfer (Regina Perlman), Grzegorz Kwas (Mietek Pemper), Vili Matula (Investigator), Stanislaw Koczanowicz (Doorman), Hans Jorg Assmann (Julius Madritsch), Geno Lechner (Majola), August Schmolzer (Dieter Reeder), Ludger Pistor (Josef Liepold), Beata Rybotycka (Club Singer), Branko Lustig (Nightclub Maitre d'), Artus Maria Matthiessen (Treblinka Commandant), Hans Michael Rehberg (Rudolph Hoss), Eugeniusz Priwiezencew (Waiter), Michael Z. Hoffmann (Montelupich Colonel), Erwin Leder (SS Waffen Officer), Jochen Nickel (Wilhelm Kunde), Andrzej Welminski (Dr. Blancke), Daniel Del Ponte (Dr. Josef Mengele), Marian Glinka (DEF SS Officer), Grzegorz Damiecki (SS Sgt. Kunder), Stanislaw Brejdygant (DEF Guard), Olaf Linde Lubaszenko, Haymon Maria Buttinger, Peter Appiano (Auschwitz Guards), Jacek Pulanecki (Brinnlitz Guard), Martin Semmelrogge (SS Waffen Man), Tomasz Dedek, Slawomir Holland (Gestapo), Tadeusz Huk (Gestapo Brinnlitz), Gerald Alexander Held (SS Bureaucrat), Piotr Cyrwus (Ukranian Guard), Joachim Paul Assbock (Gestapo Clerk Klaus Tauber), Osman Ragheb (Border Guard), Maciej Orlos (German Clerk), Marek Wrona (Toffel's Secretary), Zbigniew Kozlowski (Scherner's Secretary), Marcin Grzymowicz (Czurda's Secretary), Dieter Witting (Bosch), Magdalena Komornicka (Goeth's Girl), Agnieszka Kruk (Czurda's Girl), Anemona Knut (Polish Girl), Jeremy Flynn (Brinnlitz Man), Agnieszka Wagner (Brinnlitz Girl), Jan Jurewicz (Russian Officer), Wieslaw Komasa (Plaszow Depot SS Guard), Maciej Kozlwoski (SS Guard Zablocie), Martin Bergmann (SS NCO Zablocie), Wilhelm Manske, Peter Flechtner, Sigurd Bemme (SS NCO - Ghetto), Ethel Szyc, Lucyna Zabawa (Ghetto Women), Jerzy Sagan (Ghetto Old Man), Ruth Farhi (Old Jewish Woman), Dirk Bender (Clerk at depot), Dariusz Szymaniak (Prisoner at depot), Hanna Kossowska (Ghetto Doctor), Maciej Winkler, Radoslaw Krzyzowski, Jacek Lenczowski (Black Marketeers), Maja Ostaszewska (Frantic Woman), Sebastian Skalski (Stable Boy), Ryszard Radwanski (Pankiewicz), Piotr Kadlcik (Man in pharmacy), Bartek Niebielski (NCO Plaszow), Thomas Morris (Grun), Sebastian Konrad (Engineer Man), Lidia Wyrobiec-Bank (Clara Sternberg), Ravit Ferera (Maria Mischel), Agnieszka Korzeniowska, Dominika Bednarczyk, Alicja Kubaszewska (Ghetto Girls), Danny Marcu, Hans Rosner (Ghetto Men), Alexander Strobele (Montelupich Prisoner), Edward Linde Lubaszenko (Brinnlitz Priest), Goerges Kern (Depot Master), Alexander Buczolich, Michael Schiller, Goetz Otto, Wolfgang Seidenberg, Hubert Kramer (Plaszow SS Guards), Razia Israeli, Dorit Ady Seadia, Esti Yerushalmi (Plaszow Jewish Girls)

Plot Capsule: *The true story of how businessman Oskar Schindler managed to save 1,100 Jews from the Nazi death camps during World War II.*

1993 Academy Award winner for Best Picture, Director, Adapted Screenplay, Cinematography, Art Direction, Original Score, and Film Editing.

National Board of Review Award for Best Picture; NY Film Critics Awards for Best Picture, Supporting Actor (Ralph Fiennes), and Cinematography; LA Film Critics Awards for Best Picture, Cinematography, and Production Design; National Society of Film Critics Awards for Best Picture, Director, Supporting Actor (Fiennes), and Cinematography; Golden Globe Awards for Best Picture (Drama), Director, Screenplay.

The film received Academy Award nominations for actor (Liam Neeson), supporting actor (Ralph Fiennes), costume design, makeup, and sound.

LEFT: Liam Neeson (back row, center)
© Universal City Studios/Amblin Entertainment

Embeth Davidtz (2nd from left), Ralph Fiennes

Ralph Fiennes, Liam Neeson

Liam Neeson, Ben Kingsley

Liam Neeson

Ralph Fiennes, Liam Neeson

TOM HANKS
in *Philadelphia*
© TriStar Pictures
ACADEMY AWARD FOR BEST ACTOR OF 1993

HOLLY HUNTER
in *The Piano*
© Miramax Films
ACADEMY AWARD FOR BEST ACTRESS OF 1993

TOMMY LEE JONES
in *The Fugitive*
© Warner Bros.
ACADEMY AWARD FOR BEST SUPPORTING ACTOR OF 1993

ANNA PAQUIN
in *The Piano*
© Miramax Films
ACADEMY AWARD FOR BEST SUPPORTING ACTRESS OF 1993

223

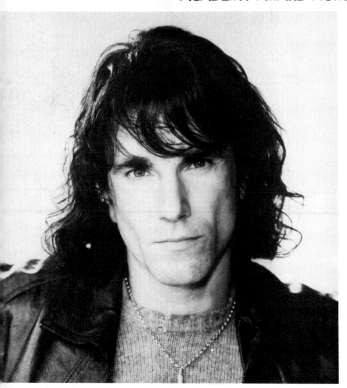

Daniel Day-Lewis in *In the Name of the Father* © Universal City Studios Inc.

Laurence Fishburne in *What's Love Got to Do With It* © Touchstone Pictures

Anthony Hopkins in *The Remains of the Day*
© Columbia Pictures Industries

Liam Neeson in *Schindler's List*
© Universal City Studios/Amblin Entertainment

ACADEMY AWARD NOMINEES FOR BEST ACTRESS

Angela Bassett in *What's Love Got to Do With It* © Touchstone Pictures

Stockard Channing in *Six Degrees of Separation* © Metro-Goldwyn-Mayer Inc.. —

Emma Thompson in *The Remains of the Day*
© Columbia Pictures Industries

Debra Winger in *Shadowlands*
© Savoy Pictures

Leonardo DiCaprio in *What's Eating Gilbert Grape* © Paramount Pictures

Ralph Fiennes in *Schindler's List* © Universal City Studios/Amblin Entertainmen

John Malkovich in *In the Line of Fire*
© Columbia Pictures Industries/Castle Rock

Pete Postlethwaite in *In the Name of the Father*
© Universal City Studios

Holly Hunter in *The Firm* © Paramount Pictures

Rosie Perez in *Fearless* ©Warner Bros.

Winona Ryder in *The Age of Innocence*
© Columbia Pictures Industries

Emma Thompson in *In the Name of the Father*
© Universal City Studios

CINEMATOGRAPHY
JANUSZ KAMINSKI,
Schindler's List

ART DIRECTION
ALLAN STARSKI (art direction),
EWA BRAUN (set decoration),
Schindler's List

Winona Ryder in *The Age of Innocence* (Best Costume Design)
© Columbia Pictures Industries

Steven Spielberg (Best Director) for *Schindler's List*
© Universal City Studios/Amblin Entertainment

DIRECTOR
STEVEN SPIELBERG,
Schindler's List

ORIGINAL SCREENPLAY
JANE CAMPION,
The Piano
CIBY 2000, Miramax Films

SCREENPLAY ADAPTATION
STEVEN ZAILLIAN,
Schindler's List

COSTUME DESIGN
GABRIELLA PESCUCCI,
The Age of Innocence
Cappa/DeFina production

FILM EDITING
MICHAEL KAHN,
Schindler's List

ORIGINAL SCORE
JOHN WILLIAMS,
Schindler's List

ORIGINAL SONG
STREETS OF PHILADELPHIA
from Philadelphia;
Clinica Estetico production, TriStar

BRUCE SPRINGSTEEN (music and lyrics)

Ben Kingsley, Liam Neeson in *Schindler's List*
(Best Screenplay Adaptation, Original Score) © Universal City Studios, Inc.

SHORT FILM (Animated)
THE WRONG TROUSERS,
Aardman Animations Ltd.;
Nicholas Park, producer

SHORT FILM (Live Action)
BLACK RIDER,
Trans-Film GmbH;
Pepe Danquart, producer

MAKEUP
GREG CANNOM,
VE NEILL,
YOLANDA TOUSSIENG,
Mrs. Doubtfire;
Blue Wolf production; 20th Century Fox

SOUND
GARY SUMMERS,
GARY RYDSTROM,
SHAWN MURPHY,
RON JUDKINS,
Jurassic Park;
Amblin Entertainment production, Universal

SOUND EFFECTS EDITING
GARY RYDSTROM,
RICHARD HYMNS,
Jurassic Park

VISUAL EFFECTS
DENNIS MUREN,
STAN WINSTON,
PHIL TIPPETT,
MICHAEL LANTIERI,
Jurassic Park

DOCUMENTARY (Feature)
I AM A PROMISE:
THE CHILDREN OF
STANTON ELEMENTARY SCHOOL,
Verite Films; Susan Raymond,
Alan Raymond,
producers

DOCUMENTARY (Short Subject)
DEFENDING OUR LIVES,
Cambridge Documentary Films;
Margaret Lazarus, Renner Wunderlich,
producers

JEAN HERSHOLT
HUMANITARIAN AWARD

PAUL NEWMAN

HONORARY AWARD
DEBORAH KERR

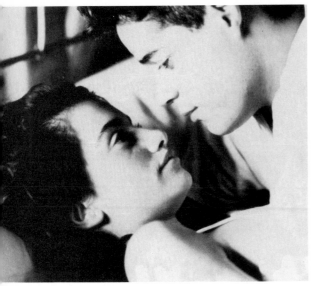

Penelope Cruz, Jorge Sanz

Jorge Sanz, Penelope Cruz

ACADEMY AWARD FOR BEST FOREIGN-LANGUAGE FILM OF 1993

BELLE EPOQUE

(SONY PICTURES CLASSICS) Director, Fernando Trueba; Screenplay, Rafael Azcona; Story, Rafael Azcona, Jose Luis Garcia Sanchez, Fernando Trueba; Executive Producer, Andres Vicente Gomez; Line Producer, Cristina Huete; Photography, Jose Luis Alcaine; Music, Antoine Duhamel; Editor, Carmen Frias; Art Director, Juan Botella; Costumes, Lala Huete; Produced by Fernando Trueba P.C., S.A. (Madrid), Lola Films (Barcelona), Animatografo (Lisboa), French Production (Paris) with the cooperation of Sogepag & Eurimages; Spanish; Cinemascope; Color; Rated R; 108 minutes; March, 1994 release

CAST

Manolo	Fernando Fernan Gomez
Fernando	Jorge Sanz
Rocio	Maribel Verdu
Violeta	Ariadna Gil
Clara	Miriam Diaz-Aroca
Luz	Penelope Cruz
Amalia, Manolo's Wife	Mary Carmen Ramirez
Danglard, Amalia's Manager	Michel Galabru
Juanito, Rocio's Sister	Gabino Diego
Dona Asun, Juanito's Mother	Chus Lampreave
Don Luis, The Priest	Agustin Gonzalez
First Soldier (Father-in-Law)	Juan Jose Otegui
Second Soldier	Jesus Bonilla
Polonia, The Madman	Maria Galiana
Paco	Juan Potau
Palomo	Felix Cubero
The Mayor	Marciano De La Fuente
Rorro	Jose Antonio Sacristan
Villager	Manuel Huete

Plot Capsule *In 1931 Spain, a young army deserter wanders the countryside where he befriends an elderly painter with four desirable daughters.*

1993 Academy Award Winner for Best Foreign Language Film
© Sony Pictures Classics

Maribel Verdu

THE OAK

(MK2) Producers, Eliane Stutterheim, Sylvain Bursztejn, Lucian Pintilie; Executive Producer, Constantin Popescu; Director/Screenplay, Lucian Pintilie; Based on the novel *Bylanta* by Ion Baiesu; Photography, Doru Mitran; Designer, Calin Papura; Editor, Victorita Nae; co-produced by La Sept, with the participation of Canal+; French-Romanian; Color; Not rated; 105 minutes; January release

CAST

Nela	Maia Morgenstern
Mitica	Razvan Vasilescu
The Mayor	Victor Rebengiuc
The Country Priest	Dorel Visan
The Priest's Wife	Mariana Mihut
The Lawyer	Dan Condurache
Nela's Father	Virgil Andriescu
Nela's Mother	Leopoldina Balanuta
Butusina	Matei Alexandru
Priest on the train	Gheorghe Visu
Mitica's Assistant	Magda Catone
Titi	Ionel Mahailescu

Plot Capsule: *Nela arrives in the Romanian provinces to begin her teaching job but finds a world devestated by violence and bureaucracy.*
© MK2

![Maia Morgenstern, Razvan Vasilescu]
Maia Morgenstern, Razvan Vasilescu

Benoit Poelvoorde

![Jacqueline Poelvoorde Pappaert, Benoît Poelvoorde]
Jacqueline Poelvoorde Pappaert, Benoît Poelvoorde

MAN BITES DOG

(ROXIE RELEASING) Producers, Remy Belvaux, Andre Bonzel, Benoit Poelvoorde; Director, Remy Belvaux; Screenplay, Andre Bonzel, Benoit Poelvoorde, Remy Belvaux, Vincent Tavier; Photography, Andre Bonzel; Music, Jean-Marc Chenut, Laurence Dufrene; Editors, Eric Dardill, Remy Belvaux; a Les Artistes Anonymes production; Belgian-French; Black and white; Not rated; 92 minutes; January release

CAST

Ben	Benoit Poelvoorde
Remy	Rémy Belvaux
Andre	André Bonzel
Ben's Mother	Jacqueline Poelvoorde Pappaert
Ben's Grandmother	Nelly Pappaert
Ben's Grandfather	Hector Pappaert
Jenny	Jenny Drye
Malou	Malou Madou
Boby	Willy Vandenbroeck

Plot Capsule: *A reporter and his cameraman follow a serial killer to capture his actions for a documentary.*
© Roxie Releasing

Hector Pappaert, Benoît Poelvoorde

Maurizio Nichetti

VOLERE VOLARE

(FINE LINE FEATURES) a.k.a *I Want to Fly*; Executive Producer, Ernesto Di Sarro; Directors/Screenplay, Maurizio Nichetti, Guido Manuli; Photography, Mario Battistoni; Sets/Costumes, Maria Pia Angelini; Animation, Gruppo Quick Sand; Special Effects, Gruppo La Rocca; Presented in association with Penta Films; Italian, 1991; Dolby Stereo; Color; Rated R; 92 minutes; February release

CAST

Maurizio	Maurizio Nichetti
Martina	Angela Finocchiaro
Girlfriend	Mariella Valentini
Brother	Patrizio Roversi
The "Child"	Remo Remotti
The Architects	Mario Gravier, Luigi Gravier
The Businessman	Renato Scarpa
The Chef	Massimo Sarchielli
The Necrophiliacs	Osvaldo Salvi, Lidia Biondi
The Taxi Driver	Enrico Grazioli
The Mugger	Mario Pardi

Plot Capsule: *A bizarre animation sound engineer named Maurizio meets Martina, a desirable "social assistant," and finds himself slowly turning into a cartoon character.*
© Fine Line Features

Maurizio Nichetti

Robert Carlyle

RIFF-RAFF

(FINE LINE FEATURES) Producer, Sally Hibbin; Director, Ken Loach; Screenplay, Bill Jesse; Photography, Barry Ackroyd; Designer, Martin Johnson; Music, Stewart Copeland; Editor, Jonathan Morris; British; Color; Not rated; 96 minutes; February release

CAST

Stevie	Robert Carlyle
Susan	Emer McCourt
Shem	Jimmy Coleman
Mo	George Moss
Larry	Ricky Tomlinson
Kevin	David Finch
Kojo	Richard Belgrave
Fiaman	Ade Spara
Desmonde	Derek Young
Smurph	Bill Moores
Ken Jones	Luke Kelly
Mick	Garrie J. Lammin

Plot Capsule: *Comedy centers on ex-con-turned-construction worker Stevie, his fellow workers at a London building site, and an aspiring singer named Susan who moves in with him.*
© Fine Line Features

Emer McCourt, Robert Carlyle

Tara Morice

Tara Morice, Paul Mercurio

Sonia Kruger-Tayler

STRICTLY BALLROOM

(MIRAMAX) Producer, Tristram Miall; Executive Producer, Antoinette Albert; Director, Baz Luhrmann; Screenplay, Baz Luhrmann, Craig Pearce; Original Idea, Baz Luhrmann; From a screenplay by Baz Luhrmann, Andrew Bovell; Photography, Steve Mason; Designer, Catherine Martin; Editor, Jill Bilcock; Music, David Hirschfelder; Costumes, Angus Strathie; Choreographer, John "Cha Cha" O'Connell; Casting, Faith Martin; a Beyond Films Ltd. production; Australian; Color; Rated PG; 95 minutes; February release

CAST

Scott Hastings	Paul Mercurio
Fran	Tara Morice
Barry Fife	Bill Hunter
Shirley Hastings	Pat Thomson
Liz Holt	Gia Carides
Les Kendall	Peter Whitford
Doug Hastings	Barry Otto
Ken Railings	John Hannan
Tina Sparkle	Sonia Kruger-Tayler
Charm Leachman	Kris McQuade
Wayne Burns	Pip Mushin
Vanessa Cronin	Leonie Page
Rico	Antonio Vargas
Ya Ya	Armonia Benedito
Terry	Jack Webster
Kylie	Lauren Hewett
Luke	Steve Grace
J.J. Silvers	Wayne Bertram
Waitress	Di Emery
Natalie	Lara Mulcahy
Clarry	Brian M. Logan
Merv	Michael Burgess
Nathan Starkey	Todd McKenney
Pam Short	Kerry Shrimpton

Plot Capsule: *Dancer Scott Hastings causes a stir at the ballroom dancing semifinals by improvising new steps. As a result he must find a new partner for the championships, reluctantly settling for the shy but determined Fran.*
© Miramax Films

Paul Mercurio, Tara Morice

Lumi Cavazos, Marco Leonardi

Marco Leonardi, Lumi Cavazos

LIKE WATER FOR CHOCOLATE

(MIRAMAX) Producer/Director, Alfonso Arau; Screenplay, Laura Esquivel, based on her novel; Photography, Emmanuel Lubezki, Steve Bernstein; Editors, Carlos Bolado, Francisco Chiu; Music, Leo Brower; Art Directors, Marco Antonio Arteaga, Mauricio De Aguinaco, Denise Pizzini; Costumes, Carlos Brown; Mexican; Color; Rated R; 113 minutes; February release

CAST

Tita	Lumi Cavazos
Pedro	Marco Leonardi
Mama Elena	Regina Torne
John Brown	Mario Ivan Martinez
Nacha	Ada Carrasco
Rosaura	Yareli Arizmendi
Gertrudis	Claudette Maille
Chencha	Pilar Aranda
Priest	Farnesio De Bernal
Sgt. Trevino	Joaquin Garrido
Juan Alejandrez	Rodolfo Arias
Paquita Lobo	Margarita Isabel
Esperanza	Sandra Arau
Alex	Andres Garcia, Jr.
Nicolas	Regino Herrera
Rosalio	Genaro Aguirre

and David Ostrosky (Juan De La Garza), Brigida Alexander (Aunt Mary), Amado Ramirez (Pedro's Father), Arcelia Ramirez (Great Niece - Narrator), Socorro Rodriguez (Paquita's Friend), Rafael Garcia Zuazua (Godfather), Rafael Garcia Zuazua Jr. (Young Alex), Edurne Ballestros (Young Tita), Melisa Mares (Baby Rosaura), Garbiela Canundas (Young Rosaura), Natalia De La Fuente (Baby Gertrudis), Neatriz Elias (Young Gertrudis)

Plot Capsule: *Because of a family tradition Tita, as the youngest daughter, must forsake marriage and take care of her mother, despite her desire to wed Paqua. To be near Tita, Paqua agrees to marry her older sister.*
© Miramax Films

Lumi Cavazos, with baby

Lumi Cavazos (L)

Bruno Ganz, Kerry Fox, Lisa Harrow

Kerry Fox

THE LAST DAYS OF CHEZ NOUS

(FINE LINE FEATURES) Producer, Jane Chapman; Director, Gillian Armstrong; Screenplay, Helen Garner; Photography, Geoffrey Simpson; Designer, Janet Patterson; Music, Paul Grabowsky; Editor, Nicholas Beauman; Associate Producer, Mark Turnbull; Casting, Liz Mullinar Consultants; Australian; Dolby Stereo; Color; Rated R; 96 minutes; February release

CAST

Beth	Lisa Harrow
J.P.	Bruno Ganz
Vicki	Kerry Fox
Annie	Miranda Otto
Tim	Kiri Paramore
Beth's Father	Bill Hunter
Angelo	Lex Marinos
Sally	Mickey Camilleri
Beth's Mother	Lynne Murphy
Janet	Claire Haywood
Susie	Leanne Bundy
Man in cafe	Wilson Alcorn
Thief	Tom Weaver
Mayor	Bill Brady
Waitress	Eva Di Cesare
Waiter	Danny Caretti
Singing Woman	Olga Sanderson
Clinic Nurse	Joyce Hopwood
Stranger	Steve Cox
Old Man (Desert Tourist)	Harry Griffiths
Desert Waitress	Amanda Martin

Plot Capsule: *Beth's younger sister Vicki returns from Europe, moves in with her sister's family and begins an affair with Beth's husband, J.P.*
© Fine Line Features

Lisa Harrow, Miranda Otto

Peter Riegert, Armin Mueller-Stahl

UTZ

(FIRST RUN FEATURES/CASTLE HILL) Producer, John Goldschmidt; Executive Producers, William Sargent, John Goldschmidt; Director, George Sluizer; Screenplay, Hugh Whitemore; Based on the novel by Bruce Chatwin; Photography, Gerard Vandenberg; Editor, Lin Friedman; Music, Nicola Piovani; Designer, Karel Vacek; Costumes, Marie Frankova; British-German-Italian; Color; Not rated; 95 minutes; February release

CAST

Baron von Utz	Armin Mueller-Stahl
Marta	Brenda Fricker
Marius Fischer	Peter Riegert
Dr. Vaclav Orlik	Paul Scofield
Grandmother	Miriam Karlin
Utz (age 18)	Christian Mueller-Stahl
Young Marta	Caroline Guthrie
Museum Director	Pauline Melville

Plot Capsule: *Drama explores the life of a Czech porcelin collector named Utz who is visited in Prague by an American art collector*
© First Run Features.

Francois Cluzet, Gregoire Colin

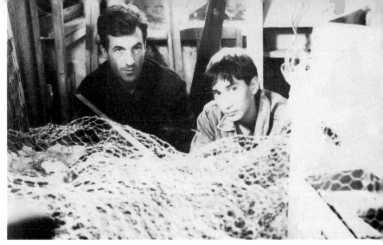

OLIVIER OLIVIER

(SONY PICTURES CLASSICS) Producer, Marie-Laure Reyre; Co-Producer, Christian Ferry; Director/Screenplay, Agnieszka Holland; Adaptation, Agnieszka Holland, Yves Lapointe; Dialogues, Agnieszka Holland, Regis Debray; Photography, Bernard Zitzermann; Art Director, Helene Bourgy; Music, Zbigniew Preisner; Costumes, Ewa Biejat; Editor, Isabelle Lorente; a co-production of Olines Productions Films A2 with the participation of Canal, Sofica Investimage 3 and Centre National de la Cinematographie; French; Color; Rated R; 110 minutes; February release

CAST

Dr. Serge Duval	Francois Cluzet
Elisabeth Duval	Brigitte Rouan
Police Officer Druot	Jean-Francois Stevenin
Olivier	Gregoire Colin
Nadine	Marina Golovine
Marcel	Frederic Quiring
Nadine as a child	Faye Gatteau
Olivier as a child	Emmanuel Morozof
Little Paul	Florian Billion
Babette as a child	Carole Lemerle
The Cop	Jean-Bernard Josko
The Neighbor	Lucrece De La Chenardicere
The Grandmother	Madeleine Marie
The Drug Addict	Francoise Lorente
Micky	Alexis Derlon
Simard	Mathias Jung
Babette	Vanessa Martin
Druot's Colleague	Luc Etienne
The Woman with the cat	Marcelle Beignon

Plot Capsule: *Nine year-old Olivier vanishes one day, driving his doting mother into despair. Six years later a teenage prostitute shows up claming to de the long lost boy. This drama was inspired by an actual incident.*

LA Film Critics Award for best music score (along with Preisner's scores for Blue and The Secret Garden).
© Sony Pictures Classics

Brigitte Rouan, Emmanuel Morozof

Gregoire Colin, Brigitte Rouan

Marina Golovine

Enrico Lo Verso, Giuseppe Ieracitano

IL LADRO DI BAMBINI
(STOLEN CHILDREN)

(SAMUEL GOLDWYN CO.) Producer, Angelo Rizzoli; RAI Producer, Stefano Munafo; Executive Producer, Enzo Porcelli; French Co-Producer, Bruno Pesery; Director, Gianni Amelio; Screenplay/Story, Gianni Amelio, Sandro Petraglia, Stefano Rulli; Photography, Tonino Nardi, Renato Tafuri; Art Director, Andrea Crisanti, Giuseppe M. Gaudino; Costumes, Gianna Gissi, Luciana Morosetti; Editor, Simona Paggi; Music, Franco Piersanti; Italian-French; Color; Not rated; 112 minutes; March release

CAST

Antonio	Enrico Lo Verso
Rosetta	Valentina Scalici
Luciano	Giuseppe Ieracitano
Martine	Florence Darel
Nathalie	Marina Golovine
Grignani	Fabio Alessandrini
Priest at the children's home	Agnostino Zumbo
Neapolitan Carabinieres	Vincenzo Peluso, Santo Santonocito
Antonio's Sister	Vitalba Andrea
Papaleo	Massimo De Lorenzo
Girl at dinner	Celeste Brancato
Police Chief	Renato Carpentieri

Plot Capsule: *A young soldier is assigned to transport two troubled children to an orphanage in Bologna after their mother is arrested. The boy, Luciano, is a melancholy asthmatic while his sister Rosetta was forced into prostitution by their mother.*
© Samuel Goldwyn Co.

Takehiro Murata, Misa Shimizu

Takeo Nakahara, Misa Shimizu,
Takehiro Murata

OKOGE

(CINEVISTA) Producers, Yoshinori Takazawa, Masashi Moromizato, Takehiro Nakajima; Director/Screenplay, Takehiro Nakajima; Photography, Yoshimasa Hakata; Art Director, Kunihiro Inomata; Editor, Kenji Goto; Music Producer, Hiroshi Ariyoshi; Japanese; Color; Not rated; 120 minutes; March release

CAST

Sayoko	Misa Shimizu
Goh	Takehiro Murata
Tochi	Takeo Nakahara
Kurihara	Masayuki Shionoya
Kineo, Goh's Mother	Noriko Sengoku
Touichi, Goh's Brother	Kyozo Nagatsuka
Yayoi, Tochi's Wife	Toshie Negishi
Tamio, the Transvestite Singer	Atsushi Fukazawa
Tsuyuki, the Bartender	Takatoshi Takeda

Plot Capsule: *A naive young girl named Sayoko meets Goh and his married male lover Tochi, and allows them to use her apartment for their sexual trysts.*
© Cinevista

Misa Shimizu, Takehiro Murata

Gong Li

Gong Li, Yang Liu Chun

Gong Li

THE STORY OF QIU JU

(SONY PICTURES CLASSICS) Executive Producer, Ma Fung Kwok; Coordinating Producer, Feng Yi Ting; Director, Zhang Yimou; Screenplay, Liu Heng; Photography, Chi Xiao Ling, Yu Xiao Qun; Music, Zhao Ji Ping; Editor, Du Yuan; Chinese-Mandarin; Dolby Stereo; Color; Rated PG; 100 minutes; April release

CAST

Qiu Ju	Gong Li
Village Head	Lei Lao Sheng
Husband of Qiu Ju	Liu Pei Qi
Mr. Li	Ge Zhi Jun
Sister-in-Law	Yang Liu Chun

Plot Capsule: *A Chinese peasant woman, Qiu Ju, is determined at any cost to seek an apology from the village chief who has injured her husband during an argument.*

National Society of Film Critics Award for best foreign language film; NY Film Critics Award to Gong Li for best supporting actress.
© Sony Pictures Classics

Gong Li

Gong Li, Lei Lao Sheng

Gong Li

LEOLO

(FINE LINE FEATURES) Producers, Lyse Lafontaine, Aimee Danis; Executive Producers, Aimee Danis, Claudette Viau; Director/Screenplay, Jean-Claude Lauzon; Photography, Guy Dufaux; Designer, Francois Seguin; Costumes, Francois Barbeau; Casting, Lucie Robitaille; French; Color; Not rated; 107 minutes; April release

CAST

Narration	Gilbert Sicotte
Leolo	Maxime Collin
Mother	Ginette Reno
Grandfather	Julien Guiomar
The Word Tamer	Pierre Bourgault
Bianca	Giudiita Del Vecchio
Psychiatrist	Andree Lachapelle
Career Adviser	Denys Arcand
Teacher	Germain Houde
Fernand	Yves Montmarquette
Fernand's Enemy	Lorne Brass
Father	Roland Blouin
Rita	Genevieve Samson
Nanette	Marie-Helene Montpetit
Leolo at six	Francis Saint-Onge
Fernand at sixteen	Alex Nadeau
Gynecologist	Louis Grenier
Geography Teacher	Richard Guevremont
Little Godin	Eric Cadorette
Fishmonger	Aaron Tager

and Luc Seguin (Latourelle), Simon Gosselin (Paquette), Luc Proulx (Fisher), Catherine Lemieux (Regina), Nick Fasano (Italian Salesman), Jade Landry Cuerrier (Young Nanette), Magalie Beauregard (Young Rita), Simon LaVigne (Baby), Amedeo Carlo Mangiu (Tommaso), Maria Petraglia (Contadina), Salvator Giuffrida (Umberto), Mikael Baillarge-Lafontaine (Diver)

Plot Capsule: *A young boy in East Montreal settles into the world of his wild imagination to escape from the realities of his strange family.*
© Fine Line

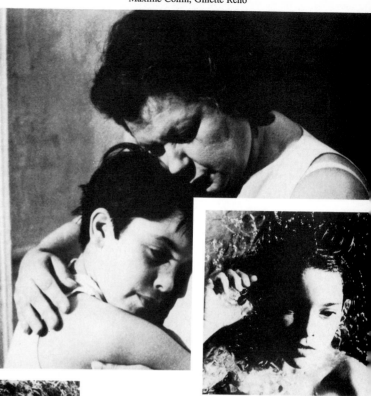

Maxime Collin, Ginette Reno

Maxime Collin

BELOW: Nathaniel Parker, Karina Lombard

Rowena King, Karina Lombard

WIDE SARGASSO SEA

(FINE LINE FEATURES) Producer, Jan Sharp; Executive Producer, Sara Risher; Line Producer, Karen Koch; Director, John Duigan; Screenplay, Jan Sharp, Carole Angier, John Duigan; Based on the novel by Jean Rhys; Photography, Geoff Burton; Music, Stewart Copeland; Editors, Anne Goursaud, Jimmy Sandoval; Designer, Franckie D; Costumes, Norma Moriceau; a Laughing Kookaburra production; Australian; Dolby Stereo; Color; Rated NC-17; 96 minutes; April release

CAST

Antoinette Cosway	Karina Lombard
Edward Rochester	Nathaniel Parker
Annette Cosway	Rachel Ward
Paul Mason	Michael York
Aunt Cora	Martine Beswicke
Christophene	Claudia Robinson
Richard Mason	Huw Christie Williams
Young Antoinette	Casey Berna
Amelie	Rowena King
Daniel Cosway	Ben Thomas
Young Bull	Paul Campbell
Drummer	Audbrey Pilatus
Nelson	Ancile Gloudin
Pierre	Dominic Needham
Benbow	Kevin Thomas
Myra	Aisha King
Hilda	Anika Gordon
Rose	Elfreida Reid

and Bobby Smith (Machete Man), Suzanne McMannus (Florinda), Pat Gooden (Margaretta), Clifford Burt (Fraser), Naomi Watts (Fanny Grey), James Earl (Man with torch), Kayarsha Russell (Cora's Maid), Jenny Wilson (Grace Poole), Helen Woods (Leah)

Plot Capsule: *Free-spirited Antoinette Cosway, raised in 1800s Jamaica, is forced into marriage with Englishman Edward Rochester, their erotic liaison resulting in tragedy.*
© Fine Line Features

Robert Joamie

Anne Parillaud, Patrick Bergin

Anne Parillaud, Jason Scott Lee

MAP OF THE HUMAN HEART

(MIRAMAX) Producers, Tim Bevan, Vincent Ward; Executive Producer, Graham Bradstreet; Co-Producers, Tim White, Linda Beath, Sylvaine Sainderichin; Director/ Story, Vincent Ward; Screenplay, Louis Nowra; Photography, Eduardo Serra; Designer, John Beard; Costumes, Renee April; Special Effects Supervisor, Richard Conway; Associate Producer, Redmond Morris; a Working Title Films, Vincent Ward Films, Les Films Ariane and Sunrise Films presentation; British-Australian-French-Canadian; Dolby Stereo; Panavision; Color; Rated R; 107 minutes; April release

CAST

Avik	Jason Scott Lee
Young Avik	Robert Joamie
Albertine	Anne Parillaud
Young Albertine	Annie Galipeau
Walter Russell	Patrick Bergin
Rainee Russell	Clotilde Courau
Clark	John Cusack
Sister Banville	Jeanne Moreau
Farmboy	Ben Mendelsohn
Boleslaw	Jerry Snell
Navigator	Matt Holland
Avik's Grandmother	Jayko Pitseolak
Chopper Pilot	Frank Verellen
Chopper NCO	Jeff Mahoney
Eskimo Woman/Cook	Rebecca Vevee
Eskimo Elder	Josape Kopalee
Anna	Reepah A...ak
Beatrice	Monique Spazia...
Newspaper Boy	Jod Leveille Bernard
Indian Patient	Edouard Kurtness
Doctor	Harry Hill
Thelma	Anick Matern
Michael	Marc Ruel
Messenger	Tyley Ross
Homeguard	Griffith Brewer
Photographer	Robert Higden
Oilman in bar	Robin Dorken
Barman	Bill Rowat
Stephen	Benoit Bissonnette
MP	Richard Zeman
American Soldier	Haden Devine
Captain Johns	Gorden Masten
Ginger	Michelle Turmel
Hotel Bellboy	Sean Hayes
Walter's NCO	Rick Manburg
Moravian Minister	Dennis St. John
Doctor on boat	Kliment Dentchev
Margarete	Tamar Koslov
Guest	Bronwen Mantel

Plot Capsule: *Sprawling drama, set between the years 1931 and 1965. Inuit Eskimo Avik, while a boy, is brought from his home in the Arctic Circle to Montreal, where he befriends, then ultimately falls in love with, a half-Indian, half-French - Canadian girl named Albertine.*

© Miramax Films

Patrick Bergin

Anne Parillaud, Jason Scott Lee

Rick Moranis, Eric Idle

Eric Idle, Barbara Hershey

Rick Moranis

Eric Idle, John Cleese

SPLITTING HEIRS

(UNIVERSAL) Producers, Simon Bosanquet, Redmond Morris; Executive Producer/Screenplay, Eric Idle; Director, Robert Young; Photography, Tony Pierce-Roberts; Music, Michael Kamen; Designer, John Beard; Editor, John Jympson; Costumes, Penny Rose; Casting, Michelle Guish; a Prominent Features production; British; Dolby Stereo; Technicolor; Rated PG-13; 88 minutes; April release

CAST

Henry	Rick Moranis
Tommy Patel	Eric Idle
Duchess Lucinda	Barbara Hershey
Kitty	Catherine Zeta Jones
Raoul P. Shadgrind	John Cleese
Angela	Sadie Frost
Butler	Stratford Johns
Mrs. Bullock	Brenda Bruce
Andrews	William Franklyn
Mrs. Patel	Charubala Chokshi
14th Duke	Jeremy Clyde
Brittle	Richard Huw
Jobson the Doorman	Eric Sykes
Nanny	Bridget McConnel
Adoption Agent	Bill Stewart
Tour Guide	Paul Brooke
Sgt. Richardson	David Ross
CID Officer	Cal Macaninch
Gita	Anisha Gangotra
Barmaid	Amanda Dickinson
Police Constable	Chris Jenkinson
Photographer	Keith Smith
German Tourist	Stephen Grothgar
Woman with dog	Madge Ryan
Vicar at hunt	Bill Wallis
Hunt Saboteur	Cameron Blakeley
Doreen	Louise Downey
Old Major	Llewellyn Rees
French Drivers	Paul Weston, Tim Lawrence
Couple at restaurant	Gary & Michelle Lineker

Plot Capsule: *Because of a mix-up while he was a baby Tommy Patel is dismayed to learn that his friend Henry is the wrongly designated heir to Tommy's title and fortune, a mistake he hopes to rectify by disposing of Henry.*

© Universal City Studios, Inc.

Denzel Washington, Kenneth Branagh, Emma Thompson, Richard Briers, Brian Blessed, Kate Beckinsale, Robert Sean Leonard

Kate Beckinsale, Robert Sean Leonard

Michael Keaton, Ben Elton

Denzel Washington, Richard Briers, Brian Blessed

MUCH ADO ABOUT NOTHING

(SAMUEL GOLDWYN CO.) Producers, Kenneth Branagh, David Parfitt, Stephen Evans; Director/Screenplay, Kenneth Branagh; Based on the play by William Shakespeare; Photography, Roger Lanser; Music, Patrick Doyle; Editor, Andrew Marcus; Designer, Tim Harvey; Costumes; Phyllis Dalton; a Renaissance Films production in association with American Playhouse Theatrical Films and BBC Films; British; Dolby Stereo; Technicolor; Rated PG-13; 110 minutes; May release

CAST

Don Pedro, Prince of Arragon	Denzel Washington
Benedick, of Padua	Kenneth Branagh
Claudio, of Florence	Robert Sean Leonard
Don John, Don Pedro's half brother	Keanu Reeves
Borachio, follower of Don John	Gerard Horan
Conrade, follower of Don John	Richard Clifford
Leonato, Governor of Messina	Richard Briers
Antonio, his brother	Brian Blessed
Balthasar, a Singer	Patrick Doyle
Friar Francis, a Priest	Jimmy Yuill
Hero, Leonato's Daughter	Kate Beckinsale
Margaret, attendant on Hero	Imelda Staunton
Ursula, attendant on Hero	Phyllida Law
Beatrice, an orphan, Leonato's Niece	Emma Thompson
Dogberry, Constable of the Watch	Michael Keaton
Verges, the Headborough	Ben Elton
The Sexton	Teddy Jewesbury
George Seacole	Andy Hockley
Francis Seacole	Chris Barnes
Hugh Oatcake	Conrad Nelson
A Boy, servant to Benedick	Alex Scott
Messenger	Alex Lowe

Plot Capsule: *At a villa in Tuscany Prince Don Pedro hopes to see his friend Claudio woo and marry the lovely Hero, and conspires to see that the ever-sparring Benedick and Beatrice realize their true love for one another.*
© Samuel Goldwyn Co.

Emma Thompson, Kenneth Branagh

Emma Thompson,
Kate Beckinsale

Robert Sean Leonard, Kate Beckinsale

Alex Lowe, Kenneth Branagh, Robert Sean Leonard,
Denzel Washington, Keanu Reeves, Gerard Horan, Richard Clifford

Andrew Kelley, Maarten Smit

FOR A LOST SOLDIER

(STRAND RELEASING) Producer, Matthijs van Heijningen; Director/Screenplay, Roeland Kerbosch; From an adaptation by Don Bloch; Photography, Nils Post; Art Director, Vincent De Pater; Costumes, Jany Temime; Editor, August Verschueren; Music, Joop Stokkermans; a Sigma Film production in cooperation with Avro-TV Holland; Dutch; Color; Not rated; 93 minutes; May release

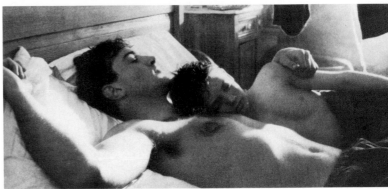

CAST

Young Jeroen Boman	Maarten Smit
Walt Cook	Andrew Kelley
Old Jeroen Boman	Jeroen Krabbe
Hait	Freark Smink
Mem	Elsje De Wijn
Laura	Valerie Valentine
Jan	Derk-Jan Kroon
Henk	Wiendelt Hooijer
Bondien	Iris Misset
Elly	Gineke De Jager
Gertie	Tatum Dagelet
Renske	Marie Josee Kouwenhoven
Chuck	William Sutton
Ventriloquist	Andrew Butling
Winslow	Andrew Cassani
Mother	Moniek Kramer

and Antoinette van Belle (Lady Companion), Rients Gratama (Vicar), Gees Linnebank (Schoolteacher), Steffen van der Kolk, Bonnie Doets, Cathelijne Lubsen, Loes Ruizeveld, Yuri Huyg, Marcel Vogelaar (Ballet Dancers)

Plot Capsule: *A choreographer reflects back on his childhood in 1945 Holland when he fell in love with a young Canadian soldier during his country's liberation.*
© Strand Releasing

Jeroen Krabbe, Maarten Smit

Maarten Smit, Andrew Kelley

SOFIE

(ARROW RELEASING) Producer, Lars Kolvig; Director, Liv Ullmann; Screenplay, Liv Ullmann, Peter Poulsen; Photography, Jorgen Persson; Art Director, Peter Hoimark; Editor, Grethe Moldrup; Costumes, Jette Termann; Danish-Norwegian-Swedish; Color; Not rated; 145 minutes; May release

CAST

Sofie	Karen-Lise Mynster
Frederikke	Ghita Norby
Semmy	Erland Josephson
Hojby	Jesper Christensen
Jonas	Torben Zeller
Frederik	Henning Moritzen
Gottlieb	Stig Hoffmeyer
Jonas' Mother	Kirsten Rolffes
Tante Pulle	Lotte Herman
Aron (age 3)	Jonas Oddermose
Aron (age 7)	David Naym
Aron (age 11-14)	Jacob Allon
Aron (age 18)	Kasper Barfoed
Rose Philipson	Sanne Granngaard
Sofie's Grandmother	Elna Brodthagen
Belse	Elin Reimer
Malle	Lone Herman

Plot Capsule: *Drama follows Sofie through her arranged marriage with Jonas, her devotion to her son and a tragic affair with her brother-in-law. Directorial debut of actress Liv Ullmann.*
© Arrow Releasing

Ghita Norby, Erland Josephson

Nick Lamont, Anthony Watson, Denise Thomas, Leigh McCormack, Ayse Owens, Patricia Morrison, Joy Blakeman

THE LONG DAY CLOSES

(SONY PICTURES CLASSICS) Producer, Olivia Stewart; Executive Producers, Ben Gibson, Colin MacCabe; Executive in Charge of Production, Angela Topping; Director/Screenplay, Terence Davies; Photography, Michael Coulter; Designer, Christopher Hobbs; Editor, William Diver; Costumes, Monica Howe; Music Supervisor, Bob Last; Casting, Doreen Jones; British; Color; Rated PG; 82 minutes; May release

CAST

Mother	Marjorie Yates
Bud	Leigh McCormack
Kevin	Anthony Watson
John	Nicholas Lamont
Helen	Ayse Owens
Edna	Tina Malone
Curly	Jimmy Wilde
Mr. Nicholls	Robin Polley
Mr. Bushell	Peter Ivatts
Frances	Joy Blakeman
Jean	Denise Thomas
Amy	Patricia Morrison
Billy	Gavin Mawdsley
Laborer/Christ	Kirk McLaughlin
Black Man	Marcus Heath
Nun	Victoria Davies
Nurse	Brenda Peters
Albie	Karl Skeggs
Bullies	Lee Blenner-Hassett, Peter Hollier, Jason Jevons

Plot Capsule: *A memory piece following the day-to-day life of a shy young boy in 1950's Liverpool who uses the movies as his escape.*
© Sony Pictures Classics

Ayse Owens, Leigh McCormack, Marjorie Yates

Ayse Owens, Leigh McCormack

ROMPER STOMPER

(ACADEMY ENTERTAINMENT) Producers, Daniel Scharf, Ian Pringle; Director/Screenplay, Geoffrey Wright; Photography, Ron Hagen; Designer, Steven Jones-Evans; Costumes, Anna Borghesi; Editor, Bill Murphy; Music, John Clifford White; Associate Producer, Phil Jones; a Seon Films production, in association with the Australian Film Commission, Film Victoria; Australian; Eastmancolor; Rated NC-17; 92 minutes; June release

CAST

Hando	Russell Crowe
Davey	Daniel Pollock
Gabe	Jacqueline McKenzie
Martin	Alex Scott
Sonny Jim	Leigh Russell
Cackles	Daniel Wyllie
Bubs	James McKenna
Champ	Eric Mueck
Brett	Frank Magree
Luke	Christopher McLean
Megan	Josephine Keen
Tracy	Samantha Bladon
Tiger	Tony Lee

Plot Capsule: *Drama exploring the violent lives of a group of Neo-Nazi skinheads in Melbourne, Australia.*
© Academy Entertainment Inc.

Daniel Pollock, Jacqueline McKenzie, Russell Crowe

Director Agnes Varda, Philippe Maron, Edouard Joubeaud, Laurent Monnier, Jacques Demy

ORLANDO

(SONY PICTURES CLASSICS) Producer, Christopher Sheppard; Co-Producers, Roberto Cicutto, Jean Gontier, Matthijs Van Heijningen, Luigi Musini, Vitaly Sobolev; Director/Screenplay, Sally Potter; Based on the novel by Virginia Woolf; Photography, Alexei Rodionov; Designers, Ben van Os, Jan Roelfs; Costumes, Sandy Powell; Editor, Herve Schneid; Music, David Motion, Sally Potter; an Adventure Pictures (London)/Lenfilm (St. Petersburg)/Mikado Film (Rome)/Rio Film (Paris)/Sigma (Amsterdam) co-production with the participation of British Screen; British-Russian-Italian-French-Dutch; Dolby Stereo; Eastmancolor; Rated PG-13; 93 minutes; June release

CAST

Orlando	Tilda Swinton
Shelmerdine	Billy Zane
The Khan	Lothaire Bluteau
Archduke Harry	John Wood
Sasha	Charlotte Valandrey
Nick Greene/Publisher	Heathcote Williams
Queen Elizabeth I	Quentin Crisp
Mr. Pope	Peter Eyre
King William of Orange	Thom Hoffman
Countess	Kathryn Hunter
Mr. Addison	Ned Sherrin
Singer/Angel	Jimmy Sommerville
King James I	Dudley Sutton
Orlando's Mother	Elaine Banham
Orlando's Father	John Bott
Butlers	Lol Coxhill, Hugh Munro, Terence Soall
Queen Mary	Sarah Crowden

and George Yiasoumi, Toby Jones, Robert Demeger (Valets), Anna Farnworth (Clorinda), John Grillo, Martin Wimbush (Officials), Roger Hammond (Mr. Swift), Peter Hayward (Harpsichordist), Anna Healy (Euphrosyne), Mary McLeod, Barbara Hicks (Women), Olivia Lancelot (Young French Woman), Cyril Lecomte (Young French Man), Sara Mair-Thomas (Favilla), Alexander Medvedev (Russian Sailor), Thom Osborn (Doctor), Oleg Pogodin (Desdemona), Simon Russell Beale (Earl of Moray), Matthew Sim (Lord Francis Vere), Victor Stepanov (Russian Ambassador), Toby Stephens (Othello), Jessica Swinton (Orlando's Daughter), Giles Taylor (Singing Valet), Andrew Watts (Counter Tenor), Jermome Willis (Translator)

Plot Capsule: *A young English nobleman lives over the course of 400 years, changing at one point into a woman.*

The film received Academy Award nominations for costume design and art direction.
© Sony Pictures Classics

JACQUOT

(SONY PICTURES CLASSICS) Producers, Perrine Bauduin, Danielle Vaugon; Director/Screenplay, Agnes Varda; Based on the memories of Jacques Demy; Photography, Patrick Blossier, Agnes Godard, Georges Strouve; Designers, Robert Nardone, Olivier Radot; Editor, Marie-Jo Audiard; Music, Joanna Bruzdowicz; Costumes, Francoise Disle; Produced by Cine-Tamaris; French; Black and white/color; Rated PG; 118 minutes; June release

CAST

Jacquot 1	Philippe Maron
Jacquot 2	Edouard Joubeaud
Jacquot 3	Laurent Monnier
Mother	Brigitte De Villepoix
Father	Daniel Dublet
Yvon 1	Clement Delaroche
Reine 1	Helene Pors
Yannick 1	Jeremie Bernard
Rene 1	Julien Mitard
Yvon 2	Rody Averty
Reine 2	Marie-Sidonie Benoist
Yannick 2	Cedric Michaud
Rene 2	Jeremie Bader
Cousin Joel	Guillaume Navaud
The Little Refugee	Fanny Lebreton

and Marc Barto, Celine Guicheteau, Aurelien Leborgne, Yann Juhel, Carole Ferron, Mathias Lepennec, Ludovic Vanneau (Friends and Children), Jean-Charles Hernot (The Worker), Edwige Delaunay (The Singer), Jacques Bourget (Mr. Bonbons), Jean Francois Lapipe (Unlce Marcel), Chantal Bezias (Aunt Nique), Marie Anne Emeriau (Grandmother), Veronique Rodriguez (The Chanteuse), Henri Janin (The Clogmaker), Marie-Anne Hery (The Clogmaker's Wife), Christine Renaudin (The Aunt from Rio), Yves De Beauvilin (The Drawing Teacher), Francis Viau (The Night Visitor), Yvette Longis (Lady in the Butcher shop), Francois Vogels (Mr. Debuisson), Francoise Lenoueveau (Madame Bredin), Philippe Lenouveau (Mr. Bredin), Jacques Demy

Plot Capsule: *Filmmaker Agnes Varda's memoir dramatizing the life of her late husband, director Jacques Demy, beginning with his boyhood in Nantes, France.*
© Sony Pictures Classics

John Wood, Tilda Swinton

Tilda Swinton, Billy Zane

UN COEUR EN HIVER
(A HEART IN WINTER)

(OCTOBER FILMS) Producers, Jean-Louis Livi, Philippe Carcassonne; Director, Claude Sautet; Screenplay, Yves Ulmann, Jacques Fieschi, Jerome Tonnerre; Photography, Ves Angelo; Editor, Jacqueline Thiedot; Costumes, Corrine Jorry; Designer, Christian Marti; a co-production of Film Par Film, Cinea, Orly Films, SEDIF, D.A. Films, Paravision International and FR3 Films production; French; Color; Not rated; 105 minutes; June release

CAST

Stephane	Daniel Auteuil
Camille	Emmanuelle Beart
Maxime	Andre Dussollier
Helene	Elisabeth Bourgine
Regine	Brigitte Catillon
Lachaume	Maurice Garrel
Madame Amet	Myriam Boyer
Brice	Stanislas Carre de Malberg
Ostende	Jean-Luc Bideau

Plot Capsule: *The friendship of Stephane and Maxime, two business partners who specialize in repairing stringed instruments, is threatened when Maxime confesses his love for a beautiful young pianist named Camille.*
© October Films

Andre Dussollier, Daniel Auteuil

Daniel Auteuil, Emmanuelle Beart

Emmanuelle Beart

LA VIE DE BOHEME

(KINO INTERNATIONAL) Producer/Director/Screenplay, Aki Kaurismaki; Based on the novel *Scenes de la vie de boheme* by Henri Murger; Photography, Timo Salminen; Designer, John Ebden; Music by various artists; a Sputnik Oy in coproduction with Pyramide Productions S.A. — Films A2 (France), The Swedish Film Institute, Pandora Film GmbH (Germany) presentation supported by the Finnish Film Foundation, The Nordic Film and Television Fund; French-Swedish-German-Finnish; Black and white; Not rated; 100 minutes; July release

CAST

Rodolfo	Matti Pellonpaa
Mimi	Evelyne Didi
Marcel	Andre Wilms
Schaunard	Kari Vaananen
Musette	Christine Murillo
Baudelaire	Laika
Barman	Carlos Salgado
Henri Bernard	Alexis Nitzer
Mme. Bernard	Sylvie van den Elsen
Lady at the second hand shop	Dominique Marcas
Gassot	Samuel Fuller
Francis	Jean-Paul Wenzel
Gentleman	Louis Malle
Doctor	Maximilien Regiani
Waiter	Daniel Dublet
Policeman	Philippe Dormoy

Plot Capsule: *Three bohemian friends, a painter, a poet, and a composer, desperately try to eke out a living in Paris in this comedy-drama.*
© Kino Intl.

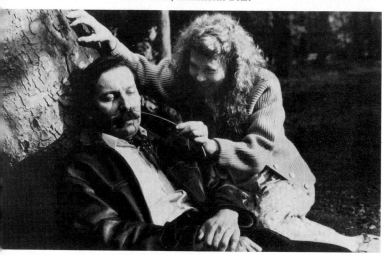

Matti Pellonpaa, Evelyne Didi

ESPECIALLY ON SUNDAY

(MIRAMAX) Producers, Amadeo Pagani, Giovanna Romagnoli, Mario Orfini; Screenplay, Tonino Guerra; Music, Ennio Morricone; Italian; Color; Not rated; 81 minutes; August release.

The Blue Dog

Director, Giuseppe Tornatore; Photography, Tonino Delli Colli; Art Director, Francesco Bronzi; Costumes, Beatrice Bordone.

CAST

Amleto .... Philippe Noiret

Especially on Sunday

Director, Giuseppe Bertolucci; Photography, Fabio Cianchetti; Art Director, Nello Giorgetti; Costumes, Mariolina Bono.

CAST

Anna .... Ornella Muti
Vittorio .... Bruno Ganz
Marco .... Andrea Prodan
Booth Girl .... Nicoletta Braschi

Snow on Fire

Director, Marco Tullio Giordana; Photography, Franco Lecca; Art Director, Gianni Silvestri; Costumes, Metka Kosak.

CAST

Caterina .... Maria Maddalena Fellini
Bride .... Chiara Caselli
Don Vincenzo .... Ivano Marescotti
Husband .... Bruno Berdoni

Additional Sequences

Director, Giuseppe Bertolucci.

CAST

Motorcyclist .... Jean-Hughes Anglade

Plot Capsule: *Three short dramatic stories each set in Northern Italy: a stray dog becomes devoted to a barber; a middle-aged man tries to seduce a young woman away from her lover; a widow secretly observes the lovemaking of her son and his new wife.*
© Miramax Films

Andrea Prodan, Ornella Muti, Bruno Ganz

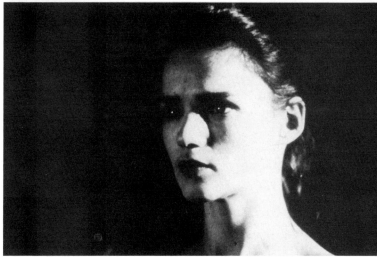

Chiara Caselli

HOUSE OF ANGELS

(SONY PICTURES CLASSICS) Producer, Lars Jonsson; Director, Colin Nutley; Screenplay, Susanne Falck; Photography, Jens Fischer; Editor, Perry Schaffer; Music, Bjorn Isfalt; Costumes, Sven Lundgren, Britt Marie Larsson; Designer, Ulla Herdin; Produced by Memfis Film and TV with SVT/TVS Gothenburg/Swedish Film Institute/Danmarks Radio/Norsk Riksrkringkastning/Nordisk Film & TV Fund; Swedish; Dolby Stereo; Color; Rated R; 119 minutes; August release

CAST

Fanny .... Helena Bergstrom
Zac .... Rikard Wolff
Axel Flogfalt .... Sven Wollter
Rut Flogfalt .... Viveka Seldahl
Fleming Collmert .... Reine Brynolfsson
Erik Zander .... Per Oscarsson
Gottfried Petersson .... Ernest Gunther
Ivar Petersson .... Tord Petterson
Eva Agren .... Ing-Marie Carlsson
Per-Ove Agren .... Jan Mybrand
Ragnar Zetterberg .... Peter Andersson
Anna Lisa Zetterberg .... Gorel Crona
Marten Flogfalt .... Jacob Eklund
Vendela Flogfalt .... Gabriella Boris

Plot Capsule: *Comedy in which a wealthy landowner dies leaving his fortune to his motorcycle-riding granddaughter Fanny whose arrival in town causes a stir.*
© Sony Pictures Classics

Helena Bergstrom, Rikard Wolff

Marie Trintignant, Stephane Audran

BETTY

(MK2) Producer, Marin Karmitz; Director/Screenplay, Claude Chabrol; Based on the novel by Georges Simenon; Photography, Bernard Zitzermann; Designer, Francoise Benoit-Fresco; Costumes, Cristine Guegan; Editor, Monique Fardoulis; Music, Matthieu Chabrol; French; Color; Not rated; 103 minutes; August release

CAST

Betty	Marie Trintignant
Laure	Stephane Audran
Mario	Jean-Francois Garreau
Guy Etamble	Yves Lambrecht
Madame Etamble	Christiane Minazolli
The Doctor	Pierre Vernier
Odile	Nathalie Kousnetoff
Frederic	Pierre Martot
Schwartz	Thomas Chabrol
Phillippe	Yves Verhoeven
Florent	Jean-Marc Roulot
Odette	Brigitte Chamanrande
The Lawyer	Raoul Curet
Elda	Julie Marbeuf
Therese	Melanie Blatt

Plot Capsule: *At a bar called The Hole, Betty, a woman down in her luck, is befriended by Laure, a wealthy widow, leading to a series of confessions and memories of Betty's earlier life.*
© MK2

TWIST

(TRITON PICTURES) Producer/Director, Ron Mann; Executive Producer, Ron Haig; Co-Producer, Sue Len Quon; Photography, Bob Fresco; Editor, Robert Kennedy; Associate Producer, Ann Mayall; Produced with financial assistance from Telefilm Canada/Ontario Film Development Corp./Canada Council/National Film Board/City TV (Toronto); Canadian; Color/black and white; Not rated; 78 minutes; August release. Documentary on the history of the rock 'n' roll dance craze, the Twist.

WITH

Chubby Checker, Hank Ballard, Joan (Buck) Kiene, Jimmy Peatross, Cholly Atkins, Carole (Scaldeferri) Spada, Joe Fusco, Gladys Horton, Betty (Romantini) Begg, Floss (Harvey) Mancini, Joey Dee, Mama Lu Parks & The Parkettes, Dee Dee Sharp, Janet Huffsmith.
© Triton Pictures

Hank Ballard and the Midnighters

Gosia Dobrowolska, Kyle McCulloch

CAREFUL

(ZEITGEIST) Producers, Greg Klymkiw, Tracy Traeger; Executive Producer, Andre Bennett; Director/Photography, Guy Maddin; Screenplay, George Toles, Guy Maddin; Story, George Toles; Music, John McCulloch; Art Director, Jeff Solylo; Costumes, Donna Szoke; Canadian; Color; Not rated; 96 minutes; August release

CAST

Grigorss	Kyle McCulloch
Zenaida	Gosia Dobrowolska
Klara	Sarah Neville
Johann	Brent Neale
Count Knotgers	Paul Cox
Herr Trotta	Victor Cowie
Blind Ghost	Michael O'Sullivan
Franz	Vince Rimmer
Sigleinde	Katya Gardner
Frau Teacher	Jackie Burroughs

Plot Capsule: *In the Alpine village of Tolzbad a beautiful young widow and her three sons are repressed by their secret desires and longings in this off-beat comedy.*
© Zeitgeist Films

Mitchell Lichtenstein, Winston Chao, May Chin

Mitchell Lichtenstein, Winston Chao, May Chin

THE WEDDING BANQUET

(SAMUEL GOLDWYN CO.) Producers, Ang Lee, Ted Hope, James Schamus; Director, Ang Lee; Screenplay, Ang Lee, Neil Peng, James Schamus; Photography, Jong Lin; Designer, Steve Rosenzweig; Music, Mader; Editor, Tim Squyres; Taiwanese; Color; Rated R; 107 minutes; August release

CAST

Wai Tung	Winston Chao
Wei Wei	May Chin
Simon	Mitchell Lichtenstein
Mr. Gao	Sihung Lung
Mrs. Gao	Ah-Leh Gua

Plot Capsule: *To cover up his gay relationship with Simon, Wai Tung agrees to marry artist Wei Wei to please his parents and assure the girl a green card. When Wai Tung's parents fly to New York for the wedding the bogus couple must carry out their deception to further extremes than they expected.*

Nominated for an Academy Award for best foreign-language film.
© Samuel Goldwyn Co.

May Chin, Winston Chao

May Chin, Ah-Leh Gua, Mitchell Lichtenstein, Sihung Lung, Winston Chao

THE LAST BUTTERFLY

(ARROW RELEASING) Producer, Steven North; Executive Producers, Boudjemaa Dahmane, Jacques Methe, Patrick Dromgoole; Director, Karel Kachyna; Screenplay, Ota Hofman, Karel Kachyna; Based on the novel by Michael Jacot; English Adaptation, Mark Princi; Photography, Jiri Krejcik; Music, Alex North, Milan Svoboda; Designer, Zbynek Hloch; Mime Sequences, Boris Hybner; Editor, Jiri Brozek; Czech; Color; Not rated; 110 minutes; August release

Tom Courtenay, Linda Jablonska

CAST

Antoine Moreau	Tom Courtenay
Vera	Brigitte Fossey
Michele	Ingrid Held
Rheinberg	Freddie Jones
Gruber	Milan Knazko
Stadler	Josef Kemr
Laub	Ludek Kopriva
Silberstein	Pavel Bobek
Petersen	Josef Laufer
Stadlerova	Drahomira Fialkova
Leroux	Rudolf Pellar
Steiner	Jiri Lir
Singer in ghetto cafe	Hana Hegerova
Gruber's Secretary	Jitka Molavcova

The Children:

Stella	Linda Jablonska
Samuel	Daniel Margolius
Heda	Kamila Hodouskova
Ester	Halberstatova
Liana	Marketa Slavikova
Otto	Jiri Malek
Ikarus	Petr Lowy

Plot Capsule: *During World War II French mime Antoine Moreau is arrested by the Gestapo and forced to perform for thousands of interned Jews in the Czech city of Terezin.*
© Arrow Releasing

Donogh Rees

Caitlin Bossley, Marcia Gay Harden

CRUSH

(STRAND RELEASING) Producer, Bridget Ikin; Director, Alison Maclean; Screenplay, Alison Maclean, Anne Kennedy; Photography, Dion Beebe; Costumes, Ngila Dickson; Editor, John Gilbert; Music, JPS Experience; from Hibiscus Films Ltd.; New Zealand; Color; Not rated; 97 minutes; September release

CAST

Lane	Marcia Gay Harden
Christina	Donogh Rees
Angela	Caitlin Bossley
Colin	William Zappa
Horse	Pete Smith
Arthur	Jon Brazier
Patient	Geoffrey Southern
Stephen	David Stott
Aunty Bet	Harata Solomon
Colleen	Caroline DeLore

and Shirley Wilson (Intensive Care Nurse), Denise Lyness, Jennifer Karehana (Physiotherapy Nurses), Phil McLachlan (Ward Sister), Wayne Roberts (Physiotherapy Patient), Alistair McConnell (Doctor), Terry Batchelor (Taxi Driver), Martin Booker (Waiter)

Plot Capsule: *Psychological drama in which Lane causes a car accident, then leaves her fellow passenger, Christina, in a coma, proceeding to the home of the reclusive novelist both women had planned to interview.*
© Strand Releasing

Marcia Gay Harden

DR. BETHUNE

(TARA RELEASING) Producers, Nicolas Clermont, Pieter Kroonenberg; Co-Producers, Wang Xingang, Jacques Dorfmann; Director, Phillip Borsos; Screenplay, Ted Allan; Photography, Raoul Coutard, Mike Malloy; Editor, Yves Langlois, Angelo Corrao; a Filmline International with the participation of Telefilm Canada in association with China Film Co-Production Corp. presentation; Color; Canadian-Chinese-French; Not rated; 115 minutes; September release

CAST

Dr. Norman Bethune	Donald Sutherland
Frances Penny Bethune	Helen Mirren
Mrs. Dowd	Helen Shaver
Chester Rice	Colm Feore
Mr. Tung	James Pax
Alan Coleman	Ronald Pickup
Dr. Chian	Guo Da
Dr. Fong	Harrison Liu
Marie-France Coudaire	Anouk Aimee
Dr. Archibald	Geoffrey Chater
General Nieh	Tan Zong Yao
Chairman Mao	Zhang Ke Yaw
Dr. Salvador	Inaki Ayerra
Shiao	Li Hai Lang
Frank Coudaire	Yvan Ponton

and Sophie Faucher (Nurse Mackenzie), Danute Kristo (Ingrid Halstrom), Beatrice Home (Mary), Nicholas Kilbertus (George Pilling), Linda O'Dwyer (Nursing Sister), Frank Fontaine (Dr. Williamson)

Plot Capsule: *The true story of Canadian surgeon Norman Bethune and his efforts to reform medical practices in war-torn China.*
© Tara Releasing

Donald Sutherland

Gabriel Byrne, Ellen Barkin

INTO THE WEST

(MIRAMAX) Producers, Jonathan Cavendish, Tim Palmer; Executive Producer, James Mitchell; Director, Mike Newell; Screenplay, Jim Sheridan; Based on a story by Michael Pearce; Co-Producers, Jane Doolan, Susan Slonaker; Co-Executive Producers, Guy East, Bob and Harvey Weinstein; Associate Producer, Gabriel Byrne; Photography, Tom Sigel; Designer, Jamie Leonard; Costumes, Consolata Boyle; Casting, Ros & John Hubbard; Editor, Peter Boyle; a Majestic Film Intl./Film 4 Intl./ Newcom presentation of a Little Bird production in association with Parallel Films and with the participation of British Screen; British-Irish; Dolby Stereo; Technicolor; Rated PG; 102 minutes; September release

CAST

Papa Riley	Gabriel Byrne
Kathleen	Ellen Barkin
Ossie Riley	Ciaran Fitzgerald
Tito Riley	Ruaidhri (Rory) Conroy
Grandfather	David Kelly
Tracker	Johnny Murphy
Barreller	Colm Meaney
Noel Hartnett	John Kavanagh
Inspector Bolger	Brendan Gleeson
Superintendent O'Mara	Jim Norton
Mrs. Murphy	Anita Reeves
Mr. Murphy	Ray McBride
Morrisey	Dave Duffy
Conor Murphy	Stuart Dannell
Birdy Murphy	Becca Hollinshead
Angela Murphy	Bianca Hollinshead
Cafferty	Owen O'Gormon
Welfare Man	Mark O'Regan
Sergeant Brophy	Phelim Drew
School Inspector	Sean Madden

and Vinnie McCabe (Video Shop Owner), Tony Rohr (Traveller), Brendan O'Duill (Barman), Dave Carey (Resident), Joan Sheehy (Woman with pram), Lana Citron (Sophie), Clive Geraghty (Smiley), Charles Ruxton (Tommo), Stanley Townsend (Rico), Derry Power (Hotel Clerk), Tim McDonnell (Shopkeeper), Joe Pilkington (Detective), Dave Finnegan (Car Man), Gladys Sheehan (Woman in lift)

Plot Capsule: *Mythical tale of how the lives of two young Dublin boys are changed when their grandfather brings them a white horse named Tir na nOg.*
© Miramax Films

Ciaran Fitzgerald, Ruaidhri Conroy

FORTRESS

(DIMENSION) Producers, John Davis, John Flock; Executive Producers, Graham Burke, Greg Coote; Co-Producers, Neal Nordlinger, Michael Lake; Director, Stuart Gordon; Screenplay, Steve Feinberg, Troy Neighbors, Terry Curtis Fox; Photography, David Eggby; Editor, Timothy Wellburn; Designer, David Copping; Australian-U.S.; Color; Rated R; 91 minutes; September release

CAST

John Brennick	Christopher Lambert
Prison Director Poe	Kurtwood Smith
Karen Brennick	Loryn Locklin
Abraham	Lincoln Kilpatrick
Nino	Clifton Gonzalez Gonzalez
D-Day	Jeffrey Combs
Stiggs	Tom Towles
Friendly Border Guard	E. Briant Wells
Maddox	Vernon Wells
Lydia	Denni Gordon
Camper	Alan Zitner
Travel Agent	Peter Marshall
Bio Scanner Guard	Dragica Debert

Plot Capsule: *Futuristic thriller in which John Brennick is sentenced to an underground desert fortress when he and his wife defy a law stating that women may become pregnant only once.*
© Dimension Films

Christopher Lambert, Loryn Locklin

LEON THE PIG FARMER

(CINEVISTA/UNAPIX) Producers/Directors, Vadim Jean, Gary Sinyor; Screenplay, Gary Sinyor, Michael Normand; Executive Producer, Paul Brooks; Photography, Gordon Hickie; Designer, Simon Hicks; Editor, Ewa J. Lind; Music, John Murphy, David Hughes; British; Color; Not rated; 98 minutes; September release

CAST

Leon Geller	Mark Frankel
Judith Geller	Janet Suzman
Brian Chadwick	Brian Glover
Yvonne Chadwick	Connie Booth
Sidney Geller	David De Keyser
Madeleine	Maryam D'Abo
Lisa	Gina Bellman
Elliott Cohen	Vincenzo Ricotta
Vitelli	John Woodvine
Mrs. Samuels	Jean Anderson
Dr. Johnson	Annette Crosbie
Art Collector	Burt Kwouk

and Neil Mullarkey (Waiter in French Restaurant), Sean Pertwee (Keith Chadwick), Barry Stanton (Peter the Vet), Bernard Bresslaw (Rabbi Hertzman), Peter Whitman (Rabbi Jolson)

Plot Capsule: *Leon Geller is dismayed to discover that his mother had been artificially inseminated, thereby making his real father a Yorkshire pig farmer.*
© Cinevista

Mark Frankel, Janet Suzman

JAMON JAMON

(ACADEMY ENTERTAINMENT) Director, Bigas Luna; Screenplay, Cuca Canals, Bigas Luna; Photography, Jose Luis Alcaine; Editor, Teresa Font; Designers, Chu Uroz, Noemi Campano; Music, Nicola Piovani; Spanish; Color; Not rated; 90 minutes; September release

CAST

Silvia	Penelope Cruz
Carmen	Anna Galiena
Raul	Javier Bardem
Conchita	Stefania Sandrelli
Manuel	Juan Diego
Jose Luis	Jordi Molla

Plot Capsule: *Silvia, daughter of the town prostitute, discovers she is pregnant by the son of a wealthy underwear manufacturer whom she plans to marry. Hoping to put an end to this alliance the boy's mother hires the town stud, Raul, to seduce Silvia.*
© Academy Entertainment

Penelope Cruz, Javier Bardem

BAD BEHAVIOUR

(OCTOBER FILMS) Producer, Sarah Curtis; Executive Producer, Sally Hibbin; Director, Les Blair; Photography, Witold Stok; Music, John Altman; Editor, Martin Walsh; a Film Four International presentation with the participation of British Screen of a Parallax Pictures production; British; Dolby Stereo; Color; Rated R; 103 minutes; September release

CAST

Gerry McAllister	Stephen Rea
Ellie McAllister	Sinead Cusack
Howard Spink	Philip Jackson
Jessica Kennedy	Clare Higgins
The Nunn Brothers	Phil Daniels
Winifred Turner	Mary Jo Randle
Sophie Bevan	Saira Todd
Linda Marks	Amanda Boxer
Joe McAllister	Luke Blair
Michael McAllister	Joe Coles
Jake Spink	Tamlin Howard
Rosie Kennedy	Emily Hill
Jason	Philippe Lewinson
Chairperson	Ian Flintoff
Priest	Kenneth Hadley
Band	Siempre Caliente

Plot Capsule: *Improvised comedy looks at the domestic life of the McAllisters, a North London couple having their home repaired by local contractors.*
© October Films

Clancy Chassay

Saira Todd, Stephen Rea

WITTGENSTEIN

(ZEITGEIST) Producer, Tariq Ali; Director, Derek Jarman; Screeplay, Derek Jarman, Terry Eagleton, Ken Butler; Photography, James Welland; Music, Jan Latham-Koenig; Editor, Budge Tremlett; Costumes, Sandy Powell; Designer, Annie Lapaz; a Channel 4/British Film Institute presentation in assocation with Uplink (Japan); British-Japanese; Color; Not rated; 71 minutes; September release

CAST

Ludwig Wittgenstein	Karl Johnson
Bertrand Russell	Michael Gough
Lady Ottoline Morrell	Tilda Swinton
Maynard Keynes	John Quentin
Johnny	Kevin Collins
Young Wittgenstein	Clancy Chassay
Martian	Nabil Shaban
Hermine Wittgenstein	Sally Dexter
Lydia Lopokova	Lynn Seymour
Paul Wittgenstein	Jan Latham-Koenig
Rudolf Wittgenstein	David Radzinowicz
Kurt Wittgenstein	Howard Sooley
Hans Wittgenstein	Ben Scantlebury
Helene Wittgenstein	Vanya del Borgo
Gretyl Wittgenstein	Gina Marsh
Leopoldine Wittgenstein	Jill Balcon
Hairdresser	Donald McInnes
Sophie Janovskaya	Layla Alexander Garrett
Schoolgirl	Aisling Magill

Plot Capsule: *An esoteric exploration of the life of philosopher Ludwig Wittgenstein.*
© Zeitgeist Films

Sinead Cusack, Emily Hill

FAREWELL MY CONCUBINE

(MIRAMAX) Producer, Hsu Feng; Executive Producers, Hsu Bin, Jade Hsu; Director, Chen Kaige; Screenplay, Lilian Lee, Lu Wei; Based on the novel by Lilian Lee; Photography, Gu Changwei; Editor, Pei Xiaonan; Costumes, Chen Changmin; Music, Zhao Jiping; a Tomson (HK) Films Co. Ltd. presentation in assocation with China Film Co-Production Corp. and Beijing Film Studio; Hong Kong-Chinese; Dolby Stereo; Color; Not rated; 156 minutes; October release

CAST

Cheng Dieyi	Leslie Cheung
Duan Xiaolou	Zhang Fengyi
Juxian	Gong Li
Guan Jifa	Lu Qi
Na Kun	Ying Da
Master Yuan	Ge You
Xiao Si (Teenage)	Li Chun
Xiao Si (Adult)	Lei Han
Old Man Zhang	Tong Di
Douzi (Child)	Ma Mingwei
Shitou (Child)	Fei Yang
Shitou (Teenage)	Yin Zhi
LiaziLI	Dan
Douzi's Mother	Jiang Wenli
Aoki Saburo	Zhi Yitong
Red Guard	David Wu

Plot Capsule: *Epic story follows the fifty year professional and personal relationship between Duan Xiaolou and Cheng Dieyi, stars of the Peking Opera, duuring China's political changes.*

The film received Academy Award nominations for best foreign-language film and cinematography.

Winner of the Cannes Film Festival Palme D'Or for Best Film; voted Best Foreign-Language Film by the National Board of Review, LA Film Critics, NY Film Critics and the Hollywood Foreign Press Assn. (Golden Globes).
© Miramax Films

Zhang Fengyi, Leslie Cheung

Leslie Cheung

Leslie Cheung

Gong Li (c), Zhang Fengyi

"Four Men on a Raft"

Orson Welles

IT'S ALL TRUE:
Based on an Unfinished Film by Orson Welles

(PARAMOUNT) Producers, Regine Konckier, Richard Wilson, Bill Krohn, Myron Meisel, Jean-Luc Ormieres; Directors/Screenplay, Richard Wilson, Myron Meisel, Bill Krohn; Associate Producer/Senior Research Executive, Catherine Benamou; Special Consultant, Elizabeth Wilson; Editor, Ed Marx; Photography, Gary Graver; Music, Jorge Arriagada; Narrator, Miguel Ferrer; a Les Films Balenciaga production in association with The French Ministry of Education and Culture, French National Center for Cinematography, Canal+, R. Films, La Fondation GAN pour le Cinema; French-U.S.; Color/black and white; Rated G; 85 minutes; October release

SEGMENTS

Four Men on a Raft
Director, Orson Welles; Associate Producer, Richard Wilson; Photography, George Fanto; with Manuel "Jacare" Olimpio Meira, Raimundo "Tata" Correia Lima, Jeronimo Andre de Souza, Manuel "Preto" Pereira da Silva, Francisca Moreira da Silva, Jose Sobrinho.

The Story of Samba (Carnaval)
Screenplay, Robert Meltzer; Assistant Director/Choreographer, Herivelto Martins; Associate Producer, Richard Wilson; Photography, Harry J. Wild; with Grande Othelo, Pery Ribeiro.

My Friend Bonito
Producer, Orson Welles; Director, Norman Foster; Story, Robert Flaherty; Photography, Floyd Crosby; Associate Producer, Jose Noriega; with Jesus Vasquez (Chico)

INTERVIEW SUBJECTS

Jose "Bafou" Pereira da Silva, Francisca Moreira da Silva, Edilson Lopes de Amorim, Luiz Juliao "Braulio" Cavalcanti, Maria do Carmo de Souza, Laria Celsa Gomes Lima, Jose "Guaiuba" Castro Meira, Raimundo de Alencar Pinto, Antonio & Francisco Affonso de Albuquerque, Jose de Lima, Maria Jose Meira Lima, Joaquim Olimpio Meira, Maria "Bahiana" Olimpio Meira, Corina de Souza Santos, Maria "Jeronimo" do Costa Lima, Luis Antonio "Garoupa" Filgueiras, Luiz Antonio de Aragao, Pedro de Castro Meira, Raimundo "Puraque" de Castro Meira, Raimunda Olimpio Meira da Silva, Raimunda Lima de Amorim, Manuel Lopes, Maria Dantas Martins, Helio "Garoupa" Filgueiras, "Grande Othelo" (Sebastiao Bernardes de Souza Prata), Pery Ribeiro, Francisca Maria de Souza, Abigail Mauricio Horta, Rogerio Sganzerla, Franklin Rodrigues de Fonseca, Aloysio de Alencar Pinto, Yacana Martins, Camilo Gomes da Silva, Luis Vitorio de Oliveira, Elizabeth Wilson, Richard Wilson, Joseph Biroc, Fred Chandler, Shifra Haran, Reginald Armour, Gary Graver, George Fanto

Plot Capsule: *Documentary on the making of Orson Welles' ill-fated multi-episode film focusing on Latin America, "It's All True," (shot in 1942) with existing footage piecing together segments of the original film.*
© Paramount Pictures

Richard Wilson, Orson Welles

FLIGHT OF THE INNOCENT

(MGM) Producers, Franco Cristaldi, Domenico Procacci; Executive Producers, Massimo Cristaldi, Bruno Ricci; Director/Story, Carlo Carlei; Screenplay, Carlo Carlei, Gualtiero Rosella; Photography, Raffaele Mertes; Designer, Franco Ceraolo; Editors, Carlo Fontana, Claudio Di Mauro; Music, Carlo Siliotto; Costumes, Mariolina Bono; Presented in association with Rocket Pictures; a Cristaldi/ Fandango production in collaboration with Raitre (Rome)-Fildebroc (Paris); Italian-French; Dolby Stereo; Color; Rated R; 105 minutes; October release

CAST

Vito	Manuel Colao
Marta Rienzi	Francesca Neri
Davide Rienzi	Jacques Perrin
Scarface	Federico Pacifici
Vito's Father	Sal Borgese
Orlando	Lucio Zagaria
Giovanna	Giusi Cataldo
Rocco	Massimo Lodolo
Vito's Mother	Anita Zagaria
Police Woman	Isabelle Mantero
Questor	Nicola Di Pinto
Scarface's Driver	Severino Saltarelli
Porter	Gianfranco Barra
Vito's Grandfather	Giovanni Pallavicino
Vito's Grandmother	Anna Lelio
Don Silvio	Beppe Chierici
Stefania	Veronica Del Chiappa
Simone	Sandro Barletta

Plot Capsule: *Ten year-old Vito flees from his village in Southern Italy, pursued by a scarfaced peasant who killed the boy's entire family out of revenge.*

Francesca Neri, Manuel Colao, Jacques Perrin

Federico Pacifici

THE SILENT TOUCH

(CASTLE HILL) Producer, Mark Forstater; Director, Krzysztof Zanussi; Screenplay, Peter Morgan, Mark Wadlow; Story, Krzysztof Zanussi, Edward Zebrowski; Photography, Jaroslaw Zamojda; Designer, Ewa Braun; Costumes, Dorota Roqueplo; Music, Wojciech Kilar; Editor, Marek Denys; Co-Producers, Mads Egmont Christensen, Krzysztof Zanussi; from Mark Forstater Productions/Tor Film Group/Metronome Prods. A/S with the participation of British Screen; British-Polish-Danish; Dolby Stereo; Color; Not rated; 92 minutes; November release

CAST

Henry Kesdi	Max von Sydow
Stefan Bugajski	Lothaire Bluteau
Helena Kesdi	Sarah Miles
Annette Berg	Sofie Grabol
Prof. Jerzy Kern	Aleksander Bardini
Joseph Kesdi	Peter Hesse Overgaard
Doctor	Lars Lunoe
Doctor's Wife	Slawomira Lozinska
Muller	Trevor Cooper
Maier	Stanislaw Brejdygant
Gelda	Beata Tyszkiewicz

and Maja Plaszynska (Baby Thomas), Peter Thurrell, Wiktor Zborowski, Krystyna Mierzejewska, Stanislav Holly, Catherine Thornborrow (Interviewees), Eugenia Herman, Piotr Wojtowicz (TV Crew), Wasia Maslennikow, Krystyna Chmielewski (Secretary)

Plot Capsule: *A young music student journies to Denmark to convince long-retired composer Henry Kesdi that his greatest work is yet to come.*
© Castle Hill Prods

Sarah Miles, Lothaire Bluteau, Max Von Sydow, Sofia Grabol

Lothaire Bluteau

James Fox

Emma Thompson, Anthony Hopkins

Darlington Hall

Emma Thompson, Anthony Hopkins

Hugh Grant, Anthony Hopkins

Tim Pigott-Smith, Emma Thompson

THE REMAINS OF THE DAY

Anthony Hopkins, Emma Thompson

(COLUMBIA) Producers, Mike Nichols, John Calley, Ismail Merchant; Executive Producer, Paul Bradley; Director, James Ivory; Screenplay, Ruth Prawer Jhabvala; Based on the novel by Kazuo Ishiguro; Photography, Tony Pierce-Roberts; Designer, Luciana Arrighi; Costumes, Jenny Beavan, John Bright; Editor, Andrew Marcus; Music, Richard Robbins; Associate Producer, Donald Rosenfeld; British; Dolby Stereo; Panavision; Color; Rated PG; 135 minutes; November release

CAST

Auctioneer	John Haycraft
Lewis	Christopher Reeve
Stevens	Anthony Hopkins
Miss Kenton	Emma Thompson
Landlady	Caroline Hunt
Lord Darlington	James Fox
Father (Stevens Sr.)	Peter Vaughan
Mrs. Mortimer, The Cook	Paula Jacobs
Charlie, Head Footman	Ben Chaplin
George, Second Footman	Steve Dibben
Housemaid	Abigail Harrison
Spencer	Patrick Godfrey
Sir Leonard Bax	Peter Cellier
Canon Tufnell	Peter Halliday
Cardinal	Hugh Grant
Trimmer	Terence Bayler
Viscount Bigge	Jeffry Wickham
Scullery Boy	Hugh Sweetman
Dupont D'Ivry	Michael Lonsdale
Baroness	Brigitte Kahn
Doctor Meredith	John Savident
Postmaster	Tony Aitken
Elsa	Emma Lewis
Irma	Joanna Joseph
Sir Geoffrey Wren	Rupert Vansittart
Benn	Tim Pigott-Smith
Wren's Friend	Christopher Brown
Lizzie	Lena Headey
Harry Smith	Paul Copley
Publican	Ian Redford
Publican's Wife	Jo Kendall
Andrews	Steven Beard
Doctor Carlisle	Pip Torrens
Prime Minister	Frank Shelley
Lord Halifax	Peter Eyre
Foreign Office Official	Jestyn Phillips
German Ambassador	Wolf Kahler
German Embassy Officials	Frank Holtje, Andreas Tons
Police Constable	Roger McKern
Waitress	Angela Newmarch

Plot Capsule: *Drama examines the staid life of Darlington Hall's meticulous butler, Stevens, who denies himself all contact with human emotion, ignoring the affections of his co-worker, Miss Kenton.*

Anthony Hopkins was named best actor for this film (and Shadowlands) by the National Board of Review and the LA Film Critics.

The film received Academy Award nominations for picture, actor (Hopkins), actress (Emma Thompson), director, adapted screenplay, original music score, art direction and costume design.

© Columbia Pictures Industries

Christopher Reeve

James Fox (left)

Peter Vaughan, Anthony Hopkins

THE SNAPPER

(MIRAMAX) Producer, Lynda Myles; Executive Producer, Mark Shivas; Director, Stephen Frears; Screenplay, Roddy Doyle, based on his novel; Photography, Oliver Stapleton; Costumes, Consolata Boyle; Editor, Mick Audsley; Casting, Leo Davis; British; Dolby Stereo; Color; Rated R; 90 minutes; November release

CAST

Sharon Curley	Tina Kellegher
Dessie Curley	Colm Meaney
Kay Curley	Ruth McCabe
Darren	Colm O'Byrne
Craig	Eanna Macliam
Kimberley	Ciara Duffy
Lisa	Joanne Gerrard
Sonny	Peter Rowen
Jackie	Fionnula Murphy
Mary	Deirdre O'Brien
Yvonne	Karen Woodley
George Burgess	Pat Laffan
Doris Burgess	Virginia Cole
Pat Burgess	Denis Menton
Lester	Brendon Gleeson
Bertie	Stuart Duine
Paddy	Ronan Wilmot

Plot Capsule: *20 year-old un-wed Sharon announces to her Dublin family that she's pregnant but refuses to name the father. Comedy-drama was originally filmed for airing on British television.*
© Miramax

Tina Kellegher, Colm Meaney

Tina Kellegher, Colm Meaney

Tina Kellegher (c), Colm Meaney,
Ruth McCabe, and family

THE TRIAL

(ANGELIKA) Producer, Louis Marks; Executive Producers, Kobi Jaeger, Reniero Compostella, Mark Shivas; Director, David Jones; Screenplay, Harold Pinter; Based on the novel by Franz Kafka; Photography, Phil Meheux; Editor, John Stothart; Art Director, Jim Holloway; Music, Carl Davis; a Europanda Entertainment B.V. and BBC presentation; British; Dolby Stereo; Color; Not rated; 115 minutes; November release

CAST

Josef K	Kyle MacLachlan
The Priest	Anthony Hopkins
Huld	Jason Robards
Leni	Polly Walker
Fraulein Burstner	Juliet Stevenson
Titorelli	Alfred Molina

and David Thewlis

Plot Capsule: *Prague bank clerk Josef K is arrested on his 30th birthday though no charge is ever specified, leading to encounters with the legal system and assorted mysterious characters. Kafka's novel was previously filmed by Orson Welles in 1963 and starred Anthony Perkins as Josef K.*
© Angelika Films

Kyle MacLachlan

Anthony Hopkins

THE PIANO

(MIRAMAX) Producer, Jan Chapman; Director/Screenplay, Jane Campion; Executive Producer, Alain Depardieu; Photography, Stuart Dryburgh; Designer, Andrew McAlpine; Costumes, Janet Patterson; Music, Michael Nyman; Editor, Veronika Jenet; Casting, Diana Rowan, Susie Figgis, Victoria Thomas, Alison Barrett; a CIBY 2000 presentation, developed with the assistance of the Australian Film Commission and the New South Wales Film and Television Office; Australian-New Zealand-French; Dolby Stereo; Color; Rated R; 121 minutes; November release

CAST

Ada	Holly Hunter
Baines	Harvey Keitel
Stewart	Sam Neill
Flora	Anna Paquin
Aunt Morag	Kerry Walker
Nessie	Genevieve Lemon
Hira	Tungia Baker
Reverend	Ian Mune
Head Seaman	Peter Dennett
Chief Nihe	Te Whatanui Skipwith
Hone	Pete Smith
Blind Piano Tuner	Bruce Allpress
Mana	Cliff Curtis
Meni (Mission Girl)	Mahina Tunui
Muturu	Hori Ahipene
Te Kori	Gordon Hatfield
Chief Nihe's Daughter	Mere Boynton
Marama	Kirsten Batley
Mahina	Tania Burney
Te Tiwha	Annie Edwards
Roimata	Harina Haare
Parearau	Christina Harimate
Amohia	Steve Kanuta
Taua	P.J. Karauria
Tame	Sonny Kirikiri
Kahutia	Alain Makiha
Tipi	Greg Mayor
Tahu	Neil Mika Gudsell
Kohuru	Guy Moana
Rehia	Joseph Otimi
Mairangi	Glynis Paraha
Rongo	Riki Pickering
Pitama	Eru Potaka-Dewes
Te Ao	Liana Rangi Henry
Te Hikumutu	Huahana Rewa
Pito	Tamati Rice
Tuu	George Smallman
Tu Kukuni	Kereama Teua

Plot Capsule: *Ada, a mute woman from Scotland, arrives in New Zealand with her young daughter and her piano to carry out an arranged marriage. When her husband allows a local settler named Baines to take possession of the piano Ada agrees to a sexual arrangement to get the instrument back.*

1993 Academy Award winner for Best Actress (Holly Hunter), Supporting Actress (Anna Paquin), and Original Screenplay.

Holly Hunter was voted best actress by the LA Film Critics, NY Film Critics, National Society of Film Critics, National Board of Review, and the Hollywood Foreign Press (Golden Globes).

The film received the best screenplay award from the LA Film Critics, NY Film Critics and the National Society of Film Critics; Jane Campion was voted best director by the LA Film Critics and the NY Film Critics; additional LA Film Critics Awards were received for best cinematography and supporting actress (Anna Paquin).

The film received Academy Award nominations for picture, director, cinematography, costume design, and film editing.
© Miramax Films

Top: Holly Hunter, Anna Paquin
Center: Anna Paquin, Holly Hunter
Bottom: Holly Hunter, Harvey Keitel

WILD WEST

(SAMUEL GOLDWYN CO.) Producer, Eric Fellner; Director, David Attwood; Screenplay, Harwant Bains; Co-Producer, Nicky Kentish Barnes; Photography, Nic Knowland; Designer, Caroline Hanania; Editor, Martin Walsh; Costumes, Trisha Biggar; Music, Dominic Miller; Casting, Suzanne Crowley, Gilly Poole; a Channel 4 Films with the participation of British Screen presentation of an Initial Film; British; Dolby Stereo; Color; Not rated; 85 minutes; November release

CAST

Zaf	Naveen Andrews
Rifat	Sarita Choudhury
Kay	Ronny Jhutti
Ali	Ravi Kapoor
Gurdeep	Ameet Chana
Jagdeep	Bhasker
Mrs. Ayub	Lalita Ahmed
Tony	Shaun Scott
Tappers	Neran Persaud, Nrinder Dhudwar, Parv Bancil
Amir	Paul Bhattacharjee
Rakesh	Dinesh Shukla
Hank Goldstein	Lou Hirsch
Yehudi	Rolf Saxon
Uncle Liaqut	Gurdial Sira
Mrs. Khan	Jamila Massey
Mr. Patel	Kaleem Janjua

and Adam and Martin Dean (Ninja Boys), Mark Anthony Newman (Ellroy), Race Davies (Receptionist), Jim Barclay (Mr. Litt), Christopher Quinn (Engineer), Kevin Elyot (Solicitor), Elaine Donnelly (Ticket Clerk), Havoc (Spook), Awaara (Bangra Band), Madhav Sharma (Ugly Abdul)

Plot Capsule: *Three Pakistani brothers in West London form a country & western band, the Honky Tonk Cowboys, and pursuade a beautiful Asian woman named Rifat to be their vocalist.*
© Samuel Goldwyn Co.

Sarita Choudhury, Naveen Andrews

Naveen Andrews

Juliette Binoche

BLUE

(MIRAMAX) Producer, Marin Karmitz; Director, Krzysztof Kieslowski; Screenplay, Krzysztof Kieslowski, Krzysztof Piesiewicz; Photography, Slawomir Idziak; Set Designer, Claude Lenoir; Music, Zbigniew Preisner; Editor, Jacues Witta; Casting, Margot Capelier; Polish-French; Color; Not rated; 97 minutes; December release

CAST

Julie	Juliette Binoche
Olivier	Benoit Regent
Sandrine	Florence Pernel
Lucille	Charlotte Very
Journalist	Helen Vincent
Real Estate Agent	Philippe Volter
Doctor	Claude Duneton
Patrice (Julie's Husband)	Hugues Quester
Mother	Emmanuelle Riva
Copyist	Florence Vignon
Flute Player	Jacek Ostaszewski
Antoine	Yann Tregouet
Domestic	Isabelle Sadoyan
Neighbor Below	Daniel Martin
Neighbor Next Door	Catherine Therouenne
Lawyer	Alain Ollivier
Gardener	Pierre Forget

and Julie Delpy, Zbigniew Zamachowski, Alain Decaux

Plot Capsule: *Surviving an accident that has killed her husband and daughter, Julie is determined to rid herself of her past and live anonymously without emotional contact.*

For this film (and for Olivier Olivier and The Secret Garden) composer Zbigniew Preisner received an award from the LA Film Critics for best music score.
© Miramax Films

Juliette Binoche, Benoit Regent

GERMINAL

(SONY PICTURES CLASSICS) Executive Producer, Pierre Grunstein; Director, Claude Berri; Screenplay, Claude Berri, Arlette Langmann; Based on the novel by Emile Zola; Photography, Yves Angelo; Casting, Gerard Moulevrier; Costumes, Sylvie Gautrelet, Caroline De Vivaise, Bernadette Villard; Set Designers, Thanh At Hoang, Christian Marti; Editor, Herve De Luze; Music, Jean-Louis Roques; French; Dolby Stereo; Cinemascope; Color; Rated R; 158 minutes; December release

Miou-Miou, Gerard Depardieu

CAST

Etienne Lantier	Renaud
Maheu	Gerard Depardieu
Maheude	Miou-Miou
Bonnemort	Jean Carmet
Catherine Maheu	Judith Henry
Chaval	Jean-Roger Milo
Souvarine	Laurent Terzieff
Rasseneur	Jean-Pierre Bisson
Deneulin	Bernard Fresson
M. Hennebeau	Jacques Dacqmine
Mme. Hennebeau	Anny Duperey
M. Gregoire	Pierre Lafont
Mme. Gregoire	Annik Alane
Paul Negrel	Frederic Van Den Driessche
Maigrat	Gerard Croce
Zacharie Maheu	Thierry Levaret
Jeanlin Maheu	Albano Guaetta
Alzire Maheu	Severine Huon
Lenore Maheu	Jessica Sueur
Henri Maheu	Mathieu Mathez
Maxime	Alexandre Lekieffre

and Yolande Moreau (LaLevaque), Georges Staquet (Levaque), Sabrina Deladeriere (Philomene), Maximilien Regiani (Pierron), Joel Petit (Bebert), Anne-Marie Pisani (La Mouquette), Andre Julien (Mouque), Solenn Jarniou (Mme. Rasseneur), Fred Personne (Pluchart), Cecile Bois (Cecile Gregoire), Delphine Quentin (Lucie Deneulin), Alexandrine Loeb (Jeanne Deneulin), Fred Ulysse (Dansaert), Frederique Ruchaud (Honorine), Maryse Moutier (Melanie), Jenny Cleve (Rose), Nathalie Hequet (Amelie), Bruno Tuchszer (Capitaine des gardes), Fernand Kindt (Secretaire de la Cie), Andre Chaumeau (Caissier de la Cie), Philippe Desboeuf (Le Docteur)

Renaud, Gerard Depardieu

Plot Capsule: *Drama from Emile Zola's 1885 novel about underpaid, overworked coal miners in the North of France who go on strike.*
© Sony Pictures Classics

THE HAWK

(CASTLE HILL) Producers, Ann Wingate, Eileen Quinn; Executive Producers, Mark Shivas, Eric Fellner, Larry Kirstein, Kent Walwin; Director, David Hayman; Screenplay, Peter Ransley; Based on his novel; Photography, Andrew Dunn; Designer, David Myerscough-Jones; Editor, Justin Krish; Music, Nick Bicat; Costumes, Pam Tait; Casting, Leo Davis; British; Dolby Stereo; Rank Color; Not rated; 86 minutes; December release

Helen Mirren

CAST

Annie Marsh	Helen Mirren
Stephen Marsh	George Costigan
Ken Marsh	Owen Teale
Mrs. Marsh	Rosemary Leach
Norma	Melanie Hill
Jackie Marsh	Marie Hamer
Matthew Marsh	Christopher Madin
Driver	Daryl Webster
Boys in car	Thomas Taplin, Joshua Taplin
Sergeant Streete	David Harewood
Chief Inspector Daybury	Clive Russell
WPC Clarke	Pooky Quesnel
Mrs. Crowther	Helen Ryan
John	John Duttine

and Joyce Falconer (Woman in Capri), Caroline Paterson (Jan), Jayne Mackenzie (Eileen), Nadim Sawalha (Bahnu), Sean Flanagan (Harry), Rachel Moores (Susan), Margery Mason (Greengrocer), Sydney Cole (Weighbridge Operator), Frazer James (Crane Operator)

Plot Capsule: *Following a series of brutal murders not far from their suburban home, Annie Marsh begins to have fears that her husband Stephen might somehow be responsible.*
© Castle Hill Prods.

Helen Mirren, Christopher Madin,
George Costigan, Marie Hamer

Katrin Cartlidge, Lesley Sharp

Deborah MacLaren, David Thewlis

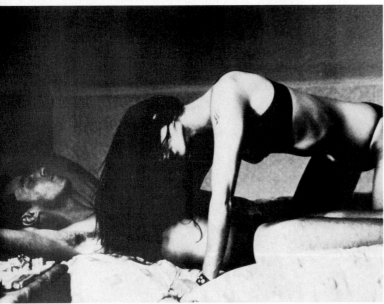

Greg Cruttwell, Katrin Cartlidge

NAKED

(FINE LINE FEATURES) Producer, Simon Channing-Williams; Director/Screenplay, Mike Leigh; Photography, Dick Pope; Designer, Alison Chitty; Editor, Jon Gregory; Music, Andrew Dickson; Costumes, Lindy Hemming; a Film Four Intl. presentation in association with British Screen of a Thin Man production; British; Dolby Stereo; Color; Not rated; 131 minutes; December release

CAST

Johnny	David Thewlis
Louise	Lesley Sharp
Sophie	Katrin Cartlidge
Jeremy	Greg Cruttwell
Sandra	Claire Skinner
Brian	Peter Wight
Archie	Ewen Bremner
Maggie	Susan Vidler
Woman in window	Deborah MacLaren
Cafe Girl	Gina McKee
Masseuse	Carolina Giammetta
Giselle	Elizabeth Berrington
Poster Man	Darren Tunstall
Chauffeur	Robert Putt
Victim	Lynda Rooke

and Angela Curran (Car Owner), Peter Whitman (Mr. Halpern), Jo Abercrombie (Woman in street), Elaine Britten (Girl in Porsche), David Foxxe (Tea bar Owner), Mike Avenall, Toby Jones (Men at tea bar), Sandra Voe (Bag Lady)

Plot Capsule: *Johnny, an angry, aimless, philosophizing drifter, arrives at the home of his ex-girlfriend, sleeps with her roommate, then takes off to wander the streets of London for a series of volatile encounters.*

David Thewlis received best actor awards from the NY Film Critics and the National Society of Film Critics.
© Fine Line Features

THE ACCOMPANIST

(SONY CLASSICS) Executive Producer, Jean-Jose Richer; Director, Claude Miller; Screenplay, Claude Miller, Luc Beraud; Based on the novel by Nina Berberova; Photography, Yves Angelo; Editor, Albert Jurgenson; Costumes, Jacqueline Bouchard; Musical Director, Alain Jomy; French; Dolby Stereo; Color; Rated PG; 110 minutes; December release

CAST

Charles Brice	Richard Bohringer
Irene Brice	Elena Safonova
Sophie Vasseur	Romane Bohringer
Irene's Lover, Jacques	Samuel Labarthe
Benoit Weizman	Julien Rassam
Sophie's Mother, Helene	Nelly Borgeaud

Plot Capsule: *In Paris, during World War II, pianist Sophie Vasseur is hired by singer Irene Brice to be her accompanist, eventually moving in with Irene and her businessman husband, thereby discovering their deepest secrets.*
© Sony Pictures Classics

Romane Bohringer, Julien Rassam

FARAWAY, SO CLOSE

(SONY PICTURES CLASSICS) Producer/Director, Wim Wenders; Screenplay, Wim Wenders, Ulrich Zieger, Richard Reitinger; Dialogues, Ulrich Zieger; Photography, Jurgen Jurges; Executive Producer, Ulrich Felsberg; Editor, Peter Przygodda; Music, Laurent Petitgand; Costumes, Esther Walz; Designer, Albrecht Konrad; Line Producer, Michael Schwarz; a Road Movies and Tobis Filkunst presentation; German; Dolby Stereo; Color; Rated PG-13; 140 minutes; December release

Otto Sander, Willem Dafoe, Solveig Dommartin

CAST

Cassiel	Otto Sander
Himself	Peter Falk
Tony Baker	Horst Buchholz
Raphaela	Nastassja Kinski
Konrad	Heinz Ruhmann
Damiel	Bruno Ganz
Marion	Solveig Dommartin
Phillip Winter	Rudiger Vogler
Himself	Lou Reed
Emit Flesti	Willem Dafoe
Himself	Mikhail Gorbachev
Kirsten	Marijam Agischewa
Captain	Henri Alekan
Jack	Tom Farell
Hanna and Gertrud Becker	Monika Hansen
Raissa	Aline Krajewski

Plot Capsule: *The angel Cassiel and his companion Raphaela roam the streets of Berlin observing various inhabitants, all the while wishing to cross over into the human world. Sequel to Wenders' 1988 film* Wings of Desire *(Orion Classics) which also featured Sander, Ganz, Dommartin, and Falk.*
© Sony Pictures Classics

Otto Sander, Mikhail Gorbachev

THE SUMMER HOUSE

(SAMUEL GOLDWYN CO.) Producer, Norma Heyman; Executive Producer, Mark Shivas; Director, Waris Hussein; Screenplay, Martin Sherman; Based on the novel *The Clothes in the Wardrobe* by Alice Thomas Ellis; Photography, Rex Maidment; Designer, Stuart Walker; Editor, Ken Pearce; Music, Stanley Myers; Casting, Susie Figgis; a BBC Films production; Developed in association with N.F.H. Ltd.; British; Color; Not rated; 87 minutes; December release

CAST

Lili	Jeanne Moreau
Mrs. Monro	Joan Plowright
Monica	Julie Walters
Margaret	Lena Headey
Syl	David Threlfall
Mrs. Raffald	Maggie Steed
Robert	John Wood
Cynthia	Gwyneth Strong
Derek	Roger Lloyd Pack
Marie-Clair	Catherine Schell
Nour	Padraig Casey
Mother Joseph	Britta Smith
Ahmed	Pierre Sioufi
Gypsy Girl	Sherine El Ansari
Margaret as a child	Annabel Burton
Gallery Owner	David Gant
Father O'Flynn	Tommy Duggan
Fatima	Maissa El Refaie
Hala	Lamia El Amir
Jennifer	Natalie Flynn
Christopher	Thomas Lawrence

Plot Capsule: *Margaret, dreaming of her first love on a past trip to Egypt, reluctantly agrees to marry the philandering, selfish Syl. Her mother's outrageous, free-spirited friend, Lili, however, senses Margaret's unhappiness and sets out to wreck the upcoming nuptials.*
© Samuel Goldwyn Co.

Joan Plowright, Lena Headey, Jeanne Moreau, Julie Walters

Debra Winger, Edward Hardwicke, Anthony Hopkins

Debra Winger, Anthony Hopkins

SHADOWLANDS

(SAVOY PICTURES) Producers, Richard Attenborough, Brian Eastman; Executive Producer, Terence Clegg; Director, Richard Attenborough; Screenplay, William Nicholson, based on his play; Co-Producer, Diana Hawkins; Photography, Roger Pratt; Designer, Stuart Craig; Editor, Lesley Walker; Costumes, Penny Rose; Associate Producer, Alison Webb; Music, George Fenton; Casting, Lucy Boulting; from Price Entertainment in association with Spelling Films International; British; Dolby Stereo; Panavision; Eastman color; Rated PG; 130 minutes; December release

CAST

C.S. "Jack" Lewis	Anthony Hopkins
Joy Gresham	Debra Winger
Warnie Lewis	Edward Hardwicke
Prof. Christopher Riley	John Wood
The Reverend "Harry" Harrington	Michael Denison
Douglas Gresham	Joseph Mazzello
Dr. Craig	Peter Firth
Desmond Arding	Julian Fellowes
Arnold Dopliss	Roddy Maude-Roxby
Bob Chafer	Andrew Seear
Nick Farrell	Tim McMullan
Rupert Parrish	Andrew Hawkins
College President	Peter Howell
Claude Bird	Robert Flemyng
Peter Whistler	James Frain
Frith	Toby Whithouse
Lieven	Daniel Goode
Standish	Scott Handy
Julian	Chris Williams
Barker	Charles Simon
Marcus	Giles Oldershaw
Fred Paxford	Walter Sparrow
John Egan	Simon Cowell-Parker
Dr. Eddie Monk	Roger Ashton-Griffiths
Mrs. Young	Pat Keen
Woman in tea room	Carol Passmore
Tea Room Waiter	Howard "Lew" Lewis
Station Acquaintance	John Quentin
College Porter	Alan Talbot
President's Wife	Heather Mansell
Mrs. Parrish	Leigh Burton-Gill

and Cameron Burton-Gill, Chandler Burton-Gill, Kendall Burton-Gill, Christina Burton-Gill (Parrish Children), Sylvia Barter (Woman in bookshop), James Watt (Boy in bookshop), Pauline Melville (Committee Chairwoman), Sophie Stanton, Ysobel Gonzalez, Ninka Scott (Lecture Committee), Gerald Sim (Superintendent Registrar), Terry Rowley (Registrar), Norman Bird (Taxi Driver), Abigail Harrison (Staff Nurse), Julian Firth (Father John Fisher), Karen Lewis (Hotel Receptionist), Matthew Delamere (Simon Chadwick)

Plot Capsule: *Famed writer-lecturer C.S. Lewis is visited in Oxford by an American fan, Joy Greshman, who soon becomes his friend and, ultimately, his wife. This true story is based on the play which opened on Broadway in 1990 and starred Nigel Hawthorne (who won a Tony Award for his performance) and Jane Alexander.*

For this film (and for The Remains of the Day*) Anthony Hopkins was voted best actor by the LA Film Critics and the National Board of Review.*

Nominated for Academy Awards for actress (Debra Winger) and adapted screenplay.
© Savoy Pictures

Joseph Mazzello, Anthony Hopkins

Joseph Mazzello, Debra Winger

Douglas Grisham, Joseph Mazzello

Anthony Hopkins

Edward Hardwicke, Anthony Hopkins

Daniel Day-Lewis, Pete Postlethwaite

IN THE NAME OF THE FATHER

(**UNIVERSAL**) Producer/Director, Jim Sheridan; Executive Producer, Gabriel Byrne; Co-Executive Producer, Terry George; Co-Producer, Arthur Lappin; Screenplay, Terry George, Jim Sheridan; Based on the book *Proved Innocent* by Gerry Conlon; Photography, Peter Biziou; Designer, Caroline Amies; Editor, Gerry Hambling; Music, Trevor Jones; Original Songs, Bono, Gavin Friday, Maurice Seezer; Costumes, Joan Bergin; Casting, Patsy Pollock, Nuala Moiselle; a Hell's Kitchen/Gabriel Byrne production; British-Irish; Dolby Stereo; Technicolor; Rated R; 132 minutes; December release

CAST

Gerry Conlon	Daniel Day-Lewis
Gareth Peirce	Emma Thompson
Giuseppe Conlon	Pete Postlethwaite
Paul Hill	John Lynch
Paddy Armstrong	Mark Sheppard
Carole Richardson	Beatie Edney
Sarah Conlon	Marie Jones
Annie Maguire	Britta Smith
Dixon	Corin Redgrave
Joseph McAndrew	Don Baker
Benbay	Paterson Joseph
P.O. Barker	John Benfield
Ronnie Smalls	Frank Harper
Prosecutor	Daniel Massey

and Alison Crosbie (Girl in pub), Philip King (Guildford Soldier), Nye Heron, Seamus Moran, Billy Byrne (IRA Men), Anthony Brophy (Danny), Frankie McCafferty (Tommo), Paul Warriner, Julian Walsh, Stuart Wolvenden (Soldiers), Jo Connor (Bin Lady), Karen Carlisle (Rioter), Maureen McBride (Mother), Jane Nolan (Girl with Baby), Laurence Griffin, Jason Murtagh (Boys in riot), Kelly McKeavney (Young Girl), Joanna Irvine (Ann Conlon), Fiona Daly (IRA Woman), Catherine Dunne (Woman on balcony), Anna Meegan (Granny Conlon), Leah McCullagh (Bridie Conlon), Saffron Burrows (Girl in commune), Jamie Harris (Deptford Jim), Barbara Mulcahy (Marian), Mick Tohill (Man in Bookies), Peter Sheridan Snr. (Manager of Bookies), Joe McPartland (Charlie Burke), Stanley Townsend (Hooker's Driver), Gerard McSorley (Belfast Detective Pavis), Tim Perrin, Tony Denham, Rob Spendlove, Philip Davis, Martin Murphy, Richard Graham, Oliver Maguire, Maurice Kehoe (Detectives), Rachael Dowling, Tina Kellegher (Policewomen), Ronan Wilmot (Paddy Maguire), Maclean Burke (Young Vincent Maguire), Joe Jeffers (Young Patrick Maguire), Alistair Findlay (Forensic Scientist), Peter Howitt, Sean Lawlor, Brian De Salvo, Luke Hayden (Remand Prisoner Officers), Aidan Grennell (Trial Judge), Bosco Hogan (Defense Counsel), Kenneth Edge (Jury Foreman), Aine O'Connor (Dixon's Wife), Guy Carleton (Prison Admissions Officer), Dave Duffy, Martin Dunne (Prison Officers), Larry Murphy (Old Prison Officer), Richard Michaelis, Mal Whyte, John Gallagher, Marcus Lynch (Cockney Prisoners), Jer O'Leary (Prisoner John O'Brien), Joey Cashman, Alan Amsby, Paul Savage, Owen Conroy, Dee Man Kole, Bernard Pellegrinetti, Emeka Okeki, Alan O'Connor, Mario McGovern, John Joe Fontana, Terry O'Neill, Joey Legaspi, Jimmie Bergin, John Higgins (Prisoners), Paterson Joseph (Benbay), Malcolm Tierney (Home Office Official), Iain Montague (Leader of Delegation), Paul Raynor (New Chief Prison Officer), Clodagh Conroy (Dixon's Secretary), Peter Sheridan (Priest), Darren McHugh (Dixon's Son), Peter Campbell (Government Official), Alan Barry (Archivist Jenkins), Jonathan Ryan (Scottish Governor), John Pickles (Procedural Court Judge), Liam O'Callaghan (Archivist), Denys Hawthorne (Appeal Judge), Tom Wilkinson (Appeal Prosecutor).

Plot Capsule: *The true story of Jerry Conlon, an aimless Irish youth wrongly accused of the IRA bombing of a British pub. Along with his father both innocent men are sentenced to a British prison all the while hoping to see justice prevail.*

The film received Academy Award nominations for picture, director, actor (Day-Lewis), supporting actor (Postlethwaite), supporting actress (Thompson), adapted screenplay and film editing.

© Universal City Studios, Inc.

Daniel Day-Lewis

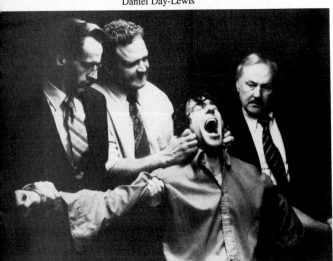

Daniel Day-Lewis (c)

Daniel Day-Lewis (r)

Pete Postlethwaite, Daniel Day-Lewis

Daniel Day-Lewis, Emma Thompson

Daniel Day-Lewis

Mark Sheppard, Beatie Edney, John Lynch, Daniel Day-Lewis

Alexander Potapov, Sam Waterston
in *A Captive in the Land* © Norkat Company

IN ADVANCE OF THE LANDING (Cygnus Communications /Cineplex Odeon Films Canada) Producer/Director, Dan Curtis; Suggested by the book by Douglas Curran; Executive Producer, Don Haig; Photography, Don Hutchison; Music, Fred Mollin; Canadian; Color; Not rated; 85 minutes; January release. Documentary on UFO's and alien contact

A CAPTIVE IN THE LAND (Norkat Company) Producers, Malcolm Stuart, John Berry; Executive Producer, Peter S. Gold; Director, John Berry; Screenplay, Lee Gold; Based upon the novel by James Aldridge; Photography, Pierre William Glenn; Editor, Georges Klotz; Music, Bill Conti; a Gloria Productions, Inc. and Gorky Film Studios/ASK Soviet American Films co-production; U.S.-Soviet; Color; Not rated; 96 minutes; January release. **CAST:** Sam Waterston (Rupert Royce), Alexander Potapov (Averianov)

Guo Liang Yi in *China, My Sorrow* © Milestone Films

CHINA, MY SORROW (Milestone) Producer, Jean-Luc Ormieres; Director, Dai Sijie; Screenplay, Dai Sijie, Shan Yuan Zhu; Photography, Jean Michel Humeau; Editor, Chantal Delattre; Music, Chen Qi Gang; Chinese; Color; Not rated; 86 minutes; January release. **CAST:** Guo Liang Yi (Four Eyes), Tieu Quan Nghieu (Monk), Vuong Han Lai (Camp Boss), Chi-Vy Sam (Bei Mao), Truong Loi (Artist), Chang Cheung Siang (Cook), Nguyen Van Thoi (Teacher), Ngo Thuon (Musician from Xun), Souvannapadith Viradeth (Sam), Su Xio Ming (Announcer), Mademoiselle Liu (Juggler)

GET THEE OUT (First Run Features) a.k.a. *Go Away!*; Producers, Rafik Zamanov, Dimitri Astrakhan; Executive Producers, Asman Bank, Nevsky Perspectiva; Director/Editor, Dimitri Astrakhan; Screenplay, Oleg Danilov, Dimitri Astrakhan; Photography, Yuri Worontsov; Music, Alexander Pantichin; Russian; 1991; Color; Not rated; 90 minutes; January release. **CAST:** Otar Mengvinetukutsesy (Motl), Elena Anisimova (Golda), Tatyana Anisimova (Beyelka), Alexander Likov (Peter), Valentin Bukin (Trofim)

FLAMING EARS (Women Make Movies) Producers/Directors /Screenplay, Angela Hans Scheirl, Dietmar Schipek, Ursula Puerrer; Photography, Margarete Neumann, Curd Duca, Hermann Lewetz,

Manfred Neuwirth; Music, Dietmar Schipek; Austrian; Color; Not rated; 83 minutes; January release. **CAST:** Susanna Heilmayr (Spy), Ursula Puerrer (Volley), Angela Hans Scheirl (Nun), Margarete Neumann (M - Chauffeur), Gabriele Szekatsch (Blood), Anthony Escott (Man with cactus), Luise Kubelka (Little Girl), Dietmar Schipek (Undertaker)

UROTSUKIDOJI: LEGEND OF THE OVERFIEND (Anime 18) Producer, Yasuhito Yamaki; Executive Producer, Yoshinobu Nishizaki; Director, Hideki Takayama; Screenplay, Noboru Aikawa; Story, Toshio Maeda; Music, Masamichi Amano; Animation Directors, Dan Kongoji, Shiro Kasami, Mari Mizuta, Kaoru Washida, Eitaro Tono; Editor, Shigeru Nishiyama; from West Cape Corp.; Japanese; Color; Rated NC-17; 108 minutes; February release. **VOICE CAST:** Christopher Courage (Amano), Rebel Joy (Akemi), Danny Bush (Nagumo), Lucy Morales (Megumi), Rose Palmer (Kuroko), Randy Woodcock (Niki), Bick Balse (Ozaki), Jurgen Offen (Sui-Kaku-Jyu)

Niki, Akemi in *Urotsukidoji* © Anime 18

DEAD ALIVE (Trimark) Producer, Jim Booth; Director, Peter Jackson; Screenplay, Peter Jackson, Stephen Sinclair, Frances Walsh; Story, Stephen Sinclair; Photography, Murray Milne; Designer, Kevin Leonard-Jones; Editor, Jamie Selkirk; Music, Peter Dasent; Creature and Gore Effects, Richard Taylor; Prosthetics, Bob McCarron, Marjory Hamlin; from Wingnut Films Ltd.; New Zealand; Dolby Stereo; Color; Not rated; 97 minutes; February release. **CAST:** Timothy Balme (Lionel), Diana Penalver (Paquita), Elizabeth Moody (Mum), Ian Watkin (Uncle Les), Brenda Kendall (Nurse McTavish), Stuart Devenie (Father McGruder), Jed Brophy (Void), Elizabeth Brimilcombe (Zombie Mum), Stephen Papps (Zombie McGruder), Murray Keane (Scroat), Glenis Levestam (Mrs. Matheson), Lewis Rowe (Mr. Matheson), Elizabeth Mullane (Rita), Harry Sinclair (Roger), Davina Whitehouse (Grandmother), Silvio Fumularo (Father), Brian Sergent (Vet), Peter Vere-Jones (Undertaker), Tina Regtien (Mandy), Bill Ralston (Stewart), Tony Hopkins (Winston), Tony Hiles (Zoo Keeper), Duncan Smith (Drunk), Tich Rowney (Barry), George Port (Lawrence), Stephen Andrews (Spike), Nick Ward (Spud), Kenny McFadden (Gladstone), Angelo Robinson (Courtney), Johnny Chico (Head Chief)

GARDEN OF SCORPIONS (Lenfilm) Director/Screenplay, Oleg Kovalov; Photography, Anatoli Lapschow; Music, Carl Orff, Bela Bartok, Dmitri Shostakovich; Includes segments from the 1955 film *Corporal Kotschetkov's Case*; Black and white/color; Russian; Not rated; 96 minutes; March release.

Timothy Balme in *Dead Alive* © Trimark

Jennifer Tilly (l), Lou Diamond Phillips (r)
in *Shadow of the Wolf* © Vision International

Wayne Bowman, Saeed Jaffrey
in *Masala* © Strand Releasing

SHADOW OF THE WOLF (Triumph) formerly *Agaguk*; Producer, Claude Leger; Executive Producer, Charles L. Smiley; Co-Producer/Director, Jacques Dorfmann; Screenplay, Rudy Wurlitzer, Evan Jones; Based upon the novel *Agaguk* by Yves Theriault; Photography, Billy Williams; Designer, Wolf Kroeger; Costumes, Olga Dimitrov; Editor, Francoise Bonnot; Music, Maurice Jarre; French-Canadian; Dolby Stereo; Cinemascope; Color; Rated PG-13; 108 minutes; March release. **CAST:** Lou Diamond Phillips (Agaguk), Toshiro Mifune (Kroomak), Jennifer Tilly (Igiyook), Bernard-Pierre Donnadieu (Brown), Donald Sutherland (Henderson), Nicolas Campbell (Scott), Raoul Trujillo (Big Tooth), Qalingo Tookalak (Tulugak), Jobie Arnaituk (Nayalik), Tamussie Sivuarapik (Korok), Harry Hill (McTavish), David Okpik (Pualuna), Patricia Eshkibok (Parted Hair), Earl Danyluk (Hatchet Jack), Glenn Verdon (Stebbins), Lucie Kadjulik, Lydia Phillips (Old Women), Jean-Michel Dortha, Gordon Masten (Sailors), Richard Zeman (Policeman), Alacie Tukalak (Arnattiaq), Sheena Larkin (Mrs. McTavish), Frederic Duplessis (Tayarak - newborn), Sam Simpson (Tayarak - one month), Estafana Chew (Tayarak - six months), Alunnigirk Airo (Tayarak - three years), Lizzie Sivuarapik (Woman in igloo), Bart Hannah Kappianak (Drum Player), Mary Iqaluk, Nellie Iqaluk (Throat Singers)

(Krishna), Sakina Jaffrey (Rita Tikkoo), Herjit Singh Pjah (Anil Solanki), Madhuri Bhatia (Bibi Solanki), Ishwarlal Mooljee (Bahadur Singh), Ronica Sajnani (Sashi Tikkoo), Les Porter (Gerald), Raju Ahsan (Babu), Jennifer Armstrong (Lisa), Wayne Bowman (Balrama), Tova Gallimore (Saraswati)

A BREATH OF LIFE (Surf Film) a.k.a. *The Plague Sower*; Producers, Massimo Vigliar, Franco Nero; Director, Beppe Cino; Screenplay, Bebbe Cino, Gesualdo Bufalino; Based on the novel by Gesualdo Bufalino; Photography, Franco Delli Colli; Music, Carlo Siliotto; a Movie Machine production with Instito Luce; Italian; Color; Not rated; 96 minutes; March release. **CAST:** Franco Nero (Gesualdo), Fernando Rey (Doctor), Vanessa Redgrave (Sister Crucifix), Lucrezia Lante Della Rovere (Marta), Salvatore "Toto" Cascio (Adelmo)

TAIGA (New Yorker Films) Director/Screenplay/Photography, Ulrike Ottinger; Editor, Bettina Bohler; Mongolian/Tuvinian; Color; Not rated; 501 minutes; March release. Documentary on the nomadic tribes of Northern Mongolia.

AMERICAN FRIENDS (Castle Hill) Producers, Patrick Cassavetti, Steve Abbott; Director, Tristram Powell; Screenplay, Michael Palin, Tristram Powell; Photography, Philip Bonham-Carter; Designer, Andrew McAlpine; Costumes, Bob Ringwood; Casting, Irene Lamb; British; Color; Rated PG; 95 minutes; April release. **CAST:** Michael Palin (Rev. Francis Ashby), Connie Booth (Miss Caroline Hartley), Trini Alvarado (Miss Elinor), Alfred Molina (Oliver Syme), David Calder (Pollitt), Simon Jones (Anderson), Robert Eddison (Rushden), Alun Armstrong (Dr. Weeks), Sheila Reid (Mrs. Weeks), Edward Rawle-Hicks (John Weeks), Jonathan Firth (Cable), Bryan Pringle (Haskell), Ian Dunn (Gowers), John Nettleton (Rev. Groves), Charles McKeown (Maynard), Roger Lloyd Pack (Dr. Butler), Jimmy Jewel (Ashby Senior)

Sibongile Nene, Farai Sevenzo in *Jit* © Northern Arts

JIT (Northern Arts Entertainment) Producer, Rory Kilalea; Executive Producers, Neil Dunn, Michael Raeburn; Director/Screenplay, Michael Raeburn; Photography, Joao "Funcho" Costa; Editor, Justin Krish; Designer, Lindie Pankiv; Zimbabwean; Fujicolor; Not rated; 98 minutes; March release. **CAST:** Dominic Makuvachuma (Uk), Sibongile Nene (Sofi), Farai Sevenzo (Johnson), Winnie Ndemera (Jukwa), Oliver Mtukudzi (Oliver), Lawrence Simbarashe (Chamba), Kathy Kuleya (Nomsa), Jackie Eeson (Gift), Cecil Zilla Mamanzi (Police Neighbor), Zanape Fazilahmed (Oliver's Wife), Taffy Marichidza (Hotel Manager), Jones Muguse (Taxi Driver), Fidelis Cheza (Barman)

MASALA (Strand Releasing) Producers, Srinivas Krishna, Camelia Friedberg; Director/Screenplay, Srinivas Krishna; Photography, Paul Sarossy; Editor, Michael Mann; Music, Leslie Winston, West India Co.; a Divani Films production; Canadian; Color; Not rated; 105 minutes; March release. **CAST:** Saeed Jaffrey (Lallu Bhai Solanki/ Mr. Tikkoo/Lord Krishna), Zohra Segal (Grandma Tikkoo), Srinivas Krishna

Connie Booth, Trini Alvarado, Michael Palin in *American Friends* © Castle Hill Prods.

DEAD FLOWERS (Wega Film) Producers, Gebhard Zupan, Michael Katz; Executive Producer, Veit Heiduschka; Director/Screenplay, Peter Ily Huemer; Photography, Walter Kindler; Editor, Eliska Stibrova; Music, Peter Scherer; Austrian; Color; Not rated; 98 minutes; April release. **CAST:** Kate Valk (Alice), Thierry van Werveke (Alex), Tana Schanzara (Grandmother), Dominique Horwitz (Willy de Ville)

Guelwaar © New Yorker Films

Tokyo Decadence © Northern Arts

GOOD EVENING, MR. WALLENBERG (Independent) Producer, Katinka Farago; Director/Screenplay, Kjell Grede; Photography, Esa Vuorinen; Editor, Darek Hodor; Swedish-German-Hungarian; Color; Not rated; 115 minutes; April release. **CAST:** Stellan Skarsgard (Raoul Wallenberg), Erland Josephson (Rabbi in Stockholm), Katharina Thalbach (Marja)

FEMALE MISBEHAVIOR (First Run Features) Producer/Director, Monika Treut; Photography, Elfi Mikesch; Editor, Renate Merck; a Hyena Films presentation; German; Color; Not rated; 80 minutes; April release. Documentary featuring Carol, Camille Paglia, Annie Sprinkle, Max Valerio

GUELWAAR (New Yorker Films) Producers, Ousmane Sembene, Jacques Perrin; Director/Screenplay, Ousmane Sembene; Photography, Dominique Gentil; Music, Baaba Maal; Editor, Marie-Aimee Debril; Wolof-French; Color; Not rated; 115 minutes; April release. **CAST:** Omar Seck (Gora), Mame Ndoumbe Diop (Nogoy Marie Thioune), Thierno Ndiaye (Guelawaar), Ndiawar Diop (Barthelemy), Moustapha Diop (Aloys), Marie-Augustine Diatta (Sophie), Samba Wane (Gor Mag), Joseph Sane (Father Leon), Coly Mbaye (Alfred), Isseu Niang (Veronique)

BLACK TO THE PROMISED LAND (Blues Prods.) Producers, Madeleine Ali, Renen Schorr, Schlomo Roglin; Director, Madeleine Ali; Photography, Manu Kadosh; Music, Branford Marsalis; Editor, Victor Nord; Israeli; Color; Not rated; 75 minutes; April release. Documentary about a group of black Brooklyn students and their visit to an Israeli kibbutz.

HARD-BOILED (Rim Film Distributors) Producers, Linda Kuk, Terence Chang; Director/Story, John Woo; Screenplay, Barry Wong; Photography, Wang Wing Heng; Art Directors, James Leung, Joel Chong; Music, Michael Gibbs, James Wong; Editors, John Woo, David Wu, Kai Kit Wai & Jack; Stunts, Cheung Jue Luh; Chinese; Color; Not rated; 127 minutes; April release. **CAST:** Chow Yun Fat (Tequila Yuen), Tony Chiu Wai Leung (Tony/Long), Teresa Mo (Teresa), Philip Chan (Pang), Anthony Wong (Johnny Wong), Bowie Lam (A-Lung), Kwan Hoi Shan (Hoi), Tung Wai (Little Ko)

Chow Yun-Fat in *Hard-Boiled* © Rim Film Distributors

TOKYO DECADENCE (Northern Arts) Producers, Yoshitaka Suzuki, Tadanobu Hirao, Yosuke Nagata; Executive Producer, Eiten Taga; Director/Screenplay, Ryu Murakami; Photography, Tadashi Aoki; Music, Ryuichi Sakamoto; Editor, Kazuki Katashima; Japanese; Tokyo Lab Color; Not rated; 112 minutes; April release. **CAST:** Miho Nikaido (Ai), Tenmei Kano (Ishioka), Kan Mikami (Client at "Mt. Fuji"), Masahiko Shimada (Client in opening scene), Yayoi Kusama (Fortune Teller), Chie Sema (Opera Woman), Sayoko Amano (Saki), Nami Nozaki (Another Callgirl)

THE EXECUTION PROTOCOL (First Run Features) Producers, Mitch Wood, Stephen Trombley; Director, Stephen Trombley; Executive Producer, Paul Baker; Photography, Paul Gibson; Editor, Peter Miller; Music, Robert Lockhart; a Worldview Pictures/West End Films Production in association with Discovery Networks; British; Color; Not rated; 87 minutes; April release. Documentary on execution procedures at Potosi Correctional Center in Missouri.

MEIN KRIEG (MY PRIVATE WAR) (Leisure Time Features) Production Director, Hans-George Ullrich; Directors, Harriet Eder, Thomas Kufus; Photography, Johann Feindt; Produced by Kanguruh-Film Berlin and WDR (Koln); German, 1990; Color/black and white; 90 minutes; May release. Documentary on six German World War II veterans who recorded the 1941 Nazi invasion of the Soviet Union.

My Neighbor Totoro © Troma Inc.

MY NEIGHBOR TOTORO (Troma) Producer, Toru Hara; Executive Producer, Yasuyoshi Tokuma; Director/Screenplay/Story, Hayao Miyazaki; Adaptation, Carl Macek; Designer, Yoshihiro Sato; Music, Jo Hisaishi; a Tokuma Group production; Japanese; Color; Rated G; 87 minutes; May release. **VOICE CAST:** Lisa Michaelson (Satsuki), Cheryl Chase (Mei), Greg Snegoff (Dad), Kenneth Hartman (Kanta), Alexandra Kenworthy (Mother), Natalie Core (Nanny), Steve Kramer (Farmer), Lara Cody (Farm Girl), Melenie McQueen (Kanta's Mom)

THE BEEKEEPER (MK2) Executive Producer, Nikos Angelopoulos; Director, Theo Angelopoulos; Screenplay, Theo

Marcello Mastroianni, Madia Mourouzi in *The Beekeeper* © MK2

Lorraine Evanoff, John Hurt in *Dark at Noon* © Sideral Prods.

Angelopoulos, Dimitris Nollas, Tonino Guerra; Photography Giorgos Arvanitis; Editor, Takis Yannopoulos; Music, Helen Karaindrou; from Greek Film Centre/Marin Karmitz Productions/ERT 1; Greek, 1986; Color; Not rated; 120 minutes; May release. **CAST:** Marcello Mastroianni (Spyros), Nadia Mourouzi (The Girl), Serge Reggiani (Sick Man), Jenny Roussea (Spyros' Wife), Dinos Iliopoulos (Spyro's Friend)

GOD IS MY WITNESS (Headliner Prods.) Producers, Manoj Desai, Nazir Ahmed; Director, Mukul S. Anand; Screenplay, Santosh Saroj; Photography, W.B. Rao; Editor, R. Rajendron; Music, Laxmikant Pyarelal; a Glamour Films production; Indian; Color; Not rated; 180 minutes; June release. **CAST:** Amitabh Bachchan (Badshah Khan), Sridevi (Benazir/Menhdi), Nagarjuna (Raja), Shilpa Shirodkar (Henna), Kiran Kumar (Pasha), Danny Denzongpa (Khuda Baksh), Vikram Gokhale (Rajput Khan), Bharat Kapoor (Aziz Mirza), Anjana Mumtaz (Salma Behn)

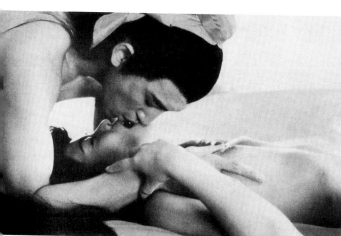

Lawrence Ng, Isabella Chow in *Sex and Zen* © Rim Film Distributors

FORBIDDEN LOVE: THE UNASHAMED STORIES OF LESBIAN LIVES (Women Make Movies) Directors/Screenplay, Aerlyn Weissman, Lynne Fernie; Photography, Zoe Dirse; a National Film Board of Canada Studio D Production; Canadian; Color; Not rated; 85 minutes; July release. Documentary in which several Lesbians talk about coming to terms with being gay; with Stephanie Morgenstern (Laura), Lynne Adams (Mitch)

BARJO (Myriad Pictures) Producer, Patrick Godeau; Director, Jerome Boivin; Screenplay, Jacques Audiard, Jerome Boivin; Photography, Jean-Claude Larrieu; Music, Hughes Le Bars; Editor, Anne Lafarge; French; Color; Not rated; 85 minutes; July release. **CAST:** Anne Brochet (Fanfan), Richard Bohringer (Charles), Hippolyte Girardot (Barjo), Consuelo de Haviland (Madame Hermelin), Renaud Danner (Michael), Nathalie Boutefeu (Gwen), Jac Berrocal (Mage Gerardini)

STEPPING RAZOR — RED X (Northern Arts) Producer/Photography, Edgar Egger; Director/Screenplay, Nichols Campbell; Executive Producers, Syd Cappe, Nicolas Stiliadis; Editor, Trevor Ambrose; Co-Executive Producer, Wayne Jobson; a David Mazor,

John Lawrence Re and Samuel MacLeod presentation; Canadian; Color; Not rated; 103 minutes; August release. Documentary on reggae musician Peter Tosh featuring Lloyd "Rocky" Allen, Edward "Bigs" Allen, Andrea Davis, Ras Leon, Ron Headley, Roy Garrick, Jahsi, Junior, Kenile, Rasta Steve, Gary Isaacs, Lawrence Mascoe, Berresford, Sandra Okiror, Thunder, Sister P., Sister Margaret, Bruce "Preacher" Robinson

SEX AND ZEN (Golden Harvest) Producer, Stephen Siu; Executive Producer, Johnny Mak; Director, Michael Mak; Screenplay, Lee Ying Kit; Based on Li Yu's *The Carnal Prayer Mat*; Photography, Peter Ngor; Music, Chang Wing Leung; Editor, Poon Hung; Hong Kong; Color; Not rated; 99 minutes; August release. **CAST:** Amy Yip (Yuk Heung), Isabella Chow (Kuen's Wife), Lawrence Ng (Mei Yeung Sheng), Kent Chang (Doctor), Xu Jin-Jiang (Kuen), Lo Lieh (Choi Run Lun)

DARK AT NOON (Sideral Productions) Producer, Leonardo De La Fuente; Director/Screenplay, Raul Ruiz; Adaptation and Dialogues, Raul Ruiz, Paul Fontaine-Salas; Photography, Ramon Suarez; Music, Jorge Arriagada; Editor, Helene Weiss-Muller; French; Color; Not rated; 100 minutes; August release. **CAST:** John Hurt (Anthony - the Marquis), Didier Bourdon (Felicien), Lorraine Evanoff (Ines), David Warner (Ellic), Daniel Prevost (The Priest), Myriem Roussel (The Virigin of Imitations), Filipe Dias (The Child), Rosa Castro Andre (Francisca), Maria Joa Reis (Ana), Adriana Novais (Paula), Batista Fernandes (Felicien's Father), Alexandre De Sousa, Laurent Moine (Doctors), Rui Mendes (Employee)

BEING AT HOME WITH CLAUDE (Strand Releasing) Producer, Louise Gendron; Director, Jean Beaudin; Screenplay, Johanne Boisvert; Based on the play by Rene-Daniel DuBois; Photography, Thomas Vamos; Art Director, Francois Seguin; Costumes, Louise Jobin; Editor, Andre Corriveau; Music, Richard Gregoire; a Les Productions du Cerf presentation in association with the National Film Board of Canada with the participation of Telefilm Canada; French-Canadian; Dolby Stereo; Color; Not rated; 84 minutes; August release. **CAST:** Roy Dupuis (Yves), Jacques Godin (Inspector), Jean-Francois Pichette (Claude), Gaston Lepage (Stenographer), Hugo Dube (Policeman), Johanne-Marie Tremblay (Inspector's Wife), Nathalie Mallette (Yves' Sister)

Roy Dupuis in *Being at Home With Claude* © Strand Releasing

Bakary Sangare, Mariam Kaba in *Samba Traore*
© New Yorker Films

Navin Chowdhry, Alexandra Powers in *The Seventh Coin*
© World's Apart Prod.

TITO AND ME (Kino International) Producers, Goran Markovic, Zoran Masirevic, Michel Mavros; Director/Screenplay, Goran Markovic; Photography, Racoslav Vladic; Editor, Snezana Ivanovic; Costumes, Boris Caksiran; Music, Zoran Simjanovic; from Tramontana (Belgrade), Ro Terra (Novi Sad), Magda Productions (Paris); Yugoslav-French/Serbo-Croatian; Color; Not rated; 104 minutes; August release. **CAST:** Dimitrie Vojnov (Zoran), Lazar Risotvski (Raja), Anica Dobra (Zoran's Mother), Predrag Manojlovic (Zoran's Father), Ljilana Dragutinovic (Zoran's Aunt), Bogdan Diklic (Zoran's Uncle), Olivera Markovic (Grandmother), Rade Markovic (Grandfather), Vesna Trivalic (Teacher), Voja Brajovic (Marshall Tito).

DJEMBEFOLA (Interama) Producer/Director/Photography, Laurent Chevalier; Based on an idea by Pierre Marcault; French; Color; Not rated; 65 minutes; September release. Documentary on South African drummer Mamady Keita.

ONCE UPON A TIME IN CHINA, PART 2 (Raw Film) Producer/Director, Tsui Hark; Screenplay, Tsui Hark, Chan Tin Suen, Cheung Tan; Photography, Wong Ngor Tai; Cantonese/Chinese; Color; Not rated; 118 minutes; September release. **CAST:** Jet Li (Wong Fey Hong), Rosemund Kwan (Aunt Yee), Mok Siu Chung (Fu), Xiong Xin Xin (Kung), John Chiang (Luke), Zhang Tie Lin (Sun Yat-sen), Yen Chi Tan (Commander Lan)

MALINA (Independent/Public Theatre) Producers, Thomas & Steffen Kuckenreuther; Director, Werner Schroeter; Screenplay, Elfriede Jelinek; Photography, Elfi Mikesch; Music, Giacomo Manzoni; Editor, Juliane Lorenz; Sets/Costumes, Alberte Barsack; German; Color; Not rated; 125 minutes; September release. **CAST:** Isabelle Huppert (The Woman), Mathieu Carriere (Malina), Can Togay (Ivan), Fritz Schediwyiwy (The Father), Isolde Barth (The Mother), Libcart Schwarz (Ms. Jellinek), Elisabeth Krejcir (Lina), Peter Kern (The Bulgarian), Jenny Drivala (The Opera Singer), Wiebke Frost (The Woman's Sister), Lolita Chammah (The Child)

SAMBA TRAORE (New Yorker Films) Producer/Director, Idrissa Ouedraogo; Executive Producers, Sophie Salbot, Silvia Voser, Les Films De L'Avenir; Screenplay, Idrissa Ouedraogo, Jacques Arhex, Santiago Amigorena; Photography, Pierre Laurent Chenieux, Mathieu Vadepied; Art Director, Yves Brover; Costumes, Oumou Sy; Editor, Joelle Dufour; Music, Fanton Cahen, Lamine Konte; Burkina Faso/Moore; Color; Not rated; 85 minutes; September release. **CAST:** Bakary Sangare (Samba Traore), Mariam Kaba (Saratou), Abdoulaye Komboudri (Salif), Irene Tassembedo (Binta), Moumouni Compaore (Ali), Krin Casimir Traore (Seydou), Sibidou Ouedraogo (Awa), Firmine Coulibaly (Koro), Hippolyte Wangrawa (Ismael), Mady Derme (The Horse Rider), Joseph Traore (The Truck Driver), Noufou Ouedraogo (The Newspaper Seller), Noel Pare, Jacques Khalifa Sanou (The Policemen), Adama Traore (The Shepherd)

PRAYING WITH ANGER (Cinevista) Producer/Director/Screenplay, M. Night Shyamalan; Photography, Madhu Ambat; Editor, Frank Reynolds; Music, Edmund K. Choi; Color; Not rated; 101 minutes; September release. **CAST:** M. Night Shyamalar (Dev Raman), Mike Muthu (Sunjay Mohan), Arun Balachandran (Raj Kahn), Richa Ahuja (Rupal Mohan), Christabal Howie (Sabitha)

POLICE STORY III: SUPERCOP (Pacific Films) Producers, Willie Chan, Jackie Chan; Executive Producers, Leonard Ho, Jackie Chan; Director, Stanley Tong; Screenplay, Tang King-Sung, Ma Mei-Ping, Lee Wei-Yee; Photography, Lam Kwok-Wah; Art Director, Oliver Wong; Editors, Cheung Yaeo-Chung, Cheung Kai Fei; Music, Lee Chun Shing; Costumes, Hung Wei-Chuk; Stunts, Tong Kwei Lai; Cantonese/Chinese; Color; Not rated; 96 minutes; October release. **CAST:** Jackie Chan (Chen Chia-chu/Lin Fu-sheng), Michelle Yeoh (Yang/Hua), Maggie Cheung (May), Tung Biao (Piao), Phillip Chan (Y.K. Chan), Yuen Wah (Panther), Tsang Kong (Chiabar)

THE SEVENTH COIN (Hemdale) Producers, Lee Nelson, Omri Maron; Executive Producers, James Nelson, Shimshon Rafaeli, Dov Strikofsky, Garry Hakim; Director, Dror Soref; Screenplay, Dror Soref, Michael Lewis; Photography, Avi Karpik; Editor, Carole Kravetz; Music, Misha Segal; Casting, Lisa London; an Orbit Entertainment/April COM Ltd. production; Israeli; Color; Rated PG-13; 92 minutes; September release. **CAST:** Alexandra Powers (Ronnie Segal), Navin Chowdhry (Salim Zouabi), Peter O'Toole (Emil Saber), John Rhys-Davies (Captain Galil), Ally Walker (Lisa), Whitman Mayo (Julius Washington)

M. Night Shyamalar in *Praying With Anger* © Cinevista

Samuel Mussen, Carmen Maura in *Between Heaven and Earth*
© Arrow Releasing

Jade Leung in *Black Cat* © Headliner Prods.

Stephen Chiau, Chang Min in *King of Beggars* © Rim Film Distributors

FRAUDS (Live Entertainment/J&M Enterprises) Producers, Andrena Finlay, Stuart Quin; Executive Producer, Rebel Penfold-Russell; Director, Stephen Elliott; Photography, Geoff Burton; Designer, Brian Thompson; Editor, Frans Vandenburg; Music, Guy Gross; Costumes, Fiona Spence; a Latent Image production in association with the Australian Film Finance Corp.; Australian; Eastmancolor; Not rated; 92 minutes; September release. **CAST:** Phil Collins (Roland Copping), Hugo Weaving (Jonathan Wheats), Josephine Byrnes (Beth Wheats), Peter Mochrie (Michael Allen), Helen O'Connor (Margaret), Rebel Russell (Mother), Colleen Clifford (Mrs. Waterson), Nicholas Hammond (Det. Simms), Kee Chan (Det. Alan), Vincent Ball (Judge), Al Clark (Barry Gribble), Martin Cooper (Lawyer)

BETWEEN HEAVEN AND EARTH (Arrow Entertainment) Producer/Director, Marion Hansel; Screenplay, Marion Hansel, Paul Le, Jaco Van Dormael, Laurette Van Keerbe; Executive Producer, Eric Van Beuren; Editor, Susanna Rossberg; Music, Takashi Kako; Costumes, Yan Tax; Casting, Greda Diddens; French; Color; Not rated; 80 minutes; October release. **CAST:** Carmen Maura (Maria), Jean-Pierre Cassel (The Editor in Chief), Didier Bezace (Tom), Samuel Mussen (Jeremy), Andre Delvaux (The Professor), Philippe Allard (The Young Man), Daniela Bisconti (Laura), Francine Blistin, Andre DeBaar, Pierre Laroche (Gynecologists), Denise De Hagen (Physiotherapist), Serge Demouli (Henri), Veronique Dumont (The Young Girl), Hugues Lepaigne (The Television Host), Johan Leysen (Hans), Patrick Massieu (The Nursey Director), Christine Michiels (The Nurse), Guy Pion (The Concierge), Pietro Pizzuti (The Guest Psychologist), Pascale Tison (Jane), Serge-Henri Valcke (Peter), Alexandre Von Sivers (The Guest Meteorologist), Jan Ackermans (The Baby's Voice)

BLACK CAT (Headliner Prods.) Producer/Director, Stephen Shin; Executive Producer, Dickson Poon; Screenplay, Lam Wai-Iun, Chan Bo-Shum, Lam Tan-Ping; Photography, Lee Kin-Keung; Music, Danny Chung; a D&B Films Co. production; Hong Kong; Color; Not rated; 91 minutes; October release. **CAST:** Jade Leung (Catherine), Simon Yam (Brian), Thomas Lam (Allen Yeung)

WICKED CITY (Streamline) Producers, Yoshio Masumizu, Koohei Kuri; Director, Yoshiaki Kawajiri; Adaptation Producer/Director, Carl Macek; Japanese Screenplay, Kisei Choo; English Dialogue/Director, Greg Snegoff; Photography, Kinichi Ishikawa; Music, Osamu Shooji; Editor, Harutoshi Ogata; Japanese; Color; Not rated; 90 minutes; October release. **VOICE CAST:** Greg Snegoff (Taki), Mike Reynolds (Guiseppe Mayart), Gaye Kruger (Maki), Edie Mirman ("Spider Woman"), Jeff Winkless (Head Black Worlder), David Povall (Gotnierge), Robert V. Barron (Section Chief)

THE ARCHITECTS (Independent/Public Theatre) Director, Peter Kahane; Screenplay, Thomas Knauf, Peter Kahane; Photography, Andreas Kofer; Editor, Ilse Peters; German, 1990; Color; Not rated; 95 minutes; October release. **CAST:** Kurt Naumann (Daniel Brenner), Rita Feidmeier (Wanda Brenner), Uta Eisold (Renate Reese), Jurgen Watzke (Martin Bulla), Ute Lubosch (Franziska Scarf), Catherine Stoyan (Elke Krug), Andrea Meissner (Barbara Schneider), Jorg Schuttauf (Wilfried Berger), Hans-Joachim Hegewald (Albrecht Wischala), Christoph Engel (Okonom Endler), Joachim Tomaschewsky (Prof. Vessely)

LA CHASSE AUX PAPILLONS (Chasing Butterflies) (New Yorker Films) Producer, Martine Marignac; Director/Screenplay/Editor, Otar Iosseliani; Photography, William Lubtchansky; Music, Nicolas Zourabichvili; Costumes, Charlotte David; a Pierre Grise Productions (France), Sodaperaga (France), France 3 Cinema (France), Metropolis Filmproduktion (Germany), Best International Films (Italy) production; French-German-Italian; Color; Not rated; 115 minutes; October release. **CAST:** Narda Blanchet (Solange), Pierrette Pompom Bailhache (Valerie), Alexandre Tcherkassoff (Henri de Lampadere), Thamar Tarassachvili (Marie-Agnes de Bayonette), Alexandra Liebermann (Helene von Zastro), Lilia Ollivier (Olga), Emmanuel De Chauvigny (Father Andre), Sacha Piatigorsky (The Maharajah), Anne-Marie Eisenschitz (Marie), Francoise Tsouladze (Yvonne), Maimouna N'Diaye (Caprice), Yannick Carpentier (Monsieur Carpentier), Otar Iosseliani (The Ghost), Alexander Askoldov (Drunk), Pascal Aubier (Quarrelsome Man)

STRICTLY PROPAGANDA (First Run Features) Executive Producer, C. Cay Wesnigk; Director/Screenplay, Wolfgang Kissel; Presented in association with Goethe House; German; Color/black and white; Not rated; 94 minutes; October release. Documentary on the Communist rule in East Germany from the end of World War II to the fall of the Berlin Wall.

Pierrette Pompom Bailhache. Narda Blanchet in *La Chasseaux Papillons* © New Yorker Films

Roberto Sosa, Claudia Becket. Bruno Bichir in *Highway Patrolman* © First Look Pictures

Miguel Bose in *Mazeppa* © MK2

Leonor Silveira in *Valley of Abraham* © Public Theatre

WHY HAS BODHI-DHARMA LEFT FOR THE EAST? (Milestone)
Producer/ Director/Screenplay/Photography/Editor, Bae Yong Kyun; Music, Chin Kyu Yong; Korean; Color; Not rated; 135 minutes; October release. **CAST:** Yi Pan Yong (Hye Gok), Sin Won Sop (Ki Bong), Huang Hae Jin (Hae Jin), Ko Su Yong (Superior), Kim Hae Young (Fellow Disciple)

NO MORE MR. NICE GUY (Cinepool) Producer, Claus Boje; Director, Detlev Buck; Screenplay, Ernst Kahl, Detlev Buck; Photography, Roger Heereman; Editor, Peter R. Adam; Music, Detlef Petersen; German; Color; Not rated; 92 minutes; October release. **CAST:** Joachim Krol (Rudi Kipp), Horst Krause (Most Kipp), Konstantin Kotljarov (Viktor), Sophie Rois (Nadine), Heinrich Giskes (Kommissar)

ONE WAY TICKET (Un Pasaje de Ida) (Independent) Director, Agliberto Melendez; No other information available; Dominican Republic; Color; Not rated; 92 minutes; October release. Cast: Angel Muniz, Carlos Alfredo, Juan Maria Almonte.

THE NORTHERNERS (First Floor Features) Producers, Laurens Geels, Dick Maas; Director/Screenplay, Alex van Warmerdam; Photography, Marc Felperlaan; Music, Vincent van Warmerdam; Editor, Rene Wiegmans; Dutch; Color; Not rated; 100 minutes; November release. **CAST:** Leonard Lucieer (Thomas), Jack Wouterse (Jacob), Alex van Warmerdam (Simon), Annet Malherbe (Martha), Veerle Dobbelaere (Agnes), Rudolf Lucieer (Anton), Loes Wouterson (Elisabeth), Dary Some (The Negro)

THE TANGO PLAYER (DEFA Studio) Producer, Herbert Ehler: Director/Screenplay, Roland Graf; Based on the book by Christoph Hein; Photography, Peter Ziesche; Music, Gunther Fischer, Julio C. Sanders; German, 1990; Color; Not rated; 112 minutes; November release. **CAST:** Michael Gwisdek (Hans Peter Dallow), Corinna Harfouch (Elke), Hermann Beyer (Dr. Berger), Peter Prager (Roessler), Peter Sodann (Schulze), Jaëcki Schwarz (Harry)

KING OF BEGGARS (Rim Film Distributors) Producer, Stephen Siu; Director, Gordon Chan; Screenplay, Chan Kin-Chung; Photography, Chung Chi-Man; Designer, Ma Kwong-Wing; Music, Joseph Koo; Martial Arts Choreographer, Yuen Cheung-Yan; from Win's Movie Production & I/E Co.; Chinese; Color; Not rated; 107 minutes; November release. **CAST:** Stephen Chiau (So Chan), Chang Min (Yee), Ng Man-Tat (General So), Chan Wai-Yee (Yee's Sister), Chui Siu-Keung (Emperor's Military Commander), David Lam (Governor)

RADIO STORIES (Independent/Public Theatre) Director/Screenplay, Jose Luis Saez de Heredia; Photography, Antonio L. Ballesteros; Music, Ernesto Halfter; Editor, Julio Pena; Spanish, 1955; Not rated; 92 minutes; November release. **CAST:** Francisco Rabal (Gabriel), Margarita Andrey (Carmen), Jose Ibert (Inventor), Angel de Andres (Thief), Jose Maria Lamea (Don Senen), Alberto Romea (Don Anselmo)

HIGHWAY PATROLMAN (First Look Pictures) Producer/Screenplay, Lorenzo O'Brien; Director, Alex Cox; Photography, Miguel Garzon; a Together Bros./Ultra Film; Mexican-Japanese; Color; Not rated; 104 minutes; November release. **CAST:** Roberto Sosa (Pedro), Bruno Bichir (Anibal), Vanessa Bauche (Maribel), Zaide Silvia Gutierrez (Griselda)

MAZEPPA (MK2) Producer, Marin Karmitz; Executive Producer, Yvon Crenn; Director/Original Idea, Bartabas; Screenplay, Claude-Henri Buffard, Bartabas, Homeric; Story, Claude-Henri Buffard, Bartabas; Photography, Bernard Zitzermann; Music, Jean-Pierre Drouet; Editor, Joseph Licide; Costumes, Marie-Laure Schakmundes, Cristine Guegan; French; Color; Not rated; 111 minutes; December release. **CAST:** Miguel Bose (Gericault), Bartabas (Franconi), Brigitte Marty (Mouste), Eva Schakmundes (Alexandrine), Fatima Aibout (Cascabelle), Bakary Sangare (Joseph)

ACLA (Intrafilms/SACIS) Producers, Pietro Valsecchi, Camilla Nesbitt; Director/Screenplay, Aurelio Grimaldi; Photography, Maurizio Calvesi; Music, Dario Lucantoni; a Cineuropa '92 and Nova Films production in colaboration with Pentafilm; Italian; Color; Not rated; 86 minutes; December release. **CAST:** Francesco Cusimano (Acla), Tony Sperandeo (Caramazza), Luigi Maria Burruano (The Father), Lucia Sardo (The Mother), Giovanni Alamia (Salvo), Benedetto Raneli (The Priest), Giuseppe Cusimano (Maurizio Rizzuto), Rita Barbanera (Concetta Rizzuto), Salvatore Scianna (Calogero Rizzuto), Ignazio Donato (Pietro), Luciano Venturino (Pino Rizzuto)

FAMINE-33 (Independent) Director, Oles Yanchuk; Screenplay, Serhij Diachenko, Les Taniuk; Based on the novel *The Yellow Prince* by Vasyl Barka; Photography, Vasyl Borodin, Mykhajlo Kretov; Music, Mykola Kalandjonak, Victor Pacukevych; Editor, Natalia Akajomova; Ukrainian; Black and white/color; Not rated; 95 minutes; December release. **CAST:** Halyna Sulyma (Odarka), Georgi Moroziuk (Myron)

CHILD'S PLAY (Independent/Film Forum) Director/Editor, Wolfgang Becker; Screenplay, Horst J. Sczerba, Wolfgang Becker; Photography, Martin Kukula; German; Color; Not rated; 107 minutes; December release. **CAST:** Jonas Kipp (Micha), Oliver Brocker (Kalli), Burghart Klaubner (Micha's Father), Angelika Bartsch (Micha's Mother)

ATLANTIS (Milestone Films) Director, Luc Besson; Photography, Christian Petron; Music, Eric Serra; Music Performed by the London Royal Philharmonic Orchestra and the Ambrosian Singers; Chief Diver, Jean-Marc Bour; French; Color; Not rated; 75 minutes; December release. Documentary of the visual wonders of the ocean.

VALLEY OF ABRAHAM (Independent/Public Theatre) Producer, Paulo Branco; Director/Screenplay, Manoel de Oliveira; Based on the novel by Agustina Bessa-Luis; Photography, Mario Barruso; Editors, Manoel de Oliveira, Valerie Loiseleux; Portuguese-French-Swiss; Color; Not rated; 187 minutes; December release. **CAST:** Leonor Silveira (Ema), Cecile Sanz De Alba (Young Ema), Luis Miguel Cintra (Carlo De Paiva), Rui De Carvalho (Paulino Cardeano), Luis Lima Barreto (Pedro Lumiares), Micheline Larpin (Simona), Diogo Doria (Fernando Osorio)

Oliver Brocker in *Child's Play* © Film Forum

Kevin Anderson

Loni Anderson

Rene Auberjonois

Barbara Barrie

BIOGRAPHICAL DATA

(Name, real name, place, and date of birth, school attended)

AAMES, WILLIE (William Upton): Los Angeles, CA, July 15, 1960.

AARON, CAROLINE: Richmond, VA, Aug. 7, 1954, CatholicU.

ABBOTT, DIAHNNE: NYC, 1945.

ABBOTT, JOHN: London, June 5, 1905.

ABRAHAM, F. MURRAY: Pittsburgh, PA, Oct. 24, 1939. UTx.

ADAMS, BROOKE: NYC, Feb. 8, 1949. Dalton.

ADAMS, DON: NYC, Apr. 13, 1926.

ADAMS, EDIE (Elizabeth Edith Enke): Kingston, PA, Apr. 16, 1927. Juilliard, Columbia.

ADAMS, JULIE (Betty May): Waterloo,Iowa, Oct. 17, 1926. Little Rock Jr. College.

ADAMS, MAUD (Maud Wikstrom): Lulea, Sweden, Feb. 12, 1945.

ADDY, WESLEY: Omaha, NE, Aug. 4, 1913. UCLA.

ADJANI, ISABELLE: Germany, June 27, 1955.

ADRIAN, IRIS (Iris Adrian Hostetter): Los Angeles, May 29, 1913.

AGAR, JOHN: Chicago. Jan. 31, 1921.

AGUTTER, JENNY: Taunton, Eng, Dec. 20, 1952.

AIELLO, DANNY: NYC. June 20, 1935.

AIMEE. ANOUK (Dreyfus): Paris, Apr. 27, 1934. Bauer-Therond.

AKERS, KAREN: NYC, Oct. 13, 1945, Hunter Col.

AKINS, CLAUDE: Nelson, GA, May 25, 1936. Northwestern U.

ALBERGHETTI, ANNA MARIA: Pesaro, Italy, May 15, 1936.

ALBERT, EDDIE (Eddie Albert Heimberger): Rock Island, IL, Apr. 22, 1908. U. of Minn.

ALBERT, EDWARD: Los Angeles, Feb. 20. 1951. UCLA.

ALBRIGHT, LOLA: Akron, OH, July 20, 1925.

ALDA, ALAN: NYC, Jan. 28, 1936. Fordham.

ALEJANDRO, MIGUEL: NYC, Feb. 21, 1958.

ALEXANDER, ERIKA: Philadelphia, PA, 1970.

ALEXANDER, JANE (Quigley): Boston, MA, Oct. 28, 1939. Sarah Lawrence.

ALEXANDER, JASON: Irvington, NJ, Sept. 23, 1959. Boston U.

ALICE, MARY: Indianola, MS, Dec. 3. 1941.

ALLEN, DEBBIE (Deborah): Houston, TX, Jan. 16, 1950, HowardU.

ALLEN, JOAN: Rochelle, IL, Aug. 20, 1956, EastIllU.

ALLEN, KAREN: Carrollton, IL, Oct. 5, 1951. UMd.

ALLEN, NANCY: NYC, June 24, 1950.

ALLEN, REX: Wilcox, AZ, Dec. 31, 1922.

ALLEN, STEVE: NYC, Dec. 26, 1921.

ALLEN, TIM: Denver, CO, June 13, 1953 W. MI. Univ.

ALLEN, WOODY (Allen Stewart Konigsberg): Brooklyn, Dec. 1, 1935.

ALLEY, KIRSTIE: Wichita, KS, Jan. 12, 1955.

ALLYSON, JUNE (Ella Geisman): Westchester, NY, Oct. 7, 1917.

ALONSO, MARIA CONCHITA: Cuba, 1957.

ALT, CAROL: Queens, NY, Dec. 1, 1960. HofstraU.

ALVARADO, TRINI: NYC, 1967.

AMIS, SUZY: Oklahoma City, OK, Jan. 5, 1958. Actors Studio.

AMOS, JOHN: Newark, NJ, Dec. 27, 1940. Colo. U.

ANDERSON, KEVIN: Illinois, Jan. 13, 1960.

ANDERSON, LONI: St. Paul, MN, Aug. 5, 1946.

ANDERSON, MELODY: Edmonton, Canada, 1955. Carlton U.

ANDERSON, MICHAEL, JR.: London,

Eng., Aug. 6, 1943.

ANDERSON, RICHARD DEAN: Minneapolis, MN, Jan. 23, 1953.

ANDERSSON, BIBI: Stockholm, Nov. 11,1935. Royal Dramatic Sch.

ANDES, KEITH: Ocean City, NJ, July 12, 1920. Temple U., Oxford.

ANDRESS, URSULA: Berne, Switz., Mar. 19, 1936.

ANDREWS, ANTHONY: London, 1948.

ANDREWS, JULIE (Julia Elizabeth Wells): Surrey, Eng., Oct. 1, 1935.

ANGLIM, PHILIP: San Francisco, CA, Feb. 11, 1953.

ANNABELLA (Suzanne Georgette Charpentier): Paris, France, July 14, 1912/1909.

ANN-MARGRET (Olsson): Valsjobyn, Sweden, Apr. 28, 1941. Northwestern U.

ANSARA, MICHAEL: Lowell, MA, Apr. 15, 1922. Pasadena Playhouse.

ANSPACH, SUSAN: NYC, Nov. 23, 1945.

ANTHONY, LYSETTE: London, 1963.

ANTHONY TONY: Clarksburg, WV, Oct.16, 1937. Carnegie Tech.

ANTON, SUSAN: Yucaipa, CA, Oct. 12, 1950. Bernardino Col.

ANTONELLI, LAURA: Pola, Italy, 1941.

ANWAR, GABRIELLE: Lalehaam, Eng., 1970

APPLEGATE, CHRISTINA: Hollywood CA, Nov.25, 1972.

ARCHER, ANNE: Los Angeles, Aug. 25, 1947.

ARCHER, JOHN (Ralph Bowman): Osceola, NB, May 8, 1915. USC.

ARKIN, ADAM: Brooklyn, Aug. 19, 1956.

ARKIN, ALAN: NYC, Mar. 26, 1934. LACC.

ARMSTRONG, BESS: Baltimore, MD, Dec. 11, 1953.

ARNAZ, DESI, JR.: Los Angeles, Jan. 19, 1953.

ARNAZ, LUCIE: Hollywood, July 17,1951.

ARNESS, JAMES (Aurness): Minneapolis, MN, May 26, 1923. Beloit College.

Kevin Bacon

ARNOLD, ROSEANNE (Barr): Salt Lake City, UT, Nov. 3, 1952.

ARQUETTE, ROSANNA: NYC, Aug. 10, 1959.

ARTHUR, BEATRICE (Frankel): NYC, May 13, 1924. New School.

ASHLEY, ELIZABETH (Elizabeth Ann Cole): Ocala, FL, Aug. 30, 1939.

ASNER, EDWARD: Kansas City, KS, Nov. 15, 1929.

ASSANTE, ARMAND: NYC, Oct. 4, 1949. AADA.

ASTIN, JOHN: Baltimore, MD, Mar. 30, 1930. U. Minn.

ASTIN, MacKENZIE: Los Angeles, May 12 1973.

ASTIN, SEAN: Santa Monica, Feb. 25, 1971.

ATHERTON, WILLIAM: Orange, CT, July 30, 1947. Carnegie Tech.

ATKINS, CHRISTOPHER: Rye, NY, Feb. 21, 1961.

ATTENBOROUGH, RICHARD: Cambridge, Eng., Aug. 29, 1923. RADA.

AUBERJONOIS, RENE: NYC, June 1, 1940. Carnegie Tech.

AUDRAN, STEPHANE: Versailles, Fr., Nov. 8, 1933.

AUGER, CLAUDINE: Paris, Apr. 26,1942. Dramatic Cons.

AULIN, EWA: Stockholm, Sweden, Feb. 14, 1950.

AUMONT, JEAN PIERRE: Paris, Jan. 5, 1909. French Nat'l School of Drama.

AUTRY, GENE: Tioga, TX, Sept. 29, 1907.

AVALON, FRANKIE (Francis Thomas Avallone): Philadelphia, Sept. 18, 1940.

AYKROYD, DAN: Ottawa, Can., July 1, 1952.

AYRES, LEW: Minneapolis, MN, Dec. 28, 1908.

AZNAVOUR, CHARLES (Varenagh Aznourian): Paris, May 22, 1924.

AZZARA, CANDICE: Brooklyn, May 18, 1947.

BACALL, LAUREN (Betty Perske): NYC, Sept. 16, 1924. AADA.

BACH, BARBARA: Queens, NY, Aug. 27, 1946.

BACKER, BRIAN: NYC, Dec. 5, 1956. Neighborhood Playhouse.

BACON, KEVIN: Philadelphia, PA., July 8, 1958.

BAIN, BARBARA: Chicago, Sept. 13, 1934. U. ILL.

BAIO, SCOTT: Brooklyn, Sept. 22, 1961.

BAKER, BLANCHE: NYC, Dec. 20, 1956.

BAKER, CARROLL: Johnstown, PA, May 28, 1931. St. Petersburg Jr. College.

BAKER, DIANE: Hollywood, CA, Feb. 25, 1938. USC.

BAKER, JOE DON: Groesbeck, TX, Feb.12, 1936.

BAKER, KATHY: Midland, TX., June 8, 1950. UCBerkley.

BALABAN, BOB: Chicago, Aug. 16, 1945. Colgate.

BALDWIN, ADAM: Chicago, Feb. 27, 1962.

BALDWIN, ALEC: Massapequa, NY, Apr. 3, 1958. NYU.

BALDWIN, WILLIAM: Massapequa, NY, 1963.

BALE, CHRISTIAN: Pembrokeshire, West Wales, Jan. 30, 1974.

BALLARD, KAYE: Cleveland, OH, Nov. 20, 1926.

BALSAM, MARTIN: NYC, Nov. 4, 1919. Actors Studio.

BANCROFT, ANNE (Anna Maria Italiano): Bronx, Sept. 17, 1931. AADA.

BANERJEE, VICTOR: Calcutta, India, Oct. 15, 1946.

BANES, LISA: Chagrin Falls, OH, July 9, 1955. Juilliard.

BANNEN, IAN: Airdrie, Scot., June 29, 1928.

BARANSKI, CHRISTINE: Buffalo, NY, May 2, 1952. Juilliard.

BARBEAU, ADRIENNE: Sacramento, CA, June 11, 1945. Foothill Col.

BARDOT, BRIGITTE: Paris, Sept. 28, 1934.

BARKIN, ELLEN: Bronx, Apr. 16, 1954. Hunter Col.

BARNES, BINNIE (Gitelle Enoyce Barnes): London, Mar. 25, 1906

BARNES, C. B. (Christopher): Portland, ME, 1973.

BARR, JEAN-MARC: San Diego, CA, Sept. 1960.

BARRAULT, JEAN-LOUIS: Vesinet, France, Sept. 8, 1910.

BARRAULT, MARIE-CHRISTINE: Paris. Mar. 21, 1946.

BARREN, KEITH: Mexborough, Eng., Aug. 8, 1936. Sheffield Playhouse.

BARRETT, MAJEL (Hudec): Columbus, OH, Feb. 23. Western Reserve U.

BARRIE, BARBARA: Chicago, IL, May 23, 1931.

BARRY, GENE (Eugene Klass): NYC, June 14, 1921.

BARRY, NEILL: NYC, Nov. 29, 1965.

BARRYMORE, DREW: Los Angeles, Feb. 22,

Drew Barrymore

Cyd Charisse

1975.

BARRYMORE, JOHN DREW: Beverly Hill CA, June 4, 1932. St. John's Militar Academy.

BARTEL, PAUL: NYC, Aug. 6, 1938. UCLA.

BARTY, BILLY: Millsboro, PA, Oct. 25, 1924

BARYSHNIKOV. MIKHAIL: Riga, Latvi Jan. 27, 1948.

BASINGER, KIM: Athens, GA, Dec. 8, 195 Neighborhood Playhouse.

BATEMAN, JASON: Rye, NY, Jan. 14, 1969.

BATEMAN, JUSTINE: Rye, NY, Feb. 19, 196

BATES, ALAN: Allestree, Derbyshire, Eng Feb. 17, 1934. RADA.

BATES, JEANNE: San Francisco, CA, May 2 RADA.

BATES, KATHY: Memphis, TN, June 28, 194 S. Methodist U.

BAUER, STEVEN: (Steven Rocky Echevarria Havana, Cuba, Dec. 2, 1956. UMiami.

BAXTER, KEITH: South Wales,Eng., Apr. 2 1933. RADA.

BAXTER, MEREDITH: Los Angeles, June 2 1947. Intelochen Acad.

BEACHAM, STEPHANIE: England, 1946.

BEAL, JOHN (J. Alexander Bliedung): Jopli MO, Aug. 13, 1909. PA. U.

BEALS, JENNIFER: Chicago, IL, Dec. 1 1963.

BEART, EMMANUELLE: Gassin, Franc 1965.

BEATTY, NED: Louisville, KY, July 6, 1937.

BEATTY, ROBERT: Hamilton, Ont., Can., Oc

Christian Bale

19, 1909. U. of Toronto.
BECK, JOHN: Chicago, IL, Jan. 28, 1943.
BECK, MICHAEL: Memphis, TN, Feb. 4, 1949. Millsap Col.
BEDELIA, BONNIE: NYC, Mar. 25, 1946. Hunter Col.
BEDI, KABIR: India, 1945.
BEERY, NOAH, JR.: NYC, Aug. 10, 1916. Harvard Military Academy.
BEGLEY, ED, JR.: NYC, Sept. 16, 1949.
BELAFONTE, HARRY: NYC, Mar. 1, 1927.
BEL GEDDES, BARBARA: NYC, Oct. 31, 1922.
BELL, TOM: Liverpool, Eng., 1932.
BELLER, KATHLEEN: NYC, Feb. 10, 1957.
BELLWOOD, PAMELA (King): Scarsdale, NY, June 26.
BELMONDO, JEAN PAUL: Paris, Apr. 9, 1933.
BELUSHI, JAMES: Chicago, May 15, 1954.
BENEDICT, DIRK (Niewoehner): White Sulphur Springs, MT, March 1, 1945. Whitman Col.
BENEDICT, PAUL: SilverCity, NM, Sept. 17, 1938.
BENING, ANNETTE: Topeka, KS, May 29, 1958. SFSt. U.
BENJAMIN, RICHARD: NYC, May 22, 1938. Northwestern U.
BENNENT, DAVID: Lausanne, Sept. 9, 1966.
BENNETT, BRUCE (Herman Brix): Tacoma, WA, May 19, 1909. U. Wash.
BENNETT, HYWEL: Garnant, So. Wales, Apr. 8, 1944.
BENSON, ROBBY: Dallas, TX, Jan 21, 1957.
BERENGER, TOM: Chicago, May 31, 1950, UMo.
BERENSON, MARISA: NYC, Feb. 15, 1947.
BERGEN, CANDICE: Los Angeles, May 9, 1946. U. PA.
BERGEN, POLLY: Knoxville, TN, July 14, 1930. Compton Jr. College.
BERGER, HELMUT: Salzburg, Aus., 1942.
BERGER, SENTA: Vienna, May 13, 1941. Vienna Sch. of Acting.
BERGER, WILLIAM: Austria, Jan. 20, 1928. Columbia.
BERGERAC, JACQUES: Biarritz, France, May 26, 1927. Paris U.
BERKOFF, STEVEN: London, Eng., Aug. 3, 1937.
BERLE, MILTON (Berlinger): NYC, July 12, 1908.
BERLIN, JEANNIE: Los Angeles, Nov. 1, 1949.
BERLINGER, WARREN: Brooklyn, Aug. 31, 1937. Columbia.
BERNHARD, SANDRA: Flint, MI, June 6, 1955.
BERNSEN, CORBIN: Los Angeles, Sept. 7, 1954. UCLA.
BERRI, CLAUDE (Langmann): Paris, July 1, 1934.
BERRIDGE, ELIZABETH: Westchester, NY, May 2, 1962. Strasberg Inst.
BERTINELLI, VALERIE: Wilmington, DE, Apr. 23, 1960.
BEST, JAMES: Corydon, IN, July 26, 1926.
BETTGER, LYLE: Philadelphia, Feb. 13, 1915. AADA.
BEYMER, RICHARD: Avoca, IA, Feb. 21, 1939.
BIALIK, MAYIM: Dec. 12, 1975
BIEHN, MICHAEL: Anniston, AL, July 31, 1956.
BIKEL, THEODORE: Vienna, May 2, 1924.

Alan Bates

Cathy Lee Crosby

Richard Benjamin

RADA.
BILLINGSLEY, PETER: NYC, 1972.
BIRNEY, DAVID: Washington, DC, Apr. 23, 1939. Dartmouth, UCLA.
BIRNEY, REED: Alexandria, VA, Sept. 11, 1954. Boston U.
BISHOP, JOEY (Joseph Abraham Gotllieb): Bronx, NY, Feb. 3, 1918.
BISHOP, JULIE (formerly Jacqueline Wells): Denver, CO, Aug. 30, 1917. Westlake School.
BISSET, JACQUELINE: Waybridge, Eng., Sept. 13, 1944.
BLACK, KAREN (Ziegler): Park Ridge, IL, July 1, 1942. Northwestern.
BLADES, RUBEN: Panama, July 16, 1948. Harvard.
BLAINE, VIVIAN (Vivian Stapleton): Newark, NJ, Nov. 21, 1921.
BLAIR, BETSY (Betsy Boger): NYC, Dec. 11, 1923.
BLAIR, JANET (Martha Jane Lafferty): Blair, PA, Apr. 23, 1921.
BLAIR, LINDA: Westport, CT, Jan. 22, 1959.
BLAKE, ROBERT (Michael Gubitosi): Nutley, NJ, Sept. 18, 1933.
BLAKELY, SUSAN: Frankfurt, Germany, Sept. 7, 1950. U. TEX.
BLAKLEY, RONEE: Stanley, ID, 1946. Stanford U.
BLOOM, CLAIRE: London, Feb. 15, 1931. Badminton School.
BLOOM, VERNA: Lynn, MA, Aug. 7, 1939. Boston U.
BLUM, MARK: Newark, NJ, May 14, 1950. UMinn.
BLYTH, ANN: Mt. Kisco, NY, Aug. 16, 1928. New Waybum Dramatic School.
BOCHNER, HART: Toronto, Oct. 3, 1956. U. San Diego.
BOGARDE, DIRK: London, Mar. 28,1921. Glasgow & Univ. College.
BOGOSIAN, ERIC: Woburn, MA, Apr. 24, 1953. Oberlin Col.
BOHRINGER, RICHARD: Paris, 1942.
BOLKAN, FLORINDA (Florinda Soares Bulcao): Ceara, Brazil, Feb. 15, 1941.
BOLOGNA, JOSEPH: Brooklyn, Dec. 30, 1938. Brown U.
BOND, DEREK: Glasgow, Scot., Jan. 26,1920. Askes School.
BONET, LISA: San Francisco, Nov. 16, 1967.
BONHAM-CARTER, HELENA: London, Eng., May 26, 1966.
BONO, SONNY (Salvatore): Detroit, MI, Feb. 16, 1935.
BOONE, PAT: Jacksonville, FL, June 1, 1934. Columbia U.
BOOTHE, POWERS: Snyder, TX, June 1, 1949. So. Methodist U.
BORGNINE, ERNEST (Borgnino): Hamden, CT, Jan. 24, 1917. Randall School.
BOSCO, PHILIP: Jersey City, N J, Sept. 26, 1930. CatholicU.
BOSTWICK, BARRY: San Mateo, CA, Feb. 24, 1945. NYU.
BOTTOMS, JOSEPH: Santa Barbara, CA, Aug. 30, 1954.
BOTTOMS, SAM: Santa Barbara, CA, Oct.17, 1955.
BOTTOMS, TIMOTHY: Santa Barbara, CA, Aug. 30, 1951.
BOULTING, INGRID: Transvaal, So. Africa, 1947.
BOUTSIKARIS, DENNIS: Newark, NJ, Dec. 21, 1952. CatholicU.
BOVEE, LESLIE: Bend, OR, 1952.

Chevy Chase

Jamie Lee Curtis

Peter Coyote

Judy Davis

BOWIE, DAVID: (David Robert Jones): Brixton, South London, Eng., Jan. 8, 1947.

BOWKER, JUDI: Shawford, Eng., Apr. 6, 1954.

BOXLEITNER, BRUCE: Elgin, IL, May 12, 1950.

BOYLE, LARA FLYNN: Davenport, IA, Mar. 24, 1970.

BOYLE, PETER: Philadelphia, PA, Oct. 18, 1933. LaSalle Col.

BRACCO, LORRAINE: Brooklyn, 1955.

BRACKEN, EDDIE: NYC, Feb. 7, 1920. Professional Children's School.

BRAEDEN, ERIC (Hans Gudegast): Kiel, Germany, Apr. 3, 1942.

BRAGA, SONIA: Maringa, Brazil, 1951.

BRANAGH, KENNETH: Belfast, No. Ire., Dec. 10, 1960.

BRANDAUER, KLAUS MARIA: Altaussee, Austria, June 22, 1944.

BRANDO, JOCELYN: San Francisco, Nov. 18, 1919. Lake Forest College, AADA.

BRANDO, MARLON: Omaha, NB, Apr. 3, 1924. New School.

BRANDON, CLARK: NYC, 1959.

BRANDON, MICHAEL (Feldman): Brooklyn.

BRANTLEY, BETSY: Rutherfordton, NC, 1955. London Central Sch. of Drama.

BRAZZI, ROSSANO: Bologna, Italy, Sept. 18, 1916. U. Florence.

BRENNAN, EILEEN: Los Angeles, CA, Sept. 3, 1935. AADA.

BRIALY, JEAN-CLAUDE: Aumale, Algeria, 1933. Strasbourg Cons.

BRIDGES, BEAU: Los Angeles, Dec. 9, 1941. UCLA.

BRIDGES, JEFF: Los Angeles, Dec. 4, 1949.

BRIDGES, LLOYD: San Leandro, CA, Jan. 15, 1913.

BRIMLEY, WILFORD: Salt Lake City, UT, Sept. 27, 1934.

BRINKLEY, CHRISTIE: Malibu, CA, Feb. 2, 1954.

BRISEBOIS, DANIELLE: Brooklyn, June 28, 1969.

BRITT, MAY (Maybritt Wilkins): Sweden, Mar. 22, 1936.

BRITTANY, MORGAN (Suzanne Caputo): Los Angeles, Dec. 5, 1950.

BRITTON, TONY: Birmingham, Eng., June 9, 1924.

BRODERICK, MATTHEW: NYC, Mar. 21, 1962.

BROLIN, JAMES: Los Angeles, July 18, 1940. UCLA.

BROMFIELD, JOHN (Farron Bromfield): South Bend, IN, June 11, 1922. St. Mary's College.

BRONSON, CHARLES (Buchinsky): Ehrenfield, PA, Nov. 3, 1920.

BROOKES, JACQUELINE: Montclair, NJ, July 24, 1930. RADA.

BROOKS, ALBERT (Einstein): Los Angeles, July 22, 1947.

BROOKS, MEL (Melvyn Kaminski): Brooklyn, June 28, 1926.

BROSNAN, PIERCE: County Meath, Ireland. May 16, 1952.

BROWN, BLAIR: Washington, DC, 1948. Pine Manor.

BROWN, BRYAN: Panania, Australia, June 23, 1947.

BROWN, GARY (Christian Brando): Hollywood, CA, 1958.

BROWN, GEORG STANFORD: Havana, Cuba, June 24, 1943. AMDA.

BROWN, JAMES: Desdemona, TX, Mar. 22, 1920. Baylor U.

BROWN, JIM: St. Simons Island, NY, Feb. 17, 1935. Syracuse U.

BROWNE, LESLIE: NYC, 1958.

BROWNE, ROSCOE LEE: Woodbury, NJ, May 2, 1925.

Pam Dawber

Tony Curtis

Mia Farrow

Tim Daly

BUCHHOLZ, HORST: Berlin, Ger., Dec. 4, 1933. Ludwig Dramatic School.

BUCKLEY, BETTY: Big Spring, TX, July 3, 1947. TxCU.

BUJOLD, GENEVIEVE: Montreal, Can., July 1, 1942.

BURGHOFF, GARY: Bristol, Ct, May 24, 1943.

BURGI, RICHARD: Montclair, NJ, July 30, 1958.

BURKE, PAUL: New Orleans, July 21, 1926. Pasadena Playhouse.

BURNETT, CAROL: San Antonio, TX, Apr. 26, 1933. UCLA.

BURNS, CATHERINE: NYC, Sept. 25, 1945. AADA.

BURNS, GEORGE (Nathan Birnbaum): NYC, Jan. 20, 1896.

BURROWS, DARREN E.: Winfield, KS, Sept. 12, 1966.

BURSTYN, ELLEN (Edna Rae Gillhooly): Detroit, MI, Dec. 7, 1932.

BURTON, LeVAR: Los Angeles, CA, Feb. 16, 1958. UCLA.

BUSEY, GARY: Goose Creek, TX, June 29, 1944.

BUSFIELD, TIMOTHY: Lansing, MI, June 12, 1957. E. Tenn. St. U.

BUSKER, RICKY: Rockford, IL, 1974.

BUTTONS, RED (Aaron Chwatt): NYC, Feb. 5, 1919.

BUZZI, RUTH: Wequetequock, RI, July 24, 1936. Pasadena Playhouse.

BYGRAVES, MAX: London, Oct. 16, 1922. St. Joseph's School.

BYRNE, GABRIEL: Dublin, Ireland, 1950.

BYRNES, EDD: NYC, July 30, 1933. Haaren High.

CAAN, JAMES: Bronx, NY, Mar. 26,1939.

CAESAR, SID: Yonkers, NY, Sept. 8, 1922.

CAGE, NICOLAS: Long Beach, CA, Jan.7, 1964.

CAINE, MICHAEL (Maurice Micklewhite): London, Mar. 14, 1933.

CAINE, SHAKIRA (Baksh): Guyana, Feb. 23, 1947. Indian Trust Col.

CALHOUN, RORY (Francis Timothy Durgin): Los Angeles, Aug. 8, 1922.

CALLAN, MICHAEL (Martin Calinieff): Philadelphia, Nov. 22, 1935.

CALLOW, SIMON: London, June 15, 1949. Queens U.

CALVERT, PHYLLIS: London, Feb. 18, 1917. Margaret Morris School.

CALVET, CORRINE (Corinne Dibos): Paris, Apr. 30, 1925. U. Paris.

CAMERON, KIRK: Panorama City, CA, Oct. 12, 1970.

CAMP, COLLEEN: San Francisco, 1953.

CAMPBELL, BILL: Chicago, 1960.

CAMPBELL, GLEN: Delight, AR, Apr. 22, 1935.

CAMPBELL, TISHA: Newark, NJ, 1969.

CANALE, GIANNA MARIA: Reggio Calabria, Italy, Sept. 12, 1927.

CANDY, JOHN: Toronto, Can., Oct. 31, 1950.

CANNON, DYAN (Samille Diane Friesen): Tacoma, WA, Jan. 4, 1937.

CANTU, DOLORES: San Antonio, TX, 1957.

CAPERS, VIRGINIA: Sumter, SC, 1925. Juilliard.

CAPSHAW, KATE: Ft. Worth, TX, 1953.

UMo.

CARA, IRENE: NYC, Mar. 18, 1958.

CARDINALE, CLAUDIA: Tunis, N. Africa. Apr. 15, 1939. College Paul Cambon.

CAREY, HARRY, JR.: Saugus, CA, May 16, 1921. Black Fox Military Academy.

CAREY, MACDONALD: Sioux City, IA, Mar. 15, 1913. U. of Wisc., U. Iowa.

CAREY, PHILIP: Hackensack, NJ, July 15, 1925. U. Miami.

CARIOU, LEN: Winnipeg, Can., Sept. 30, 1939.

CARLIN, GEORGE: NYC, May 12, 1938.

CARMEN, JULIE: Mt. Vernon, NY, Apr. 4, 1954.

CARMICHAEL, IAN: Hull, Eng., June 18, 1920. Scarborough Col.

CARNE, JUDY (Joyce Botterill): Northampton, Eng., 1939. Bush-Davis Theatre School.

CARNEY, ART: Mt. Vernon, NY, Nov. 4, 1918.

CARON, LESLIE: Paris, July 1, 1931. Nat'l Conservatory, Paris.

CARPENTER, CARLETON: Bennington, VT, July 10, 1926. Northwestern.

CARRADINE, DAVID: Hollywood, Dec. 8, 1936. San Francisco State.

CARRADINE, KEITH: San Mateo, CA, Aug. 8, 1950. Colo. State U.

CARRADINE, ROBERT: San Mateo, CA, Mar. 24, 1954.

CARREL, DANY: Tourane, Indochina, Sept. 20, 1936. Marseilles Cons.

CARRERA, BARBARA: Managua, Nicaragua, Dec. 31, 1945.

CARREY, JIM: Jacksons Point, Ontario, Can., Jan. 17, 1962.

CARRIERE, MATHIEU: West Germany, 1950.

CARROLL, DIAHANN (Johnson): NYC, July 17, 1935. NYU.

CARROLL, PAT: Shreveport, LA, May 5, 1927. Catholic U.

CARSON, JOHN DAVID: Calif.,1951. Valley Col.

CARSON, JOHNNY: Corning, IA, Oct. 23, 1925. U. of Neb.

CARSTEN, PETER (Ransenthaler): Weissenberg, Bavaria, Apr. 30, 1929. Munich Akademie.

CARTER, NELL: Birmingham, AL, Sept. 13, 1948.

CARTWRIGHT, VERONICA: Bristol, Eng., 1949.

CARUSO, DAVID: Forest Hills, NY, 1956.

CARVEY, DANA: Missoula, MT, Apr. 2, 1955. SFST.CoI.

CASEY, BERNIE: Wyco, WV, June 8, 1939.

CASH, ROSALIND: Atlantic City, NJ, Dec. 31, 1938. CCNY.

CASS, PEGGY (Mary Margaret): Boston, May 21, 1925.

CASSAVETES, NICK: NYC, 1959, Syracuse U, AADA.

CASSEL, JEAN-PIERRE: Paris, Oct. 27, 1932.

CASSIDY, DAVID: NYC, Apr. 12, 1950.

CASSIDY, JOANNA: Camden, NJ, Aug. 2, 1944. Syracuse U.

CASSIDY, PATRICK: Los Angeles, CA, Jan. 4, 1961.

CATES, PHOEBE: NYC, July 16, 1963.

CATTRALL, KIM: Liverpool, Eng., Aug.

Donal Donnelly

Barbara Feldon

Tate Donovan

Michael Dudikoff

Jennifer Grey

Griffin Dunne

Julie Hagerty

21, 1956. AADA.

CAULFIELD, MAXWELL: Glasgow, Scot., Nov. 23, 1959.

CAVANI, LILIANA: Bologna, Italy, Jan. 12, 1937. U. Bologna.

CAVETT, DICK: Gibbon, NE, Nov. 19, 1936.

CHAKIRIS, GEORGE: Norwood, OH, Sept. 16, 1933.

CHAMBERLAIN, RICHARD: Beverly Hills, CA, March 31, 1935. Pomona.

CHAMPION, MARGE: Los Angeles, Sept. 2, 1923.

CHANNING, CAROL: Seattle, WA, Jan. 31, 1921. Bennington.

CHANNING, STOCKARD (Susan Stockard): NYC, Feb. 13, 1944. Radcliffe.

CHAPIN, MILES: NYC, Dec. 6, 1954. HB Studio.

CHAPLIN, GERALDINE: Santa Monica, CA, July 31, 1944. Royal Ballet.

CHAPLIN, SYDNEY: Los Angeles, Mar. 31, 1926. Lawrenceville.

CHARISSE, CYD (Tula Ellice Finklea): Amarillo, TX, Mar. 3, 1922. Hollywood Professional School.

CHARLES, WALTER: East Strousburg, PA, Apr. 4, 1945. Boston U.

CHASE, CHEVY (Cornelius Crane Chase): NYC, Oct. 8, 1943.

CHAVES, RICHARD: Jacksonville, FL, Oct. 9, 1951. Occidental Col.

CHEN, JOAN: Shanghai, 1961. CalState.

CHER (Cherilyn Sarkisian) El Centro, CA, May 20, 1946.

CHILES, LOIS: Alice, TX, 1950.

CHONG, RAE DAWN: Vancouver, Can., 1961.

CHONG, THOMAS: Edmonton, Alberta, Can., Ma.y 24, 1938.

CHRISTIAN, LINDA (Blanca Rosa Welter): Tampico, Mex., Nov. 13, 1923.

CHRISTIE, JULIE: Chukua, Assam, India, Apr. 14, 1941.

CHRISTOPHER, DENNIS (Carrelli): Philadelphia, PA, Dec. 2, 1955. Temple U.

CHRISTOPHER, JORDAN: Youngs-town, OH, Oct. 23, 1940. Kent Slate.

CILENTO, DIANE: Queensland, Australia, Oct. 5, 1933. AADA.

CLAPTON, ERIC: London. Mar. 30, 1945.

CLARK, CANDY: Norman, OK, June 20, 1947.

CLARK, DANE: NYC, Feb. 18, 1915. Cornell, Johns Hopkins U.

CLARK, DICK: Mt. Vernon, NY, Nov. 30, 1929. Syracuse U.

CLARK, MATT: Washington, DC, Nov. 25, 1936.

CLARK, PETULA: Epsom, England, Nov. 15, 1932.

CLARK, SUSAN: Sarnid, Ont., Can., Mar. 8, 1940. RADA.

CLAY, ANDREW DICE: Brooklyn, 1958, Kingsborough Col.

CLAYBURGH, JILL: NYC, Apr. 30, 1944. Sarah Lawrence.

CLEESE, JOHN: Weston-Super-Mare, Eng., Oct. 27, 1939, Cambridge.

CLERY, CORRINNE: Italy, 1950.

CLOONEY, ROSEMARY: Maysville, KY, May 23, 1928.

CLOSE, GLENN: Greenwich, CT, Mar. 19, 1947. William & Mary Col.

COBURN, JAMES: Laurel, NB, Aug. 31, 1928. LACC.

COCA, IMOGENE: Philadelphia, Nov. 18, 1908.

CODY, KATHLEEN: Bronx, NY, Oct. 30, 1953.

COFFEY, SCOTT: HI, 1967.

COLBERT, CLAUDETTE (Lily Chauchoin): Paris, Sept. 15, 1903. Art Students League.

COLE, GEORGE: London, Apr. 22, 1925.

COLEMAN, GARY: Zion, IL, Feb. 8, 1968.

COLEMAN, DABNEY: Austin, TX, Jan. 3, 1932.

COLIN, MARGARET: NYC, 1957.

COLEMAN, JACK: Easton, PA, 1958. Duke U.

COLLET, CHRISTOPHER: NYC, Mar. 13, 1968. Strasberg Inst.

COLLINS, JOAN: London, May 21, 1933. Francis Holland School.

COLLINS, PAULINE: Devon, Eng., Sept. 3, 1940.

COLLINS, STEPHEN: Des Moines, IA, Oct. 1, 1947. Amherst.

COLON, MIRIAM: Ponce, PR., 1945. UPR.

COLTRANE, ROBBIE: Ruthergien, Scot., 1950.

COMER, ANJANETTE: Dawson, TX, Aug. 7, 1942. Baylor, Tex. U.

CONANT, OLIVER: NYC, Nov. 15, 1955. Dalton.

CONAWAY, JEFF: NYC, Oct. 5, 1950. NYC.

CONNERY, SEAN: Edinburgh, Scot., Aug. 25, 1930.

CONNERY, JASON: London, 1962.

CONNICK, HARRY, JR.: New Orleans, LA, Sept. 11, 1967.

CONNORS, MIKE (Krekor Ohanian): Fresno, CA, Aug. 15, 1925. UCLA.

CONRAD, WILLIAM: Louisville, KY, Sept. 27, 1920.

CONROY, KEVIN: Westport, CT, 1956. Juilliard.

CONSTANTINE, MICHAEL: Reading, PA, May 22, 1927.

CONTI, TOM: Paisley, Scotland, Nov. 22, 1941.

CONVERSE, FRANK: St. Louis, MO, May 22, 1938. Carnegie Tech.

CONWAY, GARY: Boston, Feb. 4, 1936.

CONWAY, KEVIN: NYC, May 29, 1942.

CONWAY, TIM (Thomas Daniel): Willoughby, OH, Dec. 15, 1933. Bowling Green State.

COOGAN, KEITH (Keith Mitchell Franklin): Palm Springs, CA, Jan. 13, 1970.

COOK, ELISHA, JR.: San Francisco, Dec. 26, 1907. St. Albans.

COOK, PETER: Torqua, Eng., Nov. 17, 1937.

COOPER, BEN: Hartford, CT, Sept. 30, 1930. Columbia U.

COOPER, CHRIS: Kansas City, MO, July 9, 1951. UMo.

COOPER, JACKIE: Los Angeles, Sept. 15, 1921.

COPELAND, JOAN: NYC, June 1, 1922. Brooklyn Col., RADA.

CORBETT, GRETCHEN: Portland, OR, Aug. 13, 1947. Carnegie Tech.

CORBY, ELLEN (Hansen): Racine, WI, June 13, 1913.

CORCORAN, DONNA: Quincy, MA, Sept. 29, 1942.

CORD, ALEX (Viespi): Floral Park, NY, Aug. 3, 1931. NYU, Actors Studio.

CORDAY, MARA (Marilyn Watts): Santa Monica, CA, Jan. 3, 1932.

COREY, JEFF: NYC, Aug. 10, 1914. Fagin School.

CORLAN, ANTHONY: Cork City, Ire., May 9, 1947. Birmingham School of Dramatic Arts.

CORLEY, AL: Missouri, 1956. Actors Studio.

CORNTHWAITE, ROBERT: St. Helens, OR, Apr. 28, 1917. USC.

CORRI, ADRIENNE: Glasgow, Scot., Nov. 13, 1933. RADA.

CORT, BUD (Walter Edward Cox): New Rochelle, NY, Mar. 29, 1950. NYU.

CORTESA, VALENTINA: Milan, Italy, Jan. 1, 1925.

COSBY, BILL: Philadelphia, July 12, 1937. Temple U.

COSTER, NICOLAS: London, Dec. 3, 1934. Neighborhood Playhouse.

COSTNER, KEVIN: Lynwood, CA, Jan. 18, 1955. CalStaU.

COTTEN, JOSEPH: Petersburg, VA, May 13, 1905.

COURTENAY, TOM: Hull, Eng., Feb. 25, 1937. RADA.

COURTLAND, JEROME: Knoxville, TN, Dec. 27, 1926.

COYOTE, PETER (Cohon): NYC, 1942.

COX, COURTENEY: Birmingham, AL, June 15, 1964.

COX, RONNY: Cloudcroft, NM, Aug. 23, 1938.

CRAIG, MICHAEL: India, Jan. 27, 1929.

CRAIN, JEANNE: Barstow, CA, May 25, 1925.

CRAWFORD, MICHAEL (Dumbel-Smith): Salisbury, Eng., Jan. 19, 1942.

CREMER, BRUNO: Paris, 1929.

CRENNA, RICHARD: Los Angeles, Nov. 30, 1926. USC.

CRISTAL, LINDA (Victoria Moya): Buenos Aires, Feb. 25, 1934.

CRONYN, HUME (Blake): Ontario, Can, July 18, 1911.

CROSBY, DENISE: Hollywood, CA, 1958.

CROSBY, HARRY: Los Angeles, CA, Aug. 8, 1958.

CROSBY, MARY FRANCES: CA, Sept. 14, 1959.

CROSS, BEN: London, Dec. 16, 1948. RADA.

CROSS, MURPHY (Mary Jane): Laurelton, MD, June 22, 1950.

CROUSE, LINDSAY: NYC, May 12, 1948. Radcliffe.

CROWLEY, PAT: Olyphant, PA, Sept. 17, 1932.

CRUISE, TOM (T. C. Mapother IV): July 3, 1962, Syracuse, NY.

CRYER, JON: NYC, Apr. 16, 1965, RADA.

CRYSTAL, BILLY: Long Beach, NY, Mar. 14, 1947. Marshall U.

CULKIN, MACAULAY: NYC, Aug. 26, 1980.

CULLUM, JOHN: Knoxville, TN, Mar. 2, 1930. U. Tenn.

CULLUM, JOHN DAVID: NYC, Mar. 1, 1966.

CULP, ROBERT: Oakland, CA, Aug. 16, 1930. U. Wash.

CUMMINGS, CONSTANCE: Seattle, WA, May 15, 1910.

CUMMINGS, QUINN: Hollywood, Aug. 13, 1967.

CUMMINS, PEGGY: Prestatyn, N. Wales, Dec. 18, 1926. Alexandra School.

CURRY, TIM: Cheshire, Eng., Apr. 19, 1946.

CURTIN, JANE: Cambridge, MA, Sept. 6, 1947.

CURTIS, JAMIE LEE: Los Angeles, CA, Nov. 22, 1958.

CURTIS, KEENE: Salt Lake City, UT, Feb. 15, 1925. U. Utah.

CURTIS, TONY (Bernard Schwartz): NYC, June 3, 1924.

CUSACK, JOAN: Evanston, IL, Oct. 11, 1962.

CUSACK, JOHN: Chicago, IL, June 28, 1966.

CUSACK, SINEAD: Ireland, Feb.18, 1948

CUSHING, PETER: Kenley, Surrey, Eng., May 26, 1913.

DAFOE, WILLEM: Appleton, WI, July 22, 1955.

DAHL, ARLENE: Minneapolis, Aug. 11, 1928. U. Minn.

DALE, JIM: Rothwell, Eng., Aug. 15, 1935.

DALLESANDRO, JOE: Pensacola, FL, Dec. 31, 1948.

DALTON, TIMOTHY: Colwyn Bay, Wales, Mar. 21, 1946. RADA.

DALTREY, ROGER: London, Mar. 1, 1945.

DALY, TIMOTHY: NYC, Mar. 1, 1956. Bennington Col.

DALY, TYNE: Madison, WI, Feb. 21, 1947. AMDA.

DAMONE, VIC (Vito Farinola): Brooklyn, June 12, 1928.

DANCE, CHARLES: Plymouth, Eng., Oct. 10, 1946.

D'ANGELO, BEVERLY: Columbus, OH, Nov. 15, 1953.

DANGERFIELD, RODNEY (Jacob Cohen): Babylon, NY, Nov. 22, 1921.

DANIELS, JEFF: Georgia, Feb. 19, 1955. EastMichState.

DANIELS, WILLIAM: Brooklyn, Mar. 31, 1927. Northwestern.

DANNER, BLYTHE: Philadelphia, PA, Feb. 3, 1944. Bard Col.

DANO, ROYAL: NYC, Nov. 16, 1922. NYU.

DANSON, TED: San Diego, CA, Dec. 29, 1947. Stanford, Carnegie Tech.

DANTE, MICHAEL (Ralph Vitti): Stamford, CT, 1935. U. Miami.

DANZA, TONY: Brooklyn, Apr. 21, 1951. UDubuque.

DARBY, KIM: (Deborah Zerby): North Hollywood, CA, July 8, 1948.

DARCEL, DENISE (Denise Billecard): Paris, Sept. 8, 1925. U. Dijon.

DARREN, JAMES: Philadelphia, June 8, 1936. Stella Adler School.

DARRIEUX, DANIELLE: Bordeaux, France, May 1, 1917. Lycee LaTour.

DAVID, KEITH: NYC, June 4, 1954. Juilliard.

DAVIDSON, JOHN: Pittsburgh, Dec. 13, 1941. Denison U.

DAVIS, CLIFTON: Chicago, Oct. 4, 1945. Oakwood Col.

DAVIS, GEENA: Wareham, MA, Jan. 21, 1957.

DAVIS, JUDY: Perth, Australia, 1956.

DAVIS, MAC: Lubbock, TX, Jan. 21,1942.

DAVIS, NANCY (Anne Frances Robbins): NYC, July 6, 1921. Smith Col.

DAVIS, OSSIE: Cogdell, GA, Dec. 18, 1917. Howard U.

DAVIS, SKEETER (Mary Frances Penick): Dry Ridge, KY, Dec. 30, 1931.

DAVIS-VOSS, SAMMI: Kidderminster, Worcestershire, Eng., June 21, 1964.

DAVISON, BRUCE: Philadelphia, PA, June 28, 1946.

DAY, DORIS (Doris Kappelhoff): Cincinnati, Apr. 3, 1924.

DAY, LARAINE (Johnson): Roosevelt, UT, Oct. 13, 1917.

DAY LEWIS, DANIEL: London, Apr. 29, 1957. Bristol Old Vic.

DAYAN, ASSEF: Israel, 1945. U. Jerusalem.

DEAKINS, LUCY: NYC, 1971.

DEAN, JIMMY: Plainview, TX, Aug. 10, 1928.

DEAN, LOREN: Las Vegas, NV, July 31, 1969.

DECAMP, ROSEMARY: Prescott, AZ, Nov. 14, 1913.

DeCARLO, YVONNE (Peggy Yvonne Middleton): Vancouver, B.C., Can., Sept. 1, 1922. Vancouver School of Drama.

DEE, FRANCES: Los Angeles, Nov. 26, 1907. Chicago U.

DEE, JOEY (Joseph Di Nicola): Passaic, NJ, June 11, 1940. Patterson State College.

DEE, RUBY: Cleveland, OH, Oct. 27, 1924. Hunter Col.

DEE, SANDRA (Alexandra Zuck): Bayonne, NJ, Apr. 23, 1942.

DeHAVEN, GLORIA: Los Angeles, July 23, 1923.

DeHAVILLAND, OLIVIA: Tokyo, Japan, July 1, 1916. Notre Dame Convent School.

DELAIR, SUZY: Paris, Dec. 31, 1916.

DELANY, DANA: NYC, March 13, 1956. Wesleyan U.

DELPY, JULIE: Paris. 1969.

DELON, ALAIN: Sceaux, Fr., Nov. 8, 1935.

DELORME, DANIELE: Paris, Oct. 9, 1927. Sorbonne.

DeLUISE, DOM: Brooklyn, Aug. 1, 1933. Tufts Col.

DeLUISE, PETER: Hollywood, Ca., 1967.

DEMONGEOT, MYLENE: Nice, France, Sept. 29, 1938.

DeMORNAY, REBECCA: Los Angeles, Aug. 29, 1962. Strasberg Inst.

DEMPSEY, PATRICK: Turner, ME, Jan. 13, 1966.

DeMUNN, JEFFREY: Buffalo, NY, Apr. 25, 1947. Union Col.

DENEUVE, CATHERINE: Paris, Oct. 22, 1943.

DeNIRO, ROBERT: NYC, Aug. 17, 1943. Stella Adler.

DENISON, MICHAEL: Doncaster, York, Eng., Nov. 1, 1915. Oxford.

DENNEHY, BRIAN: Bridgeport, CT, Jul. 9, 1938. Columbia.

DENNER, CHARLES: Tarnow, Poland, May 29, 1926.

DENVER, JOHN: Roswell, NM, Dec. 31, 1943

DENVER, BOB: New Rochelle, NY, Jan. 9, 1935.

DEPARDIEU, GERARD: Chateauroux, France, Dec. 27, 1948.

DEPP, JOHNNY: Owensboro, KY, June 9, 1963.

DEREK, BO (Mary Cathleen Collins): Long Beach, CA, Nov. 20, 1956.

DEREK, JOHN: Hollywood, Aug. 12, 1926.

DERN, BRUCE: Chicago, June 4, 1936. UPA.

DERN, LAURA: Los Angeles, Feb. 10, 1967.

Anthony Edwards   Mariel Hemingway   Dennis Farina   Marilu Henner

DEVANE, WILLIAM: Albany, NY, Sept. 5, 1939.

DEVINE, COLLEEN: San Gabriel, CA, June 22, 1960.

DeVITO, DANNY: Asbury Park, NJ, Nov. 17, 1944.

DEXTER, ANTHONY (Walter Reinhold Alfred Fleischmann): Talmadge, NB, Jan. 19, 1919. U. Iowa.

DEY, SUSAN: Pekin, IL, Dec. 10, 1953.

DeYOUNG, CLIFF: Los Angeles, CA, Feb. 12, 1945. Cal State.

DIAMOND, NEIL: NYC, Jan. 24, 1941. NYU.

DICAPRIO, LEONARDO: Hollywood, CA, Nov.11, 1974.

DICKINSON, ANGIE: Kulm, ND, Sept. 30, 1932. Glendale College.

DIETRICH, MARLENE (Maria Magdalene von Losch): Berlin, Ger., Dec. 27, 1901. Berlin Music Academy.

DILLER, PHYLLIS (Driver): Lima, OH, July 17, 1917. Bluffton College.

DILLMAN, BRADFORD: San Francisco, Apr. 14, 1930. Yale.

DILLON, KEVIN: Mamaroneck, NY, Aug. 19, 1965.

DILLON, MATT: Larchmont, NY, Feb. 18, 1964. AADA.

DILLON, MELINDA: Hope, AR, Oct. 13, 1939. Goodman Theatre School.

DIXON, DONNA: Alexandria, VA, July 20, 1957.

DOBSON, KEVIN: NYC, Mar. 18, 1944.

DOBSON, TAMARA: Baltimore, MD, 1947. MD Inst. of Art.

DOLAN, MICHAEL: Oklahoma City, OK, June 21, 1965.

DOMERGUE, FAITH: New Orleans, June 16, 1925.

DONAHUE, TROY (Merle Johnson): NYC, Jan. 27, 1937. Columbia U.

DONAT, PETER: Nova Scotia, Jan. 20, 1928. Yale.

DONNELLY, DONAL: Bradford, Eng., July 6, 1931.

D'ONOFRIO, VINCENT: Brooklyn, 1960.

DONOVAN, TATE: NYC, 1964.

DOOHAN, JAMES: Vancouver, BC, Mar. 3, 1920. Neighborhood Playhouse.

DOOLEY, PAUL: Parkersburg WV, Feb. 22, 1928. U. WV.

DOUGLAS, DONNA (Dorothy Bourgeois): Baywood, LA, Sept. 26, 1935.

DOUGLAS, KIRK (Issur Danielovitch): Amsterdam, NY, Dec. 9, 1916. St. Lawrence U.

DOUGLAS, MICHAEL: New Brunswick, NJ, Sept. 25, 1944. U. Cal.

DOUGLASS, ROBYN: Sendai, Japan, June 21, 1953. UCDavis.

DOURIF, BRAD: Huntington, WV, Mar. 18, 1950. Marshall U.

DOVE, BILLIE: NYC, May 14, 1904.

DOWN, LESLEY-ANN: London, Mar. 17, 1954.

DOWNEY, ROBERT, JR.: NYC, Apr. 4, 1965.

DRAKE, BETSY: Paris, Sept. 11, 1923.

DRAKE, CHARLES (Charles Rupert): NYC, Oct. 2, 1914. Nichols College.

DREW, ELLEN (formerly Terry Ray): Kansas City, MO, Nov. 23, 1915.

DREYFUSS, RICHARD: Brooklyn, Oct. 19, 1947.

DRILLINGER, BRIAN: Brooklyn, June 27, 1960. SUNY/Purchase.

DRU, JOANNE (Joanne LaCock): Logan, WV, Jan. 31, 1923. John Robert Powers School.

DRYER, JOHN: Hawthorne, CA, July 6, 1946.

DUDIKOFF, MICHAEL: Torrance, CA, Oct. 8, 1954

DUGAN, DENNIS: Wheaton, IL, Sept. 5, 1946.

DUKAKIS, OLYMPIA: Lowell, MA, June 20, 1931.

DUKE, PATTY (Anna Marie): NYC, Dec. 14, 1946.

DUKES, DAVID: San Francisco, June 6, 1945.

DULLEA, KEIR: Cleveland, NJ, May 30, 1936. SF State Col.

DUNAWAY, FAYE: Bascom, FL, Jan. 14, 1941. Fla. U.

DUNCAN, SANDY: Henderson, TX, Feb. 20, 1946. Len Morris Col.

DUNNE, GRIFFIN: NYC, June 8, 1955. Neighborhood Playhouse.

DUPEREY, ANNY: Paris, 1947.

DURBIN, DEANNA (Edna): Winnipeg, Can., Dec. 4, 1921.

DURNING, CHARLES: Highland Falls, NY, Feb. 28, 1933. NYU.

DUSSOLLIER, ANDRE: Annecy, France, Feb. 17, 1946.

DUTTON, CHARLES: Baltimore, MD, Jan. 30, 1951. Yale.

DUVALL, ROBERT: San Diego, CA, Jan. 5, 1931. Principia Col.

DUVALL, SHELLEY: Houston, TX, July 7, 1949.

DYSART, RICHARD: Brighton, ME, Mar. 30. 1929.

EASTON, ROBERT: Milwaukee, WI, Nov. 23, 1930. U. Texas.

EASTWOOD, CLINT: San Francisco, May 31, 1931. LACC.

EATON, SHIRLEY: London, 1937. Aida Foster School.

EBSEN, BUDDY (Christian, Jr.): Belleville, IL, Apr. 2, 1910. U. Fla.

ECKEMYR, AGNETA: Karlsborg, Swed., July 2. Actors Studio.

EDELMAN, GREGG: Chicago, IL, Sept. 12, 1958. Northwestern U.

EDEN, BARBARA (Moorhead): Tucson, AZ, Aug. 23, 1934.

EDWARDS, ANTHONY: Santa Barbara, CA, July 19, 1962. RADA.

EDWARDS, VINCE: NYC, July 9, 1928. AADA.

EGGAR, SAMANTHA: London, Mar. 5, 1939.

EICHHORN, LISA: Reading, PA, Feb. 4, 1952. Queens Ont. U. RADA.

EIKENBERRY, JILL: New Haven, CT, Jan. 21, 1947.

EILBER, JANET: Detroit, MI, July 27, 1951. Juilliard.

EKBERG, ANITA: Malmo, Sweden, Sept. 29, 1931.

EKLAND, BRITT: Stockholm, Swed., Oct. 6, 1942.

ELDARD, RON: NYC, 1964.

ELIZONDO, HECTOR: NYC, Dec. 22, 1936.

ELLIOTT, CHRIS: NYC, 1960.

ELLIOTT, PATRICIA: Gunnison, CO, July 21, 1942. UCol.

ELLIOTT, SAM: Sacramento, CA, Aug. 9, 1944. U. Ore.

ELWES, CARY: London, Oct. 26, 1962.

ELY, RON (Ronald Pierce): Hereford, TX, June 21, 1938.

ENGLISH, ALEX: USCar, 1954.

ENGLUND, ROBERT: Hollywood, CA, June 6, 1949.

ERDMAN, RICHARD: Enid, OK, June 1, 1925.

ERICSON, JOHN: Dusseldorf, Ger., Sept. 25, 1926. AADA.

ESMOND, CARL: Vienna, June 14, 1906. U. Vienna.

ESTEVEZ, EMILIO: NYC, May 12, 1962.

ESPOSITO, GIANCARLO: Copenhagen, Den., Apr. 26, 1958.

ESTRADA, ERIK: NYC, Mar. 16, 1949.

EVANS, DALE (Francis Smith): Uvalde, TX, Oct. 31, 1912.

EVANS, GENE: Holbrook, AZ, July 11, 1922.

EVANS, LINDA (Evanstad): Hartford, CT, Nov. 18, 1942.

EVERETT, CHAD (Ray Cramton): South Bend, IN, June 11, 1936.

EVERETT, RUPERT: Norfolk, Eng., 1959.

EVIGAN, GREG: South Amboy, NJ, 1954.

EWELL, TOM (Yewell Tompkins): Owensboro, KY, Apr. 29, 1909. U. Wisc.

FABARES, SHELLEY: Los Angeles, Jan. 19, 1944.

FABIAN (Fabian Forte): Philadelphia, Feb. 6, 1943.

FABRAY, NANETTE (Ruby Nanette Fabares): San Diego, Oct. 27, 1920.

FAIRBANKS, DOUGLAS, JR.: NYC, Dec. 9, 1907. Collegiate School.

FAIRCHILD, MORGAN (Patsy McClenny): Dallas, TX, Feb. 3, 1950. UCLA.

FALK, PETER: NYC, Sept. 16, 1927. New School.

FARENTINO, JAMES: Brooklyn, Feb. 24, 1938. AADA.

FARGAS, ANTONIO: Bronx, NY, Aug. 14, 1946.

FARINA, DENNIS: Chicago, IL, 1944.

FARINA, SANDY (Sandra Feldman): Newark, NJ, 1955.

FARR, FELICIA: Westchester, NY, Oct. 4. 1932. Penn State Col.

FARROW, MIA (Maria): Los Angeles, Feb. 9, 1945.

FAULKNER, GRAHAM: London, Sept. 26, 1947. Webber-Douglas.

FAWCETT, FARRAH: Corpus Christie, TX, Feb. 2, 1947. TexU.

FAYE, ALICE (Ann Leppert): NYC, May 5, 1912.

FEINSTEIN, ALAN: NYC, Sept. 8, 1941.

FELDMAN, COREY: Encino, CA, July 16, 1971.

FELDON, BARBARA (Hall): Pittsburgh, Mar. 12, 1941. Carnegie Tech.

FELDSHUH, TOVAH: NYC, Dec. 27, 1953, Sarah Lawrence Col.

FELLOWS, EDITH: Boston, May 20, 1923.

FERRELL, CONCHATA: Charleston, WV, Mar. 28, 1943. Marshall U.

FERRER, MEL: Elbeton, NJ, Aug. 25, 1912. Princeton U.

FERRER, MIGUEL: Santa Monica, CA, Feb. 7, 1954.

FERRIS, BARBARA: London, 1940.

FERZETTI, GABRIELE: Italy, 1927. Rome Acad. of Drama.

FIEDLER, JOHN: Plateville, WI, Feb. 3, 1925.

FIELD, SALLY: Pasadena, CA, Nov. 6, 1946.

FIENNES, RALPH: Suffolk, Eng., Dec. 22 1962 RADA

FIERSTEIN, HARVEY: Brooklyn, June 6, 1954.

Al Freeman, Jr.

Lena Horne

Morgan Freeman

Pratt Inst.

FIGUEROA, RUBEN: NYC, 1958.

FINNEY, ALBERT: Salford, Lancashire, Eng., May 9, 1936. RADA.

FIORENTINO, LINDA: Philadelphia, PA.

FIRESTONE, ROCHELLE: Kansas City, MO, June 14, 1949. NYU.

FIRTH, COLIN: Grayshott, Hampshire, Eng., Sept. 10, 1960.

FIRTH, PETER: Bradford, Eng., Oct. 27, 1953.

FISHBURNE, LARRY: Augusta, GA, July 30, 1961.

FISHER, CARRIE: Los Angeles, CA, Oct. 21, 1956. London Central School of Drama.

FISHER, EDDIE: Philadelphia, PA, Aug. 10, 1928.

FITZGERALD, BRIAN: Philadelphia, PA, 1960. West Chester U.

FITZGERALD, GERALDINE: Dublin, Ire., Nov. 24, 1914. Dublin Art School.

FLANNERY, SUSAN: Jersey City, NJ, July 31, 1943.

FLEMING, RHONDA (Marilyn Louis): Los Angeles, Aug. 10, 1922.

FLEMYNG, ROBERT: Liverpool, Eng., Jan. 3, 1912. Haileybury Col.

FLETCHER, LOUISE: Birmingham, AL, July 22 1934.

FOCH, NINA: Leyden, Holland, Apr. 20, 1924.

FOLDI, ERZSEBET: Queens, NY, 1967.

FOLLOWS, MEGAN: Toronto, Can., 1967.

FONDA, BRIDGET: Los Angeles, Jan. 27, 1964.

FONDA, JANE: NYC, Dec. 21, 1937. Vassar.

FONDA, PETER: NYC, Feb. 23, 1939. U. Omaha.

FONTAINE, JOAN: Tokyo, Japan, Oct. 22, 1917.

FOOTE, HALLIE: NYC, 1953. UNH.

FORD, GLENN (Gwyllyn Samuel Newton Ford): Quebec, Can., May 1, 1916.

FORD, HARRISON: Chicago, IL, July 13, 1942. Ripon Col.

FOREST, MARK (Lou Degni): Brooklyn, Jan. 1933.

FORREST, FREDERIC: Waxahachie, TX, Dec. 23, 1936.

FORREST, STEVE: Huntsville, TX, Sept. 29, 1924. UCLA.

FORSLUND, CONNIE: San Diego, CA, June 19, 1950. NYU.

FORSTER, ROBERT (Foster, Jr.): Rochester, NY, July 13, 1941. Rochester U.

FORSYTHE, JOHN (Freund):Penn's Grove, NJ, Jan. 29, 1918.

FOSTER, JODIE (Ariane Munker): Bronx, NY, Nov. 19, 1962. Yale.

FOSTER, MEG: Reading, PA, May 14, 1948.

FOX, EDWARD: London, Apr. 13, 1937. RADA.

FOX, JAMES: London, May 19, 1939.

FOX, MICHAEL J.: Vancouver, BC, June 9, 1961.

FOXWORTH, ROBERT: Houston, TX, Nov. 1, 1941. Carnegie Tech.

FRAKES, JONATHAN: Bethlehem, PA, 1952. Harvard.

FRANCIOSA, ANTHONY (Papaleo): NYC, Oct. 25, 1928.

FRANCIS, ANNE: Ossining, NY, Sept. 16, 1932.

FRANCIS, ARLENE (Arlene Kazanjian): Boston, Oct. 20, 1908. Finch School.

FRANCIS, CONNIE (Constance Franconero): Newark, NJ, Dec. 12, 1938.

FRANCKS, DON: Vancouver, Can., Feb. 28,

FRANCKS, DON: Vancouver, Can., Feb. 28, 1932.

FRANK, JEFFREY: Jackson Heights, NY, 1965.

FRANKLIN, PAMELA: Tokyo, Feb. 4, 1950.

FRANZ, ARTHUR: Perth Amboy, NJ, Feb. 29, 1920. Blue Ridge College.

FRANZ, DENNIS: Chicago, IL, Oct. 28, 1944.

FRAZIER, SHEILA: NYC, Nov. 13, 1948.

FRECHETTE, PETER: Warwick, RI, Oct. 1956. URI.

FREEMAN, AL, JR.: San Antonio, TX, Mar. 21, 1934. CCLA.

FREEMAN, MONA: Baltimore, MD, June 9, 1926.

FREEMAN, MORGAN: Memphis, TN, June 1, 1937. LACC.

FREWER, MATT: Washington, DC, Jan. 4, 1958, Old Vic.

FRICKER, BRENDA: Dublin, Ireland, Feb. 17, 1945.

FULLER, PENNY: Durham, NC, 1940. Northwestern U.

FURLONG, EDWARD: Glendale, CA, Aug. 2, 1977.

FURNEAUX, YVONNE: Lille, France, 1928. Oxford U.

FYODOROVA, VICTORIA: Russia, 1946.

GABLE, JOHN CLARK: Los Angeles, Mar. 20, 1961. Santa Monica Col.

GABOR, EVA: Budapest, Hungary, Feb. 11, 1920.

GABOR, ZSA ZSA (Sari Gabor): Budapest, Hungary, Feb. 6, 1918.

GAIL, MAX: Derfoil, MI, Apr. 5, 1943.

GAINES, BOYD: Atlanta, GA, May 11, 1953. Juilliard.

GALLAGHER, PETER: NYC, Aug. 19, 1955. Tufts U.

GALLIGAN, ZACH: NYC, Feb. 14, 1963. ColumbiaU.

GAM, RITA: Pittsburgh, PA, Apr. 2, 1928.

GAMBON, MICHAEL: Dublin, Ire., Oct. 19, 1940.

GARBER, VICTOR: Montreal, Can., Mar. 16, 1949.

GARCIA, ANDY: Havana, Cuba, Apr. 12, 1956. FlaInt 1U.

GARFIELD, ALLEN (Allen Goorwitz): Newark, NJ, Nov. 22, 1939. Actors Studio.

GARFUNKEL, ART: NYC, Nov. 5, 1941.

GARLAND, BEVERLY: Santa Cruz, CA, Oct. 17, 1930. Glendale Col.

GARNER, JAMES (James Baumgarner): Norman, OK, Apr. 7, 1928. Okla. U.

GARR, TERI: Lakewood, OH, Dec. 11, 1949.

GARRETT, BETTY: St. Joseph, MO, May 23, 1919. Annie Wright Seminary.

GARRISON, SEAN: NYC, Oct. 19, 1937.

GARSON, GREER: Ireland, Sept. 29, 1908.

GARY, LORRAINE: NYC, Aug. 16, 1937.

GASSMAN, VITTORIO: Genoa, Italy, Sept. 1,1922. Rome Academy of Dramatic Art.

GAVIN, JOHN: Los Angeles, Apr. 8, 1935. Stanford U.

GAYLORD, MITCH: Van Nuys, CA, 1961. UCLA.

GAYNOR, MITZI (Francesca Marlene Von Gerber): Chicago, Sept. 4, 1930.

GAZZARA, BEN: NYC, Aug. 28, 1930. Actors Studio.

GEARY, ANTHONY: Coalsville, UT, May 29, 1947. UUt.

GEDRICK, JASON: Chicago, Feb. 7, 1965. Drake U.

GEESON, JUDY: Arundel, Eng., Sept. 10, 1948. Corona.

GEOFFREYS, STEPHEN: Cincinnati, OH, Nov. 22, 1964. NYU.

GEORGE, SUSAN: West London, Eng., July 26, 1950.

GERARD, GIL: Little Rock, AR, Jan. 23, 1940.

GERE, RICHARD: Philadelphia, PA, Aug. 29, 1949. U. Mass.

GERROLL, DANIEL: London, Oct. 16, 1951. Central.

GERTZ, JAMI: Chicago, IL, Oct. 28, 1965.

GETTY, BALTHAZAR: Jan. 22, 1975.

GETTY, ESTELLE: NYC, July 25, 1923. New School.

GHOLSON, JULIE: Birmingham, AL, June 4, 1958.

GHOSTLEY, ALICE: Eve, MO, Aug. 14, 1926. Okla U.

GIAN, JOE: North Miami Beach, FL, 1962.

GIANNINI, CHERYL: Monessen, PA, June 15.

GIANNINI, GIANCARLO: Spezia, Italy, Aug. 1, 1942. Rome Acad. of Drama.

GIBB, CYNTHIA: Bennington, VT, Dec. 14, 1963.

GIBSON, HENRY: Germantown, PA, Sept. 21, 1935.

GIBSON, MEL: Peekskill, NY, Jan. 3, 1956. NIDA.

GIELGUD, JOHN: London, Apr. 14, 1904. RADA.

GIFT, ROLAND: Birmingham, Eng., May 28 1962.

GILBERT, MELISSA: Los Angeles, CA, May 8, 1964.

GILES, NANCY: NYC, July 17, 1960, Oberlin Col.

GILLETTE, ANITA: Baltimore, MD, Aug. 16, 1938.

GILLIAM, TERRY: Minneapolis, MN, Nov. 22, 1940.

GILLIS, ANNE (Alma O'Connor): Little Rock, AR, Feb. 12, 1927.

GINTY, ROBERT: NYC, Nov. 14, 1948. Yale.

GIRARDOT, ANNIE: Paris, Oct. 25, 1931.

GIROLAMI, STEFANIA: Rome, 1963.

GIVENS, ROBIN: NYC, Nov. 27, 1964.

GLASER, PAUL MICHAEL: Boston, MA, Mar. 25, 1943. Boston U.

GLASS, RON: Evansville, IN, July 10, 1945.

GLEASON, JOANNA: Winnipeg, Can., June 2, 1950. UCLA.

GLEASON, PAUL: Jersey City, NJ, May 4, 1944.

GLENN, SCOTT: Pittsburgh, PA, Jan. 26, 1942. William and Mary Col.

GLOVER, CRISPIN: NYC, 1964.

GLOVER, DANNY: San Francisco, CA, July 22, 1947. SFStateCol.

GLOVER, JOHN: Kingston, NY, Aug. 7, 1944.

GLYNN,CARLIN: Cleveland, Oh, Feb. 19, 1940. Actor's Studio.

GODUNOV, ALEXANDER (Aleksandr): Sakhalin, Russia, Nov. 28, 1949.

GOLDBERG, WHOOPI (Caryn Johnson): NYC, Nov. 13, 1949.

GOLDBLUM, JEFF: Pittsburgh, PA, Oct. 22, 1952. Neighborhood Playhouse.

GOLDEN, ANNIE: Brooklyn, Oct. 19, 1951.

Balthazar Getty   Helen Hunt   Giancarlo Giannini   Anne Jackson

Tony Goldwyn

Julie Kavner

David Marshall Grant

Eartha Kitt

GOLDSTEIN, JENETTE: Beverly Hills, CA, 1960.

GOLDTHWAIT, BOB: Syracuse, NY, May 1962.

GOLDWYN, TONY: Los Angeles, May 20, 1960. LAMDA

GOLINO, VALERIA: Naples, Italy, Oct. 22, 1966.

GONZALEZ, CORDELIA: Aug. 11, 1958, San Juan, PR. UPR.

GONZALES-GONZALEZ, PEDRO: Aguilares, TX, Dec. 21, 1926.

GOODING, CUBA, JR.: Bronx, N.Y., 1968

GOODMAN, DODY: Columbus, OH, Oct. 28, 1915.

GOODMAN, JOHN: St. Louis, MO, June 20, 1952.

GORDON, GALE (Aldrich): NYC, Feb. 2, 1906.

GORDON, KEITH: NYC, Feb. 3, 1961.

GORMAN, CLIFF: Jamaica, NY, Oct. 13, 1936. NYU.

GORSHIN, FRANK: Pittsburgh, PA, Apr. 5, 1933.

GORTNER, MARJOE: Long Beach, CA, Jan. 14, 1944.

GOSSETT, LOUIS, JR.: Brooklyn, May 27, 1936. NYU.

GOULD, ELLIOTT (Goldstein): Brooklyn, Aug. 29, 1938. Columbia U.

GOULD, HAROLD: Schenectady, NY, Dec. 10, 1923. Cornell.

GOULD, JASON: NYC, Dec. 29, 1966.

GOULET, ROBERT: Lawrence, MA, Nov. 26, 1933. Edmonton.

GRAF, DAVID: Lancaster, OH, Apr. 1950. OhStateU.

GRAFF, TODD: NYC, Oct. 22, 1959. SUNY/Purchase.

GRANGER, FARLEY: San Jose, CA, July 1, 1925.

GRANGER, STEWART (James Stewart): London, May 6, 1913. Webber-Douglas School of Acting.

GRANT, DAVID MARSHALL: Westport, CT, June 21, 1955. Yale.

GRANT, KATHRYN (Olive Grandstaff): Houston, TX, Nov. 25, 1933. UCLA.

GRANT, LEE: NYC, Oct. 31, 1930. Juilliard.

GRANT, RICHARD E: Mbabane, Swaziland, May 5, 1957. Cape Town U.

GRAVES, PETER (Aurness): Minneapolis, Mar. 18, 1926. U. Minn.

GRAVES, RUPERT: Weston-Super-Mare, Eng., June 30, 1963.

GRAY, CHARLES: Bournemouth, Eng., 1928.

GRAY, COLEEN (Doris Jensen): Staplehurst, NB, Oct. 23, 1922. Hamline.

GRAY, LINDA: Santa Monica, CA, Sept. 12, 1940.

GRAY, SPALDING: Barrington, RI, June 5, 1941.

GRAYSON, KATHRYN (Zelma Hedrick): Winston-Salem, NC, Feb. 9, 1922.

GREEN, KERRI: Fort Lee, NJ, 1967. Vassar.

GREENE, ELLEN: NYC, Feb. 22, 1950. Ryder Col.

GREER, JANE: Washington, DC, Sept. 9, 1924.

GREER, MICHAEL: Galesburg, IL, Apr. 20, 1943.

GREGORY, MARK: Rome, Italy, 1965.

GREIST, KIM: Stamford, CT, May 12, 1958.

GREY, JENNIFER: NYC, Mar. 26, 1960.

GREY, JOEL (Katz): Cleveland, OH, Apr. 11, 1932.

GREY, VIRGINIA: Los Angeles, Mar. 22, 1917.

GRIEM, HELMUT: Hamburg, Ger, 1940. U. Hamburg.

GRIER, DAVID ALAN: Detroit, MI, June 30, 1955. Yale.

GRIFFITH, ANDY: Mt. Airy, NC, June 1, 1926. UNC.

GRIFFITH, MELANIE: NYC, Aug. 9, 1957. Pierce Col.

GRIMES, GARY: San Francisco, June 2, 1955.

GRIMES, SCOTT: Lowell, MA, July 9, 1971.

GRIMES, TAMMY: Lynn, MA, Jan. 30, 1934. Stephens Col.

GRIZZARD, GEORGE: Roanoke Rapids, NC, Apr. 1, 1928. UNC.

GRODIN, CHARLES: Pittsburgh, PA, Apr. 21, 1935.

GROH, DAVID: NYC, May 21, 1939. Brown U., LAMDA.

GROSS, MARY: Chicago, IL, Mar. 25, 1953.

GROSS, MICHAEL: Chicago, June 21, 1947.

GUARDINO, HARRY: Brooklyn, Dec. 23, 1925. Haaren High.

GUEST, CHRISTOPHER: NYC, Feb. 5, 1948.

GUEST, LANCE: Saratoga, CA, July 21, 1960. UCLA.

GUILLAUME, ROBERT (Williams): St. Louis, MO, Nov. 30, 1937.

GUINNESS, ALEC: London, Apr. 2, 1914. Pembroke Lodge School.

GULAGER, CLU: Holdenville, OK, Nov. 16 1928

GUTTENBERG, STEVE: Massapequa, NY, Aug. 24, 1958. UCLA.

GWILLIM, DAVID: Plymouth, Eng., Dec. 15, 1948. RADA.

GUY, JASMINE: Boston, Mar. 10, 1964

HAAS, LUKAS: West Hollywood, CA, Apr. 16, 1976.

HACK, SHELLEY: Greenwich, CT, July 6, 1952.

HACKETT, BUDDY (Leonard Hacker): Brooklyn, Aug. 31, 1924.

HACKMAN, GENE: San Bernardino, CA, Jan. 30, 1931.

HADDON, DALE: Montreal, Can., May 26, 1949. Neighborhood Playhouse.

HAGERTY, JULIE: Cincinnati, OH, June 15, 1955. Juilliard.

HAGMAN, LARRY (Hageman): Weatherford, TX, Sept. 21, 1931. Bard.

HAIM, COREY: Toronto, Can., Dec. 23, 1972.

HALE, BARBARA: DeKalb, IL, Apr. 18, 1922. Chicago Academy of Fine Arts.

HALEY, JACKIE EARLE: Northridge, CA, July 14, 1961.

HALL, ALBERT: Boothton, AL, Nov. 10, 1937. Columbia.

HALL, ANTHONY MICHAEL: Boston, MA, Apr. 14, 1968.

HALL, ARSENIO: Cleveland, OH, Feb. 12, 1959.

HAMEL, VERONICA: Philadelphia, PA, Nov. 20, 1943.

HAMILL, MARK: Oakland, CA, Sept. 25, 1952. LACC.

HAMILTON, CARRIE: NYC, Dec. 5, 1963.

HAMILTON, GEORGE: Memphis, TN, Aug. 12, 1939. Hackley.

HAMILTON, LINDA: Salisbury, MD, Sept. 26, 1955.

HAMLIN, HARRY: Pasadena, CA, Oct. 30, 1951.

HAMPSHIRE, SUSAN: London, May 12, 1941.

HAN, MAGGIE: Providence, RI, 1959.

HANDLER, EVAN: NYC, Jan. 10, 1961. Juillard.

HANKS, TOM: Concord, CA, Jul. 9, 1956. CalStateU.

HANNAH, DARYL: Chicago, IL, 1960. UCLA.

HANNAH, PAGE: Chicago, IL, Apr. 13, 1964.

HARDIN, TY (Orison Whipple Hungerford II): NYC, June 1, 1930.

HAREWOOD, DORIAN: Dayton, OH, Aug. 6, 1950. U. Cinn.

HARMON, MARK: Los Angeles, CA, Sept. 2, 1951. UCLA.

HARPER, JESSICA: Chicago, IL, Oct. 10, 1949.

HARPER, TESS: Mammoth Spring, AK, 1952. SWMoState.

HARPER, VALERIE: Suffern, NY, Aug. 22, 1940.

HARRELSON, WOODY: Midland, TX, July 23, 1961. Hanover Col.

HARRINGTON, PAT: NYC, Aug. 13, 1929. Fordham U.

HARRIS, BARBARA (Sandra Markowitz): Evanston, IL, July 25, 1935.

HARRIS, ED: Tenafly, NJ, Nov. 28, 1950. Columbia.

HARRIS, JULIE: Grosse Point, MI, Dec. 2, 1925. Yale Drama School.

HARRIS, MEL (Mary Ellen): Bethlehem, PA, 1957. Columbia.

HARRIS, RICHARD: Limerick, Ire., Oct. 1, 1930. London Acad.

HARRIS, ROSEMARY: Ashby, Eng., Sept. 19, 1930. RADA.

HARRISON, GEORGE: Liverpool, Eng., Feb. 25, 1943.

HARRISON, GREGORY: Catalina Island,CA, May 31, 1950. Actors Studio.

HARRISON, NOEL: London, Jan. 29, 1936.

HARROLD, KATHRYN: Tazewell, VA, Aug. 2, 1950. Mills Col.

HARRY, DEBORAH: Miami, IL, July 1, 1945.

HART, ROXANNE: Trenton, NJ, 1952, Princeton.

HARTLEY, MARIETTE: NYC, June 21, 1941.

HARTMAN, DAVID: Pawtucket, RI, May 19, 1935. Duke U.

HASSETT, MARILYN: Los Angeles, CA, Dec. 17. 1947.

HAUER, RUTGER: Amsterdam, Hol., Jan. 23, 1944.

HAVER, JUNE: Rock Island, IL, June 10, 1926.

HAVOC, JUNE (Hovick): Seattle, WA, Nov. 8, 1916.

HAWKE, ETHAN: Austin, TX, Nov. 6, 1970.

HAWN, GOLDIE: Washington, DC, Nov. 21, 1945.

HAYES, ISAAC: Covington, TN, Aug.20, 1942

HAYS, ROBERT: Bethesda, MD, July 24, 1947, SD State Col.

HEADLY, GLENNE: New London, CT, Mar. 13, 1955. AmCol.

HEALD, ANTHONY: New Rochelle, NY, Aug. 25, 1944. MIStateU.

HEARD, JOHN: Washington, DC, Mar. 7, 1946. Clark U.

HEATHERTON, JOEY: NYC, Sept. 14, 1944.

HECKART, EILEEN: Columbus, OH, Mar. 29, 1919. Ohio State U.

HEDISON, DAVID: Providence, RI, May 20, 1929. Brown U.

HEGYES, ROBERT: NJ, May 7, 1951.

HELMOND, KATHERINE: Galveston, TX, July 5, 1934.

HEMINGWAY, MARIEL: Ketchum, ID, Nov.

Lukas Haas

Christine Lahti

George Hamilton

22, 1961.

HEMMINGS, DAVID: Guilford, Eng., Nov. 18, 1941.

HENDIRSON, FLORENCE: Dale, IN, Feb. 14, 1934.

HENDRY, GLORIA: Jacksonville, FL, 1949.

HENNER, MARILU: Chicago, IL, Apr. 6, 1952.

HENRIKSEN, LANCE: NYC, May. 5, 1943.

HENRY, BUCK (Henry Zuckerman): NYC, Dec. 9, 1930. Dartmouth.

HENRY, JUSTIN: Rye, NY, May 25, 1971.

HEPBURN, KATHARINE: Hartford, CT, May 12, 1907. Bryn Mawr.

HERMAN, PEE-WEE (Paul Reubenfeld): Peekskill, NY,Aug. 27, 1952.

HERRMANN, EDWARD: Washington, DC, July 21, 1943. Bucknell, LAMDA.

HERSHEY, BARBARA (Herzstein): Hollywood, CA, Feb. 5, 1948.

HESSEMAN. HOWARD: Lebanon, OR, Feb. 27, 1940.

HESTON, CHARLTON: Evanston, IL, Oct. 4, 1922. Northwestern U.

HEWITT, MARTIN: Claremont, CA, 1960. AADA.

HEYWOOD, ANNE (Violet Pretty): Birmingham, Eng., Dec. 11, 1932.

HICKEY, WILLIAM: Brooklyn, 1928.

HICKMAN, DARRYL: Hollywood, CA, July 28, 1933. Loyola U.

HICKMAN, DWAYNE: Los Angeles, May 18, 1934. Loyola U.

HICKS, CATHERINE: NYC, Aug. 6, 1951. Notre Dame.

HIGGINS, MICHAEL: Brooklyn, Jan. 20, 1926. AmThWing.

HILL, ARTHUR: Saskatchewan, Can., Aug. 1, 1922. U. Brit. Col.

HILL, STEVEN: Seattle, WA, Feb. 24, 1922. U. Wash.

HILL, TERRENCE (Mario Girotti): Venice, Italy, Mar. 29, 1941. U. Rome.

HILLER, WENDY: Bramhall, Cheshire, Eng., Aug 15, 1912. Winceby House School.

HILLERMAN, JOHN: Denison, TX, Dec. 20, 1932.

HINES, GREGORY: NYC, Feb.14, 1946

HINGLE, PAT: Denver, CO, July 19, 1923. Tex. U.

HIRSCH, JUDD: NYC, Mar. 15, 1935. AADA.

HOBEL, MARA: NYC, June 18, 1971.

HODGE, PATRICIA: Lincolnshire, Eng., 1946. LAMDA.

HOFFMAN, DUSTIN: Los Angeles, Aug. 8, 1937. Pasadena Playhouse.

HOGAN, JONATHAN: Chicago, IL, June 13, 1951.

HOGAN, PAUL: Lightning Ridge, Australia, Oct. 8, 1939.

HOLBROOK, HAL (Harold): Cleveland, OH, Feb. 17, 1925. Denison.

HOLLIMAN, EARL: Tennesas Swamp, Delhi, LA, Sept. 11, 1928. UCLA.

HOLM, CELESTE: NYC, Apr. 29, 1919.

HOLM, IAN: Ilford, Essex, Eng., Sept. 12, 1931. RADA.

HOMEIER, SKIP (George Vincent Homeier): Chicago, Oct. 5, 1930. UCLA.

HOOKS, ROBERT: Washington, DC, Apr. 18, 1937. Temple.

HOPE, BOB (Leslie Townes Hope): London, May 26, 1903.

HOPKINS, ANTHONY: Port Talbot, So. Wales, Dec. 31, 1937. RADA.

HOPPER, DENNIS: Dodge City, KS, May 17,

Buck Henry

HORSLEY, LEE: Muleshoe, TX, May 15, 1955.
HORTON, ROBERT: Los Angeles, July 29, 1924. UCLA.
HOSKINS, BOB: Bury St. Edmunds, Eng., Oct. 26, 1942.
HOUGHTON, KATHARINE: Hartford, CT, Mar. 10, 1945. Sarah Lawrence.
HOUSER, JERRY: Los Angeles, July 14, 1952. Valley Jr. Col.
HOWARD, ARLISS: Independence, MO, 1955. Columbia Col.
HOWARD, KEN: El Centro, CA, Mar. 28, 1944. Yale.
HOWARD, RON: Duncan, OK, Mar. 1, 1954. USC.
HOWARD, RONALD: Norwood, Eng., Apr. 7, 1918. Jesus College.
HOWELL, C. THOMAS: Los Angeles, Dec. 7, 1966.
HOWELLS, URSULA: London, Sept. 17, 1922.
HOWES, SALLY ANN: London, July 20, 1930.
HOWLAND, BETH: Boston, MA, May 28, 1941.
HUBLEY, SEASON: NYC, May 14, 1951.
HUDDLESTON, DAVID: Vinton, VA, Sept. 17, 1930.
HUDDLESTON, MICHAEL: Roanoke, VA. AADA.
HUDSON, ERNIE: Benton Harbor, MI, Dec. 17, 1945.
HUGHES, BARNARD: Bedford Hills, NY, July 16, 1915. Manhattan Col.
HUGHES, KATHLEEN (Betty von Gerkan):

Hollywood, CA, Nov. 14, 1928. UCLA.
HULCE, TOM: Plymouth, MI, Dec. 6, 1953. N.C. Sch. of Arts.
HUNNICUT, GAYLE: Ft. Worth, TX, Feb. 6, 1943. UCLA.
HUNT, HELEN: Los Angeles, June 15, 1963.
HUNT, LINDA: Morristown, NJ, Apr. 1945. Goodman Theatre.
HUNT, MARSHA: Chicago, Oct. 17, 1917.
HUNTER, HOLLY: Atlanta, GA, Mar. 20, 1958. Carnegie-Mellon.
HUNTER, KIM (Janet Cole): Detroit, Nov. 12, 1922.
HUNTER, TAB (Arthur Gelien): NYC, July 11, 1931.
HUPPERT, ISABELLE: Paris, Fr., Mar. 16, 1955.
HURT, JOHN: Lincolnshire, Eng., Jan. 22, 1940.
HURT, MARY BETH (Supinger): Marshalltown, IA, Sept. 26, 1948. NYU.
HURT, WILLIAM: Washington, DC, Mar. 20, 1950. Tufts, Juilliard.
HUSSEY, RUTH: Providence, RI, Oct. 30, 1917. U. Mich.
HUSTON, ANJELICA: Santa Monica, CA, July 9, 1951.
HUTTON, BETTY (Betty Thornberg): Battle Creek, MI, Feb. 26, 1921.
HUTTON, LAUREN (Mary): Charleston, SC, Nov. 17, 1943. Newcomb Col.
HUTTON, ROBERT (Winne): Kingston, NY, June 11, 1920. Blair Academy.
HUTTON, TIMOTHY: Malibu, CA, Aug. 16, 1960.
HYER, MARTHA: Fort Worth, TX, Aug. 10, 1924. Northwestern U.
IDLE, ERIC: South Shields, Durham, Eng., Mar. 29, 1943. Cambridge.
INGELS, MARTY: Brooklyn, NY, Mar. 9, 1936.
IRONS, JEREMY: Cowes, Eng., Sept. 19, 1948. Old Vic.
IRVING, AMY: Palo Alto, CA, Sept. 10, 1953. LADA.
IRWIN, BILL: Santa Monica, CA, Apr. 11, 1950.
IVANEK, ZELJKO: Lujubljana, Yugo., Aug. 15, 1957. Yale, LAMDA.
IVES, BURL: Hunt Township, IL, June 14, 1909. Charleston IL Teachers College.
IVEY, JUDITH: El Paso, TX, Sept. 4, 1951.
JACKSON, ANNE: Alleghany, PA, Sept. 3, 1926. Neighborhood Playhouse.
JACKSON, GLENDA: Hoylake, Cheshire, Eng., May 9, 1936. RADA.
JACKSON, KATE: Birmingham, AL, Oct. 29, 1948. AADA.
JACKSON, MICHAEL: Gary, IN, Aug. 29, 1958.
JACKSON, VICTORIA: Miami, FL, Aug. 2, 1958.
JACOBI, DEREK: Leytonstone, London, Oct. 22, 1938. Cambridge.
JACOBI, LOU: Toronto, Can., Dec. 28, 1913.
JACOBS, LAWRENCE-HILTON: Virgin Islands, 1954.
JACOBY, SCOTT: Chicago, Nov. 19, 1956.
JAECKEL, RICHARD: Long Beach, NY, Oct. 10, 1926.
JAGGER, MICK: Dartford, Kent, Eng., July 26, 1943.
JAMES, CLIFTON: NYC, May 29, 1921. Ore. U.
JAMES, JOHN (Anderson): Apr. 18, 1956, New Canaan, CT. AADA.

Viveca Lindfors

JARMAN, CLAUDE, JR.: Nashville, TN, Sept. 27, 1934.
JASON, RICK: NYC, May 21, 1926. AADA.
JEAN, GLORIA (Gloria Jean Schoonover): Buffalo, NY, Apr. 14, 1927.
JEFFREYS, ANNE (Carmichael): Goldsboro, NC, Jan. 26, 1923. Anderson College.
JEFFRES, LIONEL: London, 1927. RADA.
JERGENS, ADELE: Brooklyn, Nov. 26, 1922.
JETER, MICHAEL: Lawrenceburg, TN, Aug. 26, 1952. Memphis St.U.
JETT, ROGER (Baker): Cumberland, MD, Oct. 2, 1946. AADA.
JILLIAN, ANN (Nauseda): Cambridge, MA, Jan. 29, 1951.
JOHANSEN, DAVID: Staten Island, NY, Jan. 9, 1950.
JOHN, ELTON (Reginald Dwight): Middlesex, Eng., Mar. 25, 1947. RAM.
JOHNS, GLYNIS: Durban, S. Africa, Oct. 5, 1923.
JOHNSON, BEN: Pawhuska, OK, June 13, 1918.
JOHNSON, DON: Galena, MO, Dec. 15, 1950. UKan.
JOHNSON, PAGE: Welch, WV, Aug. 25, 1930. Ithaca.
JOHNSON, RAFER: Hillsboro, TX, Aug. 18, 1935. UCLA.
JOHNSON, RICHARD: Essex, Eng., July 30, 1927. RADA.
JOHNSON, ROBIN: Brooklyn, May 29, 1964.
JOHNSON, VAN: Newport, RI, Aug. 28, 1916.

Diane Lane

Ian Holm

JOHNSON, ROBIN: Brooklyn, May 29, 1964.

JOHNSON, VAN: Newport, RI, Aug. 28, 1916.

JONES, CHRISTOPHER: Jackson, TN, Aug. 18, 1941. Actors Studio.

JONES, DEAN: Decatur, AL, Jan. 25, 1931. Actors Studio.

JONES, GRACE: Spanishtown, Jamaica, May 19, 1952.

JONES, JACK: Bel-Air, CA, Jan. 14, 1938.

JONES, JAMES EARL: Arkabutla, MS, Jan. 17, 1931. U. Mich.

JONES, JEFFREY: Buffalo, NY, Sept. 28, 1947. LAMDA.

JONES, JENNIFER (Phyllis Isley): Tulsa, OK, Mar. 2, 1919. AADA.

JONES, SAM J.: Chicago, IL, Aug. 12, 1954.

JONES, SHIRLEY: Smithton, PA, March 31, 1934.

JONES, TERRY: Colwyn Bay, Wales, Feb. 1, 1942.

JONES, TOMMY LEE: San Saba, TX, Sept. 15, 1946. Harvard.

JOURDAN, LOUIS: Marseilles, France, June 19, 1920.

JOY, ROBERT: Montreal, Can., Aug. 17, 1951. Oxford.

JULIA, RAUL: San Juan, PR, Mar. 9, 1943. U. PR.

JURADO, KATY (Maria Christina Jurado Garcia): Guadalajara, Mex., Jan. 16, 1927.

KACZMAREK, JANE: Milwaukee, WI, Dec. 21.

KAHN, MADELINE: Boston, MA, Sept. 29, 1942. Hofstra U.

KANE, CAROL: Cleveland, OH, June 18, 1952.

KAPLAN, MARVIN: Brooklyn, Jan. 24, 1924.

KAPOOR, SHASHI: Bombay, India, 1940.

KAPRISKY, VALERIE: Paris, 1963.

KARRAS, ALEX: Gary, IN, July 15, 1935.

KATT, WILLIAM: Los Angeles, CA, Feb. 16, 1955.

KAUFMANN, CHRISTINE: Lansdorf, Graz, Austria, Jan. 11, 1945.

KAVNER, JULIE: Burbank, CA, Sept. 7, 1951. UCLA.

KAYE, STUBBY: NYC, Nov. 11, 1918.

KAZAN, LAINIE (Levine): Brooklyn, May 15, 1942.

KAZURINSKY, TIM: Johnstown, PA, March 3, 1950.

KEACH, STACY: Savannah, GA, June 2, 1941. U. Cal., Yale.

KEATON, DIANE (Hall): Los Angeles, CA, Jan. 5, 1946. Neighborhood Playhouse.

KEATON, MICHAEL: Coraopolis, PA, Sept. 9, 1951. KentStateU.

KEATS, STEVEN: Bronx, NY, 1945.

KEDROVA, LILA: Leningrad, 1918.

KEEL, HOWARD (Harold Leek): Gillespie, IL, Apr. 13, 1919.

KEITEL, HARVEY: Brooklyn, May 13, 1939.

KEITH, BRIAN: Bayonne, NJ, Nov. 15, 1921.

KEITH, DAVID: Knoxville, TN, May 8, 1954. UTN.

KELLER, MARTHE: Basel, Switz., 1945. Munich Stanislavsky Sch.

KELLERMAN, SALLY: Long Beach, CA, June 2, 1936. Actors Studio West.

KELLEY, DeFOREST: Atlanta, GA, Jan. 20, 1920.

KELLY, GENE: Pittsburgh, Aug. 23,1912. U. Pittsburgh.

KELLY, NANCY: Lowell, MA, Mar. 25, 1921. Bentley School.

KEMP, JEREMY (Wacker): Chesterfield, Eng., Feb. 3, 1935. Central Sch.

KENNEDY, GEORGE: NYC, Feb. 18, 1925.

KENNEDY, LEON ISAAC: Cleveland, OH, 1949.

KENSIT, PATSY: London, Mar. 4, 1968.

KERR, DEBORAH: Helensburg, Scot., Sept. 30, 1921. Smale Ballet School.

KERR, JOHN: NYC, Nov. 15, 1931. Harvard, Columbia.

KERWIN, BRIAN: Chicago, IL, Oct. 25, 1949.

KEYES, EVELYN: Port Arthur, TX, Nov. 20, 1919.

KHAMBATTA, PERSIS: Bombay, Oct. 2, 1950.

KIDDER, MARGOT: Yellow Knife, Can., Oct. 17, 1948. UBC.

KIEL, RICHARD: Detroit, MI, Sept. 13, 1939.

KIER, UDO: Germany, Oct. 14, 1944.

KILEY, RICHARD: Chicago, Mar. 31, 1922. Loyola.

KILMER, VAL: Los Angeles, Dec. 31, 1959. Juilliard.

KINCAID, ARON (Norman Neale Williams III) Los Angeles, June 15, 1943. UCLA.

KING, ALAN (Irwin Kniberg): Brooklyn, Dec. 26, 1927.

KING, PERRY: Alliance, OH, Apr. 30, 1948. Yale.

KINGSLEY, BEN (Krishna Bhanji): Snaiton, Yorkshire, Eng., Dec. 31, 1943.

KINSKI, NASTASSJA: Berlin, Ger., Jan. 24, 1960.

KIRBY, BRUNO: NYC, Apr. 28, 1949.

KIRK, TOMMY: Louisville, KY, Dec.10 1941.

KIRKLAND, SALLY: NYC, Oct. 31, 1944. Actors Studio.

KITT, EARTHA: North, SC. Jan. 26, 1928.

KLEIN, ROBERT: NYC, Feb. 8, 1942. Alfred U.

KLEMPERER, WERNER: Cologne, Mar. 22, 1920.

KLINE, KEVIN: St. Louis, MO, Oct. 24, 1947. Juilliard.

KLUGMAN, JACK: Philadelphia, PA, Apr. 27, 1922. Carnegie Tech.

KNIGHT, MICHAEL: Princeton, NJ, 1959.

KNIGHT, SHIRLEY: Goessel, KS, July 5, 1937. Wichita U.

KNOWLES, PATRIC (Reginald Lawrence Knowles): Horsforth, Eng., Nov. 11, 1911.

KNOX, ALEXANDER: Strathroy, Ont., Can., Jan. 16, 1907.

KNOX, ELYSE: Hartford, CT, Dec. 14, 1917. Traphagen School.

KOENIG, WALTER: Chicago, IL, Sept. 14, 1936. UCLA.

KOHNER, SUSAN: Los Angeles, Nov. 11, 1936. U. Calif.

KORMAN, HARVEY: Chicago, IL, Feb. 15, 1927. Goodman.

KORSMO, CHARLIE: Minneapolis, MN, 1978.

KORVIN, CHARLES (Geza Korvin Karpathi): Czechoslovakia, Nov. 21, 1907.

Sorbonne.

KOSLECK, MARTIN: Barkotzen, Ger., Mar. 24, 1907. Max Reinhardt School.

KOTEAS, ELIAS: Montreal, Quebec, Can., 1961. AADA.

KOTTO, YAPHET: NYC, Nov. 15, 1937.

KOZAK, HARLEY JANE: Wilkes-Barre, PA, Jan. 28, 1957. NYU.

KRABBE, JEROEN: Amsterdam, The Netherlands, Dec. 5, 1944.

KREUGER, KURT: St. Moritz, Switz., July 23, 1917. U. London.

KRIGE, ALICE: Upington, So. Africa, June 28, 1955.

KRISTEL, SYLVIA: Amsterdam, The Netherlands, Sept. 28, 1952.

KRISTOFFERSON, KRIS: Brownsville, TX, June 22, 1936, Pomona Col.

KRUGER, HARDY: Berlin, Ger., April 12, 1928.

KUNTSMANN, DORIS: Hamburg, Ger., 1944.

KURTZ, SWOOSIE: Omaha, NE, Sept. 6, 1944.

KWAN, NANCY: Hong Kong, May 19, 1939. Royal Ballet.

LaBELLE, PATTI: Philadelphia, PA, May 24, 1944.

LACY, JERRY: Sioux City, IA, Mar. 27, 1936. LACC.

LADD, CHERYL: (Stoppelmoor): Huron, SD. July 12, 1951.

LADD, DIANE: (Ladner): Meridian, MS, Nov. 29, 1932. Tulane U.

LaGRECA, PAUL: Bronx, NY, June 23, 1962. AADA.

LAHTI, CHRISTINE: Detroit, MI, Apr. 4, 1950. U. Mich.

LAKE, RICKI: NYC, Sept. 21, 1968.

LAMARR, HEDY (Hedwig Kiesler): Vienna, Sept. 11, 1913.

LAMAS, LORENZO: Los Angeles, Jan. 28, 1958.

LAMBERT, CHRISTOPHER: NYC, Mar. 29, 1958.

LAMOUR, DOROTHY (Mary Dorothy Slaton): New Orleans, LA, Dec. 10, 1914. Spence School.

LANCASTER, BURT: NYC, Nov. 2, 1913. NYU.

LANDAU, MARTIN: Brooklyn, June 20, 1931. Actors Studio.

LANDRUM, TERI: Enid, OK, 1960.

LANE, ABBE: Brooklyn, Dec. 14, 1935.

LANE, DIANE: NYC, Jan. 22, 1963.

LANE, NATHAN: Jersey City, NJ, Feb. 3, 1956.

LANG, STEPHEN: NYC, July 11, 1952. Swarthmore Col.

LANGE, HOPE: Redding Ridge, CT, Nov. 28, 1931. Reed Col.

LANGE, JESSICA: Cloquet, MN, Apr. 20, 1949. U. Minn.

LANGELLA, FRANK: Bayonne, NJ, Jan. 1, 1940. SyracuseU.

LANSBURY, ANGELA: London, Oct. 16, 1925. London Academy of Music.

LANSING, ROBERT (Brown): San Diego, CA, June 5, 1929.

LaPLANTE, LAURA: St. Louis, MO, Nov. 1,.1904.

LARROQUETTE, JOHN: New Orleans, LA, Nov. 25, 1947.

LASSER, LOUISE: NYC, Apr. 11, 1939.

Tab Hunter   Shelley Long   John Hurt   Virginia Madsen

Brandeis U.

LAUGHLIN, JOHN: Memphis, TN, Apr. 3.

LAUGHLIN, TOM: Minneapolis, MN, 1938.

LAUPER, CYNDI: Astoria, Queens, NYC, June 20, 1953.

LAURE, CAROLE: Montreal, Can., 1951.

LAURIE, PIPER (Rosetta Jacobs): Detroit, MI, Jan. 22, 1932.

LAUTER, ED: Long Beach, NY, Oct. 30, 1940.

LAVIN, LINDA: Portland, ME, Oct. 15 1939.

LAW, JOHN PHILLIP: Hollywood, CA, Sept. 7, 1937. Neighborhood Playhouse, U. Hawaii.

LAWRENCE, BARBARA: Carnegie, OK, Feb. 24, 1930. UCLA.

LAWRENCE, CAROL (Laraia): Melrose Park, IL, Sept. 5, 1935.

LAWRENCE, VICKI: Inglewood, CA, Mar. 26, 1949.

LAWSON, LEIGH: Atherston, Eng., July 21, 1945. RADA.

LEACHMAN, CLORIS: Des Moines, IA, Apr. 30, 1930. Northwestern U.

LEAUD, JEAN-PIERRE: Paris, 1944.

LEDERER, FRANCIS: Karlin, Prague, Czech., Nov. 6, 1906.

LEE, CHRISTOPHER: London, May 27, 1922. Wellington College.

LEE, MARK: Australia, 1958

LEE, MICHELE (Dusiak): Los Angeles, June 24, 1942. LACC.

LEE, PEGGY (Norma Delores Egstrom): Jamestown, ND, May 26, 1920.

LEE, SPIKE (Shelton Lee): Atlanta, GA, Mar. 20, 1957.

LEGUIZAMO, JOHN: Columbia, July 22, 1965. NYU.

LEIBMAN, RON: NYC, Oct. 1l, 1937. Ohio Wesleyan.

LEIGH, JANET (Jeanette Helen Morrison): Merced, CA, July 6, 1926. College of Pacific.

LEIGH, JENNIFER JASON: Los Angeles, Feb. 5, 1962.

LeMAT, PAUL: Rahway, NJ, Sept. 22, 1945.

LEMMON, CHRIS: Los Angeles, Jan. 22, 1954.

LEMMON, JACK: Boston, Feb. 8, 1925. Harvard.

LENO, JAY: New Rochelle, NY, Apr. 28, 1950. Emerson Col.

LENZ, KAY: Los Angeles, Mar. 4, 1953.

LENZ, RICK: Springfield, IL, Nov. 21, 1939.

U. Mich.

LEONARD, ROBERT SEAN: Westwood, NJ, Feb. 28, 1969.

LEONARD, SHELDON (Bershad): NYC, Feb. 22, 1907, Syracuse U.

LERNER, MICHAEL: Brooklyn, NY, June 22, 1941.

LEROY, PHILIPPE: Paris, Oct. 15, 1930. U. Paris.

LESLIE, BETHEL: NYC, Aug. 3, 1929. Brearley School.

LESLIE, JOAN (Joan Brodell): Detroit, Jan. 26, 1925. St. Benedict's.

LESTER, MARK: Oxford, Eng., July 11, 1958.

LEVELS, CALVIN: Cleveland. OH, Sept. 30, 1954. CCC.

LEVIN, RACHEL: NYC, 1954. Goddard Col.

LEVINE, JERRY: New Brunswick, NJ, Mar. 12, 1957, Boston U.

LEVY, EUGENE: Hamilton, Can., Dec. 17, 1946. McMasterU.

LEWIS, CHARLOTTE: London, 1968.

LEWIS, JERRY (Joseph Levitch): Newark, NJ, Mar. 16, 1926.

LIGON, TOM: New Orleans, LA, Sept. 10, 1945.

LINCOLN, ABBEY (Anna Marie Woolridge): Chicago, Aug. 6. 1930.

LINDEN, HAL: Bronx, NY, Mar. 20, 1931. City Col. of NY.

LINDFORS, VIVECA: Uppsala, Sweden, Dec. 29, 1920. Stockholm Royal Dramatic School.

LINDSAY, ROBERT: Ilketson, Derby-shire, Eng., Dec. 13, 1951, RADA.

LINN-BAKER, MARK: St. Louis, MO, June 17, 1954, Yale.

LIOTTA, RAY: Newark, NJ, Dec. 18, 1955. UMiami.

LISI, VIRNA: Rome, Nov. 8, 1937.

LITHGOW, JOHN: Rochester, NY, Oct. 19, 1945. Harvard.

LLOYD, CHRISTOPHER: Stamford, CT, Oct. 22, 1938.

LLOYD, EMILY: London, Sept. 29, 1970.

LOCKE, SONDRA: Shelbyville, TN, May, 28, 1947.

LOCKHART, JUNE: NYC, June 25, 1925. Westlake School.

LOCKWOOD, GARY: Van Nuys, CA, Feb. 21, 1937.

LOGGIA, ROBERT: Staten Island, NY.,

Jan. 3, 1930. UMo.

LOLLOBRIGIDA, GINA: Subiaco, Italy, July 4, 1927. Rome Academy of Fine Arts.

LOM, HERBERT: Prague, Czechoslovakia, Jan 9, 1917. Prague U.

LOMEZ, CELINE: Montreal, Can., 1953.

LONDON, JULIE (Julie Peck): Santa Rosa, CA, Sept. 26, 1926.

LONE, JOHN: Hong Kong, 1952. AADA

LONG, SHELLEY: Ft. Wayne, IN, Aug. 23, 1949. Northwestem U.

LOPEZ, PERRY: NYC, July 22, 1931. NYU.

LORD, JACK (John Joseph Ryan): NYC, Dec. 30, 1928. NYU.

LOREN, SOPHIA (Sophia Scicolone): Rome, Italy, Sept. 20, 1934.

LOUISE, TINA (Blacker): NYC, Feb. 11, 1934, Miami U.

LOVITZ, JON: Tarzana, CA, July 21, 1957.

LOWE, CHAD: Dayton, OH, Jan. 15, 1968.

LOWE, ROB: Charlottesville, VA, Mar. 17, 1964.

LOWITSCH, KLAUS: Berlin, Apr. 8, 1936, Vienna Academy.

LUCAS, LISA: Arizona, 1961.

LUCKINBILL, LAURENCE: Fort Smith, AK, Nov. 21, 1934.

LUFT, LORNA: Los Angeles, Nov. 21, 1952.

LULU:(Marie Lawrie) Glasgow, Scot.,Nov. 3, 1948.

LUNA, BARBARA: NYC, Mar. 2, 1939.

LUNDGREN, DOLPH: Stockolm, Sw., Nov. 3, 1959. Royal Inst.

LUPINO, IDA: London, Feb. 4, 1916. RADA

LuPONE, PATTI: Northport, NY Apr. 21, 1949, Juilliard.

LYDON, JAMES: Harrington Park, NJ, May 30, 1923.

LYNCH, KELLY: Minneapolis, MN, 1959.

LYNLEY, CAROL (Jones): NYC, Feb. 13, 1942.

LYNN, JEFFREY: Auburn, MA, Feb. 16, 1909. Bates College.

LYON, SUE: Davenport, IA, July 10, 1946.

MacARTHUR, JAMES: Los Angeles, Dec. 8, 1937. Harvard.

MACCHIO, RALPH: Huntington, NY, Nov. 4, 1961.

MacCORKINDALE, SIMON: Cambridge, Eng., Feb. 12, 1953.

MacDOWELL, ANDIE: Gaffney, SC, Apr. 21, 1958.

MacGINNIS, NIALL: Dublin, Ire., Mar. 29, 1913. Dublin U.

Mick Jagger   Penny Marshall   Dean Jones   Mary Elizabeth Mastrantonio

MacGRAW, ALI: NYC, Apr. 1, 1938. Wellesley.

MacLACHLAN, KYLE: Yakima, WA, Feb. 22, 1959. UWa.

MacLAINE, SHIRLEY (Beaty): Richmond, VA, Apr. 24, 1934.

MacLEOD, GAVIN: Mt. Kisco, NY, Feb. 28, 1931.

MacNAUGHTON, ROBERT: NYC, Dec. 19, 1966.

MACNEE, PATRICK: London, Feb. 1922.

MacNICOL, PETER: Dallas, TX, Apr. 10, 1954. UMN.

MACY, W.H. (William): Miami, FL, Mar. 13, 1950. Goddard College.

MADIGAN, AMY: Chicago, IL, Sept. 11, 1950. Marquette U.

MADISON, GUY (Robert Moseley): Bakersfield, CA, Jan. 19, 1922. Bakersfield Jr. College.

MADONNA (Madonna Louise Veronica Cicone): Bay City, MI, Aug. 16, 1958. UMi.

MADSEN, MICHAEL: Chicago, IL, 1958.

MADSEN, VIRGINIA: Winnetka, IL, Sept. 11, 1963.

MAGNUSON, ANN: Charleston, WV, Jan. 4, 1956.

MAHARIS, GEORGE: Astoria, NY, Sept. 1, 1928. Actors Studio.

MAHONEY, JOHN: Manchester, Eng., June 20, 1940. WUIll.

MAILER, KATE: NYC, 1962.

MAILER, STEPHEN: NYC, Mar. 10, 1966. NYU.

MAJORS, LEE: Wyandotte, MI, Apr. 23, 1940. E. Ky. State Col.

MAKEPEACE, CHRIS: Toronto, Can., Apr. 22, 1964.

MAKO: Kobe, Japan, Dec. 10, 1933. Pratt.

MALDEN, KARL (Mladen Sekulovich): Gary, IN, Mar. 22, 1914.

MALET, PIERRE: St. Tropez, Fr., 1955.

MALKOVICH, JOHN: Christopher, IL, Dec. 9, 1953, IllStateU.

MALONE, DOROTHY: Chicago, IL, Jan. 30, 1925.

MANN, KURT: Roslyn, NY, July 18, 1947.

MANN, TERRENCE: KY, 1945. NCSchl Arts.

MANOFF, DINAH: NYC, Jan. 25, 1958. CalArts.

MANTEGNA, JOE: Chicago, IL, Nov. 13, 1947. Goodman Theatre.

MANZ, LINDA: NYC, 1961.

MARAIS, JEAN: Cherbourg, France, Dec. 11, 1913, St. Germain.

MARCHAND, NANCY: Buffalo, NY, June 19, 1928.

MARCOVICCI, ANDREA: NYC, Nov. 18, 1948.

MARIN, CHEECH (Richard): Los Angeles, July 13, 1946.

MARIN, JACQUES: Paris, Sept. 9, 1919. Conservatoire National.

MARINARO, ED: NYC, 1951. Cornell.

MARS, KENNETH: Chicago, IL, 1936.

MARSH, JEAN: London, Eng., July 1, 1934.

MARSHALL, E.G.: Owatonna, MN, June 18, 1910. U. Minn.

MARSHALL, KEN: NYC, 1953. Juilliard.

MARSHALL, PENNY: Bronx, NY, Oct. 15, 1942. U.N. Mex.

MARSHALL, WILLIAM: Gary, IN, Aug. 19, 1924. NYU.

MARTIN, ANDREA: Portland, ME, Jan. 15, 1947.

MARTIN, DEAN (Dino Crocetti): Steubenville, OH, June 17, 1917.

MARTIN, DICK: Battle Creek, MI Jan. 30, 1923

MARTIN, GEORGE N.: NYC, Aug. 15, 1929.

MARTIN, MILLICENT: Romford, Eng., June 8, 1934.

MARTIN, PAMELA SUE: Westport, CT, Jan. 15, 1953.

MARTIN, STEVE: Waco, TX, Aug. 14, 1945. UCLA.

MARTIN, TONY (Alfred Norris): Oakland, CA, Dec. 25, 1913. St. Mary's College.

MASINA, GUILIETTA: Giorgio di Piano, Italy, Feb. 22, 1921.

MASON, MARSHA: St. Louis, MO, Apr. 3, 1942. Webster Col.

MASON, PAMELA (Pamela Kellino): Westgate, Eng., Mar. 10, 1918.

MASSEN, OSA: Copenhagen, Den., Jan. 13, 1916.

MASSEY, DANIEL: London, Oct. 10, 1933. Eton and King's Coll.

MASTERS, BEN: Corvallis, OR, May 6, 1947. UOr.

MASTERSON, MARY STUART: Los Angeles, June 28, 1966, NYU.

MASTERSON, PETER: Angleton, TX, June 1, 1934. Rice U.

MASTRANTONIO, MARY ELIZABETH: Chicago, IL, Nov. 17, 1958. UIll.

MASTROIANNI, MARCELLO: Fontana Liri, Italy, Sept. 28, 1924.

MASUR, RICHARD: NYC, Nov. 20, 1948.

MATHESON, TIM: Glendale, CA, Dec. 31, 1947. CalState.

MATLIN, MARLEE: Morton Grove, IL., Aug. 24, 1965.

MATTHAU, WALTER (Matuschanskayasky): NYC, Oct. 1, 1920.

MATTHEWS, BRIAN: Philadelphia, Jan. 24. 1953. St. Olaf.

MATURE, VICTOR: Louisville, KY, Jan. 29, 1915.

MAY, ELAINE (Berlin): Philadelphia, Apr. 21, 1932.

MAYO, VIRGINIA (Virginia Clara Jones): St. Louis, MO, Nov. 30, 1920.

MAYRON, MELANIE: Philadelphia, PA, Oct. 20, 1952. AADA.

MAZURSKY, PAUL: Brooklyn, NY, Apr. 25, 1930. Bklyn Col.

McCALLUM, DAVID: Scotland, Sept. 19, 1933. Chapman Col.

McCAMBRIDGE, MERCEDES: Jolliet, IL, Mar. 17, 1918. Mundelein College.

McCARTHY, ANDREW: NYC, Nov. 29, 1962, NYU.

McCARTHY, KEVIN: Seattle, WA, Feb. 15, 1914. Minn. U.

McCARTNEY, PAUL: Liverpool, Eng-land, June 18, 1942.

McCLANAHAN, RUE: Healdton, OK, Feb. 21, 1934.

McCLORY, SEAN: Dublin, Ire., Mar. 8, 1924. U. Galway.

McCLURE, DOUG: Glendale, CA, May 11, 1935. UCLA.

McCLURE, MARC: San Mateo, CA, Mar. 31, 1957.

McCLURG, EDIE: Kansas City, MO, July 23, 1951.

McCOWEN, ALEC: Tunbridge Wells, Eng., May 26, 1925. RADA.

McCRANE, PAUL: Philadelphia, PA, Jan. 19. 1961.

McCRARY, DARIUS: Walnut, CA, 1976.

McDERMOTT, DYLAN: Waterbury, CT, Oct. 26, 1962. Neighborhood Playhouse.

McDONNELL, MARY: Wilkes Barre, PA, 1952.

McDORMAND, FRANCES: Illinois, 1958.

McDOWALL, RODDY: London, Sept. 17, 1928. St. Joseph's.

McDOWELL, MALCOLM (Taylor): Leeds, Eng., June 19, 1943. LAMDA.

McENERY, PETER: Walsall, Eng., Feb. 21, 1940.

McGAVIN, DARREN: Spokane, WA, May 7, 1922. College of Pacific.

McGILL, EVERETT: Miami Beach, FL, Oct. 21, 1945.

McGILLIS, KELLY: Newport Beach, CA, July 9, 1957. Juilliard.

McGOVERN, ELIZABETH: Evanston, IL. July 18, 1961. Juilliard.

McGOVERN, MAUREEN: Youngstown, OH, July 27, 1949.

McGREGOR. JEFF: Chicago, 1957. UMn.

McGUIRE, BIFF: New Haven, CT, Oct. 25. 1926. Mass. Stale Col.

McGUIRE, DOROTHY: Omaha, NE, June 14, 1918.

McHATTIE, STEPHEN: Antigonish, NS, Feb. 3. Acadia U. AADA.

McKAY, GARDNER: NYC, June 10, 1932. Comell.

McKEAN, MICHAEL: NYC, Oct. 17, 1947.

McKEE, LONETTE: Detroit, MI, 1954.

McKELLEN, IAN: Burnley, Eng., May 25, 1939.

McKENNA, VIRGINIA: London, June 7, 1931.

McKEON, DOUG: Pompton Plains, NJ, June 10, 1966.

McKUEN, ROD: Oakland, CA, Apr. 29, 1933.

McLERIE, ALLYN ANN: Grand Mere, Can., Dec. 1, 1926.

Mc MAHON, ED: Detroit, MI, Mar.6, 1923

McNAIR, BARBARA: Chicago, Mar. 4, 1939. UCLA.

McNALLY, STEPHEN (Horace McNally): NYC, July 29, 1913. Fordham U.

McNAMARA, WILLIAM: Dallas, TX, 1965.

McNICHOL, KRISTY: Los Angeles. CA, Sept. 11, 1962.

McQUEEN, ARMELIA: North Carolina, Jan. 6, 1952. Bklyn Consv.

McQUEEN, BUTTERFLY: Tampa, FL, Jan. 8, 1911. UCLA.

McQUEEN, CHAD: Los Angeles, CA, Dec. 28, 1960. Actors Studio.

McRANEY, GERALD: Collins, MS, Aug. 19, 1948.

McSHANE, IAN: Blackburn, Eng., Sept. 29, 1942. RADA.

MEADOWS, AUDREY: Wuchang, China, 1926. St. Margaret's.

MEADOWS, JAYNE (formerly, Jayne Cotter): Wuchang, China, Sept. 27, 1924. St. Margaret's.

MEARA, ANNE: Brooklyn, NY, Sept. 20, 1929.

MEDWIN, MICHAEL: London, 1925. Instut Fischer.

MEISNER, GUNTER: Bremen, Ger., Apr. 18, 1926. Municipal Drama School.

MEKKA, EDDIE: Worcester, MA, 1932. Boston Cons.

MELATO, MARIANGELA: Milan, Italy, 1941. Milan Theatre Acad.

MELL, MARISA: Vienna, Austria, Feb. 25, 1939.

MERCADO, HECTOR JAIME: NYC, 1949. HB Studio.

MERCOURI, MELINA: Athens, Greece, Oct. 18, 1925.

MEREDITH, BURGESS: Cleveland, OH, Nov. 16, 1907. Amherst.

MEREDITH, LEE (Judi Lee Sauls): Oct. 22, 1947. AADA.

MERKERSON, S. EPATHA: Saganaw, MI, Nov. 28, 1952. Wayne St. Univ.

MERRILL, DINA (Nedinia Hutton): NYC, Dec. 29, 1925. AADA.

METCALF, LAURIE: Edwardsville, IL, June 16, 1955. IIIStU.

METZLER, JIM: Oneonda, NY, June 23. Dartmouth.

MICHELL, KEITH: Adelaide, Aus., Dec. 1, 1926.

MIDLER, BETTE: Honolulu, HI, Dec. 1, 1945.

MIFUNE, TOSHIRO: Tsingtao, China, Apr. 1, 1920.

MILANO, ALYSSA: Brooklyn, NY, 1975.

MILES, JOANNA: Nice, France, Mar. 6, 1940.

MILES, SARAH: Ingatestone, Eng. Dec. 31, 1941. RADA.

MILES, SYLVIA: NYC, Sept. 9, 1934. Actors Studio.

MILES, VERA (Ralston): Boise City, OK, Aug. 23, 1929. UCLA.

MILLER, ANN (Lucille Ann Collier):

Chireno, TX, Apr. 12, 1919. Lawler Professional School.

MILLER, PENELOPE ANN: Santa Monica, CA, Jan. 13, 1964.

MILLER, BARRY: Los Angeles, CA, Feb. 6, 1958.

MILLER, JASON: Long Island City, NY, Apr. 22, 1939. Catholic U.

MILLER, LINDA: NYC, Sept. 16, 1942. Catholic U.

MILLER, REBECCA: Roxbury, CT, 1962. Yale.

MILLS, HAYLEY: London, Apr. 18, 1946. Elmhurst School.

MILLS, JOHN: Suffolk, Eng., Feb. 22, 1908.

MILLS, JULIET: London, Nov. 21, 1941.

MILNER, MARTIN: Detroit, MI, Dec. 28, 1931.

MIMIEUX, YVETTE: Los Angeles, Jan. 8, 1941. Hollywood High.

MINNELLI, LIZA: Los Angeles, Mar. 19, 1946.

MIOU-MIOU: Paris, Feb. 22, 1950.

MIRREN, HELEN: London, 1946.

MITCHELL, CAMERON (MizeII): Dallastown, PA, Nov. 4, 1918. N.Y. Theatre School.

MITCHELL, JAMES: Sacramento, CA, Feb. 29, 1920. LACC

MITCHELL, JOHN CAMERON: El Paso, TX, Apr. 21, 1963. Northwestern Univ.

MITCHUM, JAMES: Los Angeles, CA, May 8, 1941.

MITCHUM, ROBERT: Bridgeport, CT, Aug. 6, 1917.

MODINE, MATTHEW: Loma Linda, CA, Mar. 22, 1959.

MOFFAT, DONALD: Plymouth, Eng., Dec. 26, 1930. RADA.

MOFFETT, D.W.: Highland Park, IL, Oct. 26, 1954. Stanford U.

MOKAE, ZAKES: Johannesburg, So. Africa, Aug. 5, 1935. RADA.

MOLINA, ALFRED: London, May 24, 1953. Guildhall.

MOLL, RICHARD: Pasadena, CA, Jan. 13, 1943.

MONTALBAN, RICARDO: Mexico City, Nov. 25, 1920.

MONTGOMERY, BELINDA: Winnipeg, Can., July 23, 1950.

Jeffrey Jones

Kelly McGillis

Louis Jourdan

Sarah Miles

MONTGOMERY, ELIZABETH: Los Angeles, Apr. 15, 1933. AADA.

MONTGOMERY, GEORGE (George Letz): Brady, MT, Aug. 29, 1916. U. Mont.

MOODY, RON: London, Jan. 8, 1924. London U.

MOOR, BILL: Toledo, OH, July 13, 1931. Northwestern.

MOORE, CONSTANCE: Sioux City, IA, Jan. 18, 1919.

MOORE, DEMI (Guines): Roswell, NM, Nov. 11, 1962.

MOORE, DICK: Los Angeles, Sept. 12, 1925.

MOORE, DUDLEY: Dagenham, Essex, Eng., Apr. 19, 1935.

MOORE, FRANK: Bay-de-Verde, Newfoundland, 1946.

MOORE, KIERON: County Cork, Ire., 1925. St. Mary's College.

MOORE, MARY TYLER: Brooklyn, Dec. 29, 1936.

MOORE, ROGER: London, Oct. 14, 1927. RADA.

MOORE, TERRY (Helen Koford): Los Angeles, Jan. 7, 1929.

MORALES, ESAI: Brooklyn, 1963.

MORANIS, RICK: Toronto, Can., Apr. 18, 1954.

MOREAU, JEANNE: Paris, Jan. 23, 1928.

MORENO, RITA (Rosita Alverio): Humacao, P.R., Dec. 11, 1931.

MORGAN, DENNIS (Stanley Momer): Prentice, WI, Dec. 10, 1910. Carroll College.

MORGAN, HARRY (HENRY) (Harry Bratsburg): Detroit, Apr. 10, 1915. U. Chicago.

MORGAN, MICHELE (Simone Roussel): Paris, Feb. 29, 1920. Paris Dramatic School.

MORIARTY, CATHY: Bronx, NY, Nov. 29, 1960.

MORIARTY, MICHAEL: Detroit, MI, Apr. 5, 1941. Dartmouth.

MORISON, PATRICIA: NYC, 1915.

MORITA, NORIYUKI "PAT": Isleton, CA, June 28, 1932.

MORRIS, ANITA: Durham, NC, 1943.

MORRIS, GREG: Cleveland, OH, Sept. 27, 1934. Ohio State.

MORRIS, HOWARD: NYC, Sept. 4, 1919. NYU.

MORSE, DAVID: Hamilton, MA, 1953.

MORSE, ROBERT: Newton, MA, May 18, 1931.

MORTON, JOE: NYC, Oct. 18, 1947. Hofstra U.

MOSES, WILLIAM: Los Angeles, Nov. 17, 1959.

MOSTEL, JOSH: NYC, Dec. 21, 1946. Brandeis U.

MOUCHET, CATHERINE: Paris, 1959. Ntl. Consv.

MOYA, EDDY: El Paso, TX, Apr. 11, 1963. LACC.

MULDAUR, DIANA: NYC, Aug. 19, 1938. Sweet Briar Col.

MULGREW, KATE: Dubuque, IA, Apr. 29, 1955. NYU.

MULHERN, MATT: Philadelphia, PA, July 21, 1960. Rutgers Univ.

MULL, MARTIN: N. Ridgefield, OH, Aug. 18, 1941. RISch. of Design.

MULLIGAN, RICHARD: NYC, Nov. 13, 1932.

MULRONEY, DERMOT: Alexandria, VA, Oct. 31, 1963. Northwestern.

MUMY, BILL (Charles William Mumy Jr.): San Gabriel, CA, Feb. 1, 1954.

MURPHY, EDDIE: Brooklyn, NY, Apr. 3,

Brian Kerwin

Helen Mirren

Aron Kincaid

1961.

MURPHY, MICHAEL: Los Angeles, CA, May 5, 1938. UAz.

MURRAY, BILL: Wilmette, IL, Sept. 21, 1950. Regis Col.

MUSANTE, TONY: Bridgeport, CT, June 30, 1936. Oberlin Col.

NABORS, JIM: Sylacauga, GA, June 12, 1932.

NADER, GEORGE: Pasadena, CA, Oct. 19, 1921. Occidental College.

NADER, MICHAEL: Los Angeles, CA, 1945.

NAMATH, JOE: Beaver Falls, PA, May 31, 1943. UAla.

NATWICK, MILDRED: Baltimore, June 19, 1908. Bryn Mawr.

NAUGHTON, DAVID: Hartford, CT, Feb. 13, 1951.

NAUGHTON, JAMES: Middletown, CT, Dec. 6, 1945.

NEAL, PATRICIA: Packard, KY, Jan. 20, 1926. Northwestern U.

NEESOM, LIAM: Ballymena, Northern Ireland, June 7, 1952.

NEFF, HILDEGARDE (Hildegard Knef): Ulm, Ger., Dec. 28, 1925. Berlin Art Academy.

NEILL, SAM: No. Ireland, 1948. U Canterbury.

NELL, NATHALIE: Paris, Oct. 1950.

NELLIGAN, KATE: London, Ont., Can., Mar. 16, 1951. U Toronto.

NELSON, BARRY (Robert Nielsen): Oakland, CA, Apr. 16, 1920.

NELSON, CRAIG T.: Spokane, WA, Apr. 4, 1946.

NELSON, GENE (Gene Berg): Seattle, WA, Mar. 24, 1920.

NELSON, HARRIET HILLIARD (Peggy Lou Snyder): Des Moines, IA, July 18, 1914.

NELSON, JUDD: Portland, ME, Nov. 28, 1959. Haverford Col.

NELSON, LORI (Dixie Kay Nelson): Santa Fe, NM, Aug. 15, 1933.

NELSON, TRACY: Santa Monica, CA, Oct. 25, 1963.

NELSON, WILLIE: Abbott, TX, Apr. 30, 1933.

NEMEC, CORIN: Little Rock, AK, Nov. 5, 1971.

NERO, FRANCO: Parma, Italy, 1941.

NETTLETON, LOIS: Oak Park, IL. Actors Studio.

NEWHART, BOB: Chicago, IL, Sept. 5, 1929. Loyola U.

NEWLEY, ANTHONY: Hackney, London, Sept. 24, 1931.

NEWMAN, BARRY: Boston, MA, Nov. 7, 1938. Brandeis U.

NEWMAN, NANETTE: Northampton, Eng., 1934.

NEWMAN, PAUL: Cleveland, OH. Jan. 26, 1925. Yale.

NEWMAR, JULIE (Newmeyer): Los Angeles, Aug. 16, 1933.

NEWTON-JOHN, OLIVIA: Cambridge, Eng., Sept. 26, 1948.

NGUYEN, DUSTIN: Saigon, 1962.

NICHOLAS, PAUL: London, 1945.

NICHOLSON, JACK: Neptune, NJ, Apr. 22, 1937.

NICKERSON, DENISE: NYC, 1959.

NICOL, ALEX: Ossining, NY, Jan. 20, 1919. Actors Studio.

NIELSEN, BRIGITTE: Denmark, July 15, 1963.

NIELSEN, LESLIE: Regina, Saskatchewan. Can., Feb. 11, 1926. Neighborhood Playhouse.

NIMOY, LEONARD: Boston, MA, Mar. 26, 1931. Boston Col., Antioch Col.

NIXON, CYNTHIA: NYC, Apr. 9, 1966. Columbia U.

NOBLE, JAMES: Dallas, TX, Mar. 5, 1922, SMU.

NOIRET, PHILIPPE: France, Oct. 1, 1930.

NOLAN, KATHLEEN: St. Louis, MO, Sept. 27, 1933. Neighborhood Playhouse.

NOLTE, NICK: Omaha, NE, Feb. 8, 1940. Pasadena City Col.

NORRIS, CHRISTOPHER: NYC, Oct. 7, 1943. Lincoln Square Acad.

NORRIS, CHUCK (Carlos Ray): Ryan,OK. Mar. 10, 1940.

NORTH, HEATHER: Pasadena, CA, Dec. 13, 1950. Actors Workshop.

NORTH, SHEREE (Dawn Bethel): Los Angeles. Jan. 17, 1933. Hollywood High

NORTON, KEN: Jacksonville, Il, Aug. 9, 1945.

NOURI, MICHAEL: Washington, DC, Dec. 9, 1945.

NOVAK, KIM (Marilyn Novak): Chicago, Feb. 13, 1933. LACC.

NUYEN, FRANCE (Vannga): Marseilles, France, July 31, 1939. Beaux Arts School.

O'BRIAN, HUGH (Hugh J. Krampe): Rochester, NY. Apr. 19, 1928. Cincinnati U.

O'BRIEN, CLAY: Ray, AZ, May 6, 1961.

O'BRIEN, MARGARET (Angela Maxine O'Brien): Los Angeles, Jan. 15, 1937.

O'CONNOR, CARROLL: Bronx, NY, Aug. 2, 1924. Dublin National Univ.

O'CONNOR, DONALD: Chicago, Aug. 28, 1925.

O'CONNOR, GLYNNIS: NYC, Nov. 19, 1955. NYSU.

O'DONNELL, CHRIS: Winetka, IL, 1970.

O'HARA, CATHERINE: Toronto, Can., Mar. 4, 1954.

O'HARA, MAUREEN (Maureen Fitz-Simons): Dublin, Ire., Aug. 17, 1920. Abbey School.

O'HERLIHY, DAN: Wexford, Ire., May 1, 1919. National U.

O'KEEFE, MICHAEL: Paulland, NJ, Apr. 24, 1955. NYU, AADA.

OLDMAN, GARY: New Cross, South London, Eng., Mar. 21, 1958.

OLIN, LENA: Stockholm, Sweden, 1955.

OLMOS, EDWARD JAMES: Los Angeles, Feb. 24, 1947. CSLA.

O'LOUGHLIN, GERALD S.: NYC, Dec. 23, 1921. U. Rochester.

OLSON, JAMES: Evanston, IL, Oct. 8, 1930.

OLSON, NANCY: Milwaukee, WI, July 14, 1928. UCLA.

O'NEAL, GRIFFIN: Los Angeles, 1965.

O'NEAL, PATRICK: Ocala, FL, Sept. 26, 1927. U. Fla.

O'NEAL, RON: Utica, NY, Sept. 1, 1937. Ohio State.

O'NEAL, RYAN: Los Angeles, Apr. 20, 1941.

O'NEAL, TATUM: Los Angeles, Nov. 5, 1963.

O'NEIL, TRICIA: Shreveport, LA, Mar. 11, 1945. Baylor U.

O'NEILL, ED: Youngstown, OH, 1946.

O'NEILL, JENNIFER: Rio de Janeiro, Feb. 20, 1949. Neighborhood Playhouse.

ONTKEAN, MICHAEL: Vancouver, B.C., Can., Jan. 24, 1946.

ORBACH, JERRY: Bronx, NY, Oct. 20, 1935.

O'SHEA, MILO: Dublin, Ire., June 2, 1926.

O'SULLIVAN, MAUREEN: Byle, Ire., May 17, 1911. Sacred Heart Convent.

O'TOOLE, ANNETTE (Toole): Houston, TX, Apr. 1, 1953. UCLA.

O'TOOLE, PETER: Connemara, Ire., Aug. 2, 1932. RADA.

John Larroquette

Dolly Parton

Spike Lee

OVERALL, PARK: Nashville, TN, Mar. 15, 1957. Tusculum Col.

OZ, FRANK (Oznowicz): Hereford, Eng., May 25, 1944.

PACINO, AL: NYC, Apr. 25, 1940.

PACULA, JOANNA: Tamaszow Lubelski, Poland, Jan. 2, 1957. Polish Natl. Theatre Sch.

PAGE, TONY (Anthony Vitiello): Bronx, NY, 1940.

PAGET, DEBRA (Debralee Griffin): Den-ver, Aug. 19, 1933.

PAIGE, JANIS (Donna Mae Jaden): Taco-ma. WA, Sept. 16, 1922.

PALANCE, JACK (Walter Palanuik): Lat-timer, PA, Feb. 18, 1920. UNC.

PALIN, MICHAEL: Sheffield, Yorkshire, Eng., May 5, 1943, Oxford.

PALMER, BETSY: East Chicago, IN, Nov. 1, 1926. DePaul U.

PALMER, GREGG (Palmer Lee): San Francisco, Jan. 25, 1927. U. Utah.

PAMPANINI, SILVANA: Rome, Sept. 25, 1925.

PANEBIANCO, RICHARD: NYC, 1971.

PANKIN, STUART: Philadelphia, Apr. 8, 1946.

PANTALIANO, JOE: Jersey City, NJ, Sept. 12, 1954.

PAPAS, IRENE: Chiliomodion, Greece, Mar. 9, 1929.

PARE, MICHAEL: Brooklyn, NY, Oct. 9, 1959.

PARKER, COREY: NYC, July 8, 1965. NYU.

PARKER, ELEANOR: Cedarville, OH, June 26, 1922. Pasadena Playhouse.

PARKER, FESS: Fort Worth, TX, Aug. 16, 1925. USC.

PARKER, JAMESON: Baltimore, MD, Nov. l8, 1947. Beloit Col.

PARKER, JEAN (Mae Green): Deer Lodge, MT, Aug. 11, 1912.

PARKER, MARY-LOUISE: Ft. Jackson, SC, Aug. 2, 1964. Bard Col.

PARKER, NATHANIEL: London, 1963.

PARKER, SARAH JESSICA: Nelsonville, OH, Mar. 25, 1965.

PARKER, SUZY (Cecelia Parker): San Antonio, TX, Oct. 28, 1933.

PARKER, TREY: Auburn, AL, May 30, 1972.

PARKER, WILLARD (Worster Van Eps): NYC, Feb. 5, 1912.

PARKINS, BARBARA: Vancouver, Can., May 22, 1943.

PARKS, MICHAEL: Corona, CA, Apr. 4, 1938.

PARSONS, ESTELLE: Lynn, MA, Nov. 20, 1927. Boston U.

PARTON, DOLLY: Sevierville, TN, Jan. 19, 1946.

PATINKIN, MANDY: Chicago, IL, Nov. 30, 1952. Juilliard.

PATRIC, JASON: NYC, 1966.

PATRICK, DENNIS: Philadelphia, Mar. 14, 1918.

PATTERSON, LEE: Vancouver, Can., Mar. 31, 1929. Ontario Col.

PATTON, WILL: Charleston, SC, June 14, 1954.

PAVAN, MARISA (Marisa Pierangeli): Cagliari, Sardinia, June 19, 1932. Torquado Tasso College.

PAXTON, BILL: Fort Worth, TX, May. 17, 1955.

PAYS, AMANDA: Berkshire, Eng., June 6, 1959.

PEACH, MARY: Durbn, S. Africa, 1934.

PEARL, MINNIE (Sarah Cannon): Centerville, TN, Oct. 25, 1912.

PEARSON, BEATRICE: Dennison, TX, July 27, 1920.

Rob Lowe

Mary Kay Place

Ralph Macchio

Martha Plimpton

27, 1920.

PECK, GREGORY: La Jolla, CA, Apr. 5, 1916. U. Calif.

PEÑA, ELIZABETH: Cuba, Sept. 23, 1961.

PENDLETON, AUSTIN: Warren, OH, Mar. 27, 1940. Yale U.

PENHALL, BRUCE: Balboa, CA, Aug. 17, 1960.

PENN, SEAN: Burbank, CA, Aug. 17, 1960.

PEPPARD, GEORGE: Detroit, Oct. 1, 1928. Carnegie Tech.

PEREZ, JOSE: NYC, 1940.

PERKINS, ELIZABETH: Queens, NY, Nov. 18, 1960. Goodman School.

PERKINS, MILLIE: Passaic, NJ, May 12, 1938.

PERLMAN, RHEA: Brooklyn, NY, Mar. 31, 1948.

PERLMAN, RON: NYC, Apr. 13, 1950. UMn.

PERREAU, GIGI (Ghislaine): Los Angeles, Feb. 6, 1941.

PERRINE, VALERIE: Galveston, TX, Sept. 3, 1943. U. Ariz

PERRY, LUKE (Coy Luther Perry III): Fredricktown, OH, Oct. 11, 1966

PESCI, JOE: Newark, NJ. Feb. 9, 1943.

PESCOW, DONNA: Brooklyn, NY, Mar. 24, 1954.

PETERS, BERNADETTE (Lazzara): Jamaica, NY, Feb. 28, 1948.

PETERS, BROCK: NYC, July 2, 1927. CCNY.

PETERS. JEAN (Elizabeth): Caton, OH, Oct. 15, 1926. Ohio State U.

PETERS, MICHAEL: Brooklyn, NY, 1948.

PETERSEN, WILLIAM: Chicago, IL, 1953.

PETERSON, CASSANDRA: Colorado Springs, CO, Sept. 17, 1951.

PETTET, JOANNA: London, Nov. 16, 1944. Neighborhood Playhouse.

PFEIFFER, MICHELLE: Santa Ana, CA, Apr. 29, 1958.

PHILLIPS, LOU DIAMOND: Phillipines, Feb. 17, 1962, UTx.

PHILLIPS, MacKENZIE: Alexandria, VA, Nov. 10, 1959.

PHILLIPS, MICHELLE (Holly Gilliam): Long Beach, CA, June 4, 1944.

PHOENIX, RIVER: Madras, OR, Aug. 24,

1970.

PICARDO, ROBERT: Philadelphia, PA, Oct. 27, 1953. Yale.

PICERNI, PAUL: NYC, Dec. 1, 1922. Loyola U.

PINCHOT, BRONSON: NYC, May 20, 1959. Yale.

PINE, PHILLIP: Hanford, CA, July 16, 1925. Actors' Lab.

PISCOPO, JOE: Passaic. NJ, June 17, 1951.

PISIER, MARIE-FRANCE: Vietnam, May 10, 1944. U. Paris.

PITILLO, MARIA: Mahwah, NJ, 1965.

PITT, BRAD: Shawnee, OK, Dec. 18, 1963.

PLACE, MARY KAY: Tulsa OK, Sept. 23, 1947. U. Tulsa.

PLAYTEN, ALICE: NYC, Aug. 28, 1947. NYU.

PLEASENCE, DONALD: Workshop, Eng., Oct. 5, 1919. Sheffield School.

PLESHETTE, SUZANNE: NYC, Jan. 31, 1937. Syracuse U.

PLOWRIGHT, JOAN: Scunthorpe, Brigg, Lincolnshire, Eng., Oct. 28, 1929. Old Vic.

PLUMB, EVE: Burbank, CA, Apr. 29, 1958.

PLUMMER, AMANDA: NYC, Mar. 23, 1957. Middlebury Col.

PLUMMER, CHRISTOPHER: Toronto, Can., Dec. 13, 1927.

PODESTA, ROSSANA: Tripoli, June 20, 1934.

POITIER, SIDNEY: Miami, FL, Feb. 27, 1927.

POLITO, JON: Philadelphia, PA, Dec. 29, 1950. Villanova U.

POLITO, LINA: Naples, Italy, Aug. 11, 1954.

POLLAN, TRACY: NYC, 1960.

POLLARD, MICHAEL J.: Passaic, NJ, May 30, 1939.

PORTER, ERIC: London, Apr. 8, 1928. Wimbledon Col.

POTTS, ANNIE: Nashville, TN, Oct. 28, 1952. Stephens Col.

POWELL, JANE (Suzanne Burce): Port-land, OR, Apr. 1, 1928.

POWELL, ROBERT: Salford, Eng., June 1, 1944. Manchester U.

POWER, TARYN: Los Angeles, CA, 1954.

POWER, TYRONE IV: Los Angeles, CA,

Jan. 1959.

POWERS, MALA (Mary. Ellen): San Francisco, Dec. 29, 1921. UCLA.

POWERS, STEFANIE (Federkiewicz): Hollywood, CA, Oct. 12, 1942.

PRENTISS, PAULA (Paula Ragusa): San Antonio, TX, Mar. 4, 1939. Northwestern U.

PRESLE, MICHELINE (Micheline Chassagne): Paris, Aug. 22, 1922. Rouleau Drama School.

PRESLEY, PRISCILLA: Brooklyn, NY, May 24, 1945.

PRESNELL, HARVE: Modesto, CA, Sept. 14, 1933. USC.

PRESTON, KELLY: Honolulu, HI, Oct. 13, 1962. USC.

PRESTON, WILLIAM: Columbia, PA, Aug. 26, 1921. PaStateU.

PRICE, LONNY: NYC, Mar. 9, 1959. Juilliard.

PRIESTLEY, JASON: Vancouver, Canada, Aug, 28, 1969

PRIMUS, BARRY: NYC, Feb. 16, 1938. CCNY.

PRINCE (P. Rogers Nelson): Minneapolis, MN, June 7, 1958.

PRINCE, WILLIAM: Nicholas, NY, Jan. 26, 1913. Cornell U.

PRINCIPAL, VICTORIA: Fukuoka. Japan, Jan. 3, 1945. Dade Jr. Col.

PROCHNOW, JURGEN: Germany, 1941.

PROSKY, ROBERT: Philadelphia, PA, Dec. 13, 1930.

PROVAL, DAVID: Brooklyn, NY, 1943.

PROVINE, DOROTHY: Deadwood, SD, Jan. 20, 1937. U. Wash.

PROWSE, JULIET: Bombay, India, Sept. 25, 1936.

PRYCE, JONATHAN: Wales, UK, June 1, 1947, RADA.

PRYOR, RICHARD: Peoria, IL, Dec. 1, 1940.

PULLMAN, BILL: Delphi, NY, 1954, SUNY/Oneonta, UMass.

PURCELL, LEE: Cherry Point, NC, June 15, 1947. Stephens.

PURDOM, EDMUND: Welwyn Garden City, Eng., Dec. 19, 1924. St. Ignatius College.

PYLE, DENVER: Bethune, CO, May 11,

Steve Martin

1920.

QUAID, DENNIS: Houston, TX, Apr. 9, 1954.
QUAID, RANDY: Houston, TX, Oct. 1, 1950. UHouston.
QUINLAN, KATHLEEN: Mill Valley, CA, Nov. 19, 1954.
QUINN, AIDAN: Chicago, IL, Mar. 8, 1959.
QUINN, ANTHONY: Chihuahua, Mex., Apr. 21, 1915.
RAFFERTY, FRANCES: Sioux City, IA, June 16, 1922. UCLA.
RAFFIN, DEBORAH: Los Angeles, Mar. 13, 1953. Valley Col.
RAGSDALE, WILLIAM: El Dorado, AK, Jan. 19, 1961. Hendrix Col.
RAINER, LUISE: Vienna, Aust., Jan. 12, 1910.
RALSTON, VERA: (Vera Helena Hruba): Prague, Czech., July 12, 1919.
RAMPLING, CHARLOTTE: Surmer, Eng., Feb. 5, 1946. U. Madrid.
RAMSEY, LOGAN: Long Beach, CA, Mar. 21, 1921. St. Joseph.
RANDALL, TONY (Leonard Rosenberg): Tulsa, OK, Feb. 26, 1920. Northwestern U.
RANDELL, RON: Sydney, Australia, Oct. 8, 1920. St. Mary's Col.
RASCHE, DAVID: St. Louis, MO, Aug. 7, 1944.
RAYE, MARTHA (Margie Yvonne Reed): Butte, MT, Aug. 27, 1916.
RAYMOND, GENE (Raymond Guion): NYC, Aug. 13, 1908.
REAGAN, RONALD: Tampico, IL, Feb. 6, 1911. Eureka College.

REASON, REX: Berlin, Ger., Nov. 30, 1928. Pasadena Playhouse.
REDDY, HELEN: Australia, Oct. 25, 1942.
REDFORD, ROBERT: Santa Monica, CA, Aug. 18, 1937. AADA.
REDGRAVE, CORIN: London, July 16, 1939.
REDGRAVE, LYNN: London, Mar. 8, 1943.
REDGRAVE, VANESSA: London, Jan. 30, 1937.
REDMAN, JOYCE: County Mayo, Ire., 1919. RADA.
REED, OLIVER: Wimbledon, Eng., Feb. 13, 1938.
REED, PAMELA: Tacoma, WA, Apr. 2, 1949.
REEMS, HARRY (Herbert Streicher): Bronx, NY, 1947. U. Pittsburgh.
REEVE, CHRISTOPHER: NYC, Sept. 25, 1952. Cornell, Juilliard.
REEVES, KEANU: Beiruit, Lebanon, Sept. 2, 1964.
REEVES, STEVE: Glasgow, MT, Jan. 21, 1926.
REGEHR, DUNCAN: Lethbridge, Can., 1954.
REID, ELLIOTT: NYC, Jan. 16, 1920.
REID, TIM: Norfolk, VA, Dec, 19, 1944
REINER, CARL: NYC, Mar. 20, 1922. Georgetown.
REINER, ROB: NYC, Mar. 6, 1945. UCLA.
REINHOLD, JUDGE (Edward Ernest, Jr.): Wilmington, DE, 1956. NCSchool of Arts.
REINKING, ANN: Seattle, WA, Nov. 10, 1949.
REISER, PAUL: NYC, Mar. 30, 1957.
REMAR, JAMES: Boston, MA, Dec. 31, 1953. Neighborhood Playhouse.
RETTIG, TOMMY: Jackson Heights, NY, Dec. 10, 1941.
REVILL, CLIVE: Wellington, NZ, Apr. 18, 1930.
REY, ANTONIA: Havana, Cuba, Oct. 12, 1927.
REY, FERNANDO: La Coruna, Spain, Sept. 20, 1917.
REYNOLDS, BURT: Waycross, GA, Feb. 11, 1935. Fla. State U.
REYNOLDS, DEBBIE (Mary Frances Reynolds): El Paso, TX, Apr. 1, 1932.
REYNOLDS, MARJORIE: Buhl, ID, Aug. 12, 1921.
RHOADES, BARBARA: Poughkeepsie, NY, 1947.
RHYS-DAVIES, JOHN: Salisbury, Eng.,.May 5, 1944.
RICHARDSON, LEE: Chicago, Sept. 11, 1926.
RICHARDSON, NATASHA: London, May 11, 1963.
RICKLES, DON: NYC, May 8, 1926. AADA.
RICKMAN, ALAN: Hammersmith, Eng., 1946.
RIEGERT, PETER: NYC, Apr. 11, 1947. U Buffalo.
RIGG, DIANA: Doncaster, Eng., July 20, 1938. RADA.
RINGWALD, MOLLY: Rosewood, CA. Feb. 16, 1968.
RITTER, JOHN: Burbank, CA, Sept. 17, 1948. U.S. Cal.
RIVERS, JOAN (Molinsky): Brooklyn, NY, June 8, 1933.
ROBARDS, JASON: Chicago, July 26, 1922. AADA.
ROBBINS, TIM: NYC, Oct. 16, 1958. UCLA.
ROBERTS, ERIC: Biloxi, MS, Apr. 18, 1956. RADA.
ROBERTS, JULIA: Atlanta, GA, Oct. 28, 1967.
ROBERTS, RALPH: Salisbury, NC, Aug. 17, 1922. UNC.
ROBERTS, TANYA (Leigh): NYC, 1955.
ROBERTS, TONY: NYC, Oct. 22, 1939. Northwestern U.

Kelly Preston

ROBERTSON, CLIFF: La Jolla, CA,Sept. 9, 1925. Antioch Col.
ROBERTSON, DALE: Oklahoma City, July 14, 1923.
ROBINSON, CHRIS: West Palm Beach, FL, Nov. 5, 1938. LACC.
ROBINSON, JAY: NYC, Apr. 14, 1930.
ROBINSON, ROGER: Seattle, WA, May 2, 1941. USC.
ROCHEFORT, JEAN: Paris, 1930.
ROCK-SAVAGE, STEVEN: Melville, LA, Dec. 14, 1958. LSU.
ROGERS, CHARLES "BUDDY": Olathe, KS, Aug. 13, 1904. U. Kan.
ROGERS, GINGER (Virginia Katherine McMath): Independence, MO, July 16, 1911.
ROGERS, MIMI: Coral Gables, FL, Jan. 27, 1956.
ROGERS, ROY (Leonard Slye): Cincinnati, Nov. 5, 1912.
ROGERS, WAYNE: Birmingham, AL, Apr. 7, 1933. Princeton.
ROLAND, GILBERT (Luis Antonio Damaso De Alonso): Juarez, Mex., Dec. 11, 1905.
ROLLE, ESTHER: Pompano Beach, FL, Nov. 8, 1922.
ROLLINS, HOWARD E., JR.: Baltimore, MD. Oct. 17, 1950.
ROMAN, RUTH: Boston, Dec. 23, 1922. Bishop Lee Dramatic School.
ROMERO, CESAR: NYC, Feb. 15, 1907. Collegiate School.

Tracy Pollan

Dudley Moore

1946.

ROOKER, MICHAEL: Jasper, AL, 1955.

ROONEY, MICKEY (Joe Yule, Jr.): Brooklyn, Sept. 23, 1920.

ROSE, REVA: Chicago, IL, July 30, 1940. Goodman.

ROSS, DIANA: Detroit, MI, Mar. 26, 1944.

ROSS, JUSTIN: Brooklyn, NY, Dec. 15, 1954.

ROSS, KATHARINE: Hollywood, Jan. 29, 1943. Santa Rosa Col.

ROSSELLINI, ISABELLA: Rome, June 18, 1952.

ROSSOVICH, RICK: Palo Alto, CA, Aug. 28, 1957.

ROUNDTREE, RICHARD: New Ro-chelle, NY, Sept. 7, 1942. Southern Ill.

ROURKE, MICKEY: Schenectady, NY, 1956.

ROWE, NICHOLAS: London, Nov. 22, 1966, Eton.

ROWLANDS, GENA: Cambria, WI, June 19, 1934.

RUBIN, ANDREW: New Bedford, MA, June 22, 1946. AADA.

RUBINSTEIN, JOHN: Los Angeles, CA, Dec. 8, 1946. UCLA.

RUBINSTEIN, ZELDA: Pittsburgh, PA.

RUCKER, BO: Tampa, FL, Aug. 17, 1948.

RUDD, PAUL: Boston, MA, May 15, 1940.

RULE, JANICE: Cincinnati, OH, Aug. 15, 1931.

RUPERT, MICHAEL: Denver, CO, Oct. 23, 1951. Pasadena Playhouse.

RUSH, BARBARA: Denver, CO, Jan. 4, 1929. U. Calif.

RUSSELL, JANE: Bemidji, MI, June 21, 1921. Max Reinhardt School.

RUSSELL, KURT: Springfield, MA, Mar. 17, 1951.

RUSSELL, THERESA: San Diego, CA, Mar. 20, 1957.

RUSSO, JAMES: NYC, Apr. 23, 1953.

RUTHERFORD, ANN: Toronto, Can., Nov. 2, 1920.

RUYMEN, AYN: Brooklyn, July 18, 1947. HB Studio.

RYAN, MEG: Fairfield, CT, Nov. 19, 1961. NYU.

RYAN, TIM (Meineslschmidt): Staten Island, NY, 1958. Rutgers U.

RYDER, WINONA: Winona, MN, Oct. 29, 1971.

SACCHI, ROBERT: Bronx, NY, 1941. NYU.

SÄGEBRECHT, MARIANNE: Starnberg, Bavaria, 1945.

SAINT, EVA MARIE: Newark, NJ, July 4, 1924. Bowling Green State U.

ST. JAMES, SUSAN (Suzie Jane Miller): Los Angeles, Aug. 14, 1946. Conn. Col.

ST. JOHN, BETTA: Hawthorne, CA, Nov. 26, 1929.

ST. JOHN, JILL (Jill Oppenheim): Los Angeles, Aug. 19, 1940.

SALA, JOHN: Los Angeles, CA, Oct. 5, 1962.

SALDANA, THERESA: Brooklyn, NY, Aug. 20, 1954.

SALINGER, MATT: Windsor, VT, Feb. 13, 1960. Princeton, Columbia.

SALT, JENNIFER: Los Angeles, Sept. 4, 1944. Sarah Lawrence Col.

SAMMS, EMMA: London, Aug. 28, 1960.

SAN GIACOMO, LAURA: NJ, 1962.

SANDERS, JAY O.: Austin, TX, Apr. 16, 1953.

SANDS, JULIAN: Yorkshire, Eng., 1958.

SANDS, TOMMY: Chicago, Aug. 27, 1937.

SAN JUAN, OLGA: NYC, Mar. 16, 1927.

SARA, MIA: Brooklyn, NY, 1968.

SARANDON, CHRIS: Beckley, WV, July 24, 1942. U. WVa., Catholic U.

SARANDON, SUSAN (Tomalin): NYC, Oct. 4, 1946. Catholic U.

SARGENT, DICK (Richard Cox): Carmel, CA, 1933. Stanford.

SARRAZIN, MICHAEL: Quebec City, Can., May 22, 1940.

SAVAGE, FRED: Highland Park, IL, July 9, 1976.

SAVAGE, JOHN (Youngs): Long Island, NY, Aug. 25, 1949. AADA.

SAVALAS, TELLY (Aristotle): Garden City, NY, Jan. 21, 1925. Columbia.

SAVIOLA, CAMILLE: Bronx, NY, July 16, 1950.

SAVOY, TERESA ANN: London, July 18, 1955.

SAXON, JOHN (Carmen Orrico): Brook-lyn, Aug. 5, 1935.

SBARGE, RAPHAEL: NYC, Feb. 12,

1964.

SCALIA, JACK: Brooklyn, NY, 1951.

SCARPELLI, GLEN: Staten Island, NY, July 1966.

SCARWID, DIANA: Savannah, GA. AADA. Pace U.

SCHEIDER, ROY: Orange, NJ, Nov. 10, 1932. Franklin-Marshall.

SCHEINE, RAYNOR: Emporia, VA, Nov. 10. VaCommonwcalthU.

SCHELL, MARIA: Vienna, Jan. 15, 1926.

SCHELL, MAXIMILIAN: Vienna, Dec. 8, 1930.

SCHLATTER, CHARLIE: NYC, 1967. Ithaca Col.

SCHNEIDER, JOHN: Mt. Kisco, NY, Apr. 8, 1960.

SCHNEIDER, MARIA: Paris, Mar. 27, 1952.

SCHRODER, RICK: Staten Island, NY, Apr. 13, 1970.

SCHUCK, JOHN: Boston, MA, Feb. 4, 1940.

SCHWARZENEGGER, ARNOLD: Austria, July 30, 1947.

SCHYGULLA, HANNA: Katlowitz, Poland, 1943.

SCIORRA, ANNABELLA: NYC, 1964.

SCOFIELD, PAUL: Hurstpierpoint, Eng., Jan. 21,1922. London Mask Theatre School.

SCOLARI, PETER: Scarsdale, NY, Sept. 12, 1956. NYCC.

SCOTT, CAMPBELL: NYC, July 19, 1962. Lawrence.

SCOTT, DEBRALEE: Elizabeth, NJ, Apr. 2.

SCOTT, GEORGE C.: Wise, VA, Oct. 18, 1927. U. Mo.

SCOTT, GORDON (Gordon M. Werschkul): Portland, OR, Aug. 3, 1927. Oregon U.

SCOTT, LIZABETH (Emma Matso): Scranton, PA, Sept. 29, 1922.

SCOTT, MARTHA: Jamesport, MO, Sept. 22, 1914. U. Mich.

SCOTT-TAYLOR, JONATHAN: Brazil, 1962.

SEAGAL, STEVEN: Detroit, MI, Apr. 10, 1951.

SEARS, HEATHER: London, Sept. 28, 1935.

SECOMBE, HARRY: Swansea, Wales, Sept. 8, 1921.

Roger Moore   Debbie Reynolds   Craig T. Nelson   Joely Richardson

Leonard Nimoy   Miranda Richardson   Phillipe Noiret   Molly Ringwald

8, 1921.

SEGAL, GEORGE: NYC, Feb. 13, 1934. Columbia.

SELBY, DAVID: Morganstown, WV, Feb. 5, 1941. UWV.

SELLARS, ELIZABETH: Glasgow, Scot., May 6, 1923.

SELLECK, TOM: Detroit, MI, Jan. 29, 1945. USCal.

SERNAS, JACQUES: Lithuania, July 30, 1925.

SERRAULT, MICHEL: Brunoy, France. 1928. Paris Consv.

SETH, ROSHAN: New Delhi, India. 1942.

SEYMOUR, JANE (Joyce Frankenberg): Hillingdon, Eng., Feb. 15, 1952.

SHARIF, OMAR (Michel Shalhoub); Alexandria, Egypt, Apr. 10, 1932. Victoria Col.

SHANDLING, GARRY: Chicago, Il, Nov. 29, 1949.

SHATNER, WILLIAM: Montreal, Can., Mar. 22, 1931. McGill U.

SHAVER, HELEN: St. Thomas, Ontario, Can., Feb. 24, 1951.

SHAW, SEBASTIAN: Holt, Eng., May, 1905. Gresham School.

SHAW, STAN: Chicago, IL, 1952.

SHAWN, WALLACE: NYC, Nov. 12, 1943. Harvard.

SHEA, JOHN: North Conway, NH, Apr. 14, 1949. Bates, Yale.

SHEARER, HARRY: Los Angeles, Dec. 23, 1943. UCLA.

SHEARER, MOIRA: Dunfermline, Scot., Jan. 17, 1926. London Theatre School.

SHEEDY, ALLY: NYC, June 13, 1962. USC.

SHEEN, CHARLIE (Carlos Irwin Estevez): Santa Monica, CA, Sept. 3, 1965.

SHEEN, MARTIN (Ramon Estevez): Dayton, OH, Aug. 3, 1940.

SHEFFIELD, JOHN: Pasadena, CA, Apr.11, 1931. UCLA.

SHELLEY, CAROL: London, Eng., Aug,.16, 1939

SHEPARD, SAM (Rogers): Ft. Sheridan, IL, Nov. 5, 1943.

SHEPHERD, CYBILL: Memphis, TN, Feb. 18, 1950. Hunter, NYU.

SHERIDAN, JAMEY: Pasadena, CA, July 12, 1951

SHIELDS, BROOKE: NYC, May 31, 1965.

SHIRE, TALIA: Lake Success, NY, Apr. 25,

1946. Yale.

SHORE, DINAH (Frances Rose Shore): Winchester, TN, Mar. 1, 1917. Vanderbilt U.

SHORT, MARTIN: Toronto, Can., Mar. 26, 1950. McMasterU.

SHOWALTER, MAX (formerly Casey Adams): Caldwell, KS, June 2, 1917. Pasadena Playhouse.

SHULL, RICHARD B.: Evanston, IL, Feb. 24, 1929.

SIDNEY, SYLVIA: NYC, Aug. 8, 1910. Theatre Guild School.

SIEMASZKO, CASEY: Chicago, IL, March 17, 1961.

SIKKING, JAMES B.: Los Angeles, Mar. 5, 1934.

SILVER, RON: NYC, July 2, 1946. SUNY.

SILVERMAN, JONATHAN: Los Angeles, CA, Aug. 5, 1966. USCal.

SIMMONS, JEAN: London, Jan. 31, 1929. Aida Foster School.

SIMON, PAUL: Newark. NJ, Nov. 5, 1942.

SIMON, SIMONE: Marseilles, France, Apr. 23, 1910.

SIMPSON, O.J. (Orenthal James): San Francisco, CA, July 9, 1947. UCLA.

SINATRA, FRANK: Hoboken, NJ, Dec. 12, 1915.

SINCLAIR, JOHN (Gianluigi Loffredo): Rome, Italy, 1946.

SINCLAIR, MADGE: Kingston, Jamaica, Apr. 28, 1938

SINDEN, DONALD: Plymouth, Eng., Oct. 9, 1923. Webber-Douglas.

SINGER, LORI: Corpus Christi, TX, May 6, 1962. Juilliard.

SKALA, LILIA: Vienna. U. Dresden.

SKELTON, RED (Richard): Vincennes, IN, July 18, 1910.

SKERRITT, TOM: Detroit, MI, Aug. 25, 1933. Wayne State U.

SKYE, IONE (Leitch): London, Eng., Sept. 4, 1971.

SLATER, CHRISTIAN: NYC, Aug. 18, 1969.

SLATER, HELEN: NYC, Dec. 15, 1965.

SMIRNOFF, YAKOV (Yakov Pokhis): Odessa, Russia, Jan. 24. 1951.

SMITH, CHARLES MARTIN: Los Angeles, CA, Oct. 30, 1953. CalState U.

SMITH, JACLYN: Houston, TX, Oct. 26, 1947.

SMITH, JOHN (Robert E. Van Orden): Los Angeles, Mar. 6, 1931. UCLA.

SMITH, KURTWOOD: New Lisbon, WI, Jul. 3, 1942.

SMITH, LEWIS: Chattanooga, TN, 1958. Actors Studio.

SMITH, LOIS: Topeka, KS, Nov. 3, 1930. U. Wash.

SMITH, MAGGIE: Ilford, Eng., Dec. 28, 1934.

SMITH, ROGER: South Gate, CA, Dec. 18, 1932. U. Ariz.

SMITHERS, WILLIAM: Richmond, VA, July 10, 1927. Catholic U.

SMITS, JIMMY: Brooklyn, July 9, 1955. Cornell U.

SNIPES, WESLEY: NYC, July 31, 1963. SUNY/Purchase.

SNODGRESS, CARRIE: Chicago, Oct. 27, 1946. UNI.

SOLOMON, BRUCE: NYC, 1944. U. Miami, Wayne State U.

SOMERS, SUZANNE (Mahoney): San Bruno, CA, Oct. 16, 1946. Lone Mt. Col.

SOMMER, ELKE (Schletz): Berlin, Ger., Nov. 5, 1940.

SOMMER, JOSEF: Greifswald, Ger., June 26, 1934.

SORDI, ALBERTO: Rome, Italy, June 15, 1919.

SORVINO, PAUL: NYC, 1939. AMDA.

SOTHERN, ANN (Harriet Lake): Chicago, IL, Aug. 28, 1943.

SOTO, TALISA: Brooklyn, 1968.

SOUL, DAVID: Chicago, IL, Aug. 28, 1943.

SPACEK, SISSY: Quitman, TX, Dec. 25, 1949. Actors Studio.

SPACEY, KEVIN: So. Orange, NJ, July 26, 1959. Juilliard.

SPADER, JAMES: MA, Feb. 7, 1960.

SPANO, VINCENT: Brooklyn, NY, Oct. 18, 1962.

SPENSER, JEREMY: Ceylon, 1937.

SPRINGFIELD, RICK (Richard Spring Thorpe): Sydney, Aust., Aug. 23, 1949.

STACK, ROBERT: Los Angeles, Jan. 13, 1919. USC.

STADLEN, LEWIS J.: Brooklyn, Mar. 7, 1947. Neighborhood Playhouse.

STALLONE, FRANK: NYC, July 30, 1950.

STALLONE, SYLVESTER: NYC, July 6, 1946. U. Miami.

STAMP, TERENCE: London, July 23, 1939.

Carl Reiner

Theresa Saldana

John Ritter

Ione Skye

UNC.

STANG, ARNOLD: Chelsea, MA, Sept. 28, 1925.

STANLEY, KIM (Patricia Reid): Tularosa, NM, Feb. 11, 1925. U. Tex.

STANTON, HARRY DEAN: Lexington, KY, July 14, 1926.

STAPLETON, JEAN: NYC, Jan. 19, 1923.

STAPLETON, MAUREEN: Troy, NY, June 21, 1925.

STARR, RINGO (Richard Starkey): Liverpool, England, July 7, 1940.

STEEL, ANTHONY: London, May 21, 1920. Cambridge.

STEELE, TOMMY: London, Dec. 17, 1936.

STEENBURGEN, MARY: Newport, AR, 1953. Neighborhood Playhouse.

STEIGER, ROD: Westhampton, NY, Apr. 14, 1925.

STERLING, JAN (Jane Sterling Adriance): NYC, Apr. 3, 1923. Fay Compton School.

STERLING, ROBERT (William Sterling Hart): Newcastle, PA, Nov. 13, 1917. U.Pittsburgh.

STERN, DANIEL: Bethesda, MD, Aug. 28, 1957.

STERNHAGEN, FRANCES: Washington, DC, Jan. 13, 1932.

STEVENS, ANDREW: Memphis, TN, June 10, 1955.

STEVENS, CONNIE (Concetta Ann Ingolia): Brooklyn, Aug. 8, 1938. Hollywood Professional School.

STEVENS, FISHER: Chicago, IL, Nov. 27, 1963. NYU.

STEVENS, KAYE (Catherine): Pittsburgh, July 21, 1933.

STEVENS, MARK (Richard): Cleveland, OH, Dec. 13, 1920.

STEVENS, STELLA (Estelle Eggleston): Hot Coffee, MS, Oct. 1, 1936.

STEVENSON, PARKER: Philadelphia, PA, June 4, 1953. Princeton.

STEWART, ALEXANDRA: Montreal, Can., June 10, 1939. Louvre.

STEWART, ELAINE: Montclair, NJ, May 31, 1929

STEWART, JAMES: Indiana, PA, May 20, 1908. Princeton.

STEWART, MARTHA (Martha Haworth): Bardwell, KY, Oct. 7, 1922.

STEWART, PATRICK: Mirfield, Eng., July 13, 1940.

STIERS, DAVID OGDEN: Peoria, IL, Oct. 31, 1942.

STILLER, JERRY: NYC, June 8, 1931.

STIMSON, SARA: Helotes, TX, 1973.

STING (Gordon Matthew Sumner): Wallsend, Eng., Oct. 2, 1951.

STOCKWELL, DEAN: Hollywood, Mar. 5, 1935.

STOCKWELL, JOHN (John Samuels IV): Galveston, Texas, March 25, 1961. Harvard.

STOLER, SHIRLEY: Brooklyn, NY, Mar. 30, 1929.

STOLTZ, ERIC: California, 1961. USC.

STONE, DEE WALLACE (Deanna Bowers): Kansas City, MO, Dec. 14, 1948. UKS.

STORM, GALE (Josephine Cottle): Bloomington, TX, Apr. 5, 1922.

STRAIGHT, BEATRICE: Old Westbury, NY, Aug. 2, 1916. Dartington Hall.

STRASBERG, SUSAN: NYC, May 22, 1938.

STRASSMAN, MARCIA: New Jersey, Apr. 28, 1948.

STRATHAIRN, DAVID: San Francisco, 1949.

STRAUSS, PETER: NYC, Feb. 20, 1947.

STREEP, MERYL (Mary Louise): Summit,.NJ, June 22, 1949. Vassar, Yale.

STREISAND, BARBRA: Brooklyn, Apr. 24, 1942.

STRITCH, ELAINE: Detroit, MI, Feb. 2, 1925. Drama Workshop.

STRODE, WOODY: Los Angeles, 1914.

STROUD, DON: Honolulu, HI, Sept. 1, 1937.

STRUTHERS, SALLY: Portland, OR, July 28, 1948. Pasadena Playhouse.

SULLIVAN, BARRY (Patrick Barry) NYC, Aug. 29, 1912. NYU.

SUMMER, DONNA (LaDonna Gaines): Boston, MA, Dec. 31, 1948.

SUTHERLAND, DONALD: St. John, New Brunswick, Can., July 17, 1935. U.

Toronto.

SUTHERLAND, KIEFER: Los Angeles, CA, Dec. 18, 1966.

SVENSON, BO: Goreborg, Swed., Feb. 1941. UCLA.

SWAYZE, PATRICK: Houston, TX, Aug. 18, 1952.

SWEENEY, D. B. (Daniel Bernard): Shoreham, NY, 1961.

SWINBURNE, NORA: Bath, Eng., July 24, 1902. RADA.

SWIT, LORETTA: Passaic, NJ, Nov. 4, 1937, AADA.

SYLVESTER, WILLIAM: Oakland, CA, Jan. 31, 1922. RADA.

SYMONDS, ROBERT: Bistow, AK, Dec. 1, 1926. TexU.

SYMS, SYLVIA: London, June 1, 1934. Convent School.

SZARABAJKA, KEITH: Oak Park, IL, Dec. 2, 1952. UChicago.

T, MR. (Lawrence Tero): Chicago, May 21, 1952

TABORI, KRISTOFFER (Siegel): Los Angeles, Aug. 4, 1952.

TAKEI, GEORGE: Los Angeles, CA, Apr. 20, 1939. UCLA.

TALBOT, LYLE (Lysle Hollywood): Pittsburgh, Feb. 8, 1904.

TALBOT, NITA: NYC, Aug. 8, 1930. Irvine Studio School.

TAMBLYN, RUSS: Los Angeles, Dec. 30, 1934.

TANDY, JESSICA: London, June 7, 1909. Dame Owens' School.

TAYLOR, DON: Freeport, PA, Dec. 13, 1920. Penn State U.

TAYLOR, ELIZABETH: London, Feb. 27, 1932. Byron House School.

TAYLOR, RENEE: NYC, Mar. 19, 1935.

TAYLOR, ROD (Robert): Sydney, Aust., Jan. 11, 1929.

TAYLOR-YOUNG, LEIGH: Washington, DC, Jan. 25, 1945. Northwestern.

TEAGUE, ANTHONY SCOOTER: Jacksboro, TX, Jan. 4, 1940.

TEAGUE, MARSHALL: Newport, TN.

TEEFY, MAUREEN: Minneapolis, MN, 1954, Juilliard.

John Savage   Meg Tilly   Campbell Scott   Lily Tomlin

1954, Juilliard.

TEMPLE, SHIRLEY: Santa Monica, CA, Apr. 23, 1927.

TENNANT, VICTORIA: London, Eng., Sept. 30, 1950.

TERZIEFF, LAURENT: Paris, June 25, 1935.

TEWES, LAUREN: Pennsylvania, 1954.

THACKER, RUSS: Washington, DC, June 23, 1946. Montgomery Col.

THAXTER, PHYLLIS: Portland, ME, Nov. 20, 1921. St. Genevieve.

THELEN, JODI: St. Cloud, MN, 1963.

THOMAS, HENRY: San Antonio, TX, Sept. 8, 1971.

THOMAS, JAY: New Orleans, July 12, 1948.

THOMAS, MARLO (Margaret): Detroit, Nov. 21, 1938. USC.

THOMAS, PHILIP MICHAEL: Columbus, OH, May 26, 1949. Oakwood Col.

THOMAS, RICHARD: NYC, June 13, 1951. Columbia.

THOMPSON, EMMA: London, Eng., Apr.15, 1959. Cambridge.

THOMPSON, JACK (John Payne): Sydney, Aus., 1940. U. Brisbane.

THOMPSON, LEA: Rochester, MN, May 31, 1961.

THOMPSON, REX: NYC, Dec. 14, 1942.

THOMPSON, SADA: Des Moines, IA, Sept. 27, 1929. Carnegie Tech.

THOMSON, GORDON: Ottawa, Can., 1945.

THORSON, LINDA: Toronto, Can., June 18, 1947. RADA

THULIN, INGRID: Solleftea, Sweden, Jan. 27, 1929. Royal Drama Theatre.

TICOTIN, RACHEL: Bronx, NY, Nov. 1, 1958.

TIERNEY, LAWRENCE: Brooklyn, Mar. 15, 1919. Manhattan College.

TIFFIN, PAMELA (Wonso): Oklahoma City, OK, Oct. 13, 1942.

TIGHE, KEVIN: Los Angeles, Aug. 13, 1944.

TILLY, MEG: Texada, Can., 1960.

TOBOLOWSKY, STEPHEN: Dallas, Tx, May 30, 1951. So. Methodist U.

TODD, BEVERLY: Chicago, IL, July 1, 1946.

TODD, RICHARD: Dublin, Ire., June 11, 1919. Shrewsbury School.

TOLKAN, JAMES: Calumet, MI, June 20, 1931.

TOLO, MARILU: Rome, Italy, 1944.

TOMEI, MARISA: Brooklyn, Dec. 4, 1964. NYU.

TOMLIN, LILY: Detroit, MI, Sept. 1, 1939. Wayne State U.

TOPOL (Chaim Topol): Tel-Aviv, Israel, Sept. 9, 1935.

TORN, RIP: Temple, TX, Feb. 6, 1931. U.Tex.

TORRES, LIZ: NYC, 1947. NYU.

TOTTER, AUDREY: Joliet, IL, Dec. 20, 1918.

TOWSEND, ROBERT: Chicago, Feb. 6, 1957.

TRAVANTI, DANIEL J.: Kenosha, WI, Mar. 7, 1940.

TRAVERS, BILL: Newcastle-on-Tyne, Eng., Jan. 3, 1922.

TRAVOLTA, JOEY: Englewood, NJ, 1952.

TRAVOLTA, JOHN: Englewood, NJ, Feb.18, 1954

TREMAYNE, LES: London, Apr. 16, 1913. Northwestern, Columbia, UCLA.

TREVOR, CLAIRE (Wemlinger): NYC, March 8, 1909.

TRINTIGNANT, JEAN-LOUIS: Pont-St. Esprit, France, Dec. 11, 1930. Dullin-Balachova Drama School.

TSOPEI, CORINNA: Athens, Greece, June 21, 1944.

TUBB, BARRY: Snyder, TX, 1963. AmConsv.Th.

TUCKER, MICHAEL: Baltimore, MD, Feb. 6, 1944.

TUNE, TOMMY: Wichita Falls, TX, Feb. 28, 1939.

TURNER, KATHLEEN: Springfield, MO, June 19, 1954. UMd.

TURNER, LANA (Julia Jean Mildred Frances Turner): Wallace, ID, Feb. 8, 1921.

TURNER, TINA: (Anna Mae Bullock) Nutbush, TN, Nov. 26, 1938.

TURTURRO, JOHN: Brooklyn, Feb. 28, 1957. Yale.

TUSHINGHAM, RITA: Liverpool, Eng.,

Mar. 14, 1940.

TUTIN, DOROTHY: London, Apr. 8, 1930.

TWIGGY (Lesley Hornby): London, Sept. 19, 1949.

TWOMEY, ANNE: Boston, MA, June 7, 1951. Temple U.

TYLER, BEVERLY (Beverly Jean Saul): Scranton, PA, July 5, 1928.

TYRRELL, SUSAN: San Francisco, 1946.

TYSON, CATHY: Liverpool, Eng., 1966. Royal Shake. Co.

TYSON, CICELY: NYC, Dec. 19, 1933. NYU.

UGGAMS, LESLIE: NYC, May 25, 1943. Juilliard.

ULLMAN, TRACEY: Slough, Eng., 1960.

ULLMANN, LIV: Tokyo, Dec. 10, 1938. Webber-Douglas Acad.

UMEKI, MIYOSHI: Otaru, Hokaido, Japan, 1929.

UNDERWOOD, BLAIR: Tacoma, WA, Aug. 25, 1964. Carnegie-Mellon U.

URICH, ROBERT: Toronto, Can., Dec. 19, 1946.

USTINOV, PETER: London, Apr. 16, 1921. Westminster School.

VACCARO, BRENDA: Brooklyn, Nov. 18, 1939. Neighborhood Playhouse.

VALANDREY, CHARLOTTE: (Anne-Charlone Pascal) Paris, 1968.

VALLI, ALIDA: Pola, Italy, May 31, 1921. Academy of Drama.

VALLONE, RAF: Riogio, Italy, Feb. 17, 1916. Turin U.

VAN ARK, JOAN: NYC, June 16, 1943. Yale.

VAN DE VEN, MONIQUE: Holland, 1957.

VAN DEVERE, TRISH (Patricia Dressel): Englewood Cliffs, NJ, Mar. 9, 1945. Ohio Wesleyan.

VAN DOREN, MAMIE (Joan Lucile Olander): Rowena SD, Feb. 6, 1933.

VAN DYKE, DICK: West Plains, MO, Dec. 13, 1925.

VAN FLEET, JO: Oakland, CA, Dec. 30, 1919.

VAN DAMME, JEAN CLAUDE: Brussels, Belgium, 1961.

VANITY (Denise Mathews): Niagara, Ont.,

Can, 1963.

VAN PALLANDT, NINA: Copenhagen, Denmark, July 15, 1932.

VAN PATTEN, DICK: NYC, Dec. 9, 1928.

VAN PATTEN, JOYCE: NYC, Mar. 9, 1934.

VAN PEEBLES, MARIO: NYC, Jan. 15, 1958. Columbia U.

VAN PEEBLES, MELVIN: Chicago, IL, Aug. 21, 1932.

VANCE, COURTNEY B.: Detroit, MI, Mar. 12, 1960.

VARNEY, JIM: Lexington, KY, June 15, 1949.

VAUGHN, ROBERT: NYC, Nov. 22, 1932. USC.

VEGA, ISELA: Mexico, 1940.

VELJOHNSON, REGINALD: NYC, Aug. 16, 1952

VENNERA, CHICK: Herkimer, NY, Mar. 27, 1952. Pasadena Playhouse.

VENORA, DIANE: Hartford, CT, 1952. Juilliard.

VENUTA, BENAY: San Francisco, Jan. 27, 1911.

VERDON, GWEN: Culver City, CA, Jan.13, 1925.

VERNON, JOHN: Montreal, Can., Feb. 24, 1932.

VEREEN, BEN: Miami, FL, Oct. 10, 1946.

VICTOR, JAMES (Lincoln Rafael Peralta Diaz): Santiago, D.R., July 27, 1939. Haaren HS/NYC.

VINCENT, JAN-MICHAEL: Denver, CO, July 15, 1944. Ventura.

VIOLET, ULTRA (Isabelle Collin-Dufresne): Grenoble, France.

VITALE, MILLY: Rome, Italy, July 16, 1928. Lycee Chateaubriand.

VOHS, JOAN: St. Albans, NY, July 30, 1931.

VOIGHT, JON: Yonkers, NY, Dec. 29, 1938. Catholic U.

VOLONTE, GIAN MARIA: Milan, Italy, Apr. 9, 1933.

VON DOHLEN, LENNY: Augusta, GA, Dec. 22, 1958. UTex.

VON SYDOW, MAX: Lund, Swed., July 10, 1929. Royal Drama Theatre.

WAGNER, LINDSAY: Los Angeles, June 22. 1949.

WAGNER, ROBERT: Detroit, Feb. 10, 1930.

WAHL, KEN: Chicago, IL, Feb. 14, 1953.

WAITE, GENEVIEVE: South Africa,1949.

WAITS, TOM: Pomona, CA, Dec. 7, 1949.

WALKEN, CHRISTOPHER: Astoria, NY, Mar. 31, 1943. Hofstra.

WALKER, CLINT: Hartfold, IL, May 30, 1927. USC.

WALLACH, ELI: Brooklyn, Dec. 7, 1915. CCNY, U. Tex.

WALLACH, ROBERTA: NYC, Aug. 2, 1955.

WALLIS, SHANI: London, Apr. 5, 1941.

WALSH, M. EMMET: Ogdensburg, NY, Mar. 22, 1935. Clarkson Col., AADA.

WALSTON, RAY: New Orleans, Nov. 22, 1917. Cleveland Playhouse.

WALTER, JESSICA: Brooklyn, Jan. 31, 1944 Neighborhood Playhouse.

WALTER, TRACEY: Jersey City, NJ, Nov. 25.

WALTERS, JULIE: London, Feb. 22, 1950.

WALTON, EMMA: London, Nov. 1962. Brown U.

WARD, BURT (Gervis): Los Angeles, July 6, 1945.

WARD, FRED: San Diego, CA, 1943.

WARD, RACHEL: London, 1957.

WARD, SELA: Meridian, MS, July 11, 1956

WARD, SIMON: London, Oct. 19, 1941.

WARDEN, JACK: Newark, NJ, Sept. 18, 1920.

WARNER, DAVID: Manchester, Eng., July 29,

Martin Short

Lesley Ann Warren

1941. RADA.

WARREN, JENNIFER: NYC, Aug. 12, 1941. U. Wisc.

WARREN, LESLEY ANN: NYC, Aug. 16, 1946.

WARREN, MICHAEL: South Bend, IN, Mar. 5, 1946. UCLA.

WARRICK, RUTH: St. Joseph, MO, June 29, 1915. U. Mo.

WASHINGTON, DENZEL: Mt. Vernon, NY, Dec. 28, 1954. Fordham.

WASSON, CRAIG: Ontario, OR, Mar. 15, 1954. UOre.

WATERSTON, SAM: Cambridge, MA, Nov. 15, 1940. Yale.

WATLING,JACK: London, Jan. 13, 1923. Italia Conti School.

WAYANS, DAMON: NYC, 1960.

WAYANS, KEENEN IVORY: NYC, June 8, 1958. Tuskegee Inst.

WAYNE, DAVID (Wayne McKeehan): Travers City, MI, Jan. 30, 1914. Western Michigan State U.

WAYNE, PATRICK: Los Angeles, July 15, 1939. Loyola.

WEATHERS, CARL: New Orleans, LA, Jan. 14, 1948. Long Beach CC.

WEAVER, DENNIS: Joplin, MO, June 4, 1924. U. Okla.

WEAVER, FRITZ: Pittsburgh, PA, Jan. 19, 1926.

WEAVER, MARJORIE: Crossville, TN, Mar. 2, 1913. Indiana U.

WEAVER, SIGOURNEY (Susan): NYC, Oct. 8, 1949. Stanford, Yale.

WEDGEWORTH, ANN: Abilene, TX, Jan. 21, 1935. U. Tex.

WELCH, RAQUEL (Tejada): Chicago, IL, Sept. 5, 1940.

WELD, TUESDAY (Susan): NYC, Aug. 27, 1943. Hollywood Professional School.

WELDON, JOAN: San Francisco, Aug. 5, 1933. San Francisco Conservatory.

WELLER, PETER: Stevens Point, WI, June 24, 1947. AmThWing.

WENDT, GEORGE: Chicago, IL, Oct. 17, 1948.

WEST, ADAM (William Anderson): Walla Walla, WA, Sept. 19, 1929.

WESTON, JACK (Morris Weinstein): Cleveland, OH, Aug. 21, 1924.

WHALEY, FRANK: Syracuse, NY, 1963. SUNY/Albany.

WHALLEY-KILMER, JOANNE: Manchester, Eng., Aug. 25, 1964.

WHEATON, WIL: Burbank, CA, July 29, 1972.

WHITAKER, FOREST: Longview, TX, July 15, 1961.

WHITAKER, JOHNNY: Van Nuys, CA, Dec. 13, 1959.

WHITE, BETTY: Oak Park, IL, Jan. 17, 1922.

WHITE, CHARLES: Perth Amboy, NJ, Aug. 29, 1920. Rutgers U.

WHITE, JESSE: Buffalo, NY, Jan. 3, 1919.

WHITMAN, STUART: San Francisco, Feb. 1, 1929. CCLA.

WHITMORE, JAMES: White Plains, NY, Oct. 1, 1921. Yale.

WHITNEY, GRACE LEE: Detroit, MI, Apr. 1, 1930.

WHITTON, MARGARET: Philadelphia, PA, Nov, 30, 1950.

WIDDOES, KATHLEEN: Wilmington, DE,

Damon Wayans

Frank Whaley

Esther Williams

Robin Wright

James Woods

26, 1914. Lake Forest.

WIEST, DIANNE: Kansas City, MO, Mar. 28, 1948. UMd.

WILBY. JAMES: Burma, Feb. 20, 1958.

WILCOX, COLIN: Highlands, NC, Feb. 4, 1937. U. Tenn.

WILDER, GENE (Jerome Silberman): Milwaukee, WI, June 11, 1935. UIowa.

WILLIAMS, BILLY DEE: NYC, Apr. 6, 1937.

WILLIAMS, CINDY: Van Nuys, CA, Aug. 22, 1947. KACC.

WILLIAMS, CLARENCE III: NYC, Aug. 21, 1939.

WILLIAMS, DICK A.: Chicago, IL, Aug. 9, 1938.

WILLIAMS, ESTHER: Los Angeles, Aug. 8, 1921.

WILLIAMS, JOBETH: Houston, TX, 1953. BrownU.

WILLIAMS, PAUL: Omaha, NE, Sept. 19, 1940.

WILLIAMS, ROBIN: Chicago, IL, July 21, 1951. Juilliard.

WILLIAMS, TREAT (Richard): Rowayton, CT, Dec. 1, 1951.

WILLIAMSON, FRED: Gary, IN, Mar. 5, 1938. Northwestern.

WILLIAMSON, NICOL: Hamilton, Scot., Sept. 14, 1938.

WILLIS, BRUCE: Penns Grove, NJ, Mar. 19, 1955.

WILLISON, WALTER: Monterey Park, CA, June 24, 1947.

WILSON, DEMOND: NYC, Oct. 13, 1946. Hunter Col.

WILSON, ELIZABETH: Grand Rapids, MI, Apr. 4, 1925.

WILSON, FLIP (Clerow Wilson): Jersey City, NJ, Dec. 8, 1933.

WILSON, LAMBERT: Paris, 1959.

WILSON, NANCY: Chillicothe, OH, Feb. 20, 1937.

WILSON, SCOTT: Atlanta, GA, 1942.

WINCOTT, JEFF: Toronto, Can., 1957.

WINDE, BEATRICE: Chicago, Jan. 6.

WINDOM, WILLIAM: NYC, Sept. 28,

1923. Williams Col.

WINDSOR, MARIE (Emily Marie Bertelson): Marysvale, UT, Dec. 11, 1924. Brigham Young U.

WINFIELD, PAUL: Los Angeles, May 22, 1940. UCLA.

WINFREY, OPRAH: Kosciusko, MS, Jan. 29, 1954. TnStateU.

WINGER, DEBRA: Cleveland, OH, May 17, 1955. Cal State.

WINKLER, HENRY: NYC, Oct. 30, 1945. Yale.

WINN, KITTY: Washingtohn, D.C., 1944. Boston U.

WINNINGHAM, MARE: Phoenix, AZ, May 6, 1959.

WINSLOW, MICHAEL: Spokane, WA, Sept. 6, 1960.

WINTER, ALEX: London, July 17, 1965. NYU.

WINTERS, JONATHAN: Dayton, OH, Nov. 11, 1925. Kenyon Col.

WINTERS, SHELLEY (Shirley Schrift): St. Louis, Aug. 18, 1922. Wayne U.

WITHERS, GOOGIE: Karachi, India, Mar. 12, 1917. Italia Conti.

WITHERS, JANE: Atlanta, GA, Apr. 12, 1926.

WONG, B.D.: San Francisco, Oct. 24,1962.

WONG, RUSSELL: Troy, NY, 1963. SantaMonica Col.

WOODARD, ALFRE: Tulsa, OK, Nov. 2, 1953. Boston U.

WOODLAWN, HOLLY (Harold Ajzenberg): Juana Diaz, PR, 1947.

WOODS, JAMES: Vernal, UT, Apr. 18, 1947. MIT.

WOODWARD, EDWARD: Croyden, Surrey, Eng., June 1, 1930.

WOODWARD, JOANNE: Thomasville, GA, Feb. 27, 1930. Neighborhood Playhouse.

WORONOV, MARY: Brooklyn, Dec. 8, 1946. Cornell.

WORTH, IRENE (Hattie Abrams):

Nebraska, June 23, 1916. UCLA.

WRAY, FAY: Alberta, Can., Sept. 15, 1907.

WRIGHT, AMY: Chicago, Apr. 15, 1950.

WRIGHT, MAX: Detroit, MI, Aug. 2, 1943. WayneStateU.

WRIGHT, ROBIN: Texas, 1966.

WRIGHT, TERESA: NYC, Oct. 27, 1918.

WUHL, ROBERT: Union City, NJ, Oct. 9, 1951. UHouston.

WYATT, JANE: NYC, Aug. 10, 1910. Barnard College.

WYMAN, JANE (Sarah Jane Fulks): St. Joseph, MO, Jan. 4, 1914.

WYMORE, PATRICE: Miltonvale, KS, Dec. 17, 1926.

WYNN, MAY (Donna Lee Hickey): NYC, Jan. 8, 1930.

WYNTER, DANA (Dagmar): London, June 8. 1927. Rhodes U.

YORK, DICK: Fort Wayne, IN, Sept. 4, 1928. De Paul U.

YORK, MICHAEL: Fulmer, Eng., Mar. 27, 1942. Oxford.

YORK, SUSANNAH: London, Jan. 9, 1941. RADA.

YOUNG, ALAN (Angus): North Shield, Eng., Nov. 19, 1919.

YOUNG, BURT: Queens, NY, Apr. 30, 1940.

YOUNG, LORETTA (Gretchen): Salt Lake City, UT, Jan. 6, 1912. Immaculate Heart College.

YOUNG, ROBERT: Chicago, Feb. 22, 1907.

YOUNG, SEAN: Louisville, KY, Nov. 20, 1959. Interlochen.

ZACHARIAS, ANN: Stockholm, Swed., 1956.

ZADORA, PIA: Hoboken, NJ, 1954.

ZETTERLING, MAI: Sweden, May 27, 1925. Ordtuery Theatre School.

ZIMBALIST, EFREM, JR.: NYC, Nov.30, 1918. Yale.

ZUNIGA, DAPHNE: Berkeley, CA, 1962. UCLA.

OBITUARIES

obituaries

DON AMECHE (Dominic Felix Amici), 85, Wisconsin-born screen, stage and tv actor, died on Dec. 6, 1993 in Scottsdale, AZ, of prostate cancer. Following his film debut in *Sins of Man* in 1936 he appeared in such movies as *Romona, One in a Million, Love is News, You Can't Have Everything, In Old Chicago, Happy Landing, Alexander's Ragtime Band, The Three Musketeers* (1939), *Midnight, The Story of Alexander Graham Bell, Hollywood Cavalcade, Swanee River, Lillian Russell, Four Sons, Down Argentine Way, That Night in Rio, Moon Over Miami, Kiss the Boys Goodbye, The Magnificent Dope, Heaven Can Wait, The Happy Land, Greenwich Village, It's in the Bag, Guest Wife, Sleep My Love, A Fever in the Blood, Suppose They Gave a War and Nobody Came, The Boatniks, Trading Places, Cocoon* (for which he won an Academy Award), *Harry and the Hendersons, Things Change, Oscar, Folks!*, and his last, *Corrina Corrina*, which he completed only a month before his death. Survived by four sons, two daughters, a brother, two sisters, 13 grandchildren, and 10 great-grandchildren.

LEON AMES (Leon Waycoff), 91, Indiana-born screen, stage and tv character actor, one of the original founders of the Screen Actors Guild, died on Oct. 12, 1993 in Laguna Beach, CA from complications from a stroke. His more than 100 films include *Murders in the Rue Morgue* (his debut, as Leon Waycoff, in 1932), *State's Attorney, The Count of Monte Cristo* (1934), *Now I'll Tell, Stowaway* (first film as Leon Ames, in 1936), *Bluebeard's Eighth Wife, The Mysterious Mr. Moto, Suez, Crime Doctor, Meet Me in St. Louis, 30 Seconds Over Tokyo, Son of Lassie, Weekend at the Waldorf, They Were Expendable, Yolanda and the Thief, The Postman Always Rings Twice* (1946), *Lady in the Lake, No Leave No Love, Song of the Thin Man, On an Island With You, A Date With Judy, The Velvet Touch, Little Women* (1949), *Any Number Can Play, Battleground, The Happy Years, Crisis, On Moonlight Bay, By the Light of the Silvery Moon, Peyton Place, From the Terrace, The Absent-Minded*

Don Ameche

died on Sept. 8, 1993 in Los Angeles. His film credits include *Navajo, Crazy Legs, All the Young Men, Unchained, Changes, Jonathan Livingston Seagull*, and *The Children of Sanchez*. Survived by two daughters and five grandchildren.

HARRY BELLAVER, 88, Illinois-born screen, stage and tv character actor, died of pneumonia in Nyack, NY on Aug. 8, 1993. His many films include *Another Thin Man* (debut, 1936), *The House on 92nd Street, No Way Out* (1950), *The Lemon Drop Kid, From Here to Eternity, Love Me or Leave Me, Serenade, Slaughter on 10th Avenue, The Old Man and the Sea, One Potato Two Potato, A Fine Madness, Demon*, and *Blue Collar*. Survived by two daughters, two grandsons, and two great-grand children.

BILL BIXBY, 54, San Francisco-born screen, stage and tv actor-director, died on Nov. 21, 1993 at his home in Century City, CA, of prostate cancer. Best known for his starring roles in the tv series *My Favorite Martian, The Courtship of Eddie's Father*, and *The Incredible Hulk*, he later directed several series episodes and tv movies. His movie credits include *Lonely Are the Brave, Irma La Douce, Under the Yum Yum Tree, Clambake, Doctor You've Got to Be Kidding, Speedway. The Apple Dumpling Gang*, and *The Kentucky Fried Movie*. Survived by his second wife.

REIZL BOZYK, 79, Polish star of the Yiddish theatre died on Sept. 30, 1993 in New York City. She was best known for her only English-speak-

Leon Ames

Bill Bixby

Professor, Son of Flubber, On a Clear Day You Can See Forever, Tora! Tora! Tora!, and his last, *Peggy Sue Got Married*, in 1986. In 1981 he received the SAG Annual Achievement Award. Survived by his wife, a daughter, a son, and two grandchildren.

JOSEPH ANTHONY, 80, former actor-turned director, died on Jan. 20, 1993 in Hyannis, MA, of undisclosed causes. His directorial credits include The *Rainmaker, The Matchmaker, Career, All in a Night's Work*, and *Tomorrow*. No reported survivors.

EMILE ARDOLINO, 50, Queens-born film and tv director, best known for the movies *Dirty Dancing* and *Sister Act*, died of AIDS on Nov. 20, 1993 at his home in Los Angeles. His other feature credits are *Chances Are, Three Men and a Little Lady*, and *George Balanchine's The Nutcracker*. A former maker of dance films he directed the Oscar winning documentary *He Makes Me Feel Like Dancing*. Survived by his companion, and his three sisters.

HALL BARTLETT, 70, Kansas City-born producer, director and writer,

Reizl Bozyk

David Brian

ing film role as Amy Irving's grandmother in *Crossing Delancey*. No reported survivors.

DAVID BRIAN, 82, New York City-born screen, stage and tv actor, died of cancer and heart failure on July 15, 1993 at his home in Sherman Oaks, CA. Following his 1949 debut in *Flamingo Road* he appeared in such movies as *Beyond the Forest, Intruder in the Dust, The Damned Don't Cry, Inside Straight, This Woman is Dangerous, Springfield Rifle, Million Dollar Mermaid, The High and the Mighty, Timberjack, The First Travelling Saleslady, The Rabbit Trap, Pocketful of Miracles, How the West Was Won, The Rare Breed,* and *The Seven Minutes.* Survived by his wife, former actress Adriana Booth.

Raymond Burr   Cyril Cusack

James Bridges

JAMES BRIDGES, 57, Arkansas-born motion picture director-writer, best known for the 1979 anti-nuclear thriller *The China Syndrome*, died on June 6, 1993 in Los Angeles of kidney failure. His other films as director and writer are *The Baby Maker, The Paper Chase, September 30, 1955, Urban Cowboy, Mike's Murder, Perfect,* and *Bright Lights Big City.* He received Academy Award nominations for his screenplays for *Paper Chase* and *China Syndrome.* Survived by his companion, his mother, and a sister.

RAYMOND BURR, 76, Canadian-born screen and tv actor, best known for his starring roles on the series Perry Mason and Ironside, died on Sept. 12, 1993 at his home in Dry Creek, CA, of liver cancer. His motion pictures include *Without Reservations, I Love Trouble, Fighting Father Dunne, Ruthless* (1948), *Pitfall, Station West, Walk a Crooked Mile, Adventures of Don Juan, Bride of Vengeance, Love Happy, Key to the City, Bride of the Gorilla, The Magic Carpet, A Place in the Sun, Horizons West, Mara Maru, Meet Danny Wilson, Fort Algiers, Casanova's Big Night, Gorilla at Large, Khyber Patrol, Rear Window, Count Three and Pray, You're Never Too Young, Godzilla: King of the Monsters, A Cry in the Night, Great Day in the Morning, P.J., Godzilla 1985,* and *Delirious.* Survived by a sister.

SAMMY CAHN (Samuel Cohen), 79, New York City-born lyricist, whose work earned him four Academy Awards, died of congestive heart failure on Jan. 15, 1993 in Los Angeles. Among his noted collaborations are "I've Heard That Song Before," "Guess I'll Hang My Tears Out to Dry," "Let It Snow Let It Snow Let It Snow," "My Kind of Town," and "Pocketful of Miracles." He received his Oscars for "Three Coins in the Fountain," "All the Way" (from *The Joker is Wild*), "High Hopes" (from *A Hole in the Head*), and "Call Me Irresponsible" (from *Papa's Delicate Condition*). He had served as the president of the National Academy of Popular Music for twenty years. Survived by his wife, son, daughter, and two grandchildren.

Cantinflas

CANTINFLAS (Mario Moreno), 81, Mexico's most famous and best loved comedian, died of lung cancer on April 20, 1993 in Mexico City. The star of over 40 Mexican films, he was best known to American audiences for his role as the valet Passepartout in the 1956 Oscar-winning *Around the World in 80 Days.* His only other U.S. film was *Pepe* in 1960. Survived by his son and three grandchildren.

CYRIL CUSACK, 82, South Africa-born Irish screen, stage and tv actor, died on Oct. 7, 1993 at his London home after suffering for a lengthy period with motor neuron disease. His many movie appearances include *Odd Man Out, The Blue Lagoon* (1949), *The Elusive Pimpernel, The Blue Veil,*

Sammy Cahn

Soldiers Three, The Man Who Never Was, Jacqueline, Ill Met By Moonlight, Rising of the Moon, Shake Hands With the Devil, A Terrible Beauty, Waltz of the Toreadors, I Thank a Fool, The Spy Who Came in From the Cold, Fahrenheit 451, The Taming of the Shrew (1967), *Oedipus the King, King Lear* (1971), *Harold and Maude, The Day of the Jackal, The Homecoming, True Confessions, Little Dorritt, My Left Foot,* and *Far and Away.* Survivors include his second wife, four daughters, all of whom are actresses, including Sinead Cusack, and two sons.

DON DeFORE, 80, Iowa-born screen, stage and tv actor, died of a heart attack on Dec. 22, 1993 in Los Angeles. Following his debut in 1937 in *Kid Galahad,* he appeared in such movies as *Brother Rat, The Male Animal, The Human Comedy, A Guy Named Joe, 30 Seconds Over Tokyo, And Now Tomorrow, The Affairs of Susan, You Came Along, The Stork Club, Without Reservations, Ramrod, Romance on the High Seas, One*

Don DeFore   James Donald

Sunday Afternoon (1948), *My Friend Irma, My Friend Irma Goes West, No Room for the Groom, She's Working Her Way Through College, Jumping Jacks, Battle Hymn, A Time to Love and a Time to Die,* and *The Facts of Life.* On tv he was best known for the series *The Adventures of Ozzie and Harriet* and *Hazel.* Survived by his wife, two sons and three daughters.

"CURLY" JOE DeRITA, 83, screen, stage and tv comedian, the last surviving member of the Three Stooges, died of pneumonia on July 3, 1993 in Woodland Hills, CA. In 1958 he replaced Joe Besser, joining original Stooges, Moe Howard and Larry Fine, in such feature films as *Have Rocket Will Travel, Snow White and the Three Stooges, The Three Stooges Meet Hercules, The Three Stooges in Orbit, It's a Mad Mad Mad Mad World,* and *The Outlaws Is Coming.* Survived by his wife and two stepsons.

JAMES DONALD, 76, British screen and stage actor, perhaps best known for his role as the doctor in *The Bridge on the River Kwai,* died on Aug. 3, 1993 in Wiltshire, England, of stomach cancer. Among his other movies are *In Which We Serve, The Way Ahead, Edward My Son, The Pickwick Papers, Beau Brummell, Lust for Life, The Vikings, Third Man on the Mountain, The Great Escape, King Rat, Cast a Giant Shadow, The Jokers, Quatermass and the Pit (Five Million Years to Earth), Hannibal Brooks, The Royal Hunt of the Sun,* and *The Big Sleep* (1978). Survived by his wife and stepson.

GORDON DOUGLAS, 85, New York City-born film director died on Sept. 30, 1993 in Los Angeles of cancer. After directing over 30 Our Gang shorts he graduated to helming such features as *If You Knew Susie, Walk a Crooked Mile, Mr. Soft Touch, The Nevadan, Kiss Tomorrow Goodbye, I Was a Communist for the FBI, Come Fill the Cup, So This is Love, The Charge at Feather River, Them!, Young at Heart, Sincerely Yours, Fort Dobbs, Follow That Dream, Call Me Bwana, Robin and the 7 Hoods, Stagecoach* (1966), *In Like Flint, Tony Rome, The Detective, They Call Me Mr. Tibbs,* and *Slaughter's Big Rip-Off.* Survived by his wife, daughter, son, and grandson.

ARTHUR DREIFUSS, 85, German-born American director died on Dec. 31, 1993 at his Studio City, CA home of undisclosed causes. His movie credits include *Secret File* (which he also produced), *The Last Blitzkrieg, Juke Box Rhythm, The Quare Fellow* (which he also wrote), *Riot on Sunset Strip, The Love-Ins, For Singles Only, A Time to Sing,* and *The Young Runaways.* Survived by his son, daughter, and two grandchildren.

JAMES ELLISON (James Ellison Smith), 83, Iowa-born screen and stage actor, perhaps best known for portraying Buffalo Bill in the 1936 Cecil B. DeMille western *The Plainsman,* died on Dec. 23, 1993 after breaking his neck in a fall at his home in Montecito, CA. His other films include *The Play Girl* (debut, 1932), *Hopalong Cassidy, Vivacious Lady, Fifth Avenue Girl, Ice Capades, I Walked With a Zombie, The Ghost Goes Wild, Last of the Wild Horses,* and *Dead Man's Trail.* He retired from acting in the 1950s. No reported survivors.

FRITZ FELD, 93, Berlin-born screen, stage and tv character actor died in Santa Monica, CA, on Nov. 18, 1993 following a long illness. His many movie credits include *Broadway, I Met Him in Paris, Bringing Up Baby, At the Circus, Idiot's Delight, Sandy is a Lady, World Premiere, Iceland, Phantom of the Opera* (1943), *The Great John L, Catman of Paris, The Secret Life of Walter Mitty, Mexican Hayride, The Jackpot, Wives and Lovers, Who's Minding the Store?, Four for Texas, The Patsy, Barefoot in the Park, Three on a Couch, The Comic, Hello Dolly!, Herbie Rides Again, Won Ton Ton the Dog Who Saved Hollywood, Silent Movie, Freaky Friday, The World's Greatest Lover, History of the World Part 1,* and *Barfly.* Survived by his wife, actress Virginia Christine, two sons and a brother.

FEDERICO FELLINI, 73, Italian film director-writer whose original, often surreal style made him one of the cinema's most controversial and influential filmmakers, died of cardiac arrest in Rome on Oct. 31, 1993. Four of his films were honored with Academy Awards for Best Foreign Language Film: *La Strada* (1956), *Nights of Cabiria* (1957), *8 1/2* (1963), and *Amarcord* (1973). He made his directorial debut in 1951 with *Variety Lights,* sharing credit with Alberto Lattuada. Later that year he earned his first solo credit on *The White Shiek.* His other films include *I Vitelloni, La Dolca Vita, Boccaccio '70* (sequence), *Il Bidone, Juliet of the Spirits, Fellini Satyricon, The Clowns, Orchestra Rehearsal, City of Women, And the Ship Sails On, Ginger and Fred,* and *Intervista.* He was given a special Academy Award in March of 1993. Survived by his wife of 50 years, actress Giulietta Masina, who appeared in many of his films.

Federico Fellini

DUNCAN GIBBINS, 41, British film and tv director, died in Sherman Oaks, CA on Nov. 4, 1993 from burns suffered in a Malibu fire while trying to rescue a cat. His movie credits included *Fire With Fire* and *Eve of Destruction.* Survived by his mother.

LILLIAN GISH (Lillian de Guiche), 99, Ohio-born screen, stage and TV actress, the last great star of the silent movie days, whose career on film spanned some 75 years, died in her sleep at her New York City apartment on Feb. 27, 1993. She achieved stardom in perhaps the most famous and influential motion picture of the silent era, D.W. Griffith's epic *The Birth of a Nation.* She later worked with Griffith on such classics as *Intolerance, Broken Blossoms, Way Down East* and *Orphans of the Storm.* Her other films include *The Scarlet Letter* (1926), *The White Sister, Romola, Annie Laurie, The Wind, One Romantic Night* (her talkie debut), *His Double Life, The Commandos Strike at Dawn, Miss Susie Slagle's, Duel in the Sun* (Academy Award nomination), *Portrait of Jennie, The Cobweb, The Night of the Hunter, Orders to Kill, The Unforgiven, Follow Me Boys, Warning Shot, The Comedians, A Wedding, Sweet Liberty,* and her last, *The Whales of August,* in 1987. She received an honorary Oscar in 1970, the Kennedy Center Honors in 1982 and the American Film Institute Lifetime Achievement Award in 1984. Her sister, actress Dorothy Gish, died in 1968. No survivors.

MICHAEL GORDON, 83, Baltimore-born movie director, whose credits include *Cyrano de Bergerac* (1950) and *Pillow Talk,* died of natural causes on April 29, 1993, in Los Angeles. His other films include *Another*

LILLIAN GISH

Stewart Granger

Kane (The Ninth Configuration), Ragtime, Firestarter, The Neverending Story, Heartbreak Ridge, and *Leonard Part 6.* Survivors include his wife, daughter, brother and three sisters.

FRED GWYNNE, 66, New York City-born screen, stage and tv actor, best known for his portrayal of the Frankenstein Monster-lookalike Herman Munster on the 1960's sitcom *The Munsters,* died of complications from pancreatic cancer at his home near Taneytown, MD on July 2, 1993. He appeared in such films as *On the Waterfront, Munster Go Home!, Luna, Simon, So Fine, The Cotton Club, The Boy Who Could Fly, The Secret of My Success* (1987), *Fatal Attraction, Ironweed, Disorganized Crime, Pet Sematary,* and *My Cousin Vinny.* Survived by his wife, two sons and two daughters.

HELEN HAYES (Helen Hayes Brown), 92, Washington D.C.-born screen, stage and TV actress, the First Lady of the American Theatre, died of heart failure at Nyack Hospital in Nyack, NY, on March 17, 1993. Best known for her long and distinguished stage career in which her triumphs included *Coquette, Victoria Regina, Happy Birthday* and *Mrs. McThing,* she also became the first performer to win Academy Awards in both the lead (*The Sin of Madelon Claudet,* 1931) and supporting (*Airport,* 1970) categories. Her other movies include *Arrowsmith, A Farewell to Arms* (1932), *Night Flight, The Son-Daughter, The White Sister, What Every Woman Knows, Stage Door Canteen, My Son John, Anastasia, Herbie Rides Again, One of Our Dinosaurs is Missing,* and *Candleshoe.* Her many accolades include three Tony Awards, the Kennedy Center Honors and the Presidential Medal of Freedom. She is survived by her adopted son, actor James MacArthur, from her marriage to the late playwright Charles MacArthur, and three grandchildren.

Helen Hayes

Part of the Forest, The Lady Gambles, Woman in Hiding, I Can Get It For You Wholesale, The Secret of Convict Lake, Portrait in Black, Boys' Night Out, For Love or Money (1963), *Move Over Darling, Texas Across the River, A Very Special Favor, The Impossible Years,* and *How Do I Love Thee?* Survived by two daughters, a son and three grandsons.

STEWART GRANGER (James Lablanche Stewart), 80, British screen, stage and tv actor, star of many action adventure films most notably the 1950 version of *King Solomon's Mines,* died of cancer on Aug. 16, 1993 in Santa Monica, CA. His credits include *Man in Grey, Fanny by Gaslight, Caesar and Cleopatra, Soldiers Three, Scaramouche* (1952), *The Prisoner of Zenda* (1952), *Salome, Young Bess, All the Brothers Were Valiant, Beau Brummell, Green Fire, Moonfleet, Footsteps in the Fog, Bhowani Junction, The Last Hunt, The Little Hut, Hary Black and the Tiger, North to Alaska, Sodom and Gomorrah, The Last Safari,* and *The Wild Geese.* Survived by three daughters and a son.

NAN GREY (Eschal Miller), 75, screen, stage and tv actress, died of heart failure on July 25, 1993 at her home in San Diego. Her film credits include *Firebird* (debut, 1934), *Babbitt, The Sea Spoilers, Three Smart Girls, Dracula's Daughter, Love in a Bungalow, Reckless Living, Girls' School, Tower of London, Three Smart Girls Grow Up, The Under-Pup, The Invisible Man Returns, House of Seven Gables,* and *A Little Bit of Heaven.* She retired in 1950 and later invented a cosmetic mirror for the near-sighted. Survivors include her second husband, singer Frankie Laine, two daughters from her first marriage, and four grandchildren.

MOSES GUNN, 64, St. Louis-born screen, stage and tv actor, died on Dec. 17, 1993 at his home in Guilford, CT, from complications of asthma. He appeared in such films as *What's So Bad About Feeling Good?, The Great White Hope, WUSA, Wild Rovers, Shaft, The Hot Rock, The Iceman Cometh, Amazing Grace, Rollerball, Aaron Loves Angela, Cornbread Earl & Me, Remember My Name, Twinkle Twinkle Killer*

AUDREY HEPBURN (Edda Van Heemstra Hepburn-Ruston), 63, Belgium-born actress, one of the most gifted and captivating performers in film history, died of colon cancer on Jan. 20, 1993 at her home in Tolochenaz, Switzerland. Following brief appearances in such British films as *Young Wives Tale, Laughter in Paradise,* and *The Lavender Hill Mob* she co-starred opposite Gregory Peck in her first American picture, *Roman Holiday,* in 1953, winning an Academy Award and becoming a star. There followed additional Oscar nominations for her work in *Sabrina, The Nun's Story, Breakfast at Tiffany's* (in which, as Holly Golightly, she introduced the song "Moon River"), and *Wait Until Dark.* She also appeared in *War and Peace* (1956), *Funny Face, Love in the Afternoon, Green Mansions, The Unforgiven, The Children's Hour, Charade, Paris When It Sizzles, My Fair Lady, How to Steal a Million, Two for the Road, Robin and Marian, Bloodline, They All Laughed,* and her last, *Always,* in 1989. In 1986 she became goodwill ambassador for UNICEF, helping to aid third world countries. She received a posthumous Jean Hersholt Humanitarian Award from the Academy of Motion Picture Arts and Sciences. Survived by her companion, former actor Robert Wolders, and her two sons from her two marriages.

INOSHIRO HONDA, 81, Japanese film director responsible for the original 1954 *Godzilla,* died on Feb. 28, 1993 in Tokyo of undisclosed caus-

Fred Gwynne

AUDREY HEPBURN

es. His other genre films include *Rodan, Mothra, King Kong Vs. Godzilla, Godzilla Vs. The Thing, Ghidra the Three-Headed Monster, War of the Gargantuas,* and *Godzilla's Revenge.* No reported survivors.

CY HOWARD (Seymour Horowitz), 77, film and tv writer-director-producer, died of heart failure on April 29, 1993 in Los Angeles. His motion picture credits as writer include *My Friend Irma, My Friend Irma Goes West, That's My Boy, Marriage on the Rocks,* and *Won Ton Ton the Dog Who Saved Hollywood.* He directed the movies *Lovers and Other Strangers* and *Every Little Crook and Nanny.* Survived by his wife and sister.

GUSTI HUBER, 78, Viennese stage and film actress, died of heart failure on July 12, 1993 at her home in Mount Kisco, NY. She was probably best known for playing Anne Frank's mother in the Broadway and 1959 film versions of *The Diary of Anne Frank.* She retired from acting in 1961. Survived by her husband, three daughters, including actress Bibi Besch, a son, and four grandchildren, including actress Samantha Mathis.

STEVE JAMES, 41, screen and tv actor, died on Dec. 18, 1993 at his home in Burbank, CA, of cancer. His film credits include *Hammer, The Exterminator, To Live and Die in L.A., American Ninja, Hollywood Shuffle,* and *The Player.* Survivors include his wife, and father.

ZITA JOHANN, 89, Hungary-born U.S. movie actress died of pneumonia on Sept. 24, 1993 in Nyack, NY. She was best known for playing the object of Boris Karloff's desires in the 1932 version of *The Mummy.* Her other movies include *Tiger Shark, Luxury Liner,* and *Grand Canary.* She later taught acting and worked with disturbed children. No reported survivors.

RICHARD JORDAN (Robert Anson Jordan), 56, New York City-born screen, stage and tv actor, died of a brain tumor on Aug. 30, 1993 at his

Moses Gunn   Richard Jordan

home in Los Angeles. Following his 1970 debut in *Lawman* he appeared in such films as *Valdez is Coming, The Friends of Eddie Coyle, Rooster Cogburn, The Yakuza, Logan's Run, Interiors, Old Boyfriends, Raise the Titanic, A Flash of Green* (which he also produced), *Dune, The Mean Season, The Men's Club, The Secret of My Success, Romero, The Hunt for Red October, Shout, Posse,* and his last, *Gettysburg,* released posthumously. He is survived by a daughter, a son, his mother, a brother and three sisters.

RUBY KEELER, 83, Nova Scotia-born screen and stage actress-dancer, died on Feb. 28, 1993 in Rancho Mirage, CA, of cancer. She was best known for her starring roles in such 1930's Warner Bros. musicals as *42nd Street, Gold Diggers of 1933, Footlight Parade,* and *Flirtation Walk.* Her other films are *Go Into Your Dance* (with her then-husband Al Jolson), *Shipmates Forever, Colleen, Ready Willing and Able, Mother Carey's Chickens* (1938), *Sweetheart of the Campus,* and *The Phynx.* Survived by five children and 14 grandchildren.

CHARLES LAMONT, 98, San Francisco-born film director, responsible for several of the Abbott & Costello comedies, died on Sept. 12, 1993 in Woodland Hills, CA, of pneumonia. His more than 100 movie credits include *Love Honor and Oh Baby, The Merry Monahans, Bowery to Broadway, Slave Girl, Ma & Pa Kettle, Abbott & Costello Meet the Invisible Man, Abbott & Costello Meet the Mummy,* and *Francis in the Haunted House.* Survived by two daughters, five grandchildren and nine great grandchildren.

Myrna Loy

ELY LANDAU, 73, New York-born film and tv producer, died on Nov. 5, 1993 in Los Angeles from complication of a stroke. His most noted productions of the 1960's were the films *Long Day's Journey Into Night* and *The Pawnbroker.* In the 1970's he created the American Film Theatre offering film adaptations of plays to subscription audiences including *Butley, The Homecoming, Rhinoceros, The Maids, The Man in the Glass Booth,* and *Galileo.* He is survived by his wife, producer Edie Landau, five children, five grandchildren, and three sisters.

WILLIAM LANTEAU (William Lanteau), 70, Vermont-born screen, stage and tv character actor died on Nov. 3, 1993 in Los Angeles from complications following heart surgery. His movies include *Li'l Abner,*

Ruby Keeler   Brandon Lee

The Facts of Life, That Touch of Mink, Sex and the Single Girl, and *Hotel.* Survived by a brother.

BRANDON LEE, 27, screen and tv actor, died from a gunshot wound in Wilmington, NC, on March 31, 1993. While on the set of his newest film, *The Crow,* he was shot in the stomach by a gun that was supposed to be filled with blanks. Son of the late martial-arts star Bruce Lee, he had appeared in the movies *Showdown in Little Tokyo* and *Rapid Fire.* Survived by his mother and sister.

MYRNA LOY (Myrna Williams), 88, Montana-born screen, stage and tv actress, one of the 1930's and 40's most-highly regarded actresses, died

on Dec. 14, 1993 in New York City. She was perhaps best remembered for her several roles opposite William Powell including *The Thin Man* (and its five sequels), *Manhattan Melodrama*, *The Great Ziegfeld*, *Libeled Lady*, and *Love Crazy*. Following a period of playing bit roles in many films including *Ben-Hur* (1925), *Noah's Ark* and *The Jazz Singer* (1927), she starred in such films as *A Connecticut Yankee*, *The Wet Parade*, *Emma*, *The Animal Kingdom*, *Love Me Tonight*, *The Mask of Fu Manchu*, *New Morals for Old*, *Topaze*, *Night Flight*, *When Ladies Meet* (1933), *Broadway Bill*, *Wings in the Dark*, *Wife vs. Secretary*, *Parnell*, *Test Pilot*, *Too Hot to Handle*, *The Rains Came*, *Third Finger Left Hand*, *The Best Years of Our Lives*, *The Bachelor and the Bobby-Soxer*, *Mr. Blandings Builds His Dream House*, *The Red Pony*, *Cheaper by the Dozen*, *Lonelyhearts*, *From the Terrace*, *Midnight Lace*, *The April Fools*, *The End*, and *Just Tell Me What You Want*. No reported survivors.

Janet Margolin

Kenneth Nelson

each for writing and directing the films *A Letter to Three Wives* and *All About Eve*. Before turning to directing in 1946, he co-wrote such films as *Skippy, Sooky, If I Had a Million, Million Dollar Legs* (1932), and *Alice in Wonderland* (1933), and served as producer on *Fury, Three Comrades, A Christmas Carol* (1938), *The Philadelphia Story*, and *The Keys of the Kingdom* among others. His films as director, most of which he wrote, include *Dragonwyck, The Late George Apley, The Ghost and Mrs. Muir, House of Strangers, No Way Out* (1950), *People Will Talk, Five Fingers, Julius Caesar* (1953), *The Barefoot Contessa, Guys and Dolls, Suddenly Last Summer, Cleopatra* (1963), *The Honey Pot, There Was a Crooked Man*, and *Sleuth*. In 1986 he received a lifetime achievement award from the Directors Guild of America. Survived by his third wife, three sons, one of whom is director-writer Tom Mankiewicz, and a daughter.

JANET MARGOLIN, 50, New York City-born screen, stage and tv actress, who came to prominence with her first film role as the star of *David and Lisa*, died on Dec. 17, 1993 at her Los Angeles home of ovarian cancer. Her other films include *The Greatest Story Ever Told, Bus Riley's Back in Town, Nevada Smith, Enter Laughing, Buona Sera Mrs. Campbell, Take the Money and Run, Your Three Minutes Are Up, Annie Hall, Last Embrace*, and *Ghostbusters II*. Survived by her husband, actor Ted Wass, and two children.

GEORGE "SPANKY" McFARLAND, 64, former child actor, perhaps the most famous and best loved star of the "Our Gang/Little Rascals" shorts, died on June 30, 1993 in Grapevine, TX. Appearing at age three in his first Our Gang short, *Free Eats* in 1932, he stayed with the series for 10 years and a total of 95 shorts. He also was seen in such features as *Day of Reckoning, Trail of the Lonesome Pine, General Spanky, Miss Fane's Baby is Stolen, Johnny Doughboy*, and *The Woman in the Window*. Survived by his wife and three children.

CLAUDIA McNEIL, 77, screen and stage actress who won acclaim for

Joseph L. Mankiewicz

ALEXANDER MACKENDRICK, 81, Boston-born director best known for helming the Alec Guinness comedies *The Man in the White Suit* and *The Ladykillers*, died on Dec. 22, 1993 in Los Angeles of pneumonia. His other works include *Whisky Galore (Tight Little Island), Mandy (The Crash of Silence), The Maggie, Sweet Smell of Success, A Boy Ten Feet Tall (Sammy Going South), A High Wind in Jamaica*, and *Don't Make Waves*. Survived by his wife and three sons.

JOSEPH L. MANKIEWICZ, 83, Pennsylvania-born director, writer and producer, one of Hollywood's top filmmakers for four decades, died of heart failure on Feb. 5, 1993 in Bedford, NY. He won a pair of Oscars

Spanky McFarland

playing the mother in the stage and film versions of *A Raisin in the Sun*, died on Nov. 25, 1993 in Englewood, NJ, of diabetes. No reported survivors.

JEFF MORROW, 86, New York City-born screen, stage and tv actor, star of such 1950's sci-fi films as *This Island Earth* and *The Creature Walks Among Us*, died on Dec. 26, 1993 in Canoga Park, CA, of unspecified causes. Among his other credits are *The Robe* (debut, 1953), *Flight to Tangiers, Siege at Red River, Sign of the Pagan, Captain Lightfoot, Pardners, Kronos*, and *The Story of Ruth*. Survived by his wife and daughter.

JEAN NEGULESCO, 93, Romania-born motion picture director, who

Rudolf Nureyev

Cecilia Parker

received an Academy Award nomination for his work on the 1948 film *Johnny Belinda*, died of heart failure on July 18, 1993, in Marbella, Spain. His other credits include *The Mask of Dimitrios, The Conspirators, Humoresque, Three Came Home, The Mudlark, Titanic, How to Marry a Millionaire, Three Coins in the Fountain, Woman's World, Daddy Long Legs* (1955), *The Rains of Ranchipur, Boy on a Dolphin, The Best of Everything, Jessica, The Pleasure Seekers*, and *Hello-Goodbye*. No reported survivors.

KENNETH NELSON, 60, screen, stage and tv actor, best known for creating the role of Michael in the original Off-Broadway production of *The Boys in the Band* and the 1970 film adaptation, died on Oct. 7, 1993 in London of AIDS. He also appeared as Matt in the original 1960 production of *The Fantasticks* and was featured in the film *The Lonely Lady*. No reported survivors.

WALTER BROWN NEWMAN, 77, screenwriter who received Oscar

Mary Philbin

Kate Reid

nominations for his work on *Ace in the Hole (The Big Carnival), Cat Ballou*, and *Bloodbrothers*, died of cancer at his home in Sherman Oaks, CA, on Oct. 14, 1993. His other credits include *The Man With the Golden Arm, Underwater, Crime and Punishment USA*, and *The Champ* (1979). Survived by his wife, son and daughter.

RUDOLF NUREYEV, 54, Soviet ballet dancer, one of the greatest and

most popular artists in his field, died of AIDS on Jan. 6, 1993 in Paris. His few movie appearances include *Don Quixote, Valentino* (1977), and *Exposed*. No reported suvivors.

CHRISTIAN NYBY, 80, movie and tv editor turned-director, died of natural causes on Sept. 17, 1993 in Temecula, CA. As an editor he worked on such movies as *To Have and Have Not, The Big Sleep,* (1946) and *Red River* (Oscar nomination). Later he turned to directing, most notably helming the classic 1951 sci-fi thriller *The Thing*. His other directorial credits include *Hell on Devil's Island, Young Fury*, and *First to Fight*. Survived by his wife, two sons, including director Christian Nyby II, and six grandchildren.

CECILIA PARKER, 78, Canada-born screen actress, best known for playing Mickey Rooney's sister, Marian, in the Andy Hardy series, died on July 25, 1993 in Ventura, CA. Starting with the first entry, *A Family Affair*, she appeared in 11 of the Hardy films ending with *Andy Hardy Comes Home* in 1958. Her other movies include *The Painted Veil, Naughty Marietta, Seven Sweethearts*, and *You're Only Young Once*. Survived by her husband, a daughter and two sons.

River Phoenix

MARY PHILBIN, 89, Chicago-born silent screen actress, best known for starring opposite Lon Chaney in the 1925 version of *The Phantom of the Opera*, died on May 7, 1993 in Huntington Beach, CA. Her other movies include *False Kisses, Human Hearts, The Age of Desire, Temple of Venus, The Gaiety Girl, Fifth Avenue Models, The Man Who Laughs, Love Me and the World is Mine*, and *Girl Overboard*. Her career ended with the advent of sound films. No survivors.

RIVER PHOENIX, 23, Oregon-born screen and tv actor, died at Cedars Sinai Medical Center in Los Angeles on Oct. 31, 1993. He had collapsed outside a West Hollywood nightclub after ingesting cocaine and heroin. Following his 1985 debut in *Explorers* he made his mark in the movie *Stand By Me*, eventually receiving an Academy Award nomination for his work in *Running on Empty*. His other movies are *The Mosquito Coast, A Night in the Life of Jimmy Reardon, Little Nikita, Indiana Jones and the Last Crusade, I Love You to Death, Dogfight, My Own Private Idaho, Sneakers, Silent Tongue*, and *The Thing Called Love*. He was shooting the film *Dark Blood* at the time of his death. Survived by his parents, and his three sisters and one brother, all of whom have acted.

VINCENT PRICE, 82, St. Louis-born screen, stage and tv actor, who became one of the movies' great horror stars through such films as *House of Wax, The Fly, House on Haunted Hill, The Pit and the Pendulum, The Abominable Dr. Phibes,* and *Theatre of Blood,* died of lung cancer on Oct. 25, 1993 at his home in Los Angeles. Following his 1938 film debut in *Service Deluxe* he appeared in such pictures as *The Private Lives of Elizabeth and Essex, Tower of London* (1939 and 1962), *Brigham Young-Frontiersman, The House of the Seven Gables, Song of Bernadette, Laura, Wilson, The Keys of the Kingdom, Leave Her to Heaven, Dragonwyck, The Three Musketeers* (1948), *Up in Central Park, The Baron of Arizona, Champagne for Caesar, His Kind of Woman, The Mad Magician, Serenade, The Ten Commandments, The Story of Mankind, The Bat, The Tingler, The Fall of the House of Usher, Master of the World, Confessions of an Opium Eater, The Haunted Palace, The Raven* (1963), *The Comedy of Terrors, The Last Man on Earth, Masque of the Red Death, Dr. Goldfoot and the Bikini Machine, The Conqueror Worm (Witchfinder General), The Trouble With Girls, Dr. Phibes Rises Again, The Whales of August,* and his last, *Edward Scissorhands,* in 1990. His

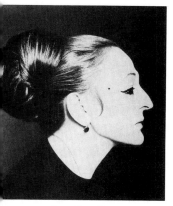

Irene Sharaff

Ray Sharkey

third wife, actress Coral Browne, died in 1991. Survived by two children.

KATE REID, 62, London-born screen, stage and tv actress, perhaps best known for her role as the bed ridden ex-moll, Grace, in the 1981 film *Atlantic City,* died of cancer on March 27, 1993 in Stratford, Ontario, Canada. Her other movies include *This Property Is Condemned, The Andromeda Strain, A Delicate Balance, Equus, Death Ship, Circle of Two, Heaven Help Us, Fire With Fire, Signs of Life, Bye Bye Blues,* and *Deceived.* Survived by a son and daughter.

DAN SEYMOUR, 78, Chicago-born screen, stage and tv character actor, who specialized in villains, died on May 25, 1993 in Santa Monica, CA, following a stroke. His more than 70 films include *Road to Morocco, Casablanca, To Have and Have Not, Confidential Agent, Cloak and Dagger* (1946), *A Night in Casablanca, Key Largo, Johnny Belinda, Rancho Notorious, Young Man With a Horn, The Blue Veil, The Big Heat, Moonfleet, Abbott & Costello Meet the Mummy, The Buster Keaton Story,*

Anne Shirley

Alexis Smith

Vincent Price

The Sad Sack, Watusi, Return of the Fly, The Way We Were, and *Escape From Witch Mountain.* Survived by his wife, two sons and four grandchildren.

IRENE SHARAFF, 83, screen and stage costume designer, died of congestive heart failure on Aug. 16, 1993 in New York. She won Academy Awards for her work on *An American in Paris, The King and I, West Side Story, Cleopatra* (1963), and *Who's Afraid of Virginia Woolf?* Her many other credits include *Meet Me in St. Louis, Yolanda and the Thief, The Best Years of Our Lives, Call Me Madam, A Star is Born* (1954), *Guys and Dolls, Flower Drum Song, Funny Girl,* and *Mommie Dearest.* No reported survivors.

RAY SHARKEY, 40, Brooklyn-born screen and tv actor, died of AIDS on June 11, 1993 in Brooklyn. His movies include *Paradise Alley, Who'll Stop the Rain, Willie and Phil, The Idolmaker, Love and Money, Some Kind of Hero, Wise Guys, No Mercy, Scenes From the Class Struggle in Beverly Hills, Wired, Rain Killer, Zebrahead,* and *Cop and a Half.* Survivors include his mother.

ANNE SHIRLEY (Dawn Paris), 74, screen actress who received an Academy Award nomination for her performance in the 1937 version of *Stella Dallas,* died of lung cancer on July 4, 1993 at her home in Los Angeles. As a child star she first billed herself as Dawn O'Day, then later adapted the name of the character she played in *Anne of Green Gables.* Her other movies include *Emma, So Big* (1932), *Rasputin and the Empress, Steamboat 'Round the Bend, Chatterbox, Meet the Missus, Condemned Women, Mother Carey's Chickens, Sorority House, Boy Slaves, Anne of Windy Poplars, Saturday's Children, All That Money Can Buy (The Devil and Daniel Webster), Four Jacks and a Jill,* and her last, *Murder My Sweet,* in 1945. Survived by a daughter and a son.

ALEXIS SMITH (Gladys Smith), 72, Canada-born screen, stage and tv actress, died on June 9, 1993 in Los Angeles of cancer. Her many films include *Dive Bomber, Gentleman Jim, Thank Your Lucky Stars, The Constant Nymph, The Doughgirls, Adventures of Mark Twain, Conflict, Rhapsody in Blue, The Horn Blows at Midnight, San Antonio, One More Tomorrow, Night and Day, Stallion Road, The Two Mrs. Carrolls, The Woman in White, Decision of Christopher Blake, Any Number Can Play,*

Ann Todd   Herve Villechaize   Sam Wanamaker   Gwen Welles

Here Comes the Groom, Sleeping Tiger, Beau James, The Young Philadelphians, Once is Not Enough, The Little Girl Who Lives Down the Lane, Casey's Shadow, and *Tough Guys.* She is survived by her husband, actor Craig Stevens.

ANNA STEN (Annel Stenskaya Sudakevich), 84, Russia-born screen and stage actress, died of cardiac arrest at her Manhattan home on Nov. 12, 1993. Following appearances in several European films she was brought to America by Samuel Goldwyn for *Nana* in 1934. Her other English-language movies include *Resurrection, The Wedding Night, A Woman Alone, So Ends Our Night, They Came to Blow Up America, Three Russian Girls, Soldier of Fortune,* and her last, *The Nun and the Sergeant,* in 1962. No reported survivors.

ANN TODD, 82, British screen, stage and tv actress, who achieved stardom in the 1945 film *The Seventh Veil,* died of a stroke in London on May 6, 1993. Her other movies include *South Riding, The Paradine Case, So Evil My Love, The Passionate Friends, Madeleine, Breaking the Sound Barrier, The Green Scarf, Time Without Pity, Son of Captain Blood,* and *The Human Factor.* Survived by two sons.

EVELYN VENABLE, 80, Cincinnati-born screen and stage actress, died on Nov. 16, 1993 in Post Falls, ID, of undisclosed causes. Her movie credits include *Cradle Song* (debut, 1933), *Death Takes a Holiday, Mrs. Wiggs of the Cabbage Patch* (1934), *Alice Adams, The Little Colonel, The Frontiersman, Pinocchio* (voice of the Blue Fairy), and her last, *He Hired the Boss,* in 1943. She was married to cinematographer Hal Mohr, who died in 1974. Survived by two daughters.

HERVE VILLECHAIZE, 50, Paris-born screen and tv actor, died on Sept. 4, 1993 at his North Hollywood, CA home of a self-inflicted gunshot wound. Best known for his role of Tattoo on the hit tv series *Fantasy Island,* he appeared in such movies as *The Gang That Couldn't Shoot Straight, Crazy Joe, The Man With the Golden Gun, Seizure, The One and Only,* and *Two Moon Junction.* Survived by his wife.

SAM WANAMAKER, 74, Chicago-born screen, stage and tv actor/director died on Dec. 18, 1993 at his London home following a long bout with cancer. After his debut in *My Girl Tisa* in 1948, he appeared in such movies as *Mr. Denning Drives North, Taras Bulba, Man in the Middle, Those Magnificent Men in Their Flying Machines, The Spy Who Came in From the Cold, Warning Shot, The Day the Fish Came Out, Voyage of the Damned, Private Benjamin, The Competition, Irreconcilable Differences, Raw Deal (1986), Baby Boom,* and *Guilty by Suspicion.* He also directed the films *The File of the Golden Goose, The Executioner,* and *Sinbad and the Eye of the Tiger.* Survived by his wife and three daughters, one of whom is actress Zoe Wanamaker.

GWEN WELLES, 42, New York City-born screen and tv actress, best known for playing the naive aspiring country singer, Sueleen Gay, in Robert Altman's *Nashville,* died of cancer on Oct. 13, 1993. Her other movies include *A Safe Place, California Split, New Year's Day,* and *Eating.* Survived by her husband, actor Harris Yulin.

FRANK ZAPPA, 52, Baltimore-born rock musician, died of prostate cancer at his Los Angeles home on Dec. 4, 1993. His movie appearances include *Head, 200 Motels, Baby Snakes,* and *Funny.* Survived by his wife and four children.

INDEX

322